1/3/2000

CW00470131

# CAMBRIDGESHIRE RECO

(formerly Cambridge Antiquarian Records Society)

# VOLUME 14

The Prince of Wales as an undergraduate 1861

# ROMILLY'S
# CAMBRIDGE DIARY
# 1848 - 1864

SELECTED PASSAGES FROM
THE DIARY OF THE REV. JOSEPH ROMILLY
FELLOW OF TRINITY COLLEGE AND REGISTRARY OF
THE UNIVERSITY OF CAMBRIDGE

## EDITED BY
## M.E. BURY & J.D. PICKLES

GENERAL EDITOR
PETER SEARBY

CAMBRIDGE 2000

Published by the Cambridgeshire Records Society
County Record Office, Shire Hall, Cambridge CB3 0AP

© Cambridgeshire Records Society 2000

British Library Cataloguing in Publication Data

A catalogue record for this book
is available from the British Library
ISBN 0 904323 14 5

Printed and bound in Great Britain by
The Book Company, Ipswich

# CONTENTS

# Illustrations

The tailpieces concluding certain years are taken from J. L. Roget, *A Cambridge Scrapbook* (1859)

# PREFACE

In the summer of 1864 Joseph Romilly, the retired Registrary of the university and a fellow of Trinity College for more than forty years, left Cambridge for Yarmouth for his usual holiday, taking with him with the last volume of the *Diary* that he had kept for much of his adult life. Before 1829 the entries had been intermittent, but he then began to write regularly and often at length and hardly missed a day. The last of his generation, he died suddenly at Yarmouth on the evening of 7 August of the heart trouble that had been evident for some years. His *Diary* was made up until the previous day and as full as ever of detail and human interest. 'A delicious record of old Cambridge' was J.W. Clark's opinion of it, and 'record' is the right word since it contains, besides a vast amount of personal information about Romilly and his relations and servants, a minute anatomy of public events in the academic life of the university, drawn by an acute observer intimately involved in its doings, and by a townsman with a deep interest in local affairs and in the lives of his neighbours. It is one of the most important, attractive, and engaging primary sources of social life in nineteenth-century Cambridge. Romilly entrusted the manuscripts to his nephew and executor, G.B. Allen, and it was fitting that in the 1930s they should return after an exile of many years when Miss R.M. Allen of Pembrokeshire presented them, together with three of his early travel diaries, to Cambridge University Library (Additional MSS 6804-42). They were not, of course, unknown before and J.W. Clark and T.M. Hughes made extensive use of them in the 1880s for their large biography of Romilly's friend, the geologist Adam Sedgwick. D.A. Winstanley also studied them carefully for his books on *Early Victorian Cambridge* (1940), and *Later Victorian Cambridge* (1947), and they have since been widely quoted. The *Diary* first became known to a wider audience in 1967 when Patrick Bury, Fellow and Librarian of Corpus Christi College, published a series of extracts entitled *Romilly's Cambridge Diary 1832-1842* and revealed the full character of an amiable, hardworking and perceptive man. On the basis of Dr Bury's further selection with some changes the present editors edited a continuation entitled *Romilly's Cambridge Diary 1842-1847* (Cambridgeshire Records Society, volume 9, 1994). Little else of what Romilly wrote appears to have survived apart from his official records; there is a handful of unimportant letters out of the thousands he sent. Of the correspondence that he received the editors especially regret the loss of letters from his nephews, especially those of E.E. Allen, which to judge from references to them were lively and amusing. His nephew G.T. Romilly told Clark and Hughes that in later years Romilly as a rule destroyed personal correspondence. After the death of his father in 1828 there is a reference to a 'private journal' which may have been written to help him come to terms with his grief.

This volume completes Romilly's story with a selection from the last seventeen years of his life. We have again confined the extracts to life in Cambridge for reasons of space but given brief connecting narratives of Romilly's movements and activities elsewhere. That these are as vivid and informative as the rest of his chronicle may be seen in the thematic volume edited by Canon Geoffrey Morris of Lampeter Velfrey whose *Romilly's Visits to*

*Wales 1827-1854* was published by the Gomer Press in 1998. Much has inevitably been omitted from the present book which spans many years and is drawn from manuscripts of several thousand pages in Romilly's small neat handwriting. Romilly's numerous and habitual contractions are silently expanded although his abbreviations 'wch' for 'which' and the ampersand '&', his characteristic spellings (except for the long 's'), and sometimes erratic punctuation, are retained. The form of dates at the beginning of each entry is standardised. The usual three points ' . . . ' signal omissions from the text within entries. Ample annotations have, as in our previous volume, been added for the benefit of local and social historians who may be interested in the customs and procedures of Romilly's day. They are not intended to be exhaustive, but rather explanatory and illustrative, and an indication of the many rich primary and secondary sources which are open to the student of Victorian life. Where it was possible we have tried to identify people mentioned in the text, and put them in an index with details which would have been out of place in the footnotes. The general index of places and subjects draws together recurring themes and events both in the text and notes.

We should like to thank Dr Peter Searby, Dr Elisabeth Leedham-Green, and Mrs Rachel Wroth for the interest they have taken in the book and for valuable advice and information. Mr Godfrey Waller and his staff at the Cambridge University Library and Mr Chris Jakes and his staff at the Cambridgeshire Collection in the city library, have, as ever, been most helpful, and Mr Jonathan Smith of Trinity College Library has patiently and learnedly answered a number of our queries. We are especially grateful to Trinity College, which provided a generous grant for the typing of the book. Sarah Cartwright carefully and cheerfully performed that exacting task while Rosemary Graham meticulously carried out our numerous revisions. The final stage in the editorial process, converting the typescript into camera-ready copy, was carried out by Vera and Alexander Hill with exemplary skill, for which we are very grateful.

# INTRODUCTION

When this third and final selection from Joseph Romilly's *Diary* begins Prince Albert had been a reforming Chancellor of the University for almost two years and Lord John Russell Prime Minister since July 1846. In July 1848 a petition was presented to Russell calling for a 'Royal Commission of Inquiry into the best methods of securing the improvement of the Universities of Oxford and Cambridge', to which the Cambridge signatories, with only one exception, were non-resident graduates. The statutes of the university and the colleges had for the most part been framed in the reign of Elizabeth I; some were ignored and many antiquated, although there was a strong sentimental attachment to them among many fellows, whilst others felt conscientiously bound to uphold them, as they had sworn to do when they were admitted. But what might have suited the sixteenth century was ill adapted to the nineteenth, and for a generation at least there had been controversy on such issues as the prohibition of married fellows, and religious tests that were designed to exclude all but members of the established church. Until 1824 when a Classical Tripos was established the only subject examined for an honours degree was mathematics, and the whole curriculum had remained narrow. Many students opted for a pass or poll degree whose standard was very low, while those who sought academic distinction depended on expensive private coaching. Trinity was one of several colleges that had attempted to rid itself of its most archaic statutes in the 1840s, and there was a feeling among the resident dons that, left to themselves, they could effect their own reforms. It is most unlikely that they would have done so. The Royal Commission reported in 1852 and was followed by a Statutory Commission in 1856 so that in the end little was unexamined and much was revised. When therefore Romilly, who as Registrary was at the heart of its administration, retired in January 1862, the university was very different from that which he had known when he was elected thirty years before, and the struggles that changed it, together with many details of his family and social life, are recorded in this volume.

Sir John Romilly, Master of the Rolls and one of the Royal Commissioners, was Joseph's first cousin and one of the six sons of Sir Samuel Romilly (1757-1818) the law-reformer and philanthropist of whom in January 1860 *The Times* wrote, 'There is no greater name than that of Romilly on the list of those refugees who were driven from their country upon the Revocation of the Edict of Nantes'. A prolific yet closely-knit Huguenot family, by the nineteenth century they had been assimilated into the Whig oligarchy and the Anglican church and amongst them were members of Parliament, lawyers, army officers, and fellows of the Royal Society like Romilly's cousin, P.M. Roget, of *Thesaurus* fame. Two of his other cousins were brothers-in-law of Lord John Russell. Joseph Romilly, born on 9 October 1791 in Frith Street, Soho, was one of nine children of Thomas Peter Romilly and his first cousin Jane Anne, daughter of Isaac Romilly, F.R.S. He was educated privately and was at one time taught by James Boyer, the fierce former pedagogue at Christ's Hospital, for whom he retained a lasting respect. In 1808 he was admitted pensioner of Trinity College, the Cambridge college to which he was to be devoted for the rest of his life. He took his bachelor's degree as fourth wrangler in 1813 preceded by (Sir) John Herschel, the astronomer, George Peacock, later Professor of Astronomy and Dean of Ely, and Fearon Fallows, another astronomer who died young; one need look no further for evidence of Romilly's academic and intellectual standing. He was elected to a Trinity fellowship two years later, taught pupils, served as junior and senior dean, and in 1840 became one of the small Seniority who with the Master governed the college. The early *Diary* shows him to be constantly sociable, rather too concerned for his health, and reluctant fully to exert himself. In fact his considerable abilities were underemployed, and, presumably recognising this, he canvassed for the office of Registrary tirelessly and without hesitation when it fell vacant in 1832. He was an administrator rather than an original thinker, and the post suited him so well that twenty-four years later he was moved to write 'I heartily bless God for having vouchsafed me health and strength to carry on for so great a length of time an employment of which I am very fond and which affords me competence and happiness'. As the most important permanent officer of the administration he soon became expert in the history and procedures of the university, and he rescued the archives from the neglect and indifference of nearly two centuries: 'His work was invaluable and can hardly be too highly praised'. (H.E. Peek and C.P. Hall, *The Archives of the University of Cambridge*, 1962, p. 22). His many duties were performed with increasing diligence. Besides acting as secretary to the governing body of the university, he translated Graces into Latin, received fees due for matriculation and degrees, took a leading part in ceremonial occasions, helped conduct the Trinity College examinations, and answered constant requests for information from inside and outside the university. It was said of his contemporary Philip Bliss, the Oxford Registrar, that men came to depend on him so much that when a question arose they would refer to him rather than make their own researches, and Romilly appears to have been similarly regarded in Cambridge.

Until 1837 he lived in college as a resident fellow; in that year his two unmarried sisters, Margaret, seven years older than her brother, and Lucy, youngest of the family, joined him when their family home in Dulwich was given up. They took a house in Hills Road, then on the outskirts of the town, and fortunately for readers of the *Diary*, Romilly thus became a householder interested in town affairs as well as an academic who retained his rooms in Trinity. The sisters were very different from each other. Margaret's portrait shows her to have been a handsome, elegant woman, who like many of her contemporaries considered it her Christian duty to be charitably employed. She visited schools, helped young girls with their reading and writing, apprenticed boys to good masters, and at home taught French, Italian, and music to would-be governesses. Margaret fell seriously ill in 1847 and despite the reassurances of the doctors died of abdominal cancer in December of that year. Soon afterwards Romilly and Lucy moved to Scroope Terrace, near the Fitzwilliam Museum, where she also died in 1854. The somewhat erratic Lucy, whose powers of mind Sir John Romilly nevertheless thought of 'a high order', was also selfless and indefatigable in working for her protégés and for sick people and ill-used animals. In the society of her equals, who found her charming, she was as shy as the birds she liberated from tiny cages, but when she thought a protégée in moral danger or saw a drayman lashing an exhausted horse or a sweep's lad in trouble, she became formidable and undaunted even when called to give evidence in court. Romilly, whose patience was often tried by her disorderly ways, was deeply distressed by Lucy's death - 'I am now left a solitary being' he wrote, no doubt acutely aware that his only brother was settled in Paris and that his married nephews, much as they tried to comfort him, had their own lives to lead. He was well cared for by his two women servants who had been with him for many years and remained until his death. To Harriet Sandfield, who twice refused to marry and leave him, he was as much a father as an employer.

In time Romilly's cheerful temperament reasserted itself and he was once more the kind, 'conversible', and witty man much liked among his colleagues and by the 'youngsters' who sometimes cheered him as he made his official way up the Senate House. Even in old age, despite heart-trouble, his interests and pleasures remained what they had always been. Above all he was a shrewd and humorous observer of people, most of whom he was disposed to like, who enjoyed the society of children and of pretty and preferably intelligent women, frequent games of whist and rarer ones of billiards, ships and the sea, and batheing even when it was cold and rough, fine hill country, looking at pictures at home and abroad, and travelling long distances however uncomfortably. He had a reputation as a coiner of puns and was, as Adam Sedgwick wrote, 'a merry genial man'. His dislikes remained constant too. As a firm Whig and reformer, though not always where his beloved Trinity was concerned, he did not hesitate when he thought it necessary to express unpopular views. Yet he was quickly bored by dinner-parties at which there was prolonged political argument or 'too much science', and firm in his disapproval of contemporary books and sermons which might unsettle religious belief. A devout middle-of-the-road Christian who distrusted 'up in the clouds' philosophising, he was steadfast in his duties of observance and charity, an admirable employer, and generous friend. He practised economy and invariably travelled second-class on the railway while his colleagues preferred to go first. Though a cultivated man, well-read in the classics and English and European literature, he remained largely unresponsive to the great poets of the day like Tennyson despite the encouragement of his friends. His chief pleasure was in paintings, and, overcoming early distaste, he came to feel strong admiration for Turner's work. He did not intend that his *Diary* should be published; it is never introspective and contains no passages of consciously fine writing, but its readers quickly become aware that its style in every way reflects the diarist. He was a small man and prematurely bald, yet with a definite presence which may be seen in the water-colour portrait of him painted by Miss Hervé in 1831 which is now in the Registry; it is reproduced in black and white in both the earlier volumes of *Romilly's Cambridge Diary* and elsewhere. He disliked being photographed and the only other likeness of him that we have found is a small and unattractive *carte de visite* at Trinity College (reproduced in this book), evidently taken late in life. He died suddenly at Yarmouth on 7 August 1864 and was buried with his sisters in the churchyard of Christ Church, Barnwell, then a poor and teeming district of Cambridge, where their family monument is one of the few that still remain.

Cambridge in 1848 was, in the idiom of the directories, a university, borough (both parliamentary and corporate), county, and market town with its own poor law union. Its population of about 25,000 and its area were gradually expanding.

'Situated on a vast level and embosomed in lofty trees, Cambridge is not seen to advantage at a distance . . . and even under the most favourable aspect the view is sadly wanting in that general succession of lofty towers and spires for which Oxford stands unrivalled. The interior appearance of the Town too is generally disappointing, and below what might be anticipated, but it is rapidly improving . . . ' (Norris Deck, *A Hand-Book for Visitors to Cambridge* (1861), p. 255). Streets in the centre were mostly narrow and filthy while the often low older houses and courts were so crowded and insanitary that a Board of Health Inspector in 1849 described them as a 'disgrace to civilisation'. Markedly in contrast with them were imposing college and university buildings that included a new university library by C.R. Cockerell, and the Fitzwilliam Museum. Also of recent construction were the County Courts on Shire Hill, a castellated gaol, the union workhouse, the Zion Baptist chapel in East Road, and the churches of St Paul's and Christ Church. Romilly, who knew from observation that the borough was growing in the areas of New Town and Barnwell, was puzzled by the 1861 census which showed that the population of Cambridge (26,351) had not increased over the past ten years; in fact people were simply moving away from the centre, and it was this redistribution and above all the foundation in 1855 of the Cambridge University and Town Water Company, under the chairmanship of Professor Whewell, which gave the poor access to clean water and led to a gradual improvement in public health. The opening of the railway in 1845 led too to the development of new employment away from the river, whose traffic declined. The town still depended to a great degree on its traditional role as the centre of an agricultural region with busy markets and good communications, and much local business and employment depended on provisioning the seventeen colleges and providing their members with such services as banking, tailoring, printing, and the law. The university had grown rapidly in numbers since the beginning of the century and its resident fellows were joined for almost two thirds of the year by more than 1,400 students. Friction between the university authorities and the town had been constant. The town had a medieval charter, and its authority had been increased by the Municipal Corporations Act of 1835. Nevertheless, the townsfolk resented outdated and unreasonable privileges conferred on the university. Its claims to exercise jurisdiction over such matters as licensing, the conduct of fairs, the provision of entertainment, and the control of prostitution were especial grounds of dissatisfaction. After tediously unsuccessful negotiations both parties agreed to the arbitration of Sir John Patteson, an eminent lawyer favoured by the government, and his Award Act of 1856 at length made possible the beginning of better relations between these old adversaries. When Romilly died in 1864 he had reason both as an academic and a householder to be cautiously hopeful that a spirit of progress in public affairs of the kind that his family had espoused was still abroad.

# ABBREVIATIONS OF TITLES USED
# IN THE FOOTNOTES

| | |
|---|---|
| Annals | C.H. Cooper, *Annals of Cambridge* (vols IV and V, 1852, 1908). |
| Chadwick | Owen Chadwick, *The Victorian Church* (2 vols 1966, 1970). |
| *Chronicle* | *The Cambridge Chronicle* (weekly newspaper). |
| Clark & Hughes | J.W.Clark and T.M. Hughes, *The Life and Letters of Adam Sedgwick* (2 vols 1890). |
| *D.N.B.* | *Dictionary of National Biography.* |
| *Endowments* | J.W. Clark, *Endowments of the University of Cambridge* (1904). |
| *Independent* | *The Cambridge Independent* (weekly newspaper). |
| McKitterick | D.J. McKitterick, *Cambridge University Library: a History* (1986). |
| *Romilly 1832-42* | J.P.T.Bury, *Romilly's Cambridge Diary 1832-1842* (1967). |
| *Romilly 1842-47* | M.E. Bury & J.D. Pickles, *Romilly's Cambridge Diary 1842-1847* (1994). |
| Searby | P. Searby, *A History of the University of Cambridge, III, 1750-1870* (1997). |
| Winstanley | D.A. Winstanley, *Early Victorian Cambridge* (1940). |

# 1848

The year 1847 had been darkened for Romilly and Lucy by the lingering death at home of their elder sister, Margaret. Yet, despite their anxieties and grief, ordinary life at Hills Road with Betsy Edwards the maid and Dosia the cook, had been recorded day by day with customary regularity. Meanwhile in college and university public affairs kept the Registry busy. After a close-run election against the Earl of Powis, Prince Albert had been elected Chancellor of the University of Cambridge and lavishly installed in July. Professor Adam Sedgwick, one of Romilly's oldest friends, had been appointed the prince's secretary for local affairs, and it was becoming clear that the future would be no idle one for the Registry and other administrative officers. Nor was the formidable Master of Trinity, Professor Whewell, who presided over the small body that ran the college, likely to become inactive. To Romilly's pleasure another old college friend, Thomas Musgrave, Bishop of Hereford, had been translated to York in November 1847; but the choice of his successor, Professor Hampden of Oxford, by the Prime Minister looked set to disrupt the church and his consecration was delayed by judicial wrangling and intemperate pamphleteering.

With such doings Lucy was uninvolved save as a spectator; her time was occupied in caring for Margaret, arranging the lives of numerous pauper protégés, especially young women, and rescuing animals from inhumane treatment. She had for years been a devoted though not always uncritical admirer of Romilly's colleague at Trinity, William Carus, the handsome evangelical vicar of Holy Trinity church which they faithfully attended. Now, despite years of protestations that he was wedded to his parish work, he was engaged to be married in earnest and his female followers were shocked. Unmarried and childless though they both were, the Romillys watched closely the progress and welfare of their wider family at home and abroad. Their twenty-four year old nephew, George (G.T.Romilly), 'our little man' whom they had brought up after his mother's early death, was still largely dependent on them and unsettled. He wished to be an artist and for that career with his uncle's agreement had left his university studies without a degree; but he was making little progress and certainly not a living, while to his uncle's relief his fiancée had lately broken off their engagement. For some time George had lived in Paris where his uncle Frank, Romilly's only surviving brother, also resided with his French wife and family. Another nephew, elder son of their dead sister Caroline was George Allen ('G.B.A.'), of whom they had seen much while he was undergraduate at Trinity, and who was becoming established as a lawyer in London. He and his wife Dora were to have many children, the first of whom the diarist christened in July 1847. George's younger brother Edward (alias 'Grim' or 'E.E.A'), an odd lad, having graduated in 1846, entered the church and became curate of St Mary's, Shrewsbury. He had engaged himself to Dora's sister Bertha Eaton in 1847, but was wilfully opposed to making a marriage settlement without which he would have control of her property in years to come. To the girl's widowed mother and uncle Joseph it was all 'very unsatisfactory'.

*Sat. 1 January.* – The opening of the new year, thank God, finds Lucy in tolerable health & spirits; & I am quite well. May God mercifully grant us a continuation of health during the year & give us the desire & the power to serve him more faithfully . . . The Bishop of Oxford has discarded his sobriquet of 'slippery Sam' by writing a Letter to Dr Hampden in which he retracts all he has said against him[1] . . .

*Tu. 18.* Bright sunshiny day: Lucy to her paupers . . . Lord Powis is dead in consequence of being shot in the thigh at a shooting party: – how fortunate it is that he was not elected Chancellor last year, as we should now be in all the tumult of a contested Election . . .

*Wed. 19.* . . . The Evening's Post brought me a letter from Mrs Eaton begging me to interfere with regard to Edward's continuing to refuse settling on Bertha all her fortune: she writes from Clifton & thinks that Edw. is coming down next week to marry her: she enclosed a copy of a letter of hers (of the 13th Inst.) to Edward in wch she tells him that unless he makes the settlement she will cast off him & her for ever: – her letter is very injudiciously violent; but Edward's conduct is obstinate, selfish and unjustifiable. – I wrote to her to decline any further interference.[2] – I read aloud M.A. Titmarsh's 'Our Street'[3] – It is very amusing & the engravings are good.

*Th. 20.* . . . A wild letter from E.E.A. asking me to marry him in 5 or 10 days time without beadle, bridesmaid, wedding-breakfast or any such absurdity. – I am highly indignant with his obstinate selfishness in refusing to settle Bertha's fortune on her: but I wrote very calmly to him & told him that I could not possibly leave Cambridge this month. I announced to him presents of 10 Guineas from Lucy, £50 from dearest Margaret & £50 from me. – After dinner read Archdeacon Churton's sermon on death of Archbishop of York . . . thought it tractarian to a very objectionable degree.[4] Began 2d Vol. of Mrs Fry.[5]

*Fri. 28.* The cold was intense last night: thermometer down at 17: – two guards on the E. Counties Rail Road nearly frozen: – there was a cutting wind. – Breakfast with George in College. – He is engaged to marry a young Lady of about 18: her name (as well as her mother's) is Meg Merriless!!! She has not a farthing: so he is again disinterested in his affairs of the heart. The Father and Mother are living in strict retirement in Paris . . . I think George is (like his cousins) mad on the subject of marriage. He wants to marry in the Summer: he has not saved a farthing yet, altho I allow him £100 a year & he has 2 of his

[1]  Wilberforce, bishop of Oxford, had become embroiled in the controversy about Dr Hampden's fitness to be Bishop of Hereford and on 16 December 1847 sanctioned a suit against him for heresy which he was soon glad to drop, assuring the world that he was satisfied with Hampden's position as he understood it. He thus acquired a doubtful reputation and lost favour at court, while his half-affectionate nickname 'Slippery Sam' in reference to his smooth manners turned into 'Soapy Sam' with a less kind overtone. See Chadwick, I, 243-5.

[2]  On marriage a woman's property and income became her husband's and her legal personality was submerged in his. In better-off families it had long been the custom to secure a wife's property in equity by a settlement drawn up in anticipation of marriage. Such cumbrous machinery proved how few parents were willing 'to entrust the welfare of their offspring to the irresponsible power of the husband, to the chances of his character, his wisdom, and his success in a profession' (Women's petition to Parliament of 1856 quoted by L. Holcombe, *Wives and Property*, Toronto, 1983, p. 237). Given Edward's eccentricities Mrs Eaton had cause to worry.

[3]  A new comic novel for the Christmas market by Thackeray under his old pseudonym and with
•  his own illustrations.

[4]  i.e. Edward Churton, Archdeacon of Cleveland, on the death of Vernon Harcourt in November 1847. Romilly's old friend Thomas Musgrave succeeded him as archbishop.

[5]  i.e. the new biography by her daughters of Elizabeth Fry (d. 1845), the Quaker prison-reformer.

own: he has not yet made a farthing by his profession: I most stoutly deprecated his marriage till he had at least made a beginning, with a prospect of getting on. – Whether he will mind me remains to be shown: – I doubt it extremely. – He dined tête-à-tête with his Aunt. – I dined at Caius College at the Celebration of their 500th Anniversary[6] ... The Master of Caius was laid up with a cold at his living of Ashdon. We met however in his Lodge, & Paget presided in his stead. He was very nervous about it & had not slept the night before. He played his part extremely well. I found this dinner extremely agreeable: I sat between Stokes & Leapingwell, & close the people with whom I was intimate ... The Bishop of Norwich spoke in his animated manner & was very well received: he said 'he would mention one great name, Harvey, at which our blood would *circulate!*'[7] – He gave the health of the Caius Wranglers of the year: they were 9: but he chose to make them 11.[8] Mackenzie (2d wrangler) returned thanks in a speech wch made every body laugh: – he said that he & his comrades had done what the circumstances of the case required ...

*Tu. 1 February.* Left Cambridge by Mail-train (10.45): I travelled in 2d Class – I bought for my amusement 'the Bal Masqué' & 'the Romance of a Mince-pye'.[9] – I lent this last (without looking at it, & seduced by its name) to a little girl of about 8 or 9 (– I think her Father, who was sitting by her, is one of Matthew & Gents establishment).[10] In about an hour the missy complained of being sick, & upon my book being returned to me I found it not at all fitted for a child: much about poisoning, suicide, & such horrors: – I must never lend a book again to a child without reading it ... At the Athenæum Blunt told me of a fresh name for Bishop Wilberforce, viz. 'The Retractarian': so he is now known by several aliases, such as 'Slippery Sam', & 'Windsor Soap'. – There is a name fabricated for the supporters of the admission of Jews into Parliament: they are called Pre-puseyans[11] ... I left Town by the Express 5.30 for Bristol:

---

[6] Of its first foundation by Edmund Gonville; its second was by Dr Caius in 1558. Dinner was on the table soon after 5 o'clock and continued all evening with speeches and toasts before a host of dignitaries. See the detailed account in the *Chronicle* of 29 January, where it is reported also that the event was also marked by the distribution of coals, bread, and money to ninety poor people.

[7] William Harvey (d. 1657), discoverer of the circulation of the blood, had been educated at Caius. His collected works were translated from Latin in 1847 for a medical printing-club, the Sydenham Society, that was run by Cambridge men.

[8] Those who sat the exacting Mathematical Tripos were divided by the examiners into Wranglers, Senior Optimes, and Junior Optimes by strict order of merit. The examination, comprising many papers of several hours each, was held in the unheated and ill-lit Senate House and was a rigorous test of both physical and mental endurance. To be Senior Wrangler was a great distinction of national importance, while even to be high in the list opened the way to prizes, fellowships, and professional advancement. For the changes by which 'Tripos' meant at first a stool and finally a system of examination see C. Wordsworth, *Scholae Academicae* (1877), pp. 16-21.

[9] *The Romance of a Mince-Pie* by Angus B. Reach, a writer for *Punch*, and *The Bal Masqué* (illustrated) by 'Count Chicard', both dated 1848, were evidently railway ephemera. Inevitably a society arose to suppress trash and immorality in railway reading.

[10] i.e. the grocery and china shop in Trinity Street.

[11] Since he was unable to take the oath 'on the faith of a true Christian' no Jew could enter Parliament even if elected, as Rothschild repeatedly was. In November 1847 the University had

I went by the 2d Class & paid 21*l*. I ought to have taken a return ticket & so saved my money, but I did not learn this liberal system until the next day when it was too late to profit by it. – The company in the carriage was very good: it was a railed-off carriage holding 10: no light! – I was about 35 Minutes getting from the Station to the Great Western Hotel. I found Edward Allen waiting for me & tea ready . . . I was delighted to find that Edward has at last (tho most reluctantly) consented to the settlement of his wife's fortune on herself.

*Wed. 2.* . . . Got up at ¼ to 7 by Candlelight: – we were to have breakfasted before the wedding: but no fire was lighted, no breakfast ready: so we deferred the matutinal meal till after the religious ceremony. – Edward, Tooke[12] & I started about 7½ to walk to Clifton . . . It was a lovely fresh morning with sunshine. We got to the Church at 10' before 8 . . . I prepared the 2 Registers & arranged myself canonically . . . Edward's conduct in the Vestry was characteristic: the Clerk asked what his father was: – he said 'lawyer': – the Clerk said 'Attorney?': – Edward by silence gave consent: I said 'O no! a Barrister': – 'what was the Lady's Father'? said the Clerk: 'Farmer' said Edward: 'O no, said I: he kept his carriage & had a park round his house: – he was a Gentleman'. – Shortly after 8 arrived on foot Mrs Eaton & her niece (Miss Hardy) in walking attire. Mrs Eaton had been married in this very church: – she begged me to come & breakfast with her after the ceremony: – I (with no very good will, as I would 100 times rather have kept my engagement of breakfasting with E. & Tooke) agreed to do so. Mrs Eaton talked to me [2½ lines are here crossed out so that they are quite illegible][13] – thing far beyond that was required, viz. a hearty affectionate reception of her daughter & son-in-law: – she tells me that she offered 50 Guas for Bertha's wedding clothes (being the sum she gave to Dora), but that it had been refused: – I recommended her paying the sum into the Banker's: – [2 half-lines similarly crossed out] have her harp: she spoke highly of his attachment to Bertha & of his integrity, but was much vext at his oddity, *which she wished me to remonstrate with him about.* I very civily & goodhumouredly told her of the impossibility of my meddling with his conduct. Edward is certainly vexatiously strange & vastly self-willed, but I think the [2 half-lines similarly crossed out]. She told me that she came in at the side door of the Church & made a circuit with her niece that there might be no appearance of anything going forward, that she thought weddings couldn't be too private etc: – I said that I could not agree with her, that the Apostle pronounced marriage honorable, & that I didn't approve of people going about it as if they were ashamed of it. – At 8½ in a fly came a Colonel Hawkshaw with the bride: – he had blundered about the time: he is a lame man (having been wounded by a cannon-ball): he is a thorough gentleman & seems amiable & good tempered. The bride was in a brown russet stuff gown, wore a very

petitioned against any relief with Romilly and others dissenting; all relief bills failed until 1858 because of opposition in the House of Lords. For Jews at Cambridge see W. Frankel and H. Miller, *Gown and Tallith* (1989).

12   A friend of Edward since their undergraduate days at Trinity, he too became a country parson.

13   Blotting out of entries is very rare. If the deletions are his, presumably Romilly felt on this occasion that his comments had been too harsh, but it is clear that he never tried to expunge such entries systematically. He came to respect Grim as a parish priest and family man.

ordinary walking bonnet & shawl, had on cotton stockings, & looked no more like a bride than Miss Hardy did like a bridesmaid. Poor thing! she has had a vexatious time of it for several months in the constant feuds [½ line crossed out]: she has not been out of the house (except to Church) for 3 months, & had lost her appetite, & looked jaded & harrassed. The bridegroom had on a shabby sort of Chesterfield & wore black gloves.[14] – I never saw such a marriage in my life, nor any body else. – Colonel Hawkshaw gave the bride away. – Both Edward & Bertha repeated their parts in clear, distinct voices: there was no sobbing, no scene at all. I have no doubt the bride was most [2 half-lines deleted] – When the ceremony was over I kissed the bride, & so did Mrs Eaton & the Colonel . . . Edward & his wife & Tooke went to the Hotel: Mrs Eaton, Miss Hardy, the Colonel & I went to Mrs Eaton's lodging . . . [2 half-lines deleted] Mrs Eaton asked if I should object to having a saucepan in the room to boil the eggs: –I said that I should like it of all things, & that I myself would boil them. – I should say that Miss Hardy seemed to me an amiable pleasing girl, tho very plain. – Mrs Eaton expressed herself gratified by my having come to perform the ceremony. – As soon as breakfast was over I posted off at the top of my speed to Bristol & there found Edward & wife & Tooke very cosily at breakfast. – I presented Mrs Edward with some cards (engraved for her at Cambridge) & took an affectionate leave of her. – I left Bristol by the 10.45 train . . . Found Lucy pretty well: she had not expected me till tomorrow . . .

*Th. 3.* . . . Also a letter from Richard Lodge telling me that my dear friend John Lodge is in a desperate state . . . he can keep nothing in his stomach: – poor fellow! his existence for the last 3 years has been a melancholy contrast to the joyous intellectual life he used to lead[15] . . .

*Wed. 9.* . . . Congregation.[16] – Barrington (grandson of Lord Barrington) came forward to take degree by Royal Consanguinity: – but was refused because his Pedigree had not circulated[17] . . . Letter from G.T.R.[18] saying that his intended has agreed to defer their marriage till he makes something in his Profession . . .

[14] The clergy and men in mourning might wear black gloves rather than white at a wedding, but Edward's choice was presumably to emphasise his determination to defy convention.

[15] John Lodge, University Librarian from 1822 to 1845 when he resigned in poor health and left Cambridge for his parish in Lincolnshire. Romilly's deep attachment to him is shown in the long and elegant inscription that he wrote in a copy of the *Graduati Cantabrigienses* given to Lodge in 1846 'in testimonium Amicitiae perpetuae'; see *Notes and Queries* 23 February 1929, p. 134. There are many references to Lodge in the earlier diaries, and an account of his work is given in McKitterick, pp. 445, 456-61.

[16] A meeting of the Senate called by the Vice-Chancellor in the Senate House once a fortnight in term to transact routine business, and especially to consider and vote on Graces (see 13 February 1849). There were also Statutable Congregations for such matters as the conferring of degrees and electing officers. See *Cambridge University Calendar* 1848 pp. 2-3.

[17] Members of the university of royal descent, having been 'examined and approved of', were entitled to proceed straight to the M.A. degree as long as they were also 'Honourable' or were the eldest sons of such men as young Barrington was. See *Cambridge University Calendar* 1848, p. 32. Since 1791 it had been necessary to present written pedigrees for inspection.

[18] i.e. George Thomas Romilly, his nephew and heir.

*Th. 17.* Arranged with Mr Fawcett to take No 3. Scrope Terrace for 3 years from Ladyday, paying £82 rent, & £4 annual for fixtures . . . Read loud Mrs Fry.

*Sun. 20.* . . . Tonight I finished the life of Mrs Fry: – her afflictions from domestic losses come upon her most severely in her latter days. – I am impressed with the deepest admiration of her piety & her energy . . . I did not know that she had visited Denmark, as well as Holland, Belgium, Prussia, etc etc. & she had had interviews with all the Sovereigns.

*Mon. 21.* . . . Tonight at the Philosophical Whewell said (in a Lecture on the Tides) 'I have received communications concerning the Mediterranean, – but I wish it to be understood that I will have nothing to do with *small seas*'.[19] As he is an expectant of the vacant Bishopric this caused a titter.[20]

*Wed. 23.* We are alas! going to lose Betsy: she is engaged to marry James Spink, brother to the lad who broke open her money-box. He is rather delicate, is 6 years younger than she is, & has the unhealthy employment of a painter: – he paints the carriages at Stratford Station. She fell in with him at Kings Chapel lately: he had come to Cambridge for a holiday: instead of minding the service he seized the opportunity of making love, – to which she willingly inclined. Indeed she has been long bent on catching some one. I wrote to Spink's present & late employers to learn his character . . .

*Th. 24.* Great excitement at Paris from the king having forbidden the Reform Banquet of last Tuesday.[21] – Congregation to complete the LLD degree of Thomas Fardell. – Asked by Sedgwick to dinner to meet the handsome Miss Pellews [sic]: his note was very characteristic 'you must come: make up to Miss Pellew: & if she says 'I will' you'll be so excited that the hair will grow on your bald pate'. – I could not have this grand excitement, being engaged to the Tookes.

*Sat. 26.* In much anxiety about Frank & George: – wrote to George sending him £10. Letters from G.B.A. & Edward Allen . . . Edward's was an account of his proceedings since his marriage. He was married on Wednesday & brought his bride to Shrewsbury on Saturday evening without having given notice at his

---

[19] The Cambridge Philosophical Society was established in 1819 – Romilly being a founder life-member on payment of ten guineas – and incorporated by royal charter in 1832 to promote and communicate scientific inquiries. Prince Albert was patron and the society was open to graduates by election for an annual subscription of a guinea, which entitled them to the use of a growing library and collections and attendance at evening meetings, held fortnightly in Full Term at its rooms in All Saints Passage. Its many honorary members in 1848 included Audubon, Faraday, von Humboldt, Buckland, Brewster, Hooker, Murchison, and Richard Owen.

[20] i.e. of Chester which had become vacant on 17 February when J.B. Sumner was nominated Archbishop of Canterbury.

[21] After a harsh winter and general economic misery in France Louis Philippe and his chief ministers were more unpopular than they thought. The opposition reform banquet in Paris had been called off, but when on 23 February in a confused mêlée a procession of demonstrators was fired on by troops events moved quickly. The king vacillated and then abdicated in favour of his young grandson, whose claim was rejected by the chamber of deputies. From the ensuing brief and fairly bloodless anarchy a self-appointed republican government emerged. It was the object of good will and hope, but totally unprepared to address the economic decline that had been evident in France for many years. Much has been written about this year of European revolutions; for the general reader R. Postgate's *Story of a Year: 1848* (1955) provides a useful introduction to public events at home and abroad.

lodgings that he was bringing home a wife: so tea was set out for *one*. He passed his wedding night at the Euston Railway: & then made a 2 days tour: the Saturday night he & his wife travelled *outside* the mail! . . . She has a most strange husband! . . .

*Mon. 28.* Declined dining with dismal Jemmy to meet a party of Ladies. – To my delight I had a Letter from Frank saying that he had kept at home & suffered nothing but the breaking of some panes of glass: he is separated from George by numberless barricades & knew nothing about him. – This revolution is marvellous for the facility with which it has been executed: the royal carriages, throne, etc burnt: the Tuileries plundered, a few hundred lives lost; – & now every thing is quiet: the Royal Family out of Paris; a democracy established. Read loud Cowley's discourse on O. Cromwell's Government[22] . . . Also read loud Mill's letter to 'the blessed Benjamin' (his son-in-law B. Webb) in attack of Hampden: it is very dry[23] . . .

*Th. 2 March.* Carus's birthday. – Lucy sent him a lovely pair of slippers (the embroidery of our niece Sophie) (made up by Bentley his shoemaker). She endeavoured to mystify him by using red wax, a seal with the letter E, an inscription in a feigned hand, & a direction by Betsy . . . she then got me to print 8 beautiful lines from Dryden's description of a Good Parson . . . The lines from Dryden were

He warn'd the Sinner with becoming zeal,
But on eternal Mercy loved to dwell.
He taught the Gospel rather than the Law;
And forc'd himself to drive, but lov'd to draw.

———

To threats the stubborn sinner oft is hard:
Wrapt in his crimes, against the storm prepar'd:
But when the milder beams of mercy play.
He melts & *throws his cumbrous cloke away.*

. . .

*Sat. 4.* . . . Letter at last from G.T.R. He is quite well but has been very busy in assisting his intended (Meg Merriless) & her Parents in quitting Paris, wch they have done successfully. – I should think he would soon follow . . . Louis Philippe (with his huge whiskers shaved off) & his Queen etc, & Guizot are all happily landed in England . . .

*Mon. 6.* . . . Had my teeth stopped by Jones: an oldish man & an undergraduate were both going to have a tooth out under chloroform.[24] I told the

---

[22]  Abraham Cowley the poet was ejected from his fellowship at Trinity during the civil war for his royalist sympathies and forced abroad. He wrote a congratulatory piece on the Restoration and in 1661 this prose discourse on Cromwell's government. Its style was much admired by, for instance, Bishop Hurd and Hazlitt.

[23]  i.e. *A Letter to a Clergyman in London on the Theological Character of Dr Hampden's Bampton Lectures* (1848). Webb was a curate at St Pancras.

[24]  Ether, hailed as a new wonder-drug only months before, was now superseded by 'an agent more readily used, more efficacious, less troublesome, less disagreeable' (*Annual Register* 1847, p. 148). According to the *Chronicle* of 4 March 1848 three amputations had been done at

youngster that I thought it unworthy of any person who called himself a man to fear a momentary pain like that of drawing a tooth: – this I said before he let the cat out of the bag that he was one of those cowards. – Whist at Skrine's.

*Wed. 8.* . . . To my great joy Dr Graham[25] is appointed Bishop of Chester: – wrote to congratulate him.

Unhappily there has been a Chartist Riot at Glasgow, & a turbulent gathering in London (beginning in an announced meeting (to declaim against Income Tax) called in Trafalgar Square by Mr Cochrane (the defeated at Westminster) & forbidden by authority: – Mr Cochrane kept away & 2 or 3 other demagogues harangued the blackguards, who eventually broke a great no of windows, robbed many bakers' shops & others, & got some of their heads broken by the Police.[26] – At night read loud Walter Scotts Woodstock.

*Sat. 11.* . . . Letter from G.T.R. saying that his intended's Father & Mother are going to live in Russia (with a brother of the Gent's), & that he George means to marry forthwith, as the alternative for Miss M. is either to become a Governess or his wife.

*Mon. 13.* Wrote to G.T.R. & Lodge. – Sent a 2d £5 to the Devonport British Female Orphan Asylum.[27] The Secretary (Lorenzo Tripe) wrote to offer to transfer £5 of the last £10 Lucy sent to my name, adding it to the £5 I sent the other day & so making me a Life Governor. I declined this jesuitical dressing myself up in borrowed plumes & sent (as above) a 2d £5 . . . North has very wisely declined a curacy in a difficult parish where Baron Rothschilds hunting establishment has dispossessed many of the poorer sort . . . Whist Club at my rooms: Skrine was in Belgium: the rest present, also Marquis & Captain Doria, V.C., Arlett, Bateson, Power (Pembroke) . . . staid till horridly late, viz. past 2.

*Tu. 14.* Dined with Lady Cotton:[28] – Sedgwick & Frere went over with me: Sedgwick was in a very growling humour from suppressed Gout & found fault with the fly, the horses & driver, & at last confessed that he was more like a fiend than a man & burst out laughing . . . Our horses were very queer, & there was so much difficulty in making them start from Madingley that I thought we should have to walk back . . .

*Sun. 19.* A very tolerable day. – Sermons for Addenbrooke's Hospital in all the Churches but Trinity.[29] Lucy went to hear Carus at Trinity where he

Addenbrooke's under 'the wonderful influence of Chloroform' without the patients being conscious of what was going on.

[25] Master of Christ's College who resigned on receiving this preferment.

[26] Chartism in Cambridge was never strong, although local magistrates were well prepared. A proposed meeting in the town on 6 April attracted a few listeners animated more by curiosity than strong convictions and it became a farce when no speaker appeared. The Chartist who took signatures for his petition on Market Hill chiefly attracted impudent boys. See E. Porter, *Victorian Cambridge: Josiah Chater's Diaries* (1975), pp. 28-9.

[27] John Romilly, the Whig politician, was M.P. for the town and his cousins subscribed to charities there.

[28] For many years Romilly had been a guest at Madingley Hall, the seat of the Cottons, presided over by the amiable widowed mother of the scapegrace baronet Sir St Vincent. In return he regularly supplied books borrowed from the University Library for the family who were voracious readers.

[29] The hospital had been opened in 1766 from a bequest of John Addenbrooke, M.D., sometime fellow of St Catharine's who died in 1719. It was one of the first voluntary hospitals for the poor

preached a dull dry sermon from John. VI. 51. .3 (2d Lesson) against Transubstantiation. She bolted out of the Church as fast as she could & came into Great St Andrews where she heard the last 10' of Sedgwicks Addenbrookes Sermon. I heard the whole of it, wch lasted 50 minutes . . . he added in extempore all the Statistics about the Cambridge Hospital, & described the blessed effect of chloroform & gave an account of 2 severe operations under its influence wch he had seen. – Parts of his sermon were very eloquently written, but I thought it far too long: & from the tenderness of his heart he almost broke down several times: – that is very distressing . . . In the Evening the grand total eclipse of the moon was invisible except quite at the beginning: thick clouds & rain. The Judges dined in Hall: but I declined being of the party[30] . . .

*Tu. 21.* . . . Frank arrived today by the 2 o'clock (in Cambridge) train: he was looking well & in good spirits: he wears a little black velvet scull-cap (called a Calotte) to hide his baldness, & has his back hair long: – he looks very much like a French Abbé . . . George (he informs us) has determined to go back again to Paris to settle every thing there & means to be married about the 11th April . . .

*Sun. 26.* . . . Miss Kelty's parcel contained a present of her Selection called 'Facts & Failings' (published in 1841), & also several copies of 2 little Tracts of hers called 'Crooked Paths & Early Training': I read them both with interest & wrote today to thank her: the story of 'Crooked Paths' is one of a young woman who joined religious society (without being really religious) & pretended to having received the addresses of a distinguished religious character: – she is exposed & dies penitent & broken-hearted: – founded on truth . . . In the Evening Frank read loud Bossuet's famous oraison funébre on the Princess Henrietta (dr of Charles 1. & wife of Philip the brother of Louis XIII): it is a glorious piece of eloquence: the description of her death 'Madame se meurt, Madame est morte' is very striking.

*Wed. 29.* All the morning indexing & arranging papers concerning St Mary's. – Mrs Scholefield called on Lucy today to see the Piano, which she accepted thankfully for the Park-house Establishment.[31] – Frank, Lucy & I went (after dinner) to Ling the Tuner, & directed him to expunge the age-betraying

outside London. It was patronised by worthies of the town, county, and university and depended entirely on subscriptions, bequests, fund-raising events such as balls and flower-shows, and church collections like those mentioned here. Romilly was one of many governors who paid a high subscription and so had the right to recommend patients and elect the professional staff. Addenbrooke's was always short of funds and its administrators in 1848 were troubled by an increasing number of patients admitted after accidents in the building and running of the new railways. The census of March 1851 was to show (besides a matron, house surgeon, and their staff of twenty-two), some 84 patients of whom a third were male agricultural labourers. See Arthur Rook et al., *The History of Addenbrooke's Hospital* (1991).

[30] By long tradition the Judges of Assize in Cambridge stayed at the Lodge in Trinity where their arrival and departure were attended with some ceremony. They did not always remember that they were guests and Whewell was not one to forget it. But serious trouble was still to come. See D.A. Winstanley, *Later Victorian Cambridge* (1947), chapter 2.

[31] The Institution for Training Young Females to fill situations as domestic servants. Advertisements in the local press of 'genteel and airy apartments' at Park Side in Park House for ladies and families wanting domestic comfort 'without the trouble and expense of servants', show on whom the young females were to practise during their two-year course.

date of 1796 wch accompanies Broadwood's name on the instrument. – rather jesuitical! – Letter from Edward Romilly to tell me of John's appointment as Solicitor General . . . In the Evening Frank and I dined in Hall, but did not *combine*. In the Evening he read loud . . . also the beginning of the new Novel 'Jane Eyre' by Currer Bell; – very clever. – We also played 3 games of chess . . .

*Mon. 10 April* . . . Today was the day appointed for a grand Chartist meeting on Kennington common to march in procession with their petition to Westminster Hall. By the wise precautions of Government the Chartist leaders were completely intimidated; not more than 15,000 (instead of the threatened 200,000) met on Kennington Common. – The mob was not allowed to cross any of the bridges in procession: Feargus O'Connor (the leader of the Chartists) recommended peacefully dispersing after a solemn act of devotion to God. – And so ended peaceably this Chartist demonstration which had created the greatest alarm: – the Queen (who had been confined only 3 weeks), went to the Isle of Wight last Saturday.

*Tu. 11.* F. & I to Town by the 8.17 train: we breakfasted at the Station. – We reached St Botolphs Church Aldgate about 11 & found G.T.R. already arrived with his friend Mr. le Vicomte de Boinville . . . he is a very gentlemanlike well-informed man who speaks English perfectly (having been at School in England & lived there many years) . . . Very punctually at 11 arrived the Bride with her Father & Mother & 2 bridesmaids: she was dressed very handsomely in white satin, had orange flowers in her hair & a long white veil, & carried a beautiful bouquet. She is very short, rather plump, with a good colour, a very large mouth & features which will become coarse: she has pretty brown hair & a very goodhumoured expression in a quiet way: she is not yet 18! Her Mother is a fine-looking woman: the father dull & stupid . . . The marriage went off very well: no crying. G.B. Allen & wife were among the Company. We all breakfasted with Mr & Mrs Mirrielees at no 3 America Square . . . a very handsome breakfast: – I gave the bride's health & afterwards that of the Bridesmaids . . . Denning gave George's health. – Mr de Boinville made a short & clever speech in honour of the Romilly name. – George & his bride afterwards went to Cambridge by 2.30 train: – they were to go on the next day to Peterboro etc. – G.B.A. & wife took Frank & me in their conveyance to the Bank: I was much pleased by this opportunity of seeing it in a state of military preparation, protected by sandbags on the battlements & at the windows . . .

*Wed. 12.* The great Chartist Petition wch was declared by Feargus O'Connor to have 5½ million signatures turns out to have less than 2 millions: a very large no are female signatures, the same name is signed repeatedly, the Duke of Wellington's 19 times, Victoria Rex once, flash names (such as Pugnose, etc) over & over again: – real signatures very little more than a million . . .

*Sun. 30.* Lucy better: – she came to Church, but did not venture to visit her paupers – (one of whom, Foulkes, is very ill indeed: – Carus preached one of his typical sermons . . . from 1 Joh. 5. 6 . . . we heard it 4 years ago. – However he was very energetic, & worked away famously & called us 'dear friends' 3 times.

*Mon. 1 May.* . . . Carus sent Lucy a copy of the Extract from Milton (Par. Lost. B 4 . L. 252) wch he set to be translated into Latin Verse. He sent also a note wch I think excellent.

10

"My dear Miss Romilly T.C. May 1/48

"Here's a beautiful account of the *earthly* Paradise – but it is only in Poetry (true poetry indeed) – & remember it is Paradise *Lost.* – I sometimes speak to you of the *heavenly* Paradise – & in very humble *proze* – but it is a glorious reality – & one I trust we shall enter upon as *gained.* Ever yr affect W.C."

... Dinèd at the V.C's at the Woodward audit:[32] an agreeable novelty, a large party of ladies at the dinner, viz Mrs French & drs, Mrs Whewell & sister ...

*Th. 4.* ... Drank tea at The Lodge to settle the Scholarships: – Mrs Temple (Mrs Whewell's sister) was there & her 2 little girls: the eldest (about 9) made a most active & charming page, helping every body. We elected 8 scholars from the 3rd year & 5 from the 2d ... of my other acquaintance Hort was the only one who did well: he must come in next time ...

*Sat. 6.* Began reading Archbishop Hare's life of Sterling: – think it a very able piece of Biography: – the religious world are indignant at his publishing the memoirs of so sceptical a person: – Sterling was his Curate at Herstmonceux for a few months. The painting No 3 Scroope Terrace begun today ...

*Wed. 10.* Cong. – 2 BD, 9 AM, 19 AB, 1 incorporated AB, 1 eundem.[33] – Address to the Q. past; also letter of Congratulation to A. of Canterbury ... Dinner to Mrs Ouvry & 2 drs, Mrs John Ouvry, Fred. Ouvry, J.N.O. North, Tooke, Roget, Jeddere-Fisher, Carus & the 3 Tutors ... Beautiful bouquets with lace-like painted paper for the 4 Ladies. Went off capitally.

*Fri. 12.* ... Dined at Magdalene lodge ... It was a very agreeable party for I sat between Lady Cotton & Miss Neville ... and was close to the Host, so I heard all his Court Anecdotes:[34]– one I thought curious: – the Duke & Ds of Montpensier called on the Queen (without having sent notice) the day before they left England for Madrid: – the Q. was at Luncheon & sent down word that when she had finished she would receive them: in the mean time she sent off a messenger to fetch Lord Palmerston: the Queen then (being instructed by him to receive the D. & Dss as ordinary visiters) went to receive them, – but they had taken their departure 10 minutes before in high dudgeon, the Duchess with her handkf to her eyes. ...

*Sat. 13.* ... Took a walk with Lucy in the Evening to deposit a pair of carpet shoes where they might be picked up by a poor person.

[32] John Woodward (d. 1728) established a chair of geology and bequeathed the nucleus of a fossil museum which since 1841 had been housed under the new wing of the University Library. An account of it appeared in the annual *Cambridge University Calendar* and was revised from time to time. The founder's will required the college heads to form a board of auditors to whom every May 'two discreet and careful persons' were to report on the condition of the collection and be paid £5 for their trouble. See *Endowments,* pp. 196-202.

[33] i.e. 2 Bachelors of Divinity, 9 Masters of Arts, 19 Bachelors of Arts, and 1 incorporated and 1 ad eundem degree. The last two refer to admission to degrees awarded already by Oxford or Dublin without further examination. The distinction between them was that an ad eundem ('to the same degree') man was not a member of a Cambridge college. See H. Gunning, *Ceremonies of the University of Cambridge* (1828), pp. 217-18.

[34] The Master of Magdalene had been a chaplain to the Queen for many years and Dean of Windsor since 1846.

*Tu. 16.* . . . Revised Kingsley's Proctorial accounts[35] . . . I went to Kingsley's rooms to look over a portfolio of Turner's Watercolours: some I admired very much, but many I thought of extravagant unnatural colouring. Kingsley is an idolater of Turner. The subjects were from W. Scotts Novels, & scenery of Palestine. – A picture of the Black Dwarf in moonlight I thought the absurdest thing I ever saw.

*Fri. 19.* Dined at 'The Family' at Warters[36] . . . Paget went away for 1½ hour to see the Fever patients in the Hospital: – there is a sad quantity of Fever at present: – 11 cases from Trumpington, – all occasioned by the pestilential effluvia of an open drain!

*Sun. 21.* Bishop of Cashel preached for the Irish Society[37] . . . his action was abundant, but not pleasing: he held his handk. in one hand, & spread out the other with all the fingers separate (as if they had quarrelled). He was abundantly in earnest & I was therefore pleased with the sermon . . .

*Mon. 22.* Declined dining at Magdalene Lodge both today & tomorrow. – Went into the Fitzwilliam; the whole of the Pictures & most of the books are now transferred[38] . . .

*Wed. 24.* Lucy took a superb Teacaddy as a present to her poor protégée (M.A. Tyler) who is in a decline: – it cost her 20/: & she has made it a most elegant cover beautiful to behold. – Grand excitement with a pig in our garden, who liked his quarters so well that no driving of his owners would prevail on him to go: at last they carried him, he making melody the whole time . . . Mrs Willis gave me a pamphlet of Professor Smyths, called 'Thoughts for the Common People': if written (as I am told) since 10th April a remarkable work for a man who has had a paralytic attack at 80 . . .

*Sun. 28.* Lucy and I went separately first to the Baptist Chapel to hear the venerable M[r] Jay . . . It was a very admirable effort of Mr Jay's: His text was Exod. XV. 27 "they found 12 wells & 70 palms". I never heard a sermon so full of quotations & of anecdotes . . . The Sermon was above an hour: but the venerable old man did not seem exhausted.

*Mon. 29.* . . . Called on Mrs Ashton to be introduced to her venerable Father Mr Jay[39] . . . He has been a Minister for 60 years & is now in his 80th year: –

[35] Both Proctors (see 17 June 1848) kept accounts during their year of office. Disbursements were small, for example, £4 each for their night-walking, but, as they collected several hundred pounds in fees, the college of the Senior Proctor entered into a bond with the university against any irregularity.

[36] A select but not exclusively academic dining club of which Romilly had been a member since 1834. See S.C. Roberts, *The Family* (1963).

[37] Its object was to disseminate copies of the scriptures in their own language among the Irish. The bishop's two sermons raised £47.

[38] Viscount Fitzwilliam of Trinity Hall, who died unmarried though not childless in 1816, had left the university his collections of books, paintings, etc. together with a vast (but not, it proved, vast enough) sum for the erection of a museum to house them. They were crammed into the old Perse School in Free School Lane, and the foundation stone of the present museum was not laid until 1837. Ten years later fitting up was still in progress though £90,000 had already been spent. See R. Willis and J.W. Clark, *The Architectural History of the University of Cambridge* (1886), III, 198-217.

[39] His sobriquet was 'the Prince of Preachers'. See *D.N.B.*

before he was 21 he had preached above 1000 sermons. Pitt is said to have pronounced him the most naturally eloquent man he had ever heard, & to have exclaimed 'what a number of votes he could get!' – He is an early riser & a great chopper of wood: he told me [he] had chopt a supply of dry wood that would last his maids for 3 years . . .

*Sat. 3 June* Meeting of V.M. & Seniors to arrange about the Examination: – the numbers are so large (366) that they cant all be accommodated in hall: we assigned 103 (viz. the 3d year) to the upper Lecture rooms.[40]

*Wed. 7.* . . . Dined with Warter in Magdalene Hall to meet T.B. Macaulay who is come down to inspect the Pepysian Library. – There was a party to do honor to him: he of course took the whole conversation into his own hands & was very amusing. . . .

*Sat. 10.* Seniority to arrange Fellowship. – Examination begins on 2d. Thompson & I begin with Greek. – The Latin day is assigned to Sedgwick & Rothman. . . .

*Sun. 11.* I preached in Chapel (for Sedgwick) a very fine sermon of Bp Andrews: I preached it 18 years ago in the same place[41] . . .

*Mon. 12.* . . . Today we gave an ad eundem to a Dr Symons of St John's Coll. Oxford: he is an interesting conversible man: he was chaplain in the Peninsular War, & buried Sir John Moore: he declares the funeral was not at midnight but at 8 in the morning[42] . . . Poor Watts (one of our Porters) today fell down in the Court & died almost instantly from an affection of the heart![43]

From 15-17 June Romilly spent a busy and enjoyable three days in London, the main purpose of which was to present a loyal Address to the Queen expressing affection, congratulation on the fidelity of Londoners during the recent threatened Chartist demonstrations and condolences on the death of the Princess Sophia, one of Victoria's three aunts living in England. On the fifteenth he bought rugs for his new house and in the evening sweltered at the Opera where Jenny Lind was admirable in Bellini's *La Sonnambula*. On the following morning he took the Address to Chester Square where the Vice Chancellor was staying, visited Frances Wilderspin and her employers and the Ouvrys and after dining at the Athenaeum was delighted by Haydn's *Seasons* at Exeter hall. He wasted no time on the morning of the seventeenth in going to the Royal Academy where apart from Landseer's portrait of his father he thought little of the Exhibition and less still of the old Masters exhibited in Pall Mall.

*Fri. 16.* Directly after breakfast to the V.C.'s (who is staying at his friend Mr Helps in Chester Sq: I took (at the V.C's request) the Address wch. the Chancellor wishes to see today . . .

[40] These were college examinations for undergraduates held in the middle of Easter Term. Those who attained first class in each year received a prize of books, and sizars also had awards of money, which must have been most important to them.

[41] He preached infrequently and, perhaps preferring quality to originality, often borrowed sermons from others, though that practice was becoming frowned upon. Lancelot Andrews (d. 1626), famed for patristic learning, had been Master of Pembroke College.

[42] Doubtless a correction to Charles Wolfe's line, 'We buried him darkly at dead of night'.

[43] He had been shifting luggage for an undergraduate. While Humphry, the medical man, gave the cause of death as heart disease the verdict of the inquest was death 'by visitation of God' (*Chronicle* 17 June).

13

*Addenbrooke Hospital, Cambridge*

*Fitzwilliam Museum, Cambridge*

Addenbrooke's Hospital and The Fitzwilliam Museum

*Sat. 17.* . . . At 2½ left the Burlington Hotel for St James Palace: I went in the same carriage with the V.C.[44] & 2 Bedells[45] (Gunning of course could not attend). The Deputation consisted of the V.C, Mr N. Grenville, Dr Webb, Dr French (these 4 kissed hands), Dr Lamb, Dr Tatham, Dr Philpott & Mr Worsley; Dr Broadley (deputy of Dr Maine) representative of Law; Dr Drosier representative of Medicine, the 2 Proctors (Baily & Williams); 2 Bedells & self. – The Speaker of the Commons, Marquis Camden, our 2 Members etc joined us in the Palace: – we had no Bishops: because the Convocation was today received by the Queen.[46] – Oxford also presented an Address. – The Convocation went up first; then Oxford; & Cambridge last: – the Dean of Windsor (Mr N. Grenville) thought this a wrong arrangement & that the Cambridge Chancellor (Prince Albert) should have claimed precedence for his University over the Oxf. Chr (the Duke of Wellington): – I think he acted most wisely in allowing the customary precedence to Oxford. – Our address was not very numerously attended: – the conduct of those present was very decorous, – no noise, little pushing. The Q. looked very well in mourning, & the Prince looked very handsome.[47] The Q. read her answer (wch was a very gracious one) most sweetly. I stood by the Prince & held the Address, wch he read with a very tolerable accent. After the Queen's answer I (as usual) presented the Deputation: – I ought at the end to have been myself presented to the Q. by the Prince or the V.C., but it happened to be omitted. On returning to the Hotel I (as on former occasions) wrote an account to the Home Office . . .

*Fri. 23.* The oil-cloth (to match the turkey carpet) arrived yesterday & was laid down. Proclaimed Midsummer Fair.[48] Lucy gave away all manner of spoils

[44] i.e. Robert Phelps, Master of Sidney Sussex. The Vice-Chancellor was elected each November from among the seventeen heads of houses. Although there were occasional upsets such 'elections' were to confirm what had been arranged long before, largely on the basis of rotation.

[45] i.e. George Leapingwell and William Hopkins. Gunning who had been an Esquire Bedell since 1789 was in poor health after a fall the previous year. These officers preceded the Vice-Chancellor on public occasions bearing silver maces, and performed other duties such as collecting fines from members of the university. See *Cambridge University Calendar* 1848, p. 6, and H.P. Stokes, *The Esquire Bedells* (1911). Writing to Philip Bliss, the Oxford Registrar, on 4 March 1852 Romilly explained that Cambridge had three Esquire Bedells, which it is proposed to reduce to two, and one Yeoman Bedell. They 'with us mix in the best society of the place... The Yeoman Bedell is merely a servant: his salary is worth from 50 to £60 a year I think.' It is to the advantage of the two universities 'to know every detail of each others customs & internal management'. (British Library, Add MS 34578 f. 550).

[46] Two Proctors or 'peace officers', chosen annually from the colleges by cycle, were the disciplinary arm of the university, with a special concern for searching houses of ill-repute and arresting suspected women of loose character, preferably before they led young men astray. For their other duties in connexion with voting and congregations see the *Cambridge University Calendar* 1848, p. 5. Mr Speaker was Charles Shaw Lefevre of Trinity. From 1604 Cambridge sent two Members to the House of Commons after election by the Senate; since 1837 these had been C.E. Law and H. Goulbourn, members of Trinity, and Camden was presumably present as his father had been Chancellor of the University from 1834 to 1840.

[47] The royal family were mourning Victoria's unmarried aunt Sophia who died on 27 May.

[48] Midsummer Fair, or 'Pot Fair', as it was familiarly called from the quantity of earthenware once sold, was held in June on Midsummer Common, when the Vice-Chancellor and his officers and the Mayor declared it open. The importance of the local fairs had diminished markedly in Romilly's lifetime and he was to say they were 'going to the dogs' (23 June 1853).

from our old house, a chest of drawers, heaps of books, etc. etc to W. How. – She & I worked away very strenuously all day at the removal of our goods . . .

*Sat. 24.* . . . Our new abode looks very comfortable although the staircase & hall are still bare, & the bedrooms are not brought into order: – my bedroom is the grandest I ever slept in: it is the back drawing-room: it has a beautiful paper: so indeed has every room[49] . . . I have reduced Barkers salary from £4 a quarter to £1 as we have little or no Garden: he told Lucy that I had broken his heart, – so I gave him coat, waistcoat & trowsers, all good. – I have given him what the gardener of the neighbouring gardens receives. – There have been awful doings at Paris from an insurrection of the 100,000 workmen: they threw up barricades: & there have been most bloody fights between them & the soldiers & the garde nationale![50]

*Tu. 27.* Lucy out before breakfast to her protégée Mrs How. Lucy has procured with much exertion a place for Caroline How: she was to go to a certain Miss Mansfield who took lodgers warranted respectable, – very highly so: these lodgers were a Mr & Mrs Brewster: the husband is a son of B. the Chemist & the wife one of the pretty flaunting drs of Wright the watchmaker: they were married about 5 weeks ago: & the lady is just brought to bed! – Lucy will not allow C.H. to wait on such people, & she is therefore to come to our house this Evening. – Lucy fitted up the Attic for Car. How, most wisely abandoning the project of putting her in the dressing room next herself . . .

*Sat. 1 July.* A very poor day indeed. – 1 MD, 1 BD, 1 LLB, 40 MA, 2 eundem. – Dined in hall: & then sat up in state fee-catching till 9½: caught only 15.[51]

*Mon. 3.* Considerable rush this morning: – a large proportion had come by this mornings or last nights trains: 1 DD, 2 MD, 1 LLB, 103 BA: so that the 2 days together are not amiss . . .

*Mon. 10.* . . . The Gilt cornices, & the muslin curtains & the gold beading put up in the drawing room: they look capitally . . .

*Tu. 11.* Worked all the morning till 3 o'clock in my office with Edleston, hunting out matters about Newton & his contemporaries . . . Bought 2 pretty Hall-chairs (2d hand) for the new house . . .

*Fri. 14.* Letter from a Captain Renaud asking particulars about his g. g. grandfather who died in Cambr where he had been fencing master for 50 years: he came over from Provence . . . Wrote to Capt. Renaud. . . . An awful storm of

---

[49] Romilly had lived in Hills Road since 1837 when his sisters came from Dulwich to live with him, but after Margaret's death he and Lucy rented a large newish house in Scroope Terrace on the edge of town.

[50] Four months of republican government had brought little but decrees and such impractical schemes as national workshops, while for the working people of Paris life was no better. Insurrection began and barricades went up. Cavaignac, the minister for war, used to dealing with native colonials, bided his time and then responded with massive force and indiscriminate carnage that left a legacy of class bitterness and fear for a generation. See R. Price, *1848 in France* (1975), 107-17, a collection of primary sources that covers the period until 1852.

[51] An important part of the Registrary's income came from the many small fees he exacted one by one at matriculation and admission to degrees. Romilly had of course inherited private means and also received dividends, which varied from year to year, from Trinity.

Thunder & Lightning: it beat down Mr Luke Jones' chimney: but nobody pitied him, as his harshness has made his 2d wife run away.

*Sat. 15.* I believe the man who wrote so many letters about the Townley Family . . . is a shaberoon: – he has never paid me the Guinea wch I charged, nor has he answered my letter reminding him of the omission. Dined at the V. Chrs to eat Venison given him by Prince Albert: it was a very snug little party of 6 . . .

*Sun. 16.* . . . Poor Lucy was made nearly mad by hearing Samuel King Webster preach at St Benets: she went there to hear our neighbour (Pullen) & found this insufferable substitute: – he preached or rather prosed upon 'Blessed is the man to whom the L. hath not imputed sin' L. thought a great deal of sin was to be imputed to him: – she was very near bolting.

*Th. 20.* . . . Went over to Audley End[52] to a grand cricket match 'Audley End' against 'Marylebone' . . . It was an unfavorable day with occasional violent showers of rain wch drove the cricketers to their tents & the spectators into the house. Lady Braybrooke had stationed a band in the Gallery wch was a great treat to us. – This match was to last 2 days: – it was won by Audley End. – The lunch was set out for 84 & looked very pretty . . . Ficklin & Capt Anderson & I returned to Cambr. by the 4½ train . . .

On 24 July Romilly travelled second class to Wisbech reading George Sands' *Haunted Marsh* whilst his companions, being Drovers, 'talked about the bullocks & the pigs in trucks behind'. He stayed with his friend Henry Fardell, the Vicar of Wisbech, and his family. They visited the girls school 'an ugly set', and Romilly, before eating a 'capital dinner served up in grand stile', visited the Cemetery where the Chapel, begun in 1843, was now finished. There he was 'amused with an Epitaph

So very suddenly I fell
My neighbours wonder'd at my Knell,
Surprised that I should be no more
The Man they'd seen the day before
I learned afterwards that this man had hanged himself'.

On the twenty-fifth he was sad to see that a sportsman had accidentally fired a very large number of shot through the principal group of figures in the 'grand painted glass East Window' of Upwell Church. 'Gale Townley bears it with extraordinary philosophy'.

*Fri. 28.* Lucy's birthday: gave her 10/- Gave 2/6 to Dosia's Mother,[53] & 2/6 to poor Betsy Barker who is desperately ill. Lucy was very active in her benevolence on this her birthday: she went to the Hospital (tho it was shut-up day) to see poor M.A. Tyler (who is no better), also to see Betsy Barker, also to Mrs Gilmour . . . & lastly she went to Mrs Newlands school (to see about Hannah Smyth whom she has put there), where she staid above an hour hearing

[52]  Lord Braybrooke's mansion near Saffron Walden where the diarist had long been a visitor, often staying for several days and acting as chaplain to the household. Lady Braybrooke was distantly related to him by marriage.
[53]  Theodosia Russell had come to the family in 1845 as a young cook when the diarist recorded 'she has a fine complexion & is very good-looking: she is short & very plump: – seems dull & slow' (*Romilly 1842-47*, p. 143).

the children sing. – She made me (against the grain) dine in hall: – I was Vicemaster . . . I put into Latin for the Master the titles & dignities of Lords Macclesfield, Cottenham, etc etc – worthies of Trinity, whose arms are to be put up in the painted glass in our Hall[54] . . .

*Wed. 2 August.* . . . Dined at Madingley at 6½: went over by myself, but brought back Paget. – A very agreeable party: but Lady Cotton was much mortified at Sir St Vincent's absence: – he is said to have lost frightfully at the Goodwood Races.[55] The party consisted of Lady & Miss Cotton, Mr Yorke, Bishop of Chester & Mrs Graham, V.C. & Mrs Phelps, Mr & Mrs George Jenyns & daughter (of Bottisham Hall), Mr & Mrs Gambier (who live with the Jenyns), & myself. Old Prebendary Jenyns (to the astonishment & indignation of the family) died many thousands (they say 40) in debt; so the Squire of Bottisham has very little to live on, & therefore the Gambiers (who are very rich) live with him, & for house-room keep up the establishment . . .

*Sat. 5.* Went to our roundabout[56] & gathered a most choice nosegay of Geraniums & Roses for Lucy to give Carus who is just returned from his month's holiday. – Today much delighted at having an autograph note from dear Lodge: it was very short, but I had not seen his handwriting for a very long while.

On 14 August Romilly, again in London, took Hoppner's picture of Lady Romilly to her son Edward in Stratton Street. At the grand wedding breakfast after the marriage of Jessy Koe on the following day he met 'Sir Charles Napier . . . the hero of Scinde: he is a delightful person full of conversation: he gave the health of the bride & bridegroom, & I made a eulogy of the Koe family & of the bride in particular'.

Five days later our diarist set out on the longest of his vacation travels. He stayed a night with Joseph Blakesley, Fellow of Trinity and Vicar of Ware, and was amused by the bashfulness of his curate who after dinner 'backed out of the room as if he had been in presence of his Bishop'. In York, despite a heavy cold and atrocious weather, he enjoyed five days with his old friend Archbishop Musgrave at Bishopthorpe where no less than 20 indoor servants attended morning prayers in the dining-room. He explored York for the first time and was especially delighted by Bishopthorpe Church where 'The Archbishop's pew is a very large one, round 3 sides of wch his household sits & his own chair occupies the middle of the 4th . . . The singing at this little Church is excellent, tho they have no organ, nor any instrument: the Clerk has a fine bass voice & the boys have been very well taught'. The weather at last relenting for Romilly's journey to Halifax, he spent two nights there with Archdeacon Musgrave, the younger brother of the Archbishop. After lunch they 'went for a walk till 6 o'clock, uphill downdale thro a most lovely country, sadly disfigured however with manufactories'. On 30 August he left

[54] For a list of heraldic glass added in the hall since the late eighteenth century see Royal Commission on Historic Monuments, *City of Cambridge* (1959), II, 227-8. Many additions had been made about 1830 but few since then.

[55] He had been helplessly addicted to gambling from his youth and had run through a large fortune. By this time his distraught but fond mother and sisters were largely funding his extravagances and his Madingley property was mortgaged. The Cotton papers in the Cambridgeshire Record Office show vividly the plight of the family and St Vincent's doomed attempts to reform. See 9 November 1855, 28 February 1857, and 2 November 1859.

[56] i.e. the Fellows' garden with its circuitous paths.

Halifax together with the Archdeacon & his wife & two maids. They 'got down at Wakefield where they had to give evidence against a young man whom they had employed to pay the milk-bills: he kept the money & forged receipts: he affected to be very pious, was very regular at Church, & used to carry home provisions (from the Vicarage) on Saturday that he might have a cold dinner on Sunday'. In London again he 'bought presents for Lucy (viz. all manner of knick-knacks in ivory, such as bodkin cases, eggs, lemons, pincushions etc), also presents for the maids (viz. Glass sugar basin & Milk jug for each) . . . Got to Cambridge at 2 & found Lucy (Thank God) pretty well' . . .

*Mon. 4 September* . . . Lucy & I have been hunting for 2 days thro Cowper, Doddridge, Watts, the 1000-hymn-book, etc: to find the lines

"Let wordly minds the world pursue:
"They have no charms for me.
"I once admir'd its trifles too,
"Till Grace had set me free".

Upon speaking to Betsy about the lines she pronounced them to be in the Cottage-Hymn-book. They were familiar to her from a minister's pronouncing them . . .
"Let wauldly minds the wauld pursue".
*Tu. 5* A basket of peaches from G.T.R. with a Letter to his Aunt. – A German beggar called on me & got 5/- for a geological tour in I. of Wight. A present of peaches & nectarines from Mrs Newland (to whose dr Lucy has just given a pound for holiday instruction to H.R. Smyth) . . .
*Sun. 10.* . . . Carus gave us a very animated sermon from the 1st Lesson . . . I thought Carus described with too evident delight the fearful murder of Jezebel: I thought too he was somewhat needlessly violent against the Roman Catholics whom he denounced as idolaters. The object of his sermon seemed almost to be to encourage persecution of the Papists. – But in spite of these faults he thoroughly riveted one's attention[57] . . . I read Voltaire's Mahomet this Evening with great admiration.[58]
*Fri. 15.* . . . Betsy's goods today removed: 14 great packages: – she has well feathered her nest . . . Left Cambridge for Audley End by the 4.55 train. Found Lady B. better . . .
*Sat. 16.* Enacted Chaplain in a *black* neckcloth (as I had been told that Mr Wix would officiate & I had drest accordingly). – At 11 I went with Mr Neville to see his Roman Villa at Chesterford: – it was the 21st of last month that he discovered it: they have now made out 20 rooms: the foundations are very few inches below the surface: – the excavators yesterday dug up a painted tile

[57] Diatribes against Catholics were commonplace and increasing at a time of conversions, trouble in Ireland, and Irish immigration into Britain. Carus was doing what hundreds of Anglican priests and almost all the dissenting ministry did, thus contributing to the anti-papal frenzy of 1850. See 5 November 1850.
[58] A tragedy written against fanaticism in religion and first acted at Lille in 1741.

19

with a womans foot on it, also the mouth of a drinking vessel with an inscription CAMICIBIBUN wch probably is the mutilation of 'hic amici bibunt'[59] . . .

*Sun. 17.* . . . Sarah Foulkes had been (apparently) at death's door last week: – today she went to Church where she had not been for a very great length of time . . . Amusing letter from Grim describing a 10 days trip with his wife into Wales: – they travelled *outside* the mail in pouring rain! She had need be strong as well as good tempered & submissive to his very odd ways.

*Wed. 20.* Mr Peyton . . . told us a ludicrous story of a man who had 7 wigs which he wore in succession for 7 days & flattered himself that nobody knew he wore false hair: – the 7th wig was of longer hair than the 1st, so that he has been heard to say when wearing the 7th wig for its last day 'ah! I shall get my hair cut tomorrow!' He told another story about wigs: – at a crowded party a servant knocked off the wig of a peculiarly well-got-up gentleman (who wished to pass for a juvenile with a fine crop) & put it on the head of a fine old gentleman who always exhibited his bare poll & was proud of it . . .

*Sat. 23.* Poor Lucy has caught an awful cold which she ascribes to a great deal of excitement about a beautiful mangle which she bought about a year ago (for above £12) & *lent* to Mrs Melbourne. Mrs M. did not communicate a distress levied on her for rates etc till the very day of the sale of *every thing* in the house: so Lucy immediately went to Elliott Smith & found she was too late to take away the mangle (tho her own property) without she paid the amount of the distress, wch she accordingly did: £4.10.11! She is justly indignant at the stupidity of Mrs Melbourne in not apprising her in time. The mangle is now lumbering our house. – At night went on with H. More.[60]

*Tu. 26.* The wedding of Elisabeth Edwards & James Spink at Little St Mary's at 10 o'clock: Elisabeth is 34 & James 24: there is obviously no love on her side, & I think she has taken up with him because she could not get any of the people she tried to catch. – Lucy was kind enough to go to their wedding: she was very well dressed in colours. – Betsy & her 7 bridesmaids were all in white & 2 or 3 of them were very pretty . . . Lucy & I took in our fly Ann Spink & Hannah Smyth: – the rest came in 3 flies: – so we made a dash & created quite a sensation in the neighbourhood . . . Lucy & the 7 bridesmaids all signed as witnesses. – Lucy has taken little Betsy How to fill up Betsy's place till a new servant comes. We had the little girl up in the Evening & I read loud for her amusement & edification several of Miss Edgeworths stories in "Early

[59] Lord Braybrooke's heir, R.C. Neville, was a keen archaeologist and excavator in Essex and Cambridgeshire. He had been elected to the Society of Antiquaries in 1847 and published numerous short reports, and several books, on his activities. There had been a large Roman settlement at Great Chesterford, near the family seat at Audley End, which Neville was the first to study closely. See *D.N.B.*

[60] One of Romilly's favoured authors in earlier years, Hannah More came under the influence of the Evangelical movement at the end of the eighteenth century and in turn influenced its development with the publication of many works aimed at the moral and religious welfare of the working classes and their children. Cobbett called her the 'Old Bishop in Petticoats' but she remained widely respected long after her death in 1833.

Lessons".[61] – I dined today in hall. Attended the Commissary's Court at Sturbridge Fair.[62]

*Wed. 27.* Wrote to Madame F.R. (£26): also to Lady Braybrooke giving her an account of yesterdays wedding. – Called on Mrs Wilkins (the coachman's widow) & Mrs Helm's nurse to apologise for having taken no notice of them yesterday: – saw them both . . .

*Th. 28.* . . . Betsy & her husband came to take leave & also to take off all the remaining possessions of Betsy . . . Betsy confessed to Lucy that her wedding supper was for 30 persons, that the table was decked out with flowers, that the company played cards & didn't break up till 20' to 3!!! – a most foolish & expensive piece of dissipation . . .

*Mon. 2 October.* 1st day of Fellowship: Greek by Thompson & myself: he taking the morning & I the afternoon.[63] I dined in Hall. – Sedgwick is returned; but I would not go up into the Combination Room with him, but came home & read to Lucy 'St Ronan's well'.[64] – I looked over 'Thucydides' etc. today.

*Wed. 4.* 3d day of Fellowship – Mathematics by Master: Latin Prose by Carus. Bateson & I went over to dine at Madingley . . .

*Fri. 6.* Last day of Fellowship. – Greek Composition & Prose & Verse by Jeremie: also Fullal by Grote . . . Lucy today called at the servants Training School & offered the handsome mangle (wch she had to buy a 2d time at the 'distress' at Mrs Melbourns): – the Matron received it most thankfully & said 'it is just what we want: – it is quite Providential'! . . .

*Sat. 7.* Lucy does not take kindly to our new maid Sarah Wood: she detected her having 'conversation cards': she saw one of them, wch was 'do you like a tender squeeze of the hand?': – the pack was condemned as heretical and burnt . . .

*Sun. 8.* Lucy caught Sarah Wood in the act of putting a piece of crimson finery round her throat: she told her that such dress was forbidden in our service. – Today Carus preached an excellent sermon for the Schools of Trinity . . . To oblige Lucy I put in 10s/, & to oblige Carus she put in five pounds . . .

*Mon. 9.* My birthday: I am now 57 complete. I am (thank God) in my usual health & Lucy is also pretty well. – Wrote to Lodge. – Last night Sedgwick fell

---

[61] Maria Edgeworth the novelist (d. 1849), one of Romilly's staple authors whom he had met in London in 1843 and found she had 'all the animation of youth' (*Romilly 1842-47*, p. 87). She had been a friend of his aunt, Lady Romilly; see S.H. Romilly, *Romilly-Edgeworth Letters 1813-1818* (1936).

[62] Stourbridge Fair was opened on 18 September each year by the Vice-Chancellor with his officials and the mayor with his. Here the Commissary appointed by the Chancellor of the university held a court of civil law (as he also did in the university and at Midsummer Fair) for cases in which privileged parties and scholars under the degree of M.A. were involved.

[63] The College had been endowed for the support of sixty fellows, chosen from among the scholars, all but two of whom had eventually to go into priest's orders. The average length of tenure of a Trinity fellowship in the period *c.* 1825-50 was twelve years. There were usually five or six vacancies a year in the number caused by death or resignation or marriage and these were filled by examination. A Trinity B.A. had three chances to compete and success at the first attempt was uncommon. Meanwhile he might take pupils.

[64] By Walter Scott, Romilly's favourite secular author.

asleep over the metaphysical papers & at last was woke up by finding them in a blaze. – Drank tea at Trinity Lodge where (after some squabbling) we elected Norris & Wilbraham of 3d year, VanSittart & Evans of 2d year & Barry of 1st. – Norris has worked himself up to very good scholarship & pleased us all: he made a very clever humorous translation from Catullus into Hudibrastic verse, wch we all greatly admired & rewarded, tho he ought to have given Prose . . . Barry (far the cleverest man of the set) was 4th Wrangler & 2d medal: – he is son of the Archit. of the houses of Parliament . . .

*Tu. 10.* Chapel at 8.45 to declare the Election. – Congregation at 10 . . . Dined with the Master & the other Examiners: Grote was poorly & staid away: his place was supplied by Atkinson who is just returned from Moscow. – Much political conversation about O'Brien's trial.[65]

*Th. 12.* Beginning of the Praelections of the Candidates for the Hebrew Professorship[66] – The 7 Electors were the V.C., the B. of Chester, Dr Procter, Dr Whewell, Bateson (vicarious of Dr Tatham), J. Brown & myself. We met in the Law Schools Gallery at [blank]. Dr Mill lectured most learnedly & well on Jacob's prophecy . . . Donaldson lectured from 11 to 12 on Deborah's song: – his lecture was clever but arrogant & presumptuous in the extreme. Jarrett closed this day's lectures: he had from 12 to 1. His subject was 'the life & doctrine of Moses': he started with a Hebrew text, & produced a most childish sermon in very bald bad Latin . . . There was not one word of Hebrew criticism. – His manner was as childish as his matter . . .

*Sat. 14.* Present of Ribstone Pippins from Mrs Willis. – To my great joy Mill was elected H.P. – He had every vote except the Provosts who voted for Harvey. – I wrote to Allott, Sedgwick & Terrot to tell them the good news.

*Tu. 17.* Letter from Fre. Romilly[67] telling he is going to marry Lady Elis. Elliott (aged 28): she is sister to Lady John Russell . . . Wrote . . . also to 2 Editors of Pocketbooks sending them correct lists of University Officers etc. Lucy took Hannah Smyth on the agreeable journey of buying her new clothes . . .

*Mon. 23.* . . . Horrid wet day! Called on Miss Page. She told me anecdotes about Mr Simeon: somebody spoke to Mr S. about the love of Angels: – he said 'Don't talk to me of the love of angels: give me the love of a dog!' . . . Her other story was of an interview wch she herself had with him. – 'I'm very glad to see you & hope you will give me something towards the Barnwell School'. 'I can't, I can't indeed: – if you were to hang me up by the heels not a shilling would drop out of my mouth: – if you were to try & bleed me not a drop of blood

---

65  After years of famine and with its leaders inflamed by continental revolution, Ireland was close to open rebellion. In July the Habeas Corpus Act in Ireland was suspended and the principal agitators were arrested and tried for high treason by a special commission. The death sentence pronounced on William Smith O'Brien, M.P. for Limerick and an old member of Trinity College, Cambridge, was commuted to transportation and he was eventually pardoned.

66  Founded in 1540 with a preference for fellows of Trinity. In August 1848 canonries at Ely were annexed to this and to the Regius chair of Greek by order in council. The electors were the Vice-Chancellor, the Master and two senior fellows of Trinity, and the heads of King's, St John's, and Christ's. See *Endowments*, pp. 153-65.

67  The diarist's younger cousin who had just retired from the army and was about to take up a political career. He married on 28 November. See Appendix 1.

would follow the lancet'. – 'But how then do you live?' 'O King Henry maintains me: he gives me food & furnishes me a lodging'. – 'Well, I hope you will profit by his good fare & get a little blood into your system & then I will apply to you again'. He gave her nothing on this occasion, & was shortly after seized with his last fatal illness[68] . . .

*Wed. 25.* The fine weather is come back, & Lucy (in spite of yesterday's work) did a good deal in visiting her paupers. She however wisely went to bed at 9 o'clock . . . I today canvassed by letters & by speech almost all the Syndics of the Press to get the large Mesman room for my Office.[69]

*Th. 26.* Polling began at 9 o'clock.[70] – at 12 o'clock it closed for an hour when the numbers were

Bateson _____123
Williams _____116

Came home at 12 to have an interview with Brown the Tailor (to whom Lucy is apprentising James How): Lucy gave him the life of Wesley, he being a Wesleian & having had his bills refused by that illiberal Brumell of St Johns on that account: – I patronised this little tailor & ordered a great coat of him.

Polling began again at 1 & went on till 5 when the numbers were

Bateson _____402
Williams _____343

To my great surprise the Solicitor General (Sir John Romilly) came down today: – he voted (of course) for Bateson: he went to call on Lucy: she was at dinner & did not see him. – I took him & J.E. Blunt to dine in hall where there was a huge party . . . At 8 o'clock the polling began again: the S.H. was well lighted with 4 Gas chandeliers. The youngsters were very noisy in the Galleries: they threw down shot & peas on the body of The S.H., but spared the dais: they concluded the evening by singing 'God save the Queen'. The Polling closed at 10 when the numbers were

Bateson _____458

---

[68] Charles Simeon (d. 1836), fellow of Henry VI's foundation King's College, and vicar of Holy Trinity, was the most influential evangelical divine of his day. Macaulay said he had greater sway than any primate. William Carus wrote a large life of him in 1847 and many anecdotes circulated about him. In fact he was a wealthy but self-denying man who spent much of his income on religious and charitable causes but who could hardly have satisfied every appeal. See H.E. Hopkins, *Charles Simeon of Cambridge* (1977), pp. 159-61.

[69] Romilly and his archives had first occupied a room in the Old Schools whence they removed in 1836 to the ground floor of the Pitt Press building. It was damp and ill ventilated and this present removal to the large room on the first floor, originally intended as a room for meetings of the Press Syndics and long given over to the Mesman collection of paintings, lately removed to the Fitzwilliam Museum, was eminently desirable.

[70] i.e. for the office of Public Orator who 'is the voice of the Senate upon all public occasions. He writes, reads, and records the letters to and from the body of the Senate, and presents to all honorary degrees with an appropriate speech. This is esteemed one of the most honourable offices in the gift of the University' (*Cambridge University Calendar* 1848, p. 5). Thomas Crick had resigned and members of the Senate were to elect his successor from names proposed by Heads of Houses. The post was unsalaried but attracted numerous fees from the common 18 pence of each B.A. to a rare 20 guineas for a nobleman's LL.D.

Williams _____ 396

It took an hour to count & read the votes & swear in the new Orator.

*Fri. 27.* Breakfast to John, Blunt, Sedgwick & Airy. – Black-Leet: – the Mayor (Foster C.F.) attended.[71] A most miserable wet day. – There was a Press Meeting today, & the Syndics to my great delight agreed to my petition for the great room with the Oriel window for a new Registry, altho both Ollivant & Blunt had applied for it for a Lecture-room, Paget for a Bird room & Dr Webb for a Syndics room (for which indeed it was built, – tho never used for that purpose: it was lately occupied by the Mesman Collection).

*Sat. 28.* . . . I should have said that at the Seniority today we decided that all the Freshman Pensioners (138 in no) are to dine at a 2d dinner at 5 o'clock. We are unusually full at present: for there are 397 remaining to dine at 4 o'clock.

*Sun. 29.* Lucy & I to Trinity Church: where Carus preached an admirable & most eloquent sermon from Ps.67.1.2: – it was a Sermon in behalf of the Church Missionary Jubilee wch is to be celebrated all over the world next Wednesday (All Saints day): Lucy & I had made up our minds to give only 2/6 a piece & took no more with us: but we were ashamed to put so small a sum in the plate of Mr Hopkins whom we knew, & we therefore deposited our beggarly contributions in the other plate wch was fortunately held by a stranger to us.

*Tu. 31.* The day for the grand changes in our academic System to be voted on.[72] I never knew so full a S.H. except in contested Elections. Considerable nos of voters came from Town, etc. All 5 of the Propositions were carried by large majorities in both houses: in the B.H. nearly 150 voted, & in the W.H. above 100 . . . Guizot & his 2 drs & Ld Northampton etc were present . . . Dined at Trinity Lodge: a grand dinner party of 20 . . . the younger Miss Guizot plaid the Piano, very nicely indeed. – Mathison also plaid admirably. – Guizot . . . speaks English with confidence, but most unpleasingly in point of accent: he spoke about the elements of Mathematics – I had the honor of being introduced to him

[71] The Black Leet or Magna Congregatio was an annual ceremony at which the Mayor and bailiffs of the town were obliged to swear to uphold the liberties and customs of the university. Such an act of subservience led to great ill-will, as is shown, for instance in the diarist's account of 1836 (*Romilly 1832-42*, p.104), and abolition was imminent.

[72] Thanks largely to Prince Albert and his right-hand man in Cambridge, the Master of St Catharine's, Dr Philpott, who had wisely enlisted Whewell, a strong syndicate had been appointed in the previous February to improve and extend courses and examinations. Romilly's friend Archbishop Musgrave warned gently of the need for caution and tenderness towards 'the opinions or prejudices of men long accustomed to a state of things under which they have grown up and prospered'. Despite mooted opposition at first the proponents of change were nervous, and they cannot have been reassured when in July a memorial to the Prime Minister insisted that the older universities had failed to reform themselves (indeed could not do so), and asked that they should be the object of inquiry. By October there had been much public argument and when the five Graces embodying the recommendations of the syndicate were presented in the Senate all were opposed. Their being approved on this day established two new honours examinations, the Natural Sciences and Moral Science Triposes, for those who already had a first degree, and also a Board of Mathematical Studies. Attendance at certain professorial lectures was also required from candidates for the Ordinary degree, and at divinity lectures by candidates for the Voluntary Theological Examination, which in practice was compulsory. The five Graces are printed in full in *Annals*, IV, 702-5. See also Winstanley, pp. 202-13, and Searby, pp. 231-3.

& conversed with him for some time about the events of the morning in the S.H. The 2 Miss Guizots seem frank goodhumoured young ladies; the elder is rather pretty: they were both drest in white, with a large white bow of ribbon at the back of their hair. Mr Fane (Ld Westmorlands son) took the youngest in to dinner, & he being a very fine handsome agreeable conversible man who has lived a great deal at Vienna & Paris she seemed to enjoy herself very much . . .

*Th. 2 November.* Highly delighted by the Master bringing to my rooms this morning Mr Guizot & son & drs & also the Chevalier Bunsen: I asked Mr Guizot to dine with me & name his day, but he goes away tomorrow. Poor Skinner has had a sad mortification about Guizot: he in the Senate House asked Guizot to breakfast & invited a party to meet him: on the morning of the breakfast he went up to Trinity Lodge to fetch Guizot: he found Guizot at breakfast with the Master, who would by no means let him go, but told Skinner he was heartily welcome to breakfast with Mr G. & have his talk with him there. Poor Skinner had to go back to his expectant guests unaccompanied by the great Lion whom he had promised to exhibit to them! . . .

*Th. 9.* . . . Trial in the V.C's Court of a freshman F.C. of Trin. (Newton), for giving a false name: sentenced to be admonished in S.H. & to repeat 200 lines of Greek.[73] – New Mayor sworn in: – his name is Charles Finch . . . Lucy (O! marvellous!) called with me on Mrs Worsley. We were received (strangely enough) in a room without a fire: we saw there a portrait of Worsley by Laurence . . . it is a very coarse unfinished picture, which I think never deserves to be finished: – we saw many excellent drawings of the Master's . . .

*Sat. 11.* . . . Dined at Caius Lodge: a large party . . . capital dinner with mock-turtle & venison. – I took Miss Thackeray down to dinner & found her very conversible: the Provost does not allow her to go to the County balls, nor even to go into the Fitzwilliam Museum!!! – Miss Chapman amused herself by making the most unqualified offer of herself to me: – I told her that I should take till Monday to think of the happiness offered me. – She is in tearing spirits . . .

*Sun. 12.* College Sacrament: Carus therefore could not preach at Trinity Church:[74] so Lucy & I went to the Baptist Meeting House & were put into Mr Ri. Foster's pew: – we heard a stranger (a Mr Squib of Huntingdon) preach & were very highly pleased with him: he had a few slight defects, he talked of the Euphrātes, had large dirty hands & omitted the h's in a dreadful manner: but he was a very powerful preacher: he was very energetic, & his sermon was full of excellent matter . . . At Lucy's request I wrote Betsy an account of this sermon. – I wrote also to Lodge. – In spite of the rain wch came down fast Lucy came to my rooms to see the rushing out of the young men from the Sacrament at Trinity at ¼ to 1.

*Fri. 17.* . . . Tonight the most brilliant Aurora Borealis I ever saw: Lucy saw it well: – as for one of Dr Clark's maids she was so frightened at it that she went into a fit. – I did not go to Mrs Prest's Evening party, but went to Pembroke

---

[73] One of Romilly's duties was to attend the disciplinary court of the Vice-Chancellor, attest its proceedings as public notary, and record them in the Acta Curiae books. During 1848 there were seven cases in all.

[74] Holy Communion was usually celebrated in college once a term on a Sunday.

Combination & lost my money: – today had been a grand feast with them in honour of their annual audit: they had supper in Hall & milk punch.

*Wed. 22.* .... Between Congregations there was a Seniority, at wch Marshall (a nephew of Mrs Whewells, was admonished previous to expulsion for not standing up at Grace, & for general irregularity.[75] – Very recently John Whewell Statter (a nephew of the Masters) was sent away for the rest of the term for getting drunk with cider cup & staying out all night . . .

*Mon. 27.* .... Letter from Miss Butcher[76] in sad despair at William Pearce having received notice at Sawbridgeworth that in a week his services will be dispensed with: I wrote to her to comfort her, & also to Geo. Fisher to beg him if possible to do something for W.P. – Had a long interview with G. Fisher who says . . . that he grieves sincerely at the sad necessity which the Company is under of reducing their establishment: Cambridge & every other station along the line is reduced. – November December & January are the 3 worst months for the Rail: – no prospect of restoring any of the rejected servants till February, – if then. – Wrote again at night to Miss Butcher . . .

*Tu. 28.* Began reading loud a novel called "Tenant of Wilderfell Hall by Currer Bell, author of 'Jane Eyre': – it is exactly in the same school, – the Hero & Heroine unamiable reasoning people: the Hero a ruffian. I think Currer Bell must be a coarse violent man.

*Sat. 2 December.* Harriet Sandfield's birthday:[77]– Lucy & I each gave her 10/- to begin an account at the Savings Bank. In consequence of our having a new servant Lucy has for the last few days dedicated herself most vigorously to setting her places to right. – She is also working hard to get Sarah Wood (our discarded servant) a place . . .

*Wed. 6.* .... Bateson made his 1st speech as Orator: it was admirable: it was delivered without the slightest hesitation & without ever referring to the paper . . . Mrs Austin (the translator of Ranke) was in the S.H: she was much pleased with this speech: she told me she had begun Latin at 4 years old![78]

*Mon. 18.* .... Bateson the Orator has given to Mrs How of 7 Doric St. one of the best of the College gifts, viz 1s weekly for life. – I today wrote to Mr Asby begging him to reform the open drains by Doric Street: – I also wrote a letter to Dr Fisher, begging him to see Hannah Smyth, wch he accordingly most kindly did: he prescribed pills, doses & plaster: she coughs a good deal & speaks so feebly that I scarcely make out a word she utters.

---

[75] The Seniority was a body of eight senior fellows of Trinity who with the Master governed the college, and which Romilly had joined in 1840. If any were absent his place was taken 'without any express appointment' by the resident fellow next in seniority.

[76] An impoverished lady whom the Romillys had helped for many years, Miss Butcher lodged with the surgeon William Pearce.

[77] Harriet was the faithful maid of whom naturally little is known beyond what Romilly relates. She was a local girl, a protégée of Lucy, and only in her twenties, who was to refuse two offers of marriage to stay with her master. See 13 February and 28 October 1862.

[78] Sarah Austin (1793-1867), translator and editor who translated Ranke's *History of the Popes* and *History of the Reformation in Germany.* She was admired by Macaulay for her 'scrupulous integrity' and received a civil list pension in 1849. See *D.N.B.*

*Wed. 20.* . . . Out walking today on the Via Lambertina[79] I fell in with the 4 Miss Helms (including Carry) & their Uncle: I turned about & walked with them back to Cambr. – Miss Betsy complained of fatigue; so I offered her my arm: she (like an ass) made scruples, but I silenced her by telling her there could be no impropriety in walking with a man old enough to be her grandfather. – There is a 4th case of cholera in Camb.: but the medical men are in no alarm . . . I should have said that yesterday the Provost of Kings & the Fellows expelled Lionel Buller from their Society: – I believe they intend making him an allowance: they have done well in casting off such an irreclaimable blackguard. Leapingwell told me a good story about Lionel Buller. He was speaking in anger about his Mother & contrasting her with a bitch, whose puppy he offered to touch & she flew at him in defence of her child: – 'ah, said his friend, it's not every bitch that whelps such a puppy as you'![80] Wrote to Broadwood for a leather cover for the Piano Forte. – At night went on with 'Vanity Fair'.[81]

*Sun. 24* . . . Lucy nursed her really bad cold, & went no where but to the Hospital before breakfast . . . Betsy (now Mrs Ja. Spink) made her appearance having got a pass ticket for her husband & self for 5 days absence . . . She was in capital spirits: her cat is passing his Xmas holidays with us! We had our Turkey today that the Maids might dine off it tomorrow. – Wrote to many people about charities.

*Mon. 25.* Very nasty wet day: – Lucy did not stir out. – I went to Benet to hear Pullen: but Mould mounted the Pulpit & preached a clever but dry Sermon on the human character of our Lord . . . Xmas Box to Lucy 10/; do to Mrs Ja. Spink; 2/6 each to the maids: I gave Hannah Smyth the Pilgrims Progress, Prayers & Precepts for every day & Sacred Songs. Wrote to F.R £15: to Jacques £5: to Madame F.R. £25, Madame Bourlet £5: – also to G.T.R sending him £10.10 for copy of my phyz . . . Read loud one of Baptist Noel's Chapel Royal Sermons . . .

---

[79] Named after James Lambert, a former bursar of Trinity, and now called Long Road.

[80] Buller had been a loose cannon at King's since 1833 (see *Romilly 1832-42*, p. 27). According to a manuscript note by Romilly in UP 17 (904) 'he had made himself very obnoxious by endeavouring to stop the college business at Seniorities'. If the fellows at King's thought they had seen the back of Buller they were mistaken. He fastened up his college rooms so they had to be broken into, and in July 1850 he was in court for threatening to shoot a porter who had ejected him. Nor was it his last appearance there. See also 26 February 1850. By July 1854 he had been in and out of asylums and gone home to Devon where his poor mother barred her doors and he was forced into the workhouse in destitution.

[81] Presumably the one-volume edition that had appeared recently, the novel having first come out in monthly parts in 1847-8.

# 1849

*Fri. 12 January.* Election of Shaw as Master of Christs: poor John Smith (who is out of his mind) was brought up to vote for Hildyard: Hildyard had 5 (or 6 Query') votes: all the rest were for Shaw. Poor Cartmell is much cut up with the disappointment of his long cherished hopes: all the supporters of Mortlock (6 in no) were willing to vote for Shaw, but not for Cartmell; so Cartmell's friends amalgamated with the Mortlockites. – Shaw was presented to the V.C. in my presence by Cartmell & Bates . . .

*Fri. 26.* The Proctors man brought the list this morning before the Servants were up, – having brought it last night after we were all gone to bed (at 11 o'clock): he clambered over the rails as the Gate was locked: – but we were inexorable & would not let him in. – The Senior Wrangler is Pell of St Johns . . . this is the 5th time of their having had the S.W. 3 successive years! no other college has ever gone beyond 2 years in succession. It is a very bad year: Pell is only 53 marks above Phear. – Porter was the favorite. – There was one really good man (a Caius man) of the year, but he broke a blood vessel & is gone to Madeira: – had he been Senior Wrangler he could not have been presented, for he was a dissenter[1] . . .

*Sat. 27.* The reading of the Supplicats[2] over in a few minutes, but the Father of St Johns & the S.W. were not forthcoming for about ¼ an hour: – the people in the Gallery behaved remarkably well . . .

*Mon. 29.* . . . Dined at Mr Fosters at Anstey Hall. The party consisted of Mr Foster & a shy plain niece . . . Mr & Mrs George Foster, a young man (unknown) a Lady unknown (some relation of Grote's), a very clever Miss Brightwell of Norwich (who etches well, & draws flowers beautifully & plaid Handel capitally), Grote & his pretty sister (a good-humoured plump young girl who sung a song in honor of the Pope, besides several other songs. – The party was very agreeable.

*Tu. 30.* Shaw & Cartmell called on me to say that he (Shaw) meant to resign the Mastership of Christs on Friday next!!! I take it for granted that it is from kindness to Cartmell who fretted sadly at his disappointment.

*Fri. 2 February.* Shaw resigned the Mastership in my presence as a Notary Public: he (by the Statutes of Christs Coll:) returns to his Senior Fellowship. Letter from G.T.R. (saying that Eastlake commends his talent, & that he is going to put up for the Royal Academy) . . . Ought to have dined at the Family today at Sidney Lodge: but I had asked J.G. Howes (Vicar of Little St. Marys) & my landlord Mr Fawcett to dine in hall to keep the last day of Christmas. – The dais

---

[1] Like Jews and Catholics nonconformists were debarred not from study but from proceeding to a degree and thereafter taking senior positions in the University, by their inability conscientiously to swear that they were members of the Church of England. The 'tests' were increasingly under attack both within and from outside but they lasted for another generation. See 25 April 1857 and 26 May 1859.

[2] i.e. formal petitions for individual degrees submitted by college praelectors. They were written on small slips of which most survive from the mid-sixteenth century until the late nineteenth.

has been extended in hall, wch is a great improvement: a complete window of painted glass has just been put up in the Hall. – My guests went away at 7: – I afterwards plaid whist & lost 6 rubbers out of 7.

*Tu. 6.* . . . College meeting at wch we agreed to give to superannuated bedmakers a pension of 7s a week: – when they are in full work (with 6 rooms) they are supposed to make 8s a week . . . Bought a Valentine for Lucy to send to her sick friend M.A. Tyler: – as I had on my cap & gown I excited a sensation. – Lucy & I yesterday & today abstained from meat.

*Mon. 12.* Miss Page begged me to do what I could at the Pitt Press for her shopboy (Pink): I called on Mr Sibley, who said that he dissuaded sending a clever well-conducted boy to the Press, for the only good situation is that of Reader: – there are 4 readers only, & no prospect of a vacancy. – I wrote to her to tell her all this.

*Tu. 13.* A strong agitation got up against the V.C.'s syndicate for revising the Statutes: Prof. Corrie & Mr Harper are the chief movers: – the complaint is that the Syndics proposed are many of them feeble creatures. – The V.C. withdraws his Grace.[3] – The Election of a new Master of Christs was this morning: – Cartmell was unopposed: – Shaw & Smith presented him to the V.C. in my presence. – At night read Macaulay.

*Sat. 17.* Trial at the V.C.'s: 3 Tradesmen (Crisp, Fruiterer, Over (Cook), Wells (watchmaker) for not sending notice to the Tutor of J.H. Puget (Trin) of their bills being over £5: – all 3 reprimanded[4] . . .

*Tu. 27.* . . . I should have said yesterday that Lucy received a present from Carus: – a prettily got up little book called 'the Pearl of Days':[5] it is an essay on the *Sabbath* written by a woman: 3 Prizes had lately been offered for essays on this subject by *Labouring* men: – above 950 essays were sent in. This able one by a woman could not gain one of the 3 Prizes, but it has produced a considerable sensation & the Q. has allowed it to be dedicated to her. – At night I read loud the Authoresse's autobiography (wch is very nicely written

---

3   Graces were formal proposals about university business to be voted on by senior members in their two assemblies, the Black and White Houses. Any member of the Caput, a six-man executive cabinet (see 8 March 1851), could veto a Grace so that it could not be put to a wider vote. In an attempt to forestall outside interference, and building on the slender proposals of an earlier committee, the Vice-Chancellor, Cookson, brought forward a Grace to appoint a syndicate to revise the statutes. Its strong liberal membership disconcerted such extreme conservatives as Professor Corrie who succeeded in having the Grace withdrawn. But a second and similar Grace soon passed unopposed, perhaps because the liberal Dr Lamb, Master of Corpus, was excluded from membership. From 14 March 1849 the Revising Syndicate was to meet regularly for several years as often as two or three times a week, and to effect many changes. Yet progress was slow, its first Report was not made until December 1851, and it soon fell under the shadow of the Royal Commission. See Winstanley, pp. 214-15, and Searby, pp. 512-17.

4   In order to control and direct undergraduates' expenses their bills for other than trifling amounts had to be paid through their college tutors. By an order of February 1847 tradesmen were required to tell a man's tutor if he ran up bills over £5 and Puget owed more than £47. The order was reissued lest anyone should pretend to be ignorant of it.

5   *Or the Advantages of the Sabbath to the Working Classes* (1848), attributed to Barbara Farquhar. Perhaps Romilly underestimated her for there also appeared under her name *Female Education: its Importance, Design, and Nature considered* (1851).

& pleased me much): – I also began the story itself, which I thought clever & pious, but it must have been greatly doctored by the Editor, who has put in long hard words which never could have been known to her . . .

*Mon. 12 March.* . . . Univ. Scholarship (Craven) today given to Whymper of Trinity.[6] Jenny Lind sang at the Townhall tonight & with her accustomed generosity sent £100 to the Hospital: – the room was not more than ¾ full: the price of common seats was a Gua, of reserved seats 1½ Gua. The bells rang in honor of her, & there was a great crowd for hours before the Bull to look at her.[7] – Whist Club at my rooms . . .

*Tu. 13.* Sedgwick gave breakfast to Jenny Lind & lionised her about the College: – a crowd flocked after her. – Letter from Mrs North . . . She tells me that her nephew Delamaine lost his left arm at the late bloody battle[8] under Lord Gough, but that Henry Ouvry was unhurt: Archdeacon Robinson's son was killed . . .

*Th. 15.* Letter from G.T.R. saying his baby is a regular long-limbed yankee & that his name is to be Francis John, & asking Lucy to be Godmother: – she declines: – I wrote to him quizzing him for not having asked me to be God-father. – Licensing day, 176 Licenses. Dined with Mrs Prest. Went on with Q. Durward.

*Sat. 17.* . . . The Classical Tripos came out today: 13 in 1st Class, 1st 6 of them & last 4 Trinity men: Coopland (Cath), Helm (Jes) & Hon. C.R. Herbert (Joh.) were bracketed equal as 7th, 8th & 9th. – Latimer Neville was 3d of 2d Class, to the great disappointment of his Family who thought he would have kept pace with Mr Herbert, – who was notoriously Captain of the Poll: – obviously a clever fellow.[9] – St Patrick's day. – Lucy sent Carus some Shamrock & Violets.

*Wed. 21.* Letter from Lady Braybrooke inviting me to dine next week: – wrote to decline. Over with Bateson to Madingley. . . . It was an agreeable small party . . . Sir St Vincent told us stories of rascals who used to travel by 'the Age' when he drove it, – particularly of a robber of the Custom House who was caught from a door slamming in wch he had left his picklock on the other side:

---

[6] Five valuable Craven scholarships, originally founded in 1649 by the will of Lord Craven for poor scholars and the founder's kin, were tenable for several years. The conditions for their becoming void or vacant were not straightforward. There is an account of them in *Endowments*, pp. 283-94, and a list of recipients since 1649 is in the *Historical Register of the University* (1917), p. 260. None of them had been poor or relatives of the founder for a long while before 1855 and the value of these scholarships was considerable, i.e. £75 a year since a chancery decree of 1841.

[7] Romilly had heard the 'Swedish Nightingale' before in opera and at Norwich when he christened her 'Guinea Lind'. See *Romilly 1842-47*, p. 224. Chater, then a young apprentice, listened to her performance from a shed-roof outside the Town Hall: 'I never heard such singing in my life – it was scarcely like a human voice, and so divinely managed' (E. Porter, *Victorian Cambridge*, 1975, p. 16).

[8] i.e. Chillianwallah in the Sikh war when victory was only achieved with heavy losses on 13 January.

[9] Below the three Honours classes of Wrangler, Senior Optime and Junior Optime, came the more numerous pass men, hoi polloi (the many), or 'poll', whence poll man. The unexacting ordinary degree, taken without shame by those who had no inclination or need to strive for honours in the mathematical and classical triposes, was also called 'the Poll' and the highest amongst the candidates the 'Captain'.

as Sir St V. says of himself – he has lived a loose kind of life.[10] – Plaid 3 rubbers & won the odd one.

*Mon. 2 April.* Delightful morning – Lucy & I went to St Edwards where H. Goodwin galloped thro the service. – Visit from Richard Rowe about a bedesman's place for an old man W. Wright formerly servant in Trin Lodge. The wife of Gray . . . came to talk to me about a Letter her husband has received from Parkhurst prison accusing him of defrauding his son of £10: – I told her that Fred had certainly been cheated: that my sister had subscribed the money solely for Fred etc etc etc: I thought myself sufficiently violent, but Lucy heard me at the door, & came & broke up all parley, denuncing future punishment against her & her husband & slamming the door in her face!! I am very glad that the Governor of the jail has written this letter to that rogue of a Gray . . .

*Fri. 6.* . . . As soon as Lucy saw Crisford & dismal Downton come into Church she took herself off & went to the new Weslyan Chapel (in Hobson St), wch was to be opened today. She heard an old man (Dr Leifchild) preach: – his text was Hosea 1.10 .11.12; it was a metaphysical sermon & had nothing to do with Good Friday . . . Lucy went again at 2½ & heard the hospitable Mr Etherage: she was greatly pleased with this thin excited wild-looking martyr-like man, & gave him all the money she had, viz 3s.8d!! . . . but the congregation greatly preferred the metaphysical Dr Leifchild whom they could not understand, & whom they applauded by crying Amen, & making the *hum* of delight & approval . . .

From 9 to 11 April Romilly was at Audley End where he found 'a very sick household'. On the evening of the first day ten people were nevertheless well enough to propose 'a great no of riddles etc . . . most of them very bad.

1.If a clock were to describe the subject of its conversation to a Parrot what would it be?
Answer. Pol-i-ticks
2. Why is the nose in the middle of the Face?
Answer. It is a 'scenter'
3. If John Kissed Betty & she objected what place of confinement would she name?
Answer. A done John
6.If a Poplar in a gale of wind smashes a window what would the wind say?
Answer. Tree-mend-us
10. Why is Louis Philippe like a wet day that mends?
Answer. Has rained: but now ceases'.

On the following day he played 'Billiards with Lord Braybrooke, Mr Oldham (the house surgeon) & the young Nevilles till Luncheon'. The weather having cleared, he walked over to Walden where he fell in with Miss Chapman and Mr Hanson the Curate of Ashdon; after dinner he 'plaid Whist with Lady B. against Charles & Latimer & lost 12s/: they play better than their Mother. – I should have mentioned that I last night looked over a game of *sympathy* plaid by Lady Elisabeth [Cornwallis] and Miss Lucy: – I thought it an amusing game of cards'.

[10] Cotton had famously driven the crack London to Brighton coach in the thirties, and a sketch of him on the box, top-hatted, whip in hand, cigar between his teeth, appeared in the *New Sporting Magazine* at that time.

*Wed. 11.* . . . 1st day of Scholarship. – Thompson & I were colleagues: he did all the duty: he set the papers, & also sat up in hall from 9 to 1: – I rather used him barbarously in this & he got very sick of these 4 hours without having his guard relieved. I went to him at 2 & released him from sorting the papers & sent him out walking: I did not get it finished till near 4. – Took away with me an Æschylus bundle: – I dined with Lucy.

*Fri. 13.* 3d day of Schol. – Mathematics by Master & Martin. – I today dined in hall, where I was glad to find Brown & Sedgwick tho they do not examine. – Poor Bowtell is in sad tribulation. His daughter Alicia (aged 32) was a Roman Catholic & had been courted by a R.C. named Smithson (a glasspainter employed at Kings Chapel): – she is said to have refused him: he has been to the R.C. Priest & has beaten him furiously with a poker, & Miss Bowtell is dead suddenly: – quære, did she take poison?

*Sun. 15.* . . . Downton is to read today for the last time, he having got some preferment! hurrah! – His last tones I thought as dismal as those of a dying swan, tho not so musical . . .

*Wed. 18.* Poor Miss Bowtell poisoned herself . . . She was found dead, & there was poison in her stomach: – the verdict was 'died of poison but whether taken volant. or ignorantly does not appear'.[11] – I dined in hall today.

*Sat. 21.* Swore in the new Scholars,. – Revising Syndicate from 12 to 2. – Declined dinner at Mr Lennards & tea at Mrs Prests. – Dined with Rothman & met a snug conversible little party . . .

*Mon. 23.* Rush was hanged this morning for the murder of the 2 Jermys: – the Eastern Counties had an excursion Train to Norwich to accommodate spectators!!!!![12] . . . Whist Club at Eyres': (Cory & Drosier not present); Mr C. Mortlock & Mr Day were there: – that horrid fellow, Walker had been at the Execution of Rush this morning! – Of course we had those eternal marrow-bones for supper! . . .

*Wed. 25.* Congregation – 13 AM, 8 AB: – lots of Graces: – one to thank the Prince for his Picture,[13] another to confirm new Fitzwilliam Resolutions[14] . . .

---

[11] She took arsenic after her suitor, Benjamin Smithson, sought to marry her privately and without parental consent. She was over thirty.

[12] One night in November 1848 Isaac Jermy, Recorder of Norwich, and his son, a Trinity graduate, were shot dead at their home Stanfield Hall near Wymondham by a masked intruder who also wounded others. Suspicion at once fell on a neighbouring farmer J.B. Rush (see *D.N.B.*) who had been at odds with Jermy. His trial, conviction, and public hanging at Norwich were closely followed throughout the country, and sackloads of special editions of the local newspapers were sent out daily with the latest intelligence. The trial is notorious among legal historians for the latitude allowed to Rush who rambled through his incoherent and largely irrelevant defence for many hours. See Owen Chadwick, *Victorian Miniature* (1960), chapter 6.

[13] Albert's new portrait by Frederick Say showing him in academical dress was placed in the Fitzwilliam Museum and removed in 1919. See *Endowments* p. 587. It has been several times reproduced, e.g. in J.W. Goodison, *Cambridge University Portraits* (1955).

[14] See 22 May 1848. The new museum building was occupied in 1848 when a syndicate was appointed to make regulations for its management. The resolutions of 25 April were based on their report. They recommended that the running of the museum should be given to a Fitz-william Museum syndicate comprising the Vice-Chancellors of the current and two preceding years and eight elected members, but did not specify any duties in detail, an omission that was to lead to trouble in 1855. No director was appointed but one candidate for the office of curator

Most fortunately Ficklin came today to ask about Lucy's arm: I happened to be at home: I told him that she was very much out of sorts indeed & that he must set her to rights: – he was very amusing & agreeable as he always is, & told no end of lies in his goodhumoured chattering way . . .

*Sat. 28.* . . . Called Congregation . . . An immensely full Sen. House to vote on the Petition against a man marrying 2 sisters: the Petition was carried by 35 to 19 in B.H. & 33 to 10 in W.H: – I did not vote[15] . . .

*Th. 3 May.* . . . Yesterday the V.C. & Orator presented the latters letter of thanks to the Prince (for his Picture by Say) at Buckingham Palace: it was a very dull affair: the Prince was in plain clothes without a gown & offered no refreshments: he was sorry they had had the trouble of bringing up the Letter, asked if the Orator was not new in his office, & whether Lectures were going on: – which questions being answered the V.C. & Orator backed out . . .

*Tu. 8.* Election of Curator of the building of the Fitzwilliam Museum: – 20 votes for Tho. Smith, & 1 for Jos. Moule: – I had signed a certificate for the said J.M. being a worthy carpenter but was much surprised to find him a candidate on this occasion against Smith (the Clerk of the works & the most fitting man that could have been found) . . .

*Th. 10.* Another miserable wet day. – I took Hannah Smyth to the Railway Station at 9: she is gone to her Aunt Mrs Cotchett (at Rothley Cottage, Loughboro) the fare by 2d Class to Syston (where she is to get down) is 15/6 paid by Lucy. I put her into the lady's carriage (wch she had all to herself), & a young Kingsman . . . who was also going to Syston lent her a horsecloth to put over her knees & said he would take care of her: – I gave her 10/- for pocket money. She exhibited no warmth of feeling either to me or Lucy: – she is as uninteresting as a girl of 17 can possibly be . . . Received from Henslow a copy of his address to his Parishioners concerning Clothing Clubs etc etc: wrote to thank him.[16] –

Mrs Gilmore called about apprenticing her son William to Talbot the Printer *without praemium*: – gave her 10/- towards the 32/ for stamps. Mrs Hatton (the Hooddy) called to ask for a hospital order for her niece (Eliza Rawlinson): I told her that Lucy was very unwell & that she could not see her.

*Sat. 12.* . . . Received from young Mr Baxendale a present of Rooks,– the 1st present of *such black* game that I have ever received. – Received from

---

asked Romilly if he thought the job 'discreditable to a University man. I said "far from it: presiding over books and pictures is always an honourable position for an educated man".'(6 August 1852).

[15] The topic had been arcane before the 1840s when several bills were introduced to legalise marriage between a man and his dead wife's sister, and in 1848 a royal commission considering prohibited degrees of affinity recommended the measure. So began a theological and parliamentary debate which begat enough printed matter to fill a library and was not resolved until 1907. See S. Wolfram, *In-Laws and Outlaws* (1987), pp. 21-51.

[16] John Henslow, absentee professor of botany but devoted priest, worked tirelessly in his populous and degraded parish of Hitcham in Suffolk. 'How active you always seem to be' wrote his pupil Darwin in admiration. And what he did he wrote about to encourage others. A school was built and its teacher paid, allotments were introduced, and numerous self-help associations (e.g. coal, clothing, blanket, and medical clubs) were formed to alleviate the poverty of the parish. See J. Russell-Gebbett, *Henslow of Hitcham* (1977).

W.F. Campbell a copy of his speech on the Jew Question: – he has (to my annoyance) dedicated it to me: I wrote to tell him I was sorry he had done so, as it did not convey my opinions, for I am in favor of the admission of Jews into Parliament[17] . . .

*Tu. 15.* Forgot to say yesterday that I as Vicemaster had to preside (in the Master's absence) at a meeting of the seniors concerning the death of a Paviour (named Shearing) to whom & others 5 bottles of wine & ½ bottle of brandy had been let down from the rooms of G. Dodson (a 2d year man of Trin.): 3 other men took part (Dobie, Dewsbery & Lambert in letting down the wine etc, & Dobie fetched the brandy from his own rooms. – We rusticated[18] Dodson & Dobie till 10 Oct., & admonished the other 2 & kept them to Gates & Hall for the rest of the term. – I wrote to the Master an account of the proceedings. – This morning the Jun. Dean (Marsh) brought 3 men before me to reprimand for bad attendance at Chapel: I did so & entered it in the Admonition Book . . .

*Th. 17.* . . . I am sorry to find that that pretty place 'the Leys' is going to be taken by Dennis the Haberdasher, who is said to give himself great airs & to cause great pain to poor Mrs G. Fisher by the way in which he speaks slightingly of the house & grounds, the favorite Alderney Cow & everything else: – low minded fellow. – Poor Mrs G.F. is reduced to take away her boys from the Charter House & send them to the Freeschool . . . Wentworth the Auctioneer has taken the Skrine's House;[19] it is very sad to see these changes! – Sarah Foulkes (who has not eaten for 3 weeks) expressed a desire for something savoury; so Lucy sent her some of our Rook pie (we dining an hour earlier to accommodate her): she ate it with relish & kept some for breakfast tomorrow!!

From 23 to 26 May Romilly stayed with the G.T. Romillys in Kensington (sleeping in 'George's Painting Room'). He christened their baby 'who is a very ugly child with a bald head & wrinkled forehead & an eruption on its skin: it is very thin & wretched, but it is only a wonder it is alive, as it was very nearly starved to death before it was discovered that the mamma's nipples were not milk-conveyors tho she had abundance of milk'. However, he was 'much pleased with Mrs Mirrielees [George's mother-in-law] and Mrs G.T.R. I think George has got just the right wife for him, very cheerful, very economical, & very obliging'. The christening over, Romilly lost no time in calling on numerous relations, seeing to his financial affairs, disapproving of the Academy exhibition and in the evening going with George to the Haymarket where the farce 'was very laughable, being full of puns & jokes'.

On the twenty-fifth he fell in with his cousins the Ouvrys who persuaded him to go to the Tower where he was greatly pleased by seeing a number of hitherto unknown

---

17  Campbell was the young liberal M.P. for Cambridge town to whom Romilly had expressed similar views in 1847, saying that he 'saw no danger' to Christianity from Jewish admission to Parliament. Campbell, however, opposed the disabilities act of February 1848 but in such feeble terms that he was castigated for want of zeal by the Tory *Chronicle*: 'there is great deal of *twaddle* in what he thinks it necessary to put before the public' (19 February 1848).

18  i.e. sent out of Cambridge for a spell, usually a term. As a punishment rustication rated between 'gating' or confinement within the College and 'sending down' or full expulsion.

19  Julian Skrine, an old card-playing crony of Romilly's, was a retired Cambridge banker and magistrate who about this time got into financial trouble and had to leave for the continent where he died several years later, probably in Paris. Mrs Skrine, a favourite with Romilly, moved in with her daughter and son-in-law Phelps, Master of Sidney Sussex.

'interesting things'. Dinner with the Edward Romillys was much less amusing. 'The Conversation was entirely in French & being almost wholly political I was rather sick of it'. And then about '11 o'clock Edw. & Prof. de la Rive entered upon a debate concerning the moral sense: – I thought it high time to be off . . . I should have said that at the Exhibition there is a picture of a dead Lion by E. Landseer: – it is placed between the portraits of Guizot & Metternich, wch creates much mirth'.

*Mon. 28.* Lucy & I walked home yesterday by the back of the Colleges: the blossom of the Chestnuts & all the foliage lovely: – in my rooms she had the excitement of feeding the sparrows & pigeons. At Kings we looked at the ground-floor rooms once occupied by Mr Simeon: – as there was a bright sun we saw his name very clearly.[20] – I was asked to 3 dinner parties today, but could not go to any of them as I had to receive the Whist Club . . . the party went off very well indeed: some of my guests staid till 2½. I won a few shillings. End of our whist Season.

*Wed. 30.* . . . We today voted a pension of £65 to Ja. Twitchett for 55 years service at the Press: We also insured the Library, & its Books etc. for £6000 . . .

On 4 June Romilly and Dr and Mrs Mill went over to Norwich to stay with Sedgwick, in residence as a Canon of the cathedral, and his nieces Isabel and Fanny. They inspected the Bishop's palace and garden, enjoyed a 'capital dinner with ice & Champagne' at the Deanery and 'climbed the Tower of the cathedral: the women were ambitious of climbing the Spire also which is mounted by a series of Ladders. – they got up part of the 1st ladder, & then most properly came down again: – Mill & I went as high as possible (rather more than 300 feet)'. On the seventh Romilly and Mill deserted the rest of the party and explored Yarmouth where they greatly enjoyed a bathe. The 'machines here are very cheap, only 6d: & you are furnished with 2 common towels & a flannel rubber'. They had missed the service in the cathedral by the time they got back to Norwich and so Romilly 'went to the Ruination Shop (Blakely's) & bought 2 Gowns & a Shawl & Collar for Lucy, & 2 gowns for the maids'. In the evening Sedgwick with his usual generosity gave another grand dinner where 'I had the Honor of taking in Mrs Opie, wch highly delighted me: she was in great force & conversed about Wilberforce, Mrs Fry, etc'. And after the guests had gone the two old friends enjoyed their usual cigar in the kitchen.

On the last full day of the visit 'We were taken over the Castle by the Governor & told every detail about Rush the Murderer. We here saw the Prisoners under different phases, some on the tread mill, some taking exercise (some with books in their hands), others sitting down where they might have one of their companions read to them'. The afternoon was spent more cheerfully in listening to the band of the 16th Lancers playing on the lawn at Thorpe and then, despite the chilly weather, 'We made a water-party' where the 'Ladies outrowed the gentlemen: – the sight was a very pretty one'.

*Mon. 11 June.* . . . Left Cambridge for Ely at 5.25 in company with G. Williams (author of the book on Jerusalem): – he showed me a Greek letter of thanks to himself from the Patriarch of Jerusalem for a Copy of his book: he showed me also Whiston our Fellows Publication concerning the Grammar-Schools attached to the Cathedrals of Rochester, Canterbury, Ely, etc.: – it is very pungent: it is extremely severe upon Peacock, & quotes his book on the

---

[20] Simeon's name would have been painted outside his rooms, as is still the practice. It had most likely been painted over but not quite obliterated when he died in 1836.

Statutes in condemnation of his toleration of the abuses etc at Ely . . . I should have said that Lucy had a grand excitement today. She saw a hole broken into Mr Asby's house & a little chimney-sweep dragged out by the leg by his brutal master (Wyot I think). She immediately sallied out, attacked the black old devil for having acted illegally in sending a boy up a flue & said she should lodge a complaint at the Station, – which she immediately after did. The ruffian behaved insolently & said 'he supposed she belonged to the Ramo*noors'*. – Lucy's spirited conduct deserved the highest praise. – The Policeman told her that she would find it hard to substantiate her charge, as the villain carried about with him a dwarfish brother of 25 whom he professes to send up the flues whenever he is charged with sending up the boy: – the Policeman engaged to frighten the Master well & also to reprimand Mr Asby (without mentioning Lucy's name): – so Lucy has let the matter drop[21] . . .

*Wed. 13.* . . . Bought a silver penny, a silver 2d & a silver 3d for Franky Kennedy: – they cost me 6d a piece. Called on Miss Page (– she is gone with Mrs Owen to Cromer), also on the Baxendales: I found Miss Salisbury (sister of Mrs Baxendale) ill with an ulcerated sore throat – I then saw the Chelsea-Pensioners exercised on Parker Piece: they performed very well.

*Sat. 16.* 2d Public day at Fitzwilliam (last Wednesday being the 1st): I went there: – the country folks behaved very well: the women were most pleased with the Taj. Mahal[22] & the men with the carpentry of the floor . . .

*Sun. 17.* . . . I wrote to nobody today. – Lucy wrote to Selina Thompson & Harriet Gilson sending them both money & begging them to write to Sarah Foulkes who is desperately ill & takes to heart not hearing from her friends.

*Fri. 22.* . . . Dined with Prof. & Mrs Miller to meet two Lady friends of theirs . . . the other guests were Prof. Blunt & Mr & Mrs Hopkins: – it was a pleasant party . . . Prof. Blunt said that he thought the purest English spoken by the lower classes was near Harwich, – more like the language of the Translators of the Bible: – they there use 'rend' for 'tear', 'weep' for 'cry' etc . . .

*Wed. 4 July.* Brown the Tailor sent us some strawberries – Sarah Foulkes a little better & now languishes for mutton chops & peas . . . Mary Edwards came today from her sister Betsy Spink's to be housemaid at the Hinds: Lucy & I both gave her advice & money without which the advice would have been of no value.

*Th. 5.* . . . Lucy was out on one of her charity missions . . . when she saw Carus whisking by in a fly, flourishing his hand to her, & exhibiting all the joy of a schoolboy going home for the holidays! – called congregation for the laggards: – 3 AM. – Called on the Outrams (our opposite neighbours) & saw

---

[21] Romilly took a keen interest in legislation to protect climbing boys, and in 1840 had tried in vain to persuade Tatham, Master of St John's, to sign a petition on their behalf. By statute sweeps were to take no apprentice under 16 nor was anyone under 21 to climb a chimney. The law was hard to enforce, however, and had to be made more stringent in the 1860s. Ramoneurs (a Frenchified genteelism) used machines of the same name. George Smith of Sidney Street, proprietor of Ramoneur chimney-sweeping machines, was presented with a silver medal in July 1851 by Lord Shaftesbury's Climbing Boys Committee which was trying to suppress the old ways ( *Chronicle* 19 July 1851).

[22] An ivory model donated in 1842 by Richard Burney of Christ's College formerly of India.

Mr & Mrs O., the youngest dr & youngest son: – my voice is so loud & shrill that Lucy heard what I was saying in the Outrams drawing room. – M.A. Tyler came to take leave of Lucy before going to Yarmouth: L. gave her 2.2–, a bottle of wine, & a camp stool: – I gave her 2/6. She was so much overcome with gratitude that as soon as she got home she wrote a letter of thanks to L. & sent it by her sister. – Called on the Searles to ask James for his Victoria votes: wrote also to Mr H.H. Harris for his: – all in behalf of Bidwell the protégé of little Brown the radical tailor.[23] Drank tea with the Marchesa ... I went away at 9¾ ...

*Wed. 11.* ... I called yesterday on the Worsleys (to thank for flowers) & found them sitting under their trees: – they are going to erect in their garden a Victoria Arch in honor of the Queens visit[24] ... Dined in Caius Hall with Stokes ... besides strawberries & raspberries we had Bananas (a present of Dr Paget's): bananas are rather like sleepy pears mixt up with pomatum: we had some fried (on the suggestion of Preston who had so eaten them at Damascus): I thought them very nice in this state. – I staid & plaid whist successfully till near 10 o'clock. – Agreeable letter from G.T.R.

*Th. 12.* Lucy a long walk (to Thompson's lane, to take some boots to little Melbourn & to see the Gilmours) before breakfast. ... The Victoria Asylum Election. Our Candidate Bidwell is defeated: – Overton has won the day. – Overton had 201 votes, Bidwell 183: – the next Candidate Freeman only 45 & Mason only 1 ... The annual school feast in Downing: – the Balloon came sailing over our house, & we heard the shouting of the children quite plain. Went on with 'Clever Boys'.[25]

*Sat. 14.* ... Lucy & I went at ¼ to 8 to meet Hannah Smyth on her return from Rothley (near Loughboro). We met with considerable difficulty in getting on to the Platform, being refused ... by a policeman stationed at the foot of the staircase: however Mr Clark heard my voice & came up & ordered our admission. We were detained above an hour, the grand excursion train (for such it was) being *greatly* behind time: – a prodigious no of carriages. – We thought Hannah a good deal improved ... Mrs Tyler & M.A. Tyler came also by the same train from Yarmouth ... I have surrendered my room to Hannah for the few days she is going to stop & sleep in college ...

*Fri. 20.* ... Dined in hall: only 4 (including myself). At 7½ Lucy walked down with me to College to see the arrival of the Judge (Wilde): when we had

---

[23] The Victoria Friendly Societies' Asylum, a retreat for infirm but respectable men and women, had been established in Chesterton Road in 1837. Romilly and Lucy were subscribers. Many charities dispensed their aid to competing applicants only after a protracted election among the subscribing patrons. The whole system of canvassing, bartering, and borrowing or buying proxy votes was as time consuming to the earnest sponsor as it must have been tormenting to the candidate. To pick a winner and see him through to victory was akin to 'any triumph on the track, the playing field or the stock market' (D. Owen, *English Philanthropy 1660-1960* (1964), pp. 481-2 ).

[24] She had attended a horticultural show at Downing during Albert's installation as Chancellor in July 1847.

[25] Presumably a juvenile tale published in 1848 by Chambers, the Edinburgh publishers. Romilly was a constant reader of books for children in his later years; he may have had an eye on suitable material for his increasing number of great-nephews and great-nieces and Lucy's child paupers.

drunk some bottled beer in my rooms & witnessed the Gambades of all the little blackguards in the Great Court news was brought that the Judge was detained at Huntingdon: – This is the only attempt Lucy has ever made to hear the Judges' trumpets: – little encouragement for her to try again. She was however much pleased with the 4 magnificent horses of the Sheriff (old Eben: Foster) which she patted & praised ...

*Sun. 22* ... Dined in Hall to receive the Judges, about 34, – just squeezed into one long table: – my Guests were the V.C., the Sheriff & my 2 neighbours Pullen & Foster ... Everything went off capitally: we all went to Chapel (including the Baptist Fosters). We had the beautiful anthem of Mozart 'Plead thou my cause'. – After Chapel introduced to Lady Wilde:[26] she is handsome & is like her Father the D. of Sussex:[27]– her parasol was yesterday stolen in the Fitzwilliam museum: – the wife of the Chief Justice should have been safe from theft ...

*Mon. 23*. ... I then escorted Lady Wilde & the 2 Marshalls (Mr Nicholson a Trinity M.A. & Mr Somerset a son of Ld Granville Somerset & Fellow of All Souls) to Trinity Library, etc. She was very gay & agreeable. On seeing the statue of Lord Byron & the Milton M.S. she said that we had committed petty larceny in obtaining them ... She was very much delighted with the Round Church.[28] I also took her to see the chalk drawing of O. Cromwell at Sidney

[26] Augusta Wilde was one of the many illegitimate and therefore unacknowledged cousins of the Queen. Her father, the Duke of Sussex, sixth son of George III, contracted (in contravention of the Royal Marriage Act) an early marriage which was declared void long before her birth in 1801. She had met Wilde while he was acting as counsel for her brother in his futile attempt to be recognised as Duke of Sussex after their father's death.

[27] Sussex (1773-1843) was singular in his family for his intellectual tastes and consistently liberal principles, which he displayed in the House of Lords to their embarrassment. He supported Catholic Emancipation and the Reform Bill. He was educated at Göttingen, received an honorary Cambridge LL.D. in 1819, and enjoyed occasional visits to Trinity afterwards. He was President both of the Society of Arts and Royal Society and was a well-liked if mildly eccentric figure in Whig circles. His large library, strong in theology, was not ornamental, and it impressed even the great Dr Parr. Sussex took offence when Parliament nominated Albert as regent in case of Victoria's death but the Prince became chief mourner at his funeral, which, in accordance with his wishes, took place not at Windsor but at Kensal Green cemetery after his body had been opened for scientific examination. See R. Fulford, *Royal Dukes* (revised edition, 1973), chapter 6.

[28] i.e. Holy Sepulchre, one of only five surviving round churches in England. Part of it had collapsed in 1841 and a drastic 'restoration' was undertaken by the vocal and energetic Cambridge Camden Society, founded in 1839 by J.M. Neale and others in the University who believed with Pugin that Gothic architecture would best lead men to worship. They encouraged the restoration of churches and their fittings in medieval fashion, and erected a stone-altar and credence-table in the Round Church which led to a lawsuit and the closing of the church. It was reopened in 1845 after several courts had examined the matter and the offending quasi-Catholic items were removed. When Romilly and Lucy visited the church on 25 April 1845 they saw that both altar and credence table 'were lying (not very decorously) in the church-yard'. Partly as a result of the battle over St Sepulchre's the 'Camdenites' were suspected of Popery and the society split, re-emerging under a new name as the Ecclesiological Society, a national body. Its influence in restoring or wrecking (depending on one's view) most English churches for the rest of the century was immense. See J.F. White, *The Cambridge Movement: the Ecclesiologists and the Gothic Revival* (1962).

Lodge: – little Edith Phelps came in, so I said to her 'this is a very great Lady, this is the Lady of the Chief Justice'; upon wch she said to Edith 'Yes, remember I am Chief Justice over the Chief Justice' . . . Lady Wilde said to me 'You Cambridge people have been great benefactors to me: – my Father had left you his library: but when you didn't elect him Chancellor he was so much vext that he altered his will: so I gained £10,000. If he had been alive when P. Albert was chosen I think he would have died of an apoplectic stroke' . . .

*Tu. 24.* An order from Home Office for a return of Admissions, B.A. degrees & pluckings,[29] & Testimonials for Orders, for last 5 years from every College. – I procured a Trinity return & drew up a report of the successful & unsuccessful Candidates for B.A. degree . . . Our maids have got the prevalent Bowel Complaint. Lucy dosed them with carminative which has done a deal of good . . . She was a good deal worried today by ceaseless inroads of paupers while she was writing her sermons . . .

*Wed. 25.* Wrote to Deighton the Surgeon about the bad state of the drains at the back of Doric St.: he has kindly promised to look into it. – Escorted Serjeant Dowling & the Chief Justice & Marshalls to our Library. Sedgwick joined us, & then did the Honors of his Museum to them & also to Lady Wilde . . . I should have said that the ruffians who assaulted Mr Glover in the Grantchester fields are transported for 7 years[30] & Smithson the lover of the unfortunate Miss Bowtell (who poisoned herself) imprisoned for 3 months for his savage assault on Mr Quinlivan the Romish priest.

On 1 August Romilly was again at Audley End and relieved to find that Mr Neville, the Braybrookes' second son, 'is so much better that he is staying in London without his Doctor'. The highlight of his stay was his walk to Strethall Hall owned by two Mr Perrys, one of whom had recently killed a man. 'I asked if I could see the house. The maid said her Masters were out, but consented to let me in. I found there a fine handsome stout young fellow dressed like a gamekeeper & carrying a gun. He acted the whole scene of the attack & defence with prodigious vividness. He planted me at the top of the staircase of 9 steps where I was to represent the Mr Perry who fired. He himself enacted chief burglar & came in stealthily thro the kitchen-door, pretending to carry a pistol in one hand & a lantern in the other. He turned halfround on seeing the man at the head of the stairs & received the contents of the gun thro his heart. He then acted falling down dead, & represented his comrades dragging off the body & escaping out of the window . . . It was this dead body wch was sent over to Paget with the pithy note 'If you would like the man who is lying in our house he is much at your service: – I'll send him over in a Cart'.

*Mon. 6 August* . . . At 7 in the Evening I went to Sedgwick's to hear him read his preface to his forthcoming 5th Edition of his Sermon: – the part he read was the attack on the Author of the Vestiges of the Creation (who is no longer thought to be Sir Hussey Vivian, but is believed to be Chambers

---

29  i.e. failed candidates, the men 'plucked' or rejected in an examination. Compare 'ploughed' which supplanted 'plucked' later in the century.

30  Josephus Glover of St John's, the Sixth Wrangler of 1848, was attacked and robbed by two local men while returning from Grantchester where he had been drinking tea with the Reverend Derisley Harding (*Chronicle* 28 July).

of Edinburgh);[31] this part is a repetition of his article in the Edinburgh Review . . .

*Tu. 7.* . . . Sent for by the V.C. who wants his Guard Books of University Papers indexed: – I undertook to do it for him. – Yesterday I copied out the trial of a Chesterton Publican (Curtis) for allowing Sunday tippling . . . I today was soft enough to show some strangers over the Public Library at the request of one of the impertinent Ciceroni: – I told him afterwards he must never ask me again. – At the Public Library one is obliged to stay all the time with the Visitors: – a mere introduction is enough at the Fitzwilliam.

*Wed. 8.* . . . Read loud the new no of David Copperfield: it is a very clever account of the embarrassments of the poor devils with whom he lodges, & also of the marriage of Barkis & Peggotty . . .

*Sat. 11.* Letter from Lady Braybrooke asking me to call on Dowager Lady Elgin & dr Lady A. Bruce[32] who are come to pass the long vacation in Cambridge: – the old Lady's son Tho. (of Jes.) is going out in January: he is now working double tides & reading with Walton & Shilleto . . . I found the old Lady a mass of flesh: she was wrapt in a loose dressing gown as if she could not bear the confinement of light drapery. She is the widow of the Elgin Marbles man: she generally resides at Paris, & was there during all the troubles of last year . . . I found her daughter Lady A. very sprightly & agreeable & quite free from the Scotch accent of her Countess Mother: – she is Lady in waiting to the Duchess of Kent . . . Sedgwick came to my office with a proof sheet for me to correct: Edleston came also to see the official document wch exempted Newton as Lucasian Prof. from the necessity of taking orders to retain his Fellowship: – it is a Royal Letter of Charles 2 dated 27 Apr. 1675 . . .

*Mon. 20.* . . . College meeting (we happen to be just 8 in College) – to pass 3 Testimonials.[33] Sedgwick brought another proof sheet for me to look over . . . A Renegade (Herbert Marshall B.A. Caius 1848) wrote to me to ask him to strike his name out of the list of A.B.s: – I answered him, that his Apostasy could not alter a fact, & that his name would remain for ever in the Registry with the names of others who like him had abjured the Faith in which he had been educated & wch he had publicly professed, but that if he wrote to his College Tutor to take his name off the boards he would doubtless be most willing to comply with his request[34] . . .

[31] The author was indeed Robert Chambers who published anonymously *The Vestiges of Creation*, a prelude in some sense to Darwin, in 1845. It had been repeatedly attacked in print and was detested by Sedgwick who inflated his new edition of *On the Studies of the University* (1850) with fulminations against it. Guessing the authorship of *Vestiges* was a drawing-room diversion for many years. See M.M. Garland, *Cambridge before Darwin* (1980), pp. 99-101, and the edition of *Vestiges* by J.A. Secord (University of Chicago Press, 1994).

[32] She was a lady in waiting to the Duchess of Kent. See *Letters of Lady Augusta Stanley: a Young Lady at Court 1849-1863* (1927)

[33] The colleges were normally asked to provide certificates of good behaviour for intending clergymen and schoolmasters. In 1834 Wordsworth, the old Master, declined to sign testimonials for Romilly's cousin Peter Ouvry, a prospective clergyman, on the grounds that he had not attended Holy Communion in Trinity chapel often enough.

[34] The authorities of a university Anglican in its tradition and usages, and a nursery of clergymen, had been embarrassed by a small but steady number of conversions to Roman Catholicism

Between 30 August and 11 September Romilly was in Paris visiting his younger brother Frank and his family for the first time for eight years. He had cut his preparations for travelling uncharacteristically fine. 'Left Cambridge by 2 o'clock train. – I arrived at the French Passport office (K. William St. London Bridge) at ¼ to 5: the office hours are from 12 to 4: – but they most civilly gave me a Passport: – by the way the Republic charges 5s for its Passport: the King used to give it gratis. – I arrived at the Bankers 5' past 5; the clerks were shutting up, but as I made very civil speeches I obtained the money I asked for (£30)'. The next morning he left 'London Bridge Quay at 11 by the Calais Boat called "The Menai": the passage cost 12s/'. As always, he got into conversation with his fellow-travellers and was the recipient of much confidential information – 'Among the passengers was a country Gentleman (named Harris) & his invalide wife & their son & a beautiful dog. Mrs Harris was ill-managed in her 1st confinement & has only one living child, having miscarried 12 times ... He is very pronounced in his opinions about uniformity: he thinks Government ought not to tolerate any Romish or dissenting Chapels & that the Duke of Wellington sullied all his victories by the Catholic Emancipation. ... At dinner on the boat I took the chair & said Grace. – We had a most beautiful passage of 9½ hours: the end of it in brilliant moonshine'.

Romilly was warmly received by his family and with them sight-saw indefatigably. It was a fascinating time in which to be in the city. 'The reminiscences of royalty are as far as possible obliterated in Paris: – the royal arms have disappeared from the theatres & all public places & the Royal names from all shops. It is most ridiculous to see "Liberté, Egalité, Fraternité" painted on the Porte St Denis erected in honor of Louis XIV, – no friend to equality. – The "trees of Liberty" are dying miserable-looking Poplars on which the ragged remains of tricolored flags (now one dingy dirt colour) are mouldering away'. Frank 'took me to see the spot where the murderous fighting took place in June 1848 (by the St Lazare enclosure): – one saw still the appearance of the loopholes (or meurtrieres) thro which the insurgents fired: – the corps de garde etc was destroyed here'. In contrast they enjoyed revisiting some of the city's greatest churches and the Louvre, took a box at the Opéra Comique where 'I found the performance insufferably long: – it lasted from 7 till near 12' and sat in the stalls of the Théatre National for the first reappearance of Rachel. Here they were in luck 'for the President (Louis Napoléon) was at the Theatre, & his box was close to us. He looks like a mediocre person who does not deserve his high position ... Not the slightest notice in the world was taken of him'. One of the most interesting dinner parties during the visit was given by Madame Alexandrine Bourlet '(Marchande de Modes to the Royal Family while Royalty existed)' and mother-in-law of Fanny, Frank's daughter. She 'showed us some of her beautiful new caps'.

On the return journey the 'steamer (wch was very small) pitched & tossed a good deal: I however was not at all qualmish, & only 2 or 3 were sick. – We got across in 2 hours. – We had to be put ashore in boats: & as the darkness was complete there was a good deal of floundering in getting down the side of the steamer, but happily the rain had now ceased'. Romilly's portmanteau and box, in which amongst other presents, were daguerrotypes of himself and Frank's family, were cleared by the Commissioner in the custom house at 7 the following morning and he was able to leave 'Dover by the Mail Train at 10' on the first stage of his journey home.

among its members, especially its junior members. Yet history was not re-written. There was no attempt to deprive them of their degrees, and resignation from the university was not provided for until the 1970s.

*Wed. 12 September.* Sallied out directly after breakfast to buy a watchstand for Lucy, toothbrushes etc. etc . . . Off by the 11.30 train to Cambridge . . . Thank God I found Lucy pretty well . . . Lucy spread out all the presents which I had brought her & which Frank & Fanny & Sophie had sent her on a table & was highly pleased with them. The presents came all safe except one of the 2 china breakfast basins sent by F. & S. – They sent also a beautiful purse with new money it in, a velvet bag with steel beads, a worked collar, & some thin velvet to tie her watch round her neck. Frank sent prints of Archb. Afra (who was killed at the Barricade last year),[35] Mr Coquerel (the Preacher at the Oratoire), & the President of the Republic (Prince L. Napoleon), 2 China figures of Liberty, a china Cat, 2 pair of spectacles, 5 bottles of Eyewater, masses of Guimauve (white & brown), a bonbonnière, a large pasteboard box of his own manufacture, an infinitude of sponge biscuits for the bird etc etc. I brought her a gold watch, a silk umbrella, drest dolls & various nicknackeries. – I brought the maids a fan and a workbox for each . . .

*Sun. 16.* An awful fire on the marketplace broke out at 12¼ last night & has destroyed 8 houses. – Lucy & I went to see the smouldering ruins just before church: I never saw more complete destruction, – the outside Walls are all gone: they must have been mere lath & plaster.[36] – Lucy staid looking on till near the end of the Litany: I went in for the beginning of the service. – Today was the 1st day of reading the prayer concerning the Cholera . . . Carus . . . said but very little about the Cholera: the principal object of his sermon was a thanksgiving for the abundant harvest . . . Lucy called on the Millegans in New Town to condole with them on the burning down of their house in St Mary's St: – Miss Millijam (Mrs M's sister) & 2 apprentices were sleeping there last night: she has always been dreadfully timid about fire & was ½ distracted when she found the house afire: – she escaped with scarcely any clothing & ran home to the New Town. – There was most happily no bodily injury endured by any one . . .

*Mon. 17.* . . . Lucy before breakfast to see the smouldering ruins: – her protégé Andrews the shoemaker (with wife & 8 children) in Pump Lane is burnt out . . .

*Tu. 18.* . . . Lucy was highly pleased with the business-like habits of an oilman named Moden who was burned out: – he has printed handbills saying he has

---

[35] i.e. D-A. Affre, Archbishop of Paris, who had been mortally wounded while attempting to pacify the crowds in June 1848.

[36] The old market place was much smaller than it is now, having a block of shops on its west side and others abutting Great St Mary's. An alarm was raised about half past midnight at Lodge's, the clothier's, and before long several fire engines were on the scene including those from Trinity and St John's, while volunteers manned bucket-chains as far as the river. But the fire took hold, walls fell, distracted folk tried to remove their goods, and a gas explosion was feared. By dawn eight houses had been destroyed and many others were damaged although no lives were lost. The police were out in force to guard tempting property from looters. After long examination a jury empanelled by the coroner returned an open verdict on the Tuesday following about the causes of the fire. After the inevitable bickering among various interested parties the Cambridge Corporation Act of 1850 empowered the authorities to reconstruct the whole site. An elaborate fountain with statues of worthies was erected in the centre of the market in 1855 and demolished in 1953. See A.B. Gray, *Cambridge Revisited* (1921), pp. 107-14 with plan.

set up shop in Falcon Yard: – Lucy sent me to buy some pickles of him by way of encouraging his new shop. – I should have said that one maidservant ran off half-naked & half distracted to her parents in Barnwell, *carrying her box*. – A child of Lucy's protégés the Andrews was very nearly burnt to death: – it had been quite forgotten, & was imagined to be with the other children: – but old Andrews in whisking off the bedclothes to save them found the little girl underneath.

*Wed. 19*. . . . Livermore (the Baker at the corner of Silver St.) attacked with Cholera. – Visit in my office from Randall concerning the licence of a house in Trin. St. (just bought by Trin. Coll.) in 1716 by the sign of the Ram: – I could find no trace of it: – the signs are not recorded regularly before 1752 . . . Isabel Sedgwick has been very ill with a bowel complaint & could not go to Birmingham to the Music Meeting & Brit. Association . . .

*Sat. 22*. . . . Poor Livermore was buried yesterday: – the coffin was lowered down from the window: – I saw it from my office. – Lucy & I had letters from Frank . . . In the Evening read loud the last no of D. Copperfield (his journey to his Aunt at Dover): – very clever.

*Tu. 25*. Took Latin paper to the Press: Carus is my colleague: he set the Poetry; I the Prose . . . Today Lucy & I wrote to poor Betsy Spink (from whom we heard this morning): she has had an attack of Cholera: & is still very weak indeed. – The Evening's Post brought a most melancholy letter from John Roget saying that Kate had had a brain fever a fortnight ago, that she had been delirious ever since & that they saw no prospect of her recovering her senses! How very dreadful: I wrote to Roget & begged him to write again.

*Sat. 29*. Walked to the Observatory to ask what time Challis would exhibit it to Lady Elgin[37] & daughter. He appointed tonight at 8 when Lady Agnes Buller (twin sister of the late Duke) is to be there . . . At 8 I went to Lady Elgin's, & proceeded with her & Lady Augusta to the Observatory. – It rained cats & dogs, & we of course saw nothing but the Instruments: – Challis gave an excellent Lecture on the Northumberland Telescope & answered an infinitude of astronomical questions with which Lady Elgin had come charged: – Lady Augusta & I talked with Lady A. Buller & her husband, who obviously cared not a straw about science. – We afterwards went into the drawing room to Mr & Miss Challis & looked over prints of nebulae etc etc . . .

*Sun. 30*. . . . Today Lucy hunted out her new protégés (the Andrews, who were burnt out at the late fire, & whose little girl of 6 years old was in great danger of being burned to death) . . . they have made a capital thing of the fire: – they have received £25 as a compensation for their supposed loss, wch they confess to have been a mere trifle, & Lucy is going to put £6 in the Savings Bank for the little girl. – Carus set on foot a subscription for the only 2 uninsured (Andrews & Wonfor) & raised £50! . . . Read loud 'Predicatoriana'.

[37] Widow of Lord Elgin of Marbles fame. Her companion, Lady Agnes Buller, was sister of the Duke of Northumberland (d. 1847) who had been High Steward and then Chancellor of the University before Prince Albert, and who in 1835 gave the Observatory a magnificent telescope made by Cauchoix of Paris and a building with a revolving dome to house it. The uninterested husband was an army man.

*Mon. 8 October.* Called on Mrs Prest to learn how to fold a great shawl of Lucy's wch I brought her from Norwich. – She told me a story about Mrs Gale Towley's unluckiness at a great dinner at Wisbech where she said 'I'm very glad that Hinds is appointed Bp of Norwich as it has kept out Dr Whewell whom all Norwich was so afraid of having fastened upon them'. – Whewell was present & must have heard her ... Carus & I went over together to dine with Mrs Adeane ... I thought the dinner a very poor affair: – no fish, no Champagne or Claret, & no Grapes at dessert ... After tea all of us (but Mrs Adeane & Mrs Ward & one daughter who was gone to bed) played at the game of 'Word & Question'. Every person writes a Question on one piece of paper, & a Noun on another: – these papers are all shaken together & each person draws one of each: – everybody then answers the 'Question' in Verse, introducing the 'Noun' ...

*Tu. 9.* I am this day 58 complete. I am, thank God, pretty much in my usual health except that I am suffering from weakness in the wrists & a more than usual propensity to perspiration ... Had a bottle of Hock at dinner for Lucy & the maids to drink my health. – I had better not have done so as it turned out. – Drank tea at Trin. Lodge with my brother-Examiners. – Mrs Whewell not returned from Lowestoff. It was the easiest election I ever recollect & the quickest. – We elected

$$\left\{\begin{array}{l}\text{Scott (University Sch.) (he wrote some brilliant Latin Verse transl. from}\\ \quad\text{Penseroso)}\\ \text{Westcott (University Sch.)}\\ \text{Walker (2nd (Wr.))}\\ \text{Hillier (4th Wr,)}\\ \text{Luard (14th Wr,)}\end{array}\right.$$

These filled up vacancies made by

$$\left\{\begin{array}{l}\text{Lawrence(Law \& married)}\\ \text{Blackburn(married)}\\ \text{Keary(married)}\\ \text{Guillebaud(Hoveringham)}\\ \text{Evatt(Cheadle)}\end{array}\right.$$

I went to Sedgwick's & smoked a cigar. Home about 9 ...

*Wed. 10.* I left home at 7½ it being a very busy day in College. – At ¼ to 9 to Chapel to complete the Election of Fellows. – At 10 the work of the term began by the Election of Middleton (Kings) as Proctor, & then every thing else in the usual routine ... Directly after the 1st Congregation (11½) was a long College meeting wch lasted till the 2d congregation. So I did not see Lucy till ½ past 3 when I found her dining off some pudding. She had been taken very ill indeed early this morning (about 8) with violent vomiting, great pain in her body & all the premonitory symptoms of Cholera. Harriet went for Mr Ficklin, but he was out of Cambridge (having gone to London to Charles Neville's marriage): Harriet then went to Mr Decks & got his remedy, which (thank God) proved effectual: – the maids had been dreadfully frightened, & so should I have been had I known of poor Lucy's sufferings ...

*Th. 11.* Lucy (thank God) is much better . . . She ascribes her illness of yesterday to the glass of Hock on Tuesday: – it may indeed have been so, as she is in the habit of drinking nothing stronger than small beer . . . Letter from J.L. Roget saying that dear Kate had borne her journey to town better than could have been expected: there are hopes that the alienation of her mind (wch seems to be connected with religious despondence) may be of an hysteric tendency & that it will in time be completely removed . . . A very agreeable letter from Mrs Tho. Smart Hughes asking me to assist her old servant (Dunn) who is a candidate for the bedmaker's place vacant by the death of G.B.Allen's old bed maker whom he hated so much (Mrs Radcliffe) . . . Mrs Radcliffe's daughter is also a candidate. My wishes are in favor of the poor dirty miserable old drudge of Mrs Radcliffe's, named Murcutt: – I fear she will not succeed, her appearance is so far from respectable . . . In the Evening read "Pickwick".

*Fri. 12.* . . . Today was observed as a day of Public Humiliation for the Cholera . . . All the shops were shut up the whole day, & there was very great external appearance of seriousness. The Churches were all thronged except Scholefields: – he had preached a very eloquent sermon on the subject last Sunday . . . Carus . . . preached in a very energetic & solemn manner on national & individual sins . . . I admired very greatly the whole attack on individual sins, but I thought him seditious & rebellious when he attacked the Queen & her Government: – his principal charges against 'the powers that be' were, the omission of 'Dei Gratia' on the Florin, the allowance of Sunday Travelling, encouragement of idolatry by grants to the Rom. Cath. colleges etc, & above all the contemplated desecration of the Sabbath by giving work on Sunday to employés in the London Gen. Post Office[38] . . .

From 17 to 19 October Romilly again stayed at Audley End 'in my usual room which I find is called the Chaplains'. He read prayers, played billiards and three rubbers with Mr Neville '(who plays villainously)', saw the pheasants being fed and learnt that the curtsying owls were dead, having been poisoned. At the grand dinner on the eighteenth he met Dr Buckland, the geologist and Dean of Westminster, who is 'wild about a book called "Antiquities of Creation" by a clergyman of the name of Gray: he said he would give me a copy if I would undertake to read it by breakfast tomorrow'. Romilly 'set to at it vigorously', thought it eloquent and well-reasoned and was given his copy. 'It praises Buckland, which may account for his great admiration of it'.

A great annual event took place on the last day. 'At 12 all the Gentlemen accompanied Lord Braybrooke to Walden Agricultural meeting: – the Ladies came in carriages after luncheon. – We went to the ploughing match, saw all the prize animals & vegetables, went over the museum (where was a white stuffed peacock), & saw the cold dinner at which Lord B. was to preside after the distribution of the Prizes . . . Lord B.

[38] Carus's sentiments are mirrored in numerous Sabbatarian and anti-Catholic writings. When the florin (or two-shilling piece) was issued in this year as a step towards eventual decimal coinage the words 'Dei Gratia' were omitted from the inscription so giving rise to the epithets 'graceless' and 'godless'. Worse still, the unhappy master of the mint was a Catholic. The issue was recalled. Maynooth was the college for training Irish Catholic clergy that was seldom free from ill-report and whose financial support by the British government was anathema to many, the more so in these days of 'papal aggression'. Sabbatarians were disgusted both by Sunday train travel and the need for workers in the Post Office on Sundays.

was very nervous & the paralytic affection of his hands was very marked: He made an admirable address . . . he touched on the happiness of the town in not having suffered from cholera: he warned the men against beerhouses, & complained of the shameful neglect of sending their children to school. – Lord B. made little speeches to each of the persons to whom prizes were given: one of them was a maid of Lady B's: – another was a woman who had had 15 children, 3 at one birth (2 of the 3 were alive & produced): – this woman had the principal prize, viz, a £5 clock from Lord B., & a scarlet cloke (which was publicly put on her) from Lady B. – Major Beresford (who is Member for the County) proposed 3 cheers for Lord Braybr. . . . The amiable Ld Nelson gave 3 cheers for the Ladies: but the few sentences he stumbled thro were a complete failure. The procedings ended with 3 shouts for the successful Candidates'. Romilly waited at Audley End until his host and other gentlemen at length returned from the agricultural dinner. He then set off for the mail train which was late and because of that and 'the no. of Gownsmen & the infinitude of their luggage' on the platform at Cambridge 'did not get to bed till near 1'.

*Sat. 20.* Sat up in state . . . at my office from 10 to 3 . . . I had prepared 300 cards: I had got a large book for the names, & had required the attendance of my Clerk. – I received one Fee only, viz for a General Ticket. – At 11 I proclaimed the market,[39] & then went to the V.C.'s to draw up an ale Licence. – At 3 Sir James Stephen was admitted by the V.C. in my presence to the Professorship of Modern History: – by the way he had not 21/ about him, so I have not received my Fee. – Today there was a Seniority to reprimand the youngsters who had disgraced themselves by their idleness & ignorance at the June Examination . . .

*Mon. 22.* Our neighbours the Hinds are queer folks: they drink no wine but have a passion for brandy & water. The other day Miss Hind thought hers too weak: so she asked for more brandy, saying with a sly look 'Man wants but little here below; but wants that little strong!' – The 5th Commandment is not obeyed in their house: the girls call their Father an 'old Humbug': & Mrs Hind speaks of her husband as 'a dirty beast' . . .

*Tu. 23.* Election of Lucasian Prof.: – no Candidate but G.G. Stokes: – there could not have been a better[40] . . .

*Wed. 24.* . . . Congregation . . . The Orator made a brilliant speech in wch he eulogised Prof. Smyth & gave a beautiful & most vivid account of his lecture on the executions of L. XVI & Marie Antoinette, & the manner in wch Smyth & all his audience were affected. He had passed on to a panegyric on Sir James' Father for his exertions on the Slave Trade when suddenly he lost the thread of his speech & remained silent for a minute or more . . . he did not produce a

[39] An annual ceremony which maintained the right of the university to supervise local trading. The Vice-Chancellor, Heads, and various officials took cake and wine in the Senate House before processing to Peas Hill where the Registrary read his proclamation which was repeated by the Yeoman Bedell. The ceremony was then repeated on Market Hill. See H. Gunning, *The Ceremonies of the University* (1828), p. 41. This right, which found no favour with the townsfolk, was abolished seven years later.

[40] The chair of mathematics, the first 'scientific' professorship at Cambridge, had been founded in 1663 out of a benefaction by Henry Lucas, the University M.P. It had been held by Newton and more recently by G.B. Airy and Charles Babbage.

paper but waited till his memory returned, when he went on admirably to the end. – Not one man in a 100 could have gone on again after such a breakdown. – The Master of Trinity exercised his disciplinarian propensities today to the sad violation of gallantry & courtesy: – he told the Jun. Proctor to turn out of the Pit an undergraduate with 2 young ladies: they had timidly come to the door & had been invited in by Leapingwell: – they were Mr Gurney (Trin) & his 2 sisters: – the rage of Leapingwell was intense: he wished the undergraduates to put on hobnail-shoes & in a body to kick his shins! ...

*Sun. 28.* . . . Betsy (Mrs Ja. Spink) came to Camb. today: she drank tea with us & sat with us till 9½: I rather astonished Lucy by kissing Betsy. I thought Betsy looking very ill from the effect of the Cholera: she made herself very agreeable, tho I would willingly have spared her sad details of the death of neighbours of hers, an old man, his son & son's wife & 3 children, – all of Cholera! – Betsy gave a ludicrous account of the Doctor looking round her room to see if her goods were valuable enough to pay him his bill. – Lucy & I each gave her 10 ...

*Wed. 31.* . . . Congregation: – no degrees. – The new modification of the Classical Tripos came on today, whereby 1st Class of Polloi are to go in to the C.T. It was carried by 43 to 31 in B.H, & by 38 to 26 in W.H.[41] – Mrs Archdall better today again. – Two chaps tantalised me by coming into my office: – I thought they were surely come for tickets: – it was to see the Mesman Pictures! ...

*Sat. 3 November.* . . . Lucy highly amused by a Lady on horseback dropping her *bustle*: the groom dismounted and picked it up! ... At breakfast today Carus told us of the funeral of young Watson (who destroyed himself): Langshaw read the service; & when he came to the words 'as our hope this our brother doth', the young man's Father exclaimed in an agony of grief 'Oh no! there is no hope for him' ... Today devoted 2 hours to looking over proofsheets for Sedgwick: the preface is dreadfully too long, above 300 pages! ...

*Sun. 4.* . . . Roget called to show me a very clever letter from poor Kate, – the 1st she had written since her illness: all the early part was written with great cheerfulness & brilliance, but I found the end very touching & mournful where she spoke of herself as being no more 'Kate the crazed', but 'clothed & in her right mind' ...

*Sun. 11.* Lovely day. – Mrs & Miss Amos in town: so we had our pew to ourselves. When we had been a few minutes in Church I observed great nos

---

[41] The Classical Tripos had been instituted in 1824 and hitherto been open only to those who had already passed the Mathematical Tripos (with the peculiar exception of the sons of peers). Mathematics was too great a hurdle for many, some of them men of intellectual distinction like Macaulay, and in April 1849 a syndicate had been appointed to consider changes in the regulations. It met stiff opposition. Whewell and others considered the Classical Tripos insufficiently testing, or testing the wrong things – especially mere linguistic skill in Greek, Latin, and English, rather than sound knowledge. The Report, issued on 20 May 1849, proposed the addition of a paper in ancient history to stiffen the content of the examination but also opened it to those who had a first class in the unexacting poll or ordinary degree. Whewell and four other Syndics declined to sign the Report. See Winstanley, pp. 216-18.

rushing out & the pew opener whispered to me that St Michaels was in a blaze.[42] Both Lucy & I longed to bolt: but we remained in church to the end. When we came out we went to St Michaels where was a great crowd, but the fire was extinguished: it had destroyed the roof: but the chancel with its beautiful stalls was little hurt. it arose from a new stove wch was heated at 7 o'cl. this morning. – Lucy afterwards to her paupers & I to St Marys . . .

*Mon. 12.* . . . Betsy . . . is going home tomorrow (having been here more than a fortnight: – she has feathered her nest famously, £3 in money, a pound of tea, a pound of cocoa, ½ dozen of wine, 3 quartern loaves (from 3 different friends); an immense piece of wedding cake (Guillebaud's our late fellow's), etc etc: she also carried off 6 boxes & baskets, having come without any! . . . I have offered to be godfather to her baby if it is a boy . . .

*Tu. 13.* Poor Dr French[43] died about 5 o clock yesterday Evening of paralysis. He was present at the Syndicate meeting on Saturday from 12 to 2 & seemed to me to be in his usual health. He was taking his lunch of chocolate in his own study about ½ an hour afterwards when he was seized with Paralysis: the case was pronounced hopeless by Fisher from the first . . . Matriculation day[44] . . . one Black (Mr Crumwell) was matriculated: I hear he has a black wife & black pickaninnies[45] . . .

*Wed. 14.* . . . Dined at the Ch. Townleys . . . Mrs Frere astonished me by doubting the guilt of Maria Manning.[46] She says that she was once in company with Sir S. Romilly & another distinguished lawyer, & that a story was then told

[42] For a bustling illustration see the *Illustrated London News* of 17 November; it is reproduced by A.B. Gray, *Cambridge Revisited* (1921), p. 104.

[43] Master of Jesus whose successor was Professor Corrie.

[44] i.e. formal admission of new undergraduates, already admitted to their colleges, as members of the university and subject to its rules and privileges. For full figures from 1800 to 1872 see H.R. Luard's *Graduati Cantabrigienses* (1873), pp. 541-2, where the annual intake is classified by status as noblemen, Fellow commoners, pensioners, and sizars. Numbers rose steadily after the 1860s.

[45] Crummell (1819-98) was a free-born ordained American episcopalian. See J.D. Twigg, *A History of Queens' College, Cambridge* (1987), pp. 168-71, and D.A. Lorimer, *Colour, Class and the Victorians* (1978), pp. 215-19. His health during his four years here was indifferent and one of his children died in tragic circumstances (*Chronicle* 7 June 1851). Later he worked as a missionary in Liberia and on his return home helped found the American Negro Academy. See 29 January 1853.

[46] After one of the most sensational trials of the age Maria Manning, a young foreigner, and her unimpressive husband (it is she who is entombed in the *Dictionary of National Biography*) had been convicted of the murder and robbery of her lover whom they buried under the kitchen floor. Acres of newsprint brought the gruesome evidence before a fascinated public. Was the elegant and self-possessed Maria a Lady Macbeth or a catspaw? Did not the law presume a wife must be under her husband's direction? See A. Borowitz, *The Woman Who Murdered Black Satin* (Ohio State University Press, 1981), reprinted as *The Bermondsey Horror* (1988). Henry Mayhew who interviewed a London seller of lurid broadsheets in 1850 discovered that they had a ready sale in Cambridge. 'The last time I was at Cambridge, sir, I hung the Mannings... We pattered at night, too late for the collegians to come out. We 'worked' about where we knew they lodged – I had a mate with me – and some of the windows of their rooms, in the colleges themselves, looks into the street. We pattered about later news of Mr and Mrs Manning. Up went the windows, and cords was let down to tie the papers to. But we always had the money first.' (P. Ward, *Cambridge Street Literature* (1978), p. 21).

to show the danger arising from implicit confidence in strong circumstantial evidence . . . She said that a boy in her fathers service when she was 10 years old was on the point of being severely punished for sawing off the tops of some park paling, when fortunately she heard of it & told her father that she was the Culprit herself. – Heard a good story about Princess Royal. Lady Lyttelton had complained to the Queen who on hearing all the various details said 'any thing more?' 'No, Madam', said Lady L.: 'then your Ladyship may retire' said the Q. – A few days after Lady L. censured the P.R. who said 'any thing more?' 'No, Princess Royal': 'then your Ladyship may retire'. – She seems to be enough to try the patience of Job . . .

*Th. 15.* Public day of Thanksgiving. We had our pew to ourselves. Carus preached . . . An excellent Sermon divided into 4 heads of thankfulness . . . He said very few words about Addenbrookes (tho this Sermon & all others at the Camb. parish churches today were for the good of the hospital, – a most appropriate thank offering on the cessation of the Cholera). After the Sermon the offertory etc was read & a collection made from pew to pew: the collectors seemed to have overlooked us, for the Prayer for 'Christs Church etc' was begun when a collector appeared at our door with an empty pewty platter, into wch we each put a sovereign, & the same wicked idea occurred to us both that he would pocket the money . . .

*Th. 22.* Letter from Miss Kelty, asking me to take some copies of a 1/ vol. of poems which a friend of hers Miss Fraser is going to publish as a livre de voyage for Emigrants: sent her 21/. – As Secretary for the Smyth Memorial sent off 25 letters to Committee to meet at Trinity Lodge on Monday[47] . . . Lucy wrote (with my pen) to the St Ann's School Brixton, to wch she means to become again a Subscriber in hopes of voting for some Cholera case. Read loud 'Family Failings': it is very clever & very amusing.[48]

*Wed. 28.* . . . Wrote also a Testimonial for Cotton (in answer to his Letter): he is undermaster at Rugby & offers himself as successor to Tait (the Head Master), just appointed Dean of Carlisle. – I should have said that last night Ann Coe inflicted herself on poor Lucy with a list of grievances . . . She told of the sickness of poor Henrietta Parry, sitting very ill by the fire, with her head shaved, & the Mother sallying out to Evening parties in search of a 2d husband who will never come . . .

*Th. 29.* . . . Two trials yesterday in the V.C.'s Court: – *W. Grey* (whom Lucy abominates for purloining the money wch she gave for his son who was transported) besides being a stablekeeper is landlord of the Tallyho beerhouse in Clement Lane, which he makes into a receiving house:[49] – He was discommuned for ever. The other case was that of G. Whitaker (who keeps a curiousity shop) & let an undergrad. run up a bill of above £50 without telling his Tutor: – he was discommuned till end of 1850[50] . . .

[47] E.H. Bailey carved the bust of the late Professor of History. He was also engaged at this time on busts of Herschel and Whewell. See *Endowments* p. 586.
[48] The recent and only (?) three-decker novel by a Miss Fisher.
[49] i.e. for stolen goods.
[50] Men in statu pupillari (i.e. all undergraduates and recent bachelors) were prohibited from dealing directly or indirectly with anyone who had been 'discommuned' or put beyond the pale

*Sun. 2 December.* A complete wet day ... Lucy had in her Pew only Mrs Amos: she let in a very damp Gownsman. She was much dissatisfied with the huge unsightly church-darkening organ of St Michaels wch has just been put up at Trinity & was played today for the 1st time ... At night read loud Whewell's thanksgiving sermon: it is very fine indeed.[51]

*Th. 6.* Bright lovely day. – Lucy out before breakfast. – Today asked to 4 dinners, viz. at my Landlords (Fawcetts), Trinity Lodge, Kings Hall (by the Senior Proctor Middleton, – their grand day), & the Vicechancellor ... At 3 o'clock to meeting in the Schools where the V.C. presided & where Captain Ibbetson (an emissary from Prince Albert) explained the Prince's pet project of a grand Exhibition in 1851 in Hyde Park of Works of Art, etc etc. Two resolutions were past, 1st to express our approbation (moved by Whewell & seconded by Bateson) 2d to make the whole of the people present a Committée (moved by Sedgwick & seconded by Paget) ...

*Wed. 19.* ... Seniority about the precedence of the new Sen. Dean (Frere): Brown & I stated that when we were in the Office we claimed no precedence (when the V.M's & Deans Tables were joined in holiday time) above the Senior Fellows. It appears that Judgson claimed to sit on the *left* of the V. Master: Thorp & Carus claimed to sit on the *right*. – We agreed that the Dean should be privileged to sit on the left of the V. Master when there was no nobleman to occupy the place, & that in going out of Chapel the Vicemaster & Dean should walk out abreast, – the V.M. on the right side ...

*Fri. 21.* Received a hare from Glostershire sent us by Elisabeth Wakefield (born Mason): she declares in her letter that it was given her by Lord Sherborne: but I think it more likely that it was poached by her husband: – she paid 1/ carriage, & we 2/, – wch was far from dear considering the distance Puss had travelled. – Lucy & I wrote to her & sent her 10/ apiece. Books returned to Library today ...

*Sat. 22.* Today Dr Fisher gave a grand dinner for a bet lost to Dr Paget concerning the birthplace of Cuvier[52] ... Sedgwick gave a most interesting account of his reminiscences of Cuvier: he had attended Cuviers Saturday soirées regularly for 2 months & had seen him in the intimacy of private life ... we sat at the dinner table till past 12: & then (the last health having been given) broke up: – 6 hours I thought an awfully long dinner.

*Mon. 24.* ... Lucy today gave a leg of mutton to Mrs How, a shoulder to Mrs Cann, & a neck to Mrs Gilmore, – varying her favors according to the no of

of official approval. This provision was of long standing and aimed at tradesmen who might take advantage of students by allowing them to run up large bills, and it had been strengthened in 1844 when any of them who took legal proceedings for debt against students without first notifying their tutors were henceforth to be discommuned (a measure overturned by Patteson's arbitration in the 1850s). In 1847 tradesmen had been warned under pain of discommuning to keep tutors regularly informed of debts more than £5. As a tool to prevent extravagance or worse it was very blunt and not wholly effective, since students were quite capable of overspending outside the jurisdiction of the university. It was, needless to say, extremely unpopular in the town.

[51] On the national day of thanksgiving for the cessation of cholera in November Whewell preached in Great St Mary's on the precariousness of life.

[52] Such dinners were traditional; see, for example, *Romilly 1842-47*, pp.166, 182.

their family. – Poor Sedgwick's horse came down with him today, & broke his unfortunate right arm close to the shoulder: his right leg is also much bruised, for the horse fell on him . . . In the Evening read loud part of Sir Ja. Stephen's 'Epilogue' (in wch he combats the doctrine of eternal punishment.[53]

*Tu. 25. (Christmas)* . . . We then went to Kings Chapel (the 1st time Lucy had ever been there by candle-light) . . . We did not dine till past 5: we had a capital turkey & Dosia exerted herself successfully in all the dinner. Lucy drank a glass of wine to Sedgwick's better health. – In the Evening we played 2 or 3 games of dominos, & I read loud as usual . . .

*Th. 27.* Wrote to Mr Headly (whose son Tanfield is residing here as an Attorney) saying I would call on his son: also to Nix about entering his son under Cooper, also to Seeley sending 44/ for remainder of my subscription for the Scott Bible: also to Miss Cotton (sending her 16 vols from the Library): also to Meares (sending him names of people who take private pupils): also to G.T.R. (in answer) . . . Dined in Trinity Hall Hall where Sir Herbert presided . . . We sat down 32 & had a magnificent dinner . . . Dreadful incendiary fire at Girton on Elliott Smiths farm: many horses, cows & pigs burnt![54]

*Fri. 28.* . . . In spite of the bitter cold Lucy sallied out for the good of her paupers, & (among other things) bought a stout great coat for James How. Dined at St Johns Lodge & met a large party of 16 . . . Heard a good story about Hudson (Railway King): when Lord Mayor of York he proposed as a toast 'Our good Dean & Moses': it was received with immense applause, for all York sided with Dr Cockburn against Sedgwick in their controversy about Mosaic Geology[55] . . .

---

[53]  i.e. in *Essays in Ecclesiastical Biography and Other Subjects* (1849), in which his latitudinarian interpretation of doctrine caused accusations of heresy to be brought against him. Stephen, formerly an influential secretary in the colonial office, had recently been elected professor of Modern History.

[54]  Incendiarism on farms and the mutilation of animals had been common in East Anglia and elsewhere since the agricultural depression of the 1830s which hit the labouring poor hard. It lasted for many years. Smith lost all his buildings and stock, but 'so little did the peasantry sympathize with the act (although these counties are notorious for wilful fires) that they worked indefatigably in subduing the flames' (*Annual Register* 1849 p. 180).

[55]  Cockburn, a former fellow of St John's, had pretensions as a cosmographer and defender of scriptural literalism; in 1838 he attacked Professor Buckland of Oxford, and later produced *A New System of Geology* dedicated to Sedgwick. Six days meant six days, the flood must be universal, and so on. Neither of the geologists believed that their theories, which contradicted Genesis, put true faith in question. When in 1844 at the British Association meeting in York Cockburn denounced Buckland's ideas as absurd Sedgwick replied in his customary uninhibited way: 'Never has a dean been exposed to such withering contempt' (Chadwick, I, 562).

# 1850

*Th. 3 January*. . . . On coming home at 10 I found to my great surprise a note from Grim saying that he had come down with his wife on a sudden thought & that he should immediately follow his note (wch arrived at more than ½ past 8). He & she did so: but Harriet said that I was dining out & that her mistress had a bad cold & was in her room & she thought gone to bed: sure enough she had rushed up into her room, but on the departure of Edward & wife to return to the Bull down she rushed & rewarded Harriet with a new shilling.

*Fri. 4*. Directly after breakfast I went to the Bull to see Edward & wife . . . settled that they were to lunch in my rooms at 1 o'cl. . . . Punctually at 1 came Edward & Bertha & Roget & the lunch, but not Lucy . . . We waited till 25' to 2 for Lucy & then began our lunch: in 2 or 3 minutes she came in quite innocently without the slightest misgiving of being late. She exerted herself very much to amuse & please Bertha & Edward, & was excellent company. She kissed her on departing & sent 'the Prince of Wales' Primer' & a bright Sovereign for little Bertha Caroline. – We both thought Mrs Edward thin & delicate: she had a bad cough & did not seem in spirits & had a hesitating manner as if she seldom had the luxury of having her own way: she seemed to us ill fitted for the exposure to weather to wch Edward subjects her in travelling outside coaches etc . . .

*Sun. 6*. Glorious sunshiny sharp frost. – Carus being gone for 2 Sundays Lucy & I went to St Edwards to hear Harvey Goodwin . . . Took Professor Miller & Tanfield Headly (a sucking attorney, – son of the surgeon) into Hall: – Miller went away before 8, but Headly was too shy to get up till every body departed at ¼ to 10: – the fire had been out for an hour & I was very tired of the party: – I shant ask him again in a hurry.

*Mon. 7*. . . . Plough Monday: the day was bright, & the ploughmen thronged the Streets.[1] – Sedgwick had a good night. He has had the Honor of an enquiry from the Queen . . .

*Sat. 12*. Sharp frost. – V.C. called on me & gave me an account of his reception at Windsor last Tuesday. He arrived there at 4 o'cl. taking with him the University Address of Condolence on the death of Q. Adelaide. – He took the University Marshall Elwood as his Servant . . . The party consisted of the Q, Prince A., the Dss of Kent, Ld Liverpool, Marchioness of Douro, Ld. Grey, the Lord & Groom in waiting, 2 Maids of Honor, etc. Mr Birch (the P. of W.'s Tutor) & the V.C. – Every gentleman takes in a Lady, offering his arm, the V.C. took in one of the maids of Honor . . . The Prince did not stay 10' after the Q. had retired. There was no music at dinner, but there was an instrumental concert each day directly after: there were cards in the adjoining room: the Queen played a round game with the Ladies & Ld Liverpool . . . The Band plays 'God s. t. Q' & then the party breaks up for the night . . . After the Q's luncheon

---

[1] On the first Sunday after Epiphany farm workers would take a plough from door to door asking for beer money before the labours of the new year began. See E. Porter, *Victorian Cambridge* (1975), p. 42 and her *Cambridgeshire Customs and Folklore* (1969), pp. 96-100.

on Wednesday the V.C. had his Audience for the presentation of the Address of Condolence . . . The V.C. was much pleased with his reception & particularly with Lord Liverpool who did the Honors of the Palace to him . . .

*Wed. 16* . . . Dined at Emmanuel Lodge; party of 12: only one Lady beside our hostess . . . Paget told us that Mrs Manning after her condemnation used to spend 2 hours a day in dressing, & that she was hanged in pink silk stockings having refused to wear what had cotton legs to silk feet. Paget's brother dissected Mr & Mrs Manning immediately after they were cut down. Ch Dickens hired a roof of a house to see the Execution; he paid 10 Guas for it[2] . . .

*Fri. 25. Besant* of St Johns is Senior Wrangler; Watson of Trin. is 2d; then come 3 Johnians. – Besant is said to have been 800 marks ahead of Watson, & the next Johnian (Wolstenholme) ran Watson very hard. – This is the 4th year St Johns has had the S.W., a novelty in the History of the University. Besant was a pupil of Parkinson; Watson (& only one other out of the 1st 6) studied under Hopkins. – Meeting at the V.C.'s at 1 to mark off the Honors, & again in the Evening at 8 to mark off the Polloi.[3] But I was not able to get to this meeting till near 9. – The plucking has been severe . . .

*Sat. 26.* . . . A nice bright frost. – The Senatehouse was crammed to suffocation: among others was our fat Theodosia who must have come out rather thinner. The V.C. read the Supplicats railroad pace, getting thro them all in 20' . . . At night went on with Shirley: – the illness of Caroline Helston is very touching . . .

*Fri. 1 February.* . . . Dined at Madingley . . . the roads were very heavy, we had but one horse & did not arrive till at least ½ hour after our time . . . Our flyman was probably drunk: he dropt his whip in the Park & passed 10' in hunting for it in vain the night being dark. – Wilkinson & I smoked all the way home. – Took with me a heap of books.

*Fri. 8.* . . . I was much shocked to hear today a report that the handsome Mrs Adeane is dead! – she had gone to town about an operation for cancer: how mournful for that large family of 12 children to be left orphans, & to have lost both parents in so short a time! – Another of the countless examples of the uncertainty of human life! . . . I hear that Miss Haggitt (who had refused Cartmell & got engaged to a Mr Edwards a clergyman of Bury), has now jilted Mr Edwards tho the day of the marriage was fixt & the bridesmaids' dresses bought: – she is now willing to marry the Master of Christs!

[2]  See 14 November 1849. The Mannings were hanged together before a raucous crowd of 40,000 of all classes and ages that had fought or bought their way to the spectacle outside Horsemonger Lane gaol. Dickens, sickened by the event, wrote at length to the *Times*: 'When the two miserable creatures who attracted all this ghastly sight about them were turned quivering into the air, there was no more pity . . . no more restraint in any of the previous obscenities, than if the name of Christ had never been heard in the world'.

[3]  See 17 March 1849.

*Sat. 9.* Congregation (called) for a Syndicate to confer with the Town concerning Police etc etc.[4] . . .

*Mon. 11.* . . . I wrote also (for Sedgwick) to Miss Meredith poor Mrs Adeane's Governess, who had written to say that she (Miss M.) was returned from Town, & that Mrs Adeane was still alive & that there was a gleam of hope. Erisypelas had come on after the operation, & she had been in that prostration of strength that she was kept alive by brandy, of wch she took ½ a bottle in 24 hours . . .

*Tu. 26.* The Baby Linen etc. (bought for Lucy by Mrs W. Clowes from the Distressed Needlewomen) arrived: – it cost £1.8.6 & there was an immense deal of it . . . Wrote also to Lionel Buller to tell him that he was rightly turned out of the Public Library, having been expelled from Kings & his name taken off the boards . . .

*Th. 28.* . . . Dinner with the Gaskins: a party of 14 . . . We spoke of the recent fall of some large trees at St Johns in fulfilment of the prophecy of their falling when St Johns has the S.W. 4 times running: the wit of Whewell was mentioned 'they fell because there were so many men at top of them'.

*Sat. 2 March.* Carus's birthday: – Lucy sent him the Cushion & my rhymes & also 10 beautiful lines from Cowpers description of a good clergyman, – to wch she put the initials W.C. – She had a fire in the drawing room, wch she put in applepie order, & drest herself all in her best to receive him on his calling to thank her: – he never came, – base man! – Revising syndicate from 12 to 2. – Sent off our British Orphan Proxies to a Lieutenant Norris in behalf of a Cholera case. – Dined in Hall. – Read loud the new No of Copperfield: – the blissful day with Dora is very comic.

*Wed. 6.* . . . Congregation today. – Jeremie took his DD by mandate: – Whewell created him: Whewell read a nice speech in wch he said that Bishop Ollivant & the present Professor (Jeremie) had both been his Pupils, 'primo avulso non deficit alter'.[5] – Bruce took his M.A. degree: Bateson made a capital speech telling of the good deeds of the young man's father (who brought the Elgin marbles), of his brother (the Governor of Canada), & of his own achievements in mathematics etc. – In the Evg read loud Mansfield Park.

*Th. 7.* There was a full Senate House yesterday afternoon to vote on the Grace concerning the Boro Police etc: it was carried by great majorities 37 to 12, & 40 to 5. – Licensing day: 181, – largest no hitherto: the V.C. & Ainslie refused Licences to the Black Bull (Sidney St) & a house in Barnwell kept by a woman named Carter: – private letters had been sent to the V.C. directed to

---

[4] The university had its own officers, the Proctors, with an ancient authority, who had perforce to work with the small town constabulary at times. Among the many grievances of the town against the university was its failure to contribute to the cost of the borough police force set up some years earlier. In 1847 a proposal to make such a payment, albeit voluntarily and on conditions, had been narrowly defeated in the Non-Regent House. Now, after careful negotiations between the town council and a university syndicate, it was agreed that if the university paid a third of the cost of the police, it should have a share in their management. The approval of the Senate which Romilly records here was, however, upset by a large majority in the Non-Regent House on 16 April (q.v.), and the problem remained. See *Annals*, IV, 687 and V, 1-8, and below 7 March.

[5] i.e. 'One being removed, another is not wanting', a Virgilian tag.

'M$^r$ Catmaul' about this latter house . . . Dined at Caius Lodge: a huge party of 18, 12 men & 6 women . . . Of course no Lady fell to my share, but I was fortunate enough to sit next Mrs Packe, so I got on very well. – Packe sat next to Whewell & opposite to Tatham, & was bold enough to ask the meaning of the sign of 'the Pig & Whistle':[6]– it is 'Boars head & Wassail bowl'.

*Wed. 13.* Trial at the Vicechancellors of Lyon the Chemist for allowing bill above £5: – his defence was the most impudent I ever heard, that part of the bill was for a venereal case: – he said he had many more such bills & begged to be discommuned at once: – the Court however did not indulge him: they could not agree upon a sentence & he was dismissed[7] . . .

*Th. 14.* . . . By the way the Master of Trinity made a scene at the Concert on the 4th: he brought in Mrs Whewell & 2 of her nieces & came to the front row, & forthwith desired some young men to make way: – they refused & very properly as they had ladies with them: – Whewell forthwith ordered chairs to be brought in & sat before the rebellious youngsters, – having no idea of acting on the Christian principle of taking the lowest room. Slept in College.

*Sun. 17.* . . . Lucy & I went to call on one of her pauper friends (named Owen): the woman is now old & twaddling & a canting methodist who talks of experiences & is always crying: she is to me utterly insufferable. But she is I believe an excellent woman: she adopted a neighbours orphan child (Selina Thompson) & has brought her up with the greatest care & kindness . . . she said she had received such a letter, so beautiful from Selina, & also a hymn: she begged me to read them, which I accordingly did, the old girl sobbing all the while. The letter was methodism run mad, & I ran mad in reading it: it begged her mother to be thinking of her sins & then gave her own experiences: she said she had had a great fight with Satan last Tuesday, but she did not say whether he appeared in the shape of a young man: that however I take for granted: – she said she conquered Satan but we have only her word for that . . . I kept my countenance, at least I thought I did but Lucy says I pulled awful long faces: however I was very civil (tho I could not find in my heart to praise the letter) & shook hands with the poor old lady . . .

*Sun. 24.* . . . Last Sunday Mill preached a high Puseyite Sermon at St Mary's from the Text 'Father forgive them for they know not what they do': he is said to have pointed out as one of the great sins wch needed forgiveness the recent judgement of the Privy Council on the Subject of Baptismal Regeneration in which the judgement of Sir H.J. Fust was reversed & the institution of Gorham (who denies Baptismal Regeneration, – as do the 2 Archbishops & all the Low

[6] Packe doubtless knew that Whewell's nickname among students was 'Billy Whistle'.
[7] The alleged patient was a Corpus graduate now a curate who had an outstanding bill of £10-7-6 from the winter of 1848-49. Half of it had gone on cigars but the Court was plainly nonplussed by the other half and wisely decided to do nothing. Lyons attributed this side of his practice to his 'having walked the hospitals', and he claimed 'the young man entreated me not to send in the bill & said he should be ruined if I did. I cannot possibly send in such accounts, as I should lose my practice with the young men, of which I have a great deal . . .'. On venereal disease in Cambridge see A. Rook et al., *The History of Addenbrooke's Hospital* (1991), p. 144, quoting the *Medical Times* of 1864.

Church party) commanded.[8] – Mill has since then put his name with those of Pusey, Thorp, & a few other redhot highchurchmen to a set of violent resolutions demanding a reversal . . .

*Sat. 30.* Lucy had a long visit from Mr Brown (the Tailor) who came begging for one of his poor Wesleian friends: – the man had borrowed £10 of the benevolent Mr Adams: – no doubt neither he nor Mr Adams had any idea of its ever being repaid: but Mr A. died unexpectedly without desiring in his will all his loans to poor people to be forgiven, & his widow (who is a miser & thought her husband mad for giving away large sums in charity) has claimed the £10 with legal expenses![9] . . .

*Mon. 1 April.* . . . Dined at the Lodge: a grand party of 19 or 20 . . . Cooper told me that I once mistook his sister for his mother & made her civil speeches about her son: – she is however a good deal older than him & taught him to read: he in return afterwards taught her Latin, Greek & German. – Mrs Willis told me with great exultation of her husband being appointed by Prince Albert & the Committee to superintend all the preparations for the great Exhibition of Works of Industry next year. – She told me also that Willis was going to give Lucy & me his letter weigher.

*Sun. 7.* Lovely day – Carus absent . . . Lucy staid at home in the morning, but went at 3 to St Pauls to the monthly christening: – little Harriet Howe was christened with a tribe of other babies: she was the smallest but far the best drest of the innocents: Lucy gave her attire & also a christening dinner . . .

*Mon. 8.* . . . I had from Henslow his recent address to his Parishioners: he declares himself most stoutly for Baptismal Regeneration:[10] – he lashes his flock for their slack attendance at the Sacrament & for their remissness in all charity. – Wrote to him in reply. – Till 4 o'clock looking over Scholarship papers. – After dinner read loud Franklins 'Poor Richard' with delight.

*Th. 11.* Drank tea at Trinity Lodge: Miss Temple was the only person beside the Master & Mrs W. + the 8 Examiners. – We had a great deal of fighting

---

8   George Gorham (1787-1857), a former fellow of Queens' College, had been much in the news since 1847 when his bishop, Phillpotts of Exeter, refused to institute him to a Devon parish and subjected him to an inquisition of several days on his doctrinal views. Forced to make known the basis of his actions in the ecclesiastical courts, Phillpotts declared that Gorham's interpretation of baptismal regeneration was unsound. Gorham appealed to a committee of the Privy Council who decided in his favour (8 March 1849), and despite long proceedings in three higher courts the judgement stood. The church was in turmoil and what Gorham believed, or what the church's teachings were, soon became less important than who should have final authority in the matter. The Evangelical party supported Gorham and others were glad to see the power of bishops checked, while yet others of a high-church persuasion were appalled that a lay power should meddle in doctrine and church discipline. The Gorham case finally propelled some churchmen, notably Manning, towards Rome. The subject was aired in dozens of books and pamphlets of which there is an account in J.C.S. Nias, *Gorham and the Bishop of Exeter* (1951).

9   A prosperous Baptist draper (and uncle of Chater the diarist), William Adams died childless in August 1848. He willed more than £4750 to institutions in Cambridge and elsewhere; they are listed in *Annals*, IV, 709. *Pace* Romilly, Chater (pp. 86-7) tells how Adams's widow spent her latter years making elaborate preparations for her own end and was particular about small legacies to poor women she knew.

10  Henslow's work is not mentioned by Nias in his study of the Gorham case (see 24 March) nor have we found it.

& ended by electing 6 of the upper year & 7 of the lower. We elected Vernon Harcourt & refused Stephen (son of Sir James): it was the last time of both . . .

*Fri. 12.* To Chapel at ¼ to 9 for Election of Scholars. – Maria and Laura Searle sent me today a beautiful chair-cover (vulgarly called Anti Macassar) worked by themselves in scarlet & white, accompanied by a very pretty note. I called to thank them, & walked with them & their Mother & their cousin (Searle of Pembroke) for ½ hour in their garden. – Lucy today saw a stout girl of 14 slapping & shaking a baby in arms: she scolded her well & threatened to call on her mistress . . .

*Sat. 13.* A fine day. – It was melancholy to see the crowds of people on foot & in carts who came streaming in to see the Execution of the Poisoners Elias Lucas & Mary Reader at 12. Happily Lucy knew nothing about it, tho she often expressed surprise at the extraordinary no of people[11] . . . At night read loud 'unprotected female' in Punch with the greatest amusement:[12]– also read loud Macaulays History.

*Mon. 15.* Lucy out before breakfast as usual . . . In the Evening came a poor little boy to sing & beg: we hardened our hearts & drew down the blinds: so he went to the Fosters: I then found his singing so touching that I gave him /6. We were highly amused at seeing him run off to the cakeshop, where he staid long enough to eat 2 or 3 pennorth: – poor child: – it seemed to him a very rare piece of good fortune. – Whist Club at Walkers: very unlucky indeed: lost 5.0.6. – Staid late.

*Tu. 16.* . . . Sir James Stephen delivered his opening lecture today to a very crowded audience in Trin. Hall Hall: several stood outside, to pick up what they could. – I was unable to go as I could not miss the Revising Syndicate where the 'Officium Registrarii' was to be discussed[13] . . . Congregation-Day: – a great fight at 2 in the S.H. on the subject of the Report concerning the Boro Police: it was rejected by 43 to 18 in B.H.H; – I was in the minority . . . Pembroke & Caius were nearly unanimous against the Report . . . Lucy to her paupers after dinner.

[11] Mary Reader aged 20 had lived with her sister Susan and her brother-in-law Elias Lucas at Castle Camps, where in the course of an adulterous affair they had poisoned Susan Lucas with arsenic in February. They finally confessed and were hanged before a huge crowd outside the gaol on Castle Hill, the first public hanging in Cambridge for seventeen years. Young Chater observed 'The town has been full all day and hundreds have been rolling about Market Street drunk, proving what a demoralizing effect public executions have upon the people.' (E. Porter, *Victorian Cambridge* (1975), p. 63). A broadsheet purporting to relate their dying words and confession was hawked about and is reproduced in P. Ward, *Cambridge Street Literature* (1978), p. 18.

[12] *Punch* was running a successful series of sketches about Miss Martha Struggles, 'gentlewoman of Bloomsbury', a good-hearted but simple spinster constantly imposed on and sometimes swindled by cabmen, Irish beggars, bank clerks, street vendors, and public officials. Romilly kept his set of the magazine and mentions it in his will.

[13] The syndicate appointed in March 1849 to revise the statutes was working carefully through them, like students of a sacred text, and had now reached the clause dealing with the office of Registrary. The re-casting of Latin phraseology, paragraph-shuffling, and drafting of new ideas, with frequent votes among the members to reach a verdict, made it a slow business, and the ill-written minutes of their proceedings (C.U. Archives MIN.VI.4) are seldom intelligible without the statutes themselves. Nothing contentious happened at this meeting.

*Th. 18.* . . . College meeting: – it was announced at this meeting that Mrs Whewell has just given £500 to found another scholarship . . . another also was founded from the donation of Francis Martin of his estate at Barrington producing £15 p.a., to wch was added the Elwes £6 p.a.:[14]– the College make up these 2 new scholarships to the same value as the other former 69 . . . Attended Sir J. Stephen's Lecture, having 1st taken a walk with him & Lady S. & daughter in the College Garden. A crowded audience: men below: gals in the Gallery: he gave a rapid sketch of the Merovingian & Carlovingian dynasties & treated the sovereigns & the people as utter barbarians . . .

*Sun. 21.* . . . Carus preached from 2d Lesson (Acts 18.24.26) on the character of Apollos. It was a horrid low church sermon which rather offended even me, & would have driven Mill mad: – Carus said that Ministers might profit by the example of Apollos, & as he learned from Priscilla & Aquila so might they also learn from laymen! – I think however that Carus would look upon anybody (whether lay or clerical) who offered to instruct him in theology [as] ridiculously impertinent . . . In the Evening I read loud the antidote to Carus's sermon; – a sermon of Mill's on the Text 'Father, forgive them, for they know not what they do': in this Sermon Mill dwells at great length & with unbounded indignation on the recent decision of the Privy Council on the Baptismal Regeneration question: this sermon of Mills has excited a great sensation . . .

Before leaving Cambridge on 24 April to stay with Sedgwick Romilly received a 'Letter from Miss Wilcox inclosing her own Proxy & another Lady's for the Governesses: – they had both put nos to Harriet Frazer: I drew my pen thro them & wrote those nos for Mary Pengree, forging the initials of the 2 signatures of Miss Wilcox and friend'. His conscience as a Notary Public apparently untroubled, he arrived in Norwich in time for a quiet dinner with his old friend, his two nieces and Miss Stanley who was mourning the death of her father. After Miss Stanley's departure Sedgwick felt able to receive other friends, amongst whom were 'Miss Brightwell (who gave me the etchings last year) & Mr Borrow: they came together: I was very glad to renew my acquaintance with Miss B. who is a sharp clever person, a great friend of Mrs Opie. I was rejoiced to make the acquaintance of Mr Borrow (author of the Bible in Spain etc etc): – he is a Gigantic man & talked very freely, which I learned from Miss Br. afterwards is not always the case . . . Mr Borrow is now very ardent about Anglo Saxon Literature & wants of all things to see a work of Gales sometime Dean of Norwich: – I shall look for it in the Public Library'.

George Borrow's call was followed by an excellent dinner and 'a large Evening party, to which a great no of pretty Ladies came' and then on the last day of the visit, after prayers at 9 and the 10 o'clock service in the cathedral, there was a long excursion. 'Sedgwick, Fanny, Isabel & I were inside the carriage & Zoe on the box'. Zoe, Sedgwick's Chinese dog, was the daughter of a bitch owned by the Queen and a keen rabbiter. They called on 'George Peacock's Father: the old Gentleman is in his 95th year: he was put into this valuable living 5 years ago as a life that would probably drop in a few months: but he seems likely to live for some years'. They walked about Lord Bayning's pretty grounds at Honingham Hall, nobody being at home and lastly drove to 'Mr John Henry Gurney's of Easton: he was out; but his wife (who is very young

---

[14] i.e. the modest income from an old gift of £100 that supported an exhibition for a scholar appointed by the Master of Trinity.

& merry & was an heiress with 10,000 a year . . . showed us over the place: the Conservatory was full of most exquisite flowers: she showed us her Zoological Collection, among which are many strange animals, wapitis, etc etc'.

*Sat. 27. . . .* Left Norwich by the 7.40 train & reached Cambridge a little before 11. Just after I had arrived came a note from the V.C. summoning me to his Lodge: Pulling the new Master of Corpus (elected this morning unanimously) was in attendance with Mould & Martin who introduced him: – the V.Ch. signed his formal deed of approbation of the Election in my presence & I attested it as Notary Public. – Poor Dr Lamb was buried in the College Chapel yesterday. Pullen read the Service. – Mould is said to be much disappointed at not being the new Master: – Pulling being the Senior was certainly the right man. Revising Syndicate as usual from 12 to 2. – Then 3 Ale Licences. I gave to Dr Ainslie a letter wch I had just received from Archbishop Musgrave in answer to my application for the Lamb family: – he promises nothing[15] . . .

*Wed. 1 May.* Distributed 13d in halfpence to the May Ladies, & 6d to little Sarah Smyth who enacted May-beggar.[16] – Letter from Betsy agreeing to next Sunday for the christening of her Baby . . .

*Sat. 4. . . .* I should have said that yesterday at dinner we had some rather warm discussion of the dreaded Royal Commission, – Stokes very violent against it & Lord John Russell, I arguing to show that Lord J.R. had no evil design against the University & that a commission of enquiry must needs come to the University as every where else[17] . . .

On 5 May Romilly christened Betsy Spink's baby Lucy Mary in a handsome church in West Ham and three days later departed from 'the magnificent station at Euston

[15] Lamb may not have been wildly imprudent. Despite his Mastership of Corpus and its revenues and the lucrative Deanery of Bristol he also had fourteen children to bring up. At the time of his death nine of them survived from a curate aged 27 to a girl of five, with one at least at college and two at school. Two sons appear to have found their way later to Australia which does not betoken overmuch luxury at home.

[16] In 1833 Romilly gave halfpennies to children who were dressed up or had dressed up dolls as Lords and Ladies of the May and in the following year he noted that the custom had been spoilt by rain. A more detailed description by an earlier Cambridge writer is quoted in Sir Henry Ellis's edition of J. Brand's *Observations on the Popular Antiquities of Great Britain* (1849), I, 221.

[17] Lord John Russell had been to neither university, was unawed by the Prince-Chancellor, and doubtless remembered the memorial of July 1848 and occasional rumblings in the Commons on the need for a commission of inquiry into the allegedly lamentable state of Oxford and Cambridge. A persistent complainer was an old Trinity undergraduate, James Heywood, M.P. who brought the subject up in the House on 23 April when Russell refused to support him, while at the same time announcing his intention to advise the crown to appoint a commission. It was to be a commission of inquiry to collect evidence and to recommend, not to regulate, though a statutory commission with plenary powers might come later. He had been careful not to warn Albert far in advance and thus invite his intervention, and the two Chancellors, Albert and Wellington, were as incensed as Victoria was. See Winstanley, pp. 221-4. When the five Commissioners were named in September it became obvious that none was a youthful firebrand. All were Cambridge men intimately associated with and well disposed towards the place, viz. John Graham (Bishop of Chester and formerly Master of Christ's), George Peacock (Dean of Ely), Sir John Herschel, Sir John Romilly (Attorney General), and Professor Adam Sedgwick.

Square' for Shrewsbury where he was to be godfather to Grim's month-old daughter. 'Grim lives in a very small house in a very shabby dirty street . . . ' but his uncle was nevertheless reassured by his visit. He seemed to be less eccentric than in his early married days, was no longer at feud with his mother-in-law, performed the ceremony of christening his daughter very well and gave a grand breakfast for twelve after the ceremony. Romilly's usual skill in making friends with children was however defeated by Grim's older daughter 'little Bertha, a very pretty blue-eyed child (16 months old this day), as fat as butter, with cheeks like a trumpeter: – she is very shy & self-willed: – she resists all attempts at familiarity & shakes her hands in a most menacing stile at those who try to coax her'. Reassuringly, her mother, also Bertha, was a welcoming and kindly hostess.

Grim also earned his uncle's approval by managing his horses very well on the 'pretty drive of 14½ miles to Prees' where they found Archdeacon Allen and his amiable wife at home and by bringing 'us in cleverly at 5½, just in time to dress for dinner'. The dinner-party was given by B.H. Kennedy a former fellow of St John's and now the great headmaster of Shrewsbury school. 'Dr Kennedy made himself very agreeable & 'to my surprise and delight' gave a rubber. It was a very enjoyable evening.

On Sunday Grim was anxious to read prayers at St Mary's 'but his fine old Rector (past 80) has no notion of being put on the shelf, & was probably desirous of showing me how well he could read at his great age . . . Mr Rowlands is very deaf, & never made out when the voluntary was over before the 1st Lesson, but seeing some strange movements among his flock he at last leaned over to me & said "has he done?": – I nodded, & he then at length got up. – He read with a very firm & tolerably loud voice. – I preached a sermon of my own composition wch I had preached 4 times at very long intervals'.

Romilly's journey back to Cambridge was strenuous. He got up at 5, was detained at Stafford for an hour by the tyre of a wheel coming off the Mail Train for which he was waiting and only just had time when home again to dress for the Woodwardian dinner at the Vice-Chancellor's. He 'found Lucy pretty well'.

*Sat. 18.* . . . Dined in Jesus Hall with Woodham: Cumming, Willis, Thacker & Edleston were also his Guests. – At 6 we all went to Chapel: the chapel & the service there are ultra-Popish. Birkett entones the service & does it extremely well: Sutton (Sir Richard's son) plays the Organ (which he gave): the choristers are also taught by him. – There is a peculiarity in this college Chapel: – the seat corresponding to our Vicemasters is never occupied while the Master is in Chapel: – women are not admitted beyond the ante-chapel. – The chapel is considered quite a gem by Pugin. – After the Service was over we escorted the Master to his Lodge (wch seems to be Etiquette) & then spent an hour in examining all the details of the Altar cloth . . . etc. etc. We then adjourned to Woodhams College rooms (wch he is still allowed to keep),[18] & a tribe of women came to tea, wch was followed by ices . . .

*Mon. 20.* . . . Today there was a Congregation to read Lord John Russell's letter (dated 8 May) to Prince Albert concerning the Royal Commission of Enquiry about Cambridge & Oxford. – It is a long affair: the jist of it is an approval of the New Triposses & all that stile of education, & a determination

[18] He had vacated his fellowship at Jesus by marriage in 1848 and would normally have moved out.

to search into appropriated Fellowships etc. etc. – I think the Commission will be issued[19] . . . Dined at Magdalene Lodge . . . After dinner the old lapdog (12 years old) was introduced & walked across the table. – The Dean of Windsor talked more than I expected: but his utterance is very indistinct & he is a mere wreck.[20] He said that the Master of Trinity is no favorite with the Queen, because when she dined here the perspiration ran off his face & fell on her plate! What things people will invent against those who are unpopular. – Shirked the Whist Club at Francis's & took gruel.

On the last day of the month Romilly began his visit to his friend Henslow, the botanist and exemplary vicar of Hitcham in Suffolk. Frances Henslow drove the last stage of the journey from Stowmarket and 'mentioned to me the shameful carelessness of an agent of her lover Dr Hooker', the eminent botanist who was to succeed his father as Director of Kew Gardens, 'who kept 7 of her monthly letters & sent them all in one packet to him! – Dr H. is now in Calcutta & is to return in the Spring'. Romilly was greatly interested by the Henslow family's activities – 'Went out walking with Henslow in the burning heat: he gave me a lecture on wild flowers as we went along. – I accompanied him to Miss Louisa's Saturday School for the grown-up daughters of the bettermost farmers: she has 6 pupils; who seem very attentive, & some of them come more than 2 miles for their weekly instruction: at the end of her lessons he made them read Geography & showed them the places in the Maps etc etc: the whole concluded with his reading one of Kelty's "Sunday Readings". On Sunday afternoon 'Henslow examined

[19] There had been turmoil in Cambridge since Russell announced the Royal Commission on 23 April. On 8 May he wrote to the Chancellor assuring him of his friendly intentions and desire to help the reform already begun, through Parliament if necessary, and after careful examination of 'obstacles which are interposed by the founders, the retention of customs and the decisions of competent authority. . .'. Albert sent this communication to the Vice-Chancellor, Cartmell, who was uncertain what to do and hoped the Prince might still exert a private influence. Meanwhile, however, he received an address about the Commission signed by fourteen Heads of Houses, most of the professors, and over 130 other members of the Senate. It argued that the university be allowed to continue its own reforms, referred gloomily to interference in college affairs 'of a kind utterly unheard of except in the worst times', predicted non-compliance with the Commissioners' requests for information, and finally urged Cartmell to 'take such steps as the emergency may appear to require'. Sedgwick did not sign, although he thought Russell had been precipitate, while Professor Sir James Stephen, who did sign, nevertheless felt constrained to write privately to the Prime Minister explaining himself and saying that the university to which he had recently returned was much improved; 'the character and spirit of the place are entirely changed' from what it had been in his youth, and 'our rulers are certainly not chargeable with languor or remissness as reformers'. Indeed – and this was surely an exaggeration symptomatic of his perplexity – he doubted 'whether their zeal for reform is not too ardent, and whether they are not moving with undue rapidity'. With open discussion of Russell's letter in Congregation on 4 May there was at least something tangible to respond to and indignation bloomed. Cartmell wrote at length to the Prince on 25 May conveying the general sentiment and inviting his closer identification with the university authorities as Wellington had done at Oxford. But Wellington was not married to the Queen. Albert was in an awkward position and immediately and publicly replied. He sympathised, he regretted the government's decision, and yet accepted that it could not now be reversed. Co-operation would be wiser than protest or resistance which would only play into the hands of enemies. See Winstanley, pp. 224-31, and *Annals* V, 11-18 where Cooper prints the chief documents in full.

[20] i.e. George Neville-Grenville, Master of Magdalene since 1813, Lord Braybrooke's brother. The wreck was sixty years old.

in their catechism those lads & lasses who were going to be confirmed (among others his own footman): he did it very well: the boys (bating the footman) said their catechism villainously, the girls very well. He also received the poor peoples subscriptions to their different clubs & gave away sacrament money. No company at dinner. Henslow carries about a snuffbox full of sugarplums, wch he gives the children under the name of a pinch of snuff' After tea Henslow exhibited some of the tidy allotments which he had fostered in the village despite the farmers' opposition and on Monday 3 June drove his friend over to the Cosford Union (of 28 Parishes) close to Hadleigh. In the Boardroom Romilly heard 'a very animated dispute about reducing the salaries of the 2 relieving Officers from £125 & £100 to £80' and then the routine business of hearing & voting on all the applications for relief. 'I went over the house, which was beautifully clean: 280 beds (out of the 400) are occupied . . . What pleased me most was the performance of the band: 8 boys played on different instruments of a military band, & were led by the son of the Master of the Union'. The boys played admirably and were rewarded by Henslow with sugar plums. Romilly thought the Master of the Union good-humoured as well as firm; his wife was matron, his son schoolmaster, his sister schoolmistress and the profit to the family '(with house and coals etc) is about £300 a year'.

A botanising expedition into the woods on the following day came to nothing because of the heat, but there was a big dinner party after which 'Mrs Knox played 2 long & very difficult pieces without book in the most finished & masterly stile. – After she was gone Mrs Henslow pronounced that that manner of playing did not at all do for the country: – she of course spoke as a Mother, who had no pleasure in hearing a performance wch utterly annihilated that of her own children'.

On his journey home Romilly dined 'off spice nuts and a glass of ale' in Bury before taking the coach to Cambridge where he was happy to catch Lucy 'just in pudding time, & I took my share'.

*Sat. 8 June.* Dined in Hall: went into Combination with Sedgwick: – he offered to come & drink tea with us, but I told him Lucy was not well enough. The Prince has asked him to be on the Commission for his Great Exhibition of 1851: – Sedgwick after a long correspondence (which he wishes to show me) has reluctantly consented. – Letter from G.T.R. sending his new Illustration . . . Went to the Fitzwilliam Museum & saw part of the Disney Collection: I didn't much like it: – the rest is not unpacked yet.[21] – Old shoes are kept at the F.M. for clodhoppers to put over their own.

Romilly was greatly pleased during his visit to London on 13 and 14 June to find Frank Kennedy, now aged 8, 'a fine tall joyous boy' and G.T.R. and his wife happily installed in their pretty house in Hammersmith. Less happy was the news of Kate Roget who was again suffering from what appeared to be religious mania. The family gathered in Stratton Street united in condemning her father's treatment of her: 'he keeps her in a house at Blackheath with one maidservant & a companion to read to her when she is well enough: all the windows are barred up, & he will not give any body her address: – he has

---

[21] John Disney of Ingatestone, lawyer and dilettante, had given to the university his inherited collection of 83 pieces of 'ancient marbles and statuary', largely brought from Italy a hundred years before. The university undertook to keep them together under his name. See *Endowments*, pp. 220-2. His name is perpetuated in the Disney chair of archaeology which he endowed in 1851.

taken away from her her bible & all religious books. It is a most melancholy case!' He was to learn, however, that by the end of the year she 'seems quite restored . . . & plaid & sang & seemed perfectly happy' when G.B. Allen visited her and her father.

*Mon. 17.* Letter from Mrs Henslow enclosing the Professor's character & my own (by Mr Warren, from our handwriting) – I am given credit for great *firmness* & courage!: I am charged with being waspish & disputatious: altogether my character is far better than I deserve . . .

*Wed. 19.* . . . Tho no great idolator of Pitt I today transferred his medallion from the entrance of the Pitt Press to place it over the door of my office.[22] – Evening party at Colonel Fullers: his daughters (one of whom is a fine handsome girl) are believers in Clairvoyance, Homeopathy, water-cure, & all such rubbish: the youngest son (aged 8 or 9) plays the organ . . .

*Sat. 22.* . . . Dined in hall: a small party: Sedgwick (just returned) presided. – Lucy & I went at 7 o'clock to Downing to gather a nosegay for Carus (who is coming back this evening): here we enjoyed ourselves seeing the haymaking. Lucy's quick eyes detected a tortoiseshell-cat lying under the Portico of the Drawing room: upon Lucy's enticing her she came out, leaving a lovely black & white kitten: she was very thin & greatly excited her compassion. Presently out came Mrs Worsley's maid to water the roses: I gave her 1s & begged her to be kind to the cat: Lucy instantly suggested her going that moment & getting some milk for Puss . . . the cat was not the house-cat, but was an unknown stranger. Lucy went into the hayfield & provided herself with hay enough to make a bed for Madam Puss, & then reluctantly tore herself away. – We filled our basket with an ample supply of roses, to which Lucy afterwards added the best of our own Geraniums, & dressed them up into a lovely nosegay. – At length (at near 9) every thing was ready & Lucy & I started for Carus's room with the said bowpot, a great jar of Walkden's Ink, a copy of Miss Henslow's 'Pat's Apology' (in wch is the charming story of the 2 Cows), & an elaborate letter of her own to him. – We gave all the presents to his bedmaker, who told us he had arrived 10' ago. – Lucy & I then adjourned to my rooms where we had a bottle of Beer & some cakes . . . didn't get home till near 10!

*Sat. 29.* Very cool – Congregation – 1 DD, 1 LLD, 57 AM, 1 incorporated – Theodosia left for 10 days –. Lucy heard last night from 8 to 9½ a very powerful sermon in the open air from Titcomb: his subject was 'Future Punishment': the locality was New Street Barnwell: the audience were of the lowest order, but they were well conducted & very attentive: he mentioned vices in the broadest manner, spoke most familiarly of the Fair, its drums & trumpets etc: said that the reward for its vices was Hell-fire: – any person would think himself very courageous who could hold his hand in a flame for an hour, – what must it be to burn for ever & ever! He alluded to 2 persons having died in consequence of the Fair (Stanley from drinking & another man from injuries in a fight there). – This is the 2d Field-Sermon of Titcomb. – He very affectionately invited to his own Church next Sunday all who do not go to any regular place of worship . . .

*Mon. 1 July.* I slept in College last night: & a great fight I had to get any breakfast this morning: just as I was beginning at 5' before 8 the crowd of fee-

---

[22]  A relief profile still (1999) in the old Syndics' Room of the Pitt building.

payers began pouring in & I was not able to finish my breakfast before 10½.[23] – A large no. of men came down by the morning train . . .

*Tu. 2.* Commencement.[24] – Nice cool day. – Jeremie made a good speech recommending moderation in Theological disputes: he entered largely into the baptismal Question . . . Fane recited his prize Engl. Poem on the death of Q. Adelaide very well, except that he said 'where were ye etc', pronouncing both the 1st words alike, & that he called Ophir Opheir (3 syllables): – his mother Lady Westmorland was present . . .

*Th. 4.* Horrid wet day: – I had a fire in College . . . Called Congregation for laggards: – 5 AM: – Fane took his degree today: – the Orator made an excellent speech. – Poor Murray (the excellent Curator of the Botanic garden) died today: – 9 days ago he was much heated when measuring for the proposed bridge across Hobsons stream & drank a great deal of cold water: – he has left a young widow & a baby[25] . . . Dined with Middleton on the dais at Kings . . . I was amused by seeing the little choristers waiting in hall . . . Away by 7½. – Read loud David Copperfield: – the childish housekeeping of Dora is most laughable.

*Tu. 16.* . . . The annual party of the Conservators:[26] I had never joined it before: I was Parker Hamonds Guest. – We started from the Great Bridge in the Conservators Barge a little after 12. At the Toll House we picked up the V.C., Paget, Mr St Quintin, etc. – Behind our Barge was one for the servants (including the Sch. Keeper & Marshall). When we had got near Ditton there came on one of the most violent storms of thunder & lightning, hail & rain that I ever saw: it lasted nearly an hour: a good deal of rain beat in because one of the windows would not draw up, & the curtain was little defence as the wind was very high. – The storm was too violent for our towing-horse & the man who rode him to bear up against, so we lay close to the Bank till it subsided into a steady & continuous rain. – We reached the Conservators House at Clayhithe at 3 & dined about ½ past 3. We sat down 21 or 22 . . . The Chairman had no list of Toasts & gave the Mayor as his 3d wch was altogether wrong: the Mayor then . . . gave the V.C. – The Chairman then gave my health, & in turn every

<hr/>

[23] The bulk of these fees were government duties imposed more than thirty years before. For an M.A. degree each man paid Romilly six guineas of which he kept six shillings for himself. There is a detailed breakdown of the rates and of those due to the colleges separately in the annual *Cambridge University Calendar.* See 18 December 1850.

[24] There were two commencements, one in January that coincided with the Senate House examination when B.A.s of the previous calendar year were admitted to their degrees, and the second, formerly a grand social gathering, in July when higher degrees were conferred. Until 1839 candidates for honours had to submit to an oral examination, a medieval survival known as 'Acts and Opponencies'. They were said to 'commence' their acts.

[25] Andrew Murray aged 45 had been curator at a busy time. The Botanic Garden had been moved after 1846 from its small, polluted site in the town (on what became the New Museums site) to large grounds on the Trumpington Road, and the job was complete by the end of 1852. Murray's successor, selected from a short-list of three after an interview with Henslow, professor of Botany, was James Stratton of the Royal Botanic Garden, Edinburgh.

[26] i.e. of the river Cam; the body empowered to regulate the river. They had lately reduced tolls from 3d to 1d a ton, and aroused anticipation by a proposal to build a substantial footbridge over the Cam at the Fort St George.

body's (except the Conservators) was drunk. – Mr Brown (who is fond of wine) was continually attacking the Chairman for not passing the bottle. Mr Brown sang with a good voice & much spirit Sheridan's song 'I'll give you a lass': Mr King with a bad voice sang a vulgar song 'the Gipsying Party' . . . A little after 7 we were all again in the barge: on its outset it was stored with wine & a variety of fruit: on its return the table was covered with wine & materials for punch. – I smoked a cigar & then played 2 rubbers of whist . . . I should have said that at Ditton & elsewhere on our return we threw cakes to boys in the water & also to those on the banks for a scramble.

*Th. 18.* . . . The Oxford Servants have beat the Camb. ones on their own ground & their own water: so I think the Cantabs must be thoroughly ashamed.[27] – The Evening being cool Lucy went with Mary Anne Tyler to her Fathers Allotments beyond the Railway: – a horrid long way off, & she was gone from 5 till ¼ to 8 . . . A genteel entertainment of Tea & cakes & br. & butter, fruit & *round* radishes! Lucy was complaisant enough to eat one horrid radish & secreted another in her glove. Mr Tyler is very angry with Cooper (Minister of St Andrews) for not letting him have a 2d allotment . . . after tea he said by way of Grace P.T.L.O.M.S, pronouncing the 6 letters as fast as he could: he means by it "Praise the Lord O my soul" . . .

*Fri. 26.* . . . Dosia has had her horrid black front teeth filed down & 2 new false ones put in: she must have been ass enough to dress like a lady & not like a cook, for that thief of a Mr Jones has charged her 50s! Lucy & I each gave her 10s/ towards it . . .

*Tu. 30.* . . . Sedgwick called: – he has now sent the last page of Copy to the Press & is in tearing spirits: – he leaves C. for Edinburgh tomorrow to be present at the British Assoc. – He & I called on Mr Harraden & saw a magnificent red parrot: he showed us some cleverish drawings of the Round Church, & what I call a blasphemous Picture of our Lord: it was intended for an improvement on Carlo Dolce! – Read loud Irving's Goldsmith.[28]

*Th. 1 August.* Letter from 'Pretty but virtuous Nancy Stone': she is of course in distress for money: she is now at Hammersmith: sent her £1.[29] – Poor

---

[27] Despite disapproval by the Oxford authorities the party of servants spent three days in Cambridge, cricketing successfully on Parker's Piece, and rowing against their Cambridge hosts on Thursday evening in a boat lent them by Peterhouse. There followed a long convivial gathering at The Hoop with toasts and songs. One of the Cambridge men composed and sang verses beginning:

> Ye sons of the Isis, in friendship we greet you,
> Each Cam-born heart swells with affection's pure glow;
> May the friendship that now warms each bosom to meet you
> Endure till the Isis and Cam cease to flow.

See the full account in the *Chronicle* 20 July.

[28] Washington Irving spent several years in England where he became secretary of the American legation in 1829, and received an honorary degree from Oxford. His biography of Oliver Goldsmith (1849) was as well regarded on both sides of the Atlantic as his earlier books had been.

[29] A mad woman who had successfully pestered Romilly for several years. In 1845 he gave her £5 'to pay her debts & take her into Wales, on condition that I was never to hear any more of her' (*Romilly 1842-47*, p.125).

Mrs Adeane buried today. – Dined with Ch. Mortlock in Mr Bumpsted's rooms at Kings . . . I sat next Mrs Clem Francis & she is indignant at the conduct of the new Master of Corpus Christi Pulling who is said to have broken off the engagement between himself & Miss Carew (Mrs Pullen's sister) by writing her a brusque letter saying it was high time to put an end to the absurd idea of an engagement between them: – very ungentlemanlike & very cruel, – if true. – In the Evening . . . the sofas etc were cleared out & there was a dance: – there was a card table placed in a window & Mrs Prest, the Colonel, Eyres & I played whist: I was very fortunate: won 59s.

*Fri. 23.* Letter from John Lodge (Jun): he does not speak of any great improvement in my dear friend[30] . . . Lucy today unluckily walked down Christs Lane where there lives a birdcatcher: she took compassion on a goldfinch wch had been kept 2 months in one of those horrid little prisons wch birdcatchers call cages: she gave 1s/9d for the beautiful bird & brought it home in a paper bag: the bag was pierced with pinholes & tied with a string. As soon as she came home she put the little fellow into a comfortable cage, gave him a dinner wch he enjoyed heartily, & we then carried him & the cage to Coe Fen & opened the door for him: he looked about him for some time before he hopped out & took his flight into a neighbouring tree: Lucy watched him for a long while & saw him come down into the brook & take a bath: he enjoyed himself vastly & is now doubtless as happy as a bird can be . . . As I was walking by the Fitzwilliam I saw Mrs Jenyns & party . . . Lady Cullum[31] amused me vastly: she is a bold dashing person who seems fond of saying startling things: she gave me the impression of having dabbled in 'the Vestiges of Creation': she talked about the countless ages before man was created, of the absurdity of the word *day* in the account of the Creation, – of the necessity of a new translation of the bible instead of our present very faulty one, etc: – I perpetually disagreed with her but I was greatly entertained. We went to Sedgwick's Museum where she expressed unbounded enthusiasm about the antediluvian beasts . . .

*Th. 29.* The mornings post brought me a letter from Mrs Lodge saying there was no hope whatever of poor Lodge: & in the evening came a letter from Dr Whittaker saying that my dear friend was no more!

*Fri. 30.* Very much disgusted with a letter from young John Lodge telling me of my dear Friend's death. He gives no particulars & expresses no grief, but speaks of accompanying his poor cousin's body to Askrigg as 'starting with him for Yorkshire' . . . I also wrote to the Butler of Magdalene directing him to write to the Master & to Warter. I communicated the sad tidings to Bowtell who was much affected . . .

*Th. 19 September.* Carus paid Lucy a visit, principally to tell of his grievances in his recent excursion to Gorlston, where he went for quiet, & endeavored to put up at a public house (the only inn of the place) but it was not the sort of an hotel that he likes: for on his ordering dinner they produced nothing but bread & butter! at night he was locked into his bedroom! . . . He

---

[30] i.e. John Lodge, the retired University Librarian.
[31] 'An espiegle clever little Irishwoman', Anne Lloyd (d. 1875), from Dublin, who had married a much older baronet, Sir Thomas Cullum of Hardwick in Suffolk, sometime chaplain to the Duke of Sussex.

brought with him Meares letter, which was very unworldly, for he Meares administered no flattery, & instead of saying that tho he did not know him personally he had always heard so much of his goodness etc etc merely mentioned his only acquaintance with him having been his signing his Exeat! The natural result is that Carus means to write him a letter of 'Christian kindness & brotherly love' & pitch him overboard[32] . . .

*Th. 26.* Horrid wet day. – rain from morning till night. – Court at 'the Great Tiled Booth' Stirbridge Fair: no Proctor attended & only one Taxor[33] . . . exactly the same number of cases as last year, viz 16, – whereby I gained £1. We walked home by the river so I missed making my customary purchase of gingerbread in the Fair: – I however bought the same quantity in the Town. – The Contest for the Representation of the University is happily ended by Cowling having retired: I think Loftus Wigram may be considered very fortunate as Cowling had the start of him by more than a fortnight[34] . . .

*Mon. 30.* . . . On enquiry at the Public Library I found that 2 Vols wch I had lent to that vagabond 'the King's Evil Lazarus Buller' had never been returned by him. As Buller is overwhelmed with debt & is in Jail for an assault I determined to go to his Lodgings . . . where I found that he had been about 3 weeks & had paid nothing . . . I then went to his previous lodgings . . . here, I saw Mrs Crowson . . . She had a lamentable tale to tell of his misconduct & base ingratitude. She said he spent considerable sums about nightingale's eggs & got such a crowd of blackguards to the house that she was quite frightened & obliged to forbid them. He owes her above £16 . . . Upon my asking . . . if he had left any books she said 'not one: but I recollect his sending 2 Vols about a month ago to Hardman the Chemist in Sidney Sussex St. – These were good tidings: so I sallied off to Mr Hardman's & to my great delight he produced the lost Vols from under his counter . . .

*Tu. 1 October.* Fellowship Examination began: – Greek day: Prose by Martin & Grote . . . I was very near forgetting the English Verse into Latin: – it never occured to me till this morning that Cooper & I had such an exercise to set: – I looked up a passage from Palamon & Arcite & another from Cowley's Complaint & got the Proof at 4 o'clock: – tomorrow is my day, – so there was no time to lose . . .

*Fri. 4.* . . . Election of Member for the University at 11: – there was no Candidate but Wigram, so the business was very soon over: the Senate House was tolerably filled, – Miss Cotton, Miss King etc. etc. were there . . . Letter

[32] It seems likely that Romilly's Welsh connexions were the basis of their acquaintance. Meares had been educated at Haverfordwest before coming up to Trinity as a sizar in 1828, and he returned to Wales for parish work. He had written to announce the death of L.B. Allen, Romilly's brother-in-law, in 1845, and in 1846 the diarist sent him three guineas.

[33] The ceremony of proclaiming Stourbridge Fair had fallen off markedly in the previous twenty years. At one time the Vice-Chancellor and other notables, having heard the Registry declare the fair open, repaired to the 'Tiled Booth' for a feast of oysters provided by the Proctors. Two other officers, the taxors, who were appointed annually to inspect and authorise local weights and measures, supplied the bread and butter. But the oyster feast was abolished in 1842 and the university's officials were unenthusiastic in their attendance thereafter.

[34] The vacancy arose after the death of C.E. Law in August. See Searby, pp. 485-92 on the university M.P.s.

from Sir John Walsham asking if he may not spare himself the expense of a Private Tutor for his son the 1st term as he does not fly at high game: – I wrote to say he might. – Read Pendennis loud till Lucy went to bed.[35] – Brace of birds from Dr Drosier.

*Sat. 5.* . . . Last day of Fellowship: Fallal by Grote; Greek Verse & Prose by Rothman: – he set an exquisite passage from 2 Gentlemen of Verona 'The current that with gentle murmur glides': but 4 of the men declared that they had seen a Greek Translation of it, so he gave them an extract from the Tempest beginning 'Be not afeard: the isle is full of noises'. . . . Sarah Foulkes returned today from her 18 weeks countrifying at the Sandfields: – she left Doric St. on the 1st of June & returned on this 5th of October: – Lucy pays 1s/ a day for her which comes to exactly 6 Guineas . . .

*Tu. 8.* Cold uncomfortable day. – Lucy came to my rooms to get 6 Guineas wch I had forgotten to give her in the morning: gave her some bottled Beer & Combination Biscuits. She did an infinitude of work in visiting sick paupers, slanging draymen, patronising asses, ordering fresh wheels for Saunders donkey cart, paying the Sandfields, etc: – she was out 4 hours! . . . I got little or no walk today, for I stuck steadily to the Examination Papers till ¼ past 3. On my return I found Lucy had gone out again to visit Sarah Foulkes (– 1st visit since her return) . . . Wrote to G.T.R; wrote also to Miss Corfield sending her Lucy's Proxy & my own in behalf of her father. – Today I tried in vain to find a pauper named Hankin: I applied to their namesake in Freeschool Lane, enquired in little St Mary's Lane (where our servants thought they lived), – all in vain: – my mind has misgiven me for refusing the poor woman yesterday morning when she came to our house: I hear that she has a sick husband: – I must try & find her out if possible.

*Wed. 9.* I am now 59 complete & am (God be praised) in good health. – Lucy is also well. – Dined with Lucy of course as it was my birthday: warned by last year did not give her any Hock to drink my health: – nothing but bottled beer. – Tea at the Lodge. – We elected Berry, Davies, Vaughan, Elwyn, Edwards & Thrupp: Berry & Thrupp were Wrangham Prizemen: – The Prizes are gold medals . . . they are given to the persons who are wranglers & 1st Class Classics & have been in the 1st Class all the 3 years of their Examination . . . £100 was given us to institute this prize: we have paid Wyon for sinking the die 100 Guineas & have laid in a stock of 50 at 6 Guineas each . . .

*Fri. 11.* Swore in the new Fellows. Violent rain in the morning. – It however cleared up at 1 and I was able to keep my engagement of escorting the 3 eldest Miss Searles & their Guest Mr Mansel (Tutor of St Johns Oxford) to the Trinity Library: – Mr Mansel did not seem to care one straw about any thing I showed him: – the young ladies however made themselves very agreeable: Miss Maria selected some German Books (for she addicts herself to such reading), & Miss Searle rather surprised me by asking me to lend her the Tale of Tub: – I said I would do so, but I cautioned her against all the alternate chapters, wch I told

---

[35] Thackeray had been at Trinity in 1829-30, done little work, and fell into the hands of money-lenders. His experiences are drawn on in the account of his hero's days at St Boniface College, Oxbridge.

her were coarse & unfit for a lady to read, tho she would not be able to comprehend the greater part of the impropriety . . . That blackguard Buller has contrived to scrape together money enough to get bailed: – so he is now out of prison. He wrote to me, stating the thiness of his shoes, etc & his utter destitution: – I sent him 10/ & desired that all intercourse between us might cease . . .

*Wed. 16.* . . . It is very amusing now meeting the Fathers with their sons: – I met Hose & Franks todays [sic], each escorting a hopeful: Nix could not spare time to come to Cambridge; he has therefore sent up his son under the escort of his brother . . .

*Th. 17.* . . . Peacock called on me to say that the Commissioners wish to recommend me to Lord John Russell as Secretary to the Commission: – doubtless the recommendation originated with Peacock: – I am very much disinclined to accepting it tho it is to be well paid[36] . . .

*Fri. 18.* . . . Breakfast at 9½ to Lord Bradford (who on close inspection is not handsome at all, – a huge nose, & face much marked with small pox) & son, Sedgwick, 2 Nixes, Walsham, Rathbone, & Searle (of Pembroke). – Sedgwick was in excellent force & was the life of the party, wch did not break up till past 11. – Sedgwick stayed after the rest were gone: he urged me to accept the Secretaryship, but I told him I had made up my mind to decline it: – I think (besides all other objections) it would not be advisable to have a 4th Trinity man (Sedgwick, Peacock & John being on the Commission) . . . Met old Counsellor Pryme who told me that Lord John Russell had just given Bailey[37] the pension of £100 a year lately held by Kidd: I was much delighted with this unexpected good fortune of the poor fellow at last after so much solicitation, & wrote immediately to wish him joy. The Evening Post brought me a letter from Bailey himself written in very good feeling indeed, asking if I would be cotrustee with Pryme, – for Lord John desires him to nominate Trustees for receiving and paying the money: – I wrote again to Bailey, accepting the Trust. – W. Cook (the Equestrian) has flown in the face of the V.C.: the V.C. refused him permission, so he has printed handbills speaking of "the distinguished patronage of the Mayor". He (W.C.) entered the town in great state today in a coach & *16* with little tom-thumb carriages, 6 bold impudent red-jacketed women on horseback, a reindeer drawing a Car, etc. etc.[38] – The V.C. has issued a decree of the Heads threatening vengeance on all undergraduates & bachelors who go to the Exhibition! . . .

*Sat. 19.* Proclamation of markets – same delightful weather. – Received a note from Clark saying that he had given up taking pupils: so I wrote to Scott begging him to call upon me: I asked him to undertake young Mr Bridgeman: he agreed to do so. – I then wrote to Mr Bridgeman begging him to call upon me that I might take him to Scott. He came & told me that he was said to have done remarkably well in the Matriculation Examination yesterday in Mathematics

---

[36] The secretaryship was eventually given to the Orator, W.H. Bateson of St John's.

[37] i.e. James 'Beast' Bailey, former headmaster of the Perse School and impecunious classical scholar. See *D.N.B.*

[38] Cooke [sic] obtained the mayor's permission for his show on Midsummer Common which in the event was well attended and free of trouble.

& that Thompson recommended him to have Scott as ½ Tutor & Walker as ½ Tutor. I told him that I thought Mr Scott abundantly capable of teaching him both Classics & Mathematics & that I would call with him on Thompson. We did so & Thompson seemed still of his former opinion but did not press it: – so I said to Mr Br. that as I understood Lord Bradford to have left the matter entirely in my hands I should recommend Mr Scott: so I took him to Mr Scott & left him to make arrangements . . .

*Mon. 21.* . . . College meeting, which I left at the end of an hour as I was summoned to the V.Ch.'s: – at this meeting we had the report of the dunces at the Examination of the Head Lecturer & Dean: – among them was Lord Muncaster. – We resolved on resisting the claim of the Town to have the College assessed for poor rates, in consequence of an elaborate report on the subject drawn up by Cooper the Town Clerk.[39] – At the V.C's I met the Proctor & Proproctors, we having been summoned for enquiry into the Equestrian Exhibition of Cook: – it appeared that every thing had been quiet & that there had not been a single undergraduate there: – so there was no trial . . . Lucy carefully gathered all the best of our grapes & wrote a witty letter to Carus: – we took the fruit & the epistle to the whitehaired rubicund divine . . . On returning home we fell in with Mr Deck (still looking very feeble after his severe illness): he told us that the Provost of Kings died yesterday in London: he said that he (Deck) had been the means of bringing about family harmony 5 years ago after the quarrel between Father & daughter in consequence of her attachment to young Kemble:[40]– Mr Deck seemed very much affected with the Provost's death, & said that he had been his medical adviser for a long while. – Whist Club at Powers . . .

*Wed. 23.* . . . Dined at 6½ in Christs Hall at the presentation of plate by the Master & Fellows to the Bishop of Chester: we were 24 of whom only 6 (including myself) were visiters . . . all the youngsters of the College dined at the same time & had wine & staid out the proceedings. The V.Ch (Cartmell) discharged his duty very fairly: – the speech of the Bishop was a brilliant specimen of his faultless command of appropriate language. Shaw had to make a speech & it was a very painful effort to him: he all but broke down . . . We didnt rise from dinner till past 10.

*Fri. 25.* Magna Congregatio, nominally at 10: but the V.C. kept us all waiting more than ½ hour. – Fire at Girton on Elliott Smith's property: there was a destructive fire there 6 months ago, manifestly incendiary: – this new fire was

---

[39] On 10 October the Cambridge town council approved a report, largely the work of its very active clerk, C.H. Cooper, on the liabilities of the university and colleges to pay parish rates. Copies were sent out inviting co-operation in a legal adjudication on this and other contentious matters.

[40] In February 1879 Fanny Kemble told Henry James of the attachment between her handsome but selfish brother Henry, and the plain, dull Mary Ann Thackeray (1818-79), only daughter and heiress of the Provost of King's. He composed a long account in his notebooks that was afterwards worked up into *Washington Square* (1880). Miss Thackeray wanted Kemble, who really wanted her money and left her when it seemed she might be disinherited, only to return after her father's death and be rejected himself. Kemble died in an asylum in 1857 and Miss Thackeray never married and died worth £45,000. See Bruce Dickins, *Times Literary Supplement* 13 October 1961.

undoubtedly incendiary also: – it was happily very soon got down, being in the day time . . .

*Sat. 26.* . . . At dinner Gibbins communicated the following enigma cypher about *Clio*: 'Divide 101 by 50 & then add a cypher: – the result will help your historical studies – I behaved very rudely in poopooing the riddle because I had not been able to guess it, C,L,I,O. – I laughed heartily at one communicated by Walmisley, 'Why is a seller of Cravats likely to become rich?', – Answer, 'Because *ties* pay the dealer'. – Gibbins proposed another 'How is a toy like a Poet'; – but he was not fortunate enough to hit my taste in this: – answer – a Poet is devoted to a-muse & delights in-fancy: – Home at 5: read loud 'Petticoat Government' till bedtime.[41]

*Mon. 28.* . . . Called on the V. Provost to get a ticket for Lucy to attend the Provosts Funeral tomorrow: much surprised at learning that no ladies are to be admitted into King's *College* even, much less into the Chapel . . .

*Tu. 29.* . . . At 11 to Kings Combination Room for the Funeral of the Provost. – Packe is joint Executor with Bishop of Lincoln & Martin Thackeray (neither of whom was present): all the work fell on Packe, who looked harrassed. – The persons present were the Heads of houses, Packe, Dr Fre Thackeray, Dr Paget, Mr Deck, Scholefield, Jeremie & Blunt & all the Society of Kings, & myself: – Sedgwick & Bateson came (uninvited) & therefore did not wear scarfs & hatbands . . . There was no wine or cake. – The procession went (about ¼ to 12) by the W. of the New Building (Gibbs's) thro the West door of the Chapel: – nobody (except the servants of the late Provost) was in the Chapel when we entered it: – the effect was very striking of the sweettoned organ accompanying the Choristers who began singing 'I know that my Redeemer liveth' as soon as they reached the steps of the door: the sun was shining brilliantly on the painted windows. – All that could be chanted in the service was . . . – As soon as I got home from the Funeral I gave Lucy my Scarf & Hatband,[42] & she took them to her protégée Sarah Foulkes who has been pining for a black silk cloak: – these 2 articles (being about 5½ yards of beautiful silk) are just enough. – So this funeral of the poor Provost is the making of her . . .

*Fri. 1 November.* . . . An old woman got into my office today, who complained of rheumatics, so I placed her in a chair close by the fire & she told me all her history . . . My Guests in Hall today vere Dr Drosier (who came without *red* gown) & T.G. Headley . . . I fortunately escaped staying for supper as Drosier went away very early, & Headley went to the County Ball: – I think Headley rather a bore & a noodle. At dinner he asked for red mullet, – there being none: then he was perpetually sighing: then he played whist most detestably; & I was heartily glad when he took his departure. Lost 1/-.

---

[41] By Fanny Trollope of whom the diarist, like many of his contemporaries, disapproved for her 'vulgarity'. Forced into authorship to provide for her family, she was turning out novels at the rate of two a year and had already alienated evangelicals and Tractarians and gained a not unwelcome notoriety. Mrs Trollope's neglected work has been reassessed by modern writers and found wholesome.

[42] The customary black mourning gifts to family and friends attending a funeral.

*Sun. 3.* A most glorious day . . . Carus preached in a most vigorous animated stile, gesticulating greatly: – his Text was Acts XV.10.11: he preached the same 5 years ago: he gave us some favorite passages from Hookers sermon on Justification. – He told us that he should say more on certain points next Tuesday (Gunpowder day) . . . I should have said that on Friday Carus paid Lucy a long visit: of course she was in a grand litter & kept him waiting sometime in a fireless room. He staid an hour & a ½ & let no end of cats out of the bag in censure of the Selwyns, the males of whom he detests, & the female's marriage with any body but himself he would think a blessing . . .

*Tu. 5.* Breakfast with Thacker who is Senior Proctor: Sedgwick etc etc there: a magnificent breakfast: at 10 we all went to the S.H. to elect the new V.C. – Corrie was elected: his speech was a denunciation of Popery & a declaration of his own intended energy against Roman Catholic pretensions:[43]– his utterance was so feeble that tho standing quite close to him I missed a great deal. He immediately afterwards preached at St Mary's: – of course he was still less heard there: – I was not present: nor do I mean to go to his wine party, for I think him a narrow-minded bigot.[44] Lucy came to my office to give her judgement about carpets etc: but that villainous Mr Smith (the Upholsterer) did not keep his appointment & we went away (after 1¾ hr) without seeing him: – Lucy amused herself with collecting dead flies for her black bird!!!!!!! Talked to Prof. Blunt about Latimer Neville: he said 'Your friend has come off with flying colours: he is very intelligent & sensible'. I was much pleased with this & wrote word of it to Latimer, sending him at the same time a copy of the Theological Tripos: – 205 went in: 1 was turned out for copying, & 10 have been plucked . . .

*Wed. 6.* . . . Carus called on me to ask me to sign a requisition to the Vicechancellor to do something strenuous in consequence of the Pope's recent appointment of Wiseman as Archbishop of Westminster & of 12 other

---

[43]  On 24 September at Rome a papal bull was issued 'in the plenitude of our apostolic power' to establish a hierarchy of Catholic bishops in England who would derive their titles from their sees. Nicholas Wiseman, head of the church and newly designated Cardinal Archbishop of Westminster, afterwards published a pastoral letter: 'Catholic England has been restored to its orbit in the ecclesiastical firmament, from which its light had long vanished'. To some the rhetoric seemed tactless; to many more it was an alarming sign of 'papal aggression' from which church and state must be defended. By November anti-Catholic sentiment had revived in a massive outburst sanctioned by a letter of Lord John Russell, formerly a champion of religious liberties, which attacked this 'insolent and insidious' attack on Protestantism, chastised the Tractarians for leading their flock to the verge of the precipice, and defended the Queen's supremacy. Wiseman and his master were burned in effigy on 5 November, scores of pamphlets fell from the press, and thousands of public meetings were held in only two months. See 30 May 1850.

[44]  Writing to Albert's secretary in January 1851, Sedgwick was to describe Corrie as 'on many points singularly narrow minded, and on all points he is, I believe, as obstinate as a mule' (Winstanley, p. 234), the words of a liberal who himself could be obstinate. Yet the kernel of truth is in them. The Master of Jesus was a shy, vastly erudite man whose conservatism in ecclesiastical, academic, and political affairs was sincere and principled, and whose life was spent fighting for and losing but never surrendering ground. His opposition to outside interference lasted into old age, when with pawky truculence he told another set of Commissioners who asked what the chief want of the university was, 'exemption from the disturbing power of Royal or Parliamentary Commissioners'.

Bishops: – I declined, saying that Corrie was quite firebrand enough without any instigation of ours. – Lucy came to my office again today & Smith kept his appointment: so we arranged about the carpets etc . . .

*Tu. 12.* . . . Revising Syndicate for 2 hours. – Walk with Sedgwick: we met 2 itinerant bears: Sedgwick produced /6d & had them dance: – fortunately it was just opposite our windows, so Lucy saw it all: – she however compassionated the Bruins & felt no pleasure whatever . . .

*Wed. 13.* Matriculation began at ¼ to 9 with 3 kingsmen. It lasted till 3 o'clock: there were 129 Trinity men . . . nobody of Downing (neither was there last year) Total nos 412: 7 less than last year. My profit £99.7.6. . . .

*Th. 14.* Congregation . . . We passed unanimously a dull & violent Address of the V.C.'s against the Popish encroachments. – Visit from Carus (to see the Address): also from his Church-wardens about warming his church with hot water): – put down my name for 5 Guineas – After 2d Congregation Drs Cartmell & Cookson came to my office (about the Rating Question) & staid till dinner time. – Present of Hare & 2 Rabbits from Sir St Vincent: wrote to thank him. Mrs Hayles wrote to me sending her Benevolent Institution proxy for Mr Corfield & 10/ . . .

On 15 November Romilly travelled from Euston to Leighton Buzzard and was lent a railway wrapper to keep his knees warm. He was going to stay with his distant cousin John Ouvry North, Vicar of Mentmore, and then with John's brother Peter whose church at Wing was to have a grand re-opening after restoration by G.G. Scott. There had been no resident clergyman at Mentmore for more than a hundred years and Romilly found the vicarage 'a tumbledown farmhouse awfully out of repair: no door nor window shuts: the place is overrun with rats' and the spare room assigned to him was so cold, despite a fire, that he went to bed with his stockings on and put his head under the bedclothes. At Wing more than 20 of the neighbouring clergy had gathered and after the service which lasted from 11 until half past 2 'there was a grand hot lunch for the whole party, which must have amounted to between 50 & 60'.

'Baron Meyer Rothschild, the great landowner here' had recently raised John North's tithes to above £300 and on the eighteenth despite pouring rain they went 'to see his kennel of stag-hounds, – fine beautiful dogs: we also had a peep at the unfortunate stags who are kept to be hunted, – but I had no pleasure in seeing them, poor beasts. The Baron keeps up a very great hunting establishment (70 horses!): he has made himself a temporary residence of the ornamented cottage class, but is going to build himself a grand house: – he is recently married to an amiable young person. – I was glad to find in my walk with John North that he had a kind word for every poor person he met: I hear that he is much liked & that his poor damp dilapidated cold comfortless church is very well attended. He must raise a subscription for setting it to rights. He is going to begin building a Parsonage in the Spring'.

*Sat. 30.* . . . Amusing letter from Grim describing his quitting Shrewsbury & his journey to Parc-glas. – At 9 o'clock I received Cartmell, Cookson & Philpott in my office (enquiry about Rateability): – at 11 to V.C. about Univ. Scholarships: from 12 to 2 Revising Syndicate: we voted that personal attendance at Creation should be dispensed with, – an important change![45] Dined

---

[45] Degrees were not yet conferred in absentia. See 9 June 1859.

in Hall: Sedgwick was acting Commissioner in Town, so I presided . . . Lucy
received a letter from Carus announcing that Trinity Church would be shut up
after tomorrow for the improvements. – Wrote to G.T.R. £10.

*Mon. 2 December.* . . . Mr Hurrell kindly called to offer Lucy & me seats at
St Mary's: told him that Carus had given us his pew. – Sealing in Chapel: – no
money however. – Today there was a meeting of the Heads summoned by the
V.Ch. concerning the Royal Commission: 14 were present. The V.C. told them
he should not ask their opinion as he had made up his mind, – his determination
was to make no answer to the Questions proposed by the Commissioners!!!
Ainslie informed me of this: he is justly indignant, & says that the great majority
of the Heads are certainly opposed to the V.C. . . .

*Tu. 3.* Letter from Miss Corfield informing us of the Election of her Father:
wrote to wish her joy. – Letter from G.T.R. saying he is going to try to get
employment as one of the Illustrators of Punch . . . Doyle (who received £600
a year from Editors of Punch) has given up in consequence of its attacks on
Popery). Lucy & I called on the Tylers to hear Mary Anne play on the Piano
Forte: – she did it very much better than I could possibly have expected: her
heart & soul are in it: – I gave her the Child's 1st music Book & a little book of
instructions (published by Easter & praised by Walmisley). – Whist Club at
Drosiers. Staid very late & lost my money sadly, viz. £4.10.6.

*Th. 5.* . . . Dined in Hall: while talking about the Address about to be pre-
sented to the Queen at Windsor Gibbins ṣaid 'I once slept in Windsor Castle';
"O! (said Thompson) on a visit to the Queen?" – 'No, said Gibbins to the
Housekeeper' . . .

*Mon. 9.* Left Cambr. by 11.5 train: my companion was Bateson, who lent me
Gordon Cumming's huntings in Africa, wch I found very amusing . . . Down at
5.35 by the S.W. from that beggarly Waterloo Bridge Station to Windsor: – my
companions were Leapingwell, Hopkins & Fenwick (the Proctor). We took near
1½ hour to perform the 25 miles. – Put up at the White Hart. – The
V.C., Thacker, etc. were there . . .

*Tu. 10.* Nasty foggy drizzling day. – Breakfasted with the V.C, Proctors
& Bedells. – The V.C. felt himself so poorly that he declined going to the Palace
& Ainslie became deputy V.C.: by the way his illness will be considered a sham
at Court as he is said to have communicated a desire of staying away being a
'family man averse to public life. – I wrote to Lucy. – Then walked out in the
fog with Leapingwell & Thacker & bought Windsor soap. In spite of the fog
I thought Windsor Castle magnificent, far more so than I had any idea of. –
I called on Lord Wriothesley[46] (who had written me a letter this morning) & saw
him & his amiable wife & 3 children (2 boys & a girl) . . . Lord Wrio. received
me in a very kind & friendly manner. He says Prince Albert is very playful
& easily amused, that he yesterday showed the Queen a caricature of Cardinal
Wiseman under the name of 'Sillyman', at which he laughed heartily[47] . . .

---

[46] Lord W. Russell, a former pupil of the diarist and brother of Mrs Charles Romilly.

[47] Albert's prejudice against Catholics was stronger than that of the Queen. Her true anger was
reserved for Tractarian 'snakes in the grass', as she described them, whose actions would 'raise
intolerant cries against innocent Roman Catholics which I should deeply deplore and regret'.
She was to write later of her distress at 'the violent abuse of the Catholic religion, which is so

The Hour appointed for our Address was 12¼: 2 others were to precede it, that of the City of London & the U. of Oxford. The V.C. of Oxford was considerably after his time (having been detained on the Railroad): the D. of Wellington reprimanded him, saying "I don't mind about myself, but you have kept the Queen waiting". – We were shown into a room with beautiful tapestry (the history of Esther & Mordecai) & a full length portrait of Mary Q. of Scots, & a painted ceiling. From this we passed thro another tapestried room into the Guardroom. In this Guardroom is a shield of the workmanship of Benvenuto Cellini given by Francis I to Henry VIII: here are several cannons in carriages, & a bust of Lord Nelson on a pedestal made of the wood of the Victory. – We remained a short time in this guardroom wch opens into St George's Hall when the folding doors opened & the Prince came to us & said that 6 were to Kiss hands as at the Oxford Address. St Georges Hall was the Throne room: the Queen & Court are in mourning for the Queen of the Belgians.[48] The Queen was attended by the Marquis of Anglesea, Ld John Russell, Sir Geo. Grey, the Duchess of Norfolk, Lady Canning & 2 Pages. One of the attendants was Lord Edw. Howard: – curious enough, he (a R.C.) & the Duchess of N. (wife of a R.C.) being in attendance at the presentation of antipapish Addresses. – The Prince read the Address with only one small boggle: the Queen read her brief reply very clearly & sweetly.[49] I thought her looking pale & too fat. – In announcing the names I omitted Dr Okes (whom I had not seen & did not know to be present): I thought I was to announce every body, but after I had named Ainslie (Dep. V.C.), Archdall, Whewell, Cookson, Cartmell, Pulling, Worsley & Broadley & all these 8 had kissed hands the Prince desired me to name no more. – I am very glad that Broadley had the Honor of kissing hands, tho neither he nor Worsley ought to have done so. – We then backed out & went into a magnificent banqueting room the Waterloo Gallery where luncheon was set out for the 3 Addresses. I was moderate, some grapes & a glass of Selzer water. – The Portraits in this Gallery are the series of crowned heads painted by Lawrence after the battle of Waterloo: the most remarkable is that of the Pope. – There was a large body of London Police at the Palace to prevent the abstraction of Forks & Spoons . . . I walked away with the Orator . . . We were well received

painful and so cruel' (C. Woodham-Smith, *Queen Victoria* (1972), pp. 322-3). The Prime Minister's description of Catholicism, the faith of almost all Ireland, as 'mummery' licensed such abuse. Victoria was, however, jealous of her prerogatives and moreover had been wrongly told that Wiseman had struck out the prayer for the sovereign from the liturgy. Russell's actions embarrassed several of his colleagues, while Wiseman's dismayed some old Catholic families like those of the Duke of Norfolk who left the church. In Cambridge a public meeting in the Guildhall on 18 December declared the new Catholic hierarchy an 'unwarrantable attack by a foreign prelate', and there was a belated protestant county meeting at the castle on 1 February 1851 on the same subject when it was proposed to address the Queen. The terminology was predictable, 'audacious invasion . . . daring attack'.

[48] She had married Victoria's beloved uncle King Leopold, and was the daughter of Louis Philippe of France who had died in exile in England three months before.

[49] The address and Victoria's short diplomatic response are quoted in the *Chronicle* of 14 December. The reporter observed that 'from the eagerness of everyone to be first' the order of the deputation was not as it should have been, a circumstance with which the Registrary was familiar after years of trying to marshal farouche academics.

by the Mob as we walked to the Castle: they hurra'd for Cambridge . . . I went to the Athenaeum to dine & had a very amusing & agreeable chat with Sedgwick & Sheepshanks . . .

Two days later Romilly was again in London staying with the Edward Romillys in Stratton Street where he found Mrs Marcet 'healthier than she has been for these 10 years.' He transacted his own and University financial affairs, bought ink and spectacles for Lucy and a railway wrapper and trousers for himself 'finding that I had accidentally brought a very shabby pair', and then 'called on my fashionable cousins in Belgravia'. As usual he got on 'famously' with their children, bar one, and on Sir John Romilly's request examined Willy, now aged 15, whose mathematics was better than his Greek and Latin. Lady Romilly most curiously had been on crutches 'ever since her last confinement; something went wrong about her milk and affected her legs'. He also looked at pictures and at the Nineveh sculptures in the British Museum where 'the magnificent winged bull and winged lion' were put up in the entrance hall, and on the seventeenth was back in Cambridge to celebrate Founder's Day at Sidney Sussex and to lose at whist, 'coming off poorer by 36.'

*Wed. 18.* Received a set of Queries about my office from the Royal Commissioners, & began working at my answer to them[50] . . .

*Mon. 23.* The Great 500th Anniversary at Trinity Hall. – I was fortunate enough to have an invitation. We dined at 6½ & sat down 84 . . . The speakers were Sir Herbert, Alderson, Talford, Cockburn (Solicitor General), Archdall, Whewell, Goulburn, Wigram, Townley & Campbell & Maine. The speakers had most wisely been apprised beforehand, so they came with speeches ready cut & dried . . . We did not get up for Coffee till ¼ to 12! I then (unwisely) went into the Combination room & played 4 rubbers (3 of wch I lost, – 19s): the heat of the hall & comb. room was very excessive: – the noise in the Combination room was astounding: – I was amused with seeing the vigorous attack wch was made on the supper after such a magnificent dinner.[51]

*Wed. 25. Christmas.* A bright lovely day. Frere summoned me to help in Chapel as Sedgwick is laid up with cold. – Lucy was highly indignant, but

---

[50] See the evidence of the Graham Commission *Report* (1852), pp. 62-71. The questions fell into six groups of which two dealt with Romilly's everyday duties and the muniments in his care. The others, which must have cost him many hours of calculating, relate to government Stamp Duties and other fees, and the number of matriculations and degrees of every kind analysed by college for a period of ten years. The Registrary's average emoluments had been £397-8-0, of which £338 came from fees at matriculation and degree time. From other sources he paid his clerk £30 a year. His answers reveal just how much he was a collector for government tax and for sums for the university's 'common chest'. He refers to a 'fruitless attempt' to increase fees in 1848 to replenish capital that had been spent on public schemes such as the Observatory and the anatomical schools in recent years, and notes that a reduction or removal of stamp duties 'would be received with great delight; but there will always be a large party among the Members of the Senate, who will endeavour to throw out any general tax which would affect their own body, as well as the Undergraduates' (p. 71). His college statistics show Trinity's predominance over all other colleges; it might be said to be half the university.

[51] An account of the speeches with their frequent references to papal aggression is given in the *Chronicle* of 28 December. So too is the menu which unsurprisingly impressed the reporter: 'the viands were of the most récherché character, and were all provided [by] Mr. Fuller, the eminent *chef de cuisine* of Gray's-inn.'

I thought I must needs leave her to go to St Mary's by herself. – a very small congregation in Trin. Chapel: Mrs Whewell, Lord Monteagle & Mr Goulburn were present . . . the Master trusted too much to his memory & made several mistakes: – as for Gibbins (who had to collect the alms) he discharged his part most bunglingly. I then called on Sedgwick, who has had a bad cold since the Address at Windsor . . . Sedgwick read me several passages from Comus, & gave very good criticisms of what he read . . . I met Lucy on her return from church: we went home, swallowed a hasty luncheon & (after she had changed Bonnet No 1 for No 2) we returned again to St Marys: Hardwick (Cath) preached in the most dull monotonous manner possible from Hebrews 1.i: – I thought Lucy must have gone mad or have quitted the church: – she did neither one nor the other, but wrote a long letter to Frances Wilderspin, – no doubt she got credit for making copious notes from the Sermon . . . We had a superb turkey for dinner, & it was capitally cooked as well as the plum pudding . . .

*Th. 26.* Nasty day; rain from morning till night: – Voice not come back a bit. – Library reopened & got out 14 Vols for Miss Cotton . . .

*Sat. 28.* Receiving Fees till 3 o'clock: business was not at all brisk: received only 72 . . . One other man signed & found himself penniless when I demanded money: a 3d (a son of Judge Coltman) had scruples about the damnatory clauses of the Athanasian creed.[52] I recommended him to think the matter over carefully & to consult some religious friend, & if at the end of a fortnight to return to me if he found he could conscientiously sign my book: – I told him that George III & many other good persons had been strongly opposed to those clauses & yet were zealous members of the Church of E.

[52] i.e. verses 2 and 42 with the phrases 'he shall perish everlastingly' and 'they that have done evil into everlasting fire'. During the next century several unsuccessful attempts were made to have the creed truncated or removed from the Book of Common Prayer. The Duke of Sussex (see 22 July 1849) is said to have written in his copy 'I don't believe a word of it'.

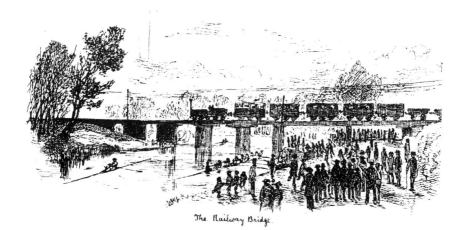

The Railway Bridge

# 1851

*Wed. 1 January*. God be praised Lucy & I are very much in our usual health at the beginning of the new year . . . New years gift of 10/ to Lucy & 2/6 to Harriet, Dosia & Anne Coe. – Brace of pheasants from T. Mortlock: wrote to thank him . . . Dined in Pembroke Hall (as the Masters Guest) where was a grand gathering in honor of the Foundress's day . . .

*Mon. 6*. A charming day: but Lucy was idle & never stirred out. Carus sent me ½ doz (– he has promised a whole dozen) of Newtown Pippins: – they may turn out palatable, but I never saw such rubbishing looking ugly apples. Lucy wrote to thank him, & to beg him not to groan so awfully as he did all prayer-time yesterday . . .

*Wed. 8*. Poor Dr Haviland died this morning at 5½! He was walking in his garden yesterday & went to bed in his usual state, but was taken with a fit soon after & never spoke again. One of his sons who was in London was fetched down by Electric Telegraph . . .

*Mon. 13*. Plough Monday. – Lucy staid at home to escape the bother of the bold beggars. Some of the mummers amused me by their straw crowns & straw jackets. At night some of them came to the door with blackened faces & rather frighted Harriet . . . Read the 19th No of Copperfield: – a charming scene where Copperfield drinks tea with Traddles & his young wife & her sisters.

*Th. 23*. Beautiful Jack Frost. – Lucy again devoted herself to birdcageglass hunting: she explored Castle End! – in vain . . . Interview with Gaskin who is desirous of bracketing together the 1st 2 wranglers: I dissuaded him: I think 40 marks difference is enough for the honor of Senior Wrangler: The marks are:

$$\left\{ \begin{array}{l} \text{Ferrers 3310 (Caius)} \\ \text{Evans 3270 (John's)} \\ \text{Yool 2884 (Trin.)} \end{array} \right.$$

I daresay I should not have felt so decidedly if Evans (a Johnian) had been highest. Went on with 'Olive': the death of the old Nurse Elspie is very dismal. Olive is too dreamy for my taste: the words I detest 'realise', 'idealise', 'objective', 'subjective', occur perpetually: – the Authoress too is an idolatress of Wordsworth & Tennyson[1] . . .

Between 28 and 30 January Romilly was again a guest at Audley End. He read prayers, enjoyed two large dinner-parties, played whist, took exercise alone or with some of the young ladies and deplored the slaughter inflicted by the men of the party on no less than '230 head of game, 180 of them were pheasants'. Meanwhile in Cambridge, Carus had paid Lucy a long visit. He described disloyally and in detail

---

[1]  This early novel of catastrophes and bombast by D.M. Mulock (Mrs Craik) was published in 1850. See the curious introduction to the reprint of 1996 in the Oxford Standard Authors series, which hardly does justice to the wretched style.

'a grand canting hypocritical scene' in the Selwyn family in public after the funeral of Maria's sister-in-law. It had ended in tearful embraces. 'Carus did not say whether any body threw himself into Miss Selwyn's arms: – he certainly would not have done it himself & would have been glad to see any body else do it . . . Miss Selwyn (Carus's Maria) has been proving herself a real Christian for she went to nurse her brothers wife (who is just dead) in her fever & is now going to keep his house & manage his boys'.

Although, surprisingly, Romilly did not deplore such animosity towards his fiancée's family, he was becoming increasingly critical of Carus. He resented the secretive manner in which he had courted a lady whom he appeared not to want to marry, the hurt done to Lucy who regarded his leaving Cambridge as a betrayal of his promises and his dependence on the admiration of so many of the ladies in his congregation.

*Fri. 31.* . . . Called on Mrs Philpott (who is confined to the house with weak ancles): she has windows of one single plate: I thought she was sitting with the windows open. – Received from Potts a present of the antipopish pamphlets (by Wickliffe etc etc) which he has reprinted & is going to circulate all over Lancashire & other parts where Romanists abound: – he says he has engaged a 'colporteur' . . .

*Tu. 4. February.* Glorious sunny day. – opening of Parliament by the Queen. To the V.C.'s at 11 for admission of Bond as Regius Professor. – From 12 to 2 Revising Syndicate. – Lucy and I went to Mr Hunnybun's to see an oak Chair of Rattee's carving which Lucy is going to give Carus for the Communion Table on the reopening of Trinity Church: – it is very solid & massive: the back is carved into Gothic Arches . . . At the Syndicate today we devoted ourselves entirely to the Faculty of Law: – it is no longer to be called *civil law*[2] . . .

*Wed. 7.* . . . Seniority & then a sealing (at wch we received 3s):[3] at the seniority the Master proposed a reformation of the dress of the waiters in hall, viz. banishing the bonnets & shawls of the women & dressing them in tidy caps: – this I think will be tried: – but the project of putting the gyps in Livery seems more doubtful. – Carus asked me if I could spare a minute & come to his rooms to see an old friend. I of course agreed & did not in the least expect any thing short of flesh & blood: – 'the friend' was a drawing of himself which had just been made & cost him 6 Guineas: it is a smirking full face, very like, but full 20 years younger than the original: – he then produced another drawing

[2] The faculty of Law was traditionally held in low esteem as 'insignificant and intended to be so' in the words of D.A. Winstanley, *Unreformed Cambridge* (1935), p. 75, who also quotes Peacock's remark of 1841 that 'the study of the civil law has continued to decline'. Teaching and examining of the subject were overhauled for a new Tripos leading to the LL.B. degree. See 4 May 1861, and Searby, pp. 192-3.

[3] The college seal was applied to legal documents in Trinity chapel in the presence of seventeen fellows including the Master (or Vice-Master) and the Seniority. Each fellow received a shilling for every document sealed (hence the 3 shillings mentioned here), unless it concerned the presentation of a benefice when no payment was made, as on 2 December 1850 above.

of himself made last term, a ¾ face not nearly so strong a likeness: – it looks like a serious footman in a religious family . . .

*Sat. 8.* . . . Letter from the University Commissioners thanking me for my return to the Questions about wch I had taken so much pains: – Bateson (the Secretary) also told me today that they were much pleased with my papers . . . Syndicate revision for 2 hours. – Cold fresh sunny day. – Lucy went to see Sarah Foulkes & Mary Anne Tyler: poor M.A.T. has completely lost her voice . . . Moral Sciences Tripos came out today: only 4 persons, all put in the 1st Class, & Whewell has given his 2 promised prizes of £15 to 2 of the men. – In the Evening read loud 'the Secretary'.[4]

*Wed. 12.* Breakfast to Tearle, Ri-Baxendale, Vernon Musgrave, Taylor, E. Prest, & Nix: – I expected Willie Prest, but his brother brought a note from him saying he didn't dare shirk lectures having been so often blown up . . .

*Sun. 16.* . . . Lucy & I after lunch profited by the glorious fine weather & walked thro Trumpington & Grantchester!!!! . . . she was charmed with the Church & read many of the inscriptions (among others that of the 2 little Miss Foys whom we used to know): – she was highly pleased with the broad gravel walk thro the fields. – In the Evening read loud the end of Bourdaloues sermon on the *sin* & danger of matrimony.[5]

*Tu. 25.* Lovely day with S.E. wind. – Lucy went to see M.A. Tyler. – After dinner she went a long excursion to Burleigh St. to buy a glass for the bird at the Fountain public house. – That ass of an Ann Coe wants to spend her quarters wages upon Lucy & me: – 1st she thought of a silver mug for each of us, then she wished to give me a gold cardcase or some gold studs: – Harriet Sandfield wisely told her that she was sure we would not accept any such costly presents . . . Dined with the Pembertons: the party consisted of Mr & Mrs Pemberton & daughters, Mrs Prest & Edmund Prest, Mrs Hamilton (born de Courcy, – of the Kinsale Family) & daughter, Wilkinson (of Kings), that dull beast Howes (Minister of little St Marys), & 3 or 4 youngsters whom I didn't know & Clem. Francis (without his wife). – I took in Mrs Pemberton & had one of her daughters on the other side: I found the party very agreeable as Mrs P. & daughters have plenty to say for themselves. After dinner came in the great pet of the Family Master Chrissy (aged 13) & a Skye terrier: I took very much to both of them: I nursed the dog for half an hour: – little Christo-

---

[4] A three-decker novel of 1850 by Colonel Richard Hort who had a hectic period as an hack-writer in that year. A useful study might be made of Romilly's reading, which he routinely recorded, and which included, besides solid fare, many now fugitive popular works such as this. The opening of the third volume tells all: ' "Surely – surely we must long since have passed the street where Lord Dropmore was to have been waiting!" exclaimed the terrified Mary, as, urged to full speed, the carriage wherein the Baronet and herself were seated dashed over the stones . . . '.

[5] The Jesuit Louis Bourdaloue (d. 1704) was the most fashionable Parisian preacher of his day whose sermons were available both in French and English translation. We are at a loss to explain Romilly's reference. Did he mistakenly write 'sin' for 'sorrow' ? Professor Peter Bayley suggests he may have been using an imperfect translation or one with a garbled list of contents.

pher is a very spirited horseboy & is allowed to hunt once a week. – As for Mr Pemberton he is too much of a coxcomb for my taste, for (as Wilkinson phrases it) he is an 'awful swell'. – In the Evening the young people played at 'running horses' with dice . . .

*Fri. 28.* . . . Went at 2 o'clock to Albert Smith's laughable entertainment called 'the Overland Mail': he starts from Suez on the journey to England: – there are 13 tableaux (of Cairo, Pyramids, Malta, etc etc), & A. Smith gives a ludicrous narrative (à la Matthews) of all the incidents, during wch he sings various burlesque songs, plays a tin fiddle, a cornopean (purposely out of tune), imitates an Englishman's detestable French 'Arretez Postillon, pour le dernier *tems*, je vous dis: je désire un petit bouteille d'amére bière etc etc'[6] . . .

*Sun. 2 March.* . . . Today Carus preached an admirable sermon on the reopening of his church after all the grand improvements of throwing back the transept arches, warming with hot water, etc etc) – by the way they boiled the water a little too much today, – the heat was oppressive) . . . all the Pews have disappeared from the Chancel: – among other changes we have recovered our carpet & hassocks that have been lying perdus ever since we left St Botolph's: – Carus has brought the singing (or rather the bawling) boys into the gallery close behind us, – for which I by no means thank him . . .

*Fri. 7.* Licensing Day in the Law Schools: – 171 Licences & 36 transfers[7] . . . Ekin has directed all his publicans to be licensed by the Town Magistrates: – all those who have Bagatelle tables are licensed by the Town. – Dined in Hall & presided at Vice Master's Table. Finished Castle Rackrent.

*Sat. 8.* . . . Syndicate for 2 hours: – the question of the Caput came on:[8]– Bateson proposed that no single voice should have a Veto: – I proposed, no

---

[6] This was in the Town Hall where seats were 4 shillings reserved and 2 unreserved with children at half-price A.R. Smith (1816-60), surgeon turned novelist, developed theatrical extravaganzas of which this is an early example before its London run.

[7] Cambridge inns had to be licensed each year by the Vice-Chancellor, the publicans being called in turn according to their parish. This privilege was much disliked among townsfolk, and no mere formality. In 1843, for example, all new applications for licences had been refused and two old ones were not renewed for one had held a Prostitutes Ball and the landlord of the other was in prison for debt.

[8] Since Tudor times the Caput had been the governing body of the university. Small, but very powerful, it comprised the Vice-Chancellor, a doctor from each of the faculties of divinity, law, and medicine, a Regent M.A., and a non-Regent M.A. It was elected annually from among nominees of the Vice-Chancellor and Proctors by a tiny electorate, i.e. the Heads of Houses, doctors, and two scrutators. The Caput had to approve all Graces before they could be submitted to the Senate for a vote and any of one its members could veto a Grace. The reform of 'the most faulty part of our constitution' (9 December 1851) was to occupy the Revising Syndicate for over a year and to lead to more violent dissension than its members had known. At its heart was who, if anyone, in the Caput should have an absolute veto on the presentation of Graces, a device dear to academic conservatives, the removal of which would emasculate them. There is an account of the lack of progress in Winstanley, pp. 238-42 which draws on Romilly's statements. Bateson's proposal that neither the Vice-Chancellor nor any other member of the Caput should enjoy a veto (8 and 11 March) was modified by Ainslie to allow him a veto with special consent of the Heads. But to this idea, Whewell, a strong upholder of the Vice-Chancellor's powers, was opposed (3 May), and he was unmollified by

single voice but the V.C.'s: – we came to no vote. – Declined dining with the Worsleys (to meet Whewell & Spring Rices). – 'The Picture of Grace' arrived by the Post: – I had been solicited by a lady to take this 2s book as a charity for a distressed clergyman: – she sent a little brownpaper pouch to hold the 2s, wch I of course sent her . . .

*Tu. 11.* . . . Heard of the death of poor E.J. Ash who married Miss Ray: – he was found drowned in a pond: he had had a polypus extracted from his nose & the bridge had given way: – poor fellow! how sad an end of so charming & amiable a man: – he & I were joint godfathers to Mrs Willis's Teddy.[9] – Syndicate as usual. – The obnoxious Caput was left in Statu quo . . .

*Mon. 17.* Rain. – Lucy not out. – Lucy received a Letter from Carus at Kirby Lonsdale expressing his regret at resigning Trin. Church for Romsey but saying that he had been prevailed on by judicious & pious friends: – he had always declared that nothing should make him give up his clerical duties at Camb: – but Lucy had told him she was sure that whenever he married he would quit Camb. – The letter was very kind . . .

*Mon. 31.* Wind very high: – Lucy not out. – Seniority (about routine bursarial business) without sealing: – we voted £25 to poor little Tom Burnaby (with 10 children): I gave also a Guinea to Martin for his benefit . . . Lucy's protégé Joseph Saunders (whom she rigged out in a new suit of clothes) went to the Industrial School today,[10] for wch he will have to pay 2d weekly: – I fear his Father has burdened his conscience with a lie: the boys are not admissible under 13, so his Father declares he will be 14 in May. – Lucy's protégée Betsy How (magnificently trousseaued) went to the Training School of Servants last Monday: – the dull girl is getting homesick already – Declined the Marchesa's Evening party. – Read Heart of Midlothian.

another and more complicated compromise of Thompson's (12 May) which was accepted after much argument (13 May) but then rejected by Whewell and three other Heads, the Masters of St John's, Christ's and Peterhouse (31 May). The issue was postponed for the summer. A new year came and it was first agreed that the Vice-Chancellor should have an absolute veto (8 November), but confirmation was again withheld (11 November) and in the end the Syndics could only report that no scheme had been agreed (9 December). See below 6 and 18 May 1852.

9   Edward Ash, formerly fellow and tutor of Christ's, had supported college reform during the 1830s, and had retired to his Norfolk livings in 1839. 'He cared for his men, and willingly took a good deal of trouble for them, in everything but the preparation of his lectures' (E.V.T. quoted in J. Peile, *Biographical Register of Christ's*, 2 (1913), 378.

10  Established by the Church of England after a public meeting in December 1847 to educate the children of the labouring, manufacturing and other poorer classes. A site was acquired in Victoria Road and more than £700 spent on building the school which opened in 1850 and closed in 1893. An industrial farm was attached. Romilly was among the thirty present at the subscribers meeting in May 1852 when Harvey Goodwin, as secretary, reported that there were 42 boys on the books, that the government inspector had reviewed their work favourably, and that the committee was £100 in debt. The *Chronicle* (8 May 1852) reminded readers that 'no gift is more acceptable to the school than cast-off clothes, shoes, or wearing apparel of any other description'. For primary sources relating to local schools see A. Black, *Guide to Education Records in the County Record Office, Cambridge* (1972).

*Tu. 1 April.* Lucy sent off to G.B. Allen a letter giving him for his son John Romilly the Dulwich house: I also wrote to him & sent him the titledeeds etc.[11] . . .

*Sun. 6.* . . . In the Evening we went again to hear Carus. – St Mary's was crammed: we arrived ¼ hr before the time & should have got no room but from Mrs Ashtons kind exertions . . . His sermon was vastly like his morning sermon: he touched but very slightly on its being his last: his voice was not tremulous. – He dismissed the Congregation with words to this purpose: – 'Live for Christ; live by Christ; live like Christ; & then you will all live with Christ for ever: – God bless you'. – It was a very fine sight & a touching one.

*Mon. 7.* . . . Went to the Industrial School at 2½ & heard Harvey Goodwin read the report (a very interesting one) to a crowded room: we afterwards went & saw the boys (there are 28) at work with the tailor & the cobbler: these artists receive 4s‑6d & 4s a day: – we saw the boys also at their hours work of writing etc. – Declined dining at the V.C's . . .

Romilly was twice away from Cambridge during the month; in London to christen George and Maggie Romilly's baby daughter, and in Norwich from 21 to 24 where he stayed with Adam Sedgwick. He found Sedgwick's nieces Isobel and Fanny staying with him and as always enjoyed meeting a great many people. There was however anxiety about Dick's curacy. Dick, who lived in his uncle's house, was curate to Mr Bland, the Rector of St Martin's and had not had his curacy renewed because the Bishop wanted Bland to resign. Mr Bland came to dinner and Romilly found him 'a most zealous & energetic young man of 28: but he has given great offence to the Bishop & all the sober Clergy by his rash headlong conduct: – he preached one day in the Unitarian Chapel (against the Unitarian tenets indeed), but still in the Unitarian chapel. He is not high church or low church, but is an Arnoldian: Sedgwick calls him a radical, & told him to his face that he thought his conduct as a Clergyman suicidal . . . Mr Bland draws an immense congregation, has set up adult schools (at wch Fanny & Isobel teach), most sedulously visits the poor, & relieves all distress with a bounteous heart'. He would, despite his resignation, have to pay Dick for half a year as otherwise Dick would be without any salary.

*Easter Sunday 20.* Bright lovely morning, quite hot: clouded over at noon, & at 5 came steady rain. – Lucy & I went to St Edwards. – H. Goodwin preached a very short sermon (of 19' only!!): he said he should address but very few sentences to them that he might not keep them long from the holy Sacrament. His Text was John VI 51...7. – He was assisted in the Sacrament by Kerrich who mumbled in a tremulous inaudible tone like a man of a 100. – At the Communion Table the good old custom was observed of repeating the words to each individual. – We then went to my rooms & had some bottled

[11] Lucy had lived with Margaret and their unmarried brother, Cuthbert, in Dulwich until his death in 1837. J.R. Allen became a civil engineer but his real love was archaeology in which he became learned. In some respects he reminds one of his great uncle: he never married and had a reputation for sardonic humour, describing his recreation for *Who's Who* as 'collecting strange oaths on golf links wherewith to address scorching cyclists'. See *D.N.B.*

beer. – Lucy went out into the Newnham fields & saw the lambs disporting to her great delight . . .

By 9 o'clock on the 24th Romilly, having caught the 7 o'clock train from Norwich 'after a most agreeable visit' was invigilating on the second day of the scholarship examinations.

*Fri. 2 May.* . . . ¼ to 9 to Chapel: I was the Senior Fellow present & of course read the Bribery Act.[12] – One of the new Scholars is named Church: he is a dwarf & therefore low Church . . . Dined at the Scholarship dinner: there were no visiters . . . At this dinner Remington did an irregular thing wch I most highly approved of & envied him for this boldness, he gave the health of Mrs Whewell as the foundress of a Scholarship. – Amused at this dinner by hearing that the small house (built by Wilkins) adjoining the Bull (occupied by Jones) was called 'the Calf' . . .

*Sat. 3.* Swearing in the new Scholars at 10. – Today the V.C. paid over to me the residue of the Professorial Ticket money[13] (after deducting Prymes 16th of the £70, viz. £4.7.6) that I might pay the other 12 Professors, Whewell, Sir James Stephen, Amos, Bond, Fisher, Henslow, Maine, Miller, Sedgwick, Clark, Cumming & Willis; the last 3 of whom had double shares. Everybody else but Sir Ja. Stephen received their little dividend thankfully, but Sir Ja. got on his hind legs & began prancing & returned me the draft saying that it was a sum wch would not be offered to the lowest menial!! wrote in reply to Sir Ja. At the Revising Syndicate today a proposal was made by Ainslie for remodelling the Caput: he proposed that the V.C.'s veto should not be absolute, but that he must previously call a meeting of the Heads & have the sanction of the majority of those present: – the Master of Trinity made a very violent attack of this scheme, & we parted without coming to any Vote. At this meeting it was carried that the V.C. might on all occasions call upon a man tendering a vote in the Senate House to declare his adherence to the subscription[14] made at his degree: I thought this very inquisitorial & voted against it: – I was in a minority of 1, not a soul agreeing with me . . . I should have said that on the 1st of May a good deed was done at Kings: it was voted

[12] Since Trinity fellows were to be elected from among its scholars, it was needful to demonstrate openly by reciting the legal sanctions against malpractice that scholarships were to be awarded only for merit. There were similar statutory provisions at fellowship elections when expulsion was threatened as the penalty for accepting any reward or present.

[13] The system of lecture tickets as a source of income was new, as the Graham commissioners explained in their *Report* (p. 71) when itemising the incomes of individual professors. All candidates for the B.A. degree whose names did not occur in the Mathematical Tripos had to procure special and general lecture tickets at £3 and £5 respectively. This would raise a sum of about a thousand pounds a year 'to be divided into 16 parts, two of which are assigned to each of the Professors of Chemistry, Anatomy, and the Jacksonian Professor [of Natural Experimental Philosophy], in consideration of the special expenses to which they are subjected in preparing their lectures and one part to each of the Professors of Civil Law, Physic, History, Botany, Geology, Mineralogy, Moral Philosophy, Political Economy, and the Downing Professors of Law and Domestic Medicine'.

[14] i.e. that he was bona fide a member of the Church of England. The proposed reaffirmation was aimed at converted Catholics though it might affect others such as Mormons.

almost unanimously (old Hunt being the only dissentient) that the Kings men should go into the S.H. examination: – a grand epoch in the History of Kings[15] . . .

*Mon. 12.* Should have said that on Saturday the Revising Syndicate sat for nearly 3 hours: Whewell came down from London on purpose to attack Ainslie's scheme . . . but neither his scheme nor Whewells came to a vote, for they were quashed by our carrying (by 9 to 8) an amendment of Thompson's that a veto should be suspensive for one term . . . Lucy out a good deal with her paupers. She is now working away for the Saunders' family: she had a rich scene on Friday or Sat. last with Thurnall (the Surgeon): who has for his 2 servants 2 children of the Saunders, viz. a boy & a girl: the girl is about 16; so Lucy thought it highly improper that so young a girl should be the only female in a profligate young Surgeon's house: she has got a place for her at the dismal Mrs Burrells. Lucy called at the Surgeons & while talking to the girl in the passage was overheard by Mr T. who followed her & asked her what business she had to interfere with his servant: – she looked him steadily in the face & said, because she thought it most improper for a young woman of that age to be his only female servant: he had the impudence to say that he didn't see it! The point is whether Mrs Saunders will have the courage & good sense to take away her daughter.

*Wed. 14.* . . . Walk with Sir Ja. Stephen: he was very amusing: he told of a dream wch Sydney Smith had in his last illness: he dreamt he was dead & taken into the Elysian Fields, where all his happiness was spoiled by seeing the Bishop of Exeter & Miss Martineau walking arm in arm.[16] He said that S. Smith used to sign his name latterly 'Croesus', after a large fortune came to him from one of his brothers will being set aside in wch he had left all his fortune to his maidservant . . . Andrews (Lucy's protégé) the bulldog[17] called

[15] Since its foundation in the fifteenth century King's College, composed exclusively of boys from Eton, had enjoyed the right of its scholars to proceed to the B.A. degree without undergoing any university examination or other test of their fitness. Indeed they were often elected into fellowships before taking their B.A. degrees. It had long been known that the privilege rested on very shaky law and it might have been surrendered earlier had not the late Provost Dr Thackeray been immovably opposed. His successor Richard Okes was in favour and Romilly already knew that he would 'make the grand reform of sending the Kingsmen into the examination' (18 February). See Winstanley, pp. 236-7. The legal instrument citing the grounds for change as 'objections that naturally attach to any such diversity of discipline' and a desire to establish 'a more perfect system of equality and unity of interest' with the rest of the university, is given in *Annals*, V, 31-2.

[16] Sydney Smith, the great wit, died in February 1845 when the incongruity of such familiarity was already comical, though this is not one of his better jokes. Bishop Phillpotts of Exeter was a litigious, high-church, pluralist clergyman of the old school and an unabashed Tory in the House of Lords. The ailing bluestocking, Harriet Martineau (1802-76), came from a unitarian family. They both wrote prolifically from dissonant positions on economic, social, and religious matters, and by 1851 Smith's vision was more ridiculous, for Phillpotts was embroiled in the Gorham controversy that he had begun and Miss Martineau had taken up mesmerism. Phillpotts was related by marriage to the Allens of Cresselly.

[17] i.e. one of the Proctors' men chosen for fitness and strength to accompany them on their rounds. 'And he had breath'd the Proctor's dogs' (Tennyson, *The Princess* (1847), Prologue).

on me to ask a loan of £8 for a week: scolded him well & lent it to him. Dined with Prof. & Mrs Miller to meet Col. & Mrs Sabine (he, the Col., is the Translator of Humboldts Cosmos)[18] . . . It was one of the most agreeable dinners I have been at for a long time, for there was abundance of animated conversation & no science . . .

*Sat. 17.* . . . Lucy has succeeded in making Mrs Saunders take away her daughter (aged 16) from Mr Thurnall the surgeon (where she was maid of all work) & has this day placed her with the dismal Mrs Burrell – I should not like to have heard the remarks made by Mr T. on this occasion. – Syndicate as usual. – Dined in hall where I presided: there were 2 Oxonians, so I went up into Combination room. – Mrs A. Thomas to the astonishment of herself & every body is again with child after an interval of 7 or 8 years. – Carus has resigned St Marys: I believe he was inducted into Romsey last Tuesday & is to preach there tomorrow.

*Sun. 18.* Breakfast without a fire. Mr Jay preached in the Baptist Chapel. Lucy . . . saw several persons come out who were overpowered by the heat, for the chapel was crammed. Mr Jays Text was Phil. 1.27 'let your conversation be such as becometh the Gospel of Christ'. The sermon was full of excellent matter & lasted 80' . . . Old Gunning was present at this sermon, being the 1st he ever heard of Jay . . .

*Mon. 19.* . . . Called on old Mr Jay. He complains of his *obesity* (as he calls it) & of his fidgets: after his sermon yesterday he had to have his legs rubbed in order to soothe his restlessness. He is now in his 83d year. His zeal makes him do too much for his strength: last Wednesday he preached in London to a huge congregation for 1½ hr & then came down to Cambridge . . .

*Tu. 20.* Seniority. – we took away the Sizarship of Edwards (who failed lately for a Scholarship) for irregularity about Chapel & lectures: the Master gave him an excellent reproof . . .

*Mon. 26.* . . . Saw the Johnians playing cricket on Parkers Piece in their boating dress (red jackets & red caps). – The day very rainy: we had a fire after dinner. – Read loud 'Lavengro'.

*Fri. 30.* . . . Lucy had a grateful letter from Susan Grounds (for £1 sent) . . . As usual on Fridays she spent all the morning with her paupers & took Henry How (son of a Cobbler) to a shoemakers & treated him with a pair of boots, he being shoeless & making that an excuse for not going to school: – he trotted down the town with L. in a borrowed pair of his brothers. William Gilmore just released from prison to wch he was sent for neglecting the work of Rattee (to wch famous wood-carver he is bound apprentice). Went on with the life of Collins: began also Ld Hollands Reminiscences.[19]

---

[18] i.e. *Kosmos: Entwurf einer physischen Weltbeschreibung* by Count Alexander von Humboldt (1769-1859), a large work that began to be published in 1845 and was available in translation. In it the polymath author, who has been called the founder of 'ecology', achieved a tour de force in his account of organic life and grasp of recent scientific progress.

[19] Presumably the *Memorials* (1848), by his son the novelist, Wilkie Collins, of the life of William Collins, R.A., a popular painter of sentimental genre pictures who died in 1847.

*Sat. 31. . . .* Wrote to G.T.R. £10. Letter of thanks from virtuous Nancy. – Lucy to M.A. Tyler who is the greatest beggar alive: she asked Lucy for a black veil, & L. (instead of refusing her) gave her 2! The last Syndicate of the Term: Whewell was very furious in refusing to sign such an organic change as the new Caput scheme: – we ended by adjourning till October tho we had fully meant to sign today. – Signed several University documents at Hydes the Solicitors. – Mr Ebenezer Foster of Anstey Hall buried today – he is said to have died immensely rich.[20] – Declined dining at the Hopkinses: – it is believed that Hopkins will be knighted (because he is one of the 'Jurors' (or prize-awarders) at the Crystal Palace & is also President of the Geological Society: – I know not how far knighthood will be compatible with his present position as Esquire Bedell & senior Wrangler Maker: as Esq. Bedell he receives about £300 a year, as S.W.M. about £3000 (he taking 40 Pupils at 70 Guas each!)[21] . . .

*Sun. 1 June. . . .* We fell in with Broadley who told us that he was going to do duty at Benet . . . Dr Broadley's reading prayers was very strange & uncomfortable & the sudden changes of his voice from quick familiar to slow sepulchral bass were very painful: I thought he would never get thro that magnificent & exulting 15th of Corinthians: – he read it as if he was going to be hanged & dreaded the resurrection . . . L. & I then walked thro Corpus & looked in at the hall (where dinner was going on): we were solicited by a little damsel to go into the Chapel, & Lucy was much pleased with the beautiful old painted glass in it. – We then paid a visit to Peterhouse . . . We walked in the Fellows garden & saw some youngsters lying on the grass drinking wine very much at their ease. We didn't get home to our dinner till 5½.

Between 6 and 9 June Romilly stayed in Hammersmith with his nephew George in order to spend two whole days at the Great Exhibition in Hyde Park 'which surpassed my expectations in spite of the great praise I had heard lavished'. And on 21 July, en route for Paris, he paid it a second visit, this time with Maddison, the Vicar of All Saints, who in the train from Cambridge 'sat on my tail & tore it: so I had to go into a tailors to have it mended'. They walked to the Crystal Palace from Pimlico Pier to which they had come by steamer and made for the machinery section where they 'had the centrifugal pump exhibited to us by a very clever mechanic'. After refreshing themselves with a bottle of ginger beer and a slice of ginger pie Romilly 'had the luxury of a good wash for wch I paid 2d because I had a towel to myself: – the common jacktowel is allowed to penny washers. There are here retiring places for wch you pay

Holland (1773-1840) was a Whig politician, who with his wife hosted a brilliant social and intellectual salon. He had worked closely with Sir Samuel Romilly.
[20] The Fosters were a Cambridge family of Baptists prominent in banking and commerce. Ebenezer who died on 26 May aged 74 had been councillor, mayor, and magistrate.
[21] Hopkins was not knighted but secured fame as the coach of such men as G.G. Stokes, William Thomson (Lord Kelvin), and James Clerk-Maxwell. A prestigious prize for advanced work in mathematics and physics was founded in his memory in 1867. See *D.N.B.* and Searby, pp. 633-5.

a penny or a halfpenny . . . The people behaved very quietly & I was much amused with seeing them at their meals: they came furnished with large baskets carrying provisions plates & glasses etc: they were accommodated with tables & seats in the various open courses adjoining the refreshments rooms . . . there was no appearance of any person being tipsy: – in spite of stories I had heard I perceived no smell of spirits.' The most entertaining of the novelties 'was a bed wch compels its tenant to quit it at a fixt time: – we saw a man get into it: & when the right time came a violent spring acted & shot him out in the middle of the place: the spectators roared of laughter, but the man rubbed himself & looked considerably disconcerted'.

*Sat. 14.* Lovely day & not at all hot: – so our sightseeing prospered. – Took L. & Carry to see the Senatehouse: also to our kitchens & cellars: we each drank pale ale out of a stoup: – the cellars were exhibited to us as if we had been Royal people, the exhibiter (with 2 lighted Candles) walking backwards the whole time: – he told us the largest butt of Audit contained 108 Gals: – we also examined all the plate at the Butteries . . . Sedgwick made himself very agreeable at tea, & Lucy plaid her part very well. Of course Carry never spoke but when spoken to.

*Sun. 22.* Cool; almost chilly. – Lucy & I at 10½ to Hobson St. Chapel to hear Mr Vasey a London Wesleian preach in behalf of Missions. This was my 1st visit, but Lucy had been there before. It is a very comfortable well-ventilated chapel: it was not more than ¾ full, & of those present many gave nothing: – the Wesleyians are poor & uninfluential in Cambridge . . . Lucy gave 3s.8d½, taking great trouble to rummage up all the halfpence from the corner of her pocket. I was content with giving 2/6 tho I greatly admired the preachers eloquence & felt vext at the probable smallness of the Collection . . . We then walked thro our walks by the backs of the Colleges sitting down on various benches, & into Queen's Garden (having borrowed the Key at the Porters Lodge) where we gathered a pretty nosegay . . .

*Tu. 24.* Weather cool. – Lucy to St Edwards Church: congregation of 10 women & 1 man: the reader fortunately was not Kerrich. – Lucy then went to Barker's (to pay him his quarter), to the Tylers, & to Brown the Tailor. Her object in this last visit was to get a place for little Saunders, a boy who has just been dismissed by Thurnall the Surgeon. He is not turned away for any alleged fault: Lucy thinks it is because she took away his sister (whom she has placed at Mrs Burrells). She learned from Mr Brown that the Wesleian preacher whom she admired so much was not the Mr Vasey announced, but a makeshift for that great gun who had been unable to arrive in time . . . Lucy & I went with M.A. Tyler (drest all in her best) at 5½ to their allotment of ½ acre close to the East end of the new Botanic Garden: – we there met her Mother & Lavinia: – I amused myself with putting 6 pence in one of the flowerbeds for Lavinia to dig up. – Mr Tyler has erected a summer house, which he has decorated with oyster shells nailed in front & behind: – it is impossible to imagine any thing in worse taste. Lucy & I went with the determination of being pleased, so we praised every thing we saw with more goodnature than sincerity.

*Sat. 19 July.* Very rainy day indeed. – Lucy today prentised Tom Saunders (age 19, son of the ass-owner, late errand boy of Thurnall the surgeon) to

William Gillingham, cabinet maker for 4 years: – she paid £20, the lad is to be slept & is to receive 3s a week the first year, & an additional shilling each year. – Old Saunders had the sense to say 'I'm quite lucky to have lit upon such a friend' . . .

Romilly's detailed description of his last Long Vacation holiday with his brother Frank and his family fill no less than 40 pages of the Journal. He sight-saw indefatigably in Paris and on expeditions outside it, was enchanted by Rachel's acting in Racine's *Phèdre* and at an evening at the opera, attended by the President, enjoyed *Les Nations*, 'a medley of dancing & singing composed in honor of the Great Exhibition . . . Half of the house had been taken for the English'.

On 8 August Romilly was surprised to find that Frank on parting with him 'kissed me as if I had been a Frenchman' – a prelude to so rapid a journey, despite very rough seas, that Lucy was out when her brother arrived home two days before she had expected him.

*Sun. 10 August.* . . . A very amusing thing has happened in my absence: Messrs Hunnybun & C.E. Brown (Churchwardens of Trinity) wrote to Lucy to say that they were sorry not to receive from Mr Carus among the other subscriptions the magnificent one which they had heard she intended giving: – the letter commemorated the munificence of a certain Miss Cook also. – Lucy wrote in reply that the moment she knew of Mr Carus's proposed departure she had written to him to say she should not contribute at all to the organ. she added that she had already disposed of the sum which she had destined to that purpose & that she did not mean to have any more connexion with the Parish (wch was not her own). – Very spicy!

*Th. 14.* Harriet Sandfield returned from her 12 days leave of absence: she brings a bad account of Betsy Spink who seems to have caught cold since her confinement. – Carus called today in a Fly at Lucy's dinnertime & was not admitted. – I met Peacock & wife & 2 friends . . . in the streets: – Peacock asked if I would take him & Mrs Leach into Hall: – I most readily agreed (having already intended to dine there, it being a feast day). I offered to receive the ladies in the gallery & send them choice dishes: – they declared they had already dined . . .

*Mon. 18.* Sent 4 bottles of Port wine to poor Betsy . . . Bought a cotton umbrella of old Hinds by way of charity: cost 4/6 & was worth about 2/: – his g. daughter has a doll made by a one-armed young man: the doll has no arms at all. – Read loud Sense & Sensibility . . .

*Tu. 26.* . . . Mrs Scholefield called on Lucy about 'the Training School' to explain why Pashley's daughter could not be admitted, she being a dissenter, too old, dressing too smart, etc: – Mrs Scholefield said that I had said to Mr Ashton that I thought the refusal on Mrs Scholefield's part *very illiberal*: Mrs Ashton said this to Mrs S – I have no recollection of having said so, but if I did it was clearly very treacherous & illbehaved of her to repeat it. After dinner we had a fire. – Finished Sense & Sensibility. The dénoument is most absurd . . .

*Wed. 27.* . . . Lucy paid a visit to Mrs Gilmour . . . her son William is giving her no end of trouble: he is apprentice to Rattee (the Wood carver) but neglects his master shamefully. – Willis & wife & Margaret are just returned from Paris (whither he went as one of the Jurors of the Great Exhibition): the little girl is highly delighted: – the Willises (like so many of the other Excursionists) were separated from their clothes for 3 days . . .

*Fri. 5 September*. Lucy has given to M.A. Tyler all our hassocks, Cushions & carpet that came from Church: – she worked all day (without stirring out) at covering the Hassocks. – I went on with 'Junior Proctor's Book', comparing it with 'Old Proctors Book', Markaunt, etc. etc.[22] . . .

*Sun. 7*. Lucy & I went to St Michaels & sat in Mrs Lestourgeon's pew with herself & her 2 ugly girls. – We got tired to death of Scholefields sermon . . . I never heard him hesitate so much: he must have felt that it was a poor performance. – We then got from the Porter the key of Mr Carus's rooms & spent rather more than an hour in going over every nook & corner of the rooms & garden: there is nothing left but one shabby chimney glass, 2 or 3 rubbishy bookcases, one large table (with mahog. legs & deal top), & 2 packing cases full of goods. We found the place filthily dirty & miserably out of repair; – the dry rot in the floor of the dining room. – We then came to my rooms & had some bread & ale . . .

*Sun. 14*. Lucy received very agreeable letters from Frances Wilderspin, M.A. Tyler (at Royston) & Hannah Smyth. This last was very satisfactory as it expressed much gratitude for the presents & stated her recovery from her illness. – Lucy & I started at 10.25 to go to St Peters Church: but we found that Witts (the Clergyman) is out of Cambridge & that the Church was shut up: a little girl told us that there was never any Sunday service, but constant weekday service. We then went into St Giles[23] . . . We were put in a nice pew (with an old Gentleman & a dull carrotty haired girl) just before the marvellous parabolic sounding board: it is a curious old church with odd ladders from one corner of the gallery up to the roof; there is a holy water place at the entrance & a poorbox in the inside. Dodd *intoned the prayers & the Communion*. I was surprised at finding so high a churchman as Dodd used Simeons hymns . . . We were out of church by 12.20 (the sermon having been only 28'). – We then (in spite of the very considerable heat of the day, for there was a bright sun & cloudless sky & but little wind) walked to Chesterton . . . We crossed the river at one of the ferries where the boat runs on a chain: – Lucy had never seen such a boat: so today was a day of novelties, for she was never at Chesterton or at St Giles' Church. – We tried the echo in Jesus meadow but it was in the sulks & wouldn't talk . . .

*Tu. 23*. . . . I went to the Fitzwilliam to see the 2 pictures just given by Mr Vint of Essex: one of them is a very dirty ugly picture of Prometheus & the

[22] On official occasions the Proctors still carry copies of the statutes since these had at one time been found in their 'books'. Thomas Markaunt was Junior Proctor in 1417-18. For the contents of the items mentioned see Dorothy Owen, *Cambridge University Archives: a Classified List* (1988), pp. 57-60, 189-90. Romilly dated his index attached to the Old Proctor's Book 1 October 1851.

[23] This small and unimproved church, parts of which dated from the eleventh century, was aisleless and galleried. It was demolished in 1875.

Vulture: they call it Titian: the other is a fine picture by Spagnoletti: the subject is a dead St. Sebastian with 2 female figures . . . Ficklin drove me over in his gig to dine with the Charles Townleys: there was a slight mizzling of rain, but not enough to put up an umbrella: – also slight rain at our return at 11½. Ficklin told me plenty of anecdotes about all manner of people . . . he says that the quantity of ale drunk by Hind & Shilleto is quite appalling.[24] He told me a curious story of Miss Sutton (the school mistress) having called upon him in a most towering passion the other day . . . "What did you mean by advising a child to be taken from my school?". – Ficklin answered "I have advised Mrs Shilleto to take away her little girl & I shall advise every body I know to take away their children from you till you give up your medical treatment of them: I know no person whom I would more recommend for teaching a child if you would confine yourself to that". – Ficklin says that Miss Shilleto is a healthy little girl whom he has examined carefully & that she has no affection of the spine: – Miss Sutton has (without consulting any medical man) laid the child on boards for 2 hours a day for 2 months, & given the child a globule every morning & evening & a homeopathic dose every alternate day!! . . . Ficklin told me that his horse Jemmy was out at grass near the railway, & . . . became suddenly scared by some puffs of steam & rattling of carriages & broke out from his field & galloped to where he was (near the Station with some friends) & nestled his head against him & seemed to think himself as secure as a child under its mothers protection . . .

*Th. 25.* . . . Dined with Mrs Prest who has just had £150 left her by General [blank]: it will help her in setting up Willy for a soldier. His reading at Bonne lasted for only 5 weeks & he then set out touring & made up his mind that he would go into the Army: he is now cramming for the military examination on the 1st of October: his mother clearly thinks he will break down. – The Ensigncy is to cost £450 & the outfit £100 . . .

*Th. 2 October.* Second day of Fellowship – Latin by Cooper & Remington: – Eng. Verse & Latin Verse by me. Visit from old Gunning (who wanted one of my Gracebooks): he told me that old Peacock (the Dean's Father) is just dead at the age of 96 . . . his own daughter Mrs Alger (she has been twice married) is a horrid drunkard & frightens him out if his wits when she is staying at his house because she reads in bed late at night . . . This

---

[24] Shilleto is a pattern of academic failure. A scholar of exceptional gifts he had married young (see 6 May 1862), so disqualifying himself from a fellowship. He toiled as a coach to support a growing family and this and a lack of advancement led him to drink. Heitland describes him as 'a pathetic figure' though 'the first Greek scholar in England', and 'at night, when I saw him, a pint pot of beer stood handy on a pedestal. When it was low ebb in this vessel, he placed it in a pigeon-hole close to the door, and rang the bell. Soon a stealthy hand withdrew it and put it back refilled. So much liquid refreshment entailed other embarrassing phenomena.'(W.E. Heitland, *After Many Years* (1926), p. 130). By the time of his election to a fellowship at Peterhouse in 1867 when he was passed over in the election to the professorship of Greek his addiction was cruel; the nadir of his fortunes must have come in November 1871 when he entered the town library drunk and dirty, refused to leave, and assaulted Pink the librarian (*Chronicle* 16 December 1871).

morning a tame hawk answering to the name of Tilly got into my bedroom: his master (a Trinity man) was in despair when he missed him & sent the towncryer to cry him: my bedmaker with the assistance of a man caught him without difficulty, & received 1/ from his Master . . . Two or 3 of the men staid ¼ hr beyond the time (4 o'cl.) at my paper in hall: & one (Taylor) staid till near the ½ hour. Dismal Jemmy[25] said to me afterwards 'of course you'll vote against him'! Mr Senior dined in hall with me. Sedgwick presided: a good party of us (Sedgwick, Remington, Thompson, Rothman, etc etc) went upstairs. Sedgwick was in great force & we staid till 8¼. Cooper told me that Carus is to be married on the 7th *in London* at Hanover Sq (St George's) by *Jeremie*: he asked Bishop of Winchester to marry him; but the Bishop is obliged to go to Geneva. Lucy went to the hospital taking with her some toys (a windmill etc) to an ugly little protégée of hers. – No reading loud this Evening.

*Tu. 7.* The day of Canon Carus's commencing captivity. Worked as usual all the morning at Fellowship papers. Fell in with Pryme who told me that Carus had declared to him directly after Mr Simeon's death that he meant to imitate him & never marry & never quit Cambridge . . .

*Th. 9.* I am this day 60 years complete, & am (God be praised) in the enjoyment of my usual health. Received from M.A. Tyler a pair of very pretty slippers as a birthday present, & a kind note accompanied the present. Drank tea at the Lodge . . . We then proceeded to election & with little or no fighting elected 2 classics of the Upper Year (Rowe son of the winemerchant) & H. Taylor, both pupils of Thompson), & 2 mathematicians of the middle year (Watson & Westlake, both Pupils of Cooper. – It was very odd that of the 19 Candidates none belonged to Atkinson . . .

*Sun. 12.* . . . We sent off our Blind Proxies, I mine (by promise) to C.E. Long: she hers to an anonymous application for a girl blinded by firearms. The day being very mild we walked to Trumpington: the church both outside & inside looks beautiful after the recent restorations.[26] We saw poor Antony Gordon there: he was at the Communion Rails with a person to take care of him[27] . . . We had a large pew (with a large hole in the floor) to ourselves . . . Grote did the whole duty. He said that as it was Sacrament Sunday he should give them a very short sermon: & he kept his word for he preached for 12' only, being the shortest sermon I ever heard . . . Lucy found the sermon very dry & the church damp & cold. We then walked to Grantchester & examined the tombstones & walked round the lovely church. We here met Mr Deighton who has been living during the summer with his family in the tumbledown vicarage where I had Pupils in 1813: he told us that these 2 last nights thieves had tried to get in . . .

---

[25] i.e. J.A. Jeremie, fellow of Trinity and Regius Professor of Divinity from 1850, who was regarded as sensitive, fastidious, and indecisive.

[26] Trumpington was a Trinity living. Restoration, including woodwork by Rattee, evidently took several years. See *Chronicle* 4 February 1854.

[27] Chaplain of Trinity who had gone out of his mind (see *Romilly 1842-47*, p.186).

*Tu. 14.* Lucy did infinitude of pauperising . . . Meeting in Chapel at 12 to elect a successor to Carus in the Seniority: we passed over Moody & Sheepshanks (agreeably to letters of theirs) . . . we then proceeded to the election of Whiston who was present, & willing to take the Oath: he will be admitted tomorrow. By the way Whiston's trial before the Bishop is expected to come on at Christmas.[28] – At this meeting we reswore & readmitted our 4 new fellows, the V.C. having (correctly) declared their former admission irregular because it took place before their signing the 36th Canon at his Lodge. The new fellows were reminded that they ought to write letters of Thanks . . .

*Wed. 15.* Left Cambridge by 7.15 train 2d Class: Kingsley (one of the Jurors) & Wiseman (an exhibitor) were my companions.[29] Deighton was afraid of catching cold & went in 1st Class . . . the place was immensely full: the Crystal Fountain had been removed to make room for a Platform for Prince Albert & the Commissioners: – a throne was set for the Queen, but she did not make her appearance. – Punctually at 12 the Prince arrived: the accommodation was not good for seeing, & of course hearing was out of the Question: – I could however see the heads of all the people on the Platform. When the Prince entered the building two verses of 'God save the Q' were plaid: at the end of his speech the National Anthem was sung, & the whole proceedings closed with the performance of the Halleluiah Chorus with a full band & choir: the effect was beautiful . . . I should have said that the proceedings on the Platform began with the reports of the Chairman of the Jurors (Lord Canning) wch was followed by a very dry address read by the Prince: after wch the Bishop of London offered up a prayer . . . I dined at the Athenæum & afterwards went to the Adelphi to see the Yankee Actor (Seelsby) whom I thought very clever indeed . . . After it was a piece called the Follies of the day, in which appeared 12 women in Bloomer costume: a Bloomer Lecture

[28]  Robert Whiston, fellow of Trinity and master of Rochester School had published a pamphlet exposing the administration of the Dean and Chapter who, he believed, were appropriating an undue share of the cathedral revenues, and in particular failing to provide adequate scholarships at Oxford and Cambridge. This led to a series of legal processes and airing of linen which ended with his final reinstatement at the school in January 1853. Whiston's case was one of several that brought the anomalies or unconsidered abuses that might attend archaic trusts to the attention of an amazed public (and to Anthony Trollope). Its implications for Oxford and Cambridge were not hard to discern. See Chadwick, I, 513, and R. Arnold, *The Whiston Matter* (1961).

[29]  Wiseman won no prize at the Great Exhibition for his Bible bound in scarlet morocco with illuminated fly-leaves, but another Cambridge binder, E. Budden, got £10 for an elaborately ornamented binding of an album. According to the official catalogue of the exhibition Cambridge had eight exhibitors there (Oxford had 27), of whom another was J.P. Papera, a sculptor of historical figures, whose seven works included the Saviour and Sir Robert Peel. The university had its own committee to communicate with the Commissioners for the exhibition when it was being set up in the previous year and their minutes survive (University Archives, Min.VII. 63).

was given & the Bloomer Polka danced.[30] I came away before the concluding piece, being thoroughly tired & exhausted with the extreme heat of the theatre wch was crammed to suffocation – Slept at the Golden Cross, wch is now a good hotel. – my bedroom looked on St Martins Spire.

Between 18 and 20 October Romilly stayed in London for the christening of Betsy Spink's baby, his godson and namesake. Betsy showed Romilly 'her very pretty neat new house' in Stratford and he thought the church in which he had 'to hollow as loud as I could to be heard' above the screeching of the second baby he christened 'beautiful both inside & out'. In the evening he walked from the Athenaeum to Bishopsgate Street along the Strand where 'there was at one part an almost impassable crowd, from a belief of thieves having got into a house: – I buttoned my coat to secure my watch & purse & elbowed my way thro' without being robbed'.

*Tu. 21* . . . Paid all the 12 Professors their dividend of the receipts of the Professorial tickets for the last Academic year: Sir James Stephen (the 13th) declines receiving so paltry a sum . . .

*Fri. 7 November.* Lucy's usual day of rambling: – she went to M.A. Tyler etc etc. She took Hannah Saunders to buy her a pair of Boots: – she has now shod Father, Mother & all the children: – there remains no creature to be shod except the Donkey, for whose sake she patronised the whole family. – Letter from Cruttwell enclosing a draft for £21.3.4: this will be her last receipt as she is going to give her Bath house to G.B.A. for his eldest son . . .

*Sat. 8.* . . . Revising Syndicate today: fullish meeting (19): Cartmell's proposal of revising our decision 'about the Caput on the basis of the *absolute* veto of the V.C.' was carried by 9 to 8 . . .

*Mon. 11.* . . . Seniority, at wch the Master read the searching queries (about our revenues, charities, etc etc) sent by the Royal Commission to the Master & Fellows: – they are certainly very inquisitorial & will not be answered in any detail. Then to the Revising Syndicate: we fought furiously & ended by refusing to confirm the last minutes, so Cartmell's proposition (of discussion on the basis of the V.C.'s absolute Veto) falls to the ground . . . Went into Corpus Library 5' before 4; so I saw but little of the M.S.S. (which were this day inspected):[31]– soon after 4 I dined in Corpus Hall, where was a grand party & a magnificent dinner. Whewell, Corrie, Blunt etc etc were of the party . . .

---

[30] Amelia Bloomer's attempt in the early fifties to introduce rational dress, a short skirt worn with loose trousers gathered at the ankle instead of women's cumbersome crinolines, provoked ridicule in her native America and Britain. Journalists, cartoonists, and moralists made 'bloomerism' the topic of 1851 and quickly triumphed over the few women daring enough to wear the outfit in public. Mrs Bloomer later dropped the campaign as it distracted attention from more serious issues of women's rights. See C.N. Gattey, *The Bloomer Girls* (1967). A Bloomer disciple, Miss Atkins, lectured in Ely and intended to proceed to Cambridge in November but was warned off and never appeared.

[31] It was cannily provided that the library should be inspected each year by representatives of two other colleges, Caius and Trinity Hall, and that if serious losses were discovered the whole collection should pass to the inspecting colleges, and so on in circular perpetuity. Of course no serious losses were ever found.

*Th. 13* Breakfasted in College at 8¼. – To the Senatehouse at 8.45 & staid till 3.20. The matriculation was good; 444 in all; viz. 1 Nobleman (Cavendish), 10 Fellow Commoners, 390 Pensioners, 43 Sizars . . . it was not the year for Downing to have a man[32] . . .

*Mon. 1 December* . . . Dined in Hall & presided, but shirked Combination. Finished 'Coelebs' & began that vulgar Mrs Trollopes new novel 'Mrs Matthews'. – The beginning I find very amusing, & warmhearted: – it describes the Heroine marrying at 50 entirely from affection to her Father. – Read to Lucy (out of 'the Times') a long & brilliant criticism of Tennyson's poems (called 'In Memoriam') on the death of A. Hallam.[33] – Absurd letter from Bailey talking of resigning his Perse Pension & throwing himself on the mercy of Caius Coll.

*Wed. 3* . . . Passed all the morning working out statistics about degrees . . . for Gaskin as Moderator[34] to send up to the Royal Commission . . . Shocked to hear of there having been a revolution at Paris: – Louis Napoleon has dissolved the Chamber, dismissed the Ministers, proclaimed Paris in a State of Siege, proposed Universal Suffrage & sent Changarnier & all the leaders opposed to him to Vincennes. Happily no bloodshed: – but matters are not ended yet.[35]

*Mon. 8.* Sat up in State from 10 till 2 to exhibit to all comers the Questions of the Royal Commissioners concerning the Press & the University Revisions & also the Opinions of Sir F. Kelly & Mr Cowling in July & November 1850: only 5 came. – Letter from Frank: very satisfactory . . . Sophie was constituted Commander in chief at the house, & allowed nobody to go to the windows. The barricades have all been carried by the troops: many lives have been lost: but Paris is now quiet . . .

*Tu. 9* Sat up again at my Office to exhibit the Commissioners' Queries from 10 till 12: I had about 20 visitors. At 12 to the Syndicate Meeting: we sat till 2½ & a clause was introduced expressing *regret* at our not having concurred upon any proposal to recommend to the Senate concerning

---

[32] Downing, the most recent College foundation, had been unable to admit undergraduates before 1821 and their numbers remained negligible. According to the *Cambridge University Calendar* of 1848 (p. 391) Downing had the fewest members of the Senate (35) and the fewest undergraduates (11).

[33] Noting that of modern poets Tennyson has perhaps 'met with the fewest obstacles on the highroad to reputation', in a piece headed 'The Poetry of Sorrow', a reviewer in *The Times* (28 November), while he acknowledges certain felicities, dilates on the 'enormous exaggeration of the grief' for Hallam, the disquieting 'amatory tenderness', and obscurity of expression.

[34] Two moderators were appointed each year by Grace to conduct university examinations and to class the candidates.

[35] Louis Napoleon, having progressed from membership of the republican National Assembly to its presidency during 1848, restricted the press, deprived General Changarnier of command of the National Guard, and laid plans for a coup d'état on 2 December. The legislature was dissolved and troops occupied Paris. Napoleon at once engineered his election as President of France for ten years and after a further plebiscite he was declared emperor on the first anniversary of the coup.

a modification of the constitution & power of the Caput: – Great opposition had been made by the Heads & their supporters to this expression of regret, but they gave way & I expressed my readiness to sign. It is a most unfortunate termination of our labours that we have not amended the Caput, wch is the most faulty part of our constitution, & a change in which has been confidently expected from us by the Senate . . .

*Wed. 10* . . . Congregation day . . . Cope (Father of Trinity) presented a Supplicat for Geo. Dodson (the man who was tried for bringing a written paper into the Senatehouse & acquitted, tho his case was pronounced one of very grave suspicion):[36] A very long discussion took place in the Caput & the degree was refused (on the ground that his Examination & Approval had not been signed by the Moderators etc . . . Among the Graces of today were 2 concerning the Royal Commission: the 1st 'to authorise the V.C. to answer in his own name the Queries of the Commissioners'; the 2d 'to authorise the Press Syndics to answer according to their own discretion the Queries of the Commissioners' . . . Two of the Heads (Corrie & Webb) voted against these Graces . . .

*Th. 11.* Lucy wrote to G.B.A. & made his son J.R.A. a present of her Bath House: she gave her Dulwich house to the same boy this year.

*Mon. 15.* . . . Heard an amusing account of Paget's marriage: Dr P. made a speech on the reciprocal duties of forbearance in husb. & wife, & his brother James made such a flaming eulogy of him that all the young Ladies burst into tears.[37] Miss Chapman told me some of the senior Fellows of Caius came over to the wedding & plaid at 'Blind man's Buff' for the luxury of having young ladies fall into their arms! Read loud Christian Knowledge 'Bear & forbear' (dull & preachy).[38]

*Tu. 16.* . . . At 11 to Chapel for the Commemoration of Benefactors: Mate preached in a most lacrymose manner on 'the fulness of time': – the matter seemed to me good but the delivery would have done credit to an undertaker, & he read every benefactor as if he had died before his eyes in dreadful agonies. – Then to the Hall to see the Prizes distributed: a man of the name of Benson came up 6 times for Prizes! he made the 2 Prize Declamation in Latin & English: the Latin one was the eulogy of Barrow, the English that of G. Herbert[39] . . . We have partly revived our Commemoration magnificence: –

---

[36] Dodson had appeared before the Vice-Chancellor's court on 7 November when he asserted that, far from bringing papers into the examination to copy, he had made a copy there of his original paper, thinking there was a mistake in it. His tutor did not feel his word could be relied on, but the court, though suspicious, would not convict. Dodson took his B.A. in 1853.

[37] On 11 December Paget married Clara, youngest daughter of Thomas Fardell, Vicar of Sutton in the Isle of Ely.

[38] Probably a new improving book for the young by Mary Elliott who worked in that vein for forty years.

[39] Isaac Barrow (1630-77), divine and mathematician, was Master of Trinity at the end of his life; see M. Feingold (ed.), *Before Newton: the Life and Times of Isaac Barrow* (1990). George Herbert, the poet and a fellow of Trinity, was Orator of the university from 1619 to 1627.

there was a superb dinner in hall, & the V.C. & 4 other Heads (beside the Master) were of the party: – the Doctors did not wear scarlet & there was no band. – Grace was sung as usual . . .

*Th. 25. Christmas Day* . . . L & I went to Great St Andrews where we were separated till the sacrament . . . she had not found Cooper's sermon long as she amused herself by copying out a very interesting inscription on the Favell monument,[40] – 2 brothers dying in the field of battle, one in Holland, one at Salamanca & one at Toulouse . . . Lucy then called on Caroline Fordham & gave her a Christmas box . . . We had a Turkey & Ham for dinner & Lucy gave legs of Mutton & Shoulders to the 4 families of Cann, How, Gilmour & Sanders . . . After dinner read loud a Sermon of Coquerels 'Le gain du fidèle'.[41] – That insufferable Ann Coe inflicted herself upon us in the Evening & talked us nearly mad in reward of our giving her 2/6 a piece. After tea read a Christian Knowledge Book 'Penny saved is a penny got': – it is a recommendation of Provident Clubs.

*Fri. 26.* Lucy answered Carus's very kind & affectionate letter . . . Library reopened today: sent off *14* Vols to Miss Cotton & wrote to her. Agreeable letter from Grim thanking us for our promised subscriptions to his schools. – Walk with Sedgwick: he wears a respirator:[42] Miss Murphy quizzed him about it three days ago saying it was merely to excite the compassion of tenderhearted women: he said that it was to keep his beautiful lips from being kissed by the women: – she met him again today & said 'Ah! I see you still wear an antimaykisser!!' . . .

[40] See Bruce Dickins, 'The Favells of Petty Cury', *Proceedings of the Cambridge Antiquarian Society*, 56/57 (1963-4), 103-114.
[41] There were two modern French Protestant divines with this name.
[42] A wire or gauze device to prevent the inhalation of dust and smoke. It had been patented and improved by an army surgeon, Julius Jeffreys, who wrote on its use and on pulmonary complaints. Romilly bought Lucy one in January 1854.

Reading the list of names of those who passed

# 1852

*Tu. 6 January.* Lucy had the laurels taken away from our front garden, a great improvement. – Lucy went to Hebelwhite's to buy a cloke for Hannah Saunders, but being dissatisfied with the nice sober new ones there she went – to a Pawnbrokers!!!! & there bought a flaunty 2d hand cloke which she didn't like half as well, & for wch she paid more!! – rather crackow! But it was her 1st visit to a Pawnbroker & I hope will be her last: – Miss Ainslie rode by as she was in at 'my uncles', but no recognition took place: – L. was partly induced to buy at the Pawnbroker's because she had interrupted him at his dinner . . .

*Th. 8.* Wrote to Hannah Smyth to complain of her not acknowledging the £5 & the letters. – Lucy had a letter from Mr Titcomb about Sarah Fordham's case: she wrote saying that she would pay anything he recommended . . . Dined at Catharine Lodge: a grand party with 2 brides (one of them (Mrs Paget) drest in bridal white, the other (Mrs Pulling) in celestine blue) . . . I took down Mrs Skrine & had Mrs Paget on my other side: I think her delightful, she is so gentle & so conversible & so very pretty: she past 5 days of her honeymoon at Paris & went away the 1st day of collecting the Votes for Louis Napoleon's 10 years Presidency . . .

*Fri. 9.* Spent 1½ hr in my office without a fire writing out all I could discover about the Election of *Assessors*[1] . . . Dined in Hall: – Sedgwick came in at ¼ past 4 (that having been the time for the last 3 days while the Examination was going on in the Senate House). Sedgwick was highly excited & sent for the Hudsons: they were not forthcoming, but the Clerk came & Sedgwick let forth his indignation upon the change of hour without authority from him: 'it was a great piece of impertinence on the part of Mr Hudson', said Sedgwick to the affrighted clerk: – I think S. was altogether in the wrong . . .

*Sat. 24.* Lucy . . . received today Rattees bill (£8.10s.) for the Communion Chair made for Carus's Church (Trinity) last March: ordering it for Carus to use was very agreeable, but paying for it for Clayton to sit in is vastly different: however she satisfied herself with bemoaning her hard fate & didn't go off into a fit (as Lady Dacre used to do when her bills came in) . . .

*Mon. 26.* . . . Went to Rattee's to pay for the Chair: saw in his workshop some beautiful book-stands etc: they are very costly: the price of a little book-stand to put on a table was £3.10.–! it had 2 small figures of men carved on it . . .

*Fri. 30.* . . . Peterhouse is covered with glory: – they have the 1st 2 viz. Tait & Steele: – Steele was the favorite of Hopkins & was fully expected to beat Tait: – he is of course greatly disappointed: – the Johnian champion Godfray (a married man who had been a schoolmaster) is only 3d: he fainted

---

[1] Such research was needed since between 1805 and his death on 6 January the office of Assessor, who assisted the Vice-Chancellor in his court, had been held by one man, William Hunt, the 'most notorious drunkard' of Gunning's *Reminiscences*. See 31 March and 15 May 1852.

away one day of the Examination. – The moment the Peterhousians heard of their glory they issued invitations for a grand dinner tomorrow & sent me a card . . .

*Sat. 31.* Breakfasted with Cope & his 88 sons: he beats Priam hollow.[2] – A most awful jam in getting into the Senatehouse: the youngsters behaved far worse than they have for many years, hooting & halloing, whistling Whewell, & doing everything offensive: – we got out of the S.H. about 1½. The riot doubtless arose from the V.C. having sent instructions to all the Tutors to have up the young men & exhort them to good conduct: – about the most likely thing in the world to make them go wrong. – The V.C. put up extra barricades in the Pit, wch were very serviceable. – Lucy not out. – Dined in Peterhouse Hall: – a capital dinner. The heroes of the day Tait & Steele sat on the right & left of the Master: I sat next Steele. There was only one speech & that of course was by the Master in honor of the 2 young men: Tait returned thanks in a very modest manner, saying he was in quite an unexpected position. – I believe Steele was always ahead of him in former examinations, & was considered the stronger Mathematician by Professor Thompson & by Hopkins the Senior Wrangler maker . . .

*Tu. 17 February.* Archdeacon & Mrs Musgrave called. – I was out. – Met Mr Titcomb who told me to tell Lucy that he thought Sarah Fordham might have a chance by taking an unfurnished lodging at 1/6 per week if Lucy would furnish it, & that she might get occasional employment by going out washing. – Letter from Miss Butcher begging me to write something in praise of Emigration to Australia as Louisa's younger brother Henry Pearce (bred a farmer) is determined to go (as he can get no employment here)[3] . . . Letter from Mrs Leach telling me that she is obliged to communicate with her brother John thro an attorney as he will not perform his executorial duties: wrote to her in reply. Whether my dear friend's property was left in a very entangled state or not I cannot tell. – but at all events John shows himself to be a very negligent if not dishonest Executor[4] . . .

*Wed. 18.* . . . Congregation Day: 2 Hon. A.M, 4 AM, 1 LLB. – I made a slip in my Latin 'commoraverint' for 'commorati sint': the V.C also objected to 'iterum' for 'again' & not for 'a 2d time'. – The Grace about the Kingsmens degrees & Examinations past without opposition[5] . . .

---

[2]   Cope was college praelector or 'father' to the undergraduates. Homer's Priam was credited with a mere fifty sons.

[3]   For some years Australia had ceased to be merely a criminal sink and become a magnet for immigrants, especially after the gold rush of 1851. The *Chronicle* has numerous references to local emigrants, and carried advertisements for vessels. A Mr Brice, author of *Australia As She Really Is*, packed the Town Hall on consecutive days in December 1851 with his 'dioramic lectures' showing 80 views on thousands of feet of moving scenery, and Sir St Vincent Cotton paid the passage for men from Madingley who left with tearful farewells. From the village of Waterbeach alone some 80 people went to Australia (whose population was no more than that of Liverpool) in two years. See 13 April 57.

[4]   We have not found Lodge's will. His three modest estates were divided among relatives, and small bequests included a Bible and 'other books' bound in blue morocco to Romilly, and £100 to Magdalene College (7 January 1851).

[5]   See 3 May 1851.

99

*Fri. 20.* . . . A bad fire broke out in Trinity Hall this morning at 6 & burnt till 9, gutting the East side of the Court[6] . . . My poor little goddaughter Katie died today: the Dr had given good hopes of her, but a relapse came on & carried off the poor little sufferer . . .

*Sat. 21.* . . . I went to look at the Trinity Hall Débris: it appears that about 12½ Mr Nunn went to the closet (where fire revivers etc. are kept) to put his cat to bed in there: – he had been smoking but don't recollect whether he then had a cigar in his mouth . . .

*Th. 4 March.* . . . Lucy had a letter from Hannah Smyth saying that (beyond all expectation) she had just heard that the result of her Examination at Whitelands[7] is her gaining a Certificate: it is not very grand, being 2d Division of 3d Class: still it is a certificate, & she seems as happy with this small affair as Tom Thumb's Mother who prayed for a child if it was no bigger than her thumb. Lucy wrote to her saying she should be glad to receive her for a week at Easter. – I was busy & didn't go to a Seniority today at wch Willan one of our Bachelors was rusticated for giving expensive noisy parties & for allowing an undergraduate to sleep all night on his sofa . . .

*Tu. 9.* . . . Refused a Mr Webb (to whom I had once sent money) who is in trouble. – Letter from Harvey Goodwin begging for his Industrial School New-Buildings-debt: sent him £5, & Lucy gave 3.3. . . . Mr Geldart this day elected Master of Trinity Hall:[8]– learned a curious history of Mr Geldarts gaining his fortune: – he saved a person from being run over: the person turned out to be named Gildart & to have the same arms: having no relations he left all his fortune (£6000 a year I hear) to his preserver . . .

*Fri. 12.* . . . I declined the Judges' dinner: – greatly to my own comfort: it was at 8½!! – There is but one Judge (Lord Campbell): the other (Crompton) was taken ill. – Dined at the Family at Warters: the party consisted of Warter, Phelps, Cartmell, Sir St Vincent, Power, Martin, Stokes, Bateson, Paget & self. Played 6 rubbers & won 13/ . . . Sir St Vincent said that just after he became a member of Brookes (at the age of 22) Lord De Ros played a rubber with him against Anson & Sefton (the 2 reputed best players in London) & he (the Bart) carried off £995 upon that one rubber!! what awful gambling. – We broke up at 11¼: – I caught a sore throat at this party.

*Sat. 20.* . . . Wrote to Betsy sending her a draft for £7, the last remainder of her Saving Bank Money, except 2/5 for interest. Wrote also to Swinny declining his London Orphan Asylum[9] case: also to Mordecai (giving him 5/). – Lucy walked a little in the Garden by herself. I took a solitary walk: I was sorry to find that the Johnians have stript off the ivy from many (too

---

6   The east range fronting the lane was rebuilt within two years with an extra storey to Anthony Salvin's design at a cost of about £4,800.

7   A training college in Chelsea for women teachers founded in 1841 by the National Society for Promoting the Education of the Poor in the Principles of the Established Church. It was to blossom under the patronage of Ruskin and Miss Burdett Coutts.

8   Sir Herbert Jenner Fust (for whom see *D.N.B.*) had died on 20 February.

9   Founded in 1815 by the Congregationalist minister and philanthropist Andrew Reed (see *D.N.B.*). It had large premises at Clapton in Hackney opened by the Duke of Cambridge in 1825, and catered for some 300 orphans.

many) of the trees in their Fellows' Garden. – Package of old clothes & new cakes from George R. & wife: – Lucy very wisely gave away all the old clothes within an hour of their coming into the house: the principal receiver was T. Saunders (whom she apprentised to Gillingham). – We had a visit from Ann Coe in the Evening: she brought L. a present of violets, & me some Gingerbread: – she has been this day 9 years at Miss Apthorps . . .

*Wed. 24.* Lucy very poorly indeed: – got some physic from Deck: she didn't go out at all . . . I had a letter from Waud begging for charities on the wholesale that he might exchange or London Orphan & Idiot Proxies for Deaf & Dumb proxies for his protégé: wrote to tell him that we had already promised all these Votes . . . Mrs Walker wanted to canvass me in behalf of her monthly nurse Mrs Levett who is putting up for the Victoria! Neither Mr or Mrs W. or her sister subscribe to the V. Asylum!!! I told them that of course we couldn't help them & strongly recommended their immediately subscribing (– the thoughts of which seemed like wormwood to them), telling them they would not run the remotest chance in any Charity without they were sufficiently in earnest to subscribe to it . . .

*Th. 25.* . . . The Classical Tripos out today (– *after* the Medals by way of Novelty): the first 5 are Trinity men . . . I find that young Nix is very susceptible to mesmerism, electrobiology[10] & such rubbish: any body with firmness can control his bodily movements: at a breakfast party today his host defied him to lift his fork to his mouth, & so completely fascinated him that he couldn't. – The Electrobiologist (the Reverend Theop. Fiske of U.S.) instructed a class of 16 (among whom were 3 or 4 Trinity Fellows) at a Guinea a head in the mysteries of the Art . . .

*Mon. 29.* . . . A grand scene about a Mrs Leeson (with whom Sarah Tyler has been in service for 2 or 3 months): the said Mrs Leeson went away this Evening, wishing Sarah to remain alone in the house with her son!!! (who is going in for his degree next term). Mrs Tyler applied to us & we told her that she must of course fetch away Sarah instantly: – the young man is an ill-conditioned fellow who does not scruple at swearing at his Mother . . .

*Wed. 31.* . . . At 12 waited on the V.C. taking with me Edleston & Atkinson: – the V.C. had with him Dr Ainslie. Ainslie said that he had recommended the V.C. to bring forward the Grace for the Election of Amos as Assessor. He & I were the arguers of the Question, but very few words being said by the V.C. & my 2 comrades: – I strongly urged the right of the Senate to have an open Poll for the Election of its officers, & urged the contested 'more Burgm' Election[11] for the High Steward[12] in 1840 & for the Assessor in

[10] A new and impressive sounding word for hypnotism and auto-suggestion which were in vogue not least because they puzzled scientists.

[11] i.e. in the same way as for the election of university M.P.s. A member of the Senate voted by writing down the name of the chosen candidate and his own, and giving the paper to the Vice-Chancellor. The procedure was also used in elections for the Chancellor and certain professors, and in nominating clergy to benefices in the gift of the university as a corporate body.

[12] The office was largely an honorary one for a prominent member of the university who often held it for life. The High Steward had power to try scholars impeached of a felony within the

1790 as irresistible precedents. Ainslie spoke of the want of courtesy in not acceding to the V.C.'s wishes in the Election of an Officer so closely connected with him as the Assessor . . . The conference was conducted in perfect good humour on both sides & we parted at 1½ confirmed in our original views . . .

*Th. 1 April.* . . . Called on Mrs Ashton to ask her Victoria Votes for Bidwell: walked with her round her garden: – she said Mr Carus had sent her a little cream jug (like that sent to Lucy & Mrs Hoskin) & in his note spoken about 'the sincere milk etc etc.' (as also to Lucy). Miss Watson was the bearer of these little jugs: – she had staid a week with Carus at Winchester & declares that he has fitted up his houses very quietly & that he is a poor man & that tho he is allowed £100 p a. by his mother he has only £500 a year to live on as he makes nothing by Romsey! She says that he is occasionally lowspirited & that one day directly after his wife had left the breakfast room he said to her with tears in his eyes 'that little woman has done all this'! Mrs Ashton very properly told Miss Watson she was very wrong in communicating such anecdotes as they might do great hurt to Mr Carus if repeated by his enemies . . . I said to Mrs Ashton 'our excellent friend Mr Carus made a great mistake in not marrying early in life as he wd have escaped a good deal of the dangerous flattery wch is administered to handsome unmarried popular preachers' . . .

*Fri. 2.* . . . Dismissal of term: 1 eundem. – Trial of Labouchere of Trin (turned out of Senate House for suspected copying at Little Go)[13] for having circulated a printed letter accusing Proproctor Barnard Smith & the Examiners of unfair treatment. – The young man behaved in a reckless discreditable manner during the whole trial (leaning his elbow on the table, interrupting the V.C. etc etc) wch lasted from 11 to 3½: he is a bad subject: he is said to have betted £300 on getting thro this Examination: he bets at horseraces etc etc: – his sentence was 'Admonition & suspension from degree for 2 years': – he asked 'is there no higher court I can appeal to?'[14] . . .

*Sat. 2 May.* Letter from J.P. Gell about Mandate DD: wrote to Gell[15] . . . Dined at the Woodward Dinner. It was very unnatural for Sedgwick was absent: – the dinner was unfortunately fixt for 6 o'clock & he was going to Norwich by the Evening train. The party however was a very agreeable one, for Worsley talked very amusingly & well about the fine arts: Mrs Okes dined with us: her quiet gentle manners are very winning. – I began the 3d No

limits of the university (i.e. a mile in any direction from any part of the town), and to hold a court leet. But no cases had been tried in living memory and the 1852 Commissioners found that his powers were 'merely nominal'. Lord Lyndhurst, sometime fellow of Trinity, M.P. and Lord Chancellor, had been comfortably elected in November 1840 (see *Romilly 1832-42*, p. 204).

[13] i.e. the Previous Examination in classics and divinity which all undergraduates were obliged to take in their fifth term. Its standard was low.

[14] The bad subject became a controversial journalist and M.P. and was always 'a rebel against constituted authority' (*D.N.B.*). For Labouchere's own unedifying account of his Cambridge days see the *Life* by A.L. Thorold (1913), pp. 20-6.

[15] Gell had unusually proceeded M.A. 'by Royal consent' in 1840 only a year after his first degree before leaving for Australia. He was never awarded a doctorate.

of 'Bleak House'. Another blank day for Victoria Votes, for that clumsy Searle has sent his 2 votes & Mr Nashe's 2 to Bidwell.

*Sun 2.* Lucy & I both had letters overflowing with gratitude from Grim for our £5 each for his schools: he told us that we had built 100 perches of wall (of 8 foot by 1 foot), amounting to a wall 48 ft long & 16 ft high . . . Lucy had a letter from Frances Wilderspin about quitting her place at the Surgeon Menzies: she is very fond of the little children, & likes her Master & Mistress, but there are 2 cursing foulmouthed profligate grown-up sons. Lucy wrote a letter to Frances recommending her leaving, & I sent her 10/ . . .

*Th. 6.* Bidwell & wife called to give account of the Election: the Votes were as follows, Rooke 299, Bidwell 139, Levitt 70, Abbott 0, Haggis 0 . . . Today we had a meeting of the Revising Syndicate: not a soul at our end of the table approved of Ainslie's scheme of reference to Bishop Turton, Sir E. Alderson & Sir J. Pattison for a new scheme of a Caput, so he withdrew it . . .

*Fri. 7.* . . . Went to the Annual meeting of the Industrial School: there was a good meeting: Cookson was in the Chair, & H. Goodwin read a very interesting report, stating the gloomy part as well as the encouraging: the gloomy part was a debt of £100, & the wickedness of the boys on Sunday (when they do not come to the Asylum); – one of them (for whom a grant had been promised to enable him to emigrate) has committed an atrocious villainy (robbery, I suppose) for wch he will probably be obliged to emigrate in the degraded position of a transported felon. – Harvey Goodwin subscribed £10, Cookson, Baxendale, Col. Glover & I each £5; – £75 was raised. – Prof. Henslow & son Leonard, Atlay & I over to Madingley together. The Baronet was not well enough to make his appearance: a party of 9 . . . The young lady with ringlets fell to my lot: she is not yet out: she is a young teetotaller: I found her very gay & conversible: she was drest very decorously up to the throat, but her sister who is come out thought she might make a larger display of her person . . .

*Sat. 8.* . . . Met W.H. Thompson escorting Mrs Pollock: he is hospitable enough to receive her & her husband into his rooms for 3 or 4 days, where they sleep just as in a private house. Letter from S.O. Meares about a youth (named Jones) son of a pupil of his: – he wants the lad to be admitted at Trinity for next October tho our no is full, & we never take more without the supplicant is something out of the common way: – this lad seems to be a very commonplace mortal . . .

*Sun. 9.* . . . Lucy went to Bene't Church at 3 & had the misfortune to hear Dalton preach a long insufferable sermon from 'Love not the world'. As she was going to Church she met Esther Bailey (who had formerly been a Pupil of hers) & who has been weak enough to follow the Example of her Family in going over to the Mormonites: – Lucy made a most animated attack upon the immorality & the blasphemy of their doctrines: – to wch Esther answered quite coolly that they had never been proved wrong!!.[16] – Lucy wrote to Hannah

[16] Two local Mormons, noting that 'Cambridge is a seat for much learning, but alas, she is blind', asked for missionary help in 1848. It came in the shape of Elder Flanagan from America, who found her 'one of the strong priest-manufacturing holds of Satan's empire' (K.J. Goates, *William Goates*, privately printed (1991), pp. 16-17). The ecclesiastical census

Smyth. – She went out for an hour in the Evening to take that poor old Guly to bathe: she was rewarded by hearing the nightingales in full song. – She tonight left off fire in bedroom.

*Wed. 12.* . . . There being no prospect of a rubber I went at 9½ to the University Concert & heard the overture to the Freyschütz, some good Glees ('Welcome bounteous May' by Spofforth, & a drinking Glee of Bishops), and a trio of Beethoven. – I had a fire in the Office today, & copied out all the Graduands of 1600 & 1601 from the original Supplicats.

*Th. 13.* Old May day:[17] 4 nice little Chesterton May-ladies with chaplets of flowers on their heads made their appearance in our garden and enticed 6d from us . . . The V.C. printed 100 cards for each of the following 5 persons Dr Dinsdale (born Trotter) Mr Mills, Dr Broadley, Prof. Pryme & Mr Tozer: – the 1st 2 however are not candidates. . . . The Polling began at 10 & went on to 1: at wch hour the nos were Broadley 46, Tozer 42, Pryme 5. – The polling was resumed at 2 & closed at 5 when the nos were Tozer 83, Broadley 76, Pryam [sic] 7. So poor Broadley after all the excitement of several months has lost the great object of his anxiety! I am heartily sorry for him. I think Broadley was ill used by the Trinity men: Edleston & Atkinson had accompanied me in the Deputation to the V.C. wch ended in this open poll, & were imagined sure supporters of Broadley: – neither voted for him . . .

*Sun. 16* Thompson told on Friday the story of Archdeacon Allen examining a school at Cambridge upon the Parable of the Good Shepherd: – Thompson (as he says) asked one child who the Porter was, & the child answered 'Please, it's the man that sweeps the college walks!' . . . Lucy & I started at ¼ to 3 (as if we were going to Church!) for a walk till dinner: the weather was quite delicious tho the sun was rather overpowering: – we staid out 2 hours lounging along the Trumpington Road & listening to the Nightingales . . . We were greatly entertained by the Gambols of Saunders little ass (a week old today): its mother lay down in the middle of the road & the frolicsome fole galloped round her in a good large circle a dozen times at least & once jumped over her back! – Seeing a poor jaded woman on the tramp I gave her 4d: – whereupon a strapping young fellow (apparently belonging to her & seemingly half drunk) held out his hand to me & said 'Excuse my hand, I love you'. – Read loud two very interesting letters (sent by Miss Wilcox) of a Mr Wilson who is a prodigious benefactor to the Candle-factory schools of Belmont Vauxhall: one is to the Boys, the other to the Men: – he has set up Cricket & established annual excursions (to Herne Bay, etc. etc.) . . . The labour at this Factory

of Sunday 30 March 1851 listed 222 places of worship for Mormons in England and Wales. One was in Cambridge where there were 150 sittings and that morning 38 people had attended worship. Any admiration that may have been felt for the energy of the Mormons was quite lost by their espousal of polygamy. The *Chronicle* of 15 May 1852 reports the explosion of a steamer at Lexington in April. Among the passengers killed on their way to a Mormon settlement were three unmarried Cambridge women including Lois and Marianne Bailey, 'deeply lamented by their parents'. The editor could not forbear to observe that this 'salutary caution' might save the misguided 'from a step which cannot but end in their irretrievable ruin, females more especially'.

17 i.e. the original May Day before the calendar reforms of 1752.

is 12 hours, alternate weeks of night & day work from 6 to 6: – great nos attend the schools, chapel & the cricket ground.[18]

*Tu. 18.* . . . At 10 o'clock to Pemb. Lodge: the subsyndicate (consisting of Ainslie, Philpott, Cookson, Bateson, Sykes & self) sat till 1½, agitating a scheme (of Sykes & Batesons) for appointing a Board of 16 in wch all measures not relating to degrees should originate, no person in this Board having a Veto: – the Caput to be left as it is for Degrees: – the Board to consist of V.C. & other 3 Heads, 3 Doctors, 3 Professors, 3 Non Regent & 3 Regents[19] . . . In our Library I met Sir James Brooke (Rajah of Sarawak)[20] & was introduced to him by Harvey Goodwin . . .

*Wed. 19.* Lucy don't seem to get on. – She had a visit from Brown (the Schneider) about apprentising Henry Andrews to a Gardener at Bourn for 5 years: the premium is large, £40: £10 is to be paid by the boys Father & Uncle: Lucy will pay the £30 – but the youth is to be lodged, boarded & washed: – a fight is to be made for some small weekly payment to the poor lad. – Congregation: 1 Mandate D D (Bishop Vidal), 10 A M, 1 LLB, 4 AB & 3 eundems: one of the ad eundem was Rajah Brooke (LLD Oxf.): – he was well received by the youngsters who gave him 2 or 3 rounds of applause. – The Senate house was well filled with Ladies . . .

*Th. 20* . . . I . . . (at Lucy's request) asked Broadley to dine with me in Hall. – There was a large party; our 2 Noblemen (Ld Muncaster & Ld Cavendish) were in their gaudy gowns: – the Dean of Ely etc of the party: Leapingwell was the only Doctor who had been correct enough to come in his scarlet gown. I presided. – About 8 o'clock in came Shilleto with Mr Scott (the Lexicographer) & of course I welcomed them as if Shilleto had not done a very irregular cool thing. I gave Mr Scott's health: he made a short & smart reply beginning 'As a Dictionary-maker I must not say that I am at a loss for words'. – The conversation turned on jokes & puns. Mr Scott asked if we could read off the following letters K I N I into a line of Hamlet: – nobody could: – the answer is 'A little more than kin & less than kind' . . .

*Mon. 24.* Just heard that Frederick Romilly & his Colleague Mr Smithe (Members for Canterbury) fought a duel last Friday: Smithe used some

[18] See the *Quarterly Review* 92 (1852-3), 1-18, which describes the work of James Wilson, managing director of Price's Patent Candle Company at Vauxhall 'who thought it possible, without loss or hurt to the texture of the candles, to humanise and Christianise "the hands" that made them'. From small beginnings since 1847, when boys were taught to read and write after work in an atmosphere of self-help, the education and recreation of the workers bloomed.

[19] The Senate was divided into two houses, the Regent or White Hood House of Masters of Arts of less than five years' standing and doctors of less than two (who wore hoods lined with white silk), and the Non-Regent or Black Hood House of other M.A.s and doctors. Romilly uses the terms Black and White House on 2 February 1853. Graces were read in the Non-Regent House, and voted on if any member declared that he was opposed (non placet); an uncontested Grace or one approved by vote in the lower house (placet) was then taken before the Regent House and the process was repeated.

[20] In a startling private enterprise Brooke had assumed the government of Sarawak in 1841. This same evening he addressed the Borneo Church mission in a crowded Town Hall and was rapturously received.

offensive language & on refusing to retract was called out by Fred: – shots were exchanged harmlessly: – there is a ludicrous account of the affair in the Times of today:[21]– I have stuck it in my 'University Papers' Book. Two trials at V.C.'s: – the 1st was the adjourned one of Death: – he did not appear: – he was discommuned till the end of October. – The 2d was that of Dixon (a Sizar of Queens) for copying at the Little-Go . . . he was suspended for 2 years[22] . . . Dined at Corpus Lodge: – a grand party of 18 . . . The V.C. told me that at a dinner at T. Mortlocks in honor of 2 married daughters of the Bishop of Lincoln one of the dull husbands (an Oxford man) said to him, 'pray Sir is not Mr Romilly the wit of the University?': – Miss Chapman was at that dinner & she & I had some skirmishing in nonsence talking . . .

*Th. 27.* . . . Meeting of the Revising Syndicate: our new Scheme was proposed: – as an addition or corrective Cookson proposed as a 17th member of the Council the exvicechancellor, & also that if the V.C. differed in a measure before the Council there must be 9 members of the Council opposed to him in order to defeat him . . .

*Fri. 28.* . . . wrote to G.T.R. sending him next months remittance: – he has been ill for 3 weeks with cough & relaxt uvula, but is now better . . . Syndicate meeting from 12 to 3: we adopted the amended Scheme, & everybody signed. – Ainslie wrote on a bit of paper & handed to me a slight variation from Horace's

'stupens

Demittit atras bellua centiceps

'Aures'.　　Od. 2. xiii. 34

He changed centiceps to sexticeps, & it applied nicely to the defeat of the Caput[23] . . .

*Tu. 1 June.* Lucy to St Edwards: Kerrich read prayers to 6 people! Lucy to the Hospital: I met her as she was coming out & we walked over Mr Kings house (lately Mr Pembertons): we went into every room: the place is undergoing a thorough repair, which it wanted amazingly. – We then walked over all the gardens to wch we could get access: – discovered that I had lost my keys: – found them in a bed of groundsel where I had been gathering for the Canary!!!

Romilly returned on 17 June from a three-day stay with his hospitable old friend Sedgwick at Norwich. It included a visit to a shawl factory where the heat and noise were very oppressive and 'between 5 & 600 hands were employed'. In addition to his customary presents for Lucy and the maids he brought home a joke. This concerned the

---

[21]  This is often said to be the last duel in England. Duelling in earnest had been suppressed even in the army and was widely regarded as abhorrent or ludicrous; in this case neither man seriously intended any harm to the other.

[22]  John Death, horse dealer and liveryman, was owed £143 by C.J. Vernon of Trinity. C.A. Dixon cut a sorry figure, having been caught in the Senate House in March with notes on Euclid hidden under his blotting paper. First he said 'an enemy had introduced them on purpose to harm him', but later argued that a friend who wished to serve him could have put them there without his knowledge.

[23]  Horace alludes to Cerberus: ' No wonder that the hundred-headed brute droops his dark ears, enchanted by those songs'.

Crystal Palace which was being re-sited at Sydenham. 'What 2 historical characters would answer the question "Who is to put on the roof for us"? – Answ. "Wat Tyler Will Rufus"'.

*Mon. 21* . . . Dined in Hall to celebrate the Queens accession: I presided: a small party of 11. I went into the Combination room, where we were foolish enough to give the healths of one another: Edleston (to my surprise) made a most affectionate eulogy of me. – The 2 Dr Fishers (W.W. & Anthony) were of the party: a great deal of wine was drunk & I didn't get away till near 9. – I then read loud some of 'the Armourer of Munster'.[24]

*Wed. 23.* . . . Proclamation of Pot Fair: – Cartmell kept us waiting nearly ½ hour: he was deputy for Dr Okes (whose brother Johnny of Cherry Hinton is alarmingly ill. – I heard a good sporting joke: 'What are the Politics of the V.C.?' – Answer 'With the present Ministers, for *the Okes follows the Derby*.[25] – An impudent Fellow at the Fair cried out 'speak up': I did so with peculiar emphasis & pleasure as the coming passage was against 'those of ill life or suspected of the same'. – Saw from my office window the funeral of Dr Frederick Thackeray: – he was buried in the Family vault at St Botolph: – it was a walking funeral: *the ladies of the family*, (Mrs Thackeray, her Sister Mrs Preedy, 2 Miss Thackerays) Dr Mill etc attended. – Heard (from Mrs Leapingwell) that poor Gunning is in a violent state of madness at Brighton[26] . . .

*Sun. 27.* . . . Our last adventure was going over his hired garden with Leapingwell: Lucy was vastly gracious to him & admired every thing: he amused me by his underrating the vines & all the fruit trees & everything left by Mr Pemberton: – Leapingwell pays £14 a year to Peterhouse for this garden & hot house . . .

On 29 June Romilly patiently travelled by omnibus, rail, stagecoach and ponychaise to Hitcham in Suffolk to stay once more with the Vicar and Professor of Botany John Henslow. He found his host examining the girls of Stowmarket school 'in wild-flower-botany: they passed an excellent examination, & rattled out the long-tailed Greek words in a stile that astonished me'. The following day again saw the Henslow family and Romilly in a school – King Edward's, Bury St Edmunds, where the brilliant classic and former Fellow of Trinity, Dr J.W. Donaldson, was headmaster. 'At 1 the distribution of Prizes & the recitation of the Prize Compositions & of scenes etc in Greek, Latin & English'. In contrast, the last day of Romilly's visit was spent in the open air, 'quite

[24] On the following day he finished the novel whose subtitle was *A Page from the History of Fanaticism*, one of a series by Robert Bell entitled *Hearts and Altars* (3 vols, 1852). Its subject is the historical John of Leyden (1510-36), an Anabaptist crowned king of Munster whose story, ludicrously altered, also supplied the plot of Meyerbeer's *Le Prophète* which Romilly had admired at the opera in Paris on 30 July 1851.

[25] Lord Derby was prime minister in a Tory administration from February to December 1852. Hippophiles will not need the joke explained.

[26] Gunning's declining years are chronicled in a series of letters written from Brighton (where he had gone in May) to Sedgwick by Miss Beart who took care of him. They were printed in the *Cambridge Review* of 1912 and separately in the same year as *Gunning's Last Years*. Insanity ran in the family but he had lucid intervals and an adamantine constitution.

beautiful from morning till night' which contributed greatly to his enjoyment of the annual flowershow in Henslow's garden. 'The Master of the Union (Mr Pattison) brought over his band of workhouse boys'. The flower and vegetable exhibits were so good that a number of extra prizes were given and Henslow gave 'a very clever Lecture . . . on the weeds of Agriculture: he concluded with good advice to the Allotment-Cultivators, & recommended a few of them to try the new system of sowing with a fallow layer between, so that only ½ of the usual seed corn is sown'. After tea for 300 men, women and children, sports and 'God save the Queen' played by the band, cheers were called for: Romilly was especially glad to cheer Henslow's servants who had 'all got up at 3½ this morning. – A person from the mob then gave 3 cheers for the Professor (wch he wd have deserved if they had been 300) . . . At 9¼ the premises were clear & the 2 policemen were gone & the old mare Kitty had trotted off with a Waggon containing the Band (11 in no) & the Master of the Workhouse & an old toothless gay-hearted dame of 85 out of the Union: she was bent double like Lady Cotton but seemed quite happy: she said that a contented mind was a continual feast! – The day went off most delightfully'.

*Sun. 4 July.* Another letter from Beast Bailey (about his books in pawn): sent him £5 . . . Lucy and I went to St Michaels where Perowne read prayers & Scholefield preached . . . Then to my rooms & had some beer & biscuits. – Afterwards we went into the Trinity walks & paid our respects to Coopers mare & fole. We sat for ½ hour on the bank opposite the brewhouse in company with a nursemaid (with a beautiful sleeping & snoring boy) & an old man pretending to read a book: – presently to my great surprise I saw two young boys bathing in the horsewatering place of Garret-hostle-bridge: – on my exclaiming against the impropriety as well as the novelty of their conduct the old man got up & threatened the lads with the Porter & his whip: – they bounced out of the water & put on their clothes. Presently a Mrs Moule came & sat down next to me & entered into conversation in a canting hypocritical stile about faithful ministers & about our utter sinfulness without God's Grace etc . . . After dinner I wrote to Francisca,[27] to Sophie (Kennedy), to G.T.R. & to Frank (£10). – While I was doing this Lucy sat in her room with Sarah Saunders (who was too much tired to go out with the maids) & heard her read a Chapter of the Bible etc. which she did very dismally . . .

*Mon. 5.* Breakfast in College: a great fight to get any at all from the constant tide of visitors. – Today the following degrees, 1 Hon A M (Adeane), 101 AM, 1 LLD, 1 MD, 1 BD, 2 LL B (1 p.b.) & 1 AB. – A good average year; – 233 AM altogether: last year there were 230. – What with writing out the degrees for Johnson & collecting information about Tuition Fees for Bateson I had not a moment to myself till past 4 . . . After dinner began reading the new no (5) of Bleak House . . .

*Th. 8.* The Cambridge Town Election today. – Lucy walked with me at 8 o'clock to the Hustings: I gave a plumper for Adair. . . . The Election went all the day against Adair & Mowatt: – the final nos at 4 were Macaulay 821, Astell 804, Adair 737, Mowatt 637 . . . Lucy made some little children (with the Whig colours) happy by giving them some pence & prompting them

---

[27] His second cousin once removed, Francesca or Francisca Ouvry, who later took an active interest in family history and wrote three novels with a Huguenot background. See Appendix 1.

to shout 'Whigs for ever' . . . Very sorry to find that John lost his election for Devonport . . . Frederick has lost his election at Canterbury[28] . . . On passing by the '½ moon' (Lamberts) this afternoon at 2 I said to Shaw (whom I happened to meet at that moment) 'that is not the state of the poll I should like to see': upon wch the Landlord said 'I suppose you would like to throw off your gown & introduce 'popery': – I was foolish enough to get excited & to tell him that it was a most impertinent speech for him to make to a clergyman of the Church of England'. – I passed him again an hour afterwards & he shouted out 'No Cardinal Wiseman: we're for Church & state'. – After dinner read Vicar of Wakefield: – in the cool of the Evening we watered the garden.

*Fri. 9.* Lucy walked before breakfast: the V.C. knocked the term on the head. – Miss Chapman dressed herself up in the tory colours (pink & white) & went about with the dashing Mrs Macaulay in an open carriage: – she was cheered several times by name. – The Clarks have exhibited their Toryism by hanging 2 laurelled pink & white flags at their gates. – L. & I went to a very pretty exhibition, the feast of the Barnwell Sunday School in Peterhouse grove: there were more than 1100 children present, besides the Teachers & the Visiters: there was a band: the boys & girls were divided: the boys played football, trapball, etc. etc: – the girls danced, etc. They seemed vastly happy tho occasionally overpowered with thirst: there was a throng of children with their little mugs rushing to the *watering* place: the benevolent butler supplied some with small beer . . . at 8½ they sang some hymns & concluded with G. s. t. Q: – they gave 3 cheers for the Master & Fellows. – There was a kite placed against the Grove gate with devices & mottoes on it: – such as 'We wont part with the Bible: we love it': – 'Little children, love one another': – 'We love Him because He first loved us' – 'neque semper arcum 'Tendit Apollo': – 'inter Sylvas Academi'.[29] – I thought the gay assemblage dancing & playing under the trees the prettiest sight I had seen since I was at Versailles . . .

*Sat. 10.* Letter from Sophie (in answer to mine): she says that John might have come in without opposition for Edinborough & Frederick for the Ayr Boroughs: I wonder that Fred. did not accept the offer as he must have known that his chance at Canterbury was very questionable . . . Unopposed Election of Goulburn & Wigram for the University: – Lucy took a good walk before breakfast & paid Mary Anne a visit: – Mrs Tyler told her interminable stories about her own integrity & her husbands, & how upon one occasion the Tory bribers put £10 in her hands wch she immediately took to the Whig Committee-room who returned it to her & told her to keep it. – In the Senate house at the Election this morning was Lady Catherine, the wife of Wigram: she is a very pretty woman, a daughter of Lord Selkirk. – I find that at Devonport they made caricatures of John's canvassing the Electors, with the words 'The Master of the Rolls begging his bread from door to door' . . .

[28] Sir John had been M.P. for Devonport since 1847 and was the last man to be allowed to combine membership of the Commons with the office of Master of the Rolls. Neither he nor his brother Frederick sought election again.

[29] i.e. 'due relaxation is necessary' and 'amid the woods of Academus [to seek for truth]', both from Horace.

*Sun. 11.* . . . We went next into Queens walks by the usual little gate: thro the kindness of Clark (of Qu:) we gained admission into the Fellows Fruit- & flower-garden: we were struck with admiration of the ancient mulberry tree: the stem has disappeared & the branches seem to be growing out of a small central mound: these branches are kept together with iron collars & supported by numerous wooden props. In this garden is a square very little pond with gold fish in it: you descend to it by 3 stone steps: – the garden was gay with an astonishing profusion of larkspurs. We then went into their adjoining Grove & staid till past 4 admiring the swans & refreshed by the cool air & sitting under the shade of the trees by the edge of the river . . .

*Th. 15.* . . . The Devonport paper (sent by Sophie) arrived, giving the account of the speeches of John & the other Candidates before & after the Election: – John has been shamefully used: – there is no doubt of bribery on the part of the Government Candidates[30] . . . Dined in hall: a very small party, viz. Sedgwick, myself, Hedley, Thrupp & the young Prince of Schleswig Holstein: – I asked him if he went out on the river: – 'no, said he, I do abominate the Cloaca Maxima'.[31] – I came directly after dinner. – Lucy took a little sickly Saunders (named Hannah) out shopping from 6½ to 8¾: she treated her with a pink frock etc etc . . .

*Sun. 18.* Two of Lucy's gowns being at the Mantuamakers as patterns she had none that she liked to go to Church in . . .

*Wed. 21.* . . . Breakfast to Captain Ouvry[32] & Prince Frederick of Schleswig Hostein. – I afterwards escorted Henry (i.e. Capt. O) to the Public & Trinity Library & also to the Library of Kings: he was in search of a Persian manuscript of Yusuf & Zuleika: he found it indeed in the *Catalogue* of Kings Coll, but the M.S. itself could not be produced by the Librarian (Piper), who evidently knew but little of the treasures wch he guarded: – this small library has only 10,000 volumes . . . Dined in Hall to be ready for receiving the Judge: – it was a small party, viz. Self, Prince Frederick, Henry, Mate, Hedley & an unknown. Just as the Pastry was coming on the Judges' trumpets sounded & we rushed out (thro the Lodge) to receive Chief Baron Pollock: – Sir James Parke was to come later in the day: – there was a ludicrous contrast between the heights of Sir F. Pollock & the undersheriff (Clem. Francis) & the puny stature of the socalled High Sheriff Parker Hamond. – Lucy was snugly ensconced in my rooms to see this ceremony of the Fellows meeting the Judge in the middle of the Court & there cootooing to him: she had never seen it before. – She brought with her Sarah Saunders. – When we had ushered the Judge into the Lodge & seen him drink the cup of welcome we returned into

[30] The whole election was marred by allegations of malpractice and in some 24 seats (but not at Devonport) the result was declared void.

[31] i.e. the greatest sewer. Cambridge as a whole and particularly the river, which received all manner of filth on its short course through the town, stank on hot days and continued to do so till long after Romilly's time. See 21 October 1857 for the 'very soft' river water, presumably from upstream, used in Trinity's beer.

[32] For Romilly's soldier cousin (1813-99), on leave from India, who much later published military books and translations from Sanskrit, see F. Boase, *Modern English Biography* VI (1921), 335.

hall to finish our dinner. – The moment it was over I went to do the honors of my rooms to Lucy & Sarah: – I gave them bottled beer & lemonade & biscuits . . .

*Th. 22* . . . I should have mentioned yesterday our going over Thompsons rooms (late Carus's): they are full of workpeople: – he seems to be sparing no expense & to be doing every thing in capital stile: – he has metamorphosed the 3 bedrooms into 2 rooms, a sitting room & a bedroom . . . The following doggrel is posted on the walls, in allusion to the Town Election,

> The man who sells his rights for gold
> > would sell his wife or daughter:
> We have your names: they shall be told;
> > And then you'll cry for quarter.

This outburst of Election purity is headed with a deaths head & cross bones . . . Dined with the Judges (Pollock & Park [sic]) . . . We walked up & down Whewells garden for ½ an hour waiting for Judge Parke: the garden is very prettily laid out, & there is an aviary for gold pheasants. – Dined at 7¼ & got away at 9: we had turtle soup & turtle by itself. We had (as usual) no dessert or coffee & were dismissed with the customary toast of 'Prosperity to the *Norfolk* circuit', – wch one of the blundering Marshals gave out as the *Northern*: this created a general laugh as The Northern is thought abundantly too prosperous by the other circuits.

*Sat. 24.* Lucy out before breakfast: a lovely morning with a gentle breeze. – Dined in Hall & presided: Baron Parke & the High Sheriff etc (about 36) dined: it was a very agreeable party in spite of the painful effort necessary to catch the few low mumbled words of the High Sheriff (Parker Hamond) . . . The conversation turned a good deal on law matters & Elections: the story was told of Rothschild having said 'I am the choice of the people', – & one of his opponents exclaimed 'So was Barabbas' . . . Sir James . . . spoke to me highly in praise of the talent of Tozer (the Assessor), which I immediately repeated to him . . .

*Tu 27.* Breakfasted in College . . . Our servants & Sarah went to the marriage of Miss Marshall to a Birmingham schoolmaster named Bull: it was a dismal affair: the bridegroom cried like a bull-calf & his old Father (who performed the ceremony) was so overcome that he could scarcely get thro the service: he omitted the prayer for children!![33] . . . While we were at tea at 9 o'clock in came Sedgwick & made himself most agreeable by talking about his recent visit to the Queen . . . When Colonel Grey sent Sedgwick the Invitation he told him to put a sermon in his pocket, & that the Queen did not like long sermons. Sedgwick read prayers, but was told that the Queen would dispense with the Sermon as the heat was so oppressive. Sedgwick stayed from Saturday 17th to Monday the 19th when the Queen & Prince & 4 children embarked at 9½ A.M. for a cruise. – When little Prince Arthur (age 2 y. 2 m.) saw Sedgwick he said 'Who are you?.' – Sedgwick's 1st sight of the Q. (on this visit) was of her Majesty & the Prince on horseback: – they both wore wide-

---

[33] Romilly had been cross on this account before: 'I wonder what young people marry for except to have children' (*Romilly 1842-47*, p. 173).

awakes. The Queen was in excellent spirits . . . Lord Geo. Lennox told S. of a letter wch the Q. wrote to him on his daughters marriage, 'wishing her as happy as herself, tho that she considered impossible' . . .

*Mon. 9. August.* Lucy got up at 5 having to stow away all her dresses etc etc etc which have been lying about for months & of course could only be arranged the last morning. I got up at 7. By dint of great bustling we contrived to do every thing & took an affectionate leave of Dicky & consigned him to the especial care of Dosia. At 9 came an Omnibus for us, wch was outrageous: so I told the driver to send the next 20' later. I suffered for this as two of the dirtiest labourers (but not illbehaved) were inside this 2d omnibus. As it was we had to wait for ¼ hour. Lucy had the pleasure of seeing some very ragged miserable Paddies on the platform & astonished them & all the bystanders but myself by giving 2s to the 2 most miserable. – By the way at most of the stations on the road we observed congregations of such objects: doubtless, as beggars find it profitable to ply at bridges so these poor creatures do something more than merely satisfying their curiosity by besetting the railway stations . . .

The Long Vacation continuing, Romilly and Lucy, with Harriet and Sarah to look after them, left Cambridge on 10 August for a five-week holiday in Yarmouth. Despite 'an extract from the Cambridge Chronicle giving rather a sprightly account of Yarmouth & saying that flocks of Cambr. folks are there from the University Registrary down to the College Gyps' they saw very few people whom they knew. They took long walks, Lucy frequently getting up at 5 and strolling along the beach before breakfast, they visited the silk mill which employed 500 hands, of whom 450 were women, they climbed up two of the 5 lookouts near their lodgings, admired the 'very pretty national schools' and the handsome 'Dutch' appearance of the Quay and talked to boatmen and women mending nets. Lucy patronised a thin grey mare and donkeys galore and made friends with a blind sand-carrier in whom she continued to take an interest after her return to Cambridge. Bathing was a complicated business unless one could swim as Romilly often did 'among the Savages: – one man (in a state of nature) road his horse into the sea like a Neptune'. Lucy's bathing 'was very characteristic: I had engaged a machine for her, for wch we waited an hour, but in the mean time she observed the machine horse to be in very bad condition so she declined bathing with that set of machines (Bowles) & went to the other company (Brown) where the horse was in much better plight'. Lucy must have been glad to hear that a policeman had told her brother 'that the Inspector of the Society for suppression of Cruelty to Animals is in Yarmouth at this moment'.

On Sundays they attended services in various churches, approving especially of the 'Methodists New Connexion' chapel which was 'crammed' and also spent hours in churchyards transcribing inscriptions which interested or amused them. On weekdays Lucy often enjoyed herself shopping. She enclosed small presents in her frequent letters to Dosia, the Romilly's cook, but nevertheless had to 'set to vigorously after breakfast' on their last morning when she 'packed very carefully all the glass & crockery & treasures of every kind: this took up 3 hours or more: – she then went & bathed: – the water was so rough that she was obliged to be dipt by young Mr Brown (his Father the old dipper being ill)'. There being no third class on their fast train the maids had to travel expensively by second, but they were in Cambridge 'at 7½ thankful for a health-improving stay at Yarmouth & for a prosperous journey home'.

*Sat. 18 September.* Lucy went with me to the Public Library & selected two well-printed vols of old Divinity, viz Bishop Andrews, – but alas modernised. – on parting with her I went to proclaim Sturbridge fair: as the rain came down in torrents I cut my 3 proclamations rather short. Leapingwell told anecdotes about the Gunning family Lunacy: Frederick G. had the delusion that he was a Serjeant: old Gunning has the delusion of being D. of Bridgewater: the other day a few grapes were offered him wch he rejected with scorn & asked if they were fit for a man who had 50 acres of glass[34] . . . The beastly rain of course caught the unfortunate Lucy who tho she had an umbrella never thought of going home at once. She 1st took refuge at Lilleys & Edens & laid out 8/6 for things she didn't want in return for the shelter. – She then took refuge in the entrance to Mortlocks Bank . . . Mr Mortlock himself came & carried her off into his dining room with a bright fire & offered her lunch . . . he made a good deal of interesting conversation & when called out on business lent her a vol. about the Slave Trade (of wch she could not read a word the type being diamond[35]) & the Art Journal Engravings of the Crystal Palace. – He acted completely like a Sir Charles Grandison for he drove her home in what *he called* his own close carriage & escorted her to the door . . . I of course could not resist hunting for her . . . in vain . . .

*Sun. 19.* . . . I went to H. Goodwins & heard him preach from Matthew 6. 24. 25 ('Ye cannot serve God & Mammon'): I should not have expected any éloge of the Duke of Wellington in such a sermon: but the conclusion of the Sermon was the declaration that he had been while he lived the greatest man in the World . . .

On Monday 20 September Romilly again left Cambridge for a four-day visit to his old friend Thomas Musgrave, Archbishop of York. Bishopthorpe was the scene of constant arrivals and departures and of large dinner-parties, but Romilly found time on his first visit to York to establish that his dear friend Lodge's will had not been proved there. And on his second he heard an excellent concert given by the children of the Wilberforce Blind School and sat in on a class at which the boys were being taught arithmetic with the aid of a board pierced with holes and ingeniously designed plugs. 'Some of the advanced boys were doing long division with considerable rapidity'. They also saw a girl thread a needle with her tongue.

*Sat. 2 October* . . . 2d day of Fellowship: – Latin into English by Grote: English Verse into Latin Verse by myself from 1½ to 4. One of the Candidates came to me & said 'That piece of Milton is translated in the Musae Oxoniensis': – 'Oh, said I, I didn't know that: but I daresay you will do it quite

---

[34] Miss Beart (see 23 June) wrote to Sedgwick on 9 October to say that 'you and Mr Romilly have been the frequent subjects of his conversation and of his affectionate and grateful remembrance both in his lucid and rambling intervals'. On a later letter (21 March 1853) that was shown him Romilly wrote 'How very sad is poor Gunning's condition. He is drinking out the dregs of the cup of life. Death would be far preferable.'

[35] Which is smaller than this.

as well'. – Martin told me that he also had set it 14 or 15 years ago & that Osborne (the Univ. Scholar) did it capitally. Finished that dismal 'Uncle Tom's Cabin' & returned it with a letter of thanks to Mr Mortlock[36] . . .

*Sun. 3.* After Church Lucy & I . . . investigated Pembroke Coll. & had a conference with that goodtempered fellow Cory. Lucy & I then climbed that curious staircase leading to the rooms over the Hall: we walked in the gutter of the battlements as if we had been cats: – a bedmaker fastened herself upon us & begged to show us Mr Brown's rooms (wch are over the Hall): I submitted but gave her not a sous . . .

*Mon. 4.* 3d day of Fellowship: – Mathematics by Master: – English Prose & Latin Prose by Humphry: he set that beautiful account in Southey of the news of the death of Nelson: – a most appropriate selection while Wellington lies unburied.[37] – A college meeting for 1½ on Bursarial business: – we agreed to purchase books for our Library (to the value of £30) bought by the Master at Frankfort the other day . . .

*Tu. 5.* . . . 4th day of Fellowship: Mathematics by Martin: Metaphysics & *Natural History* by Master & Sedgwick. – Sedgwick prevented Lucy having a walk today, for just as I was starting to *drive* her out at 2 he called & begged me to walk with him. – I of course agreed: we called on Preston at 'Makamat Mansion': – to my astonishment we found Preston had not yet begun fires . . . He told us that he had been 3 times chloroformed, twice for having a tooth out, & once for lancing an absess on his shin (wch he called an Aleppobutton, & says that all the people who visit A. invariably have it). – The waters were a good deal out & had flooded the road on the other side of Chesterton: a woman kindly offered us her pattens, but we declined & turned about . . .

*Wed. 6.* Wrote to lady Cotton (to thank for a brace of birds). – Feeling very dyspeptic declined dining as Drosiers guest at the Caius Feast. – 5th day of Fellowship: English Prose & Verse into Greek Prose & Verse: set by Martin & Thompson: – two awfully dull pieces the Verse from Tennyson, the Prose from Locke: – the examination concluded with a general paper set by Grote & Rothman . . .

*Fri. 8.* . . . To Trinity Lodge at 6½ to tea: – We soon agreed upon electing 4 out of these 5, Schreiber, Beamont, Hort, Lightfoot & Yool: the 1st 3 being of the 3d year, & the 2 last being of the 2d: – by the way there was only one candidate of the 1st year, viz. Benson (a 1st rate scholar, whom Martin & myself put at the head in the Classical Examination). – Lightfoot is an

36 He later admired and re-read Mrs Stowe's sententious and fascinating book whose success was prodigious. It was translated worldwide and became the most read novel of the century. Macaulay found it 'disagreeable' and yet 'the most powerful addition that America has made to English literature'. The Cambridge Theatre Royal put on a stage version on 8 October by which time it was indeed hard to escape Uncle Tom who appeared in the newspapers, in public readings, and even advertisements.

37 Wellington had died on 14 September and surprisingly (for he was over eighty) caught everyone off guard. There had been no advance planning and now amid much confusion several authorities were claiming a share in the elaborate state funeral.

admirable Scholar, whom Thompson preferred greatly to all others: Yool was 3d Wrangler & 2d Smith's prize but his neglect of every thing but Mathematics we thought discreditable. Ultimately (to my great contentment) we rejected Yool: – Schreiber & Lightfoot were both Senior Med. & Beamont 2d: – Hort is a very clever hardheaded man who does well in everything & has distinguished himself in the Moral Sciences Tripos . . .

*Th. 14.* At 10 o'clock went to the Bull Hotel to see John & his son William (who is only 17½ having been born on 14th of April 1835 . . . ) . . . He has merry twinkling little dark eyes, & looks to me as if he never would stick steadily to any thing. John professes a good deal of alarm about him on the score of his idleness, but says he is not addicted to gaming or any vice he knows of. I nearly died of suffocation from suppressed laughter at seeing 2 cards of Brown's the little tailors lying on the table of John's sitting room at the Bull: – I of course instantly knew that Lucy must have called upon the Schneiderlein yesterday & suggested this artful dodge to him . . . I took John & Willy to the Hostel to see the rooms & they both professed themselves pleased . . . I afterwards . . . took them shopping to Brown, Matth. & Gent, & Shallow: – at Brown's I was amused by the tailors making the most of his good fortune, for he equipped Willy with a surplice as well as a Cap & Gown!! . . . John consulted me about an allowance for Willy: I thought £250 (independently of private Tutor) quite enough: John means to pay 250 by quarterly payments from Childs to Mortlocks & opened an account at Mortlocks today with the 1st quarter . . . Took John & Willy into Hall: – Willy of course went to the Freshman's table & John dined with me at the high table (the only one) under my presidency. By the way John's sharp eyes detected that one of our pieces of painted glass in the Hall was in honor of William Pitt High Steward: – it is one of the most recent: – it is rather misplaced as Pitt was a Pembrochian . . .

*Sat. 16.* . . . Today was the Freshman preliminary Examination: – Willy thinks he acquitted himself well. – I took Willy to order table, chairs etc., as his predecessor (Jeffcoatt) will on Monday take away everything but the curtains & carpet. – A french beggar (sent by 'le Professeur Fisher') made several fruitless attempts yesterday & today to catch me: – he was vigorously repelled on 2 occasions by Lucy: – I by no means thank 'le Professeur' for sending begging Frenchmen to me: – I have a peculiar horror of them at this moment from reading Southeys life of Nelson, for that great man hated a Frenchman like the devil . . .

*Wed. 20.* . . . I received from John Romilly a copy of the Report of the Cambridge Commission . . . It is the *Report* only, & not the *Evidence*, etc . . . Wrote to John to thank him: I told him at the same time that I feared he very greatly overestimated Willy's Classical attainments, that I thought his knowledge of Greek sadly inaccurate, that I was much surprised to find he had not looked at either the Eumenides or the book of Thucydides (wch are the freshmen Greek subjects), & that I thought he could not have got on at all on equal terms with other young men if he had not a Classical private tutor. – Received from Sayle the Undertaker a Scarf & hatband & pair of gloves accompanied by a card of wch this is a copy 'In Remembrance of the late Mrs Anna Horlick Potts of Cambridge who died on the 11th Instant aged 40 years & was this day interred at the Cemetery. With the family's respects. –

Cambridge Oct. 19. Rob. Sayle Undertaker'.[38] . . . Lucy has learned that poor Christiana Howe is just going to be dismissed from St Lukes as she has been there a 12 month & her case is thought hopeless: – it is a very mournful tale: it is plain that she lost her understanding from a young man making love to her & deserting her (without any fault whatever of hers): her late father was a respectable coach builder, & her brother is a well conducted young man who makes velocipedes etc & supports his Mother . . .

*Tu. 26.* . . . Highly amused with Leapingwell's account of Dalton's marriage to Miss Meller. The Lady's affections were excited by his conduct at Exeter Hall & she sent her maid after him on his quitting the Hall: – the maid soon came back & said 'He is a son of Belial: I saw him go into a Ginshop'. – However Miss Meller met him a few days afterwards at a T.P. party, & he completely recovered the ground he had lost by his visit to the Ginpalace. – Dalton appears to be the vainest man alive: – he thinks the Evangelical interest would immediately fall if he left Cambridge. He has quarelled with the dwarf Falkner, & has either resigned the Curacy of St. Sepulchre or been dismissed from it . . . I had a long chat with Willy & pumped him as much as I could. I do not think (from his manner) that he much likes his Mathematical Coach Yool: but he seems pleased with the Classical Coach Henry Taylor Fellow of Trinity . . . He passed 2 years in University Hall[39] (the new redbrick building close to Gordon Square): this institution seems to be any thing but thriving: it was built to accommodate only 30, & only 18 are actually there: in Willy's time the no was only 15. He seems to have made no progress in his 2 years attendance on the Lectures here . . . the prayers (wch seem to be attended very slovenly about 3 or 4 times a week) are contrived so as to have nothing wch can shock a Unitarian!!!!! – indeed the great majority of the students are Dissenters & very many of them Unitarians . . . He was 6 years at the University School before he went to the Hall . . .

[38] Mrs Potts (d. 1852), wife of the Trinity coach, wrote and sometimes published occasional poetry. There is a pleasing mural tablet to her in Holy Trinity with some of her own verse. For Potts's second marriage see 24 February 1854.

[39] Part of University College, a constituent member of the new University of London. The college was established to provide a literary and scientific education at moderate expense (like the Scottish universities rather than Oxford and Cambridge), and its foundation stone was laid by the ubiquitous liberal Duke of Sussex. Divinity was deliberately excluded from its studies together with religious tests and compulsory Anglican chapel, which were as obnoxious to some as rarefied mathematics and classical drudgery were to others of a utilitarian bent. University Hall, erected in 1849, made some compromise and offered general lectures in theology. Perhaps Sir John sent Willy there and not to the avowedly Church of England King's College to make a point and please his political friends. On British universities generally see Searby, pp. 423-30.

*Senate House & University Library Cambridge.*

*University Press Cambridge.*

Rock and Co, Views of Cambridge, c. 1851.  The Pitt building where Romilly had his office.

*Fri. 29.* . . . Dined at the Family at Powers . . . From Bateson I heard that Sedgwick was so tenderhearted that he broke down in reading his own Peroration to the Commissioners . . . Thompson gave us the rich story of Dick Sedgwicks marriage. Dick has distinguished himself by being Captain of the Poll. But he has also made himself memorable in the abduction line. Six years ago he ran away with a very pretty young girl the daughter of a solicitor named Woodhouse: but before he got to Church he was overtaken by the constables & torn away from the damsel. This last summer Dick fell in with a bagman who talked to him about Bolton-le-moors (the fair one's place of abode): Dick found that the Father was thriving, the mother dead, one son & the eldest daughter married, but the 2d, Mary) still unmarried tho she had had several good offers: on asking why she had refused them, he learned that she was pining after a parson from the South with whom she had been desperately in love 6 years ago. This constancy deeply touched Dick, – who had not been as true a lover for he had twice offered to other ladies & been refused. Dick had been an immoral undergraduate: he kept a girl, & getting tired of her dismissed her: on her waylaying him as he came from his tutor he committed an Assault for which he was tried before the town magistrates: Cooper defended him & passed him off as Richard Wedgwick[40] . . . Dick renewed his addresses . . . Professor Sedgwick readily gave his consent & £50 & the loan of his house: he went down also to Lancashire & tacked the loving couple together: the same constables who formerly stopt them now cleared the way for them to go to Church: – a great crowd assembled & the rabble shouted 'the young'uns have won, the young'uns have won, long life to the young'uns' . . .

*Sat. 30.* Breakfast to Willy, Nix, Vernon Musgrave & his agreeable handsome cousin Mr Taylor, & Crompton (friend of Willy) . . . Hearing from Bateson last night that he had received from the V.C. an invitation for the Duke's Funeral I wrote to the V.C. stating my claims as a constituent member of all deputations of the University for Installations & Addresses to the Crown & mentioned also that I was sure Lord Charles Wellesley would wish me to be present as I had been his private Tutor. The V.C. did me the Favor of having an interview with me & told me the whole state of the case: nothing in the world could be more kind & amiable than the whole of his conduct . . . Meeting of the Revising Syndicate. Ainslie gave us a very interesting abstract of the contents of the Commissioners Report & read us many extracts expressing high praise of our proceedings & also most of the principal recommendations: – Whewell was very angry at the republican impertinence of a recommendation to discontinue the carrying of maces before the V.C: – the Commissioners approve of our proposed reduction to 2 Bedells. – Poor Christina Howe was brought home by her brother today . . .

*Sun. 31.* . . . we walked as far as St Mary's where we saw a good many persons going in. Upon enquiry it turned out that Harvey Goodwin was going to preach at St Mary's this morning. Lucy immediately resolved to go to St Mary's: so she was deposited in a pew & I rushed to College to get my cap &

---

[40] Compare this blatant cover-up with the harsh treatment meted out to T.G. Headley who also kept a girl (15 and 16 February 1854).

gown. Today was the Commemoration & therefore a Scarlet day: – all the Doctors wore a black scarf over their red gowns. – H.G.'s Text was Romans XII. 1 ' . . . a living sacrifice wch is your reasonable service'. – It was a most able & well reasoned sermon, showing the danger of this age from the calm declaration of sceptics that the present enlightenment from science etc supersedes Christianity wch was a religion adapted for less instructed times: – he maintained that the Church of England allowed & encouraged all scientific & learned research & the most acute exercise of the reason, & that the profoundest reasoners were among the sincerest Christians . . . Lucy declined sitting among the Professors' wives as the Verger intended her by way of honor: – this pew is behind the pulpit . . .

*Wed. 3 November.* Letter from G.B.A. announcing his wifes 5th confinement, – a girl: poor Mrs Houghton had the mortification of arriving 9½ hour too late. Wrote to wish him joy . . . Went to the Public Library to look out books for Sir St. Vincent Cotton: selected 7 & wrote to him. – Poor old Bowtell is heartbroken at being dismissed for old age: – he is allowed a retiring pension of £100 p.a. I do not think he will enjoy it long; for tho he declares he has never been happy since dear Lodges resignation (from Powers treatment of him), yet his existence has been identified with the Library for nearly 40 years & he will certainly pine away when excluded from it. – Sent our Infant Orphan proxies to Mrs Blake. – I should have begun this day by saying that I went to Senate House before breakfast to hear the speech of Dr Okes on quitting office: – it was in choice Latin, & there was a great deal (playfully & elegantly written) about the 'Great Blue Book' of the Commissioners . . .

*Th. 4.* Excellent breakfast at Clarks of Christs the Senior Proctor . . . Senatehouse at 10 for Election of V.C: – the new one is Pulling. Clark made a very good speech in nice Latin: – a good deal about the Royal Commission. Pulling made rather a pious one with 2 or 3 prayers in it in very indifferent Latin: – it was very modest . . . the tone of his speech was very conciliatory. – Mrs Arthur Saville (Lucy Neville) was in the S.H. with her ugly mean-looking fat little husband . . . To the astonishment & disgust of everybody Caius has elected *Guest*!! I believe he had 7 votes out of the 12 tho he is not a Norfolk man, & so the practice of Centuries has been departed from: Stokes means to protest against the legality of such Election. I am glad at all events that Sir E. Alderson is not elected, for Guest has this recommendation that he is a Senior Fellow: – however I am heartily sorry for Paget who must be dreadfully disappointed[41] . . .

*Fri. 5.* Seniority at wch a 2d year man named (Thorpe) would have been rusticated for bad chapels, gates & lectures: I however was struck by his penitent manner & begged for him to be allowed another trial, so he was reprimanded & gated: – at this Seniority 2 of the quire (the Tenor

---

[41] The founder's statute demanded that the Master be a Norfolk man, like Paget or Alderson, both of whom were eminent enough to have filled the office. But the statute was most unpopular among some of the fellows of Caius who had resolved to act. There were three ballots in the last of which Guest was elected by his own vote. Grumbling, pamphlets, and appeals to the college visitor did not unseat him. See C.N.L. Brooke, *History of Gonville and Caius College* (1985), pp. 213-14.

& Countertenor) Eastes & Miller were well jobed by the Master for absence
from the Hall on 1st of November: – in consequence no anthem was sung: –
that coxcomb of Eastes said that in the hurry of business he had forgotten it; –
Miller's defence was that he had come ½ hour too soon & then walked about
till he was too late: – the Master took that opportunity of censuring the stile of
singing *Amen* in Chapel: – Eastes said 'Indeed the *young man that reads*
(meaning the Chaplain!!) ends the prayers in so strange a manner that it is very
difficult to get into tune immediately!' . . .

*Sat. 13.* Breakfast to Willy tête à tête: he made himself very agreeable &
talked away . . . Matriculation from 8.45 to 3.15: the race of Fellow
Commoner is nearly extinguished – only 5[42] . . . Trinity had exactly ¹/₃ of the
whole, viz 136 (1 N, 3 F.C., 123 P, 9 S) . . . Dinner with Sedgwick to meet
his niece the bride & her dull husband Dick . . . The bride has a face as round
as an apple, very rosy cheeks, blue eyes, dark dangling ringlets, a plump little
body & a merry countenance: she talks away without fear or restraint . . .

*Mon. 15.* . . . To my great delight a ticket for the Duke's Funeral was
given me today: it was done in the most amiable manner imaginable: the donor
of it said 'I heard you say you were at Lord Nelson's Funeral & would much
like to be at the Dukes: so I wrote for a ticket for you, but not knowing
whether I should succeed I never spoke to you about it'. I was charmed with
this most graceful act of kindness, but was stupid enough not to recognise the
performer of it: – It was Mr Marley (a Fellow Commoner of Trinity) whom I
met at Sedgwicks at Norwich. – Took Lucy to see the inundations at the back
of the Colleges: she was much pleased: the meadow at Queens from Erasmus'
Walk up to the rails by Mr P. Beales was one sheet of water: – the left bank of
the river between Kings & Clare was overflowed . . . as the rain now began
we sat down in St Johns Hall for a good halfhour & warmed ourselves at the
Charcoal fire . . .

*Tu. 16.* Letter from G.T.R. saying that he was in negotiation for a successor to Harriet Gillson & therefore couldn't take Francis Wilderspin. – he
& Maggie tried in vain to see the lying in state at Chelsea: – the crowd was
intense: – some lives lost . . . Revising Syndicate for 2¼ hours: – we couldn't
agree about 10 year men & Licentiates in Theology:[43]– we are to have a grand
palaver on Saturday week. – I went to see the inundation of Jesus Piece: – it
was one of the prettiest sights I ever saw: – the expanse of water looked like
a very large lake: – there was one 8 oar (with redcoated crew), several 4 oars

---

[42]  This verdict was premature but numbers had fallen in recent years both absolutely and as
a proportion of total matriculations. See the statistics in Romilly's second edition of the
*Graduati Cantabrigienses* (1856).

[43]  The statutes provided that a man of mature years who had been a member of a college for
at least ten years and had resided for three terms during the last two years might proceed to
the degree of Bachelor of Divinity. There were never many 'ten-year men' at one time, but
they had long been despised in the university whose authorities wished to be rid of them. See
Winstanley, *Unreformed Cambridge* (1935), pp. 69-72. The Revising Syndicate favoured their
abolition as did the Graham Commission, albeit reluctantly, but existing rights were protected
so that the last man of this class took his degree as late as 1870. The proposed new title of
'Licentiate in Theology' for mature students who might ultimately take the B.D. was
an evident compromise to retain the ten-year men under another name and it was dropped.

& very many smaller boats, & 3 or 4 with sails, – all spread over Jesus Piece!! . . .

On the seventeenth, despite queueing for 3 hours Romilly was too late, as were G.T.R. and Maggie on the previous day, to see the Duke lying in state in Chelsea hospital. He did however make sure of being in good time at St Paul's where provided with 'sandwiches for refreshment in the Cathedral' he arrived at 6·45. The doors opened three quarters of an hour late, there were no numbers on seats despite tickets being numbered and 'there was of course a scramble for places'. He was however 'fortunate enough to get into the 2d row, where I saw admirably' and passed the waiting hours reading *She stoops to conquer* and Wieland's *Oberon* which he had taken with him. The funeral ceremony was intensely moving. 'Nothing could be more solemn . . . The appearance of a grave in the middle of the pallbearers by the disappearance of the coffin filled one with awe. The rehearsal of the long list of titles by the Herald, the breaking his wand, & throwing it into the Grave, & the discharge of a single cannon concluded the sublime ceremonial'.

Romilly ended the long day at the Athenæum where he 'dined with Jeremie, Thorp & Worsley & passed 2 hours most agreeably in talking over the great event of the day. By the way neither Archdall nor Phelps used his ticket: – a great pity they didn't make up their minds earlier'.

*Sat. 20.* . . . Syndicate from 12 to 2¼; we fought about the Taxors Office & the Inspector of Weights & Measures: we agreed to defer this matter till the Privileges Syndicate have reported upon it: I was for abolishing the Taxors & leaving the Inspector entirely to the Town[44] . . .

*Sun. 21.* Blunt preached in Honor of the Great Duke before the University at 10½ . . . & Cooper before the Mayor at 11 at Great St. Andrews. I went to Great St. Andrews & was very much pleased with Coopers Sermon. His Text was 1 Corinthians 4. 2. 'required in Stewards that a man be found faithful'. He divided his sermon into 3 Topics: 1st what the Duke had *done* for us; 2dly what he *was*, 3 dly the Application to ourselves. *First*, he had been Gods instrument to save the country from foreign invasion, – God had raised him up to deliver us from the tyrant Bonaparte . . . Cooper then touched on his conduct as a Statesman. *Secondly* the Duke had always acted 1st on the principle of *Duty*, 2dly with impartial *Justice*, 3dly with complete freedom from selfish & interested motives. Thirdly: – Cooper applied the subject to all present, & 1st to the Mayor etc, recommending them to follow the Dukes example by acting on a paramount sense of *duty*, and to behave with forbearance & temper to their opponents: Cooper then addressed all the other members of the Congregation as *Stewards* & as *Christians*: – he added a few words for the 'old Schools', – for wch there were sermons in most of the Churches today. – Lucy never stirred out. – I congratulated Clem. Francis on

---

[44] Two taxors, appointed annually by the university, had authority under various charters to supervise weights and measures in Cambridge, a privilege warmly resented by local tradesmen and the corporation. The Graham Commission recommended that they be abolished and their functions be transferred to the borough magistrates. The university conceded the point and it was accomplished in 1856 when the parliamentary act confirming Sir John Patteson's arbitration of town and gown disputes was passed.

the birth of his little girl, – he told me she was dead: – I was much shocked . . .

*Wed. 22*. . . . I should have mentioned the want of tact of Miss Austin the other day: she preferred (in talking to Lucy) the preaching of a young Mr Chalmers to that of Carus! – so Lucy will not attend any more of her recitations. – Glad to hear that Prince Albert very graciously wrote to the V.C. saying that he begged to be Godfather to his baby tho it was born before he came into office: – accordingly the little one was christened with the name of Albert . . .

From 30 November to 3 December Romilly was a guest at a grand house-party at Audley End. He played billiards, whist and chess (badly), tried to answer Lady Braybrooke's riddles, observed the exploits of the truffle dog and listened to the Bishop of Rochester's anecdotes about 'the great world'. He said quite seriously that one of George the third's 'fits of madness arose from his punctuality: he had been hunting & had got wet thro & fearing he should be too late for his levee he didn't pull off his wet cotton stockings but pulled some silk ones over them, & stood 2 hours at his levee: – he caught a bad cold which flew to his head'. Mr Hanson curate of Ashdon, Essex and of the late Dr. Chapman, Master of Caius, said 'that for the last days he had been in stupor, but that just before that he had the delusion of having been buried & asked how it had all gone off: – his mind had obviously for some time previous been dwelling on his own death: e.g. – on being told that the Dr was come he said "O ask him to the Funeral". – He left £50 to each of his servants and £2 for each year they had been in his service . . . . He left money to everybody, £10 to the Churchwardens, £100 to Mr Hanson, £2 to the Sexton!!'. Romilly was home again by the early afternoon of Friday 3 December but not before enjoying Lord Braybrooke's tale of a 'cockney's account of the cold air in a building & the necessity of a heating apparatus "there is a cold hare running about the place & we must eat it"'.

*Wed. 8 December.* . . . Grace for raising Wootton's salary from 70 to 80 Guineas on his reelection for 5 years: – Wootton is much disappointed at not being raised to the Salary of Bowtell (who leaves at Xmas). – Crouch (the Yeoman Bedell) asked me to lend him 3 Guineas: refused. – Lucy not out. – Declined dining with Willis: dined with Harvey Goodwin to drink the health of his baby Frances Wycliffe: the party consisted of 11 . . . The dinner was very badly cooked & nearly cold, but the party very gay & agreeable there being an incessant fire of conversation. The most amusing anecdote I thought was one of Goodwins: – a woman complained to him of the number of her children & he said to her 'God never sends a fresh mouth without sending enough to feed it'. – 'Yes, said the woman, but the fresh mouth is sent to me & the means of feeding it to you' . . . I should have said yesterday that Paget told us a great deal about the modern system of treating mad people without any coercion: – he says that agricultural work is found the most conducive to the recovery of intellect: he says that in some of the Lunatic Asylums a great quantity of washing & ironing is done by the women: – dancing & amusement promoted. If a person is very violent he is put into a solitary room, the walls of which are padded[45] . . .

*Tu. 14.* Seniority & then a sealing at wch I received 3 shillings. – Mrs Gilmour & Agnes (who is Lucy's Godchild) came to take leave previous to settling in London. We gave Agnes 2/6 each: – as for William Gilmour he would not work at Rattees & the indentures were cancelled: – he is an unmanageable youth, – used perpetually to run away from School . . .

*Th. 16.* Dismissal of Term . . . Lucy has bought the best 3/6 edition of Uncle Tom's Cabin to give to William How: – she (in spite of her resolution to abstain from reading it) could not help reading the melancholy death of Eva. – Lucy had a letter from Thomas Grounds saying that his wife Susan has been confined to her bed these 6 weeks: – I wrote to him & sent Susan a Sovereign.[46] – Dined at the 500th Anniversary at Corpus. There were about 135 guests . . . We were received before dinner in 4 different places, one at the Masters Lodge, one (to wch I belonged) at Mr Moulds) & the other 2 at the rooms of 2 other Fellows. I was not dignified enough to sit at the upper table . . . The dinner was excellent, but the waiting was bad & it was not easy to get anything. I should have said that the Commemoration service was in the Chapel at 5: I did not attend & am glad I didn't for there was no music & Fenwick's narrow-minded sermon (in wch he attacked the Royal Commission) would have enraged me. – the V.C. did not take the trouble of learning his speeches by heart but read every word of them! – stooping down very clumsily in order to do so. The great speech of the night was Sedgwick's (as commanded by the Prince) . . . At the high table they drank ale out of the great horn[47] & Blunt clumsily deluged his neighbour Mr Mould (who had to go out, – so wet was he): – Whewell made them all roar by saying that Blunt if he

[45] As in other areas of life many Victorian reformers were full of religious energy and humane optimism, believing that right thinking and right laws would solve most problems. It was no longer tolerable to exhibit the mentally ill as freaks crowded together indiscriminately. The comfortable classes to which Sedgwick's nephew Dick (see 14 August 1863) belonged had always been better cared for privately, but to care well for those without means was new. They must not be treated like prisoners, coerced and restrained, but given supervised work in clean and if possible pleasant surroundings, fed and nursed properly, and supervised professionally. After legislation in the 1840s asylums were built throughout the country; that at Fulbourn near Cambridge was opened in 1858 and it has left an impressive record in its annual reports. See 27 Feb. 1860. To read the eulogy on Fulbourn delivered at Caius College in 1862 is to conclude that, exaggerated though it may be, for many such places must indeed have been asylums. See 'The Progress of Psychological Medicine' in the *Journal of Mental Science* (1862), pp. 204-5

[46] Lucy had saved Susan Grounds (née Chune) from entering the workhouse in 1839, brought her home, and sent her into service. She was an ailing young woman who later lived with the Romillys again, being in and out of Addenbrooke's Hospital, before marrying Grounds 'a mason by trade, a sober, steady man' in 1846.

[47] A medieval loving cup. See G.H.S. Bushnell, *Letter of the Corpus Association*, 52, (1973), 28-30, and the illustrations facing pp. 297-8 in vol. I of J.J. Smith, *The Cambridge Portfolio* (1840).

didn't moisten his clay yet had wetted the mould. – Lord Monteagle made a lively clever speech, – after wch (it being now 10½) I retired.[48]

*Fri. 17.* Lucy did the amiable & called upon Miss Austin to thank her for the little Almanac: – she was so unfortunate as to find her at home . . . Finished reading the life of that great hero Rob. Blake. – The burst of indignation of his biographer (Dixon) against Charles 2d for digging up his bones is very fine.[49] Began reading loud 'Uncle Tom's Cabin'.

Romilly's last expedition of the year took him for two days to London. As usual, he met relations and friends at the Athenæum, decided that the cleaned Claudes in the National Gallery 'now don't look as well as the magnificent Turners next them', admired the Nineveh sculptures in the British Museum, had his books examined at the Stamp Office and spent an afternoon in the Gallery of Illustration. This was 'formerly Nash's beautiful house in Regent Street' and on show were a series of dioramas representing 'the scenes and incidents of all the D. of Wellington's battles from that of Assai to that of Waterloo'. Views were also 'given of the exterior of Walmer Castle, of the room the Duke died in, of the lying in state, of the Procession (as seen at Trafalgar Square) & of the interior of St Pauls'. He returned to Lucy, travelling economically, as he preferred to do, 'with some well-behaved female servants of the higher grade & one Governess'.

*Christmas Day.* Lucy & I to St Edwards, where we were put into the Pew of Mr & Mrs Eaton (with their folio prayer book & reading stand: we found the pew (like most at St Edwards) very inconvenient for kneeling down, & we went into another for the Sacrament . . . We then paid a visit to our Hall & examined the sideboards made by the one-armed man: we also went into the butteries & made civil speeches & handshakings with Mr Claydon & drank some beer out of stoups. We next visited our Roundabout (– having failed in our search for flowers in the Bowling Green) & fairly stript it: we gathered a very pretty nosegay & brought away some winter Aconites (mould & all) to transplant into our garden: – we brought away also some variegated holly to deck our room . . .

[48] The College of Corpus Christi and of the Blessed Virgin Mary had unusually been founded by two gilds of the town. There is a long account of the dinner and speeches in the *Chronicle* of 18 December when the reporter complained that Sedgwick had been hard to follow owing to 'his habit of dropping his voice at the end of his sentences'. See P. Bury, *History of Corpus Christi* (1952), pp. 64-7, who reprints the sumptuous menu of some fifty dishes. What some of them were and how they were prepared (e.g. pâtés à la Sefton, Bene't creams, côtelettes à la Wyndham, and Mansfield puddings) would be an entertaining labour for the culinary historian to discover.

[49] Admiral Blake was given a state funeral and buried in Westminster Abbey in 1657 but disinterred with others at the Restoration. According to W.H. Dixon his remains were 'cast into a pit'.

# 1853

*Tu. 4 January.* . . . Meeting of V.C., Provost (late V.C.) & Proctors & myself concerning the Standing of Candidates for Honours in the Examination beginning today: lasted from 11 to 1½. – It was found Wentworth was not (according to the new regulations of April 1852) entitled to go in for Mathematical Honors because he takes Honorary degrees (without Little Go of course) & has resided *10* terms (1 too many): – after sending for Philpott & a very long discussion it was allowed to pass[1] . . .

*Sat. 8.* . . . Read loud (at Lucy's desire) for the 2d time the clever money scene between George & Mrs Bagnet (in the last no of Bleak House). – Lucy has taken up an enthusiastic passion for 'Uncle Tom': she today bought a 2d copy of the best 3/6 edition: this one she is going to give to Tom Saunders: she has also bought a clever Abolitionist publication called 'Uncle Tom's Almanac': it is full of Engravings . . .

*Mon. 10.* Plough Monday: a prodigious no of mummers: – the lads who were drest up as women had open sleeves & carried white pocket handkerchiefs. We made ourselves iron & brass & gave to none of them . . . At the office all day till 4 o'clock marking the Kingsmen who did not come from the Foundation of Eton. The most modern man was in October 1810 (Clement Tudway).[2] This year a Kingsman (James) has voluntarily gone into the Senate House Examination, having previously passed the Little Go: – he is the 1st . . .

*Sat. 29.* The V.C. made the Congregation an hour earlier, viz. at 9: so I missed the Father's Breakfast at Trinity . . . The Senate House was crowded & the youngsters didn't make more than an average noise . . . The youngsters gave me 3 Cheers; they also cheered 'Topsy'[3] & to my great surprise there were 3 cheers for Frank Smedley. Gaskin was twice saluted with 3 Groans. – The only witty things was giving 3 Groans for 'the fallen Angel'! – afterwards they gave him some ironical cheers, '3 cheers for the Spoon, & for Spoons in general'[4] . . . Poor Johnson the Schoolkeeper is in despair at the printing the

---

[1]  T.F.C.V. Wentworth, grandson of the Marquis of Ailesbury, who matriculated in 1848 went out M.A. 1853, having been (quite needlessly in respect of his degree) a Senior Optime in the Mathematical Tripos. Noblemen might proceed to the higher degree after examination without taking a B.A.

[2]  Tudway attended Sherborne school in the 1790s and went up to Merton College, Oxford from where he migrated to King's at the age of twenty-eight. His history was therefore odd and that perhaps accounts for his omission from the published register of King's admissions. The college was not hasty in admitting men from schools other than Eton, and the first three (in 1865-66) had elder brothers who had been to Eton before entering King's. Etonians predominated for many years.

[3]  i.e. the black, Alexander Crummell (see 13 November 1849), who was almost certainly the first of his race to be admitted to a Cambridge degree. The event was less pleasant than Romilly relates since Crummell was greeted by a voice – at once shouted down – crying 'Three groans for the Queens' nigger' (J.D. Twigg, *A History of Queens' College* (1987), p. 270.

[4]  Cambridge vernacular had many humorous terms for those who had scraped through their degrees or had a specific place in the class-lists, and some are listed by Christopher

Lists of Degrees having been (for the 1st time) taken from him whereby he loses £12! . . .

*Tu. 1 February.* . . . To the Audit of Dr Okes' accounts: – I was not detained more than ½ hour. Saw the beautiful Gold cup given by Prince Albert to little Pulling his Godchild: it has 2 figures of guardian angels holding infants & a relievo of our Lord blessing the children: – I thought the taste of the cup excellent: the inscription was 'Robert Pulling from his Godfather Albert' . . .

*Wed. 2.* Lucy went to St Edwards & found the church very cold: H. Goodwin rattled thro the Service full gallop. Congregation . . . The Carus Prize Grace passed today: no opposition in Black House: in White House Wolfe of Clare & 7 others voted against it: the division was 22 to 8.[5] The Graces about requiring tickets[6] from Honormen who are plucked or gulfed[7] were thrown out by great majorities in the Black House, Marsh of Trinity Hall being the great Agitator: 47 to 6 in the case of Gulf; 38 to 16 in case of Pluck. Bateson made a brilliant speech in presenting his 3 sons: he opened with a playful exultation at his having 3 at a birth: he greatly eulogised an ancestor of Lord Bradford's son (Orlando Bridgeman) . . .

*Wed. 9.* . . . Lucy had yesterday a very desponding letter from Betsy (in answer to hers): she says she has no wish to live. Her rascally husband was seen at the Emigration Office *a fortnight ago*: he has not written to her, nor does she know where he is . . . We both wrote to Betsy & I sent £5. – A collector for the Soup Fund caught me & extracted £1 from me . . .

*Th. 10.* . . . Seniority, at wch we raised the little living of Shillington[8] from £150 to 400 p.a.: we also voted ⅔ of £50 if St Johns will pay ⅓d towards apprentising Robinson as a Musical pupil to Walmisley: – Robinson (son of a poor Cambridge tailor) was the best singer in our Quire: – the usual premium for a Musical Apprentice is £200, but Walmisley is generously content to take £50 . . .

Wordsworth in *Scholae Academicae* (1877), pp. 56-7. 'Fallen angel' is not among them, though it was current Stock Exchange slang for a bankrupt or defaulter. The 'spoon' or 'wooden spoon' was from about 1800 (until 1909 when the regulations were altered) the last of the junior optimes in the Mathematical Tripos. Besides the obvious sense there is play on 'spoon' meaning 'simpleton'. 'Wranglers are said to be born with golden spoons in their mouths, the senior optimes with silver, and the junior with leaden ones' (*Lexicon Balatronicum* (1811)).

[5] Friends had raised £500 to found annual prizes 'for the encouragement of the accurate study of the Greek Testament' in honour of Carus. He himself added another £500 in May, and forty years afterwards £100 was added by an old member of Trinity in thanks for his instruction 'especially in his Sunday-evening addresses in the room over Trinity Gate'. See *Historical Register of the University* (1917), p. 323. For the Black and White Houses see 18 May 1852.

[6] See 3 May 1851.

[7] 'To be gulfed' or 'gulphed' was to be allowed a pass degree only, the fate of those not bad enough to be plucked completely and not good enough to be placed in the Tripos lists.

[8] A Bedfordshire parish. Trinity was the patron of more than sixty livings, which of course were given to its own members; half were in the counties of Bedford and York. College patronage (about 290 parishes in all) is listed in the annual *Cambridge University Calendar* from which it is clear that few were in the expanding cities.

*Mon. 14.* . . . Lucy was till past 3 preparing work for Mrs Redmore: she then (the brightness of the day being nearly over) went to Mrs Redmore & some other paupers – We heard the history of Louisa Watts tea party at wch poor Christiana was present: it was a party of 10 & they played a 5 farthing game called Snip, Snap Snorum at wch Christiana was grandly successful & carried off 90 farthings: she was in such spirits that she sang them several songs: – she has a sweet voice. – Finished the Index of the V.C.'s Guard Book: Grand day for Professorial Tickets, – 9 of them. – The Moral Sciences Tripos published today: – none but *Middle* Bachelors sat: so Whewell has no opportunity of giving his 2 £15 prizes[9] – Visit from Willy who borrowed 2 books & asked my advice about attending Whewells Lectures: I of course advised him to do so . . .

*Tu. 15.* Lucy to the Hospital (taking a picture book painted by herself for little Hannah Lion): she also charitably went & sat with Mrs Tailor (who has an affection of the lungs & of whom she buys ready-made clothes for her paupers – e.g – she yesterday bought a pair of trowsers for old Saunders to go to his daughters wedding) . . . Harriet is convinced that she saw today that scoundrel James Spink (disguised indeed & shunning observation) walking with one of his thievish brothers. – Today there was a beautiful celestial phenomenon. – two false suns: 4 were seen by many people, but only 2 were pointed out to us – the prismatic colors of one were quite vivid . . . First day of the Revised Statutes Graces: – 2 were thrown out in the Black House . . . The 'Council' was carried, & also the abolition of Tenyearmen, of Compositions & Cautions, of Sermons in long Vacation, etc etc.[10] . . . Maddison today distributed bread in his vestry: he stopped 14 loaves & sent for the Baker who confessed that some of the loaves were *high-baked* & that they might lose as much as 3 oz. in weight thereby: he was shown that several of his loaves were short by 8, 10 & as much as 15 oz!!! What a rogue in Grain! . . .

*Sat. 26.* At 10 o'clock to Kings Lodge to admit a Scholar (Tremlett) with an impediment in his speech. At 11 to a trial at what they are now pleased to call 'A meeting of the V.C. & Heads': – I was instructed to make a separate book for such meetings & Whewell suggested lettering it 'Forum Domesticum'. The case was that of W. Cox (a liverystable keeper who can't read or write!) for allowing an undergraduate to run up a bill without etc etc: – 2 mortal hours I thus consumed: – the culprit was cautioned as to his future

[9]  Middle Bachelors were presumably so called as they had already satisfied the requirements for their first degree and were on the road to the M.A. They had to have passed a tripos before taking examinations in the new Natural Sciences and Moral Sciences triposes that were held in Lent term. Whewell's various prizes in Moral Philosophy were not continued when he resigned his professorship in 1855. See *Historical Register of the University* (1917), p. 322.

[10]  There were congregations of the Senate on this and the following three days to deal with a plethora of Graces arising out of the Reports of the Revising Syndicate dated 10 December 1851, 23 March, 28 May, and 30 November 1852. They are set out in *Annals*, V, 108-9. Among the rejected proposals were those to abolish the privileges of Commorantes in Villa, to admit graduates of other universities than Oxford and Dublin to titular degrees, and to reduce the Esquire Bedells from three to two.

conduct. – My poor bedmaker has caught a most awful cold, so I gave her a bottle of sherry to make whey & 6 d to her little grand child whom she had in her arms . . .

*Tu. 1 March.* Went at 10 o'clock to the Rose & Crown (Russell St) to give my vote for 'the Free Library'.[11] – Wrote to Mrs John Hildyard (of Ingoldsby) to decline voting for her pauper. – The Election-Committee sat yesterday & Saturday upon the Cambridge Bribery case: as there were above 100 witnesses producible the sitting members Astell & Macaulay have resigned: – so the bells have been ringing merry peels & the Whig bands have paraded the streets playing 'O! dear! what can the matter be' etc.[12]

*Sat. 5.* . . . Betsy How called to announce the Training School having found her a place at Cottenham (where 5 servants are kept) . . . Having been fortunate enough to get Villette (by Miss Bronte or Currer Bell as the Authoress calls herself) I read it loud for an hour before dinner, & all the Evening afterwards. The opening of the book is excellent . . .

*Tu. 8.* Lucy not out. – She had a letter from M.A. Tyler who is still in London, staying with the Greens: she asks for Lucy's consent to her continuing in town. – She hopes to get work by making nets for the hair at 4/ a dozen: she will find her work paid at a very different rate from L's magnificent stile. – I worked all the morning at arranging for the Bookbinder all the College Examination Papers for the year 1852. – Went on with Villette . . .

*Wed. 9.* Licensing 173 publichouses from 10 to 2½ in the Divinity Lecture Room: Ainslie was the Assessor. The new system (of no bondsmen) made the proceedings quieter, but (to my surprise) didn't expedite matters in the least: – The Black Bull, the Hearts Ease etc were refused . . .

*Fri. 11.* . . . Congregation Day . . . One of the Graces was for a Petition against the Jew Bill: the Petition is exactly in the same words as in 1847, 1849, expressing 'consternation & alarm' wch can be felt by very few. The Grace was carried: Black House 30 to 13, White House 21 to 9. Dined at the Family . . . The party consisted of all the Family except Phelps, viz Stokes, Tatham, Cartmell, Paget, Power, Shaw, Martin, Thompson & Clark & myself & Bateson: – Thurtell made the party up to 12: he very much likes Edward Romilly who is his pupil, & says he is very gay & lively & that his Father

11   The vote of the burgesses to adopt the parliamentary act allowing the town to raise a rate for a public library and museum was 873 in favour and only 78 against. Romilly subscribed £10 to the book fund when the library was being established as did Sedgwick, Guest, Geldart, Phillpott and others. A printed list of these names is reproduced on p. 12 of B.D. Hutchin, 'A History of Public Libraries in the City and County of Cambridge 1850-1965' (Fellowship thesis of the Library Association, 1972), of which there is a copy in the Cambridgeshire Collection of the city library. When the library opened on 28 June 1855 in the old Quaker meeting house, 'very suitable, being at once central and yet retired' (*Chronicle*), there was seating for 120, a stock of 1,500 books, and a place for workmen to wash before they used it.

12   In fact a committee of the House of Commons had already declared the recent Cambridge election void. A commission of inquiry in June examined almost 300 witnesses and in August issued a damning report reprinted in *Annals*, V, 111-32. The history of elections for fifty .years was examined and corruption by the candidates' agents, liberal and conservative, was found to be general. Among those who declined to give evidence was the diarist's old friend Lord Monteagle. See 30 March 1857, and Searby, pp. 479-82.

greatly exaggerated his deficiencies. – Played 8 Rubbers & won 6 of them carrying off 31/ . . .

*Tu. 15.* . . . Lucy & I went to inspect *Merton House*: a very tidy maid told us that the Family (named Smith) were in the house, & that she didn't know of its being to let, & modestly suggested the neighbouring place 'Merton *Hall*' wch was to let . . . There are 3 tenements here with the name of Merton, viz. Merton Cottage, Merton House (built by Prof. Farish), & Merton Hall, – all on the estate bought in the reign of Henry 3d by Walter de Merton Bishop of Rochester & founder of Merton College Oxford. – The remarkable part of Merton Hall is the ancient building called Pythagoras's School (now used as a Granary)[13] . . . only a portion is to let: – a mere dolls house with very small rooms & very low ceilings: – wouldn't in the least do for us . . . Finished the Life of W.S. Walker by Moultrie: I was surprised & amused by finding myself commemorated as an 'agreeable rattle' at a soirée of the Marchesas[14] . . . Latham told me about Headley (son of my late surgeon) having been dismissed from Trinity Hall where he was a Fellow Commoner; he has just been turned out of the Senate House for copying at the Little Go. He was very unpopular & gave great offence to the fastidious by his greediness in the matter of eating generally but more particularly in his insatiable passion for fat . . .

*Wed. 23.* . . . Our Landlord Fawcett called just as we were getting ready for Church: so Lucy ran away into the fireless Library for the 10' he stopt: – his object was to say that he had not been able to suit himself & that I must turn out at Midsummer . . . Mr Fawcett is ready to hang himself (& I should not much mind if he did, I shouldn't break my heart if he so broke his neck) at having lost Mr Pembertons house. He offered to take a lease of 7 years (at 100 p.a.) if he were allowed 2 yrs rent to put the place in repair . . .

*Th. 24.* A little before 8 came Mr Fawcett's groom with a double knock: – he brought a note from my Landlord offering to call on me today if I had not already arranged with Mr Warren: I jumped out of bed, rushed downstairs in my dressing gown & my bare feet thrust into slippers & wrote to Mr. F. appointing from 1 to 2 . . . We had a fire in the Library for Mr F's reception & L. set out the room in Applepie order for him: he came at 1½ & delighted me by saying that Mrs Fawcett was very reluctant to move from Newnham . . . & that I need take no steps till I heard from him again: I told him that he had made me very happy, that I considered myself as certainly his Tenant for another year & hoped that I should be his Tenant for 20 . . . so we parted very

[13] This, the oldest secular building in Cambridge and one of only a dozen of its kind in the country, had been owned since the thirteenth century by Merton College, Oxford. See Royal Commission on Historic Monuments, *City of Cambridge* (1959), II, 377-9, and J.M. Gray, *The School of Pythagoras* (1932).

[14] Walker, poet and Shakesperian critic, had been a fellow of Trinity 1820-9 where John Moultre was a near contemporary. This edition of his *Poetical Remains* (1852) with a long memoir quotes several references to Romilly in letters to Walker's mother: 'Greenwood speechified briefly and drily, and Romilly pleasantly, and Sedgwick inimitably' (May 1827); 'Romilly with his natural courtesy and inexhaustible stream of delightful rattle' (March 1829). The Marchesa was the lively and hospitable Scotch wife of the Marquis di Spineto, teacher of Italian; they are often mentioned in earlier diaries.

good friends & I now feel more charitably than I did yesterday about him hanging himself . . .

*Tu. 29.* . . . Lucy did a great deal today: she went to the Training Institution & saw the Upper Matron (Mrs Butler): she paid her for Betsy How £2.12. – (being a weekly 6 pence for 2 years) as the customary contribution to the outfit of a girl when placed out from the Institution. She showed Mrs Butler a very agreeable letter of Betsy How's to her mother in wch she expresses herself as being very happy at Mr Banks at Cottenham; – they are very kind to her, she is not overworked, lives well & has a beautiful garden . . . Mr Deighton was kind enough to lend me the new no of the Ecletic: so in the Evening I read loud to L. Todhunters article on the Cambridge Commission: it contains a bitter tirade against Peacock as a non-resident Professor, & also an invective against Mills dangerous theological opinions[15] . . .

*Fri. 1 April.* 3d day of Scholarship – Mathematics by Thacker from 9 to 1. – There should have been a 2d paper at 2 (from Thompson): but he forgot all about it . . . I met Greaves Townley & learned from him that Mrs Whewell was accompanied in her recent trip to Kreutznach by the amiable Miss Ainslie & by one of Sir J. Herschel's daughters (a Genius of 13). – We had a grand visiter today, little Miss Finkel out of the workhouse:[16] the living there agrees with her for she is as rosy as a fullblown piony & as fat as a pig: – we of course gave her money. – Went on with 'Leonora' at night.[17]

*Sat. 2.* 4th day of Scholarship. – English Verse & Latin Verse by me from 9 to 11 . . . As far as I have seen the papers of the 3 Candidates for the Cambridge Scholarship, Challis, Clark & Piper they have done villainously: I have indeed only seen their Homer & Euripides: Clark did both most bunglingly:

---

[15] The article in the monthly *Eclectic Review* (1853, I, 257-78) was unsigned. Todhunter, the son of a dissenting minister, was Senior Wrangler of 1848 and a fellow of St John's, whose criticisms of unnamed persons (like Professor Corrie), and of the weakness of what really went on at Cambridge and of changes it was proposed to make, are adroit. Much of his drift is anti-clerical, yet he also mounts a strong defence of private tuition against Whewell. It would be a pity to dilute his vitriol on Dean Peacock and Professor Mill. The Lowndean professorship 'is at present held by an ecclesiastical dignitary not resident in the University. The salary exceeds £400 a-year, and during the last ten years we believe only one course of lectures has been delivered, and, as we understand, the quality was by no means a compensation for the rarity. Our readers will be surprised to learn that this languid professor is himself a member of the commission, and has for a long period simulated the character of an academical reformer' (p. 262). 'The University may well be proud of her professor of Hebrew, endowed as he is with all the treasures of Eastern and Western learning, yet the homage rendered to his attainments and character should not be allowed to extend to his opinions and proceedings . . . and if there be any truth in the maxim which judges of a man from his friends, or any wisdom in making the past and the present serve as indications of the future, Cambridge may soon contend, and not unequally, with her sister university, for the glory and the shame of supplying the Romish church with her most illustrious convert' (p. 278).

[16] The Union workhouse with which some of Lucy's protégées were acquainted had been built in 1838 on Mill Road, conveniently near to working class Barnwell and with a doleful proximity to the new parish burial grounds. Its records survive in the Cambridgeshire Record Office awaiting detailed examination.

[17] Maria Edgeworth's novel of 1806, not *Leonora: a Love Story* by Mrs Nisbet (1848).

Piper did no Euripides & Challis no Homer: – What they answered was very bad indeed . . . A dismal letter from G.T.R. complaining of his 2 pictures being badly hung, & talking of giving up the profession: – Lucy suggests that he had smoked too many cigars & drunk too much ale. – Lucy staid at home till past 3, vainly expecting a Lark which she bought yesterday, & for which she had lined a cage & prepared abundant food: – it did not come till past 7!!! . . .

*Sun. 3.* . . . Lucy & I to the Hobson Street Chapel. One of the great guns among the Wesleians (W. Jackson) officiated: he is a handsome man in the vigor of life with the greatest power of bellowing possessed by any animal since the bulls of Basan . . . he was the very antipodes of that tame dull drowsy Howes of Little St Marys. His text was I Peter.1.8.9. 'Whom having not seen ye love, etc'. He was very eloquent & in extraordinarily fine condition, for he held forth for 45' with occasional bursts of vehemence like the firing off a gun he only once wiped his brow. He impressed one with the conviction of being a good man & feeling deeply the joy in Christ which he described in such glowing characters . . . Mr Jackson is now a great gun at Sheffield: – he went from *Cambridge* about 10 years ago . . .

*Mon. 4.* Worked till 3 at Scholarship papers. – Lucy went today to the Trumpington woods on a slave-emancipating expedition. She started before 1 o'clock & took the wild fluttering Mrs Lark in a basket which she had carefully lined & padded & furnished with a soft bed of grass . . . The moment the basket was opened off she flew with the speed of lightening . . . Began reading loud Francis's 'Chronicles of the Stock Exchange' with much interest: – it is written in a sparkling stile à la Macaulay:[18]– Miss Cotton recommended it to us). – Read also a chapter in Bleak House: we thought the scene of the visit to Mr Skimpole very amusing.

*Th. 7.* . . . Could not dine at the Audit dinner at the V.C's at 6½ as I had at that very hour to drink tea at Trinity Lodge. It was a grief to miss Mrs Whewell & to know that she was absent from ill health. – The 1st business was electing a Cambridge Scholar: there were 5 Candidates, Perkins of the 3d year, Alston of the 2d year, Challis, Clark & Piper freshmen . . . Perkins did very respectably in all the Classical Exercises but did not send in a Mathematical paper: this very nearly ruined him, & if I had not made a great fight for him he would have been thrown overboard . . . The rest of the Election went off tolerably smoothly, 7 men of the 3d year & 7 of the 2d were chosen (independently of Perkins) . . .

*Fri. 8.* . . . Dined at the Scholarship dinner: we were all present. – The Master astonished me by saying that Archbishop Whately is a believer in Mesmerism: the Archbishop called on him today & gave a minute account of 2 cures of himself by Mesmerism, one from a swelled face & the other from gout! Whewell told the story of 2 rival shoemakers: one put up in his window

---

[18] John Francis's *Chronicles and Characters of the Stock Exchange* (1849) which had gone into a second edition.

'Mens conscia recti':[19]– the other replied by 'mens & womens conscia recti' . . .

*Mon. 11.* . . . Miss Cotton sent 2 bunches of violets by her Groom who knocked double as if he had been a Gentleman . . .

On 14 April Romilly again stayed for two days at Audley End. The enjoyable and by now familiar pattern of his visits was varied by Lord Braybrooke's wish to consult him about the Mastership of Magdalene. The Master, Lord Braybrooke's brother, George Neville-Grenville had in 1846 been appointed Dean of Windsor and had been anxious to resign the Mastership '2 years ago, & again quite lately. The Statutes require the Master to be 30 or thereabouts: but the Visitor has the power of dispensing with the Statute & such dispensation was resorted to in 1813 at the appointment of the present Master: now Latimer (Lord Braybrooke's fourth son), 'is 2 years older than his uncle was at his appointment. – Is there any likelihood of the Fellows objecting? I will have a confidential conference with Bright, & also ask him whether late Fellows in this year of Grace have any voice in the matter'.

*Sat. 16.* . . . Walked with Lucy to the Hospital . . . She also had an interview with Sarah who is dismissed by Miss Marshall, partly (it is probable) from indignation of that young lady at her having worn red velvet round her throat & wrists like herself. She also called on Mrs How & learned the fate of the Guinea wch she gave William How the other day at the expiration of his apprenticeship: – he gave it to his fellow workmen who each added 1/ & they had a merrymaking at which William presided: – it seems to be the general practice for prentices at the expiration of their time to give a treat . . . a letter from G.T.R. telling me that Frank's cough is nearly well & that his pictures have been praised in the Spectator[20] . . .

*Sun. 17.* Lucy & I to St Marys at 10½ to hear Venn (formerly Tutor of Queens) preach a funeral sermon on Prof. Scholefield . . . Lucy did not at all like the sermon & thought the preacher did not seem in earnest. So she posted off to St Michaels where we arrived in the middle of the 2d Lesson. The Church was very full, the pulpit lined with black, but the great mass of the congregation not in mourning, at which Lucy (who had put on mourning for the occasion) was surprised & indignant. – We were both highly pleased with Perowne's sermon which showed deep earnestness & a genuine veneration for the object of his panegyric . . . he dwelt with great tenderness on the Patience which S. exhibited in the decline of life, in the severe trial of being by physical infirmity shut out from the spiritual labors in which he delighted, & in the calmness & serenity of his last moments. Perowne made an address to his congregation [in] which he entreated them to reflect whether they had made a fitting return in their conduct to so faithful a minister whose decline of life they had filled with anxiety by their feuds & dissensions & opposition to him,

[19] i.e. a mind conscious of its own rectitude.
[20] The reviewer of the exhibition of the Society of British Artists liked little and did not mince his words. George got off lightly. 'A few other small subjects are to be distinguished from the herd – chiefly by their singularity . . . Over-timid particularity and want of subject clog, but do not quite repress, quiet truthfulness in 'Contentment and Regret' and 'Grace after Meat' by Mr. Romilly' (*Spectator* 2 April 1853, 326-7).

& he begged them now to offer up to his memory the tribute of a return to brotherly love among themselves . . .

*Mon. 18.* . . . Conference with Bright (about Latimer Neville): he has been lately at Butleigh, & no expression of desire of resignation was then made by the Master or his Family: that certainly when made Dean of Windsor he was willing to resign but had been persuaded not to do so . . . Two years ago Lord Braybrooke had a communication with Warter when Lord B. wished his brother to resign & (according to Warter's belief) the Master was unwilling to do so: – certain it is that Warter told Lord B. he must not expect to appoint Latimer in the same way now as his Father had done the present Master in 1813, for that the College would certainly oppose him. – The then Lord Braybrooke wrote a letter to the College saying 'Dr Gretton being dead it is my intention to appoint my 2d son George & to use the power wch I possess of dispensing with the statute concerning the age of *triginta aut* circiter' . . . The Statutes certainly want reforming: there seem to be numerous interpolations by Kelk & other masters & they are all of the most despotic nature possible: the Statutes give almost unlimited authority to the Master & to the Visiter. – Warter's letter on this matter to the Royal Commission is important. Warter thinks (and so do his friends) that he ought to be the new Master.[21]

*Tu. 19.* Had another interview with Bright: he has had a talk with Hughes: – they are not desirous of *inducing* the Dean of Windsor to resign, but if he should resign are most willing to accept Mr Latimer if Lord B. nominates him on the ground of his degree, his attainments & his having been Fellow, & they would be willing to give a wide interpretation to '30 years or thereabouts', but they utterly object to Lord B's [illegible word] on the alleged right of dispensing with the statute. – Bright put the substance of this on paper; – I copied his statement, & added a little more of my own in my letter to Lord B . . .

*Fri. 22.* . . . A very grateful letter from Lord B. who says that he will nominate without claiming the right of dispensation . . .

*Fri. 13 May* . . . Very good tidings from Betsy Spink. Her worthless husband returned to her a fortnight ago, & has got work at a Coach proprieters. She had the honesty & good sense instantly to send for the Treasurer of the Benefit Club & to have the accounts looked into thoroughly: – happily it turns out that instead of £43 (as stated by his enemies) the defalcation is only £10: – she immediately parted with some of her most dispensable goods & paid off £5, & he has since paid £1 from his wages. – He professes to have been at Cambridge ever since he deserted her in December last: – he walked up to Town. – Lucy & I both wrote to her & I sent her £5 . . .

---

[21] The Magdalene fellowship under Neville Grenville was with few exceptions undistinguished. Warter, remembered as 'most kind and painstaking, and as a good rider to hounds' seems to have been above the average, but his wish for the mastership was not granted. Lord Braybrooke gave it to one of his younger sons, Latimer, whose birth was his only recommendation and who for fifty-one years ruled amiably a society reputed to be the home of dull, raffish, and largely aristocratic sportsmen, many of whom had been rejected by other colleges. See P. Cunich et al., *A History of Magdalene College* (1994), pp. 206-212.

*Sat. 14.* . . . I had no time yesterday to read Sophie's charming letter: –
I read it today with great pleasure: she tells a pleasing anecdote of Franky's
kindness to the servants at Mr Faithful's: – he gave slices of his cake to the
Servants as well as to his comrades. He is much liked by every body, being
generous, affectionate & good tempered & obligeing. He writes 4 times a week
to his mother: she sent me a long letter of his of 6 pages (– his last): a most
creditable performance in every way. Sophie apprised me that the moral
sentiments in it were rechauffés of passages in her own letters, such as 'I shall
try all I can to grow up a good man & become worthy of all the kindness
shown me'. It appears that all the Dalquharran[22] tenants celebrate his birthday
always with great demonstrations of joy . . .

*Whit Mon. 16.* Began leaving off fires in the morning. Harriet went off
with her Mother by the Excursion Train: Lucy sent by Harriet 6 Books as
a Present to Hannah, viz. Enfields Speaker, Our Cousins in Ohio, Gems of
Literature, Moral Songs, Cottagers of Glenburnie & Sacred Poetry . . . I paid
a visit to Dr Guest & sat ½ an hour with him: – he is awfully sensitive to the
E. wind: the new Hall is to be begun immediately at Caius: the Architect is
Salvin.[23] – I utterly forgot the annual meeting at the Industrial School this
Morning: I hope H. Goodwin will forgive me . . .

*Wed. 18.* . . . Rather a droll thing happened today. The Post brought me
the 1st nos of Vol. 6 of the Philological:[24] as 5 nos of Vol. 5 have not yet
arrived I wrote to Dr Guest to ask him to be kind enough to procure them for
me: – he told me at dinner that I had been unconsciously slapping his face for
he is the occasion of the deficient nos, having promised papers & never having
found time to write them!

*Sat. 21.* Lucy went to see Sarah Fordham . . . she gave the old great grand
mother . . . (aged 80 & upwards) 1/; the old dame hobbled out of the house
& came back not long afterwards very merry; during her absence
a crossquestioning from the old womans grand daughter . . . brought out
Lucy's avowal that she had given the aged crone 1/: – 'you should never give
her money, Ma'am, she is sure to get drink with it: – then she never goes
to Church: – I wish you would speak to her about her wickedness'. – Lucy
accordingly remonstrated with the beldam & told her that she ought to
remember at her great age how uncertain life was: '– ah! said the greatgranny
quite cheerfully, people die at all ages'! . . .

*Sun. 22.* . . . I should have said yesterday that Frere is a believer in that
rubbish called Electrobiology: – he declares that he was one of 4 persons who
laid their hands all touching each other in the prescribed form of mummery
upon a certain round table & that after a short time it began spinning round

---

[22] The seat of the Kennedy family in Ayrshire until the 1930s.

[23] 'The poet Longfellow described a visit to Caius in 1868 and "its amiable and excellent Master
Dr Guest who had a mania for building".' (Christopher Brooke, *History of Gonville and Caius*
(1985), p. 214). See 19 September 1854.

[24] The society was established in 1842 thanks in great measure to Guest of Caius who acted as
its secretary. Membership was rather exclusive and entailed sponsorship and balloting, and
some members liked to tag M.P.S. or even F.P.S. after their names. Most of the officers
in the early years were Cambridge men.

with great rapidity!!!!! I asked if it was after dinner: – but the insinuation was repelled . . . Lucy has a principle that when she has declined giving an intended sum to some Charity it must be given to some other: so she proceeded after St Marys . . . to see Sarah Fordham who now lives at a very industrious family's in Jesus Lane (named Hinson): – these people keep three schools, 2 of them in their nutshell of a house – the 3d in the garden: – besides this laborious teaching they let a room . . .

*Wed. 25.* Very busy day indeed . . . The 1st Congregation lasted till 1½! – The 2d till 3½!! There was fierce fighting (– altogether unexpected by me): Walker (Cai), Todhunter, etc. are all furious against the new Spinning-house scheme: it was thrown out in Black House by 15 to 11: the objections are supposed to be, the largeness of the salaries to the Matron etc, – there being no male in the Establishment. – & the non-production of the Estimates. – Ainslie (who has been working at this matter for 20 years) was so angry that he resigned, & Phelps & Worsley declared they would do the same[25] . . .

*Fri. 27.* . . . Letter from Grim saying he would come by the 11.30 train today. – Seniority & Sealing . . . Grim arrived a little after 2 at my office. I did not think him looking well: – he is as yellow as a Guinea & very thin: he has acquired a very odd habit of winking perpetually as if the light were too strong for his eyes . . . We (i.e. Grim & I) dined at 'the Family' at 5 . . . The dinner was magnificent: – white bate & all luxuries: – ice after dinner . . . Slept on my sofa, having given up the bed to Grim . . .

*Sat. 28.* Walk half way to Coton before breakfast. Breakfast to Grim & Willy. Willy told me that the accounts of his mother were better: – Sir John escorted her to Paris, & from Paris she took care of herself & 4 children (viz Anne & the rest except Willy, Fred & the 2 youngest) all the way to Geneva. Willy is going out as one of a reading party to Heidelberg. – Called Congregation to pass the modified Grace for *building* the New Spinning House: – all the part about *salaries* is dropt. There was a very large gathering in the Senate House, but no nonplacet was given tho there was much grumbling . . . Took Grim to dine in Hall: I presided. We went into the Combination room & were accompanied by Thompson (to whom I gave a copy of the Armorial bearings awarded to the Greek Professor in 1590) etc etc. – We went to Chapel & heard a beautiful Anthem of Mozarts from the 103d Psalm. A 2d painted window has just been put up in the Antechapel: one half

[25] After the national debate following the death of Elizabeth Howe in 1847 it was to be expected that the university gaol for loose women would receive continued examination, if not by the authorities responsible. A self-appointed Special Commissioner of the *Morning Chronicle* for 2 January 1851, having been denied official information, mounted an unanswerable attack; the supposed regulations are a dead letter and the present deputy governor who doubles as gaoler, cook, porter, and chaplain, runs his own tailoring business in the Spinning House. And the very basis of arrest which precedes a repugnant form of trial is flawed since it needs no overt act on the part of the accused, but merely suspicion by the Proctors who have inflicted on many respectable women 'the ordeal of an examination from which every modest woman would shrink with abhorrence'. The university had to be seen to do something and eventually it did, without surrendering its power and its final justification that the Proctors (mostly) knew well who the bad girls were. See 14 December 1859.

of it is a memorial window of Dean Hemery, & the other of George Herbert . . .

*Sun. 29.* . . . Grim & I dined in hall, where I presided. I did a prodigiously stupid thing in the Combination room. We got on the topic of sermons & I expressed my most decided dislike of Mills manner which I pronounced utterly insufferable: – after I had committed myself or in the middle of my doing so Thompson pulled my sleeve: – the "blessed Benjamin"[26] was there by all that was unlucky!! – he of course took no notice, & we immediately talked of other things, – but I felt my head swimming round as fast as one of the mesmorised tables . . .

*Mon. 30.* . . . Began reading again W. Scotts Woodstock: – I found it as charming as ever. I always return to Walter Scott with tenfold zest after having travelled thro any of his successors . . .

*Wed. 8 June.* . . . I heard from Cartmell that Whewell has taken out Mirza, the Pony-chaise, & her dog to Mrs W. at Kreuznach: so he shows himself a kind attentive husband . . . About 6 o'clock Dr Clark called again without Johny.[27] He is immensely enraged at Johny being in the 2d Class: – he says it is robbery: his son had a right to be in the 1st Class: that he was 15th in the Examination: that it is contrary to the practise of very many years to make so small a 1st Class as 13: – that it is disgraceful to the College; that it is infamous on the part of the Examiners; – that it was carried by 5 Examiners against 4 after a debate of 2 hours; that it was the arbitrary conceitedness of non-resident ignorant examiners, that the college deserved to go to the dogs after such a proceeding: that he regretted Whewell wasn't here to blow up the Examiners: – that Johny felt he was robbed, & talked of migrating. I soothed the irritated & disappointed Father as well as I could . . . For my part I think Johny is in his proper place & I never expected him to be higher . . . With regard to the Classes Willy (in spite of his 2 coaches) is only in the 4th; – indeed I should have been surprised if he had been higher . . .

*Wed. 16.* Began wearing a gauze flannel waistcoat, kindly ordered by Lucy. – Lucy went before breakfast to see Mary Anne Tyler who was a trifle better . . . On our return I met Miss Chapman walking with Miss Croker & her fiancé John Croker (a quiet-looking young man without fortune or profession) . . . Mrs Prest now came up & said 'It's all too late now: I heard Miss Chapman once offer to you': – I answered 'More fool I for not having snapt her up at once'. Miss Chapman said 'It's not irremediable yet: I will give you my direction': – I said 'What is that when you can't give me your heart?' . . . Lucy & I refreshed ourselves by going into Downing & sitting on the Bench & watching the haymakers, & then visited the sheep in their pen opposite Dr. Fisher's . . .

*Sat. 18.* . . . Letter from Master of Rolls (John) about the character etc etc of E.E.A: – his brother-in-law Strutt (as Chancellor of Duchy of Lancaster has the Perpetual Curacy of Needwood Forest at his disposal: it is only worth

---

[26] i.e. Benjamin Webb, Secretary of the national Ecclesiological Society in London (formerly the Cambridge Camden Society).

[27] He was to be Romilly's successor but one as Registrary and a great Cambridge figure of the late nineteenth century.

£150 p.a., the parsonage is in a miserable state, & delapidations unattainable as the last Incumbent was insolvent: – Strutt requires information on 2 points; viz. whether E.E.A is a *Puseyite* (wch would be fatal) & a *Gentleman* (wch is indispensable): – it appears that the neighbouring gentry are fashionable men of the world who hate highchurchism[28] . . .

*Sun. 19.* Wrote to Sir John, telling him that Edward is a Gentleman & no Puseyite: – Lucy suggested my adding the epithet *Christian* to Gentleman as a slap-in-the-face to the Socinian Strutt. – John laments over Willy's having been only in the 4th class & thinks he might with exertion have been in the 2d. – Letter from Miss Kelty asking for aid for a baby of sin (5 months old), the mother being truly penitent & going into service, & 5/6 per week being wanted for nursing the little boy: – Miss Kelty wants an admission into the Foundling, hopes I will beg of my friends, etc. – Wrote to her saying that she need not send any such cases to Cambridge as they were 'coals to Newcastle' or 'Owls to Athens', that I had no interest at the Foundling & that I never begged of my friends, – but sent her 3 Guineas . . . That goodnatured Ann Coe brought a present of shrimps: our tea being over they were kept till this morning, when they were bad & had to be thrown over the wall.

*Th. 23.* Had a fire at breakfast & kept it up till bedtime. Lucy nursed her cold & never went beyond the garden. – Proclamation of Midsummer Fair at 11. – the fair (like all other fairs) is going to the dogs. At 2 o'clock to a Seniority at wch Sedgwick presided . . . The object was to bow the stubborn neck of the Puseyite Kinder. – His supposed patron Martin received an unsatisfactory letter from Mr Kinder yesterday & very readily agreed to an Order for the future conduct of Uttoxeter School: – the children are not to be taken to Church at all on Saints days or any weekdays, Mr K. is to make a selection of prayers from our liturgy & submit it to the College for approval, & on the Sundays is not to compel any but the 8 foundation Scholars to go to Church, & finally he is to Communicate these Rules to the Parents & Guardians of all the children, dissenters or churchmen[29] . . .

*Th. 30.* . . . I had a long conference with Potts about Carus . . . he is coming to Camb. in Sept. to spend a week & to preach sundry sermons. He was surprised at not finding among the subscribers to the Carus Testimonial some of his dearest friends: – the Scholefield & Spence factions caused this. The Report is coming out immediately: it is written by W.B. Hopkins who wanted to ignore in it the Committee of young men who originated the whole thing!! . . .

*Sun. 3 July.* . . . Lucy went to St Pauls at 3 & heard some screaming children christened by Nicholson (– one of them was only 'received into the Church') . . . I went to Clare Hall piece to see if there was any parade: the old pomp of the promenade of Commencement Sunday is entirely gone: – not a

---

[28] E.J. Strutt's wife and Lady (John) Romilly were sisters. In his youth he had been an intimate of such unchurchmanlike thinkers as Bentham and Mill. He was now briefly the dispenser of patronage as Chancellor of the Duchy of Lancaster. See 18 June 1854.

[29] Trinity appointed masters to four schools. The Reverend John Kinder (B.A. 1842) had been at Uttoxeter since 1846 but after this contretemps went in 1855 to New Zealand to pursue his career and remained there.

single Dr's red gown was visible . . . Poor old Yuly (aged 16) died today in a fit to Lucy's great grief: the Groom told me of it & had the tact to say 'Miss R. will be very sorry that the old white dog is dead who used to come to her door'.

*Mon. 4.* . . . The degrees today were 1 DD (Bishop Colenso), 1 LLD, 2 LLB, 123 AM (the largest number I every had in one day), 1 eundem. – The AMs this year amount to 257, a number never surpassed: – there was the same no in 1842 . . . In the Senatehouse was the pretty Mrs Bunbury whom we admired so much as Miss Horner: Sedgwick brought her to my table to speak to me: this is the fascinating young lady whom Sedgwick at the wedding breakfast compared to Venus, but said that her husband tho a very good sort of a fellow was certainly not an Adonis! – he is an ugly dwarfish man.

*Wed. 6.* Lucy went to the Hospital to see Harriet . . . Lucy wrote a long & very amusing letter to Dosia, saying nothing (at Sarah's especial desire who is as pleased as Punch at being lady paramount) about Harriets illness. By the way Ann Coe paid us a visit this Evening & Sarah (before introducing her) said to Lucy 'she is come to offer to cook for you, – but pray don't let her') . . .

*Th. 7.* Lucy found a frog in the Area: – She took him into the Garden & made much of him . . . A called Congregation: 2 DD, 6 AM, 2 eundems, a very unusually profitable day for me: one of the DDs was a Mr Cole (a horrid 10 year man at Clare): he gave great offence by preaching against Sedgwicks Geology last Sunday:[30]– he is a most conceited blockhead: – Broadley & some other people suggested to Jeremie that he ought to refuse to admit him: Jeremie consulted me & I told him to make no demur about it . . .

*Tu. 12.* Letter (at last) from Grim, saying he has been to Needwood & written most gratefully to Sir John & to Strutt to decline it: – the net value is only £123, & the immediate expenses on the house & farm buildings would be about £300: – he gave a vivid account of his excursion from Narberth to Needwood – 220 miles. – I wrote to say how thoroughly L. and I approved of his decision.

*Mon. 18.* . . . Letter from George Romilly who left London last Wednesday Afternoon 4 o'clock per Steamer for Yarmouth: – they had one of the most rainy & tempestuous passages ever known, were within an ace of running down a vessel, had to come to anchor, & didn't arrive till noon on Thursday, several hours after their time: – Almost everybody desperately ill except George himself who was only qualmish & Franky who enjoyed himself & was not ill at all. George & wife & son have taken up their quarters at the Crown & Anchor on the Quay . . . they find the accommodations good & cheap, 20 s each the women, 25s/ each for men, & nothing for Frank . . .

---

[30] Geology in the first half of the nineteenth century was a battleground between science and religion which left few of its soldiers unscathed. An extreme example is that of Philip Gosse, in whose mind traditional literalist belief and recent research could not coexist, so that he was forced to conclude that God put fossils into rocks to test men's faith. Attacks on Sedgwick, which he had endured for many years, are not without a pathetic irony, for he was a conservative thinker in many ways and increasingly out of sympathy with recent developments. See Searby, pp. 212-17 and Chadwick, I, 558-68.

*Th. 28.* Lucy's birthday – Thank God she is quite well. – Gave her 4 vols of Bradleys Sermons[31] . . . A little girl named Dawkins said to me today 'Have you found a Shilling?': 'No indeed! have you dropt one!' – 'Yes: father lives at back of Downing Terrace: he is a shoemaker & sent me to buy some leather & I lost the money!' – She had got a bit of new leather in her hand: I gave her ½ her loss. – Hoppetts brother (of Silver St) called on me to ask assistance, he having fallen into trouble: – I gave him nothing, – not knowing him from any other son of Adam – Read a great deal of 'Young Heiress'.[32]

*Fri. 29.* . . . By the 1½ train to Ely . . . After lunch Peacock exhibited the Cathedral: the improvements are quite marvellous: the new skreen is beautiful: & the removal of the Organ a very great gain: – the statue of Bishop Allen I thought pleasing[33] . . . Curious story of wedding performed by the Dean: (I think the Bride's name was Darwin): towards the end of the service 2 ladies rushed up to the communion table looked the bride anxiously in the face & ex-claimed 'it's not she': – they then rushed out again. It turned out that the runaway whom they sought had been married in that same Church an hour before . . . Thompson mentioned a joke of Tom Taylors on the Trinity Arms – (a lion between 2 Books): – 'lions interrupt reading'. – There was a great deal of conversation between Mr Leach & Thompson on German Literature, wch was very clever but very dull . . . this Mr Leach is helping Peacock in the long-promised life of phenomenon Young[34] . . .

*Sat. 30.* Either the German Metaphysics or the hashed venison (it must have been the former) disagreed with me & I slept wretchedly – Mrs Peacock read prayers & did it very well . . . The Dean sent the Marchesa, Meggie & me to the Station in his carriage: – we reached Cambridge a little after 2 . . .

*Sun. 31.* Wrote to G.T.R. (£10). – Lucy & I to *Corpus Chapel* where the Bene't Parish assemble because the Church is repairing. We were in the Stalls & Mrs V.C. lent us a hymn book. Pullen preached an unintelligible Ordination sermon on the indwelling of the Holy Spirit . . . The sermon lasted only 20' & was delivered with great energy, but Mrs Haviland, Mrs Prest etc etc slept soundly. There was a substitute for an organ in the shape of a piano forte in the Vestibule: – the playing & singing were very agreeable & the Psalms

---

[31] Charles Bradley (1789-1871), vicar of Glasbury in Brecknockshire, published several volumes of sermons that were often reprinted. He belonged to the evangelical school of the church and his sermons, commended as pithy and practical yet dignified, were preached from pulpits throughout the English-speaking world.

[32] A new novel by Fanny Trollope.

[33] Professor Peacock became Dean of Ely in 1839 and with the advice of Robert Willis undertook a comprehensive restoration and refurbishment of the interior of the cathedral that lasted thirty years. G.G. Scott was appointed architect in 1847 and was responsible for the choir, screens, and carving, the whole exercise being unofficially but imperatively monitored for catholic propriety and medieval correctness by the Ecclesiological Society. The *Chronicle* of 2 June 1860 contains a description of their work by Scott and Willis when Ely was visited by members of the Architectural Society, and Scott's further reminiscences with a chronology were published in Charles Merivale's *St Etheldreda Festival* (1873).

[34] The book appeared in 1855. Thomas 'Phenomenon' Young (1773-1829), infant prodigy and sometime member of Emmanuel College, made important contributions to knowledge in medicine, physics, and Egyptology.

beautiful . . . We then walked in Peterhouse grove, where we met the vulgar Matron of Addenbrookes Miss Bishop drest in the extreme of fashion . . .

*Fri. 5 August.* . . . Mrs Willis's son (Charley I think) has been before the magistrates for kicking the cook: the cook told him that he was not Master, that he was a nasty snap: whereupon he was brutal enough to kick her: – it appears that the cook refused to let the groom have some water & that Charley very cavalierly ordered her to give it him. The case was heard by Dr Phelps & he fined the boy 10/ . . .

On 6 August Romilly left London for Gloucester where he had been subpoenaed to bring his degree books into court in the case of a horse thief being tried for perjury and forgery. He was not called into court on the first day and was delighted to discover a small pin manufactory in the city although the main trade was now transferred to Birmingham. He saw all the processes which he describes in detail – 'the last process is whitening them, wch is done by boiling them 4 hours in water with tin filings & the lees of port wine wch are imported for that purpose; I bought here half a pound of mixt pins for 1/3 & a paper of pins for /6'.

En route for home on the eleventh he 'went by Croydon Railway to the Sydenham Crystal Palace which was not yet finished and where there was nothing to be seen but a large collection of sculpture'.

*Fri. 12.* Awoke by the Barber knocking at my door: 'Want Barber or Hairdresser?' – Directly after breakfast sallied out to make purchases: bought for Lucy a Brussels Lace Collar 20/ & a pair of sleeves 4/6: – bought for the maids 6 pair of stockings 7/6 & for self 3 shirts 21/ & a carpet bag 3/. – Off by the Mail to Camb. at 11.30: – I had taken a 2d Class ticket, but meeting Bateson I exchanged for a 1st that I might travel with him. – Found the establishment flourishing & Harriet returned to us . . .

*Sun. 14.* Our household was rather scattered this morning: – Harriet & Hannah went to Corpus Chapel . . . Dosia & Sarah went to St Pauls & heard Mr Scott. Lucy & I went to Great St Andrews & heard a villainously dull reader-of-prayers Mr Payne, but a capital preacher (Calthrop the Trinity Chaplain) . . . After Church we had some beer & biscuits at my rooms, & I then did the honors of Trinity Hall Lodge: – we found fires in all the rooms: they were much wanted, for the new walls were very damp . . . This Lodge will be most commodious & handsome.[35] – At the Porters Lodge Lucy spied a Canary & she gave him her stock of groundsel: – Mrs Portress told her that the bird (tho 6 years old) was very nervous & when the cage was being cleaned would fall into a fit: – Lucy told her that she should have 2 cages & never clean the cage while he was in it: – she gave her 1/ towards a new cage – After our Lunch of Chocolate we took Hannah to King's Chapel. We sat in the Stalls: next me were Dr & Mrs Geldart (whose lodge we had been examining) . . .

*Fri. 19.* . . . Today came into the Town an Equestrian company: – it was a pretty sight: a car was drawn by 10 pair of horses of all manner of fantastic

---

[35] Salvin had just remodelled and enlarged the lodge at the Master's expense. See R. Willis and J.W. Clark, *Architectural History of the University* (1886), I, 224.

colours & spots: the mistress of the establishment drove a pair of cream-colored: – one pet black pony ran along without rider or driver. – I worked at the Office till 4, & Lucy took Hannah from 3 to 4 into the Botanical Garden, where H. told her the story of 'the Female Jesuit'[36] wch seems to have interested her greatly. – Hannah dined with us . . .

*Sat. 20.* Lucy wished to give Hannah 'Sarah Martin':[37] I went to every bookseller in Cambridge to get a Copy: but in vain: – I gave her a copy of Burders Village Sermons & 20/ to pay her expenses. Lucy gave her a Coverdale Medal,[38] a Muff, fur cuffs, a parasol etc. & 11/. – Hannah took her departure for Ely at 1.30. – Lucy sent some Port & Chicken to poor Christiana whose life seems to be ebbing away. – Lucy did not get beyond the garden, & I worked in my office steadily till dinner . . .

*Sun. 21.* . . . On coming to Queen's Bridge we were highly amused at seeing 3 Cows swimming over from Sheep green, & on speaking to a Milkwoman she said it was their constant habit & that the Calves swum like ducks. – The Maids called on Christiana Howe, who said that she thought L. a very good woman & that I must sing well! that last rather a bad shot. – Wrote to Thompson about Fellowship Papers.

*Wed. 14 September.* Lucy received (as a mark of gratitude) from Miss Hawes the ugliest heaviest purse ever seen: its steel beads will hereafter fetch something for their weight as old iron . . . Lucy then called at my office to ask me to escort her to the Fitzwilliam into wch visitors were pouring in strange profusion: – These excursionists had a harsh band: they picnic'd on Christs piece: – 1001 Visitors at Fitzwilliam today (I was not at my Office, being in College looking out passages in Aristophanes & Pindar): – it appeared afterwards that these visitors were an Excursion train of 500 members of Temperance Society from Lynn . . . Lucy & I walked for 1½ hour before dinner in our favorite Botanical Garden. – After dinner we used Mrs Worsley's key & went into Downing to see the Barnwell 850 Sunday Scholars have their annual treat: – our maids & Miss Theobald were among the spectators. – We were much pleased with the familiar good sense of Mr Titcomb's address to the children: he said that people could not always mow without wetting [sic] their scythe, for that they would be tired & the scythe would be so blunt that they would make but bad work of it: – so, boys & girls must sometimes sharpen their wits by good hearty play. Mr Titcomb set his brother-in-law Mr Senley to pitch the Psalm, & miserably he did it: – he has no voice: – the children sang 'the blackbird' – a very pretty song, 'the stately homes of England' – an absurd song for pauper children, 'away with needless sorrow' – very good – etc etc & G. s. t. Q . . .

[36] *Or The Spy in the Family* (1851), a sensational anti-Catholic novel by Mrs Jemima Luke.
[37] i.e. the life of the prison-visitor of Great Yarmouth who died in 1843 and attained posthumous fame for her charitable work. A sketch of her life by the Religious Tract Society sold tens of thousands of copies and even appeared in a French version in 1860. Bishop Stanley of Norwich said 'I would canonize Sarah Martin if I could'. See *D.N.B.*
[38] The tercentenary of Coverdale's English translation of the Bible was celebrated in October 1835 when many medals were struck in his honour, and presumably it was one of them that Lucy gave as a present.

*Mon. 19.* . . . Letter from Mr Morris asking for a few shillings as he is afraid of distress for rent unless he pays £1 today: sent him £1 & wrote him word that I would never help him again . . . Lucy . . . had a visit from Raby (out of the Union) whom she wishes to apprentice to a Barber: – she found him utterly ignorant of the proceedings of his Father & the Master-Barber (Perry): – she gave him 1/ to stump over to Hauxton to see Mr Williams (the Clergyman) who has been exerting himself in the matter . . . Tonight finished 'Haydon's life': the account of his distress of mind at the rejection of his Cartoons & the failure of his exhibition of 'Aristides' ostracism' & 'Nero's burning Rome' is very touching: – these were 2 of the 6 pictures which he intended painting as fit decorations for the Houses of Parliament; – these 2 were to show the evil of Republicanism & Tyranny. I ought not to have read the account of poor Haydon's suicide at night for it made Lucy & me uncomfortable & disturbed our sleep[39] . . .

*Wed. 21.* . . . Lucy got (from Mr Scott at Woodley's) a rich story: on Sacrament Sunday (for wch Cooper returned to Cambridge) some admirers of Calthrop had the want of delicacy & tact to say to him we've called to ask the favor of your lending your Pulpit today to Mr Calthrop: – Cooper answered 'I shall do nothing of the kind: I think you make a great deal too much of him' . . .

*Fri. 23.* . . . Lucy out for 4½ hours Carus-shirking . . . As I was in Trinity Great Court I met Carus: he is looking remarkably well, his eyes less pinky, his stomach less projecting, his face a shade less rosy, & his hair a purer white: – I congratulated him on his healthy appearance. He says that he is obliged to wear Spectacles at night. I told him that since he deserted us we have given up Trinity Church & should never go there again. He said his mind misgave him sometimes about having given up Cambridge: that it was completely against his will: – that the Bishop of Winchester had insisted on it . . . I childishly put my bunch of keys on my stick to have a shy with them as I was passing thro Kings: – not having my glass I hunted for them more than ½ hour in vain, shuffling up & down with my feet close together that I might kick them up. At last came a Gardener who deliberately put boots on a horse that he might drag a machine for mowing & rolling the grass: the horse can't bear his boots & began kicking as soon as they were on. I communicated my loss to the Gardener & promised him a Shilling if he found my keys & brought them to my Office: – he was not long about it, for he came in a few minutes after me . . .

*Sat. 24.* . . . Carus packed off his wife (– who seems by the small glimpse Lucy caught of her fair & pasty-faced, shortish of stature, springy in her walk, & elegant in her dress) by the 2 o'clock to her old Father at Hemingford: – I wondered whether the phrase 'good riddance of bad rubbish' occurred to him . . .

---

[39] The book was edited by Tom Taylor of Trinity in 1853. The painter had cut his throat like Romilly's uncle Samuel whose fate is often mentioned in Haydon's diaries. See A. Hayter, *A Sultry Month: Scenes of London Literary Life in 1846* (1965).

*Sun. 25.* Heavy continuous rain during the night & early morning. Wrote to Frank (£15): so did Lucy . . . Read the Lessons etc to Lucy & (by way of sermon) Mrs Scholefields history of William Wimmera (a pious little Australian Savage (brought over by Mr Lloyd Chase) who died at the age of 11 in England 11 months after sailing from Melbourne): – the dream which he had of Heaven is really very beautiful: – there is every appearance of the story being accurately told without embellishment: – Mrs Scholefields address at the conclusion to the Training School is very good & practical: – she quotes the good life & death of a girl trained there. This story of little W.W. was a great favorite of Professor Scholefields[40] . . .

*Tu. 27.* . . . Lucy did a very ingenious thing: she went with me to my office at 10¼ & staid there till 3: she did me great service in putting my place to rights & airing some books before the fire: her serious employment was reading Bradley's sermons. – I had to attend Sturbridge Fair at 11: there was no Proctor present, so Nind (Senior Taxor) did the Proctorial duty of keeping the accounts: he & Bashforth & I & Ventris made the Court . . . While we were out Carus called & left a P.P.C.:[41] he left also a present for Lucy (viz. Stephenson on the 23d Psalm): – he wrote an affectionate record of his present on a Fly-Leaf . . .

*Fr. 30.* . . . 1st day of Fellowship: Greek by Thompson & me. He has a bad cold so I relieved him from 11 to 12½ & then had my own turn in Hall from 1½ to 4½ . . . I had a fire lighted in the hall: – the Master (just come from Lowestoff) looked in & had a little chat with me: – he expressed astonishment & horror at my sitting close to a charcoal fire. – I told him I was more afraid of being chilled with the cold if there were no fire than of being asphixé by its noxious vapors. – One of the best Scholars (Whymper) made an odd mistake: – he thought the Examination didn't begin till tomorrow, so he arrived in Cambridge the middle of the day & missed all the Greek Verse set by Thompson: – he came in for the Greek Verse set by me: I told him he must whip up his horses. – There are 7 Fellowships to fill & only 20 Candidates . . .

*Sun. 2 October.* Lucy still but poorly: – I would not let her go to Church. – Went to Corpus Chapel & heard Mason read prayers in that strange way of drawling out all the last syllables. Pulling preached in his ultra melancholy stile: – His text was Hebrews IV. 3. (the rest of God): – it ought to have been a cheerful subject, but he contrived to make it double dismal: – he said all in

[40] Mrs Scholefield's very rare *Short Memoir of William Wimmera* (Cambridge, 1853) records how her husband listened to his story 'with increasing interest. The last time it was read to him was in the evening of the Sunday on which he preached his last sermon in Ely Cathedral, and while resting on a sofa, being much exhausted. When it was finished he said, "It is very sweet".' (Preface). The child's mother was shot by settlers in 1846, and he was brought to England for missionary training but succumbed to loneliness, cold, and consumption. To their great dismay Mrs Scholefield's book was read to Willie's people in May 1860 by missionaries unaware of the connexion. See 'W. Wimmera' in the *Encyclopedia of Aboriginal Australia* (Canberra, 1994). We are indebted to Dr Pierre Gorman of Melbourne for his help with this note.

[41] i.e. pour prendre congé, a leave-taking note.

the world was unrest: – if we had rational pursuits & domestic endearments we got satiated with them, etc etc: – my impression was that he would go home & hang himself . . . Prepared making a 'Wellington' Vol. of Engravings from the 'Illustrated London News' . . . Read loud also a favorite child's book of the Saints called 'the Peep of Day':[42]– I disapprove however of talking to children under 5 years of their dying & being put into a pit: – it is nasty and revolting to all the innocent natural feelings of childhood.

*Sat. 8.* . . . At 6½ to Trinity Lodge to settle the Fellowships . . . . Mrs Whewell is still staying at Lowestoff: she happily has a niece stopping with her. – The conversation turned principally on the wonderful news of the day, – the solution of the problem of 300 years – the actual discovery of a N.W. passage.[43] – Our 7 vacancies were – 4 by marriage – 3 by superannuated lawyers . . . We rejected poor Whymper of the 3rd year tho he had been University Scholar: – he did no Mathematics, & his escapade about the 1st days Examination was of great disservice to him. I was however very sorry at his rejection both for his own sake & his mother's . . . Finished 'Rob Roy'.

*Mon. 10.* . . . Took a walk with Mrs Archdall & spouse: he is furious from an attack of Whiston's on Dean Pellew: – I told him he would meet with no sympathy from me as I was a friend to routing out all abuses.[44] – Met Mrs Paget escorting her little son in his donkey-ride: – by the way Paget has set up a Brougham, wch looks like getting practice. – Dined at the Fellowship dinner: the Master was in great force & very amusing: – Sedgwick also was very good company. The Master made a pun about daguerrotype drawing wch made us laugh: he said he had seen 2 men on the bridge *daguerre-drawing*. He told us of a French hatter who invited his customer to look at himself in a glass: – in that short interval a daguerrotype likeness was struck off wch he presented to the purchaser to stick in his hat: – the Master told us a charming story in ridicule of phrenology: – a subject had well-developed organs of music & domesticity: – these were put in strong agitation simultaneously & the effect was – the man sang 'Sweet Home' . . .

*Tu. 11.* The Master being absent Sedgwick admitted the new Fellows: – he made them a capital speech expressing regret at the good Candidates we had been obliged to pass over & cautioning the successful ones against imitating his example & retaining their Fellowships to old age . . . I asked Mrs Ashton

[42] *Or a Series of the Earliest Religious Instruction the Infant Mind is capable of receiving* by F.L. Bevan (Mrs Mortimer). She wrote other books of the same kind, long forgotten, but deserves a line in the annals of sub-literature for hitting on the generic title 'without Tears', as in *Reading without Tears* (1857).

[43] The finding of a northern passage was the grail of navigators; it had been sought repeatedly when the ending of the Napoleonic wars again permitted geographical exploration. The disappearance after July 1845 of Sir John Franklin's officially sponsored expedition caused an intense international search which almost incidentally led to the discovery of the North West passage by Robert M'Clure, who named it after the Prince of Wales in October 1850. The news did not reach England for nearly three years.

[44] Pellew, Dean of Norwich since 1828, had written a pamphlet on cathedrals as long ago as 1836. Whiston (see 14 October 1851) accused the authorities of other cathedrals than Rochester of neglecting to act lawfully, though he had nothing particular to say of Norwich which unusually had no cathedral school at all.

about Mrs Carus; she thinks her like a tallish schoolgirl, with nothing interesting in her looks or conversation; whenever she speaks in her husband's presence she looks up to see whether he approves: – she is obviously an idolatress of Carus, – wch is the only circumstance in the case wch will at all reconcile him to his 'marriage forcé'. Mrs Ashton amused me by saying that she should be miserable if she were Carus's wife, – he is such a fidget . . .

*Wed. 19.* Lucy I think a little less languid. (Wet day from morning to night). No possibility of her getting an outing. – Congr. 2 AM, 1 LLB, 1 AB. – Then a Seniority at wch we voted £1200 for buying the field close to the Spring wch supplies our fountain: we afterwards had a sealing at wch I enacted Vice Master. (Sedgwick having staid at home to take physic): received 11/6 for Sealing Money. Edleston told me that last night Walmisley was unable to go on playing the Organ (– cette malheureuse passion pour le vin & l'eaudevie), that one of the singers had to play the rest of the service & that there was no Anthem.[45] – Edleston asked me if I or Lucy knew of any poor people to recommend, because (as Steward) he had 2 pieces of preferment at his disposal. I recommended Mrs Snarey, & in the Evening Lucy wrote a letter in behalf of Mrs Saunders wch will be copied out & sent to Edleston tomorrow . . .

*Th. 21.* Letter from Lady Braybrooke asking me for next Wednesday till Saturday: – wrote to decline . . . Mrs Saunders called on Mr Edleston & received from him £1 & is to have £1 quarterly!!!! Old Howes called to ask me to recommend him to the Fitzwilliam Syndicate as a successor to Traylen. I declined. – Went to the Museum & learned all the particulars: Traylen & Todd were 2 supernumeraries who mounted guard in the Picture rooms, Traylen's beat being the Taj Mahal room: the pay was 15/ a week. Traylen leaves tomorrow, having been promoted by Bateson (who is Librarian of St Johns) to attend in the Library (with a salary of £70!!) & also to be his Secretary . . . Lucy is trying to get Walter Watts into Traylen's shoes at the Fitzwilliam. I wrote on his behalf to the V.C. . . . but the V.C. told him he was too late . . .

*Sat. 22.* . . . I called on Mrs Clark to thank her for her present of Normanton Pippins. I found her at home & had a regular gossip with her: she opened her heart upon the 2 subjects nearest to it, for love or hatred, her Son & the Servants . . . she thinks her 3 discarded maids were 3 devils, the Cook being the archdevil . . . Cook has been giving away her provisions for years to a young man (a journeyman tailor without a farthing . . . ) & that the other servants tho often pinched in consequence were afraid to tell: – during this last vacation she gave great teaparties to . . . a heap of Magdalene bedmakers etc etc in the drawing room, – that the company used sometimes to sit out on the lawn, the journeyman tailor occupying the Doctor's easy chair & smoking at his ease . . . The gardener resisted all temptations to join any of these festivities & doubtless was the informer . . .

---

[45] T.A.Walmisley had been elected organist of St John's and Trinity at the age of only 19, and professor of music at 22. He was a prolific composer and much of his work remained unpublished until after his death, hastened by drink, in 1856. Several of his pieces remain in the repertoire of cathedral and college choirs.

*Mon. 24.* . . . The Rev. G. Williams (of Hauxton) called twice today . . .
He has managed the 'William Raby' apprenticeship at last: – he has with great
difficulty raised from his miserable parish about £3. 5. –, so the Indentures
have been drawn whereby W.R. is apprenticed to a Barber (named Perry) for
the præmium of £5 (to be paid by Lucy): Lucy had also offered if necessary to
pay £1 for the indentures: – but that is needless, being included in the £3. 5.–
. – I paid Mr Williams in shining gold & heaped upon him a profusion of
thanks for the trouble he had taken & the great kindness he had shown, & said
how greatly my Sister would regret not having had the pleasure of shaking
hands with him & thanking him in person. He is hideously ugly, tall & gaunt,
wears a wig all awry, & had red whiskers. – I don't wonder Miss Pearce
wouldn't marry him . . .

*Tu. 25.* . . . 1st Whist Club of the Season at Brights . . . Two of the Club
were absent, Day (who has shot off his thumb joint) & Power (who was
summoned to his uncle (the Librarian's) sick bed. – At supper the novel of
'Ruth' was discussed: it is by the author of Mary Barton (Mrs Gateskill or
some such name): – they say it is intensely pathetic: – a story of a girl who is
seduced by a manufacturer, – she is true to him – & is reclaimed by the hero of
the book a deformed dissenting minister: – I shall not read so dismal a book.

*Mon. 31.* . . . Had my guests in hall Sir James Eyre & Dr Abdy. Sir James
is the most ludicrously vain man I ever saw: he is a coarse-featured ugly
vulgar-looking man who is not immaculate in his *hs*. He told me that if he had
made music his profession he should have been most distinguished for he was
gifted with a very fine voice & the most delicate ear imaginable. He said that
when he was Mayor of Hereford he appointed his venerable father his
Chaplain, & that his Father said at a public dinner 'if your new officer gives
you the same satisfaction as Mayor wch he has always given me as a son you
will find him *perfection*'. he was so much beloved by everybody that at the
Accession of William IV Lord Somers (the Lord Lieutenant) requested the
King to knight him . . . His poor Father was overcome by his delight at being
his Chaplain & died during the Mayoralty . . . Sir James showed me a list of
120 people who had subscribed ½ Guinea for a portrait of his ugly face, –
headed by his dear friend the Archbishop![46] – I did not offer to put my name
among the subscribers . . . In the Combination room Mr Selwyn (of
Hemington) sat next to me: I talked with him about his son-in-law Carus. He
says that Carus is certainly out of his element at Romsey & not half so happy
& so useful as at Cambridge: – there is no society except Lord Palmerston: –
as for Mrs Gerald Noel[47] she has been a thorn in Carus's side, for she is ultra-
high-church if not tractarian: – & the Bishop of Winchester was doubtless
desirous of getting Carus to counteract her puseyite tendencies. – Mr Selwyn
(or his host Dr Jeremie) told an amusing story as coming from the mouth of the
Bishop of Oxford 'an obsequious timeserving Clergyman used to wait till the
Squire of the Parish was seated: – one Sunday he mistook another man for the

---

[46] i.e. Musgrave of York, formerly bishop of Hereford.
[47] Widow of the former vicar of Romsey whose nephew Lord Camden had gone over to Rome
in 1851.

Squire & began 'When the wicked man': – upon wch the Clerk stopt him: – 'No! that a'n't he: he ben't come': – But as this story comes thro Bishop Wilberforce perhaps it is not true, for his Father used to say 'I never can get Sam to speak the truth'.

*Tu. 1 November.* The Cholera very bad at Soham: 10 have died out of 40 attacked:[48]– 2 cases also at Ely. – Letter from Miss Cotton saying the Bart is confined to his room & wants more books. – Wrote to her saying that he must wait patiently till tomorrow as today is a holiday at the Library. – Present from Sir James (who left this morning) of a copy of his book on the Stomach (– wch Paget says is very trashy): – wrote to thank him . . . Dined in Hall & had for my guests my landlord Mr Fawcett & Harvey Goodwin . . . the principal topics of conversation were the Cholera, the robbery of an undergraduate of Jesus (Owen)[49] of 55 sovereigns wch he had in his waistcoat pocket, & W.B. Hopkins loss of his portmanteau containing valuable bursarial papers. The robbery of Owen is somewhat mysterious: – it was on Jesus Piece between 6 & 7 in the Evening directly after a wine party in Portugal place by 2 men crape-faced & pistol-presenting: – Woodham (who always thinks the worst of everybody & everything) believes that the young man was after some wickedness in spite of the good character he bears . . .

*Fri. 4.* Breakfast at the Senior Proctor *Theeds*: he lives in Mr Simeon's rooms: – the handrail on the stairs was made by Mr Simeon's *order*. At 10 came on the Election of the new V.C. (Geldart): he has a nose & chin intensely like Punch, & at Melton he used to be called Punch: – his speech was good but rather too much blowing his own trumpet: – he talked about his own 'mens conscia recti', & of his resolution to work indefatigably. – I believe he will do one part of his duties admirably, viz. the hospitality: – he has ordered 20 lbs of grapes for his wineparty today & is said to have contracted for ice at all his parties during his year of office. I was amused by his wife's hearty gaiety: she declared it was the happiest day of her life & that she felt so proud . . . Lucy today went to take a frock to little Becky. – I fell in with her & took her to see the new Spinning House. We were getting on very nicely under the guidance of a goodhumoured maid when she was unfortunately superseded by the Keeper himself (Mr Wilson, a round dwarfish tailor, who was not quite sober & had an extravagant opinion of his own merits): the Spinning house has now 19 cells besides receiving & lock-up rooms: they are on 2 stories: there is a gloomy chapel (at wch the Keeper acts as Clerk & professes himself highly delighted with Peill's Sunday sermon wch is invariably from the Epistle of the day: – he

[48] Cholera began late in October when a poor man named Bye died in the space of five hours, his hands shrivelled like 'those of a washerwoman after a hard day's labour' (*Chronicle* 29 October). Within a week there were forty deaths, chiefly of farm labourers earning a meagre ten shillings a week and existing in cottages served by 'disgusting' privies. Nothing, the medical man Dr Lewis told the newspaper, would serve but 'a thorough, comprehensive, and well-devised system of drainage under the Public Health Act'. The epidemic lasted a month.

[49] The thieves appear to have evaded capture. According to the *Chronicle*, Owen, who was on his way across Midsummer Common from college to his lodgings, had been accosted by a couple who asked him for the time and then put a pistol to his head.

said it was like '*sweets* to him'): there is also an infirmary, a largeish kitchen & a laundry: – the paved yard is to be decorated with a border of flowers. – Mr Wilson made a prodigious clatter in exhibiting the stove wch heats the whole building: – every cell has a gas-light in it, a fixt little table, with a fixt 3 legged stool: the inmates sleep on a hammock wch is taken away in the day time. Each cell is furnished with a bell, wch causes a gong to strike, & makes the no of the cell start out from the wall so that the ringer is immediately known & visited. The place is admirably ventilated by airbricks & airtraps. – The arrangement is copied from the model prison at Pentonville. The inspector of Prisons was here today & expressed complete satisfaction. – Gas was burning in every cell & the Stove threw out a great heat: – there are no inmates in the cells. & will not be till the Prison is considered perfectly fit for their reception: – at present the unfortunates are committed to the Town Jail . . .

*Mon. 7.* . . . Passed all the morning settling the years accounts of the Registrary: – drew up my Bill for the V.C. & took it to Pulling who paid me without looking at it– I used for the 1st time one of the new penny Receipt Stamps on my receipt to Pulling. These stamps are separated by a lace-like division, wch tears without the necessity of scissors: – the Inventor of this novelty is said to have received £4000 for it!!!!![50] . . .

*Wed. 9.* . . . Congregation day: – 1 BD, 5 AM, 1 ML, 1 LLB, 2 eundem. – Got from Babington the rules of the Caucuss[51] Club: – it was born in February (– just before the voting on the Revised Statutes), – it sits the day before every Congregation, – it has a fresh President every term: – its existing President is Neptunian Adams: his 2 Predecessors were Clark (Christs) (the late Senior Proctor) & Ferguson (Pemb) (late Junior Proctor): – Ferguson was the 1st President – The Caucussites agitated successfully on this occasion & threw out the Grace for appointing a University-man Curator of the Fitzwilliam with a salary of £200: The Votes were 22 Non Placet, 19 Placet: I did not vote: if I had I should have voted among the Non Placet: – Lucy was strongly opposed to this Grace. – Lunch at the V.C.'s previous to swearing in the new Mayor (Brimley the Grocer). – Off at 5 for Audley End: I travelled with Mill & wife: I learned that the 3 grandchildren as well as their Mother Mrs Webb & 'the blessed Benjamin' are all well . . . Mill is as crooked as if he had been a feeble young girl who had carried a heavy child. – At Audley End station I got into the Omnibus & travelled with 2 Quaker Ladies who befriended me & thou-&-thee'd me . . .

Romilly again enacted chaplain during his four days at Audley End, and was once more the only man not to turn out 'to a battue' where 'all the 7 gentlemen . . . killed

---

[50] A machine to perforate stamps had been invented by one Henry Archer in 1847, and its praises were so often sung in the Commons by Muntz, the Birmingham Member, that the patent rights were bought for the Post Office.

[51] A very early and semantically important use in a thoroughly English context of the original American meaning , i.e. a preliminary meeting of the leaders of a group to pick candidates and settle plans of action before a main assembly is convened. Compare 24 February 1854 and 5 November 1856. *Caucussites* (below and at 23 November) appears to be Romilly's own coinage, with a whiff of disapprobation.

287 head of the game, wch were spread out on the Lawn'. Life in the great house followed much the same pattern as usual, but Romilly's last evening was exclusively devoted to a pastime immensely enjoyed by him and a great many of his friends. 'In the Saloon after tea we guessed the riddles in the New Pocket Books: Mrs Neville & Lady B. were far the best guessers. – Lady B. told me that many years ago herself & sisters were commemorated in a Pocket Book as having guessed all the riddles: – not very long ago they guessed all the riddles at Audley End & Whewell sent up anonymously a poetical answer containing their guesses: – the 1st Prize was awarded to him'.

*Tu. 15.* . . . Sedgwick has been attacked by a dizziness in the head & great bleedings at the nose: – he has not (I hear) lectured since Friday the 4th: he has had leeches applied abundantly by Paget, & violent doses of calomel: – Paget reports very favorably of him. –

To my great surprise about 2½ in the intensity of the horrid fog I was haled from the other side of the road by Lucy who was taking a very sickly palefaced pauperess – (name Haggar – age 6 or 7) to the shoeshop . . . Lucy rigged her out with new boots, a petticoat etc etc . . .

*Wed. 16.* Congregation day for Election of Perpetual Curate of Acton Round: – the voting was from 10 to 11 & from 3 to 4.[52] There were 11 Candidates: among them were the notorious Dr Bartlett (Clare) (who at Kelly's election in 1842 brought down £1000 in his portmanteau to bribe the town, an Oxford DD (Rowley) & an Oxonian AM (Houghton). The existing Curate (John Gibson B.A. Dublin) won easy . . . Dined at Mrs Havilands: I believe it was her first dinner since her husband's death: everything was in very good style . . . Plaid 2 rubbers of whist with Phelps against Mrs Prest & Peacock: I won them both & carried off 5/. – I however created a scene which I peculiarly detest: – Phelps led a suit which had already been renounced by both his adversaries, – certainly the worst play in the world. I (in perfect goodhumour but with a great want of civility) said 'Well I think it was impossible to play worse that that': – he turned as black as thunder & said that people didn't make such observations as that in public: I made the warmest & most energetic apologies possible– but I would have given £10 not to have given him such deep offence. – We are in the habit at the Whist Club of expressing unqualified terms of disapprobation. – If Phelps & I ever play together again he may be certain that I shall not find fault. – Home a little after 10.

*Sat. 19.* . . . To the V.C.'s concerning a degree to the Duke of Brabant who comes here on Tuesday with Prince Albert: – the Duke is of course a Roman Catholic but that will not interfere with his taking a *complimentary* degree[53] at the hands of his Royal Cousin the Chancellor, – without subscription oaths or fees . . .

---

[52] This meagre living of £85 p.a. was in Shropshire. Its patron, a Roman Catholic, was debarred from presenting to it by an act of James I which gave the rights of such a 'popish recusant convict' to the two universities. Cambridge had rights in 27 counties. Curiously the gentleman penalised on this occasion was the future Regius Professor of History and Honorary Fellow of Trinity whose applications to Cambridge colleges were refused in his youth.

[53] i.e. an honorary degree.

*Sun. 20.* . . . Agreeable letter from Grim. – Wrote to Frank – Read loud the Lessons etc etc etc to Lucy. – In the Evening read loud Allen's Modern Judaism & Horne about burial & embalment.[54] – Lucy never stirred out & I followed her example: – I wrote the headings of hymns etc. for Sarah's copybook. – Drank tea with V.C & Mrs Geldart: – they very agreeably surprised me by saying that they thought me the most important officer in the University & tho their table would hold only 24 they would give me a Card: – wch Mrs Geldart (who is the Secretary) immediately wrote out, whereupon I kissed her hand as if she had been a Queen & made her a pretty speech. – I was highly delighted with this unexpected honor.

*Mon. 21.* Lucy never stirred out, I having been far too busy to come & stir her up. – Got 600 cards printed for Wednesday . . . Cross the Coachman called upon me & showed himself a very great fool. He wished me to obtain for him the means of seeing the Prince that he might remind him of the Poems he had sent him (handsomely bound): – I told him that it was altogether out of the question . . . Might he call on Dr Whewell about the business? – I most strongly dissuaded so rash a piece of impertinence: – I afterwards learned from Lucy that this cidevant Coachman bears a very bad character & has been 4 times in prison! He is Candidate for a place in the Fitzwilliam Museum[55] . . . Lucy is doing all she possibly can for Walter Watts – whom she greatly compassionates since his failure in business . . .

*Tu. 22.* . . . At 10½ to Trinity Lodge to receive Prince Albert & his Cousin the Duke of Brabant & their suite Colonels Grey & Gordon, Count Lannoy & Mr Vande Weyer. – They did not arrive till 11¼: – We received them at the Master's Hall door & after having duly kootoo'd followed them up into the drawing room: – in a minute or 2 we all took our departure. Two Royal Coaches with magnificent bayhorses, short fat legless apoplectic-looking coachmen, & gigantic footmen (two behind each coach). The masters Groom on horseback headed the procession. I afterwards heard from Dr Geldart that the Prince gave a sort of shudder as if he thought he was going to be smashed when the Carriage turned into our beggarly lane: – it entered thro the Queen's Gateway. By the way Trinity Lane is the only approach to the V.C.'s: – Garrett-Hostle Lane is the last part of the carriage approach to Trinity Hall Lodge: – pretty work for huge State Coaches to go down two such miserable Lanes: – however no accident happened. – The Prince etc were lionised about Trinity by the Master till Sedgwick's Lecture at 12. The great people didn't come till 12¼: they were received with loud applause by the assembly . . . Sedgwick's Subject was one of the most amusing of his course (– it was the

---

[54] i.e. a work on Jewish tradition and custom since the time of Christ published in 1816 by John Allen, a dissenting schoolmaster. Horne is probably the very prolific Thomas Hartwell Horne (1780-1862), a ten-year man awarded his B.D. degree in 1829.

[55] Cross was a local 'character' of some education who, having lost his living as a stage-coachman because of the railways, had turned to hawking his own poetical compositions of a religious and historical kind. Not devoid of merit, they attracted the attention of dons and undergraduates. In 1855 he was to be runner-up to Pink for the new post of town librarian. In his *Autobiography* (1861) Cross includes an anecdote that shows Romilly more kindly disposed towards him; see *Romilly 1842-47*, p. 94.

Lecture in order, as he assured us): it was about the Megatherion & Myloden & other Gigantic members of the Sloth family. He attacked (in glorious language) the daring impiety of Buffon in having ventured to say that any animals had parts unfitted for the place assigned them by God: he lamented that Cuvier in this one solitary instance had also been guilty of the same want of reverence. He showed (from Waterston's experience) that the Sloths were seen in their proper state of enjoyment when they were clinging to the branches among wch they lived & hanging with their body downwards. – At the end of his very amusing & eloquent Lecture he thanked the Prince for his condescencion in coming to his Lecture & dwelt with fervid admiration on the Prince's discharge of all his high duties: he introduced also warm expressions of attachment & loyalty to the Queen. He then turned to the young Duke of Brabant & told him that the nation felt great interest in him as the son of a Monarch who was so much beloved by them & who had been connected with their dearest hopes: he hoped it would be long before he held the reins of monarchy & that when he did he would tread in the steps of his illustrious father & rule his country in peace & prosperity. – The young duke was a good deal touched by this address: – he shook hands with Sedgwick & thanked him for the manner in wch he had spoken of his dear Father: – Sedgwick didn't dismiss us till near 1½: – certainly far too long. After his Lecture he accompanied the great people in their sightseeing & then lunched with them at Trinity Lodge. I think in the sightseeing the Prince & the Duke & the V.C. & Whewell were in the 1st carriage, Sedgwick & the suite in the 2d. – My attending Sedgwicks Lecture made me sadly late at the Pitt Press where I had professed to deliver tickets from 1 to 4. I found a very large assembly awaiting me: – a good many however had no business there, being undergraduates (who required no tickets for themselves & who (as I told them) were considered as *friendless* by the University & not allowed a ticket for a friend . . . Hoppett gave me great pleasure by an act of kindness: – he provided me with a piece of gingerbread & a glass of water. – He kept the door for me for an hour & more, to drive back the ignorant undergraduates. At 4½ I had a basin of peasoup in my rooms. I then drest for 'the Reception' at Trinity Lodge at 5. I was the Lord in waiting & had to announce the names. Canon Selwyn violated etiquette in a strange way: – after I called his name instead of passing on he said 'I am desired by the Master of St Johns to express his Gratitude for your R.H's condescencion in sending to Enquire after him'. – The Prince said 'I was sorry to hear of his accident & hope he is going on well'. – This accident was from Dr Tatham climbing the outside staircase for the Undergraduate Gallery of the Senate House & falling down: he received a hard blow on the head & his face was much scratched & bruised– it bled profusely. – He was promptly attended to & is doing well. – The 'reception' went off so rapidly that a considerable number (– a large batch of Queensmen among them) were too late: – after the Reception (& my presentation by Whewell) the Prince did me the Honor of shaking hands with me & asking a few questions about his own mode of conferring the degree on the Duke of Brabant. – I should have mentioned that the V.C. desired me (very properly I think) to introduce him as 'Master of Trinity Hall'. – Whewell & Sedgwick & the Duke & Suite stood by the Prince during the Reception. – When the

Reception was over I went & sat with Sedgwick a little. He is in very good force & doesn't seem at all knocked up by his excitement: he has declined dining with the V.C. but he & Willis will drink tea there at 9. – I had the Honor of dining with the V.C. & Mrs Geldart: the hour was 7.30, the party consisted of 24, viz. Dr & Mrs Geldart, the Prince Albert, the Duke of Brabant, Count Lannoy, Mr Vande Weyer, Colonels Grey & Gordon, Drs Webb, Whewell, Philpott, Okes, Cookson, Guest, Corrie, Cartmell, Pulling & Phelps, Mr Worsley, Bateson, Senior Proctor (Theed), 2 Bedells & myself. – Philpott (the Chancellor's Chaplain) said Grace before dinner: but there was none after, – the V.C. forgetting to ask Philpott. – The Prince took in the Mistress of the house, – offering her his arm wch she of course took. She was beautifully drest & wore diamonds . . . The dinner was magnificent: – Mrs Geldart kindly allowed me to take away the Bill of Fare (wch was a specimen of beautiful writing).[56] Three Royal footmen attended, wearing épaulettes: – they made the ordinary attendants look quite mean. – English was spoken, with the exception of a short sentence in German by the Prince to Mr Vande Weyer & his reply: I didn't hear the words. Whewell told some anecdote in wch there was a good deal of French, & I think he spoke a few words of German to Count Lannoy. – Mrs Geldart backed out of the room quite admirably: both the Prince & the Duke of B. turned round & looked at her all the time she was backing. – I should have said that the Grace-cup was handed round in this manner: the V.C. presented it to the Prince who gave it to Mrs Geldart: he then drank it & it was handed to the D. of Brabant: then it went round regularly to Philpott, Okes, myself, Leapingwell, etc. etc.: – the table was too wide for it to be zig-zagged across. – Col. Gray approved of it highly & lamented that he had not taken a longer draft. – We didn't stay long after Mrs Geldart's departure. The Prince & the Duke went immediately into the Drawing Room to Mrs Geldart & had tea & coffee handed to them: – every body else (including Sedgwick & Willis who were now come) had tea in the Library (the intermediate room between the Dining & Drawing Room). – I afterwards learned all about this from Mrs Geldart. She had asked the Prince's Page to inspect all her preparations: she had intended the Prince & Duke to drink tea with all the rest of the company in the Library, & had set 2 grand chairs for them by the fire: Mr le Page however said that it would be better for her to have the P. & the D. by themselves in the Drawing room. – The Prince & the Duke were exceedingly affable to her & examined her pictures carefully & praised them: the Prince's favorite was Barroccio's Holy Family, the Duke's Dominichino's Magdalene . . . The Prince departed about 10 – (but not to the Observatory as intended, there being a dense fog): we all departed immediately after. I went home & took off my Cassock & went to the Whist Club at Headlams . . . By the way I should have said that Phelps today took me aside & expressed great contrition for his outbreak at Mrs Havilands: I told him that

---

[56] Geldart had a reputation for hospitality, so much so that the only anecdote of him that survives in the folk-memory of Cambridge is that on his deathbed in 1877 his wife complained that 'poor dear Charles' was not interested in the funeral arrangements, but murmured at the end 'You will let the undergraduates have some of the old sherry' (C.W. Crawley, *Trinity Hall* (1976), p. 147).

the fault was entirely mine in having been rude enough to find fault & that the apology was entirely due from me: I hoped he would show that all was completely right between us by playing a rubber with me at 'the Family' on Friday. – On breaking up from the Whist Club a great fire was lighting up the sky: – as it was in the direction of my Office I was in great alarm lest it should be there or at Scrope Terrace: – it proved to be Charles Finch Foster's Mill on Sheep-Green. It was a most beautiful sight: – no neighbouring houses caught, but the Mill itself was utterly destroyed. – I got back to College a little after 2, & gave permission to some Trinity men to go to the fire, tho I strongly advised them to go to bed & told them they could do no good.

*Wed. 23.* After all the excitement of yesterday I slept very badly & didn't feel half alive when I got up at 8. – Shoals of people came for tickets: – to my surprise an unknown unescorted female came & tho neither young nor pretty said quite gaily & confidently 'A Lady applicant for a Ticket': – I rewarded her boldness by giving one . . . The Plucked men were sadly mortified at not being allowed their degrees in the morning from the hands of the Prince . . . The only degrees which the Prince admitted were the complimentary one of LLD to the Duke of Brabant, & 4 Oxford adeundem . . . Certainly Willy Romilly is a Laodicean: he didn't *take the trouble* of going to the Senatehouse!! – The Galleries were thronged but the Pit would have held more without much inconvenience. – The youngsters did me the favor of giving me 3 rounds of applause & one cheer more as I walked up the Senate house: – Mrs Geldart said afterwards in allusion to this kind greeting that she should like to see a portrait of me with my books in my arms. – When the Prince & the Duke came there was cheering long & loud & most hearty: – they both seemed pleased. – The Orators speech was admirable: he began on very slippery ground, namely the Prince's Election (he Bateson having been the great supporter of Lord Powis): he said, that 6 years ago after mature deliberation the University had committed to him the guardianship of her rights & privileges & had found ever since that he had responded mostly nobly & faithfully to that trust; he then spoke of the honor of the visit, & the interest he exhibited in our working system by attending 2 of our Lectures: – he then addressed the young Duke & spoke warmly of his Mother's attractions & virtues & the high talents & noble conduct of his Father as a King: – he rather surprised us by making no allusion to the young Dukes marriage. – The Duke was highly amused with his Doctors Cap & fairly laughed when it was put on his head: – the Prince smiled at his glee. – I afterwards heard from the V.C. an anecdote about the Duke's scarlet gown. – The V.C. asked him yesterday if he wished to take away his Gown: – 'Oh yes! said he, I shall put it on & walk with my cap in my hand into the drawing room at Windsor to surprise my Duchess'. – The V.C. sent for a tailor, – & he sat up all night to make the Gown. – Directly after the Senate House proceedings the Prince in his Chancellor's gaudy gown & the Duke in his newly acquired scarlet one went to Willis's Lecture: – I went to this Lecture & am glad to have heard any thing so clever: Willis discretely made it very short: the subject was Rope-making: – the Prince was pleased with it & clapped his hands, – wch was taken up by the rest of the audience. The Prince also begged Willis to come to the lunch at Trinity Lodge. – The Prince then visited the Anatomy Museum[57] (exhibited by Clark), the Library (exhibited by E. Atkinson, the deputy of poor Power), the Observatory & some Colleges & took his departure at 4. Both he & the Duke gave Elwood £5. – There was one very unfortunate omission in this hurried visit: the Chancellor forgot to call at Corpus Lodge: – Mrs Pulling was of course languishing to present his god-child to the Prince, & perhaps thinking he would condescend to kiss the bantling. – & the Nurse was all in her best pinners both days: – but no Prince came. – Caius, Pembroke, Magdalene, Emmanuel & Downing were not visited: – one of the Fellows (Mr Anderson) gave lunch to a party of young ladies & one old one (Miss Apthorp) that they might see the Prince walk about the college: – they staid till pitch dark & long after the Prince had left Cambridge in vain expectation. – The Prince pleased the V.C. by sending him word that he was going sight seeing in his *black* gown: the V.C. of course rightly interpreted this into a hint to him to put off his scarlet & come also in black. – In the Evening read loud 'the Persian Princes'.[58]

*Th. 24.* Lucy not out again. – After setting my office to rights & clearing away all the Cards of the late applicants for Tickets I worked away steadily (with closed doors) in my office at a List of Taxors for 150 years & of Proctors for 70: – Sent off my 2 Lists to Mr Hardy of the Record Office in the Tower[59] . . . Dined at 'the Officers' dinner at the V.C's: – Bateson was the most dignified person there & took in Mrs Geldart: I sat on her other side. – She was in diamonds & gave real turtle, 2 sorts of ice & all as if we had been Princes. – Bateson afterwards bantered me on the warm praise I administered to our hostess: – but I think she deserved every tittle of it, & one cannot too greatly admire a lady of delicate health who professes (& I believe truly) to act on this great principle, 'it's my duty & therefore I shall do it: – I shan't break down, because I know its my duty to go thro with it' . . . Harvey Goodwin was at this dinner: he & I were speaking about his Church: I said 'there are but 2 things interesting about it, that Latimer preached there in the days of old & that H.G. preaches there now'. – He laughed & said, – 'that's just like the Perse School: 'Jeremy Taylor was educated there & Charles Clayton, – & no other person is named between' . . .

*Sat. 26.* . . . I have accidentally omitted one or 2 matters about the Prince's visit: e.g. – Mrs Geldart told me that if she had previously known the Prince she would have had Mrs Pulling's baby & nurse at her house because the Prince *ought* to have seen it. – The Prince spoke highly of the conduct of

---

[57] Properly the 'Anatomical Museum' of specimens used by the professors of anatomy and physic to illustrate their lectures. Its accommodation in a corner of the former Botanic Garden had become quite inadequate, and plans were afoot to redevelop the whole area for museums, laboratories, and lecture rooms. See Willis and Clark, III, 159-65. The regulations of this and other institutions with details of their staff and opening were revised each year in the *Cambridge University Calendar.*

[58] An account of a royal visit by J.B. Fraser published in 1838. Romilly had read it before.

[59] Doubtless Thomas Duffus Hardy, the archivist, who became Deputy Keeper of the Public Records.

the young men in the Senatehouse, – their remaining perfectly quiet as soon as the actual business began. – The Prince went to Christs so very long after the time expected that all the Fellows (except Shaw) had deserted the Master: – the Prince did not go into the Lodge: – Milton's admission was exhibited to him; he visited Milton's mulberry tree.[60] – He went to Catharines & went up into Mrs Philpotts drawing room & shook hands with her. – At 8.45 this morning to the Chapel to elect a Senior in the place of Campbell: – Moody & Wilkinson (both Senior to Thompson) & Thompson were present: – Moody & Wilkinson both declined: – we elected Thompson unanimously & (as tomorrow is Sunday) swore him at once . . .

*Sun. 27.* . . . I afterwards went to St. Mary's to hear H. Goodwins concluding sermon . . . the church was crammed: – by the way he was greatly applauded in the Senate House on Wednesday. – His subject was the call of St Matthew: he dwelt at great length on the call wch a Candidate for Ordination professes, '*moved* by the Holy Ghost, *called* by Christ: he said that a man might conscientiously so declare when he was impressed with the sacredness of his duty & resolved to do it to the best of his ability, feeling that the choice of Parents, his own inclination etc were all marks of God's having pointed out the Ministry as his career. He said that 5/6 of the young men before him were probably destined for the Church, & he trusted that no one of them would be impelled by so base & unholy a motive as seeking after the fleece instead of saving the lost sheep . . . Our Harriet is in despair at St. Johns Coll. intending to reduce her Mothers salary as a Laundress by £40!! – It appears that that is only 1/3d of her annual receipts for these last 35 years. – It will be a sad loss to her.

*Mon. 28.* . . . Bowtell (the Bookbinder) called on me about getting an allowance from the Hobson Trustees for prentising his son (as his uncle had given £500 towards that Charity[61]): – I advised him to go directly to the Spinning House: – he caught the Trustees sitting & they instantly granted him £10, with wch he will apprentise his son to a brother Bookbinder (Armstrong) . . . I had an interview with Willy today . . . 'How does your Father stand his work?'. 'O! very well, I believe: – have you read the attack of him in the Press for having given the place of Clerk of Enrolment to a Mr Wright: they say that when on the Commission he proposed correction of abuses for the Court of Chancery to which he would have no chance of being promoted, but none for the Rolls which he was certain of getting: – & that his present appointment of Wright is the result of his original sin'. – From an interview I had with Mrs Challis it turns out that on *the Tuesday night* altho

---

[60] The tree at Christ's may have existed in Milton's time but it was not associated with him at all until the late eighteenth century. The earliest dated picture of it is an etching of 1838 in J.J. Smith's *Cambridge Portfolio* (1840) accompanied by several pages of fanciful sugary prose and an appalling sonnet. See D.E. Combe, 'Of Milton and Mulberries', *Christ's College Magazine* (1987), 15-20. Joseph Shaw of Christ's (d. 1859) mentions a tea-caddy made of the wood from this tree in his will.

[61] John Bowtell (1753-1813), stationer, historian and wealthy bachelor, bequeathed a large sum to Addenbrooke's Hospital and a more modest one to the Hobson trustees specifically to apprentice boys to useful trades. See *D.N.B.*

there was a complete fog in Cambridge yet it was clear at the Observatory at ½ past 9 & Saturn was peculiarly beautiful, – a double star also was visible, – & Neptune with Adams to exhibit his foundling – but a little before 10 came a message saying that the Prince was not coming in consequence of the Cambridge fog. – The Prince went next day & saw the instruments, especially that for wch Challis gained the Crystal Palace prize.[62] – The Prince seemed pleased at exhibiting every thing to his Cousin.

*Tu. 29.* . . . I learned from the V.C. the history of the unvisited colleges: – the Prince at an *unexpected* time went thro *Clare* & tho the V.C. sent forward a messenger as soon as they got into the avenue the Master etc were not in attendance & the Prince walked thro without seeing any thing: – on returning from the Observatory by Magdalene the Prince said 'We will not get down here, for the great object of interest is the Pepysian Library & it is too late & too dark to examine its treasures': – the Prince could not make time to see Corpus Christi, Emmanuel, Caius or Downing, tho he had promised to visit Worsley: – as for Caius Dr Guest was unwell with influenza & had declined the honor of a visit. – At the visit to Christs college the V.C. said to Col. Grey 'Will you tell his Royal Highness that I fear he will be too late if he lingers here?' Col. Grey declined & the V.C. stept forward to do it himself: the Prince immediately said 'I perceive you are going to tell me I must not stay any longer'. . . . The Duke of Brabant was very gracious to the V.C. at taking leave & said (with a warm long shake of the hand) 'I have been so happy, I shall like very much to come again: – you must come & see me in Belgium' . . .

*Th. 1 December.* . . . I had an interview with Mrs Challis: she told me that the Bidwells are intensely happy in the Victoria Asylum & that they say 'they don't know what to call it but being in Paradise' . . . I learn that Theed has been ousted from the Viceprovostship: – This is a Puseyite movement got up by Williams: Bacon is one of the highfliers. – *Bacon* has been elected by a majority of 1: Kirwan (the firebrand who is at feud with the Provost the Patron of the dull amiable inefficient Theed) was the abetter of the Plot: – the Number of 7 voters could not be raised for any one Candidate by the Senior Fellows, so the Juniors were called in to the discomforture of Theed . . .

*Fri. 2.* Lucy (thank God) seems better. – She made the most of this bright day. She paid a visit to Mrs Shedd & promised Mary Kelly the dirty squinting little maiden of all work (age 16) a frock at Christmas if she stays in her place: – the love of finery will doubtless work her . . . she also went to see M.A. Tyler & had the spirit to send back a jacket wch M.A. professed to have rectified, but it was all wrongified. All this (& more) she did before my return to walk with her. – At 1½ she started with me in her best bonnet to visit the Fitzwilliam, or rather to wish Massey joy of his raised salary: – she has a feeling that Massey has been useful & may continue to be useful to her in her pet scheme of getting an Assistants place for Walter Watts. She shook hands with him & was very civil: she allowed him to show her some prints of Natural history (particularly a portrait of an Ant-eater), Salvator Rosa's etchings,

---

[62] Challis had been awarded a medal for calculating the corrections for a transit instrument.

Callot's beggars, the oldest Engraver Schooen, & facsimile of papyrus writing given by Duke of Northumberland. We both (& she particularly) pretended to be deeply interested in what he exhibited: – he favored us with the history of his fall from a ladder in the Library with a minute account of the injury done to his leg & his side. – We then proceeded to see the débris of the houses pulled down for the enlargement of the market: – a glorious opening: – Lucy had here the satisfaction of ascertaining from a waggoner that an old horse wch she had often seen with his tongue out of his mouth as over-worked was perfectly happy & always had that habit from a fole of lolling his tongue out: she gave the Waggoner /6. – We then went to Ladds where Lucy bought a pretty blue Pellisse for little Fordham. – Finding that for the last 2 days I walked with pain in consequence of a very small lump under the sole of my foot I went to Ficklin's: he was examining some candidates for the Militia (of whom he passed 7 & rejected 1) . . . Letter from G.T.R. saying there were prospects of another child – wrote to wish him joy.

*Sat. 3.* . . . At Lucy's desire I got Welsford to write 10 Cards for Walter Watts (Candidate for Assistant Place in Fitzwilliam Museum): – he wrote them beautifully . . . Broadley paid me a long visit about his Testimonials . . . He told me that several Ladies declined going into the Senate House when the Prince was here because the V.C. in his notice about Tickets only spoke of *persons* & did not mention *ladies*: – they didn't like to be called *persons*!! I suppose we must call them *jenny-asses*! . . . I learned yesterday from Patrick Beales that both the Kings mill & Newnham mill were occupied by C. Finch Foster, that C.F. Foster thinks Newnham mill was destroyed by combustibles thrown into the windows, – but the workmen & Beales & every body else thinks it was Friction of the machinery. – In Patrick Beales Office I perceived a strong smell like rotten cheese: he told me that it came from the salvage flour after the fire wch he had harboured for a short time in his warehouses . . .

*Sun. 4.* . . . I then went to the ruins of Newnham mill: – I was surprised to find them still smouldering. – In the Evening read loud the 1st of Harvey Goodwins short Sermons for the Sacrament: – it was a hard mischievous sermon suggestive of difficulties, – speaking of the impossibility of God revealing himself to man except as man.

Romilly spent three days, 8-10 December, in town. Waiting on Cambridge station for the 9.30 express to London he identified no less than six Heads of Houses, one of whom, Webb, 'seemed bent on private business for he was carrying a large tin filthy oil-can'. Romilly's private business was more salubrious. He bought a dozen calico shirts, stockings for the maids, flannel waistcoats for Lucy and himself and 'toothbrushes and powder etc. etc'. He stayed with Sophie and Kennedy and was delighted to find a 'very radiant and happy' Frankie just home for the holidays; the news from his other cousins the Edward Romillys was much less good because of his mother-in-law's violent states of excitement. Edward was honest enough to confess that Mrs Marcet's death would be the greatest relief to him and Sophy. However the old lady continued to live in Stratton Street until 1858 when she died aged 89.

*Sun. 11.* Lucy & I didn't go to Church: she never stirred out: – I read the Lessons etc to her & in the Evening H. Goodwin's Sermon 'Wherewithal shall a young man cleanse his ways'? . . . By the way Lucy did a thing today that met my warmest approbation: – she saw an Irishwoman & husband & children: she gave plenty of Maggie's cakes to the little beasties, & a quantity of old shawls etc & 11d in money to the Mother. – At Lucy's suggestion I wrote to Philpott to ask him when the Assistants would be appointed by the Managing Syndicate & how many: – he very civilly called after St Mary's & said that he had jogged the V.C. already & would jog him again tomorrow . . . A propos of writing, Lucy had suggested to Mrs Sandfield calling upon Dr Tatham (touching the proposed reduction of her Salary as Hall Laundress) from £120 to 80 p.a.): he received her very kindly, said he knew nothing about it & sugggested her writing him a Letter: – she confessed she was no scholar, so he advised her to get somebody to do it for her: Mrs Sandfield is not learned even in her own craft for she didn't know whether she was a Laundress or a Laundry!! – Harriet in the course of the Evening wrote a very good letter in her Mothers name: – her Mother will leave it tomorrow. – I today wrote also to Col. Glover telling him I had neither time nor inclination to read controversial Theology & returning him 'the Catholic Layman' & 'Achilli's Herald':[63]– I afterwards met him & he asked me what would have been the state of religion if Luther had been like me . . .

*Wed. 14.* . . . My bedmaker gave me a Thermometer & a blotting paper roller left her by one of her gentlemen: – I gave her 2/6. – Lucy made an escapade today which made me uneasy: – She started for a ramble at 20' to 3 about a brooch for Sarah & then made a 2d start at 3½ in the cold fog to buy boots for a little Carter: – she didn't get home till ½ past 4, & was greatly chilled & had scarcely any breath in her body. She wisely had a hot mixture of spiced beer with a little portwine & afterwards had her bed warmed . . .

*Fri. 16.* Lucy not out. – We this morning received a letter from Philpott saying that the Election of 2 Assistants had taken place at the Fitzwilliam Museum & that Watts was not elected. – that there had been 20 Candidates, many of them very good ones. – Philpott was very sly & never mentioned that one of the successful Candidates was Frisby (*his own butler*) who had put up for the Curatorship of Pictures: – the other was Ellwood a brother of the Marshalls: – he had been acting as a supernumerary: therefore his Election was quite natural & proper: – Frisby may also be a fit man, but it looks like a job . . . Wrote to Walter sending him £5 as salve for his disappointment: – gave Lucy also a very little salve (to the amount of £1). – knocked term on the head at 10. – At 11 to Chapel for the Commemoration Service: – I never saw the Chapel so empty on this occasion . . . Sedgwick gave me an account of the death of his sister Isabel just 30 years ago: the night she died Isabel (his niece) was born. He looks on the death of this favorite sister as the greatest domestic calamity of his life: – she had never had an hours illness till she met with an accident in Portsmouth dockyard from the effects of wch she died in 6 months . . . She seems to have been of a most sweet temper, utterly fearless, & the greatest tomboy alive: – she would ride astride & would climb the tallest

---

[63]  i.e. the *Achill Missionary Herald and Western Witness* (Co. Mayo) and the *Catholic Layman*, a Dublin journal that ran from 1852 to 1858.

trees to look into magpies' nests. – Dined at the grand Commemoration Dinner, wch is revived with something of its pristine splendor: – but we had no band in the gallery as in the days of old. – I read Grace with the Master . . .

*Sat. 17.* . . . Summoned to the V.C.'s in consequence of a Letter from Lord Palmerston asking what we are doing in compliance with the suggestions of the Royal Commission: – a Convocation is called for Friday & I have agreed to be in my Office from 12 to 2 all the preceding days to show the Letter to all Members of the Senate.[64] – A grateful letter from Walter Watts. – I should have mentioned before that Mrs Sandfield's letter to Dr Tatham proved a complete failure (tho suggested by himself): he afterwards informed her that he had ceased having anything to do with College Accounts & Mr Hiley (whom she again visited) told her that the reduction would begin from Christmas . . .

*Mon. 19.* Not nearly so cold, as there was no wind: – but not a day for a delicate creature like Lucy to venture out . . . She had a long interview with Harvey (Collector for the Victoria Asylum) & gave our usual 5/ for a Xmas dinner to the Asylum. – Sat up in state at my office from 12 to 2 to exhibit Lord Palmerston's Letter to Prince Albert: the 5 Points of it (– for it is like Calvinism & the Charter in having 5) are these: 1st – Improved representation of our different orders; 2dly – Extended education to poorer students: 3dly – destruction of bye-Fellowships & all appropriations: 4thly curtailing the tenure of Fellowships without people will come & reside & take active part in public education or *in private study*!! – 5thly –abstracting from the College funds for the support of Professors etc. –

As for No 2 I utterly abominate the idea of swamping us with poor beggarly students who ought to be tinkers & tailors. – Finished the Life of Abernethy & began the life of Toussaint L'Ouverture.[65]

*Wed. 21.* Lucy alas! don't get a bit better & won't see a doctor . . . At the Office from 12 to 2 showing the Letter. That tiresome Broadley inflicted himself on me for 2 mortal hours! – he took over that loutish eldest Shilleto all thro the snow with him in an open gig to hear him (B) do duty at Arrington: –

64 Unlike Lord John Russell, the Home Secretary was well acquainted with Cambridge University, where he had been educated and which he had represented in Parliament between 1811 and 1831. His letter dated 12 December to the Chancellor was typically ceremonious yet firm; as the Commission report had appeared more than a year ago, some formal and wide-ranging response was now expected. Rather pointedly he rehearsed the main topics that the government wished to see addressed and legislated for, i.e. the constitution should be changed; the number of students should be increased with proper regard for those of limited means; rules about fellowships and scholarships should remove restrictions and open competition; fellowships should not be sinecures but either be held for a limited time or continued only for the active; and finally the colleges should give financial support to the general purposes of the university. The letter is printed with the report of the syndicate that framed a reply (to the first two points only), that was unanimously confirmed by Grace on 13 January 1854, in *Annals*, V, 135-48. See also Winstanley, pp. 274-8.

65 Both books were new, i.e. J.R. Beard's account of the Haitian black who resisted Napoleon's attempts to reimpose slavery and died in a French prison in 1803, and G. Macilwain's *Memoirs* of John Abernethy (d.1831), the first surgeon of his day, whose reputation was kept alive by tales of his cantankerousness and eccentricity.

the idea of encountering stormy weather to hear such a preacher proves the lad an idiot. Broadley told me a story about the Bishop of Worcester wch highly amused me: – 'The Bishop saw an Omnibus-driver ill-using his horse & reprimanded him sharply, whereupon the Coachman slanged him & was impertinent: – but a man sitting by the Coachman said "do you know that was the Bishop of Worcester whom you abused so?" – "No! was it? I would not have done it for £100 had I known it for all his servants etc go by my buss & I bring no end of parcels to the Palace": presently the Bishop turned into his own gate: so Jarvey resolved to run after him & apologise: – so he pulled up sharp, gave the reins to a man, & *whip in hand* ran after the Bishop: – the Bishop seeing him thought the insolent Coachman was coming to horsewhip him, took to his episcopal legs & ran for dear life & got into his house before Coachee overtook him'. – Began reading 'Legend of Montrose'.[66]

*Fri. 23.* . . . Convocation concerning Syndicate to answer Lord Palmerston's Letter: the Caucussites presented a request (there being 40 present) to add the words 'such remarks having been 1st submitted to the Senate for their approval'. – The V.C. very wisely agreed to their Petition & the Grace was carried 'nem. con.' . . .

*Sat. 24.* I followed Lucy's advice & planted myself at the Library-door 5' before 10: there were congregated about 20 persons waiting for the opening of the door . . . I placed myself quite close to the door, & Rusby told me that I must run upstairs as hard as I could, for that every body would try to pass me: – so away we went helter-skelter I keeping ahead: I rushed into compartment Y & seized on 'Lewis Arundel' & then turned to catch 'Heir of Redclyffe', – but it was snapt up & so was 'My Novel': – I rather hope that Rusby carried off 'Heir of R'. as he said he was come to get a novel beginning with R for a Lady. – Skinner (every action & every word of whom is always unpleasing to me) was humbug enough to say 'whenever I find another person wants the same book as myself I give it up to him'!! If so what possessed him to come to get the 1st chance?[67] . . .

*Sun. Christmas Day.* Lucy very much the same: not well enough (alas!) to go to Church, wch seems so unnatural & so uncomfortable on this double Festival. – Gave her 10/ by way of Xmas Box: 2/6 to Harriet & Dosia & 1/ to Sarah . . . We had an excellent Turkey & Ham for dinner & Dosia dressed them admirably . . .

*Mon. 26.* Today kept as holiday for Xmas day. – I shut myself up in my office & worked steadily till 4 in spite of kicking & rattling at my outer door . . . I hear that Mr Girdlestone is benevolently going to set up a Baker to sell flour to the people at this time of dearness for 2/6 instead of 3/11: what an

---

[66] By Walter Scott.

[67] By virtue of its copyright accessions the University Library held an expanding quantity of popular fiction to be carried off promptly by senior members for themselves or their friends and thumbed to bits. The opening of the town's Free Library in 1855 did not relieve this demand as its small budget was reserved for serious work of an improving sort, and borrowing was not permitted at first. As the University Librarian grumpily reported in 1865, 'for years the principal work of the Library has been to compete with the circulating libraries to the waste of assistants' time and of money spent on rebinding'.

admirable clergyman he is ! . . . In yesterday's history I should have mentioned that I preached in Chapel for Sedgwick (who is still prisoner with a bad cold): I preached a Sermon of Mr Boyer's wch I preached in the same place in the years 1844 & 1849. The Master was absent: there were not 20 people in Chapel: – Mr Glover & I required no help in administering the Sacrament . . . I was amused by 2 boys coming this Evening from the Pitt Press: they had collected 3/ towards a dinner next Wednesday: – I gave the poor urchins a shilling to help it on . . .

*Tu. 27.* . . . Seniority at Sedgwick's rooms: present the Master, Sedgwick, I, Thompson, Moody, Cooper, Monro, Mate & Hedley. We discussed 2 matters: 1st Edlestons Petition & then Lord Palmerston's letter.

With regard to the Petition Moody thought it ought to be an entirely amicable suit, that we ought to pay Edlestons expenses, that we ought immediately to retain Bethel & Roundel Palmer: – & that he thought we (the supporters of Thompson) should be defeated.[68] –

With regard to Lord Palmerstons Letter the Master is for giving increased advantages to resident fellows & for paying more to the Officers (Steward, Head Lecturer etc etc), for diminishing the tutorial £10 per pensioner to £4 & giving the other £6 towards paying college lecturers on new subjects & to University purposes. – I was summoned at 3 to the Vice Chancellor's. He told me that poor Mill died on Sunday, & wished me to tell him what he had to do: he also wanted to know about the Matriculations of the Dean of Windsor & Latimer Neville: He wished me to write him 2 official separate notes on these points: – wch of course I afterwards did: – Geo. Neville was matriculated a Nobleman & sat in Golgotha among the Noblemen on the right of the V.C.: – Latimer Neville was matriculated a Pensioner: he is to have no precedence . . . Mr Deighton today paid me a visit to ask a great favor. His son (a freshman at Christs) was highly provoked at the account wch his Father gave of the insulting manner in wch he had been treated by Mr Edmund Foster: – so he rose abruptly from the dinner table & went in search of E.F: – he met him on Kings Parade, called him a d–d liar & an insolent blackguard & afterwards struck him!!! Any thing more brutish one cannot conceive. – Mr Deighton says that Mr E.F. has always behaved very ill to him in the matter of the St Michael's Rate (in wch he Deighton is £200 out of pocket) & that he recently brought an action against Mr D in the Counties Court for part of the salary of the organist but that Mr E.F. was nonsuited because of a misnomer . . . Mr E.F. has given notice that young Deighton is to be tried at the Quarter Sessions next Monday. The favor Mr D. had to beg was that I would call on Mr Edm. F. & intercede for mercy on the promise of the young ruffian making any abject apology that E.F. shall dictate. – I expressed myself to Mr D in round terms of abomination of his son's conduct, but undertook to call upon Mr E.F. – I did so at his office in Green Street: I pleaded earnestly for mercy, saying that imprisonment would be a blot on a collegian's character

---

[68] Joseph Edleston, the uncomfortable fellow of Trinity, was about to appeal to the Queen as visitor of his college complaining that W.H. Thompson, the new Regius Professor of Greek, had been allowed to keep his fellowship and emoluments contrary to the Elizabethan statutes. See 6 March 1854 and 3 December 1857.

from wch he could not recover, – that it would break his heart & his fathers, & that a kind-hearted & religious man like himself would be most reluctant to push the punishment to so extreme a length. – I obviously softened him: he said that he would consult with his brothers & let me know the result . . .

*Th. 29.* I looked at our out-of-doors thermometer before Breakfast & to my horror found it at 7!! 25 degrees of frost . . . I had charity letters from Lord Bayning etc wch required answer & one from poor Mill's son-in-law (Benjamin Webb) inviting me to the Funeral next Sat. in Ely Cathedral: – I wrote as kind & sympathising a letter as I could & said that I was detained in Cambridge on Sat. by 'Subscriptions'.

Put on (for the 1st time) a pair of India Rubber clogs: – vastly comfortable . . . Some hours later came a letter from Mr E.F. saying that all his brothers were of opinion that the case was beyond an apology, as young Mr Deighton had stated before the Magistrates that E.F. had repeatedly insulted his Father, & that neither of the Deightons had retracted this assertion or exprest any contrition . . .

*Fri. 30.* . . . Lucy had a Letter from 'the Indigent Blind Visiting Society':[69]– I believe she has given this Society before: but as her eyes are weak & her pity strong she gives to all such Institutions: she wrote an autograph Letter & sent 5 Guineas. – I wrote to George Romilly & sent him £10 – . I also wrote (for Lucy) to Mrs Bernard who wants (if you please!) to know what society will help her in sending up her son (age 21) & wanting to be a Clergyman) to College: – I told her there was no such society: she must send him in the cheapest grade to the cheapest college, – a Sizar to St Johns: – there is nothing lower than that . . . Very severe weather for poor Mrs Mill & Mrs Webb to attend the Funeral.

[69] Established in 1834 it continued under this name into the present century.

Proctorising

# 1854

*Th. 5 January.* Saw a sleigh pass by. – See by the Newspaper that the Queen drives out in a sleigh. – Great deal of snow – Poor Lucy has caught an atrocious cold & sore throat.

*Fri. 6.* Lucy passed a bad night & most wisely consented to see a medical man *if he didn't come too early*: she selected Lestourgeon as *an old woman*: I sent a note to him at 11 stating her shortness of breath, her very bad cold & affection of the throat. – About 12½ he called on her: she had got herself & the room in apple-pie order: she was pleased with him, finding him kind & cheerful & a man who didn't frighten Mr Dick. He asked her very few questions & seemed to think he understood her case perfectly & spoke encouragingly about setting her up. – He told her immediately that there was an affection of the heart: he listened to its beating but she told him he ran no chance because she wore so many clothes: – she thought he judged by the color of her lips, – in which she showed much observation: – for he afterwards called upon me & described her case minutely: he said that the purple colour of her lips showed a wrong circulation in the heart, that he saw no necessity whatever for sending for Bond, that he should dissuade her mounting many stairs to her bedroom, & that he would watch her case most carefully, that she must eat what is digestible & abstain from veal & pastry. – She took this intelligence most cheerfully . . . She very discretely agreed to exchange bedrooms with me for the present . . . Saw a letter from Miss Beart communicating poor Gunning's death last Wednesday: – he died calmly & without pain: – shortly before his death (I know not whether on the very day) the Dr said 'Can I do any thing to give you relief'?: to wch he answered 'God alone can give me relief' . . .

*Mon. 9.* Lucy very much the same; possibly a little better in spite of her sad cold & wheezing cough: – her ancles have swelled; which Lestourgeon considers part of the same complaint, & also a painful, suffocating sensation in the throat: – God grant these ills may gradually be subdued . . . Seniority in Sedgwick's rooms at 10: we sat for 2½ hours & our emendations are to be printed & ready for us at an adjourned meeting at 6½ this Evening: – Martin has suggested & we have adopted 2 grand improvements; the 1st is giving prizes to the Sizars and Subsizars, £25 if they are in the 1st class, £15 if in 2d, & £10 if in 3d; – the same prizes after they become Scholars: – the 2d is agreeing to commute the 3 annual Westminster Scholarships[1] into Exhibitions

---

[1] The Elizabethan Statutes of 1560, stated that boys from Westminster School should be preferred to other candidates for scholarships, and that the Dean and Chapter of Westminster 'may frame statutes with the consent of Trinity College and of Christ Church, Oxford, as to the studies to be prosecuted in the said school, and the mode of electing the head master and under master thereof'. Trinity had become aware that Westminster scholars were often inferior intellectually to other scholars and therefore welcomed the Royal Commission's recommendation that scholarships appropriated to particular schools should be converted into exhibitions. See Winstanley, pp. 341-3, and a fuller history in W.W. Rouse Ball, *Cambridge Papers* (1918), pp. 48-70.

of £40 p.a., these exhibitioners to be eligible into Scholarships: we shall thus gain 12 open Scholarships . . .

*Tu. 10.* . . . At 12 to the Senatehouse to declare the Vacancy of Esquire Bedell[2] . . . Consulted Leapingwell about fees of this B.A. Commencement: he is of decided opinion that those paid before Gunnings death are due to his Executor: – I am very glad of this as 2 bedridden deranged sisters of Gunnings are still alive & without any means of support now their brother is dead. – When Gunning gave that grand dinner 2 or 3 years ago (wch cost him £50) he was quite deranged: – he had (as Leapingwell tells me) drawn out £400 (of the £500 from an insurance on his life) & had taken a farm and stocked it!! . . . Sedgwick seemed sleepy at the Seniority. – After it was over he went to the Marchesa's & was there seized with one of his distressing bleedings at the nose: – the Marchesa & Meggie accompanied him to his rooms & begged him to send immediately for Paget, wch he did . . . Bought for Lucy (at her desire) a Respirator: – the new Patent, very clever & very cheap, only 2/6 . . .

*Wed. 11.* Lucy very much the same . . . Sedgwick called on me upon his way to the Marchesa: Paget gave him 5 gr. of Calomel yesterday & he is a deal better: Paget prescribes mental idleness, so he has taken to Scott's Tales of a Grandfather . . . At tea time she [Lucy] said 'Just look in the tea-kettle & see whether that untidy Sarah has left in it the cloth with which I was cleaning its inside when she came & took it away in a hurry': – I immediately seized the toasting fork & plunged it into the kettle with all the eagerness wch was displayed by the sons of Eli in fishing for meat in the cauldrons: – to my infinite amusement I found a coloured duster! it would have served Sarah right to have made her wear it all day as a turban . . .

*Tu. 17.* . . . Mr Barron today asked me to write to Thacker about A.N. Bates' debt of £1. 11. 9: I declined, Barron admitting that he had already had a personal interview with Thacker . . .

*Wed. 18.* Lucy perhaps a little better . . . The new Master of Magdalene vastly happy etc. Today A.N. Bates paid me his fees, so I thought this was an occasion to urge him to pay his debt to Barron: I did so pretty stoutly: – he no doubt was greatly astonished & somewhat frightened: – he said he had never seen the man, he affected to call him Barrow, said that he had bothered him with letters: – I told him it was very natural he should have done so, that the sum was important to a petty tradesman, etc etc: – he promised me that he would pay. – It turned out comically enough that Lucy at the same time was exerting herself for Mr Barron . . .

*Th. 19.* . . . At 9 I went to the Law Schools for the Election of an Esquire Bedell: – Liveing of St Johns watched for Godfray, & Shilleto for Roberts . . . St Johns & Jesus Colleges were the greatest supporters of Godfray; Roberts had a majority of Trinity. Lord Braybrooke & Charles Neville & Arthur Saville & Lord Charles Hervey voted for Roberts: – so did all Magdalene except Hicks. – I was glad to learn when I got home that Bates kept his word: – he has paid Barron . . .

---

[2] On the letter from Miss Beart announcing Gunning's death Sedgwick wrote, 'My dear Romilly, – I have just received this letter. 'Tis all over with this world's life of our warm-hearted old friend.'

*Fri. 20.* Lucy very much the same. – An end to my early exits so we had our breakfast in peace & quiet. – We fully expected Lestourgeon today & when he went in at the Fosters made sure of his coming to us, – but he was treacherous. – A most curious incident occured at my rooms today: a man came & wrote down the name of Weston of Emmanuel presenting a professorial certificate & offering 3 Guineas: I having no papers for such a man put a few questions, when it turned out that the subscriber was not Mr Weston, but that he had come to do a kindness to his friend: – I told him that he had committed a most serious offence, that he had been guilty of no less an enormity than forgery & cautioned him most gravely against ever again daring to sign another man's name. – I received a visit from Godfray: I congratulated him most cordially & he expressed much gratitude for my support. He is going to publish the Poll: so I told him to send to my house for the Cards at 4[3] . . . Wrote to Betsy in answer to a most kindhearted affectionate letter of hers about Lucy: her children are recovered & she is looking forward to her approaching confinement . . .

*Sun. 22.* . . . In my walks I fell in with Philpott who has just been visiting the Queen & preaching in Windsor Chapel: – he says the Queen & Prince are good Church & Chapel goers: that the Chapel at Windsor holds about 70 & is very gay with the uniforms of a large proportion of the congregation: – the Prince of Wales & Princess Royal have a gallery to themselves, & the rest of the Royal children are with the Queen & Prince . . .

*Tu. 24.* . . . Alston (the Grocer) who patronises his nephew *John Manser* for the London Orphan, called this morning . . . he came all gratitude to announce the Election of John Manser (who came in last with 195 votes): – I shook hands with him & heartily congratulated him . . . What a contrast in point of numbers with Maria Blencowe whom Lucy with immense exertion brought in at the head of the Poll with more than 10,000 votes![4] . . .

*Wed. 25.* Lestourgeon came: – Lucy complained of the medicine being too powerful: so he has directed her to take only ½ the quantity each time & has not increased the number of times: – recommends Sal. Volatile if the Medicine makes her faint or sick . . . Today arrived from Ficklin & Bumpsted a bill to Lucy for July 1852!! On referring to my accounts & also to my journal I of course found that I had paid it at the time . . . Letter from George Romilly stating his religious feelings & consulting me about his returning to College & becoming a Clergyman: – Lucy & I laid our heads together & produced a long elaborate letter stating my utter disapprobation of the scheme, on account of the annoyance of the Little-Go, Great-Go & Voluntary Theological,[5] my utter want of interest in the Church, – the difficulty of

---

[3] Publishing the details of elections (that is who voted openly for whom) to such offices as those of the Chancellor, Registrary and Librarian, had been a monopoly of Gunning for most of the century.

[4] See 5 July 1849. In 1833 at Dulwich Lucy spent months determinedly canvassing for her protégée, Maria Blencowe, and secured 3,000 votes more than any of the rival candidates for charity.

[5] One of the more patent anomalies of Cambridge studies until recent times had been their failure to offer appropriate training for the large numbers of men intending to become Anglican priests. How indeed could it be said that the admission of dissenters would enfeeble

*beginning* parochial work at his time of life, – the fatigue & anxiety of a parish etc etc: I hope & trust that we shall have completely settled this matter . . .

*Fri. 27.* . . . I yesterday flew at a Clarehall man named Faught for his dilatoriness, – he not having yet applied to Sir James Stephen for his Certificate: – I told him that if he had been as slow in preparing for his degree his chance of success was small, & that in after life he would be left behind in every profession. – To my very great surprise he made his appearance today with the certificate in his hand: – I immediately shook hands with him most heartily, said that he had completely reinstated himself in my good books by his energy of himself going to town & having an interview with Sir James Stephen & that I heartily hoped he would pass thro the Examination: – my good wishes were not however realised, for he was plucked! . . .

*Sat. 28.* Lucy I thought a little better. – She & I both had letters from pretty Nancy: – but we burnt them without answering . . . Breakfasted at Munro's 'paternal' breakfast:[6]– I sat between Dr Kennedy & Maxwell our highest man (2d Wrangler): – Maxwell is said to be the cleverest man of the year, & it is prophecied that he will be a great philosopher.[7] – Dr Kennedy gave me an account of the 'Monitor' row at Harrow: – a son of Baron Platt (as Monitor) chastised severely another boy; Lord Royston interfered & Platt said he would thrash him: – Ld Royston wrote to his Father to ask if he was to submit: Ld Hardwicke said in reply that of course he was, – it being the discipline of the school; – Dr. Vaughan however considered Platt to have behaved harshly & degraded him to the bottom of the Monitors: – whereupon Baron Platt came & fetched his son away. – Lord Palmerston a short time ago wrote an official letter of enquiry concerning the system of Monitors[8] . . . I learned a rich story in the Senate House about Harvey Goodwin: some ladies were coming to visit him: in the same railway-carriage were Clayton & one of the Perownes: they lamented with long-drawn faces over the mischievous tendency of H.G.'s writings, considered his views to be Gnostic, & thought the defection from Evangelical views truly lamentable in the son of a sincere Christian. They were disagreeably surprised by H.G. meeting these ladies on the Cambridge

the university as a seminary for the church? The only requirement was a certificate of attendance at a quota of the lectures delivered by the Norrisian Professor of Divinity that was presented before ordination. During their term as Vice-Chancellor both Graham and Archdall failed to devise an acceptable scheme, but in the teeth of opposition from Professor Corrie a 'voluntary theological examination' was instituted in 1842. When Whewell characteristically alerted the bishops to its desirability and importance the pretence that it was at all voluntary fell away and the number of candidates exploded; in 1843 there 14 and in 1850 more than 200. See Winstanley, pp. 168-74, and Searby, pp. 265-8.

6   i.e. it was given by the college praelector or 'father'.

7   He was, being James Clerk Maxwell.

8   Although brutality of many kinds had long been rife in the old public schools and has been minutely chronicled, this case seems more than usually vicious. For 'cheek' on the sports field the victim was thrashed 31 times across the shoulders with a heavy cane and needed medical attention. Vaughan's demoting Platt from his position as monitor was to no purpose when both boys wrote home and the press soon heard the story. It was a rare lifting of the veil, and Palmerston, an old Harrovian, felt obliged to interfere. See J. Chandos, *Boys Together* (1984), pp. 239-44, and for a contemporary survey of reaction, the *Eclectic Review* 1854 (1), 596-611.

Platform and escorting them to his house . . . The conduct of the youngsters in the Senate House was very riotous & discreditable: – they coupled H. Goodwins name very pointedly with the ultra-high-church party, giving 3 cheers successively for the Bishops of Exeter & Oxford & H.G. – By the way there is a severe article in the Record, pulling to pieces H. Goodwins last University Sermons. – A Trinity man (Rokeby) was wooden Spoon: – a gigantic one was dangled by a string from the Gallery. – The principal imitative sounds were barking of dogs, crowing of cocks, & mewing of cats (for the Catharine Hall men & the Puseyites). – One blackguard youngster gave '3 cheers for the old woman in Scarlet' – meaning the V.C. . . . the V.C. made me guardian of his snuff box while he was conferring the degrees: – I plied him with snuff the moment his work was over . . .

*Mon. 30.* . . . By the way Hopkins star is in the ascendant this year: the Senior & 2d & 3d Wranglers, the 6th, 7th, 8th & 9th are his Pupils: – last January his highest man was 8th, & his servant is reported to have said of him "Master an't placed this year!" – Our neighbours the Fosters had a servants dance tonight: – an annual custom: – Lucy found the noise rather a nuisance . . . Dined with the V.C. & Mrs Geldart at 6½ . . . I pumped Philpott a good deal about the life in a Royal Palace: – the Queen & the Prince breakfast & lunch by themselves & (unless a special audience is vouchsafed) are not seen till 8 o'cl. at dinner: the Queen leaves the Saloon at 11 & every body retires to their own room. There are no Evening Prayers: morning prayers are at 9 in the Chapel: – nobody but the Chaplain (Gerald Wellesley) can see whether the Queen is in her Gallery or not . . . There are 2 different breakfast parties for the guests, one of the ladies & certain officers of the household, the other for equerries, chaplains etc . . . Mrs Geldart told us the following anecdote about the wilfulness & incorrigibility of the Princess Royal: – the Queen lectured her for the haughtiness she had displayed to her young comrades at a child's party & said 'I shall shut you up in the long gallery at the top of the Palace': – 'O! Mamma, that's just where I have been longing to be ever since I can recollect' . . .

*Fri. 3 February.* . . . Visit from Willy . . . he is as poco-curante about his family as ever . . . The matter wch seems really to interest Willy is a Protest of the Questionists against the badness & dearness of the dinners in Hall wch cost 2/ : – he says that at the Eating houses near University College he used to get an excellent dinner of meat & pudding for 1/-, – & at Christmas turkey & mince pie at the same price. – The Smith prizes given today: Routh & Maxwell are pronounced equal. – Dined at the Family at Martins . . . Whewell's anonymous publication on 'the Plurality of worlds' was discussed at great length: – his arguments are to show that all our ideas of moral responsible beings have reference to *men*, & that therefore as such creatures as ourselves cannot (from want of atmosphere, etc etc etc) exist in any of our Planets it is most probable that they at least cannot be inhabited by moral responsible beings[9] . . .

[9] *Of the Plurality of Worlds: an Essay* (1853) was written to prove that we have no reason to believe in the existence of inhabited worlds other than our own, although at that time 'belief in the plurality of Worlds was nearly universal' (I. Todhunter, *William Whewell* (1876), I, 185). The book was widely reviewed and discussed, many distinguished scientists opposing

*Sun. 12.* . . . Wrote to H. Goodwin & gave him £5 for his ragged School. – Lucy's letter to F. Wilderspin was a regular trimmer: it appears that she avails herself of poor Mrs Furnivalls non-interference (– she being out of her mind) – with her servants to dress in a very unbecoming flashy stile. –

At 2 o'clock to St Mary's to hear Eyre's 2d Sermon . . . it was an attack upon the indulgences of sense. I thought him indecorously minute in his details of profligacy. He applied very finely the text from Job 'Thou settest a print on the heels of my feet'. He spoke of a young man going to a certain street, & a particular house & an individual chamber & thinking that the dew or the rain had obliterated all traces of his footsteps, – but they are indelibly stamped in the eternal records of God . . . The sermon was above an hour: – it was listened to with breathless attention. He attacked over-eating & drinking, & addiction to sports & amusements: – but these were not the powerful parts of his sermon . . .

*Mon. 13.* Lucy much the same . . . George's pictures were unpacked: the small one called 'We fly by night' is the most hideous thing I ever saw as far as concerns the flying spirits: – there is a dull leaden tone wch is frightful . . . The large picture is in 2 Compartments & is called Contentment & Regret: – it is a clever well-painted picture: – 'Contentment' is his own wife knitting: – 'Regret' is a female figure who looks as if she was seasick . . .

*Tu. 14.* Valentine Day . . . Met Mr & Mrs Hoskin (who returned to Camb. at 11 last night: she told me that after 3 weeks retirement by the seaside in a snug sheltered spot she found her husband didn't get at all better, so she called in medical aid: – the Surgeon immediately pronounced the lungs to be right but looked down the throat (– wch Humphrey *that wretched general practitioner* (as dismal Jemmy calls him) had never done), pronounced the Uvula to be far too long . . . cut off ½ an inch (– not giving any pain to speak off) & Hoskin is now getting all right, tho he is still advised not to preach for another Sunday. –

The negotiation between the Town & University is painfully broken off: the bone is the insisting on Proctors & Pros being brought before the Town Magistrates for harsh exercise of their authority . . .

*Wed. 15.* . . . The V.C. told me I should have to attend 2 trials tomorrow: one of Parfitt (for sending to the tutors only *parts* of bills) & the other of Headley of Trinity Hall (son of my former Surgeon). – Headley (besides being a glutton & a blackguard & a dunce & a cheat who was plucked at the Little Go for copying) is an impudent profligate. He has taken 2 sets of Lodgings one in the name of Headley, the other in that of Hyde: under the name of Hyde he lives with a woman whom he calls Mrs Hyde . . .

*Th. 16.* . . . Headley's case came on: – he was expelled: – he behaved in a most dastardly manner & with tears intreated for mercy, confessing his *fault* committed in a *moment* of infatuation . . . The Lady (who seems to have behaved quite quietly while here) wisely took her departure last Tuesday, – the Senior Proctor having suggested the prudence of such conduct: – Miss Smith's virtuous indignation broke out very ill-advisedly at her departure & she rejoiced at such people leaving the house: – whereupon Headley said 'that

Whewell's views. See chapters 4-7 of M.J. Crowe, *The Extraterrestial Life Debate 1750-1900* (1986).

comes with a good grace from you who used to sleep every night last term with your Queen's Lodger, & that I can swear before any Magistrate. – This dastardly lie he had to eat afterwards before Miss Smith & the Proctor, when it was declared that he should be confronted with the said Queensman. – Happily my old friend the Surgeon is dead & cannot witness the infamy of his son. – He attempted at 1st to brazen it out to Theed that he was not a University man, but Theed said 'Why! I remember your dining in Kings Hall & know your name to be Headley'. – I don't think Theed's bulldog (Jonathan Smith) – the letter of the lodgings in Botoph Lane – gets well out of the scrape: – he ought to have made out that his lodger was identical with Mr Headley living (within a stone's throw) at Livermore Thurley's: – this discovery was made by Martin (the good old bulldog) . . .

*Sat. 18.* Gave breakfast to Willy, Clark, youngest Nix, Crompton, & Lloyd (friend of Mrs Koe) . . . To the V.C.'s at 10 for the trial of Parfitt the Tailor – he was discommuned till the end of next term for his shameful conduct in the case of a Clare Hall undergraduate (Chambers) to whom he has just sent in a bill of more than £50 for clothes in 5 different quarters, of wch he gave no previous bill either to the Tutor or the young man . . .

*Mon. 20.* Lucy very much the same, but very cheerful under her long stay-at-home-ativeness . . . At 9 I was in the Schools for the Election of the Arabic Professor. – Watson appeared as Vicepresident of Queens: he was refused as no deputies are allowed at this Election: – Drs Cookson & Guest stayed away: – of the 14 present 10 voted for H.G. Williams (nominated by the V.C.) the 4 for Preston were Whewell, Phelps, Worsley & Latimer. – Preston (incomparably the best Arabic Scholar) has lost this election as he did the Hebrew from the rumours spread abroad against his moral character. – He expressed himself to me afterwards as much disappointed at this 2d failure: – the 1st he bore perfectly well, thinking the University had a very good Hebrew Professor in Jarrett . . .

*Tu. 21.* Lucy much the same – She wrote a letter (very amusing) to Harriet Gillson in answer to her announcing the confinement of Mrs G.T. Romilly . . . I have promised to be Godfather & have sent a present of £20: the names are to be Samuel Joseph Maclean . . . A man came to my office today (for whom I copied out gratuitously the Matriculation & degrees of M. Newcomen) & forgot to take off his hat, – I requested him to do so: – he had his revenge in a quiet way: as he was going away he said 'I think you will lose one of your Papers' & pointed to my head where was sticking on the bald crown a paper wch I carried in my hat: – I burst out a laughing at the absurdity . . .

*Fri. 24.* Lucy much the same. – Wedding cards of Mr & Mrs Robert Potts!! he has been ass enough to marry en secondes noces a very young girl of 20 . . . Shilleto has written the following doggrel upon this marriage,

'Why is Jeanetta Barmaid, & to Sots?

Because with ardent spirits she fills Potts'. –

. . . the new Mrs Potts was Jeannette Fison. – I hear there are 11 brothers & sisters: one sister married the purblind Mr Waring: – queer marriages they make with their pretty faces![10] . . . I was amused today by Babington (one of the chief of the Caucusses): – he told me a story about Cartmell (– whom he nicknames 'our friend James'): – some one said in Cartmell's hearing 'Now that the 3 nominating Heads have selected Hardwicke & Harold Browne out of the Candidates for the Norrisian Professorship, the Senate will have to make the choice'. – 'O dear no, (said friend James with uplifted hands & eyes in holy horror) the Heads'. – The following have now announced themselves as Candidates for Burwell;[11] – Dr Bromby & Mr Russell of St Johns, Harvey Goodwin, Cockshott (the fearless Cholera-visiting Curate of Soham), Hulbert, Milton, Thornhill . . .

*Sat. 25.* . . . Letter from the Stamp Office asking a return of Matriculations & Degrees for the year ending Dec. 1853: – this looks well for the abolition of this Knowledge-Tax as the letter was in obedience to an Order from the House of Commons. – I made the following return – Matriculations 436. – Degrees – 3 Mandatory, 5 Hon AM, 260 AM, 5 DD, 3 LLD, 1 MD, 10 BD, 16 LLB, 0 MB, 2 ML – 339 AB: – i.e. 8 at £10; 297 at £6; 339 at £3: – making £436 for Matriculations & 2879 for Degrees: total £3315 . . . I went over the new houses opposite to us: – they are not nearly so good as ours: the only really good room is the drawing room, wch is very handsome: – the approach to the gardens is between 2 high brick walls running for 70 or 80 yards . . .

*Fri. 3 March.* . . . Wrote to Mr Winthrop (of Boston U.S.) expressing at least as much admiration for his Lecture on Archimedes & Franklin as I felt.[12] – Leapingwell said to me today: 'You'll have a good dinner at Phelps' today. – no thanks to his daudling useless wife who can't even keep the Laundress's accounts, much less look after the kitchens: – Phelps orders & looks into every thing about the house, & is a capital hand at frying an Omelet'. – I certainly found the dinner excellent, tho there was no Omelet of his frying . . . Certainly Mrs Phelps conversation is very fiddle-faddle: it consists almost entirely of 'Yes' 'No': – I suspect it is from paucity of ideas & not from compliance with the injunction of 'Let your communication be Yea! Yea! Nay! Nay!'.

*Sat. 4.* . . . I had a letter from a Mr Burd begging for 1/- towards restoration of his miserable tumble-down church: – he is going to write 1000 letters in order to raise £50!! . . . went hunting after young Bowtell to give him a book binding job: – he has left Green St & gone up to Shelleys Row Castle End: – he is obviously a complete pauper: his wife grieved me by saying that old Mr B's affairs at Yarmouth are in a very sad state . . . A bear & a cub were exhibited before our house by a jabbering Frenchman . . . Highly pleased today with a visit from Mr Cockshott: I received him most cordially, shook

---

[10] Potts was twenty years older than his bride whose brother, Lorimer Fison of Caius, studied with him before leaving after 'a boyish escapade', to attain some celebrity as a missionary and anthropologist in Fiji and Australia.

[11] When a vacancy arose in this Cambridge parish the university Senate elected two candidates, and the Earl of Guildford, whose ancestor had secured such patronage, presented one of them. The Senate also elected to the living of Ovington in Norfolk.

[12] *A Lecture introductory to a Course in the Application of Science to Art* (Boston, 1853). Romilly had met Winthrop, 'a well informed conversible man', in 1846 (*Romilly 1842-47*, p. 218).

him most heartily by the hand, told him I took the warmest interest in his success & how greatly I had admired his truly Christian fortitude in the time of Cholera at Soham – my Clerk Welsford (who is a Laodicean) was in my room & must have been astonished at my enthusiasm. – Lucy had an interview with a pretty little Miss Carter & gave her oranges & money for herself & Ale for her sick mother.

*Sun. 5.* No Doctor – Lucy much the same – Read the Lessons to her – Wrote out headings to Sarah's Copybook. – Wrote to Grim in answer to a letter of his containing a paragraph of his own composition on the publication of a Liberal Newspaper called 'the Telegraph': – I thought it rather exaggerated & like bad hustings–declamation. – He told the story of Jeffery having been bored by questions about the Arctic expeditions & cursing the *North Pole*: – Sidney Smith put on a sympathetic face & said 'I have heard him before speak disrespectfully of the Equator'. At 2 to St Mary's: I fell in with Col. Glover at our door & gave him my arm all the way to Church. He told me he was going at 3 to Christ Church Barnwell to hear Mr Titcomb's Children-Lecture wch is always on the 1st Sunday in the Month . . . The Church presented a most interesting spectacle being filled principally with children: – it was intensely full . . . The Service concluded with a pretty hymn (from 'Infants hymns') of thanks for being brought to church. – I was highly pleased with the whole service. Such men as Mr Titcomb are the salt of the earth . . .

*Mon. 6.* . . . Seniority in consequence of Judgment of Lord Chancellor last Saturday that Thompson's Fellowship was vacated when he became Greek Professor. – The Master gave a calm statement of the facts & appointed next Saturday for the Election of a Senior.[13] – Edleston was present at this meeting: Sedgwick expressed himself with great warmth & even acrimony upon the breaking up of brotherly feeling by such an action, & of the peculiar offensiveness of Edleston's having employed such an Attorney as Cooper . . . Munro & I then went to Sedgwick's rooms where he relieved himself by a fresh outbreak against Edleston: – Munro told a story of the dry sarcastic uncomfortable stile of Thompson to Edleston: – Edleston (who has great memory for peoples degrees etc) was asked the date of a man in last century: – he said he didn't know & one couldn't know every thing: – 'Oh, said Thompson, I thought you would have known that because it is so unimportant & useless' . . .

*Fri. 10.* Lucy much the same – no Doctor – Licensing 168 Alehouses from 10 to 2 . . . One amusing thing happened at the licensing: a publican came & was so prepared to swear that after Crouch had mumbled the customary form 'A.B. you are bound etc etc' he seized hold of a dirty book of Crouch's & began kissing it! – The V.C. told me that he had made a most unfortunate oversight at the Levee on Wednesday: after kissing the Queens hand he did not

[13] See 27 December 1853. Lord Cranworth, taking the Queen's part as Visitor, after surveying the Trinity statutes of Elizabeth, Charles II, and Victoria, decided against Thompson and the College. Thompson had ceased to be a fellow in more than name when he was admitted to the professorship of Greek, he had no right to any college dividend while holding the chair, and his election as a Senior was void. All costs had to be met by the College. Thompson intended to resign but was dissuaded. The various statutes are reprinted in *Annals*, V, 160-4.

observe that the Prince did him the honor of holding out his hand (covered with a *black glove*) to shake hands with him. Dr Locock reproved him for this want of vigilance having prepared him to expect such a Courtesy: Dr Ainslie (the V.C.'s assistant Magistrate) suggested that the Prince wore a glove to show his hand was not to be kissed. – There was a Turk at the Levee: as he could not show respect by taking off his turban he uncovered his feet & appeared in stockings without shoes! . . .

*Sat. 11.* . . . Before breakfast to Chapel to elect a Senior. To my utter astonishment it turned out that Thompson this morning communicated to the Master his resignation of the Greek Professorship: – we all utterly disapproved of this step. The Master has begged him to reconsider his resolution & has appointed next Monday for the Election of a Senior . . . called at Willy's . . . Shortly after he made his appearance in my rooms & said he would bring his mother & brother from Cromptons where they were resting . . . I found Edward a very frail unhealthy-looking shy lad who seems likely to have an early passport to the skies. Lady R. begged to examine my rooms . . . she spoke of the possibility of Willy's being plucked for the Little Go, & her fear of his being tinged with German Rationalism, & of his going into the army. I told her that I thought him free from vice; but a victim to the Romilly disease of indolence: – that I thought it impossible he ever could gain any honors in the University, & that his going into the army now in a time of active service would be the best thing for him. She lamented over his unlikeness to both his grandfathers who were most laborious[14] . . . I took a great deal of notice of Edward & talked about his entomological pursuits . . . we then walked (with Sedgwick) to Jesus College (her Father's College) . . . The Chapel is decorated in the Romish stile & Lady R. said 'I have great difficulty in abstaining from crossing myself' . . .

*Wed. 15.* . . . I was pleased today at meeting Lucy's protégé Mr Andrews in a bright new scarlet coat: I immediately concluded that he was made Towncrier: – he is vastly happy, for it was a touch & go affair: his competitor & he had each 17 votes & the Mayor gave him the casting vote. – I shook hands with Andrews & heartily wished him joy.[15] – Read loud a little of 'Heir of Redcliffe': – pleased with it.[16]

*Th. 16.* Bond came punctually at 9: he was surprised at learning that she had never been sounded before: he rather hurt her by his poking. – He sat with me some time afterwards: he said he detected today what he could not perceive

---

[14] i.e. Sir Samuel Romilly and William Otter, Bishop of Chichester. Willy left with no degree and was for a time a lieutenant in the 23rd Foot. He roused himself enough to be called to the bar in 1864 and to find unexacting employment as 'Clerk of Enrolments in Chancery'. One suspects that his father eased his way.

[15] Isaac Moule, town-crier and bill-poster for many years, died on 18 February aged 77, his duties having lately been discharged by deputy. In considering his successor the corporation stipulated that he should pay Mrs Moule ten shillings a week for life. The Town Crier 'still wears officially, on his left arm, a fine silver badge bearing the town-arms etc. and stating the fact that it was made in the year 1723 . . . ' (H.P. Stokes, *Proceedings of the Cambridge Antiquarian Society*, 20 (1915), 39). See 1 May 1856 and 9 March 1857.

[16] Charlotte Yonge's new romance strongly flavoured with Tractarian piety. Keble had vetted it and the large profits went towards missionary work.

while she was drest, that there is alas! some valvular defect: – but he says it is very slight: she needs great watching . . . She was determined she would not miss offering him his fee so she kept it all the time tightly grasped in her hand: – he however declined. – He spoke to me in great praise of the talents & judgment of Lestourgeon, but said that he does not *do himself justice*: what does he mean? – He said that the practice of a physician would be very mournful if it were not for the Hospital where cases of all kinds were to be found: that he & Paget thought the hospital was sadly overstocked with maidservant-patients, that their mistresses immediately sent them in for any trifling headache or pain in the side (– 'I never knew a woman without a pain in her side'), – but he didn't exhaust the funds of the hospital by giving them expensive medicines!

He told me that Mrs Whewell's internal tumour is incurable: she was relieved by a surgical operation: but it is swelling again: – this is very sad . . .

*Mon. 20.* . . . Dined at Trinity Lodge: it was a party of 15 . . . no ice, no champagne. – There was plenty of amusing talk, for Milnes (who, as Smyth long ago said of him, is a very good fellow tho a great coxcomb) talked a good deal about Lamartine, the King of Prussia & other celebrities whom he knew familiarly . . . Whewell was in capital conversation: – he told the anecdote of Bishop Blomfield's observation on Mrs Carpenter's picture of him with his hand on a bust of Newton, 'Whewell confirming Newton' . . . The great talk of the day is Professor Blunt's having refused the Bishopric of Salisbury. – Lord Aberdeen has offered 3 pieces of Preferment to Cambridge men who have all declined: – Bishopric of Salisbury to Blunt, Deanery of Peterborough to Sedgwick, & living of St James' to Witts. – Blunt is now looked on as a prodigy by all Clergymen: he is not 60, but considers himself too old for a Bishop.

*Th. 23.* Lucy very much the same as far as I can observe. – Both Bond & Lestourgeon happily consider her better. – Bond came about 11¼: he missed a good steel pen put out for him & began writing with a bad quill one, which was a failure: for after having made blots & blurs he got up to throw his prescription in the fire: – upon wch L. presented him with the good steel one & all went smoothly . . . Called at Trinity Lodge & had a good chat with Mrs Whewell: – she says she does not consider Mrs Carus so shy, but says that certainly during the 2 days she staid with her she talked to nobody but her husband when he was present, – that Mrs C. was taken to Church & placed in a good position for *looking up* to her husband . . . that Mr Carus had been delivering the Astronomical Lecture all over Hampshire, – that he had no liking for Parish work & couldn't bear being at Romsey . . . We got talking about Monkton Milnes: – I said he talked republicanism & was a believer in Spirit-rapping: – Whewell said 'We call him the Red Republican & he likes every opinion that is outrageous: Smyth once told him 'that of all the men whose minds he had endeavoured to guide his was the most extravagant'[17] . . .

[17] Milnes had been Whewell's pupil on his admission to Trinity in 1827. He was one of those unfortunate young men who 'bolted' when faced by examination, but was an original 'Apostle' of diverse talents, and became a traveller, bibliophile and poet, connoisseur of erotica, M.P., and social reformer. By the 1840s no fashionable gathering was complete without him and his

*Sun. 26.* Lucy slept very badly in her new sleeping room (the Library), partly perhaps from the change but principally from the great strength of the medicine (to check the swelling at her ancles wch has unhappily returned): this horrid physic makes her very faint & miserable – inclined to vomit tho nothing is actually thrown up: – all this is very distressing: – She is however (as she has always been) very cheerful . . . I went to St Michaels: the appearance of the Church was most melancholy – such a contrast to Scholefield's time: – I don't think I ever saw a Cambridge church so empty in service-time . . .

*Tu. 28.* Lucy still slept very indifferently . . . Dr Bond . . . recommended also Harriet sleeping in the same room in case any thing should be wanted in the night . . . She today had letters from Agnes & Mrs Gilmore telling of Agnes's arrival at the Home & Colonial School yesterday:[18] Agnes had to pay £6. 7. 2 on entrance: we had sent a draft for £6. 7. (the original sum) & are mystified by the 2d over . . . Harriet Gillson called: her nose looked frightful as if it had a bad chilblain: however it is not so bad as formerly: – Humphry undertakes the case & treats her as an outpatient . . .

*Th. 30.* . . . Trial at the Vicechancellors in 'the Forum Domesticum' – Henry Lyon (the Chemist) who had been before the Heads in 1850 was the culprit: he had let an undergraduate run up a bill of above £20 (principally for cigars) without any notice to the Tutor (Gunson). He behaved in the most impertinent way imaginable & said 'I suppose I may sit down': – the V.C. said 'if you wish': – he said 'will you advise me how I am to get in my debts from 180 undergraduates': – Whewell exclaimed 'We are not here to advise you': – Philpott said 'I will give you a piece of advice, – comply with the regulations of the University'. – He was discommuned sine die: – he took it very coolly & said 'You ought to punish the young man'. – The vagabond has given notice of actions against all the University men in his debt. – Left cards for L. & self at Mrs Harvey Goodwins: mother & babe going on well . . . A most kindhearted & excellent letter came from Betsy Spink, lamenting over L's sad illness: it was full of piety & sound sense. – I wrote in reply . . . I should yesterday have mentioned a Seniority . . . One interesting measure of Cooper's was carried, viz. raising the allowance of the bedmakers during the dearness of bread, at the rate of 24s where they used to have a pound: it is understood that the poor helps are to come in for some advantage. – Sedgwick called today to ask after Lucy: – a great no. of paupers had also the grace to do so. – Today I declined dining at Catharine Lodge: – a party of 8 women & only 4 men . . .

*Mon. 3 April.* . . . In the morning a little languor & drowsiness, but much better than yesterday: so I am more happy today: – the Dr has prescribed a very odd beverage broom-decoction: – schoolboys would tingle at it . . . Shocked to hear of the death of Vance of Kings: he is said to have been brought home a corpse about 2 o'clock this morning from a disreputable house: – it is said that 2 other Fellows of Kings were also in the house. – I am told that he died of a heart complaint . . .

sobriquet was 'The Cool of the Evening'. He was portrayed in novels both by his friend Thackeray and Disraeli. See J. Pope Hennessey, *Richard Monckton Milnes*, 2 vols (1949-51).

[18] Founded in 1836 to train governesses and teachers.

*Tu. 4.* Lucy was very restless on being made up for the night: she passed a most disturbed night & was so ill early in the morning that she allowed Harriet to go for Dr Bond: – he arrived before 8: he thought poor dearest Lucy was sinking & prescribed stimulants, a mustard poultice, brandy, – Ether every hour. – There was that degree of chilliness about her that he recommended flannel wraps – She preserved her characteristic unwillingness to give me pain by seeing her suffer & insisted on my going out of the room: – indeed dismissed me till 2 o'clock. I of course continued in the Parlour . . . When I came in to see her at 3 she dismissed me almost instantly & told Harriet & Dosia & Nurse Martha i.e. Deighton not to let me come in again. So I was not present when her soul took its flight to Heaven as it most assuredly did, for she was a sincere Christian relying solely on the merits of her Saviour, & her life was spent solely in doing good to creatures animate or inanimate. She used often playfully to say that if there were brute creatures in Heaven (as Tucker thinks there will be) she hoped it would be her duty to feed them & take care of them. – I went in the moment all was over & kissed her lips & commended her soul to her most merciful Saviour. There was her Mothers sweet smile on her countenance & a truly heavenly look. Hers had always been a steady & firm faith which she cherished in her heart & did not show by talking about God . . . May God give me Grace so to live that by my Saviours mercy I may enjoy her society for ever in Heaven. – Read prayers as usual to the Servants & took a dose of Sal. Volatile when I went to bed. – I am now left a solitary being, but O how great a blessing it is that my dearest Sister always had a companion & a protector in myself & that my life has been prolonged so as to have been a comfort to her: – I am very thankful for this great mercy.

*Wed 5.* Before breakfast went into the mysterious chamber of death & kissed my dear Sister & prayed for God's Grace. – Had an interview with Peck (the undertaker): wrote to Mr Titcomb (about burial in my vault in his Churchyard): sent a notice to the Camb. Chronicle & wrote to Lestourgeon.[19] – I wrote a vast no. of letters during the morning & at night . . .

*Th. 6.* . . . I passed the Evening in reading Law's Serious Call & Jeremy Taylors Holy Living. – The more I think of dearest Lucy the more I admire & love her: hers was a very remarkable & very noble character: there was a purity of heart & a high devotion of herself to rescuing others from danger & from sin which I have never seen equalled: – her powers of mind were of a high order & were always so considered by her cousin John: – her tenderness to me & her care of the poor & her fondness for brute beasts marked her as one of the dearest of God's servants.

*Fri. 7.* . . . Very kind call from the V.C. before breakfast to ask after me: – he left a very kind letter to me. I received an excellent letter from dear old Lady Cotton: a very affectionate & tender one from John speaking in the highest terms of Lucy's talents & her goodness: I had also a very good & kind letter from G.B.A. (offering to come to the funeral – wch I wrote to refuse as I did also to John who begged to attend). G.T.R. also wrote a very amiable and excellent letter . . .

---

[19] In the *Chronicle* Lucy's death is attributed to 'a heart-complaint'.

*Sun. 9.* Very much overcome at giving my kiss this morning. – The more I think of my dearest Sisters transition from incurable illness to the joys of Heaven the more I feel reconciled to my own sad loneliness & only hope that I shall have Grace so to live as to join her hereafter. – The Post brought letters from Francisca Ouvry . . . Betsy & Sophie: these 2 last did me good for they made me cry heartily . . .

*Mon. 10.* My dearest Sisters funeral – To my surprise Willie Romilly came: – I had [sic] glad he did so, as these solemn scenes cannot but make some impression even upon the most worldly minded young man: – I talked to him affectionately on the matter nearest my heart as an old man to a very young relation. – My letter had travelled after him to Town & he came down by last nights Mail . . . I observed that the shops opposite were shut up in respect to my dearest sister. – The service was read very touchingly by Mr Titcomb; & now my 2 most dear Sisters lie in the same vault . . . I took a long walk round thro Coton & Granchester. – After dinner wrote to the Master: wrote also to Mr Titcomb (asking if I could have a sitting in his Church): – also to Mills giving up the Whist Club . . . Little did I think this day week that I should now be the lonely creature that I am!

*Tu. 11.* . . . I asked Bowtell (the bookbinder) today about his Father: he said 'Well! he a'n't very well': – 'At Yarmouth still?' – 'No – I believe in London' – 'Indeed! what takes him to London?' 'Well! I believe he's in prison for debt'. – 'Ah! I exclaimed: it is his sons that have done that for the good old man'. – This was in the hearing of Mr Sibley, who said (as soon as Bowtell had sneaked off) 'that's quite true' . . . Letter from G.T.R. saying they had thought it best not to wait & the baby was christened last Friday (he George standing for me) . . .

*Good Friday.* A very tender & most sensible letter of Miss Wilcox's . . . Also a letter full of the most passionate grief from M.A. Tyler: – it did credit both to her head & her heart . . . I went thro Granchester & Trumpington. I have learnt that the Vicarage (where I had Pupils in 1813) is occupied by Mr Widnall (only child of the great Florist): the large house built by his Father is unoccupied – (it was lately occupied by a Mr Fowler who died there) . . .

*Easter Sunday 16 April.* An extremely kind letter from Carus inviting me to Winchester: – I of course declined . . . I went to Barnwell Church & avoided sitting in the Pew of Mr Titcomb: – I learned afterwards that Harriet & Dosia & Hannah Smyth & Mrs Carpenter & Hoppett were at this Church: – all of them except Hannah had been at the Funeral.

*Easter Monday the 17th of April* . . . I wrote the following Epitaph on my dearest sister

Sacred to the Memory of
Lucy Mary Romilly
youngest daughter of Thomas Peter Romilly Esq.
of London & Jane
Anne his wife

Born 28 July 1797 – Died 4 April 1854

> She was governed by two great principles,
> love to her Saviour & love to all living creatures.
> In spite of very delicate health she passed
> much of her time in the houses of the poor.
> The only sufferings she ever forgot were her own.
> She was always calm & resigned, & in her last
> illness did not murmur a complaint . . .

*Wed. 19.* . . . Frank spoke very feelingly in his letter of the great happiness that Lucy's reconciliation had been to him & of the religious amendment it had led to . . . I received a very excellent consolatory letter from a quarter where I did not expect, – from Art. J. Russell: – I was much touched by his kindness & wrote to thank him. – Worked in the office till 2½ & then walked to the Red-Cross Turnpike & so round thro Cherryhinton: the country looked beautiful from the highground – At night read the Testament in French & some prayers in German: also Jeremy Taylor.

*Wed. 26.* (Day of Humiliation)[20] . . . At 11 to Christ Church Barnwell: Mr Titcomb preached very vigorously from 2. Chronicles 20. 15. 'the battle is not yours but the Lords' . . . He spoke of the sins of Russia, France & England having called for punishment from God: – the sin of ours that he dilated upon was the over-exultation in our prosperity & thinking that no harm could befal us. – He said that at night he should dwell upon the *hopes* of the enlargement of Christs Kingdom from this crisis. – At 2 I went to St Mary's & heard a most brilliant sermon from Jeremie . . . He then dwelt on the horrors of war, – beginning with expressing our sensations at a single murder & showing how war produced the same misery & desolation but infinitely multiplied. He next spoke of the consolation we might feel in the consciousness that England had done all she could to avert this awful scourge . . . He then spoke of our present Visitation & the duty of deep humiliation. He then pleaded most beautifully for our charity in behalf of the families of those who were going to shed their blood for us . . . I should have said that coming out of Christ Church Barnwell we were played out with 'God s. t. Q' – to my great pleasure: – but I heard a lady observe 'what bad taste! to play God. s. t. Q. on a fast day'! – I (like a Quixote – for what did it concern me?) said 'I can't agree with you Ma'am: in the church service we have been praying for success to the Queen's cause & I think the National Anthem most appropriate on such a day' . . . I today read with great pleasure Isaac Walton's life of Donne. I also read Mr Winthrop (of Boston U.S.)'s brilliant lecture on Algernon Sidney.

*Wed. 3 May.* . . . Letter from G.T.R. saying that Maggie is going to wean her baby & that she suffers great pain while suckling: he has been alas! unsuccessful in his attempt at employment in the Crystal Palace Illustrated Catalogue, & other projects, & his Picture has been uncomfortably half accepted in the Exhibition & hung in a bad place: – he offers (or rather

---

[20] For God's aid in the 'just and necessary war' against Russia. The text of the royal proclamation of 21 April appointing the day is printed in *Annual Register* 1854, p. 65. It was interdenominational with collections for the families of soldiers, and was also observed in parts of the empire. About £330 was raised locally.

declares his intention) to run down & see me for a few hours to take a walk with me!! – I wrote to beg him to do nothing of the kind, for I very greatly preferred being left entirely to myself: – I desired him to paint a small 30 Guineas Picture for me & to chose his subject. – Great fighting in the Senate House: – all the new proposals about the Little Go, & the Triposses of Theology, Moral Sciences & Natural Sciences were thrown out: – the Classical-Tripos-Degrees passed, but they were opposed in both houses. – A Fly sheet of considerable merit by Hort, attacking them all[21] . . .

*Mon. 8.* Opened dearest Lucy's will: it is dated as far back as 1840: it leaves £100 to 'Disabled Missionaries', £50 to Propagation Gospel in Foreign parts, £25 to Carry Hudson, £10 to Susan Chune: appoints me sole Executor with Legacy of £100; & leaves every thing to poor dear Margaret: – in a Codicil £52. 10/ is left to John as a remembrance . . . After Prayers I gave Dosia & Harriet £5 each & desired them to put it in the Savings Bank: – I told them I felt sure that if my dearest Sister had made a Will recently she would have left them a remembrance.[22]

*Wed. 10.* . . . On going to College I found Letters from Law (of Orwell) asking for Charity votes) & from Sir John acknowledging my 1st letter (about G.T.R.). This letter of Johns was very kind indeed . . . John asked me in confidence how Willy had done at the Scholarship: I therefore wrote a note to Martin who most kindly gave me full particulars; – 'Herodotus – very respectably; Thucydides very poorly,⌐
                              unfinished⌡ Homer, very poorly, full of words left untranslated: – Æschylus, not attempted . . . Mathematics only 13 marks: – General Paper 0'. – I told John that I thought a Scholarship morally impossible & that without Willy became 10 times more diligent I despaired of his getting a Junior Optime: – I thought he was doing no good at College: – he has this term dismissed his private Tutor Yool . . . Present from Whewell of his pamphlet concerning the Oxford University Bill . . . His facility in writing is marvellous: it seems to cost him no more trouble to send forth a large pamphlet than it does other people to issue a small fly sheet.[23]

*Fri. 12.* Letter from Sir John containing the particulars of the little living of Millom: its value is £196. I hastened off to the real Post Office with a letter to E.E.A. in which I enclosed these particulars: – the Post Office shuts at 9.10,

[21] The Studies Syndicate in a report of 21 March proposed thirteen Graces, but of these only four were accepted. The text of all thirteen and the voting figures for each are in *Annals*, V, 171-5.

[22] Lucy's failure to revise her will after Margaret's death is typical of her, as is Romilly's evident failure to interfere in her private affairs. It was to cause a little trouble (see 11 June 1854) since Margaret's lapsed legacy had to be rightly apportioned among her two surviving brothers, who had £1,113 each, and nephews.

[23] Whewell's pamphlet of 36 pages dated 1 May 1854 seems to have been for private circulation. In it he disapproves strongly of proposals in the Oxford bill which might be made at Cambridge, and especially the providing for university funds by suppressing college fellowships. Were this to happen at Trinity and St John's, leaving the smaller colleges untouched, 'all persons interested in the improvement of the University would regard such a proceeding as enormously mischievous and perverse'. See I. Todhunter, *William Whewell* (1876), I, 213-14.

so I was only just in time . . . The post also brought half a dozen notices of his 'Humiliation' Sermon from Edward Miller, but fortunately no letter: – he has not the tact to perceive that brother Clergymen care but little about each other's sermons: – they generally think they could have done as well themselves . . .

*Sat. 13.* . . . That dear good A.J. Russell having seen me in the streets looking out of spirits has written me a 2d very very long letter of Christian consolation: I wrote to thank him: but hope he will not send me a 3d. – Letter from John saying that I am right & that dearest Lucy's estate will have to be divided into 4 parts . . . Meeting of Master & Seniors: – among other matters we discussed C.B. Scott's long statement complaining of the dinners in Hall, the system of waiters etc. etc. etc: he says that the Head waiters (who farm the tables & sell the remaining victuals) make nearly 300 a year!! Edleston (the Steward) doubted the accuracy of many of Scotts details, so he was requested to report to us on the matter . . .

*Mon. 15.* . . . I was glad to receive a letter from Grim saying he had accepted the living of Millom: it was an exceedingly sensible letter . . . in the Evening George Allen made his appearance . . . I found him looking extremely well: but he is marvellously bald: – he has also acquired a trick of constantly saying 'yes' like Mrs Phelps, – but not from a corresponding paucity of ideas. – After tea we looked a little into my melancholy duties as Executor & he gave me very good instructions. – We took pen & paper & made out that the probate will have to be taken for between 4 & 5 thousand pounds. – Had prayers at the usual time, & to bed about ¼ to 11.

*Tu. 16.* George & I worked together till 11½ . . . George paid a visit to his old Coach Walton & came to me in the office at 3 . . . Dosia gave us a very good dinner & in the Evening he amiably proposed calling on old Mrs Murcutt (– help to his bedmaker Mrs Radclyffe): – by dint of Harriet's instructions to go to Adam & Eve Row we found from a neighbour her present abode: – she was not at home; but we saw her sister & George left 2/6 for her . . . Mrs Murcutt had touched his heart some years ago from her being in tears at her exclusion from a feast given to the bedmakers (– she being only an unhappy Help) – We didn't get home to tea till 9.

On 18 May Romilly and a party of some 25 other men from Cambridge had dinner at the Mansion House. Their invitation was due to the hospitality which W.M. Gunson, the distinguished Tutor of Christ's College and others, had given to the Lord Mayor, Thomas Sidney, some months earlier. 'The Lord Mayor is obviously fond of making speeches & if he didn't drop the *h*'s & was not too prolix he would be a very good speaker'. However, 'Like most public dinners it was too noisy & far too long'. Earlier in the day Romilly had spent an hour at the Royal Academy where George's picture 'seemed to me pretty & better coloured than usual: – but it was at the top of the room & very difficult to see at that height'. Another disappointment awaited him in the Athenæum where he was grieved to learn that his favourite cousin's husband, Thomas Kennedy has been dismissed from his office for harshness to the subalterns: – this is sad news, – for independently of the deep annoyance it is a great pecuniary loss'.

Before returning to Cambridge the next day George Allen, who practised in the Temple, was very helpful to his uncle in accompanying him to his Proctor where he swore his affidavit as executor of Lucy's will.

*Fri. 2 June.* . . . Matriculation rather good for this term, 3 Fellow Commoners & 3 Pensioners . . . Barron very civilly sent me a 2d nosegay – Walked round the Via Lambert. – met old Harraden the Artist: he stopt me & spoke to me in a kind & feeling manner – Index at night . . .

*Sun. 11.* Fire at breakfast – Large package from G.B.A. containing the Probate, & all the papers from the Stamp Office: – he has been most kind & energetic & has taken a very great deal of pains for me: – he has settled every thing at the Stamp Office, has paid £153. 17s. 6d duty for all the Legacies & has sent me all the Legacy papers (filled up – except the signatures of the Legatees – wch I shall get from each as I pay the Legacy) . . . George . . . says he does not know how far I shall be affected with regard to the furniture dear Lucy & I held in common: – if my interest was under £100, clearly not at all . . .

*Th. 15.* Letter from Betsy . . . Wrote to her, saying I should be glad to see her when ever she could come: I begged her to christen the baby at once as I should decline doing it . . . Worked in the Office till ¼ to 4. – Went to look after Willy's place in the Classes: he is in the 5th. – Lord Belmore is posted: Lords Dunglas, Dunlo, Hervey & Rollo are in the 8th Class: so the Nobility don't shine. – I also went to Caius to see how Bob Willis had done: – I am truly sorry for Prof. & Mrs Willis: – Bob was posted in Classics: – & will probably be posted in Mathematics as Croker tells me he is last but 3!

*Sun. 18.* There has been a change in the Ministry: – Lord John Russell is now *President of the Council*: Ld Palmerston *Home Secretary*; Ld Clarendon *Foreign Secretary*; Sir George Gray *Colonial Secretary*; Duke of Newcastle *War Secretary*: – Lord Granville *Duchy of Lancaster*. – Poor Strutt has unceremoniously been set aside without any fault committed: – Grim therefore was right in accepting Millom as Strutt has no longer any patronage. – Letter from Sir John asking me to pay a visit to Cabalva: – it was a very kind letter & I wrote to accept for a week in August . . . I met Mrs Clark coming out of her house & began talking with her about her own son John (whom she idolises) & her nephew Bob Willis (whom she hates): she says that Bob was turned away from Marlborough: – his offences there were general misconduct & insubordination: – but the last flagrant act was swearing at the Master who reproved him for flinging bread across the table. – The maids had leave out till ¼ to 9: Dosia went to St Pauls: Harriet walked thro Granchester & Trumpington . . .

*Th. 22.* . . . Received Kennedy's pamphlet concerning his dismissal from Woods & Forests: – I read it & wrote to him to express my indignation at his treatment: – he has been too stern a reformer for those who lived by the old corruptions.[24] – Wrote also to M.A. Tyler as kind a letter as I could, praying

---

[24] T.F. Kennedy had married the diarist's cousin Sophie Romilly in 1820. A strong Whig, he had been an active M.P. before retiring in 1834 on account of debts inherited from his father, but in 1837 he was given a post as paymaster to the civil service in Ireland which he

her to be resigned under her sickness & not to be hankering after a school, the duties of wch would certainly be too much for her delicate health. – Wrote also to Agnes Gilmour (– who is at home with her Mother for her holidays) . . . I found great fault with her bad spelling: – I told her to send the School bills to me as I always mean to pay them . . .

*Wed. 28* . . . to London by the Express 9·30 . . . Went to Witherby who escorted me to the Bank: I received 4 Dividends of dearest Lucy's stock . . . Mr Witherby then went to the Stock Exchange & sold out the £600 B.S. at 206 producing £1236: his commission & the stamp amounted to 27/: so he paid me £1234. 13. – During the ½ hr he was in the Stock Exchange I went shopping & bought myself a pair of Silk Gloves, a Silk Stock & 7 Silk P. Hands (costing £2 · 1 ·) . . . I then went to G.B.A.'s Chambers & paid him his Legacy of clear £540. 1s. 10d (after having deducted the Legacy duty wch I had paid): – I also paid him the same sum for Grim. – I afterwards walked with him for an hour: – we had a look at the handsome Record Office (by Pennethorne) & went to the Northern Railway Station (Kings Cross) wch he admires greatly & so on to old St Pancras Church wch I used to know as a child so well . . . All this Northern part of London was quite new to me: – new squares, many new Churches & the effect very striking . . .

*Sun. 2. July.* . . . I avoided the Commencement Sermon at St Mary's even tho it was preached by H. Goodwin. – Strolled about till chocolate time & then went to hear Mr Titcombs sermon to the children . . . Mr Titcomb's subject was David as a soldier . . . His divisions were: 1st good cause: 2dly right purpose: – 3d successful result. – 1st *good cause*: it is not a good cause for you children to fight when you want to get other childrens tops or marbles, it is not a good cause to fight as the Emperor Nicholas is now doing against the Turks: – – but ours is a good cause for war: – who are we fighting against? – 'The Russians' exclaimed many little voices. – Well, the Israelites were not fighting against the Russians were they? 'No'. – 'against whom?' – 'the Philistines' . . .

*Wed. 5.* . . . Being invited to the Royal Luncheon I thought I could not do otherwise than lay out a Guinea upon an Archaeological ticket.[25] The Prince . . . came into the Senate House about 10' before 12 (in red gown – preceded by Bedells: no applause was given to him. – Directly he had sat down in his Chair looking *towards* the dais the President of the Archaeological (Lord Talbot de Malahide) directed Dr Guest to deliver his lecture: – it was principally on the 'Ichenel de weg' or 'High way of the Iceni' . . . then up got

exchanged for a commissionership of woods and forests in 1850. After a dispute with a subordinate he was forced to retire in 1854 without a pension, and he published his account of the affair in an open letter to his old friend Lord John Russell who was a member of the cabinet. See 18 March, 18 and 24 May 1855, and for Kennedy's later life *D.N.B.* His papers relating to the years 1853-5 are in the British Library.

[25] The annual meeting of the Archaeological Institute was held this year in Cambridge from 4 to 11 July. A gentleman's ticket cost a guinea, but ladies, whose tickets were transferable, paid half. A temporary museum was arranged by Isaiah Deck in Trinity, and besides excursions there were many lectures on such topics as rebuses, Celtic remains in Ireland, the life of King Harold, stained glass in King's College chapel, and the need for an *Athenae Cantabrigienses.* (*Chronicle* 8 and 15 July).

Willis & gave a most admirable lecture upon the comparison of Cambridge as in Caius description & Loggan's maps with Camb. as it is now:[26] the parts about Pembroke, Benet Church & Jesus Chapel were peculiarly interesting: he was listened to with great admiration & rapturously applauded . . . All this lasted till a few minutes to 2 when we went to the V.C.'s Lunch: it was set out for his usual number of 24, but there were 2 or 3 vacant seats: – there were not many heads present, Guest, Whewell, Cookson, Ainslie & Cartmell only (I think): the Orator & myself were the only University Officers: – no Bedells: Dean Milman was of the party; so too were Lord Talbot & Albert Way. The lunch was delicious, especially the ice: – we broke up before 3 considerably & went to the Museum in our Lecture Rooms . . . The Museum is full of choice treasures: – the gold plate of Caius, Corpus & Christs looked very beautiful. I was most struck with some curious little watches, one in the shape of a snail, another of a dog . . .

*Th. 6.* This was the called Congregation for the laggards: – there was one very important Grace today, – that for agreeing to Lord Palmerston's recommendation of referring the University & Town disputes to Sir John Patteson: it was unopposed.[27] – There were 3 AMs (including Harris whose bride was looking on) & 1 LLB & 13 ad eundems. The V.C. had (I know not how) learned that a Mr Stoddart was coming forward & that he was highly objectionable (having held Mormonite views): the V.C. desired me to ascertain from somebody who knew him whether this was the Mormonite, & Dr Okes (who is on the Caput) pronounced that this was the gaunt gigantic man for he remembered well having seen him at Eton . . . Dr Bond stood the mans friend & brought (at 2 o'clock) printed testimonials to show that he was now a staunch churchman & had renounced the heretical opinions which he had once held. So he was at last allowed by the V.C. to be admitted. – This business made a great bustle & worried me very much in the morning as there were the other 12 applicants for ad eundem crowding round my table & waiting to sign my book. – I am afraid that I wished the V.C.'s spy as well as all the Mormonites at the bottom of the Salt Lake . . .

*Sun. 9.* . . . At 2 to St Marys to hear Whewells Sermon for the Propagation of the Gospel . . . The Archaeologists are in such force that St Mary's Pit was well filled . . . The Sermon was full of brilliant eloquence; but it had two great faults: it lasted an hour & he paid his audience the bad compliment of thinking they were all utterly careless & heartless about the spread of the Gospel: – indeed he told them that they were also constantly thoughtless about their daily comforts & blessings & privileges . . .

[26] Dr Caius wrote a history of the university down to his own times. David Loggan's careful and detailed engravings of plans and views of the principal buildings in the 1680s, *Cantabrigia Illustra* [1690], were of great value to Professor Willis and J.W. Clark in their *Architectural History of the University*.

[27] In letters to the Vice-Chancellor and mayor Palmerston proposed to settle their many long-standing differences by arbitration, and proposed a member of King's College, Sir John Patteson, who had retired from the bench owing to deafness. He was becoming known as an arbitrator and both sides agreed to his appointment in a joint reply to Palmerston in December.

*Mon. 10.* Rain & very cold. – The Archaeological day for Ely . . . Today between 11 & 12 the Archaeologists Museum was open to Servants: so, I went to see them enjoying themselves: it was well crammed . . .

*Mon. 17.* Declined Mrs Prest's family dinner to meet Bob Wale & pretty little wife: – the said Bob is waging war (till last Saturday under the masked battery of anonymousness) against John Ingle about having had in his Cathedral School of Ely a book of Popish tendency called 'the Catechism of the Incarnation'. – For breakfast a Yarmouth Herring given me by Mrs Walter Watts. – Mr Titcomb kindly wrote to tell me that his Sunday-School-Treat would be in Downing this Evening . . . At 4½ I went to Downing & gave my arm to Mrs Hoskin . . . in our walk we met her husband & I had some talk with him about his Parish. He is anything but satisfied with his flock: there are 5 Beershops besides the one regular Alehouse, & there is a large Paper-Mill wch employs 300 hands & wch he looks upon with only one degree less horror than he does upon the Beershops: – his amiable wife takes a more cheerful view of things & described to me with satisfaction her adult class of more than 20 persons. – I did not see much of the proceedings in Downing: – the Sports were all over (having begun at 2): I heard the Grace sung before Tea & saw the 800 children falling to on the provisions with a hearty good will . . .

*Th. 20.* Dosia went (by Excursion Train) to Ely with her friend Miss Topping: her 1st visit there. Called on Maddison & took him to Leapingwell: they both witnessed my signing my will: – I afterwards told Harriet that it would be found in the drawer of my desk if anything happened to me . . . At 1 o'clock to Trinity Lodge to be in readiness for receiving the Judges . . . I went into the Judges Kitchen (for the 1st time in my life): a capital one it is: Pryor (the tinman) exhibited to me the Pewter plates & saltsellars etc (date (1736)) wch are always brought by him for the Judges' Servants: – their cloth was laid in the Servants Hall (wch also I had never seen before) – At ¼ to 2 the Judges arrived: after seeing them decline the mulled wine & after having invited them to dine in hall on Sunday we took our departure when the V.C. & Heads were announced . . . Returning from the Post I found a little boy crying bitterly: – I learned from other 2 children that he had fallen out of a Cart: – I enticed them to my house promising to give them all a cake & the tumble-down child a penny: for fear of jealousy I gave them all a penny: – the tears ceased. – Met the Workhouse girls & gave 1/- among them. – I astonished the diggers of a drain before Scrope Terrace by giving them 1/- because they had not begged. – Sarah Saunders called: I had her up in the parlour & was glad to find her looking very healthy . . . She pleased me by producing ½ a Sovereign wch she brought for her Savings Bank in my hands. – Finished the 1st Vol. of Gunning[28] & read a little of the 'Old Curiosity Shop'.

Lucy's death inevitably meant that the pattern of Romilly's life and of his 'Journal', as he liked to call it, changed. He no longer describes Lucy's doings almost as fully as

[28] Henry Gunning's *Reminiscences of the University, Town, and County of Cambridge from the Year 1780* had been dictated in old age and edited and published by his amanuensis Mary Beart (by subscription 1854, popular edition 1855). The subscription list is curious for the many names not in it.

his own, though he works conscientiously for her protégés and the charities in which she was especially interested. He can no longer comment on the books he read to her in the evenings or record her shrewd comments on their relations and friends. Instead he works longer hours in his office and the diaries increasingly describe the details of his registrarial duties or, as in the following entry, the research needed to answer questions about members of the university long since dead.

*Th. 27.* . . . George Williams (of Kings & Columba) . . . wanted to learn all particulars about the degree of John Pearson (the famous Bishop): he was matriculated at Kings in Dec. 1632 and *subscribed* for AB in Jan. 1635/6: upon the strength of wch Richardson in his Catalogue enters him as AB of 1635: – I presume he was (according to the King's fashion) *admitted* AB at Kings but there is no 'Placet' for him as a Fellow of Kings nor any supplicat (wch would have been required if he had not been a Fellow.) Williams says that he certainly was Fellow & that his name was on the boards at Queens before his coming to King's: – I don't comprehend this as he was on the foundation of Eton . . . I didn't get my dinner till near 6 . . .

*Sat. 29.* . . . I expected Betsy by an early train as I thought Excursion trains always left at early hours: however she didn't make her appearance until 4½. She brought with her her baby (now 6 months old): he is a very healthy chap with blue eyes & a large head & pale face: he wears no cap & is called George Edward. – I had a long & very agreeable chat with Betsy till dusk; the baby is very good & does wonderfully little in the way of crying . . .

*Wed. 2 August.* . . . Only a walk on the Coe Fen before dinner. After dinner I walked up & down the garden reading till dusk. I finished 'Old Curiosity Shop' & admire Dickens the more I re-read his works –. I also began Gunning's 2d Vol. The eulogy of old Peate Musgrave[29] is most hearty & will please the Archbishop & his brother . . .

*Th. 3.* . . . Worked in the Office till 5.20 at the drawer of Representatives. – Then home via Coe Fen . . . Read a good deal of Gunning: his account of the immorality of the Seniors of Trinity is very Curious.[30]

*Sat. 5.* Betsy very wisely agreed to stay a little longer: – she is better this morning . . . Tried in vain from the Baker M.S.S. to work out whether Tom Crouch was Fellow of Trinity: – but that period between 1640 & 1660 is lamentably deficient in all University & College records: – as for the University records there was a disgraceful Statute for destroying all the

---

[29] Father of Romilly's old friend, to whom he had been chaplain, Thomas Musgrave, now Archbishop of York. He died in 1817 and lies buried just by the south door of Great St Mary's.

[30] Gunning was an undergraduate at Christ's in the 1780s when the resident fellows of Trinity were notorious for their eccentricities and sexual frailties, which are related in the second volume of his *Reminiscences*. Unmarried they were obliged to be, but not chaste. Still, as Winstanley observes, they were probably not much worse than their contemporaries, and 'scandal being better copy than tales of edification, and therefore far longer lived' posterity remembered the bad rather than the good. (*Unreformed Cambridge* (1935), p. 258).

Cromwellian records[31] . . . Mr Jones the Dentist has just had a wedding in his Family: Amelia his 2d daughter is married to a Mr Edmund Wilson. I believe his deaf & dumb daughter was reduced to that state by a foolish nurse who drest up a sort of bogle & set it at the foot of the child's bed to keep it quiet!

*Sun. 13.* . . . To Trinity Church hoping to hear Calthrop but I heard Clayton . . . As for his sermon it was a mischievous ultra-calvinistic effusion from Revelations 7. 9: – he said he could not comprehend the *great* multitude spoken of by St John without indeed it consisted of the souls of infants who died before the commission of sin: he seemed to lay down that scarcely one of his flock would be saved & then made a great tirade against good works as a ground of hope: – the sermon was utterly detestable . . .

*Mon. 14.* . . . Heavy shower from 7 to 7½ in the Evening. When it was over I walked to Trumpington in the delicious freshness. – On my return I passed 4 women walking together: – one of them exclaimed 'there's Mr Romilly: I'll consult him. – Of course I stopt: 'Will you be so good as to protect me into Cambridge? – my friends are going back to Trumpington & I'm afraid of walking by myself & had made up my mind to go & sleep with them'. – 'O! I shall be very happy to escort you: – it is not proper for ladies to walk alone at night especially at Harvest time when so many labourers are about'. – Tho the light was imperfect I could make out that my companion's beauty was not sufficient to make my position equivocal. – She talked away like a magpie . . . She said her name was Ingram & she was governess of the little Millers: – she praised them & Mrs Miller very much . . .

On 19 August Romilly left London for his main Long Vacation holiday. He enjoyed a quiet, domestic and delightful eight days at his cousin John's country house *Cabalva* about nineteen miles from Hereford. Lady Romilly and their five younger children were there, the weather was beautiful, John's conversation was 'most amusing & instructive', there were carriage drives and walks in lovely country and an ascent of Cliro hill with three of the children and two ponies. 'We laid down among the Gorse for ½ an hour: it was in beautiful flower, but John says it blossoms more or less all the year, & that it was said to be like kissing – always in season'. Ten days later Romilly began the cross-country journey to Parcglas near Narberth, Pembrokeshire where 'Grim', son of his late sister and brother-in-law Baugh Allen, his wife and numerous Allen relations were on their home ground. George's and Grim's wives were sisters and there was constant intercourse between the two families and at this holiday-time their nine children. 'Grim's girls are far finer, fatter and prettier than George's'. On Friday, 8 September before beginning the journey home 'Grim amused himself at the Narberth Road Station by weighing Bertha, himself & me: she is under 8 stone: to my surprise I weighed more than Grim: – he made my weight 10 st. 13 lbs, – a stone heavier than I thought myself'.

*Sun. 17 September.* . . . Called on Captain & Mrs Needham & found Ficklin there . . . They came over last year (then unmarried) from India & touched at St Helena: – their room was hung with drawings of Longwood etc.

---

[31] The records of the Protector's dealings with Cambridge during the 1650s were burned at the Restoration as part of the return to normality and to confirm their illegality in royalist eyes. A few charred fragments remain.

Ficklin had also been at St Helena both when Bonaparte was alive & also just after his death. He gave a very amusing account of his last visit: – he & a large party went over Longwood & bagged various articles as reminiscences of the Emperor: – Ficklin pocketed a little soap-dish (to oblige a lady), one man took a pen, & others took something or other, one Lady in particular filching a great number of knick-knacks, – They had not got very far from the house & were walking with the Governor when a servant addressed the Governor 'Please your Excellence several articles have disappeared since this party left the house': – to their shame & confusion the Visitors had to restore their booty, – Ficklin 1st beginning by laying down his soap-dish: – one officer had to restore a *beautiful China plate with one of B's battles painted on it*!! . . . In the Evening read 2 of Jeremy Taylor's sermons. on the day of Judgment: – the 1st is truly sublime.

*Tu. 19.* Two marriages: – Mrs Hoskins' maid (an excellent young woman who has been with her 9 years) married to a worthy young man: Mrs Hoskins gave her £10 & a genteel breakfast – they are to be gyp & bedmaker at Caius: – Mr & Mrs Hoskin attended. The 2d wedding was of a less respectable person, Miss Barron (sister to the Grocer): she has had 2 or 3 children! & she has not communicated her disgrace to her intended . . . Letter from Medical Directory (about degrees etc.): wrote to them: they asked (inter alia) if Paget was Linacre Lecturer: Paget being out of Cambridge I called on the Matron (Miss Bishop) to ask her: – I was amused at seeing the manner in wch dinner was laid for her & the house surgeon & one other, – napkins & *3* silver forks by each plate. – Walked in the Botanic garden: – the glasshouses all glazed. Also went to Caius new Hall: getting on fast.[32]

*Fri. 29.* . . . First day of Fellowship Examination: Greek Prose by Martin 9 to 12½: Greek Verse by me 1½ to 4½. – I dined in hall & of course was president: I went up into the Combination room for an hour. – There are 21 Candidates for 5 Fellowships. – Read Burton's Anatomy of Melancholy during the 3 hours watching in Hall . . . Looked over 2 sorts of papers before 11¼, viz. Theocritus & Pindar.

*Sun. 1 October.* . . . Today is the thanksgiving for the glorious harvest. Mr Titcomb . . . spoke of the war & the cholera as *clouds* that God had brought upon the earth, – but the rich harvest was the cheering *rainbow*: – one part of his sermon put me in mind of Defoes history of the Plague, – it was a vivid description of the horrors lately occasioned by the Cholera in London[33] . . .

[32] Large parts of the College were rebuilt during Guest's mastership. For the new hall he employed Salvin, the preferred architect in Cambridge in the 1840s and 50s, who, it will be remembered, was engaged across the road at Trinity Hall. The syndicate appointed to develop the Old Botanic Garden site had recommended in December 1853 that its designs be entrusted to Salvin, whose work at Trinity Hall and Caius already gave 'proofs of his especial skill in the planning of complicated and commodious buildings upon sites limited in space, awkward in form, and connected with previous structures'.

[33] The text which was to be read in churches through the land is quoted in the *Annual Register* 1854, pp. 168-9. There was an optional paragraph to be added for cholera districts where there must have been less to be thankful for and people needed comforting.

*Mon. 2.* . . . In the street today a pretty nurse crossed over to me with an ugly baby in her arms; – She was sent (very civilly) by her mistress Mrs Nedham: I of course kissed the baby & praised it & gave the nurse 1/. – The news has arrived of a great victory gained by the English & French in the Crimea over the Russians: it is expected that Sebastopol must have been taken also.[34] – The bells rung all day, & there were squibs & bonfires at night on Parkers Piece. – Began fires in College. – Looked over Fellowship papers till 4. – In the Evening went on with Monte Christo . . .

*Mon. 9.* My birthday. I am now 63 complete & have so passed over the grand Climacteric. I have reached the greatest age attained by any of my Father & Mothers 9 children: – dearest Margaret was 63 when she died. – Gave Harriet & Dosia 2/6 each. A most kind & amiable letter from Betsy (Mrs James Spink) on my birthday: it was accompanied by a basket containing a pot of marmalade, a chicken & some French beans & Potatoes from her own garden: – she also wrote to Dosia to tell her to steam the Potatoes. Wrote to thank Betsy. – Excepting the irritation in my legs I have every reason to bless God for the health wch I enjoy. – The Return of the 26 officers killed at Alma was published today . . . I received another birthday-gift today: – M.A. Tyler sent me a blotting-paper book & a remarkably well-written affectionate grateful letter. – Tea at Trinity Lodge at 6½: I thought Mrs Whewell looking quite dreadfully . . .

*Tu. 10.* In chapel at 8.45 to complete the Election of Fellows. – The beautiful carving of the Posts in the oriel of the dining room of the Lodge (finished this summer) is costly: – £160!! the Master is to pay ½ & the College ½ . . . Dined at the Fellowship Dinner at 5: it was only too good a dinner: – the Masters conversation (describing scenes at the recent British Association at Liverpool) was very amusing . . .

*Wed. 11.* At 10 o'clock the swearing in of the 5 new Fellows: – the Senior of them Seeley is sandyhaired & hideous, the other 4 (particularly Hawkins) very goodlooking . . . Mrs Prest a little mending: – she now lends me the Times daily. – I past the Evening in reading it & in studying the Voluntary Theological Paper set today to the 240 candidates.

*Th. 12.* The Caput Election took place at 1. – This year the Norrisian Professor (E.H. Browne) for the 1st time takes part in the Voluntary Theology: – there are 3 days of Examination, one for each of the 3 Divinity Professors: – the average of plucked men is about 30, i.e. reckoning the numbers at 220 14 p.c. – Worked diligently at the Office till 4½ & finished letter A in rewriting my Graduati[35] . . . fell in with Worsley & had a long chat with him: he is just come from Filey Bay, where Archbishop Musgrave & Archbishop Cardinal Wiseman were staying also & exciting great notice: –

---

[34] Despite the defeat of Russian forces at the Alma on 24 September allied commanders failed to press home their advantage. Sevastopol held firm through a frightful winter for its besiegers and was not taken until September 1855.

[35] He had in hand a revised and enlarged edition of the *Graduati Cantabrigienses* which listed alphabetically the names of graduates from 1760 together with their Colleges and degrees and included other historical lists. It was a labour of immense usefulness (nothing comparable exists in this age of computers), and it appeared in 1856.

the Archbishops were in the same lodginghouse. Worsley told me of his interview in bygone days with Wiseman at Rome about printing at Rome a Sermon preached there by Julius Hare: – Wiseman had expressed great admiration of the sermon thinking Rome was in it called 'the *faithful* city', but when he found the epithet to be *fateful* (– very Julian!) he waxed cold & did not gain permission for printing it . . .

*Mon. 16.* . . . Received a very agreeable tho not a very cheerful one from Sophie: she is a good deal affected by the death of her cousin Arthur Walsham (who was killed at Alma): – I never saw him, tho I knew very well his brother who took his degree last January: – she says that Kennedy can't bear parting with Franky: so while they are condemned from poverty to exile in Scotland the poor boy is taken from Mr Faithfull's where he was so happy & getting on so nicely: Sophie has the sole charge of his education & the classical part is entirely set aside: – this is sad & is an irreparable mischief . . .

*Th. 17.* Met one of the little Carters; she declared her Mother had given her a shilling to buy dripping & that she had lost it: – I fear she lied: I scolded her for her stupidity (affecting to believe the tale) & gave her 6d. – Library opened today: the Library in a very comfortable state from the new system of warming: – all the books have been dusted & look very nice, & that admirable person Heun has done Wonders with regard to a new Catalogue.[36]

*Sat. 21.* Most kind & affectionate Letter from Sedgwick offering me his Idiot Votes: – he is just returned from Paris with Isabel & Fanny: they enjoyed themselves thoroughly, but he suffered from a feverish cold. – Rather a demand for Professorial Cards today: one man got into the house at forbidden hours (viz. after dinner), not for a card, but to learn how he might do without one!!! – Today was Proclamation of Markets: – only one Esquire Bedell (of course Leapingwell): the V.C. was disposed to send for the other 2, but spared them. By the way he has done a very gracious & kind act: he has just given a magnificent dinner to the Mayor & Corporation: – I hope the Custom will be kept up by future V.C.s. . . . Harriet returned this morning, having thoroughly enjoyed her 8 days holiday. – Present from Mrs Hoskin of a little Tract (called 'Dig deep') written by herself last May: I met her with it in her hand & she told me it was a child of her brain: I read it after tea & wrote to thank her: it ends with an anecdote of a Negress who on her deathbed pointed to the Bible & said 'Jesus is there', – to Heaven & said 'He is there' & then touched her heart & said 'And He is here also': – a beautiful little story.

*Tu. 24.* Called on V.C. – Prince Albert has just announced his intention of giving an annual Gold Medal for the encouragement of Law[37] . . . Left for Audley End by the 5 o'clock train: – my companions were 5 disgusting blacklegs just come from Newmarket. – Staid ¼ hr or more at Audley End Station waiting for the down train as the Omnibus does not start till its arrival:

---

[36] See 26 November 1859.

[37] The prince was following tradition. His predecessors the Dukes of Newcastle and of Gloucester had instituted gold medals for classical learning and English poetry in 1751 and 1811 respectively. The new medal 'for Legal Studies' was first awarded in 1857 to Hugh Shield who had taken firsts in the classical and moral sciences triposes. There was indeed a strong legal component in the latter, which included jurisprudence and English law.

we were a goodly party of 7 in the machine; one was an invalid Lady who was lifted in by her companion. – At Audley End I was very kindly received by Lord & Lady Braybrooke who are both pretty well, tho in a dreadful state of anxiety about Henry & Grey who are both taking part in the siege of Sebastapol . . . We made talk till bedtime (11): Lady B. taking the principal share & conversing (as she always does) very cleverly & amusingly. – One riddle was proposed: it was 'When is a man hereditarily fishy?'. – Ans. 'When his Mother's a dear good soul & his Father a little common-place' . . .

*Sat. 28.* . . . I met Mrs Willis today & she offered to walk with me: I of course accepted: I talked to her very earnestly about the children, particularly about Robert's disgraceful career last year & the necessity of talking most stoutly & earnestly to him: – she didn't at all like the conversation & said it was no use talking & some young people would not read: – I said that then they ought to be reasoned with & talked to most seriously & even sternly. – She is obviously a fond mother who has not the slightest control over her children. – She made me come in & I saw the said Robert & spoke to him seriously (tho not harshly): – Mrs Willis filled my pockets with her delicious apples. – After dinner I pasted in University papers & read the News.

*Fri. 3 November.* . . . Seniority: – we gave away the King Wm. Prize to Swanston & directed him to be summoned from Twickenham by Telegraph as he has to recite the Essay tomorrow.[38] We discussed the Patriotic Fund for the Widows & Orphans of those who fall in the war: the College gives nothing as a College: – there is however a list opened at the Butteries: – the Master gave £20, Sedgwick £10, Martin & I £5 . . . I amused myself by drawing up Statistics of the average tenure of a Mastership at the different Colleges . . . the shortest average being at St Johns: the longest at Emmanuel: The average (taking all the Colleges) is 13·86 or nearly 14 years . . .

*Sat. 4.* Met blind Peter: he had had a *franc* given him for a Shilling: I of course changed it for him. – Breakfast with Edleston: – a superb breakfast, as that of the Senior Proctor by immemorial usage is. – He made a short & terse speech in the Senate House in praise of Geldart & Guest. Guest (the new V.C.) made an excellent one (very short): it was delivered oratorically & *by heart* (a happy novelty in a V C's speech): – he seemed to dread the forthcoming Government Measure touching this University:[39]– his principal topic was an eulogy of Sir J. Patteson (– the Arbitrator in the Controversy between Town & University) – Hoppett very much better. – There was an intense row last night in the Townhall at the lecture of a paltry foolish man who ventured to declaim against smoking in its headquarters[40] . . .

---

[38] Ten pounds was awarded annually from money given by a local squire to a junior B.A. of Trinity who wrote the best essay on the conduct and character of William III.

[39] Doubtless the Statutory Commission.

[40] The would-be speaker, one Thomas Reynolds, founder of the British Anti-Tobacco Crusade and editor of the *Anti-Tobacco Journal*, was met by a rowdiness of students with pipes and cigars. Two Johnians were afterwards fined for assault on the police who had helped the Mayor and Proctors to clear the place and the riot attracted much comment in the national press.

*Sun. 5.* . . . (tho I put on a good deal of steam) did not get to St Marys till 4 or 5 minutes past 2: Bp Selwyn had begun his prayers: – the place was crammed: many stood the whole time: – Bright kindly squeezed me into a place where I sat bodkin. – Selwyn's voice & appearance are magnificent: his sermon was most eloquent & was listened to with the attention wch Melville used to command . . .

*Th. 9.* . . . Went to the Poultry Exhibition: it cost only 1/-: I also sent the Maids & M.A. Tyler (on whom I called & found plump but out of spirits). – I was much pleased with the beauty of several crested Fowls, & greatly amused with the row wch the Cocks made.[41] I met all the little Bonds here & their Mother: I put myself under the guidance of the two youngest & saw all their favorites. – Worked at the Office till 5: – prepared a Table of Syndics, Examiners etc etc as I did last year (for the 1st time) . . .

*Fri. 10.* . . . Dined at the Family . . . There was a good deal of conversation about New Zealand & its excellent Bishop . . . The Bishop ascribes the diminution of the aborigines (among other causes) to the introduction of Indian Corn & Blankets: the Maize is too heavy for the infants stomachs & kills them, & the Blankets overheat the wearers far more than their original mats. – An amusing anecdote was mentioned: – the Missionaries of course preach against polygamy: – one chief (who had 2 wives) said they had so much convinced him that he had eaten one of them![42] . . .

*Sat. 11.* Breakfast to Willy & his agreeable clever friend Crompton (one of our new Scholars) & to the dull uninteresting freshman called Onslow. – I had asked John Clark & young Challis & Wyndham Neville: – the 2 former (tho they didn't mean to come) hadn't the manners to write & say so till on the 3rd day after their invitation I sent Hoppett to them: – in my invitation I had expressly desired an answer: – I can't help thinking I shall never invite them again . . .

*Sun. 12.* . . . At 10' to 2 I took up a position (– a very bad one) at St Mary's: I ought to have been 5 or 10' earlier: – nos were turned back. – The Bishop preached from 'Kings shall be thy nursing Fathers & their Queens thy nursing Mothers': – parts were very brilliant, especially one about the war in

---

[41] Held at Parker's Carriage Repository in St Andrew's Street this was the first show of its kind in the town and had an impressive number of patrons headed by Prince Albert. Competitors came from as far away as the West Country, and their fowls were carried free by the Eastern Counties railway. Many rare and expensive breeds were shown and they attracted the social elite. Mortimer Ford, an old Etonian and undergraduate of Trinity, took first prize in one class and third in another. See *Chronicle* 11 November 1854.

[42] After the treaty of Waitangi in 1840 British colonisation proceeded promptly and Selwyn was appointed to his vast diocese in 1841. The country was not pacified, however, for many years and Selwyn was one who considered that the Maori population were unjustly treated especially by English land companies. On the early connections between Cambridge men and New Zealand see J.A.W. Bennett, *The Eagle* (St John's College), 69, Easter 1981, pp. 8-10. He reminds us that Samuel Marsden (Magdalene 1790) first preached the gospel in New Zealand in 1814 and sent Maoris to Cambridge to help with a dictionary of their language. Romilly may have seen them and have known of Baron de Thierry (Queens' College 1820), who proclaimed himself sovereign of New Zealand in 1835, landed there with a posse of Australian street-loafers in 1837, and ended his days as a music teacher in Auckland.

the Crimea, & another about God in the tumult of nations having taken a young girl & seated her on our throne to sway the destinies of the world . . .

*Wed. 15.* . . . letter from Lady Braybrooke telling me that Grey had been knocked off his horse in the thick of the battle & had received 4 stabs while on the ground: one only (– from a lance) was thought serious, it had passed through the shoulder & hurt the lungs: – the Surgeons however give good hopes . . . Worked in the Office till 4½ on the drawer of 'Sewers and Drains', – important in these times of Cholera.[43] – A dozen delicious Marie-Louise Pears sent by Dr Phelps: I sent ½ of them to Mrs Prest: – the Maids & I consumed the rest . . .

*Sun. 19.* . . . The Service having been over at 12½ (Mr Jessop reading intensely fast) I found my own gate still locked, – the maids not being returned: so I walked for ½ an hour on the London Road, & had some conversation with diverse parties, viz. Col. Glover, Miss Francis, & Prof. Blunt & charming little daughters: – on my return the gate was still locked, but as it was raining & I had no umbrella I clambered over in my cap & gown, wch I daresay will have been seen by some idle gossip & commented on as most unseemly behaviour on a Sunday . . .

*Tu. 21.* A very grateful letter from Betsy: her heartless husband took away my little namesake's shawl! – he is a pitiful scoundrel. – Letter from a Mrs Drury asking my Governess votes for an unfortunate Miss Bayley – her 20th attempt! – She also asked me to help her in founding a new Annuity: – I refused both her petitions . . . Began working at the 'Plague' drawer: the weather being awfully wet & the pestilential character of the paper I was arranging induced me to smoke a cigar. – After dinner worked at 'Graduati'.

*Sun. 26.* Letter from Lady Braybrooke in answer to mine: she says 'We are heart-broken at present: our dear departed Hero is indeed a void not to be replaced. Thanks be to God he passed the 9 hours between his mortal wound & his (at last) fearful end among his own people & now lies buried with his comrades, – in a distant clime it is true – but that matters not. In the midst of our grief we have a ray of comfort: our dear Grey writes himself he was doing well the 10th. Alas! ere now he knows the dreadful loss he has sustained: he has none to comfort him' . . . After Chocolate I hurried off to St Mary's & got comfortably seated at 20' before 2: Dosia went & got in. – Harriet & her sister Louisa went about 2 o'clock: – of course they couldn't get in . . . The Bishops Text was John XVII. 21. – He preached against disunion: a sermon that did my heart good, but had Mill been alive to hear it he would have gone into a fit. – He recommended all the most learned high-church people who can find no rest here where the Church is torn to pieces by disputes to go out as Missionaries: they would soon learn that they must give up all subtle refinement & preach the Gospel in the plainest simplicity . . .

*Tu. 28.* Letter from Mrs Geldart asking for linen for Miss Nightingale & her Nurses in the Crimea: Harriet undertook to make up a parcel & take it . . . Bright told me a most melancholy piece of news: poor Grey Neville has

---

[43] For the seventeenth-century court of sewers see D. Owen, *Cambridge University Archives* (1988), pp. 102-3; of more immediate relevance were the files from 1822 of a syndicate on drainage of the town (University Archives, classmark Min.VI.1).

died of his wound! an overwhelming calamity to Lord & Lady B. thus to lose 2 sons by this bloody war.

*Wed. 6 December.* . . . The V.C. forgot to bring with him into the Senate House today the Latin Graces: he had left them in a drawer: – he 1st sent his servant, & afterwards Mr Mackenzie to fetch them: they both failed: – he then doft his red gown put on his black one & fetched them himself: they were exactly where he had described them & where the blind buzzards ought to have found them: – he consulted me 1st whether the Congregation would be vitiated by his going out: I pronounced decidedly that it would not . . .

*Sat. 9.* . . . I received today the Governess's Report (M.E. Horrocks) of Agnes Gilmour: – it is favorable: see Fly leaf . . . They lead but a contentious life at Kings: last year they displaced Theed from being Vice Provost & set up Bacon: this year there was a strong party in favor of Barrett, but it has ended in the election of the ultra High Churchman George Williams (who as Warden of St Columba's behaved so obnoxiously to the Archbishop of Armagh the Patron & great benefactor of the Institution: – ultimately the Archbishop (after G. W's refusal to resign) stopped the supplies.)[44] . . .

*Sun. 10.* . . . At 2 I went to St Mary's (a very thin congregation) to hear Rowland Williams. – I saw at once that he would develop very pronounced opinions for he gave out his Text from the 2d Epistle *ascribed* to St Peter . . . It was a clever sermon but the most presumptuous I ever heard. He spoke of the folly of considering the Bible in all its parts a book for all ages: – he said that God's inspirations were according to the time, & that he revealed nothing whatever about Astronomy & Natural History etc., that he did not give perfect & full inspiration to the Apostles – that the Apostles interpreted some Scriptures wrongly – that the prayers of modern Bishops were so feeble from their being made centos of quotations from Scripture – : – He insinuated that the writings of men of this present time under God's inspiration were as valuable as the writings of St Paul. – He treated with contempt Jonah's whale . . .

*Tu. 12.* . . . At 6½ dined at the V.C.'s: a grand dinner with ice for 20 . . . After the women were gone Cartmell eulogised Rowland Williams' sermon of last Sunday as the most masterly performance he had ever heard: – I immediately flamed up & denounced it (in spite of its cleverness wch I abundantly allowed) as the most startling & mischievous sermon I had ever heard. – Skinner (with whom I never agree) said that he was himself absent & that his wife had been delighted . . . Skinner then said that Origen[45] had said things quite as strong as Williams on the subject of Inspiration: I said that Origen one might read or not as one pleased, that I had no copy of him & never meant to read him, but that I could not help hearing what a preacher

[44] For Williams see *D.N.B.* Many thought that the religious instruction of St Columba's at Rathfarnham near Dublin, where he had been warden since 1850, smacked too much of modern innovation to be palatable to Irish Protestants. He returned to Cambridge.

[45] Third-century ascetic and theologian most of whose writings are lost or represented only at second-hand. The teachings attributed to him were condemned as heretical by the medieval church, and his allegorical exegesis and Platonic speculations belong to the scholar's study. Few Anglican clergymen of the 1850s can have known much about them.

poured into my ears from the pulpit at St Mary's.- I was not wise in all this violence, – wch may get round in an exaggerated shape (wch is not necessary) to Rowland Williams. – In the Evening came Maggie Willis & brothers & a singing lady friend of Mrs Willis: – Maggie is not yet out, but Mrs W. is following the advice of Worsley in bringing her as much as she can into society to prevent gaucherie & shyness . . .

On 22 December Romilly left Cambridge for four nights in London. He put up at the *Golden Cross*, took his large new matriculation book to the Stamp Office, enjoyed dinners with George and Maggie Romilly and George and Dora Allen and their young families and on Christmas morning 'went to St Martin's which is close at hand . . . I particularly disliked some pews with sash windows'. The weather was foul and the streets unusually filthy and he failed to get a cab or an inside place in an omnibus going to Hyde Park Terrace where the Master of the Rolls was to celebrate the Day in great style. At three o'clock there was a dinner party after which 'conversation sprang from mention of an allusion in a London paper to the offence given by R. William's sermon at St Marys'. And two hours later, when the grown-ups and children invited to the children's entertainment had arrived, 'John & Willy exhibited a magic lantern very successfully'. 'After that came the grand attraction, the illuminated Tree hung with all manner of beautiful objects: there was a profusion of toys & bijouterie etc etc. & every child was laden with treasures: – the old people too were not neglected'. The day ended with four rubbers of whist and 'at 10 with supper and very merry it was'. It was fortunate for Romilly that on this first Christmas day since Lucy's death Lady Romilly's health had been equal to organising a celebration which left him little time for sadness. By the following year she had written to say that her health was 'so very bad that she thinks it will certainly be her last Xmas dinner' and our Diarist, himself unwell, ate a solitary meal 'for the 1st time in my life'.

*Tu. 26.* . . . Found the Maids quite well: – their Christmas dinner (to wch Harriets family & Anne Coe came) went off very nicely . . . Mary Edwards & little Lucy Spink are here on a visit to Mrs Milligan, who however cannot sleep them: – I had an interview with them & begged Mary to sleep here & stay as long as ever she liked . . . after tea I worked at 'Graduati'.

*Fri. 29.* Rather a run for Professorial Tickets: – I worked till 4½ at verifying Matriculations & Little-Gos: – sufficiently dull employment it must be allowed . . . Dined at C.C.C. Lodge to meet the Father of Mrs Pulling (Christopher Hodgson – brother of John, Douglas & Hugh who took their degrees in 1818 & 1819) . . . The party was very agreeable (as is generally the case where Paget is a guest). – I plaid 4 rubbers & won them all, carrying off 20/ . . . Whilst sitting out I amused myself with guessing Pulling's puzzles at which I was very successful: – he has great talent at concocting charades etc & writing light poetry. – The following 3 were among the puzzles. – the underlined words are transposed letters of the answer

> (1) 'Deemed it *not pleasant he alone* to dwell
> Far from the noisy world he loved so well.
> For him that peaceful valley had no charms
> From costly pomp remote & clash of arms'
> Ans. 'Napoleon at St Helena'

(2) 'He, mighty sage, *saw in Creations* laws
   Sure indications of a great First Cause'
Ans. 'Sir Isaac Newton'

(3) *'Lines to honor* a Hero brave
   whose home was on the mountain wave'
Ans. 'Horatio Nelson'

*Sat. 30.* . . . I know not why, but I slept remarkably ill. – Breakfasted punctually at 8½ that I might be ready at my announced hour of 9: – nobody came however till 10: I went on receiving till 3½ & had visits from 136 youngsters: – 9 of whom had also to take Professorial Tickets . . . Dined at Trinity Hall festivities as the guest of long Latham. – I had some talk with Sir James Stephen before dinner: – he is (to my taste) a very disagreeable man . . . with Roupell I had a good deal of talk about Sir Alex. Cockburn (Attorney General), formerly Fellow: Cockburn was much mortified at not being elected Master on the death of Sir H.J. Fust: – the position would have given some support to his character wch is very bad indeed in the point of profligacy[46] . . .

[46] In the mastership election of March 1852 the fellows of Trinity Hall had preferred Geldart, an amiable but otherwise insignificant man, to Sir Alexander Cockburn, a rising lawyer much in the public eye. He was already an honorary Life Fellow of his college and was unlikely to be a cipher. He did not endear himself to some when he had earlier pressed to the vote and carried an 'un-English' proposal that postprandial toasts should be drunk in claret instead of port, causing the old Master, Jenner-Fust, to leave in anger. Though loaded with public honours, Cockburn was again passed over for the mastership in old age in favour of Sir Henry Maine.

Trinity Ante-chapel after service on Sunday evening

# 1855

*Mon. 1 January.* God be praised I begin the new year in very good health: – the servants also are well & Mary & Betsy's little daughter. I gave Dosia & Harriet a new shilling each, & the child a new sixpence. – Master of Downing & Mrs Worsley called to wish me a happy new year: Mrs Worsley brought me some pots of Apricot . . . Worked at the Shrine of Mammon (fee-receiving) from 9 to ¼ to 4 . . .

*Fri. 5.* . . . Letter from Mynors Bright telling me of an article in the Westminster Review attacking the University Fees & especially the immense sums for Degrees & *Cautions* paid to *the Registrary, whose duties might be discharged by a Clerk with a salary of £200.*[1] – Wrote to Bright, saying I had no intention of refuting the falsehood: – that the Cambridge Commissioners had already published in their Blue Book my Report concerning Fees etc[2] . . . A great fire at Girton tonight: 3 farms blazing!

*Th. 11.* Letter from G.T.R. wch filled me with surprise. Thro the kind exertions of his friend Mr MacLean (who is in the Ordnance) he has got a *temporary* place as Clerk in the Ordnance (in the department of Royal Carriages) at Woolwich: – the hours are from 10 to 10 (with an interval of 2 hours for dinner): the salary £120 . . .

*Mon. 15.* College meeting at 11: – the principal business was the proposed enlargement of St Mary's Street & St Mary's passage by curtailing the Churchyard: – things are at 6s & 7s: – the improvement Commissioners & the parish can't agree: – we hold our judgement in suspense . . . Read the French letters: I was much pleased with those of Fanny & Sophie: they were cleverly composed & seemed written from the heart . . . Wrote to Frank (£10): the foreign postage is now reduced to 4d (– from 10d) . . .

*Mon. 17.* Sharp frost: ground white. – Prettily written letter from Martha Bye who is returned to School. Letter from George Romilly at Woolwich: he had overstated his hours of work: they are from 10 to 4½: he is the lowest clerk: he likes the other clerks, particularly the elder married ones: he finds them all gentlemen . . .

*Fri. 26.* Dosia was at prayers last night: – she is a little better. – Last night that wicked woman Mrs Spink called . . . Dosia spoke stoutly to her about Jem's wickedness in deserting his wife: – his Mother said 'I don't blame him at all: he can't live with her, she's such a bad temper' . . . It appears that the worthless fellow is staying with his worthless mother . . . The Combination room presented a curious sight yesterday: a Samaritan (a real one not a figurative one) dined in hall: he wears a red cap, talks nothing but Arabic, believes in nothing but the Pentateuch: – Preston brought him into hall, & also one of our Consuls who spoke Arabic. The Samaritan seeming uncomfortable

---

[1] A long anonymous article (vol. 63, 154-86), one of many that appeared in serious journals as university reform developed through the 1850s.

[2] i.e. Romilly's evidence to the Royal Commission set out in its official report.

195

he was asked if he would like a pipe: – he joyfully assented: whereupon Sedgwick etc etc lighted Clay pipes & smoked bravely . . .

*Mon. 29.* Delightful letter from Grim, giving a humourous account of his Cumberland Savages & speaking about Cannibalism, Tattooing, etc. He has communicated to me a word new to me – 'brogging': – it means setting up posts in the sea sands . . . In my Office I had a visit from my Gyps son: he brought back the Arithmetic & Algebra books I had lent him: – he has collected from them a large number of examples & expressed much gratitude: I was pleased with his conduct & think he deserves to get on well . . .

*Tu. 30.* . . . Visit in my office from Miss Poole the public reader: – she is a tall dark very good-looking woman (apparently about 25) who has a good colour in her cheeks, very white teeth & wears spectacles . . . I took one of her tickets (for tonight's reading of King John & a tale of Mrs Hemans, & Crabbe etc) wch cost only 2/6. – She told me that she confined her recitations to rhyming poetry & blank verse: – that she had been advised by Bishop of Peterboro to recite hymns, but she had shrunk from it: that if she had confined her readings to Shakespeare she should not have succeeded at all as there was a strong feeling against stage plays, – tho that had diminished since Mrs Butlers readings: – that she was much patronised by Dissenters (particularly Quakers) as well as Church-people . . . I said I wished heartily she would teach our Clergy to read, as many of them marred an admirable sermon by poor delivery. – She said she had been called on (for instruction in reading) by several young Clergymen, but (being unmarried) had declined giving them lessons[3] . . . dined at V.C.'s . . . The Master of Trinity's Conversation was brilliant: – he spoke of Sartor Resartus as by far the best work of Carlyle (whom he & Hallam & Macaulay hold cheap) . . .

*Fri. 2 February.* . . . Seniority: – the principal matter was a letter from poor Julius Hare's widow offering us all his German Books, & all the Books of Councils & Fathers wch we do not already possess: she says that she knew her late husband had always wished these books to be presented to Trinity Library: – a noble gift[4] . . . To day the Smith's prizes were decided: Whewell told me the Candidates were the worst by far that he had ever examined, – that they knew nothing of the History of Mathematics, had not read Newton, & knew nothing but Cram MSS:[5]– no one deserved to be 1st Smith's Prize, so the Senior Wrangler & 2d were marked =. Ellicot called on me at ¼ to 4 & we walked together to college & to the grand dinner – Sedgwick

---

[3]  Miss Poole eludes us. Mrs Butler was Fanny Kemble, the actress, who had taken up public readings after her divorce some years before.

[4]  The Reverend Julius Hare, philosopher, linguist, and churchman, had died in January 1855. He held a Trinity fellowship from 1818 to 1844 before retiring to his parish where he amassed a large library especially strong in German works. Searby (pp. 352-70) describes him as 'perhaps the most bookish and erudite Cambridge man of his day', and observes that he introduced Coleridge's ideas to his pupil F.D. Maurice, who in turn diffused them through the church. His bequest to Trinity is unsurprising for he was a friend of Whewell and Sedgwick, but its arrival was one of the great accessions of the nineteenth century that destroyed the spacious elegance of the Wren Library.

[5]  i.e. cribs and digests.

presided – Ellicott has plenty to say for himself: he is a very studious man in theology, works hard at Hebrew & Syriac, & has already published one Vol. on 'Galatians'. He is very intimate with Cookson, who, he tells me, (in spite of natural shyness & coldness) has gradually become a laborious parish priest. He spoke also a good deal about Captain Doria, whose marriage he brought about: he thought the Captain leading an idle disreputable life & advised him to marry; asked him to his Fathers parsonage that he might there meet the daughter of one of his parishioners, a wealthy medical man: he went, spoke & was accepted: his bride has a fortune of between 5 & 600 p.a: – the Captain is now a Magistrate & keeps his 2 horses & is greatly improved every way . . .

*Fri. 9.* In the Office finished Queens College Documents. Seniority today: Sedgwick had a cold & was absent: we rusticated a youth (named Hoblyn) who slept in a friends room last night: – he had been dining with him & became *ill* (– euphemism for drunk): – this was his third offence in sleeping out of his lodgings . . . Ld Palmerston succeeded yesterday in forming a ministry: – Gladstone, Ld Panmure (Fox Maul), Layard etc are members of it: – Duke of Newcastle, Lord Aberdeen & Lord John Russell are not[6] . . .

*Sat. 10.* Letter from G.T.R. asking my advice about taking a *permanent* Clerkship at Woolwich; Mr Maclean is making great exertions for him, & the Seniors in the Office are highly pleased with his conduct: – I wrote recommending him to jump at the permanent place if he can get it altho at the outset his salary will be reduced to £90 . . . I told him that (agreeably to his desire) I had written to Sir John stating his precarious position: – I had received no answer & did not think the great man wld be able to do anything for him . . .

*Mon. 12.* . . . There was to be a cricket match on Emmanuel pond today, but I preferred going to Chesterton to see Drosier skate: close by the railway are 2 ponds, called "Great Ballast Hole" & "Little Ballast Hole": – I fell in with Cope (who was going to skate) & walked with him to the scene of action. It was a gay spectacle: there were plenty of spectators male & female & also orange vendors etc.[7] . . . A very keen N.E. wind that took away one's breath . . .

*Wed. 14.* . . . Visit . . . also from Calverley (the Craven Scholar): he cannot get the Trustees of the Craven Estate to recognise him as a Scholar, they counting 5 Cambridge ones without him: – I made him civil speeches about his Tripos verses wch were so much admired & wrote him out the statistics of the Craven Scholarship for the last 6 years, mentioning whose Scholarship each new Scholar filled up . . . the sun was shining brightly, so I

---

[6] Lord Aberdeen's government foundered in the face of attacks on the conduct of the Russian war. Both Russell and Lord Derby failed to form administrations, but Palmerston succeeded and remained Prime Minister (with a brief interval) until his death in 1865. A few weeks later it was discovered that members of the administration were largely unchanged and they were the same people with different hats. Austen Layard, who had no office, told the Commons on 19 February that what the country wanted was youth and energy, not more 'septuagenarian experience'.

[7] Owing to the flatness of the fens ice-skating had been brought to a high skill in Cambridgeshire. See N. and A. Goodman, *Handbook of Fen Skating* (1882).

started for a walk: I went to see the skating on Emmanuel Pond, & then at the ferry bridge (Jesus Piece): – this last was a very gay scene: – the ice was thronged with sliders & skaters . . .

*Tu. 20.* Seniority – Some persons (Cooper particularly) wish to have the Commination Service[8] read in Chapel: it never has hitherto: – I lifted up my voice against it, & said that I wished the service rejected from our Liturgy: – Sedgwick was not present, but the Master said he also was opposed, using as an argument his objection to the prefatory Rubric wch says 'it is highly *desirable* to revive penance': – Atkinson voted with me (I having voted first): the Masters leaning was clearly against the innovation: – my argument was, that College Chapel service was of the nature of Family prayers & therefore that a service of cursing was inappropriate: – several of the Seniors (– Edleston among them) gave no opinion: – for the present at all events the Commination is staved off . . .

*Fri. 23.* . . . Worked in the office till dressing time at Christs College Drawer. 'The Family' dined with me: all the members were present (& one Honorary member Stokes – all the way from Denver): – the Club now consists of the following 12 members, Drs Tatham, Phelps, Cartmell & Paget, Shaw, Bateson, Thompson, Power, Martin, Clark, Frances & myself. Peacock & Stokes are Honorary members . . . Paget's eldest child is droll for his age (of about 2 or 3): he was today to go out & spend the day with a little boy of his own age (whose birthday it was) . . . He began by saying that he should not come home till morning: – he then asked whether he might pinch his friend: on being told 'certainly not' he asked if he mightn't slap him? – There were 2 card tables: one broke up at 10½: the other persevered till 12. – I lost 23/.

*Sat. 24.* College meeting – we refused our consent to the Town Commissioners proposal of making the railing in St Mary's passage parallel to the tumble down houses & not to the church. – Wrote to John Cooper declining to take shares in his Lodging Houses: by the way I am much pleased with the superscription over each door 'Peace be to this House' . . . After dinner I read the report of the proceedings before Sir John Patteson in the Arbitration between the University & Town: – Bateson spoke very ably for St John's Coll. (on the Rating Question), but the information & the cleverness of C.H. Cooper (who represents the Town) are quite admirable. – The further hearing is put off till after the Spring Assizes. – I pasted the Report into my Book & did a little 'Graduati'.

*Th. 1 March.* College meeting at 11 . . . We voted £30 towards a Central Boys' school. We had long discussion about Hare's books: the 1st instalment (above 2000 volumes) is arrived & I was amused with the difficulties about stowing them away: the turn of the debate was as if we were suffering from an intolerable affliction! I certainly shall leave no books to the College[9] . . .

---

8 'Or Denouncing of God's Anger and Judgments against Sinners', a service of 1549 in the Book of Common Prayer for use after morning prayers on Ash Wednesday and at certain other times.

9 Romilly did not change his mind and the books mentioned in his will (see Appendix 2) were for the family. He, however, presented a 'considerable' number of volumes to the University Library soon after Lucy's death, rather than 'leaving them all in a lump in my will'. The bulk

*Sat. 3.* The Emperor Nicolas is dead! He was born in June 1796 & was in his 59th year: – his death is most sudden, like that of many of his race: apoplexy is assigned as the cause . . . His 2d & abler son is notoriously ardent for the war: the eldest is an advocate for peace . . . Fell in with Ficklin: I was very glad to hear from him a better account than I expected of Sir St Vincent: – his recent illness was influenza & not a fresh attack of apoplexy: – he is a most rebellious patient, but is getting on gradually in recovery: Ficklin restricts him to 2 pipes a day: – so his servant fills all his pipes every morning & lays them in a row, – the Baronet tickets the 1st as Ficklin, the last as Bumpsted: – all the intervening ones he counts for nothing! . . .

*Th. 8.* . . . That excellent person Mrs Julius Hare has offered 18 Pictures of her late husbands to the Fitzwilliam if the Fitzwilliam will pay £1000 wch he meant to raise on the Pictures for his school at Hurstmonceux: the pictures are worth far more[10] . . . An evil of non-residence in Professors became glaring today: – Henslow ought to have examined for the Natural Sciences Tripos: but he never made his appearance . . .

*Fri. 9.* . . . The V.C. was talking to me today about Dr Davy's detestation of the Cockerell wing of the Library which darkened his garden: he said 'I should like to see Whewell & Willis dangling from its roof':[11]– the V.C. also told me of a joke of the partisans of J.J. Smith (in the contest between him & Power for the Librarian's place) 'do you want Power without work, or work without Power?'. In the Evening worked at 'Graduati' & read the history of Russia from Paul Ist's death.

*Sat. 10.* . . . Seniority at 12 to discuss (among other things) the arrangement of Hare's Books: – I offered to give 3 hours a day from 12 to 3 to cataloguing them (except on Congregation days): Munro offered to give 2: – Edleston, Hort etc will help . . . Visit from V.C. to bring the List of Hares 18 pictures & the valuation: the valuation is £1960: 2 of the Pictures (a Madonna & Child by Raffael – £500, a marriage of St Catharine by Basaiti £200) are to be kept by Mrs Hare during her life. The V.C. told me of Dr Okes' pleasantry (when V.C.) to J.C. Adams (Proctor): 'when you perambulate the streets at night you rarely see the Constellation Virgo' . . . Wrote to a William Peacock (at Luxembourg Hotel Paris) who wants to teach Chinese at the University!! – Wrote advising him to stay where he is . . .

*Wed. 14.* . . . Visit from Eliza Hawes (to whom dearest Lucy used to be so kind): she will be 20 in June: she looks many years older, for she has lost most of her teeth: they dropt out in her severe illness: she goes daily from 9 to 9 to a Milliner in Fitzwilliam Street: – I gave E.H. an *out-door* order for Adden-

---

of his library was sold at The Hoop on 4 November 1864 when many were bought by Robert Potts for the University Library. The sale-catalogue names several sets of works by major authors and numerous reference books besides many job lots.

[10] For the nine pictures that came to the Fitzwilliam, all but one being of New Testament subjects, see J.W. Goodison and G.H. Robertson, *Catalogue of Paintings, II: Italian Schools* (1967), p. 197.

[11] Martin Davy, Master of Caius, who died in May 1839, lived to see much of the southern part of his college overshadowed by Cockerell's tall new Library begun two years before. Willis, a fellow of Caius, and Whewell sat on the syndicates responsible for its erection.

brookes & sent her a bottle of Port. – This was a grand day on my part for Hospital Orders: I gave another *out* for a W. Smith of Barnwell: – & an *in* for a Mrs How of the same genteel neighbourhood: – & afterwards was asked by Mathison to give an *indoor* for a Pauper of his: – I declined . . . Extra Matriculation: – 1 Pensioner – In the Senatehouse today there were 2 AM, 1 BD, 1 Mand. DD (Pulling): Jeremie made an eloquent speech & amused me by praising the *constantia* of Pulling, who was known as the *Lady Killer*. – There was a grand fight at 2 o'clock in the Senate House about the £1000 for Mrs Hare's Pictures; Long (Kings), Kingsley etc. strongly opposed . . .

*Sun. 18.* A very affectionate charming letter from Sophie: – she says 'we have at last got the Treasury Minute containing a most complete & I should say humiliating apology from Mr Gladstone & Mr Wilson, saying that they did not *mean* what they said when they called in question Mr K's honor etc: so far as 'character' goes nothing can be better & I would not change places with those 2 Gentlemen for all their wealth – poor as I am – for we have yet another Treasury Minute containing the Queen's warrant dismissing Mr K. whose only offence (as is acknowledged on all sides) is that he served the Public too faithfully' . . .

*Wed. 21.* I should have mentioned yesterday an interview with Walmisley about the Organist's place. – He has only one competitor a young Fiddler whom he holds very cheap . . . Walmisley wants 2 things, viz. to be Organist to the University & to have the salary raised from £50 to £80. I threw cold water upon his money hopes. I afterwards looked up in the Grace Books & Audit Books all I could find on the subject of Organist. – The 1st mention of a Salary is in 1704 . . .

*Sat. 24.* Wrote to Madame F.R. (£25) . . . Then to a Seniority: 2 of our men were thereat rusticated for next term on account of scandalous behaviour in Chapel: their names were Baldwin (2d year) who brought a lighted cigar into Chapel, & Eschelaz who repeated the responses in a very loud tone: they were accused of having made profane remarks, – they utterly denied this: – the accusers (some sizars behind whom they sat) begged not to be brought forward or even named, – so the Prosecutors were the Deans & Ingram the Chaplain: – a 3d youth was let off with a reprimand. – Dr & Mrs Bond have just lost their 4th daughter (aged 14): – I sent my card . . .

*Sun. 25.* . . . Went to St Pauls to hear Bp Perry: the Church was gloriously filled: – extra benches & chairs were brought in, but many gownsmen etc had to stand the whole time . . . The Bishop spoke but a very few words on the Providential leading of himself & the Congregation since he last addressed them 7 years ago. – This was characteristic of him for he never used in former days to speak about himself: – I think however the congregation would most gladly have heard some details of his life in Australia & his ministrations there[12] . . .

---

[12] Charles Perry (1807-91), sometime Senior Wrangler and fellow of Trinity until his marriage in 1841, was a popular vicar of St Paul's, Cambridge, where the Romillys sometimes worshipped. His interest in missionary work led to his consecration in 1847 as the first bishop of Melbourne. For his career there see *Australian Dictionary of Biography* 5 (1974).

# MISS KATE KIRBY WILL DANCE HER POPULAR IRISH JIG.

After which the Interlude of

# IS HE JEALOUS.

Mr. Belmour, a Studious Man............Mr. HOOPER

Mrs. Belmour....Miss WYATT——Harriet....Miss CUT ISS——Rose....Miss MANNERS

## Herr NICOLO DEULIN and his SONS

WILL DANCE THEIR EXTRAORDINARY

# STILT POLKA.

In the course of the Evening the CAMBRIDGE

# AMATEUR CORNET BAND,

Who have kindly offered their powerful aid, will Perform their most favourite
OVERTURES, WALTZES, POLKAS, &c. &c.

To conclude with for the first time here, the Drama of

# UNCLE TOM'S CABIN.

Governor..Mr. FITZROY—Mr. Legree..Mr. UNDERWOOD—Uncle Tom..Mr. HIGGIE
Mr. Shelby..Mr. UNDERWOOD—Haley..Mr. G. WATSON—Tom Loker..Herr DEULIN—Manks..Mr. BOWTELL
Vau Tromp..Mr. COLEMAN—George Harris..Mr. CLARKE—Sam..Mr. JAMES—Andy..Mr. WILLIAMS
Eliza Harris ...Miss CUTTRISS——Charity Prudence....Madame SIMON

*Doors open at Half-past Six, Performance to commence at Seven o'clock precisely.*
Dress Circle, First Price, 3s.; Second Price, 2s. Upper ditto, First Price, 2s.; Second ditto, 1s. 6d. Pit, 1s.;
no Second Price. Gallery 6d.; no Second Price.
Box Office at Mr. MARTIN's, Tobacconist, Sidney Street, where Tickets and Places may be had from 11 till 2

**STAGE MANAGER, Mr. FITZROY.—TREASURER, Mr. LANCASTER**

NAYLOR AND CO., PRINTERS, "CAMBRIDGE CHRONICLE" OFFICE

The end of the bill for the Theatre Royal, Cambridge, 8 October 1852

*Th. 29.* . . . Poor Mr Rattee (the distinguished Wood-carver is dead[13] . . . Catalogued Hare's Pamphlets as usual: then to the Office till 5: – I today began the Index to the 1st Vol. of my own Catalogue of the Muniments. – In the Evg wrote a long letter to G.T.R. containing £10. I also worked at 'the Graduati'.

*Wed. 4 April.* The anniversary of my dearest Sisters death. – God give me Grace to endeavour to follow her good example . . .

*Easter Sunday* . . . At 2 to St Mary's where Harvey Goodwin preached with great animation a most acute & able sermon on the Resurrection from Acts XXVI. 8. – attacking the notion of the *impossibility* of a Resurrection . . .

*Wed. 11.* Shocked to hear of a young woman having tried to drown herself in the Hobson-stream last night: – she was saved. She was a servant at Barrett the Chinaman's: she will give no account of herself: – she was taken to the Female Refuge. Letter from Grim announcing the birth of his 5th child (a boy) on the 7th April. 'Bertha yesterday produced a boy under the most favorable auspices & is going on most favorably. The whelp is one of the regular rough & tough English bulldog breed with a round compact bullet head that might have come into the world in the camp at Sebastopol ready to rough it with our poor fellows there. We had no doctor, but managed every thing ourselves snug & comfortably with the attendance of a canny Scotch Mrs Gamp who is a cer-tificated professor of the obstetric art. I had been with her in her room all day as she felt slightly indisposed & at 5 o'clock I went down to get some tea & sent her up a good bowl full which she mopped up & when I came up again soon after 6 I found her as well as possible, not even perceptibly pale with her whelp as big as a goodsized tomcat simmering in a basket before the fire' . . .

*Th. 12.* . . . Looked over Scholarship papers till 5 o'clock: I saw 3 (out of 4) of Willy's Greek Exercises, viz Homer (utterly deplorable) Sophocles (very bad) & Thucydides (most indifferent): – he can't run the remotest chance in the world . . . Beset with violet-selling little girls: took one halfpenny bunch & gave them 7d. – In the Evening did a great deal of my Index.

*Fri. 13.* . . . Letter from Martha Bye in very pretty language & beautiful writing. – her schooling is nearly over & she is to be dressmaker under a Miss Turner: – wrote & sent her a New Shilling. – At 1 o'cl. to the Hall to set the Latin Prose. In a great stew at finding that they had stupidly printed only 50 copies (– there being 58 Candidates): I was obliged to beg a few to have a paper in partnership: – went to the Press to get more copies & to grumble at the stupidity. – Fortunately the type had not been broken up & I got 50 more worked off . . . Letter from Potts giving me the account of the Election of the Librarian to 'the Free Librarian' [sic]: there were 6 Candidates . . . Dr Cookson (the Chairman) gave the casting vote for Pink: Pink & the 2 Crosses were always at the head.[14] – Potts has been to town to see Mannings Bust

---

[13] James Rattee awaits a biographer. In his short life he established himself as the greatest wood-carver of the day and worked locally, for instance in the chapels of St John's and Magdalene, at Westminster Abbey, Eton College, and in hundreds of churches.

[14] John Pink (1833-1906) was a local youth, assistant to Dixon the bookseller in Market Street, and was appointed at a salary of £63 a year. See W.A. Munford, 'John Pink', *Library*

of Mr Simeon: the materials for the Bust having been slight the Sculptor wisely read the Memoirs of Mr Simeon to impress his character on his mind: – the bust will be exhibited at the Royal Academy: – Potts thinks it successful.[15] – Wrote to Potts. – In the Evening 'Index'. – I was surprised to hear from Bateson that poor Lady Cotton (who died on the 5th) is not yet buried: she is to be buried tomorrow & Sir St Vincent means to be carried into the Church. No person has been asked to the Funeral & Bateson was doubtful whether he should go: I told him I certainly should not . . .

*Mon. 16.* . . . Looked over 3 sets of papers, viz Xenophon, Virgil & Livy: I was sorry to find the wonderful inaccuracy of Willy – who is in fact no scholar at all . . . he has a certain command of good English, – & voila tout . . .

*Fri. 20.* At ¼ to 9 to Chapel for the Election of Scholars: – a larger crowd than usual waiting for the result at the door . . . After breakfast I wrote a long letter to Sir John about Willy's inaccuracy & want of scholarship: – I told him if Willy goes in (as he proposes) to the Classical Tripos he can't be higher than 3d Class: – my own private fear is that he will be plucked for Classics: – his performances in Mathematics are desperately bad (– he only got 12 marks for Math. & 9 for General Paper) . . .

*Sat. 21.* Visit from Mrs Edleston . . . she came to consult me about a house of hers in Silver Street, next to the Pitt Press Steam Engine: her Tenant (Alison the Grocer) can't pay his rent because people won't stay in his lodgings on account of the vibration from the Steam Engine: – she is desirous of selling the house to the University. I recommended her sending her brother (Mr Hazard) to call on the V.C. with a statement of her proposed price: – I however told her that I thought the Press not in such a state as to be able to buy any houses . . . Much shocked at hearing that this year's Senior Wrangler (Mr Savage) was found dead this morning at Comberton: he had been missed for 2 days: – a son of Earnshaw (the S.W.) told me that poor Mr S. had been annoyed at not being elected Fellow . . . Wrote to Mills saying that my health seems to have given way & that I must (reluctantly) decline rejoining the Whist Club.

*Mon. 23.* . . . Much delighted with receiving a letter from George saying that after all the appointment at Purfleet is to be given him: – this seemed utterly hopeless after Sir John's letter wch said it had been actually given to another person. – He is almost entirely indebted for it to his excellent friend Mr Maclean who talked the Secretary over . . . George is to succeed the Senior Clerk (who will shortly be superseded) whose minimum is £140 & maximum £170 p.a. with house & allowances! . . . I wrote to Sir John to tell him this good news, & also to George telling him very truly that no event since my own election in 1832 had given me so much pleasure. – In the Evening worked at 'Graduati'.

---

*Association Record* (August, 1954), pp. 289-94, which contains many details about the library to which Pink gave distinguished service until his death.

[15] The bust by Samuel Manning the younger was paid for by subscription and accepted by Grace on 30 May. It is now (1999) in the Old Schools, and there is a small photograph of it in J.W. Goodison, *Catalogue of Cambridge Portraits* I (1955), plate XXIIII.

*Tu. 24.* . . . Received from Whewell a copy of his reply to 'the Remarks upon the Government Cambridge Reform Bill' (– by the way are those remarks by Bateson?): the Master brings one strong objection to the Vicechancellor being any other than the Head of a House, viz. that it would make the Master inferior to one of the members of his College. The Masters pamphlet is not only vigorous but I think it an able answer to the Author of 'the Remarks' on all points except 'Nomination'.

*Fri. 27.* Letter from Mrs Smith about the burial of poor old Mrs Grounds in Hoxton Churchyard. – Read with great interest the eloquent speech of Ld Lyndhurst on the Lord Chancellor (Cranworth)'s Bill for the University: it was like a Commemoration Sermon. The Commissioners proposed are to be 7, viz Lord Burlington, Bishop of Chester, Lord Monteagle, an unnamed Lord, Baron Alderson, Prof. Sedgwick & John Lefevre: – possibly 2 others will be added.[16] – Wrote to Mrs Smith (saying she need not send the account of the funeral expenses) . . . Dined with Paget . . . Much talk about Donaldson's 'Book of Jasher':[17] it is written in very choice Latin Thompson says, but is wild & indecent: it has already been reviewed (disparagingly) by a German (Ewald I think) . . .

*Sun. 29.* Very amusing (slangy & quaint) letter from Grim: he speculates upon the future career of his 2 sons. 'Baugh will be the swell, very exact in coat boot & hat with aspirations towards Almacks & the Italian Opera; while the nameless one will probably take to the low slang or varmine line, sport a wide awake a short pipe & velveteen perhaps with a live rat or two in the pockets & a thorobred bulldog. The former will no doubt speak of me as 'A aw's the Governour?', the latter as 'the old un", perhaps as 'the clerical buffer who claims the honor of my paternity'. – He proposes also some questions for Fellowship Examination . . . Shocked to hear of Barton (the coach builder) having hanged himself: I believe the bailiffs were in his house . . .

*Th. 3 May* Letter from William Williamson asking votes for a poor Idiot named Hornett: wrote to say I could not vote for her & hoping she wouldn't sting me: – she had above 2000 votes last time so she is pretty sure of success . . . Mrs Carpenters daughter (Susan Haylock) is not appointed to the vacant bedmaker's place, but the *widower* of the late Bedmaker is expected to have it: – he-bedmakers used to be female in the days of old in the University . . . There is to be a Grace tomorrow about Medical-Degrees-Reform Syndi-

---

16  As Lord Chancellor, Cranworth (B.A. Trinity 1812) brought before the House of Lords a bill to appoint a Statutory Commission for Cambridge University. On 24 April he had received a letter critical of it from four of the ex-Royal Commissioners (Peacock, Herschel, John Romilly, and Sedgwick), which was based on the anonymous flysheet (see 24 April above). Cranworth, who had himself found weaknesses in the bill, asked that it be suitably amended, and in amended form it returned to but was later abandoned in the Commons (7 August) for want of time in the session, and a fresh bill had to be introduced the following year. See 26 March 1856.

17  A lost Old Testament book supposedly narrating the deeds of Israel's heroes. Discussion of it had been bedevilled by an eighteenth-century forgery reprinted as lately as 1827. Donaldson sought to reconstruct the book by reassigning to it many passages from existing Old Testament books, and perhaps inevitably his views were not accepted.

cate,[18] the Home Secretary having sent down 2 bills for our observations: – but who is the Home Secretary? after some trouble I made out it is Sir Geo. Grey. – Latinised the Grace by introducing Sir G.G. & avoiding 'Her Majesty's Secretary of State for the Home Department' . . . wch however was required by the Caput . . . Dined at Sidney Lodge Audit dinner: – a large party of 20 . . . The only ladies at dinner were Mrs Phelps, Mrs Prest, Mrs Prof. Miller (very big with child), Mrs Clem. Francis, Miss Wilkins & a Lady who seemed to me to be the Phelps Governess. – I took in Mrs Clem. & had the talkative Mrs Miller on the other side: – she says that her husband often dines out & that when he does so she never has any thing but bread & cheese!!! what next? . . .

*Mon. 7.* Wrote to Frank £15 . . . Met the staring madwoman who (as usual) stopped me: I gave her 1/ but told her that she must not stop me any more. I also took compassion on the old sweep at the Backgate of Kings: I told him that I believed I had never given him any thing in my life so I gave him 1/. – To my surprise when I thought my indexing the Hare pamphlets was come to an end a fresh batch was brought in: – I worked at them steadily till 2. – I declined going to the Public Meeting in the Arts Schools at 2 today called by the Proctors (Edleston & Drake) to discuss the Parliamentary Bill for reforming the University[19] . . . A grand cricket match today between 11 University men & 11 strangers (3 Lords among them) who call themselves I Zingari[20] . . .

*Tu. 8.* . . . At the Meeting called yesterday by the Proctors R.A. Grant (our Fellow) proposed the resolution of dissatisfaction with the Parliamentary measures of Reform (on account of the nomination resting with the Heads) & J.C. Adams (the discoverer of Neptune) seconded it. – The energy of Grant in this matter surprised me prodigiously. – The Petition was brought to me today & I signed it . . . After dinner had a visit from Wasse of Magdalene: I was very polite to him & gave him every assistance, but he is marvellously helpless. – In the Evening read with the greatest admiration Andersons 'Kleine Seejungfrau': the whole story (particularly the scene with the sea-witch) is most imaginative.

*Wed. 9.* . . . I was unfortunate enough to give great offence to Abdy by making my customary observation on one of the LLB being plucked for Little Go '– of course as he goes out in law': – Abdy made a great outbreak: – I told him most truly that I was very much grieved at having given him pain, & that it was as far as possible from my intention to do so . . . This has put an end to

---

[18] On repeated changes to the Cambridge medical course since 1821 see Winstanley, pp. 160-6, and Searby, pp. 199-202. Medical training and qualifications were under parliamentary review that resulted in the Medical Act of 1858, the setting up of the General Medical Council, and the publication of the first official *Medical Register* in July 1859.

[19] About a hundred members of the Senate attended but no Head of House, the group under attack since the ex-Royal Commissioners had aired their doubts (see 27 April). The bill was roundly attacked for its failure to ensure a freer constitution or curtail the power of the Heads, and the petition which Romilly signed the next day with 120 others was sent up to the House of Lords. See Winstanley, p.50.

[20] i.e. 'Gypsies', a peripatetic club of wealthy amateurs founded in 1845.

my idle chaffing about the LLBs Little-go exploits, at least when Abdy is on the Caput . . .

*Fri. 11.* . . . Worked steadily in the Office till dressing time & am thankful to God for having granted me to finish the Catalogue of my Muniments about wch I have been so long engaged . . .

*Fri. 15.* . . . Letter from G.T.R.: – he is now settled at Purfleet: he finds his house very pleasant, tho too small to hold all his furniture & books (some part of wch is stowed away in an adjoining unoccupied house). He has a beautiful view of the river & the shipping. – His duty is to superintend powder-proving every 3 weeks or so . . . he has to register the ranges of the 3 mortars & to strike an average . . .

*Fri. 18.* . . . Saw in the Times of yesterday (under the heading 'End of the great Kennedy case') a letter of Mr Kennedy's accompanied by a testimonial from an unnamed benefactor who settles on him £1200 a year for life in consequence of his public services & his private worth: – Mr Kennedy has accepted it . . .

*Mon. 21.* . . . Visit from Philpott (to return borrowed papers): he expressed himself very well satisfied with the conduct of Cooper in the hearings before Sir John Patteson. These hearings are now over & Sir John says he shall work hard at the case . . . Bateson . . . is just returned from Town where he was summoned to the Lord Chancellor's to meet Philpott, Ld Monteagle & Ld Burlington to discuss the 'Camb. U. Bill': he told the Chancellor very distinctly his view about the Council & about nomination by the Heads. He says it is obvious that Philpott has had a great deal to do in framing the Chancellor's Bill . . .

*Th. 24.* . . . In the Evening I received a delightful letter from Sophie in answer to mine. She says their benefactor is the excellent Scotch Judge Lord Murray, who is the only person from whom Mr Kennedy would have accepted such a favor as he was quite certain he was obliging Ld Murray by the acceptance. Sophie & all the family are highly indignant at Lord Lansdowne: – Lady L.'s death has produced a great change in him: she was his guardian angel. Sophie is naturally annoyed at Ld Lansdowne having taken part against Mr. Kennedy, – he having originally brought about her marriage with Mr K, having been her Guardian & Godfather to her only child. – Ld L. has seen every thing in the most unfavorable view for Mr K. & has acquiesced in his daughter's husband having Mr K's place! . . .

*Sat. 26.* . . . Dined at the grand party in Christ's Hall to meet the Bishop. I sat between Bateson (the Orator) & a cidevant Fellow named Wilkinson. – Cartmell made a very good chairman & had got up his topics carefully . . . The great speech of the day was the Bishop's: Archdall spoke with great fluency as he always does: Jeremie in a tender tone of regret of the loss of his great friend & patron Bishop Kaye: Shaw (in a choked tearful voice) a few words about the affectionate Kindness of Bishop Graham to himself . . . & the Master of Trinity gave us all great pain by an intemperate harangue against those who were breaking down time-sanctioned authority etc etc, palpably directed against Bateson . . . Greatly surprised on reaching home to find G.B. Allen, who had never written to announce his visit. The maids had given him tea . . .

*Mon. 28.* Up at 6! Breakfast at 6½ as G. was to return by the early train. – I was pleased at the knowledge of Virgil wch he showed: – he was looking at one of Amos's amusing clever Examination papers & he immediately pounced on a false quotation . . . He says he is now more than covering his expenses: – he has a Pupil, – whom he prepared last year for a law Examination at Oxford . . .

*Tu. 29.* . . . . Wrote to Maddison sending him £5 towards the enlargement of the King Street schools. – I of course shirked the grand dinner in Trinity today – 'Oak-day':[21]– for want of rain the oak leaves are most scarce. I omitted in the account of yesterday's dinner 2 or 3 anecdotes about School-examinations: les voici. An Examiner was holding forth about miracles . . . he said to a boy 'Now if you were to see the sun in the middle of the night what should you say?' – 'Why I should say, Father it's time to get up'. – They now examine children scientifically – as to a place being agricultural, manufacturing etc: an Inspector was examining at Cambridge & asked a little girl what Cambridge was: she answered 'manufacturing': – 'Oh indeed! & pray what do they manufacture here?' – 'Ministers, please'. – the Examiner was fairly beaten. – That begging Mrs Scott came to college today with thorough begging purposes: she brought a bottle to be filled with wine, & a ragged grand daughter for whom she begged 2/ for clothing: I complied with all her requests, told her she was an outrageous beggar (– wch she bears with equanimity) & gave her the usual monthly allowance: – I gave the little grand daughter 6d wch I charged her to keep for herself. – Then came the gaunt old night-nurse Mrs Snarey & wheedled me out of 3/ by praising dearest Lucy. This loquacious dismal giantess nearly talked me mad . . .

*Wed. 30.* . . . Mrs Walker (my neighbour) ran across the road in the rain & dirt to beg me to change my mind & come to her party tonight: – I could not be so ungallant as to refuse. – There was a huge gathering & a great many pretty young women whom I did not know . . . the great attraction was the fiddling of a young musical prodigy named Hudson, who is only 16 . . . I went away at 11¼ when dancing was beginning: – little Miss Bee (age 4) still up!

*Wed. 6 June.* . . . Visit from Bateson who kindly brought me a copy of Letter No 1 to the Chancellor . . . Bateson told me that an angry correspondence has taken place between Whewell & Sedgwick about these 2 Letters to the Chancellor. Whewell accusing S. of having deceived him & saying that he would never have recommended him to be one of the new Commissioners if he had thought him capable of being a party to these 2 letters etc etc.[22] – Bateson is highly pleased with the conduct of Sir John Romilly with

[21] i.e. the celebration of the birthday and restoration of Charles II who had hidden in an oak after the battle of Worcester. Sprigs of oak were worn, and the Book of Common Prayer still contained an act of worship for the day that was expunged in 1859.

[22] Whewell felt not unreasonably that he had been betrayed. When he supported Sedgwick's appointment to the Statutory Commission he had not expected him to join the other three ex-Royal Commissioners in retracting their earlier position vis-à-vis the constitution and government of the university (see 27 April 1855), and writing openly about it. In May Whewell sent out one of his private tracts on the subject and in effect accused Sedgwick of bad faith. What he said now was not what he had said and been understood to say before.

regard to the Chancellor's Bill . . . Letter from M.A. Tyler: – she writes in better spirits: her Mother has been to see her Father, – he is a little better . . . M.A. returns the novels of Walter Scott which I lent her. – Poor thing! she has aspirations far beyond her powers of mind & body: – she says she is attending very much to French & wishes there may be a college open for young women as well as young men! She is now teaching her brother English (that's his name not his study). – She wants 'the Popular Educator': I never heard of the book, but shall try to get it for her: – she says Mr Green (her brother-in-law Schoolmaster at Royston) lent it to her for a short time.[23]

*Th. 7.* . . . Seniority . . . We also talked about the Master's pet project of improving the approach to Trinity by throwing the walls behind the Limes: I said I was quite willing that the change should be 1st made on my side: – I said the only objection I knew was the facility wch would be acquired for getting into College by climbing the trees & so getting over the wall. – Atkinson & I then went with Hotham into his garden: his limes were pollarded by Johny Brown & are not half as handsome as mine. – I then exhibited my garden to them. – Met C.H. Cooper & asked him if the report of a new number of his Annals was true: he said it was & that he would send it to me[24] . . .

*Fri. 8.* . . . At 10 o'clock to Kings for admission of a Scholar into his Fellowship (Stone): the Provost, Heath, Theed, Witts & Evans were present: any thing more disagreeable than the conduct of Heath is inconceivable: – he perpetually stopt the Provost while reading, – said it was unstatutable to have so few Fellows present, – that the Visitor ought to be applied to, – etc etc: – such cantankerous conduct was peculiarly objectionable before a stranger like myself, who must necessarily be distressed at these family jars . . . Found 2 letters & a book and a card on my table: they had been left by the *Honorable* Josiah Quincy Junior son of *the Hon* Josiah Quincy Senior (who wrote the history of Harvard University)[25] . . .

Sedgwick fumed and twisted and the ensuing correspondence (quoted by Winstanley, pp. 54-7) grew acrimonious. Seeking an apology that never came for 'a very grave offence against the invaluable courtesies and charities of life', Sedgwick was in high dudgeon all summer. See 11 August 1855.

23 'Another form of most praiseworthy exertion on behalf of popular education. It is distinguished from 'The Leisure Hour' in being more scientific, and in addressing itself to a class somewhat more advanced in years. It is freely illustrated, and has obtained, we are informed, a very large circulation' (*Eclectic Review* 1853, I, 369).

24 Charles Cooper (1808-66) was the most learned historian of Cambridge in his generation. His *Annals*, published in four volumes between 1842 and 1852, told the story of town and gown from mythical beginnings to recent years, and he began work on a fifth for the period 1850-56 which was not completed and published until 1908. Many within the university disliked his activity as Town Clerk at a time when the corporation was determined to air its grievances, and seem to have feared his erudition and what it might reveal.

25 Romilly was plainly struck, not to say amused, by the title 'Honorable' as it was used in the United States. It had come into widespread, almost indiscriminate use among public officials. See H.L. Mencken, *The American Language* (1963 edition), pp. 324-6. The elder Quincy had sent Romilly his history of Harvard University where he was President in 1843.

*Sat. 9.* . . . I was greatly surprised at finding Mr Quincy was travelling with wife & daughter & a young lady with sandy hair about the daughters age (i.e. 24 or 25): Mrs Quincy is lame: she & her daughter are both awfully plain, & the friend positively hideous. Mr Quincy is a fine tall clever-looking man with his hair nearly white: I found the party extremely conversible & completely free from form & ceremony: we got on capitally. I was soon informed that the Ladies knew Latin: & Mrs Quincy told me that all their females were very highly educated & that they were on the 'go-ahead' system. Mrs Q. being a bad walker a carriage was ordered. The 1st place I lionised to the party was my own office, where I showed the signatures of Newton & Milton, Queen Elisabeth etc etc etc. We then went to the Fitzwilliam Museum: – their observations on every thing were those of persons on the sharp look out for gaining knowledge. I then took them to Trinity Library & showed all the treasures (except the Principia, wch was out). – Afterwards I took them into Hall (tho there were still the fag ends of the examinees at their papers) & exhibited the Sir Joshua.[26] – Mrs Q. being now tired went home & took the young ladies with her . . . At 4 we dined in hall where I presided. A good party went into the Combination room. Mr Q talked very agreeably & well. He told us he had been in company with Joe Smith (the founder of the Mormons): J.S. proceeded immediately to exhibit hieroglyphics etc etc wch he interpreted with the utmost boldness relying on the ignorance of every body present . . . Some person asked him 'if he wouldn't preach to Mr Quincy?'. – 'O yes': he then preached with extraordinary volubility & an immense command of Texts on the words 'Go teach all nations'. – When speaking of Baptism being necessary to salvation he said 'that the penitent thief was no exception for we didn't know but what he was baptised before he became a thief: – besides this Gentleman (turning to Mr Q.) will tell you that Paradise in the original Greek don't necessarily mean a place of beatitude, but the abode of the dead'. – I was amused with a bold exaggeration truly American: 'they (the Americans) have vessels with so little draught that they can get on where it is at all damp' . . .

On 12 June Romilly left for an eight-day holiday in Norwich and Cromer. In the train he 'read "Handy Andy" with much amusement, having bought that lively book of Lovers at the station'. He found Sedgwick in great form, though he was sad that Richard, who with his wife Mary lived in part of his uncle's house, 'has that melancholy discontented look still which suits so ill with the husband of so joyous & pretty & loving a wife as he has & the father of such charming children'. As usual, there were drives in the country, calls on Sedgwick's many friends and comfortable cigar-smoking hours in the kitchen after the ladies had gone to bed. One evening he took 'a solitary stroll thro some of the wretched parts of Norwich (St. Pauls & St Saviours beyond the Barracks): the churches here are wretched to look at: they look as if

---

[26] i.e. Reynolds's fine portrait of the Duke of Gloucester, later Chancellor of the University, in academical dress, aged 14 when he was admitted to Trinity. For details of how it came to the college see *Romilly 1842-47*, p. 125. The painting is reproduced in the Fitzwilliam Museum's *Cambridge Portraits* (1978).

they were made of mud: – there was great appearance of poverty & wretchedness & the cholera always makes ravages here'.

Sedgwick's conversation was, as so often, a delight and during this visit Romilly particularly enjoyed his account of 'bringing into the Combination room the intelligence of one of the great peninsular victories & the cheering & shouting with wch it was received: also his bringing home (at Dent) the news of the battle of Waterloo he having met the postboy covered with ribbons riding full speed his foaming horse'.

On the sixteenth he left for Cromer by Omnibus: 'we were close packed inside: we were licensed for 10 & had 10 full-grown people & 3 children (of about 8 or 9 years old). The Hebrew Professor Jarrett was one of the travellers: he made himself very agreeable . . . & talked away very amusingly'. Romilly thought Cromer 'a beggarly-looking place', but despite this and failing to find the learned Miss Gurney at home, he thoroughly enjoyed his walks by the sea and explorations inland.

*Wed. 20.* . . . I found a profusion of letters . . . My poor friend Col. Glover is dead, Mr Herbert of Ickleton is dead, & Henry Griggs Andrews (to whom dearest Lucy was so kind is dead! A sad mortality among my acquaintance. – It makes me the more grateful to God for the continuation of my own life. – It should teach me also to endeavour to live as one whose turn may very soon come.

*Th. 21.* Left Cambridge by Express Train 9·35 for London. – Latimer Neville was in the same carriage with me. He had declined the dinner at the Mansion house (on account of the recency of his poor brothers' death): the V.C. (Dr Guest) also declined because he didn't like making a speech. – I tacked myself to the skirts of Leapingwell: we went in the same cab from Shoreditch & I put up at his hotel (Feuillades in the Opera Colonnade). – We went to the 2 Panoramas of Alma & Sebastapol: – I was much interested with both of them: – at the Alma we had some talk with a private (named Bennet) who had fought at Alma, Balaclava & Inkerman, & lost one arm: he has been taken great notice of by Duke of Cambridge. – I now parted company with Leapingwell & went to the Royal Academy Exhibition . . . I disliked the 2 pictures wch are most talked of, viz Mellais' [sic] *Rescue* (– a fireman enveloped in red light giving her rescued child to a ghostlike woman) & Maclise's 'fight of Orlando with the Duke's prizefighter':[27]– the bust of Mr Simeon looked frightful where it was placed . . . Leapingwell & I (he red-robed & I cassocked) made our appearance at the Mansionhouse at 6·20: – we were this year admitted at the grand facade (last year at the side entrance). – A party of 250: – profusion of Ladies & Bishops: I spoke to only 4, viz. London, Oxford, St Davids & Melbourne . . . There were only 4 Cambridge Heads of Houses present, viz Whewell, Cookson (& wife), Geldart, & Worsley (& wife). A very large gathering of Oxford Heads . . . each man sat by his wife or daughter: all the Bishops & their families sat together: all the Oxford people together, & all the Cambridge people together: – not a judicious arrangement. I sat between Bateson (the Orator) & a vulgar Sir Charles Crossley (Sheriff): he was knighted (I believe) at the same time as the Mayor (Moon) was baronetted, viz. immediately after the Emperor & Empress

---

[27] The most recent of his paintings on Shakespearian subjects by Daniel Maclise, R.A.

lunched in the City. – We sat down to dinner about 7 o'clock. – My vulgar neighbour (who like the Mayor can't pronounce the letter *h*) was very good natured & offered me the services of his servant, apparently for the sake of the sweet & novel sounds 'Yes Sir Charles' . . . Bateson & I thought the Oxford ladies who sat opposite to us very unattractive. – Of all the bad speakers I ever heard I think Sir F. Moon the worst: his manner is intensely vulgar & there is neither thought nor amusement in what he says . . . The speeches in general were very mediocre, at least what I could hear of them . . . the Master of Trinity spoke a few clever sentences wch were well heard: he said that the University of Cambridge could sympathise with the City of London in its veneration for old usages, & (like it) was prepared to make reforms wch would not injure its powers of doing good . . . I did not find this party at the Mansionhouse so agreeable as last year's.

*Fri. 22.* Leapingwell & I went to Kew (by the Waterloo Bridge train): we arrived at 11 expecting the gardens to be open all day: we found they do not open till 1. I immediately proposed calling on Sir William Hooker (as I know his son Dr H. who married Fanny Henslow): Sir William was reported to be inaccessible, being in the Gardens: – but the Dr (who resides at Richmond) was fortunately in Kew: so I went in quest of him. I found him in the red brick house wch used formerly to belong to the Duke of Cumberland before he became King of Hanover: – the house is now given up to scientific purposes . . . we were shown some of the treasures of the establishment, viz. the portfolios of plants etc & the rare books on Botany: Dr H. sent a young Gentleman with us to the Museum: here we were highly pleased: one division contained flax & then all stages of the manufacture of linen: similarly for paper, india rubber, gutta percha etc etc etc: there were also specimens of all sorts of grain, fruits, & woods. I could have spent many hours there with pleasure, every thing was so systematically arranged from the simplest natural substance to the most finished manufacture from it . . . Some parts of these gardens are very picturesque: one sees the red-brick palace wch was such a favorite with George III & Queen Charlotte: – I was told that it is unoccupied . . . We . . . returned to Cambridge by the 5 o'clock Express in company with the V.C., Bateson, etc. all in the same carriage . . . We have met with a sad reverse in attempting to storm Sebastapol.

*Sat. 23.* . . . Mrs Leapingwell told me an anecdote about Lord Mayor Moon wch highly delighted me . . . When the Mayor was fêté at Paris he was taken to Fontainebleau & was shown the apartment of Henry 2d's Mistress *Diane* de Poictiers wch is decorated with moons: – he was greatly excited & was overheard saying 'very kind – very flattering': – the dolt thought they were in honour of himself. – At 11 to the Proclamation of Midsummer Fair: – probably the last time it will be proclaimed by the University . . . Wrote to Madame F. Romilly (£25) giving her a full account of the Lord Mayors Dinner: – also to the Master of the Rolls about Willy's being in the last class, saying that after that I thought there was no chance of his getting thro in Honors, & that without he turned over a new leaf he would be plucked for the polloi: – I recommended consulting his Private Tutor . . . The new wall bounding my college-garden is very nearly finished & the trees are now seen outside: it is a vast improvement . . . After dinner cut up the paper & pasted extracts in my University Book.

*Wed. 27.* . . . Letter from Sir John in answer to mine: he is full of trouble about Willy who has not returned home, & who seems to be going on very ill. On going to College I made enquiries of Hoppett. It appears that he went to Norwich on Monday the 18th saying he should stay 3 days & then go home to London. Hoppett says that he gives no noisy parties . . . & that he always finds him in bed of a morning. I was unable to confer with Blore his private tutor, he having left Cambridge. – I wrote the purport of all this to John . . .

*Fri. 29.* I am now so languid & have such pains & weariness in my legs after a few minutes crawling that I cannot get to college without resting ½ way & sitting down on the chains at Catharine Hall. – At 12 o'clock there was a great gathering in the Senate House for the Election of a Margaret Professor: Cowie, & Dr Hall having retired as well as W.W. Harvey there remained only 3 Candidates, viz *William* Selwyn, Edward *Harold* Browne, & Henry John Rose. By the way Selwyn said to me 'the contest is between William & Harold, but I fear it will not be William the Conqueror': decidedly sprightly. – All the Electors were called within the barrier & (according to printed notice) were sworn. . . . The V.C. immediately consulted his assessors about the meaning of 'ad tunc': they of course agreed with his interpretation of its meaning *continuity of name on boards* & therefore excluded DD per Saltum . . . the V.C. however said that tho such was his opinion he would accept such votes[28] . . . While the V.C. Dr Guest was conferring with his Assessors Whewell rushed to the table to remonstrate at the delay wch wd be occasioned by taking the votes according to juniority (– I having just begun according to the V.C.'s instructions to call the Junior BD according to a list wch I had drawn up): – the V.C. was immensely annoyed, told him he was engaged on a most important discussion & could listen to nothing else. – Whewell then seems to have left the Senate House. – The conference ended with his assessors the V.C. agreed to the custom of higgledy piggledy voting. – A little before 2 . . . the votes were added up & were Selwyn 43, Browne 43, Rose 17: whereupon the V.C. (who had not voted previously) gave the casting vote to Selwyn & declared him duly elected. The Registrary then began reading the Deed of Foundation: to our astonishment (while the reading was going on) up came the Master of Trinity & tendered a vote: the V.C. behaved with great spirit: – he said the Election was declared & he refused the Vote: – Whewell remonstrated, saying the V.C. had not complied with the custom of announcing the time of the close of the Poll. – The curiosity was that Whewell's vote being for Browne would have given him the election if offered in time! – So much for the effects of impatience . . .

*Sat. 30.* . . . The proceedings in the Senate House began with another fight, – peculiarly uncomfortable to me who am so languid & lackadaisical. – Whewell (having failed in his former attempt to get Okely elected Travelling

---

[28] Such a degree excused non-resident M.A.s from performing the required exercises for this higher degree if they had had a distinguished undergraduate career, as it was assumed that since then they had been occupied with other duties. Hence they took it 'at a leap'. See Winstanley, *Unreformed Cambridge* (1935), pp. 73-5.

Bachelor – there being a tie of 6 votes) came forward & presented Okely & Pomeroy.[29] – Edleston protested against the proceeding till a certificate of the resignation of Browning (Catharine) elected on the presentation of Dr Corrie for Dr Whewell was produced: – the V.C. decided on accepting the present nomination of Dr Whewell, the Trustees having apprised him that there was a vacancy & that Dr W. was to nominate: – Edleston refused to administer the oath to Dr. W, Drake also refused: – the Registrary administered it. At the polling 26 voted for Okely, & 1 (Hopkins Esquire Bedell) for Pomeroy: Edleston didn't vote . . . Letter of thanks from Betsy . . . the children are well & Jem (at work in London) comes home every Saturday night . . .

*Th. 5 July.* . . . Received from Miss Neville a very touching & very pious mémoir of her own composition of her 2 poor brothers Henry & Grey: – I read it with the greatest interest, & wrote to her. Letter from G.T.R. recommending a visit to Purfleet by way of change of air: he tells of a story of a poor man's child admiring Franky's little percussion gun & asking who gave it to him. 'Papa': – 'ah! if I had a Papa perhaps he would give me one, but I have only a "Father"'. – After dinner I plaid chess & read in the Garden (wch looks beautiful with all its roses) . . .

*Fri. 6.* Dismissal of term at 10. – Visit in my office from Edleston – about items of Proctors profits: – he says that he expects St Mary's will claim the 4d on each AB & the 2d on each AM:[30] – I believe this has not been done for a long while: – the other degrees pay nothing to St Mary's. – I gave Edleston an account of the profits of his future Office of Taxor (to wch I presented him this morning), viz. £33. 10. – Corrected the list of Degrees for the Cambridge Chronicle: – while I was doing it I fed the imp of a boy with pic-nic biscuits (just fresh) & then gave him a penny to buy marbles: – he seemed very happy at these delicate attentions . . .

On 9 July Romilly and H.A.J. Munro, the classical scholar and fellow of Trinity, went over to 'Lowestoff' to visit the Whewells in their house there. Two Miss Okes, daughters of the Provost of Kings had been staying with the Whewells for a fortnight and Cooper presumably joined them at bed-time. Whewell took the menfolk into the lighthouse built when Pepys was Secretary to the Admiralty and the whole party visited Sir Samuel Peto's 'superb' newly built mansion of Somerleyton. Romilly, who loved the sea, also managed to have some hours to himself during which he bathed and enjoyed the sands and pier. He approved of the changes at Lowestoft, 'so much altered in the 3 years since I was here that it was scarcely to be known again'. He approved too of the brilliance of Whewell's conversation and noted that he was 'violently opposed to the war with Russia & we had some animated discussion on the subject after dinner'. On the eleventh Romilly escorted the Provost's daughters back to Cambridge and was rewarded by a lift home in the Okes' waiting carriage.

---

[29] By the will of William Worts of Catharine Hall dated 1709 £100 a year for three years was to be given to each of two B.A.s from different colleges for study-travel in foreign countries. The Bachelor must ensure that he did not proceed to a higher degree if he wanted to qualify for the 'pension'.

[30] i.e. traditional payments made to the university church. For its history and the ceremonies performed there see W.D. Bushell, *The Church of St Mary the Great* (1948).

*Mon. 16.* . . . Wrote a note to Bond asking him to call. – He listened to my heart & said he found nothing wrong there: he said that my pulse also was good: he thought I was redder in the face than I used to be & much fatter: he recommended my eating more meat & less bread & pudding (farinaceous food being more fattening than nourishing): – he said I thought too much about my ailment: – he did not seem to think there was any thing vitally wrong: – so his visit cheered me a good deal. He will call again on Wednesday. – I took an egg in the middle of the day instead of my usual biscuits. – Dr Bond wrote a prescription of Muriatic Acid, Nitric acid & Taraxacum[31] . . . Began reading again Dickens' D. Copperfield: it is charming. – Did a vast quantity of 'Graduati'.

*Tu. 17.* Dosia went off (for a month's holidays) by the 11 o'clock Excursion Train, just before the rain began . . . Babington told me a great deal of Gossip: – poor Henry Staples Foster is in confinement, two brothers of his are also out of their mind (one of them a harmless Idiot whom I know & speak to): my neighbour Mr. Edmund Foster is separated from his brother Ebenezer who did not approve of him as a Partner. Babington told me also that the V.C.'s Assessors (Ainslie & Phelps) have given their Judgment concerning Dr Webb's affairs, viz. that he still owes the College £3000 & that he is without assets: he did owe £8000 but has wiped off £5000: – he was so utterly ignorant of the state of his accounts that he thought there was a balance in his Favor!! . . .

*Sun. 22.* Up at 7 & after a little cup of coffee walked in the garden for ¾ hour. – I felt more sick & giddy & headachy today & did not venture to Church either morning or afternoon. I have to bless God for not having been kept away from Church by illness for many years . . . Letter from John saying that Willy is now a soldier, he is gazetted in the 23d Foot (a distinguished regiment now before Sebastopol) & will shortly join: – John proposed coming down to look about his furniture etc etc: I wrote . . . that I & Hoppett could manage every thing, – that he should write to Willy's Tutor to take his name off . . .

*Sat. 4 August.* Up at 7. – Rather alarmed at the griping diarrhoea I have had these 3 days. Wrote to Bond to ask if he meant to produce such an effect: – he called & denied any such meaning: he said he would give me some stuff (for two days) to check it . . . I should have mentioned in my account of Sir Johns visit yesterday that Willy escaped all Examination for his Commission in the 23d Fusilleers on the strength of his having been in 1st Class Little-Go!!! Willy was also spared all stripping for surgical Examination: – I believe he would have stood such an Examination fearlessly for he is strong built & is in the perfection of health.

---

[31] 'My strength gave way 2 years ago & I have entirely renounced all society. But by Gods blessing I am able still to discharge the duties of Registrary with comfort to myself & to the satisfaction of the University. I have not like you the great happiness of having a tender & affectionate wife, for I am still that unsociable monster a Senior Fellow of a College. I have however abundance of friends & full employment for every hour of the day & am free from pain: – so I should be a monster of ingratitude if I were not deeply grateful to God' (Romilly to Philip Bliss, 16 February 1857: British Library, Add. MS 34580 f. 543).

*Th. 9.* . . . While I was lounging in the garden Dr Bond was announced: I had not expected him till Saturday. – He listened to my heart, & said he saw no disease there, but that the action was very feeble. He has now prescribed me some pills (& no drinking stuff) 3 times a day: he recommends sponging with cold water (& not tepid as I have been using) & sleeping with the dressing room window a little open . . .

*Sat. 11.* . . . Wrote to the V.C. asking for his Subscription Book & then worked strenuously (off & on) till 20' to midnight verifying the names in my Graduati marked as Fellows. – Sedgwick called about 2½ & found me strolling about the Garden: he is just returned from Lowestoff where he was passing 4 days at the Hotel, – for he won't visit Whewell till he apologises for his letter to him (about 'Remarks on Cambridge University Bill'): – by the way the Bill has been dropt for this Session in consequence of the public dissatisfaction . . .

*Fri. 24.* . . . Letter from G.T.R. telling me that Baby has had the ague but is getting better . . . I was shocked to hear from him that Mr Smith (of Dulwich & Long Acre) (whose daughter he was in love with) is ruined: – I thought he had been a wealthy prosperous man . . .

*Sat. 25.* . . . Dr Bond (9th Fee) came: he took great pains with me . . . he said . . . 'What I am desirous to see is an amendment in the strength of your legs: as term time is not very long off you must be braced up by going to the seaside for 3 weeks or a month: – less will be of no use: – I should recommend Cromer . . . I asked if he thought I ought to resign the Registraryship: he said 'O dear no: – but you keep your College rooms I hope, as it is a long way to walk to the Senate House' . . .

*Tu. 28.* Up at 6½: – walk in Botanic Garden between 8 & 9. – Tore up great quantities of letters etc, to save my Executor trouble hereafter. – Wrote to the Master & Martin to tell of my not intending to examine for Fellowships: wrote also to Hotham asking him to be my Deputy at Sturbrich Fair . . . Packe called & I admitted him. He & his wife have been spending a month at Vichy, – washing & drinking: – he was recommended by Bright the great authority in cases of Gravel etc: Bright has alarmed him by saying that he has a tendency to Diabetes & that he must give up sugar & farinaceous food & port wine, but may eat as much meat as he likes & drink 2 glasses of Claret daily . . . I was glad to have a chat with him as he is a kind amiable man . . . I roamed about (between 3 & 5) behind the Colleges, where I fell in with Patrick Beales riding to his farm (– he farms 300 acres) . . .

On 1 September Romilly departed for the Belle Vue hotel in Cromer where he occupied the delightful bedroom 'I had in June looking full on the sea'. As always when by the sea his health improved and he devoted no less than 102 cheerful pages of his journal to the people he met, the books he read and the events of each day of his five-week stay. He took walks of increasing length, entered into conversation with people on the sands and jetty, watched two Trinity young men and their ladies riding races on the shore, was invited to lunch and whist and enjoyed seeing Professor Selwyn and his wife and their niece Dudu, whose parents were in India, almost every day. Romilly's devotion to the six-year-old Dudu dated from this holiday. They went for drives in an open carriage and on one occasion saw the lifeboat launched at Sheringham. 'It was amusing to see the great boat descend the cliff into the sea, & it was a grand sight to see her riding over the heavy surf & then one moment at the top of a huge wave & then the next disappearing in the trough'. Selwyn invited Romilly and Vice-Chancellor Wood, the chancery judge, to come with him in the boat but 'we stoutly refused'. When the huge boat was 'hauled up the steep cliff: – V.Ch. Wood, Selwyn & all the men & boys of the place helped pull'. On 24 September Romilly was himself almost in need of rescue 'When I had got about a mile from Overstrand I bathed: – the waves were much too rough for the water to be cold: – I found the sousing (tho I had the greatest difficulty in keeping on my legs) very pleasant. – I then went on more than another mile & reached the *Sidestrand* waterbreak where I sat down a good bit gazing at the glorious breakers . . . these are Spring tides, it was high water & the N.E. wind blowing strongly in shore. In getting round 2 or 3 headlands I got wet ½ way to my knees: but in attempting to get round that at the farthest Cromer breakwater the water wetted me almost to my hips & the waves dashed so furiously against the cliff that I was in alarm lest I should be overpowered: so I dug my hands & knees well into the dirt cliff & scrambled up far beyond the reach of the water: – I don't think I was ever so foully dirty in my life'.

On Sundays Romilly approved of the services of the Vicar of Cromer, Mr Fitch, and occasionally helped with them. He also enjoyed the catechising of the children on Sunday evenings though Miss Selwyn, the Professor's sister, 'thought too that such a public examination was likely to puff up the children with vanity'. 'Miss Selwyn is an admirable person: besides being most pious & charitable & fond of teaching she knows Latin, Greek & Hebrew as well as French, German & Italian: she would be a fit companion for Miss Gurney'. Miss Selwyn must have been glad to be escorted home after the children's service as at night 'Cromer is not lighted'; after a party at the Fitches Romilly and other guests 'were guided by a lass with a lantern'.

Romilly's thoughts during his holiday appear only once to have turned to University affairs, but he returned home on 8 October delighted with the summary in the *Times* of Sir John Patteson's award in the matter of differences between the University and the Town. 'It is admirable: it takes away from the U. all jurisdiction in Markets & Fairs, all swearing in of Mayors etc etc, all granting of Ale-licences: it declares all the Colleges to be rateable & sets out the parishes in wch they are: – it allows wine licences (but without fee), it confirms the Proctorial Power & does not allow the Proctors, Proproctor & Servants to be had up before the Town Magistrates (– the very point on wch the negotiations between G. & T. broke down). It confirms also the Discommuning. The Award alters the University Quota from ²/₅ to ¼. – I hope the Award will satisfy the Town: – indeed they have gained almost every thing they wished.' The Quota was the annual sum raised by the University as its contribution to the expenses incurred by the Cambridge Improvement Commissioners or Local Board of Health.

*Mon. 8 October.* Up at 6½: – breakfasted at 7½: – no time for a walk . . . Read a good deal of Göthe in the Railway carriage: – arrived at Cambridge a little before 2 & found Dosia, Harriet & the bird quite well. – Wrote to Dr Bond to say how much better I was . . . I introduced into the prayers at night a thanksgiving for my recovery of health.

*Tu. 9.* Up at 6½ – Out at 8 & walked in the Botanic Garden. – This is my birthday & I am now 64 complete . . . To my great surprise & also pleasure Betsy made her appearance directly after breakfast: she brought my namesake with her: – they are both looking well. She had remembered that it was my birthday & brought me as a present from herself a very fine pair of soles etc etc. & a pot of marmalade as a gift of her sister Mary's . . .

*Wed. 10.* . . . Opening of Term – 7 AM – 1 AB & 2 AB p.b.

– Then a Seniority for 2 mortal hours: – it was a stormy meeting, Edleston & Thacker being violently opposed to a proposed scheme for widening the street opposite All Saints by making a path inside our newly exposed trees & allowing the free use of this path to the Town: – the matter deferred . . .

*Sun. 14.* . . . God be praised I am now well enough to go to Barnwell Church, where I have not been these 3 months . . . At 3 I went to St Paul's: – Mr Nicholson read prayers & a spectacle-wearing young man preached in the most drowsy unprofitable manner imaginable, & the matter was as dull as the manner . . . I understand that the sleep-compelling young man is Batty (Fellow of Emmanuel) (Curate at Great St Andrews): he was 2d Wrangler in 1853 . . . I have always thought that such preachers (however good at heart) do immense damage to the cause of religion, wch they utterly fail in bringing home to a man's conscience . . .

*Mon. 15.* Up at 6½. – I walked 3 times round the Botanic Garden & the circuit seems to me to be just ½ mile . . . Drake (late Proctor) called on me concerning Proctorial Accounts etc etc: he told me that he had a wife all ready if a decent living would but fall vacant. – Tried again at my Registrarial Accounts without detecting the error. – Fell in with David Stewart who is just arrived. – he looks as young & as handsome as ever. – Walked round the Via Lambertina, – slowly indeed, but without any desire to rest. – I was joined by Dr Archdall who turned about & walked home with me. – He is furious at Browne's not having been elected Margaret Professor, & particularly angry with Cookson & Philpott for having voted for Selwyn & so contributed to the Johnian monopoly of the Margaret Professorship . . . Archdall considers Selwyn's Election utterly informal & invalid & will never look upon him as rightful Professor till he is reelected at the end of 2 years. – I kept as cool as a Cucumber & was amused at the quantity of steam he worked off. – He is also furious against an article in the Edinburgh Review (on the correspondence between Jerome & Napoleon) because the Reviewer attacks Napoleon & refuses to admit his claim to be a great man. – Archdall showed an utter ignorance of the indolence & insouciance of my character when he begged of me to write a sharp letter of remonstrance to the Editor who so recklessly trifles with the feelings of our Ally Napoleon the 3rd!! . . .

*Th. 18.* . . . At 9·45 to the Station to look out for Grim . . . At 1·30 Grim arrived, saying that he had missed the 8 o'clock train by just 4 minutes & had laid out 1/6 in telegraphing his mishap: – he has several times used the Electric Telegraph, once to recover Bertha's Parasol . . . we went to the Station & got his communication (the 1st I have ever received) from the Electric Telegraph Office . . . At 5 Grim & I dined: – Dosia had catered capitally & produced an excellent dinner: & for dessert we had Mrs Willis's apples & *my own* grapes! After dinner I sent for Betsy & Joey to come up & see Edward . . .

*Sat. 20.* Up at 6½: – walked to Trumpington. – Betsy & Joey went off at 10 by Parliamentary Train . . . At 11 I went by Rail to Foxton: it was the 1st time I had ever been on the Royston line. – Dudu & her Swiss Maid Louise were there to receive me: – we were very soon joined by the Professor & his dog Duke. – The scenery (in a quiet way) is very pleasing . . . The house wch Selwyn took in May 1853 for 4 years was built for a Mr Hurrell: – there are 4 gardens . . . we went to see all Dudu's pets, viz. her 2 rabbits, the 2 calves, the 18-year old pony, the 2 hives of bees, the poultry (the handsomest cock & hen were her own private property) . . . Lunch was to be at 1·30: – so I got Dudu to read loud to me a few pages of Miss Edgeworth's 'Barring out', wch she did with a good deal of spirit: – at her uncles suggestion she also read & construed a couple of verses from the French Testament very fairly . . .

*Sun. 21.* . . . I deserted my Church & went to Gt St Andrews to hear a famous Birmingham Preacher J.B. Marsden (B.A of St Johns in 1827) . . . His Text was Acts VIII.8. He compared our great manufacturing towns to Samaria in their ignorance of God: he spoke of the immense good now done by the Lay Readers & particularly eulogised a Lay Reader & his wife at Birmingham. – I have not been so much pleased with a sermon for months. – I came home for my Arrow Root. – At 2 I went to St Mary's to hear Harvey Goodwin: his was an excellent sermon in praise of *real* science as a handmaid to true religion . . . St Mary's was crammed: – Goodwin particularly addressed the Freshmen . . . Declined Mrs Prest's invitation to coffee this Evening to meet Dr & Mrs Willis (– the lady's cold manners are to me peculiarly disagreeable: – she looks as ill as if she had been under her husbands homoeopathic treatment) . . .

*Mon. 22.* . . . I fell in with Harvey Goodwin who said that I might make the fortune of the people of Cromer by sending them 2 portraits of myself, one as I was before I went there & the other as I was when I quitted it.

*Tu. 23.* . . . The day being sunless I thought it a good opportunity for going to London by the 9.25 Express. – I of course was ½ an hour too soon on the Platform: but I fortunately found Johny Okes (of Cherry Hinton) & his daughter equally early: So I walked up & down with them. He is one of the Hobson Trustees & talked to me a good deal about the Conduit wch is now building: he is desirous of some public inscription to commemorate Hobson's benefactions.[32] He spoke of Hobson & Cocker both having given rise to Proverbs – 'Hobson's choice' & 'according to Cocker' . . . My only object in London was to receive my Dividends wch were sadly in arrear . . . I dined at moderate cost at the Athenæum, viz. for 1/: for wch I had 2 mutton chops. – I then walked thro St James Park to the Houses of Parliament: – the Clock Tower is nearly finished & the Victoria Tower getting on: – I am an idolater of Barry. – I now got into a twopenny steamer which took me from Westminster Bridge to London Bridge. – I arrived at the Shorditch Station 40' before my time: but I saw 2 other trains start, & the bustle & confusion prevented the time seeing [sic] long. I travelled back by the 5 o'clock Express & got into

[32] Thomas Hobson (d. 1631), the wealthy carrier immortalised by Milton, subscribed to the making of the invaluable 'New River' to bring water from Nine Wells to Cambridge, and left an endowment for its upkeep. The conduit scoured the foul King's Ditch and carried piped water to a handsome fountain of 1614 on Market Hill. In 1856 this was re-erected at the end of Lensfield Road and replaced by a neo-Gothic structure. See W.D. Bushell, *Hobson's Conduit* (1938), and the summary in Royal Commission on Historic Monuments, *City of Cambridge* (1959), II, 307-9.

C. a little after 6·30. – I had an egg with my tea. – Letter from Captain Montague (of Psalm-versifying memory) wishing me to distribute copies of the 2nd Edition of his 'No Popery' pamphlet. I wrote to decline, & told him I apprehended no danger to the young men from Popery but a good deal from scepticism & rationalism.

*Fri. 26.* . . . The V.C. & the Privilege Syndicate decided that there should be no 'Magna Congregatio' today: – indeed the Town Clerk had written to the V.C. to say that he should not summon any body to attend . . .

*Tu. 30.* . . . Letter from Luard about rusticated men going in for honors: – wrote telling him 'certainly'. The rusticated men must have been only *one* term. Mathison to put cases about Honorary Degrees etc: – I solved his difficulties. – The Voluntary Theological is come out: – 173 are passed: 31 plucked. I hear from the Examiners that the Candidates were in general deplorably ignorant, & that 30 more deserved to be plucked . . .

*Wed 31.* . . . Congregation day – 1 BD, 5 AM, 1 AB. Also 12 Graces unopposed: One of them was to thank Mr Halford (the Benefactor to the Library) for a Guido (Salome with John Baptists Head): another to confirm Sir John Patteson's direction in his award that we should receive no more annual payments for Wine-licences, & to return the money received since the Award . . . Wrote to Whewell attacking the principle of appointing a coadjutor to *each* of the 13 Professors examining for Certificates: – my argument was that some of them had nobody at all to examine . . .

*Wed. 7 November.* Up at 6½: – walked in Botanic Garden. – Breakfasted with the Senior Proctor (Wolfe): a small agreeable party. – There was a storm expected in the Senate House: but happily it came to nothing: Caucuss took no part in the business: Edleston was supposed to be the stoutest of the malcontents, & Sedgwick, Professor Thompson, & Leapingwell were hostile also against Whewell: – but no one came up to the scratch. – Philpott had been nominated with Whewell: – 13 votes only were tendered & they were all for Whewell[33] . . .

*Fri. 9.* . . . Today was the Election of Mayor: Patrick Beales declined (on the score of his wife's bad health): Mr Ekin was chosen. – The V.C. did *not* swear him in. That offensive privilege is now gone for ever. – The V.C. (Whewell) was asked to the new Mayor's dinner: – but he was engaged . . . While I was out Miss King called in Miss Cotton's carriage & left a letter & a package from Miss Cotton: – the letter was a very kind & a touching one, taking leave of me before her departure next Tuesday & begging me to accept as a memorial of her Mother an engraving of her brother Sir Charles Rowley . . . & regretting that there was no engraving of Gainsboro's beautiful picture of her. Miss Cotton had just seen her nephew Col. King, who is returned from the Crimea wounded. – Miss Cotton is going . . . to settle at Hastings . . . Clark communicated the following very indifferent joke about the very large Princess *Mary* of Cambridge who is

[33] i.e. to serve as Vice-Chancellor for the coming year.

supposed to be on the look out for a husband: – 'What one man would be bold enough to take ⎰ so vast a Poll ⎱ !'
⎱ Sevastopol ⎰ [34] . . .

*Wed. 14.* . . . Selwyn told me that his Lecture Room (the Arts School) is so crowded with youngsters to hear his Lectures on Genesis (– the difficulties concerning the Mosaic account of the Creation etc) that many can't get seats: – about 300 have sent in their names . . . Selwyn told me that in his last illness Dobree used to get his bedmaker to read the bible to him & was so humble as to tell her to select as she knew the bible much better than he did![35] . . .

*Fri. 16.* . . . I am sorry to hear that Mrs Marlow (of the King St. School) – & Mother of Mrs Coppin) is found unequal to the present requisites of a Mistress & is to be dismissed: – she takes it greatly to heart: – she is to have a pension of £15 p.a; – she used to have £50 or £60 . . .

*Tu. 20.* . . . The Master has most kindly asked me to meet the Duchess of Cambridge & Princess Mary at Lunch tomorrow; I accepted with much pleasure . . .

*Wed. 21.* . . . As I was walking to Trinity Dr Cookson called out to me to get into his fly wch I did most willingly . . . In Trinity Court we saw the Duchess of Cambridge's carriage standing near the Chapel: the Duchess, the Princess Mary (so-vast-a-Poll), etc. were inside the Chapel & the Organ was playing: – there was a concourse of people in the Court. – I thought Trinity Lodge drawing room (the Henry VIIIth room) looked beautiful, with its gilt chairs, its magnificent carpet (bought from the 1st Crystal Palace), & filled with distinguished guests. It was however a great drawback that poor Mrs Whewell was not well enough to be present. All the Heads (but no Headesses) were asked: the Vice Master & the other Seniors of the College, Dr Jeremie & our young noblemen (Lds Althorp, Belmore & Royston) were the only other Cambridge guests. The Doctors were all in Scarlet & the Noblemen in their gold gowns. The Guests from Wimpole were Lord Hardwicke (who wore his red gown), Lady Hardwicke & daughters (I think), her sister Lady Barrington & daughters, the Duchess of Cambridge & the Princess Mary (who is goodlooking & merry & not so large as I expected), Lord Stanley (M.A. of Trinity in 1849) (who has just declined being Secretary to the Colonies), Lord Cardigan (with portentous moustache) etc etc etc. The Belle was Miss Barrington. The Duchess is on a large scale; she talks a good deal & with a foreign accent. The Master desired Sedgwick & me to sit at top & bottom, he himself sitting in the middle. Sedgwick had the handsome Miss Barrington sitting next him: – I had no such luck, – only 2 Heads of houses. Unfortunately

---

[34] She 'is so big now again – much worse than she was – and whose manners and I grieve to say conversation too, now – are not refined . . . I fear there is no hope for a husband. All this with her figure is too much' (R. Fulford, *Dearest Child. Letters between Queen Victoria and the Princess Royal* (1964), p. 142, 27 October 1858). Her cousin Victoria was long exercised with settling 'poor Mary' Cambridge and succeeded in 1866 when she married the Duke of Teck.

[35] i.e. Professor P.P. Dobree (1782-1825), the foremost Greek scholar in Cambridge after Porson's death. He left Trinity a thousand volumes and books with his own manuscript notes to the University Library which included them in a *Catalogue of Adversaria* (1864).

there was not room for all the party to sit down: so Doctors Okes, Pulling & Jeremie, Martin & Atkinson remained standing in the oriel, – uncomfortable & tantalising. – The Master begged me to get them to sit down as soon as we had risen: – the Provost however declined, saying he had lunched before. – This want of room was a sad mishap, but it couldn't have been helped without a side table, & nobody would have liked to sit there. – The Master took his guests into the hall before lunch, & after lunch exhibited the Newton Letters etc etc from our Library in the drawing room . . . At Trinity Lodge there was a very costly rug, wch hurt my eyes from bands (with the College motto Virtus vera Nobilitas) slantingwise . . . the border representing coats of arms I admired . . . The Fitzwilliam Museum was shut against the public today for the sake of the Duchess of Cambridge & the Princess Mary: but they didn't arrive there till 4 o'clock when the daylight was pretty well gone.

*Sat. 24.* Up at 6½. At 9 to the Selwyns to meet Bishop & Mrs Perry, Mr Jenyns (Vicar of Melbourne in England), Dudu & myself. Afterwards came Dr Paget & John Cooper & 2 nephews of Mrs Perry's. – The prayers began with the Psalm of the day, then the Confession etc – all from the Prayer Book. Dudu made herself most useful at breakfast by acting page . . . The Bishop told a comical story of a man threatening to drown his wife if she persisted in saying 'Scissors': – he kept his word, but as she was sinking she raised 2 fingers to look like a pair of Scissors. – I told the well-known one of Talleyrand saying to Madame de Stael (who had asked him wch he would save from drowning, herself or the beautiful —, if he could save only one) 'Vous savez nager sans doute' . . . At 25' past 2 arrived Maggey [sic] & George, more than ½ hour after the usual time. – They were exceedingly well . . . At 5½ we dined, – a party of our 3 selves. Both Maggie & George plaid the piano in the Evening: – she does not sing: – they both plaid by heart. After much searching George found out (in 'Punch' of 1850) 2 slang ballads of Thackeray's, one about Elisabeth Davies (a servant lass deluded into receiving a housebreaker for a lover) & the other of a Doctor having a baby palmed on him in a Railway Carriage. – George read them both aloud. – Bed soon after 10.

*Mon. 26.* . . . I gave to Maggie all the silk dresses wch had belonged to dear Margaret & Lucy & also the muff & furs. I escorted George & M. to Pembroke to show them the bust of Pitt.[36] I then trusted them with the key to my rooms (wch they wished to revisit) & went to my office. – Gave them lunch at 12½. Maggie not having tasted Champagne since her wedding breakfast I produced a bottle –: she is marvellously temperate at meals & well observes 'the rule of not too much in what she eats & drinks'. – G. & M. went away by the 1·35 train, & professed themselves greatly pleased with their visit . . .

*Fri. 30.* . . . Wrote to Maggie (enclosing £10 for George & announcing hamper of Audit): she had written to me to describe their safe arrival & the

[36] Done in 1833 by Sir Francis Chantrey. Romilly could have compared it with the Nollekens statue in the Senate House, a terra cotta bust by Gerrard in the Fitzwilliam Museum, both dated 1808, and a medallion at the Pitt Press (see 19 June 1850).

warm reception from baby & Franky: – baby was unwilling to go to bed as if afraid of a similar slippery trick of desertion . . . In the Evening an amusing letter from Grim describing the grinning of his savages at the sight of eatables from Fortnums & Masons: – he makes his wife sing the Ratcatchers daughter & speaks of her pathos in the stanza 'So 'e cut 'is throat with a pane of glass

> And stabbed 'is donkey arter:
> So 'ere was an end of Lilly white sand
> Donkey & the Ratcatchers dorter'. –

I wrote Grim a long letter in reply.

*Sat. 1 December* . . . A man came to my office for a Professorial Card: it turned out that he was already A.B, but wished to attend Clark etc economically: I of course told him the cards were meant for undergraduates: – he remonstrated & was greatly disappointed: I told him that if he wished to attend any Professor he must pay whatever that Professor charged. – Dr Cookson suggested to me the propriety of having a notice-board at my entrance-door of the Pitt Press, as he had himself climbed the 50 steps & all in vain: – I immediately acted on this suggestion, fetched my 'At Home' board from college, drove a nail into the downstairs door & hung up my board from 2½ (after Congregation) till 5 . . .

*Sun. 2.* . . . There has been an enthusiastic meeting in London in honor of Miss Nightingale: the tribute agreed on is the education & training women to be Nurses for the Sick. At this meeting a warm eulogy was passed on the late Mrs Moore (widow of a gallant Officer who died so lamentably) for exertions like those of Miss Nightingale: I think this must have been Mrs Willoughby Moore (born Clark & sister of the fascinating Caroline Clark who married 1st a Mr Dickens & then John Guthrie . . .

*Mon. 3.* . . . Visit in my Office from Hopkins (Esquire Bedell): he wanted to learn what persons who had taken Honorary Degree were entitled to a place in Golgotha:[37]– he thought Lord Arthur Hervey was: – I gave my judgement against him, & laid down as the law that *younger* sons of Noblemen were not entitled *unless they had been entered as Noblemen*: it is most rare for them to be so entered: – but the late Dean of Windsor – (the Hon. Geo. Neville) tho a younger son wore a Nobleman's gown as an undergraduate & was therefore always entitled to a seat in Golgotha among the Noblemen . . .

*Wed. 5.* . . . In the street I was accosted by Alderman Finch (Father of the walk called by his name): he is very anxious to transfer the old Conduit from the Market-place to the beginning of the Wranglers walk: he is collecting subscriptions: – I very gladly gave him a Guinea. He told me that the new Conduit (from a design of Mr Hill) will cost £600, & that a few years ago about £600 was spent in new pipes for Hobson's stream . . . Learned from Atkinson that the new work "Cambridge Essays" is edited by W.G. Clark (–

---

[37] i.e. the eighteenth-century gallery across the chancel of Great St Mary's, reserved for doctors, noblemen, and *heads* of houses. Hence the name in allusion to Matthew 28, verse 33. So powerful was the influence of the ecclesiologists that the destruction of this gallery and other Georgian fittings was imminent, and the church today bears almost no resemblance to what was there in 1850.

Gazpacho),[38] that Clark is a contributor, that Watson (grandson of the Bishop) (who lives over the water with his Father) has an amusing article on Molière, & Brimley an article on Tennyson:[39]– Watson was a candidate for the Disneian Professorship, but his being only B.A. was fatal to him. – Letters from Paris: they will keep till the 16th when they will be read & answered.

*Mon. 10.* . . . Treated myself with "Cambridge Essays". In the Evening read W.G. Clark's article on Classical studies. he is violent against the dishonesty of petty tradesmen: he utterly deprecates the Moral Science & Natural Science Triposes as thorough failures: – he writes with rather a strong tory reverence of the wisdom of our Fathers: – the concluding eulogy of Latin & Greek is animated . . .

*Fri. 14.* . . . In the evening a very amusing letter from Grim. It contained a collection of 21 Hymns 'selected & *revised*' by himself for Millom Church: Bertha is forming a choir & has got a *harmonium* . . . He tells me that he has not introduced Oliver Twist into the Village Library because one of the best & most influential parishioners is named Bill Sykes! . . . Grim's letter enclosed a little note from Bertha the Less: 'dear Uncle Joseph how are you: I dont like living at Millom: – believe me your affectionate niece B.C. Allen'. – I wrote her a long letter & put it in a Cover to herself: – I also wrote a long letter to Grim. – Triumph for Russia – Kars has fallen: – thro famine.[40]

*Wed. 19.* . . . I was shocked to hear that poor Mrs Whewell is dead: she died yesterday: she underwent a severe operation on Friday & Mr Humfrey & Mr Lestourgeon thought most unfavourably of her state: she became much worse on Sunday, & on Monday no hope was left. Happily her sister Lady Monteagle was with her: I hear the Master is greatly overcome . . .

*Th. 20.* . . . My neighbour Mr Dennis of the Leys told me that Barrett (the Glassman) is dead & is reputed to have been worth £100,000! He was (teste Magistro Dennis) a great Screw who never parted with a farthing & gave no portion to his 2 daughters (his only children) on their marriage! . . .

*Mon. 24.* Up at ¼ to 7. – On my walk to College at 8 I fell in with Grote who was come over to attend poor Mrs Whewell's funeral. – It was nominally to be at 8½: – Sedgwick & Grote & I went into the diningroom of the Lodge at 8½ & there saw Lord Monteagle, Cooper & Hedley: these last 2 were to officiate in Chapel . . . Besides Lord & Lady Monteagle the Mourners were Mr & Mrs Worsley, & James & Arthur Marshall. – The Funeral began about 9:

[38] Nickname of W.G. Clark since the publication of his amused and amusing little book with this title about his summer ramble in Spain in 1849.
[39] The other contributors were C.A. Bristed (on the English language in America), Francis Galton (on modern geography), Charles Buxton (on limitations to severity in war), G.D. Liveing (on the transmutation of matter), Fitzjames Stephen (on the relation of novels to life), and R.E. Hughes (on the future prospects of the British navy). Three more miscellaneous volumes comprising 21 papers under the title *Cambridge Essays* appeared in 1856-8; they included papers by Maine, Hort, Luard, and Hopkins. Authors and titles are listed in R. Bowes, *A Catalogue of Books printed at . . . Cambridge* (1894), p. 397.
[40] The Asiatic frontier saw severe fighting during the Crimean War. In 1855 the Russians under Mouravieff, despite losing over six thousand men, encircled the British-Turkish garrison on the heights of Kars. Under Lieutenant-General Williams it held out for five months despite cholera, intense cold, and eventually starvation. See 6 July 1857.

Drs Geldart, Cartmell, & Cookson, Jeremie & Munro & the small no of resident Fellows were waiting in the antechapel. – Lady Monteagle came in leaning on the Masters arm. – I thought Cooper & Headley read very well. – Dr Geldart had a carriage & offered to take me to the Cemetery . . . Maddison (Clergyman of All Saints) read the service in the Churchyard in a clear & consolatory voice. – It was very cold while our heads were uncovered, for there was a keen wind. – Afterwards Cooper called on me. He told me that he & Arthur Marshall (her brother) are poor Mrs W's Executors. She has left £9000! to the College (the Master having a life interest): this £9000 (if not otherwise bestowed for the good of the College by the Master) is to go to the Pigott Fund.[41] What a noble benefaction! . . .

*Christmas Day*. Up at ¼ to 7. A very dark morning: – a very little rain. – Up to Huntingdon Turn Pike. I found the women & girls in a great state of excitement up at St Giles, & no wonder, for 3 weddings were going on . . . I had a grand Turkey & Ham for dinner. – all by myself! – the 1st time in my life I have eaten a solitary Xmas dinner: – such solitude is a sad penalty of old age & a remembrancer of preparing for my own departure . . .

*Sat. 29*. . . . From 10 to 2½ received fees of the Questionists: 139 came (without a moments cessation): 10 of them I also had to furnish with Professorial Cards. At one time a batch was insubordinate & would not comply with Hoppett's injunction to stay in the dining room till my bell rang & then to come in (according to my desire) only 6 at a time: – they came thronging about the drawing-room door . . .

---

[41] John Pigott, sometime fellow, gave Trinity £12,000 in 1811 to augment the income of its poorer parishes.

A Breakfast Party

# 1856

*Sun. 6 January.* . . . I was greatly amused with an impudent handbill on flaming red paper wch I saw today on a wall in Barnwell: *Heresy!!!* 'With the permission & under the patronage of the V.C. & the Mayor will be burnt on Sunday Evening in the square before Trinity Great Gate by the Rev. J. Cooper & Rev. C. Clayton the *Book of Jasher*, Reynolds London, & the Liber Expurgatorius'[1] . . .

*Sat. 12.* Up at ¼ to 7. Thermometer at 30° – Walked to Trumpington. Allot told me yesterday of the monstrous sinecure held by Dr Percy (Bp of Carlisle): he is Prebendary of Finsbury, & every 7 years receives a fine of £49,000!! He says 'the Times' has not shown him up (probably from ignorance of the fact) tho they attack Archdeacon Hale for being Master of Charterhouse, etc etc altogether about £3000 p.a. – This Prebend was an 'Option'[2] of Archbishop Sutton's & he gave it to his son-in-law Percy. – 'Options' are now abolished . . . The List of approved for Mathematic Honors came out this morning: our best Trinity man 'Dunning' is to have an aegrotat degree:[3] 6 men are plucked – two of them (Goodhart & Morgan) are Trinity men: 33 are reduced to Polloi (– 12 of these are Trinity men!): – so Trinity Coll. will cut a sorry figure in the Mathematical Tripos . . .

*Sun. 13.* . . . Rich letter from a Mr Theophilus Berigni, asking for a *friend* (quaere himself?) who wants a degree in a 12 month as he has the offer of a living: – he begs a personal interview, & that every thing may be confidential, & he is prepared to deposit a good sum of money!!! – Wrote in reply that we did not sell degrees. – Kind letter from Mrs Hoskin accompanying a present of a 2d tract wch she has just published: it is called 'My Jesus' or the power of prayer. – Her former Tract was called 'Dig Deep'. This is a very touching true story of a young girl who had worked in the mill at Whittlesford, & whom Mrs Hoskin had attended in Addenbrooke's Hospital & upon her death-bed at Whittlesford. The tract is well written & deeply interesting . . . At 11 to Barnwell, where Mr Monk (the Curate) read prayers & Mr Titcomb preached vigorously . . . The end of the sermon was an appeal for 'the Savings Club' & for 'the Adult Mens School' (at wch only 40 men have attended:) Mr Titcomb wished to raise £16 from this & 2 other sermons

---

[1] The *Chronicle* of 12 January, unlike Romilly, found the joke 'a piece of thoughtless work, regretted by every sensible person'. Placards throughout the town advertised the burning of *Jasher* (see 27 April 1855), *Mysteries of the Court of London* by the radical journalist G.W.M. Reynolds, and other 'heretical and hateful works'. The presence of the mayor and police ensured that the large crowd which gathered by 8 p.m. behaved quietly, and accompanied the only conflagration – that of a copy of *The Times* – with shouts of laughter.

[2] i.e. the right of an archbishop when about to consecrate a bishop of choosing a benefice or preferment in the see to which he could act as patron when it fell vacant. Archbishop Sutton died in July 1828 soon after Percy, who had married the eldest of his ten daughters, had become in rapid succession Bishop of Rochester and Carlisle.

[3] Literally 'he is ill'; hence a certificate saying that a student is too unwell to attend lectures or be examined. An aegrotat degree was awarded if the examiners were satisfied that he could have passed when well.

to be preached at Christ Church today: – the great mass of well-dressed substantial-looking people flocked out of church without giving a farthing[4] . . .

*Wed. 16.* . . . A poor pretty sickly girl (named Lucy Newman) called on me with an in-door Hospital Order: – I gave her 2/6 to buy tea & sugar in the Hospital: – all her family are in the Union: she herself had been taken out of the Union by Mrs Wotton (wife of the sublibrarian) to be her maid . . . I also had some talk with Philpott (Deputy V.C.) about the Election of Atkinson: – he told me that the 2 Scrutineers (the Senior & Junior Fellow) escorted Atkinson to Catharine Hall, that he (Philpott asked if all had been done statuably & if there was a majority: – they exhibited the 19 signatures (every Fellow Senior & Junior having been present: – Philpott then (standing) made Atkinson kneel on a chair, took his hands between his own & admitted him 'in magisterium, curam & regimen Aulæ de Clare'. – I entered all these details in a Memorandum in my office[5] . . .

*Sat. 19.* . . . Letter from Archbishop Musgrave; asking mode of proceeding for Dr Wesley to become Prof. of Music in case of poor Walmisley's death . . . Afterwards in a walk behind the Colleges I met Mathison who told me that poor Walmisley is dead: he died at Hastings: his brother (a Clergyman) was with him & administered the Sacrament to him: his illness had brought him into a good frame of mind . . . Dr Wesley (now Organist of Winchester; having succeeded Clarke Whitfeld at Hereford, then gone to Exeter, then to Leeds & now to Winchester) is reputed the finest Organ-player in the Kingdom, but is so illtempered & quarrelsome that nobody can get on with him. – In consequence of this information I wrote a 2d letter to the Archbishop (my 1st being already posted) . . .

*Sun. 20.* . . . Letter from Power giving interesting details about the Clare Fellowships . . . He tells me that the 1st Act of Atkinson's Mastership was assuming the designation of *College* for Clare: – in the statutes the foundation is called 'Domus, sive Aula, sive Collegium' . . . From 3 to 5½ walked. – This was a longer walk than I had intended, but I met Potts & his sister-in-law Miss Fyson & I found their conversation so agreeable that I walked with them a long way on towards Shelford . . . We happened to be talking about the great coarse Saunders of Sidney & Potts said that he used to be known by the name of 'Backy, Beer & Bible', pipes & a tankard & a Bible being always to be found on his table . . .

[4] The *Chronicle* of 24 May 1856 reports fully the first anniversary meeting of the Working Men's College of which Harvey Goodwin was principal. In his speech he described the setting up of an adult school to act as a feeder to the college. They would have been satisfied to have thirty or forty persons 'prepared to pay fourpence a week, for instruction after their day's toil, in the three R's . . . but the day after the school opened they were so overwhelmed with pupils that it was necessary to move to larger premises', and now a hundred pupils were taught on four nights of the week from 8 to 10 o'clock by members of the university. For want of space no more than forty pupils could have been accommodated before the move to Maddison's schoolroom.

[5] Atkinson's was the only election to the mastership at Clare between 1814 and 1915 when he died having long outlived his faculties.

*Wed. 23.* . . . From 10 to 12½ at Caput at Trinity Lodge: I had got the papers in excellent order & I never knew the work got thro nearly so quickly . . . I was very glad to find that Whewell could laugh & tell jokes: – one of our Questionists was Hudson of Magdalene – I said 'he is son of the Railway King': – 'ah! said Whewell & used during his reign to be called *Prince of Rails* & after his fall *Wreck of the Royal George*' . . . The case of Sir J. Stephen's certificate was an amusing one: – the youngster had not (as required) attended one whole course, but Sir J.S. goodnaturedly read to him afterwards 3 Lectures. – Of course the Caput allowed the slight informality to pass . . .

*Fri. 25.* . . . As was expected St Johns has the Senior Wrangler: – the 1st 6 are

| | |
|---|---|
| Hadley _____ | (Johns) |
| Rigby _____ | (Trinity) |
| Clark _____ | (Queens) ⎤ |
| Ellis _____ | (Sidney) ⎬ æq: |
| Smith (Horace) ____ | (Trinity) ⎦ |
| Hardy _____ | (Trinity) |

. . . Seniority at 11 . . . Whewell was amused at Clare renouncing its appellation of *Hall* & says it spoils the Poetical associations

'As many quit the streams that murmuring fall
To lull the sons of Margaret & *Clare Hall*,
Where Bentley late tempestuous wont to sport
In troubled waters but now sleeps in port.
Before them march'd that awful Aristarch,
Plow'd was his front with many a deep remark:
His hat, wch never veiled to human pride
Walker with reverence took & laid aside'
Dunciad – Book IV. –[6]

There was a sealing afterwards at wch we received 4/. – Whewell's kind attempt to get the Honor List published at 8 failed: – the Examiners refused to comply & said the Grace of the Senate appointed 9. – I hear that all the Fitzwilliam managing Syndicate have resigned because Whewell directed the walls of the Gallery to be painted red, they preferring green! – what a squabbling world![7] – Dined in hall, the 1st time since the summer. I was in

---

[6] The three Halls (Pembroke, St Catharine's and Clare) all dropped that designation during the nineteenth century and adopted 'College' instead. Partly perhaps the reason was that in various publications the grouping of halls as something other than colleges implied a difference and inferiority which had not existed for two centuries. Trinity Hall had no option but to stay as it was.

[7] The Syndics had much graver reasons for resignation than a choice of paint, and it is hard to side with Whewell as Romilly did. He had taken the opportunity of the closure of the museum for partial redecoration to hang recently acquired pictures and rehang others, and Worsley who had visited unexpectedly wrote that he had done so on his 'own single authority, and without the consent, or even the privity of the Management Syndicate'. With his usual seeming confidence, defiant and unrepentant, Whewell published a *Vindication* in which he

the Vice Master's chair . . . I went up stairs for ¾ hour. – We discussed the Grace & Benson asked if I would authorise his altering the punctuation on the Grace Board from 'Domine Sancte, Pater Omnipotens etc' to 'Domine, Sancte Pater, Omnipotens etc': I willingly gave my consent . . .

*Sat. 26.* Up at 7: took 3 turns in our walks: it rained hard all the time. – Declined the breakfast of the Father (Hedley). – A little before 9 to the Senatehouse, – then only ½ full: – among the visitors was Dosia (with a friend): the weather now cleared up & the Senate House was soon crammed to suffocation. – There was no delay: the reading of the Supplicats by the *Caput* was considered complete last night: – the reading by the Scrutineers (I acting for Bright) began at once. I was rejoiced to see Whewell warmly applauded by the galleries: I received 3 cheers as Registrary & 3 more on going out as 'old Fellow Romilly!' – The work was got thro by 20' to 12 . . . At night a visit from a Mr Brunyee (Clare) just come into Cambridge & anxious to attend Amos's Examination on Monday: told him he might, in spite of this late notice: – lucky for Amos: – now he & his Assistant Examiner will have 2 men to examine, a man apiece![8]

*Mon. 28.* Up at 10' to 7: Ground white with hoarfrost: thermometer at 30. – Walked in Cherry Hinton Road. – Letter from G.T.R. & Maggie. He tells me that his prospects seem brightening, for the retirement of the Storekeeper Greensitt (who has been his great enemy & has poisoned the mind of Col. Askwith against him, – Geo. having believed the Col. to be most friendly to him) is expected very soon to take place. – Maggie's was a very agreeable letter: I was much pleased with the following passage about the children 'Your little godson is the picture of health . . . never passes a soldier without making himself as big as he can & saying "Arms". Frank has made up his mind to be a Clergyman & to have 2 services at the Garrison Chapel instead of one. We have therefore decided that Frank shall be Archbishop of Canterbury & Baby Commander in chief!' . . . I learned from Mrs Willis that her husbands order of the Legion of Honor was conferred in the most distinguished manner by the Emperor himself: – only 14 others had that marked compliment. It is however not Etiquette for Willis to wear the Medal in England without leave from the Queen, & leave will not be granted without it can be shown that his services were purely for France & in no way related to England[9] . . .

*Tu. 29.* . . . Whewell's Vindication of himself in the matter of the painting the walls, new hanging the Pictures etc this vacation came out today . . . I think it very able: – the Protest also of 7 Fitzwilliam Syndics & their final Resignation (on the 21st) was today sent me by one of the Resigning Syndics

argued that the museum should reopen as soon as possible but refused to suspend his alterations. See Winstanley, pp. 139-47, and 29 January.

[8]  Andrew Amos, Professor of the Laws of England, whose examination papers Romilly found 'very entertaining', examined Nathaniel Brunyee for a professorial certificate on 28 January. For the proportion of candidates to examiners in the Moral Sciences Tripos see Searby, p. 249.

[9]  Professor Willis was a Vice-President of the Paris Exhibition opened by Napoleon in May 1855.

(Philpott): the other 6 are Guest, Worsley, Long, Blore, Cooke & Searle. – I am very sorry that Whewell should meet with all this fash. – After dinner read Macaulay . . .

*Wed. 30.* Up at ¼ to 7. Bright frost. Thermometer 28° – As I was walking in the road I heard a noise & turning round sharp saw some horses within a few yards directly behind me: – I cannot be too thankful for my Providential escape: the horses were going like mad, having run away with the cart: – the driver was a long way behind, running after them: – had I not instantly jumped aside I must have been run over & perhaps killed . . .

*Th. 31* . . . After my tapioca I went into the Fitzwilliam (wch was today reopened after the new painting & new hanging wch has caused the resignation of the Syndics). – I thought it looked beautiful, & I thought Whewell's hanging the Pictures very clever indeed; but I regretted his horror of undraped figures having made him put the Titian's Philip & Princess of Eboli in a dark corner: & I thought the placing the beautiful Paduanino high up over a door & covering it with a green curtain purely ridiculous: – so too thought Mrs Willis & drew up the Curtain to have a look.[10] A Mr Scharf has given 4 or 5 admirable casts. – Whewell has certainly violated the Constitution of the Fitzwilliam Museum by throwing the Syndics overboard, but he has done his work like a man of genius . . .

*Mon. 4 February.* . . . Visit in my office from V.C. to talk about special Constables etc etc with reference to the approaching Election. After he was gone I looked into the accounts of Dr Philpott in the grand year 1847 & also the great contested Election for the Representatives. I found special Constables for 1st but not for 2d[11] . . . I called at Miss Apthorp's & left cards for her & Mrs Parry. – I hear that an impudent relation of Mrs Parry gave (when she was in the Senate House at the Bachelors Commencement) 3 cheers 'for the ladies who want husbands & cant get them'!: – Mrs Parry was highly indignant . . .

*Wed. 6.* . . . I was exceedingly glad of one thing today: – the Caput passed Lord Hervey's supplicat & he was duly admitted with Lord Belmore & Lord Rollo, standing, as Noblemen by the V.C.: the other 2 Hon. degrees Hon Mr Fielding & Sir I.B. Guest were admitted on their knees . . .

[10] Although Whewell's name has been especially remembered for it, criticism of immorality in exhibitions was not new. In the supplement to *The Record* of 23 January 1854, for example, a pseudonymous correspondent warns of allowing young members of the university and 'astounded rustics from the adjacent villages' to contemplate pictorial and plastic naughtiness. 'Vile contamination is thus spread amongst all classes. Surely now is a time for withdrawing from the public eye such impure objects and loathsome subjects.' In his own *Vindication* Whewell observed that 'the exhibition of nude figures in a public gallery is always a matter of some embarrassment' and 'since in recent times we have opened the Fitzwilliam . . . to very young persons of both sexes it appears to be quite necessary for the credit of the University that it should be possible to pass through the gallery without looking at such pictures'. Romilly misspells Padovanino; the picture was called 'the Sleeping Venus'.

[11] The Queen and Prince Albert came to Cambridge in July 1847 when he fulfilled his Commencement duties as the newly elected Chancellor (*Romilly 1842-47*, pp. 213-17). As usual on occasions of extraordinary excitement in the town numbers of special constables were sworn in and to these were confided the keeping of the streets. C.E. Law and H. Goulburn were elected M.P.s for the university on 3 August after five days of polling.

*Th. 7.* . . . Took voting cards, V.C.'s Oath etc etc into Senatehouse before breakfast. – 1st day of Election of a Representative: the Candidates are Walpole & G. Denman . . . Polling began immediately after the preliminaries were over (wch commenced at 10): – the 1st of these preliminaries was reading the Writ, wch now for the 1st time was not from the Sheriff but from Charles Romilly (Clerk of Crown Office as I believe): then came bribery oath, & lastly the V.C.'s oath as returning officer . . . A very ardent Tory named Potchet (AB 1798 Johns) voted for Walpole: he is allowed by his host Maddison to be one of the most fiery & furious politicians alive & of ungovernable temper in all things: – he quarelled with old Lord Huntingtower of reprobate memory, who said to him 'What'll you take to reverse the syllables of your name?'.[12] – Selwyn afterwards introduced me to this red-hot Tory: – I was extremely civil to him & said you & I, Sir, have many points of resemblance: we are both elderly, were both 4th Wrangler, & are both ardent politicians'. After 6 hours polling the numbers were Walpole 297, Denman 160. . . . Lord Jermyn & his son Lord Hervey voted together: all the Herveys voted for Walpole. – Lord Belmore & Lord Rollo tendered votes (1st for Walpole & 2d for Denman) but were refused as Minors. – I was amused by a decently dressed man stopping me to ask if Prince Albert might vote at this Election if he pleased: – I assured him he couldn't . . .

*Fri. 8.* . . . I went to the Office & ordered 500 more cards for Walpole, there having been a hue & cry for cards last night: – the Walpolites have polled 329, but the 500 cards I put on their table are all gone! . . . The Polling began at 10: the undergraduates were excluded from the gallery: – everything went on very quietly till about 3 when there was shouting & halloing outside the rails for about 10' . . . At 7½ to the Arts Schools for the Evening polling: – there were squibs flying in all directions & something of a gathering, but I apprehended no mischief. Presently however an infuriate rabble of the scum of Barnwell (mixed up doubtless with undergraduates) burst the barriers & got to the doors of the Schools (if not into the schools themselves): they shouted & screamed like so many incarnate devils. The Proctors declared they could do nothing: they had gone to the door & spoken to the men but they wouldn't mind or stir an inch in the way of retiring. The brutish mob doubtless thronged the V.C. & impeded his getting into the Schools where there were 53 voters (armed with cards) who were in a very excited state about there being nobody to receive their votes. Trevor jumped on a table & proposed there should be a deputation from the 2 committees to go to the V.C. & demand of him the reason of his delay! This foolish proposal however met with no encouragement: – about ¼ hr after the time the V.C. made his appearance – in a very excited state as was to be expected: but in my opinion he behaved like a man of immense energy & of resources to overcome all difficulties. He called upon the MAs present to exert themselves so as not to allow the voting

---

[12] Time has veiled the private life of Sir William Manners (1766-1833), alias Lord Huntingtower, a married man with twelve children. Perhaps the reference is to his rackety but very much living heir Lionel (born 1794) who was examined in bankruptcy in November 1842 with liabilities of £200,000 after passing himself off as a horse-dealer and being involved with bill-discounting.

to be interfered with. And when there was a smash of glass in the old Court of Kings – some undergraduates clambered over the wall by King's Old Gate, undid the bars & let in the mass – Lamb of Caius & Dr Drosier (at V.C's request) went to them & cleared the Court – & there seemed to be a danger of the mob breaking in thro the windows he demanded of them that they should support his authority by going to the different windows. He was indeed received with "3 cheers for the V.C." when he got into the Schools, but the MAs present seemed generally afraid of going to the windows. One person was overheard by the V.C. saying to Undergraduates 'come in': – Whewell immediately with great dignity & great vehemence combined challenged the person if a M.A. to give his name: – the man had not the courage. – The voting was got thro within the limited time 8½: the votes were 37 for Walpole & 16 for Denman, making the total for Walpole 631 & for Denman 316: – as nearly as possible 2 to 1. – The V.C. on closing the Polling said 'I am now going to my Lodge & I call upon you to protect your V.C.'. – A large no of us accompanied him to the gate: – there was no hindrance, tho a considerable rabble-rout flocked along the street hooting like wild beasts. – Some elderly people are fonder of excitement than I am . . . To me this uproar & hubbub were most painful & distressing & I was grieved for Whewells sake . . . The Evening post brought me a very amusing letter from Grim describing a supper of his to 11 singers (3 female & 8 male): 'We had 2 tables lengthwise in an outer room & these we laid with the best silver & cutlery & with the following dishes, pâté de lapins foudroyant, thundering rabbit pie blazing hot, a leg of mutton, a ham & a dish of sausages all hot: these were removed by an apple-pie, a plumpudding, mincepies & tartlets. I took the head of the table & did the honors & after the substantials had been done ample justice to we wound up with a jug of steaming hot bishop' . . .

*Sat. 9.* Up at ¼ to 7 – Thermometer at 50". – Very delightful morning. – Went to look at the scene of last night's disgraceful outbreak. I met the Master at Kings Old Gate & told him how highly I approved his spirited conduct. He said that when he got into Trinity Court (after the night polling) there was a Trinity M.A. (Bentinck) smoking with undergraduates: – he had the impudence to say to the Master who remonstrated with him 'Sir, you are behind the times!'[13] . . . Polling began on this 3d day at 10 (as usual) . . . Denman's academic distinctions were talked about: he was Captain of the Classical Tripos, Captain of the Poll (– tho very singularly he was not 1st in Classics in that Examination but ran far-a-head in Mathematics – not his line), Captain of the Trinity Boat & won the Sculls. – By the way Lord Redesdale made a joke thereanent t'other day: he said 'Walpole is a good head, & Denman a good scull' . . . Maddison was vastly amusing today: a queer man of the name of Beavor came to vote & Maddison said his Father was a fighting parson, – who was continually boxing with his parishioners: – the son was wild & unclerical, – so that a wag said 'In Norfolk there are 3 sorts of creatures, men,

[13] Whewell disapproved of smoking which was increasingly frowned on in some circles and especially in clergymen, even though returning troops from the Crimea were spreading the habit. Nor would he approve of an M.A. fraternising with mere undergraduates. See also the riot of 4 November 1854.

women & Beavers' . . . Whewell was apparently none the worse for yesterday's excitement: he told the story of a man biting off another's nose & being bound over to keep the piece: – he observed when the 3 *Heaths* (of Trinity) voted that we had now done with the *Heathen*. When it was observed that the mustachio-wearing people generally voted for Denman he said 'it was a prima facie presumption in his favour' . . . I was highly amused by the 3 Divinity Professors going up together to vote for Walpole: – a Cerberus bark. – The V.C. amiably again produced an Orange for me. At 1 we had a cessation of hostilities for ¼ hour & that amiable fellow Day of Caius took me to lunch in their Combination room & fed me with Tongue & Chicken . . . At 4 the numbers were W. 886, D. 419. – Mr Titcomb's 3 little girls (all voting for Denman in their hearts) were with their father in the Senate House (he did vote for us): – Mrs Prest, etc etc were there. – but the show of Ladies was small . . . Whewell circulated today a notice wch he drew up & wch all the votetakers who sat at his table signed: viz Dr Pulling, the 2 Proctors, myself, & the scrutineers for the 2 Candidates: – the notice was to say that the undergraduates in the galleries had made such a noise that we could not hear the names of the voters & that we approved of the V.C.'s conduct in excluding them. Most of the Colleges mean to gate their men to night. – At 7½ went down for the Evening Polling & found to my delight that Denman had resigned & therefore there would be no meeting in the schools: – all the college gates were open & the streets perfectly quiet: – a most happy contrast to last night. – By the way there was a hooting & hallooing crowd followed the V.C. to Trinity at 4 . . .

*Tu. 12.* Called in good time, up at 6½: – dowdy & damp & muggy . . . Translated my Graces & with them sent to the V.C. a letter expressive of my agreeal with the Reasons wch he has today printed in vindication of his turning out the undergraduates from the Galleries: – in this paper he warmly eulogises the conduct of the young men when the Queen was here & speaks hopefully of them for the future. – Shilleto has printed some Greek verses on the Election, violently attacking the Master & Martin[14] . . . I did a great deal of Registrarial work today, wch had been thrown into arrear by the horrid turmoil of this vexatious election. By the way Martin told me that Mr Walpole dined in Hall yesterday, & that Sedgwick made a beautiful speech . . .

[14] Professor N.G.L. Hammond has kindly translated and commented on the verses which he considers a scholarly tour de force both metrically and in their recherché vocabulary. 'Who was the originator of the uproar in his love of horrible internal strife? it was Eupsithyros [i.e. good-slanderer, Whewell], a quarrelsome fellow, altogether bitter, loving strife and ready for a fight. When many were in strife, and when those entitled to vote, as well as those whose age did not yet given them the right to vote, were whistling and making an uproar . . . he all by himself took control of the mob of lads. Granta rang with hissings'. Chrematolumes [i.e. corrupt in money matters, Martin, the bursar of Trinity], is next loaded with malicious phrases, and the piece concludes 'O Zeus the king, fill us entirely with the flavour of friendliness and put an end to internal strife. And thereafter make an agreement with the lads not to bear malice but to put an end to Eupsithyros'. Whewell and Martin evidently took all this in their stride, for, as Shilleto's obituarist noted (*Chronicle* 30 September 1876), his pieces were regarded as witty and playful with 'no trace of malice'.

*Th. 14.* Up at 20' to 7. – On sallying out of the Botanic Garden I met Dudu & her uncle: she was looking very pretty & highly pleased with a party last night at Clem. Francis's where there were above 20 children . . . After breakfast Selwyn read me several stanzas of Tennyson's on 'the Brook': – I was greatly pleased with them & liked them better than any thing I ever read of the Laureat's . . . Went to the Amateur Artist Exhibition at the Red Lion: – it is for the benefit of the families of the Crimean Army. I was much pleased with it . . . There are several contributions by Charles Jenyns: – one of them is a Gem: – it is a view of the castle of Amboise. There are several of Worsley's water colours, & 4 or 5 of Phelps' of a high order of merit. There were some paintings of Mrs Leapingwells (her copy of the Carlo Dolci was one) & Miss Hopkins' . . . Dr Whewell sent a drawing (or is it an Engraving) of Prince Albert in armour: on the frame is an inscription of its having been given to Mrs Whewell by the Queen[15] . . .

*Fri. 15.* . . . I have learned from Martin that Shilleto's attack upon him is for his (Martin's) having seized an undergraduate on the Friday Evening just as he had broken the lamp at the entrance of the Schools: there was a grand tussle, both Martin & the youth were rolled on the ground, Martin's spectacles were broken & his cap lost, & ultimately the culprit was rescued . . . Dined at the Family at Clark's . . . We were talking about 'Objective' & 'Subjective' & I was expressing my utter abhorrence of the introduction of such mystification in Sermons (wch ought to be addressed to the heart more than to the head): Mr Francis said Mr Ruskin was entirely of my opinion & he read loud (& so well that I complimented him) an exquisite banter of Ruskin's upon these up-in-the-clouds words & upon the Germans who use them[16] . . . Power has printed a letter in the Times repelling the insinuation that he had voted for himself at the recent Election of Atkinson: he tells me that Atkinson will make a valuable Head of a house, that he is the most deeply read person he knows (especially in Divinity), that (tho shy) he thinks for himself & has a will of his own. – I played 8 rubbers & won 1s . . .

*Sat. 16.* Up at 7 – Breakfasted in College – my poor Bedmaker Mrs Carpenter is in great trouble from the death of her daughter Mrs Harris: I think her death a most happy release, for she had gone out of her mind on her husband's enlisting for the Crimea: she had had 3 children, but they are all dead: – gave Mrs C. £1 . . .

*Sun. 17.* . . . After my Tapioca I went to St Mary's and was highly delighted with a sermon of Mr Woolley's from 1 Timothy IV. 12–16. He said this was an appropriate day for addressing the future Candidates for the Ministry as they had been praying every day of the past week for those who

---

[15] Mr Jonathan Smith of Trinity tells us that the picture no longer appears to be in the college; presumably it remained in the family when Whewell died. There is an account of the show in the *Chronicle 16* February.

[16] 'German dulness, and English affectation, have of late much multiplied among us as two of the most objectionable words that were ever coined by the troublesomeness of metaphysicians – namely "Objective" and "Subjective". No words can be more exquisitely, and in all points, useless . . . '(*Modern Painters* III (1856), opening of chapter XII; cf. also Appendix II, pp. 343–5 on 'German Philosophy'.

were to be ordained today. He spoke with great force of the necessity of a learned Clergy in these days of German Rationalism & of appeals to the discoveries of science. But above all he enforced the necessity of practical holiness in a Clergyman, as his life would be far more persuasive than the best sermons that ever were penned . .

*Tu. 19.* . . . From 12½ to past 2 at a College meeting: we rusticated 'sine die' an ill-conducted idle reckless vagabond named Moore – he had been gated, but he broke gates, shirked Sunday Evening Chapel & went to a Hotel to drink & smoke till they shut up the house & turned him out:[17]– we did a good deal of Bursarial work. – It was too late to go home for my Tapioca: so I ate a sausage roll at the pastry-cooks & went to my office to work. – Here I had a visit from the Master of Caius (Guest) to whom I lent sundry documents relating to the charges against Dr Branthwaite (Master of Caius) in 1617. Dr Guest . . . was very amusing in his conversation about Göthe, with whom he was most intimate during a year he spent at Weimar: he was present at Göthe's celebration of his Jubilee, 50th year of some Court appointment at wch all the distinguished people from far & near did homage to the great Genius . . . Guest used often to act as a kind of secretary to Göthe, & gratified him much by 1st telling him of Shelley's translation of one of his works 'the ascent of the Brocken' (wch translation he gave to Göthe). – Guest found Göthe a sceptic with little sympathy for any body – In the Evening I read a good deal of Macaulay & was highly delighted with his brilliant account of the barbarous state of the Highlands in 1689.

*Tu. 26.* . . . Today at 2 o'clock there was an Exhibition by Hoffman of his Organophonic Band of 9 men who imitate instruments: I sent Harriet & Dosia & Anne Coe. – One of the performers was a short black, the other 8 were well-grown men who looked like Hungarians. I have not been so much amused with anything time out of mind: they produced the effect of a full band & you seemed to hear drums & cymbals distinctly, & in one piece they imitated most successfully a musical snuff-box . . . their masterpiece was the song of old Towler, with imitation of a hunting horn & hounds in full cry[18] . . .

*Sat. 1 March* Didn't get up till 7½. No walk before breakfast. Received from Whewell an admirable sermon of his preached in the Chapel on the 3d of February from 1 John III 3 'Every man that hath this hope purifieth himself even as He is pure'. – The loss of poor Mrs W. obviously gave the whole tone to the composition. Wrote to Whewell thanking him. Whewell has generously given £100 & more for the conveyance of the Saurian Fossils just presented by Mr Hawkins:[19]– he also magnanimously threw into the fire a list of rebellious undergraduates (in the recent Senate House disturbance) saying 'The Election

---

[17] G.W. Moore achieved a ninth class in the college examinations in 1853 and in 1854 had still not passed his Previous Examination half way through his third year.

[18] 'These entertaining performers . . . represent by the human voice, a complete orchestra, both wind and stringed instruments; even the drum, cymbals, musical box and bagpipes are imitated with a correctness that would deceive the most acute ear' (Advertisement in the *Independent* of 23 February). They lived up to the claim and were rewarded by brief but enthusiastic notices in the same newspaper and in the *Chronicle* on 1 March.

[19] See *Endowments* p. 525.

is over: they will behave better another time'. But he is not yet in smooth water about the Fitzwilliam Museum: – he is unwilling to propose the reelection of all who resigned; – he asked Philpott, but he declined unless all the rest are asked. – What a squabbling world it is! . . . I found today in Carters History of Cambridge (published in 1753) that there used to be *special music* in Kings Chapel on Ladyday & that till quite lately the special music used (after the Sermon was over) to play from the leads of the Chapel . . . I went down to the river, wch was swarming with 8-oars: one of them (carrying a little blue flag) was the picked crew that are to row against Oxford.[20] The river was rather choked with barges . . . My unfortunate bedmaker is suffering from sick headache.

*Tu. 4.* . . . From 10 till 3 (excepting an interval of ¼ hour from 1 to 1.15 when I devoured a sausage roll) the Election of a Music Professor in the Arts Schools: Bennett ran ahead the whole time. I was highly amused at the Corpus men almost invariably voting for him . . . Read the new no of 'Little Dorritt: it is very clever: there is a touching scene between L.D. & Mr Clennam: also a very rich interview between Mr Clennam & his former flame (Flora Casby) now a widow of great magnitude & of great appetite, full of affectation & desirous of making scenes.

*Th. 6.* Up at 6½. – Walk in the Botanic Garden in the rain & without umbrella: there being (as usual) not a soul there but myself & I having unluckily my best hat on I walked with my handkerchief over it . . . Covent Garden Theatre has been burned to the ground!! it was last burnt in 1808: – Drury Lane in 1811. – At 10 past 4 went to Corpus Christi Chapel: it is a beautiful little chapel & beautifully got up in all its details of Organ, Eagle, Chandeliers with twisted stems etc: – the Organ is a Novelty: it is played by an undergraduate: they have a regular choir of singing boys: – there was an anthem. – I afterwards dined in Hall as the Master's Guest: – the V.C. (Whewell), Atkinson (Master of Clare), Leapingwell & Maddison etc etc were there. It was Dr Spencer's audit: – he wrote 'de legibus Hebræorum': he gave the College an Estate producing more than £400 a year.[21] – The dinner was excellent; the V.C. talked brilliantly & was excellent Company. Home at 8.

*Sun. 9.* . . . Just opposite my own door I met Cissy Goodwin & 3 more of them on the look out for Papa & Mamma: so I took hold of the hands of Cissy & her little sister (who is pretty & quiet & good & loving but not clever, – she can't get Geography etc into her head) & professed my intention of walking up & down with them till we met P & M, – wch in about 10' we did. – Harvey Goodwin astonished me by telling me that he teaches his little girls to play whist! He communicated to me the following conundrum: 'What is the cause of the Potato disease?' – 'The rot-tator-y motion of the earth': I must

[20] The first Oxbridge boat-race was rowed in 1829 but it did not become an annual event until the 1850s. By this time too light blue and dark blue were established as the sporting colours of Cambridge and Oxford, having most likely been borrowed respectively from Eton and Harrow. There are other explanations.

[21] John Spencer, Master of Corpus 1667-93, was a Hebraist whose work on Jewish ritual law controversially traced its connexions to that of other Semitic peoples.

tell it to Lady Braybrooke. H.G. also mentioned the old joke of calling the uglier of 2 men a Carpenter because he is a 'deal plainer' . . .

*Tu. 11.* . . . I was grieved to hear that Heun (the principal Underlibrarian) who has worked so admirably in the Public Library is gone out of his mind: he had far too much work to do, & did it with intense energy: – he had the delusion of thinking he was going to be married & bought several white waistcoats: then he purchased a gun: then he subscribed £100 to some charity: – poor Fellow! they have found it necessary to confine him[22] . . .

*Tu. 18.* Up at 6½. – Dull but not cold. – They are beginning the new buildings (for propagating plants) in the Botanic Garden . . . Wrote to G.T.R. advising him to bow the head to the storm & write a letter to Mr Godley expressive of great sorrow at having given dissatisfaction & promising the greatest exertions in order to gain his good opinion. – I greatly fear that he will not humble himself in this way. My letter was occasioned by one from him saying that his friends were exerting themselves to get him to Weedon & that he should not use my letter to Frederick without they failed . . . Into my office today got a young bit of contraband, viz. Lucy Newman (about 15 or 16) who used to be Mrs Wootton's little maid: she has a bad cough & is an out-patient at the hospital: she is not now in regular service but is staying with her sister & helping her in her place. I told her she must come to my house & never again to the office: she is gentle & genteel-looking & dangerously pretty for her station (– her mother being in the Union) . . .

*Sat. 22.* . . . After my tapioca when I was reading (as usual) the morning lesson in Hebrew a lad was announced as Master *Broughton*: he is a dull loutish chap (about 14) whose ideas flow as slowly as his indistinct utterance: – he turned out to be the son of James *Brogden* (who left Cambridge – as he always did every place – in great embarrassment): this stupid boy (after an immense quantity of pumping) told me that he is the eldest son, but that there are 9 of them (boys & girls): his Father (who in panic terror fired at night at a supposed burglar some years ago) resides on his Living of Deddington & teaches his own children, having no other Pupils. – From the Clergy-List I find that Deddington is worth only £150 p.a. & has a population of 2500. – I don't wonder that he should always be in difficulties, for I presume his 'Catholic Safeguards' brings in no regular income.[23] This lumpish lad has only been a very short time away from his Father: – he is now at school at Huntingdon with John Fell (B.A. Trinity 1818) . . . He had walked over the 16 miles from Huntingdon with a boy a year younger than himself,

---

[22] Oscar Heun of Leipzig joined the staff of the library in 1852 and became Principal Assistant in December 1853. Overwork on the catalogue broke him down and by the winter of 1855-56 he was seriously unbalanced and in need of medical attention for which the university paid. He resigned the following October but never fully recovered. See McKitterick, especially pp. 520-2. Heun published a weird pamphlet on the German church in 1858, and his annotated copy survives in the University Library.

[23] i.e. James Brogden's, *Catholic Safeguards against the Errors, Novelties and Corruptions of the Church of Rome*, 3 vols (1851). This 'ample treasury' abstracted from the writings of seventeenth-century divines though commended by the hierarchy must have been caviare to the general.

whom he had left outside. I immediately fetched him in & was much pleased with his girl-like modesty & gentleness. – I opened a bottle of Constantia[24] for them & produced biscuits & gave them 2/6 each. – I am glad that I was at home, for they must have wanted refreshment sadly: they intended walking back! I hope they will take a lift in a market cart . . .

*Easter Sunday. 23.* . . . This very day of March 24 years ago I was elected Registrary & I heartily bless God for having vouchsafed me health & strength to carry on for so great a length of time an employment of which I am very fond & which affords me competence & happiness. Went to Christ Church: the old Church was reopened today: but I did not know of it[25] . . .

*Wed. 26.* 1st day of Scholarship Greek by Grote & Cooper . . . The new Professor of Music is in doubt how to proceed: he wants a degree, but will not submit to sending a Musical Exercise to any person whatever for approval: – I told him he might be certain that any exercise (Canticum) wch he would compose & perform would be received as a qualification without the sending it to any tribunal for approval . . . I told him that there would be no difficulty in getting a Mandate: – but he didn't relish that idea at all . . . Prof. Bennett is a thin, sallow, uncomfortable-looking man. – At 2 to Catharine Lodge for 3 Ale Licences. – Bouverie's University Bill proposes an important change in the Election of the Council: the sectional elections are given up, & the Elections to be thrown open to all *members of The Senate*.[26] – Not sleepy tonight.

[24] A Cape wine.

[25] The old church of St Andrew the Less in Barnwell, far too small for the expanding population of the parish, had been disused for about sixteen years and the much larger Christ Church in Newmarket Road had been built in 1839. The old church had now been restored under the superintendence of the Cambridge Architectural Society.

[26] The University Bill of 1855 had been so retarded by amendments that it was withdrawn, but now a new bill, much the same as the former in its amended state, was introduced into the Commons on 14 March by Edward Pleydell-Bouverie, yet another old Trinity man. It was a symbolic choice, his father having been that Earl of Radnor who had vainly tried to interest Parliament in university reform a generation before. There was little controversy this time; despite reservations all the main players who had been so much at loggerheads - Whewell, Sedgwick, Bateson, and Philpott - agreed that it needed little alteration. Philpott was alarmed to find, however, that further delay might be caused by the government's timetabling of legislation and alerted Prince Albert who in turn wrote to the Prime Minister, now Lord Palmerston. On 30 May 1856 the Commons went into committee and got through all the clauses with only two major changes; the Lords passed it with a major amendment requiring members of the Senate to declare themselves members of the Church of England, and the bill so amended went speedily through the Commons and into law as 19 & 20 Victoria c. 88. Henceforth no declarations or subscriptions of faith were to be made for college scholarships and the like, while religious tests were abolished for all but divinity degrees and the M.A.; the Caput was abolished with effect from next November to be replaced by a Council of the Senate (see 7 November 1856) with the authority to promote Graces and to nominate to vacant offices; the Vice-Chancellor's power was circumscribed. Eight Commissioners were appointed to revise all university and college statutes. Until January 1858 they had to take into account the views of the Council and of the college Governing Bodies but after that had a freer hand.

*Th. 27.* . . . Letter from Betsy acknowledging the £5: she gives a good account of the health of Jem & their 4 children & of Mary: my godson & little Lucy are fond of the Baby but George slaps his face & pokes his finger in his eyes! a young jealous villain. – Betsy feels very weak in her back . . . A charming letter from Sophie . . . Lady Elisabeth Romilly has produced her 3d son: he is to have the name of Hugh, Lord Fortescue having asked to be Godfather & having sent a present of £100. The Duke of Bedford has generously given his sister (Lady Georgina Romilly) £10,000 in proof of his admiration of her mode of living on a small income[27] . . . Sophie tells the following anecdotes of Fred's son Henry (age 6): upon the birth of the baby he asked Lady John Russell where the baby came from: she said 'All Babies come from Heaven': – 'O then it's a miracle: I suppose it will be the last as I was told miracles were over' . . . Franky came home thin & weak: he calls the Doctor 'jolly': he orders him 2 dinners a day one with porter the other with port. He does 2 Propositions of Euclid daily with Sophie . . . I worked steadily (without headache) at Scholarship Papers till 11 at night: I looked over 3 sets of Sophocles, Xenophon & Terence.

*Mon. 31.* . . . News is arrived of Peace having been yesterday signed at Paris! – The Bells rang, cannons were fired, & at night a band played round the town: 4 banners were carried, & a mob followed shouting & throwing squibs: – the band played well . . . G.T.R. has bought a photographic apparatus: so I shall have portraits of his children & Maggie.

*Th. 10 April.* . . . Letter from Power (The Librarian) saying that he shall not be able to dine at 'the Family' tomorrow as he is laid up at his Fathers at Atherstone with a bad influenza wch puts him in mind of the Charade 'Why is the influenza like the House of Commons?' – 'Because sometimes the Ayes have it & sometimes the Noes' . . . Whewell brought Salvin, who is to make the alteration in Newton's rooms etc: – Salvin will exhibit his drawings at the V.C.'s tonight . . .

*Fri. 11.* . . . Visit in my office from Sedgwick who came to ask me to lunch: we had a good chat & smoked a cigar. He was going to give a lecture to Lady Affleck (sister to poor Ellis the Senior Wrangler),[28] Miss Grote & Mr & Mrs Curtis. – I came to the Museum towards the close of his Lecture & was highly delighted with his history of the structure of the fossil Elk etc etc . . . Sedgwick's lunch was excellent & his conversation very brilliant & very entertaining: – he gave us the history of the Kangaroos & the marvellous process by which the young are supplied with their Mothers milk when they can neither suck nor swallow . . .

*Mon. 14.* . . . At 1½ to Magdalene Lodge to meet Lady Braybrooke & Lord John Fitzroy. – I had not seen Lady Braybrooke since her great misfortune of losing her 2 sons Henry & Grey: she was very much overcome

---

[27] i.e. Elizabeth, daughter of the Earl of Minto, and Georgiana, daughter of the Duke of Bedford and half-sister of Lord John Russell, the wives respectively of Romilly's cousins Frederick and Charles. See Appendix 1.

[28] i.e. a brilliant former fellow of Trinity, R. L. Ellis, who was to die young. Lady Affleck had been widowed in 1854 after a marriage of twenty years; she became Whewell's second wife in July 1858 and died before him.

at 1st speaking to me . . . After lunch Mr Latimer took Lord John & myself to see the Chapel etc etc: the Chapel is quite a Gem. When I went to College & for many years after the Chapel had a flat ceiling & there were sets of rooms over it: the ceiling is removed, the East window filled with Glass in admirable stile (à la Antique), the adjoining South window is also of painted Glass: I thought it very pretty . . . the Carvework is all by Rattee: there is a beautiful Lectern, & everything in the highest state of finish: – Lord John nearly fell on the polished encaustic tiles – there are no curtains to the stalls of the Master & President. – We then went to see the College Library wch is in the old Lodge, & the Pepysian Library wch is in poor Mr Grey Neville's rooms. In the Pepysian our host exhibited to us a memorandum book of Sir Francis Drakes, Pepys's original Diary, M.S. of Pepys from the dictation of the King when he resolved on flight, etc etc . . . In the Evening did pasting work etc etc.

*Wed. 16.* . . . Lunch (or rather dinner) at 4½ with Sedgwick to meet 5 Miss Adeanes (Alethia, Lucy, Amabel, Jane & Constance) & Mathison. – There is another Miss Adeane: – all 6 & 4 other young ladies were bridesmaids at Miss Emmeline Adeane's marriage the other day. – Sedgwick was in great force: – he had accused Miss Jane (who is a tallish & very pretty lass of about 14) of being a grown-up woman: – she resisted the charge & volunteered coming & sitting on his knee. – Numbers of Riddles etc etc were told by the men folks. – Mathison communicated the following. – 'Why do the Scotchwomen talk so much?' A. – 'Because you cant prevent the deerstalking in Scotland' . . .

*Sun. 20.* Up at ¼ to 7. Walked in the Cemetery: I saw there a monument to Colonel Glover in such old-fashioned letters that I had the greatest difficulty in making them out. I saw also the monument to dear Mrs Whewell: it recorded simply 'Cordelia the wife of W.W. Master of Trinity College: age 52': there were also in a circle the words 'to live to die': also 'thro the grave to life everlasting' – on a cross was the representation of the Sower sowing the seed; – certainly in her case the seed was sown in good ground . . . Fell in with Kingsley (riding to Newton & Hauxton at both of wch he does duty): – he tells me that Jelinger C. Symonds (the noodlish School-Inspector) who denies the rotation of the moon on her axis) is in my Graduati wrongly given to Sidney Coll: he was of Corpus Christi. – On my asking him about Renouard (aged 75) who keeps him out of the best living (Swanscombe) he said that he was alive though ailing: he was reported to have been thrown into the sea by the collision of 2 steamers wch carried off the water-closet where he was[29] . . . I afterwards walked saunteringly by the Via Lambertina. I fell in with Emery of Corpus & had ¼ hours talk with him. He is very anxious that there should be a Sermon every Sunday in every College Chapel: it is so at Corpus,

---

[29] Renouard, formerly professor of Arabic, survived until 1867 in his college living in Kent but the disappointed W.T. Kingsley (a cousin of the novelist Charles) proved even more durable. Sidney presented him in 1859 to a Yorkshire living which he held until his death in 1916 at the age of 101 when he was probably the oldest Cambridge man in any office. He had interests in music and astronomy, was a friend of Turner and Ruskin, and is said to have offered 'to go to Africa as a missionary after one of Livingstone's lectures, but was rejected on medical grounds' (*Cambridge Review* 18 October 1916, p. 33).

Catharine, Queens, Jesus & 2 more: he thinks if Trinity would take it up then all the remaining Colleges would immediately join in . . .

*Mon. 21.* . . . Letter from Maggie in answer to mine: happily her ague has not attacked her the last 5 days: she says my godson treats his frock as if it was a tailed-coat, lifts it up, puts his hands behind him & so stands with his back to the fire . . .

*Sun. 27.* . . . To St Mary's at 2 to hear H. Goodwin: I was much surprised at seeing him in the Pitt. – a Mr Ogle BA 1845 of Jesus preached. His Text was Romans 1. 16. – It was a completely Evangelical Sermon: it was a denunciation against being ashamed of Christ. The preacher rather astonished me by his eulogy of Wesley for seceding from the Church of England . . . Coming out of Church I was joined by Harvey Goodwin & wife: they told me that the Sermon was preached expressly against him (H.G.). Harvey Goodwin says that there has just appeared in an Evangelical Magazine a severe article against himself, & he presumes Mr Ogle has been horrified against him thereby.[30] – H.G. had written to Mr Ogle very courteously saying that his turn came in the middle of the official Sundays of the Hulsean preacher & that he should be most happy in paying the 3 Guinea fine if he would allow him to go on with his course. Mr O. wrote in great indignation at this offer & said that it would be most inconvenient to him to come, but he would willingly bear much greater inconvenience & pay a much larger sum than that a preacher whose doctrine he condemned should occupy the pupil [sic] in his stead!

*Tu. 29.* . . . The Cambridge papers say the Funds of Addenbrookes are £500 in arrears: so I gave £10 today: Nurse of Martha-ward and another nurse have been dismissed for giving away remains of patients' provisions . . .

*Th. 1 May.* . . . Peace was proclaimed yesterday in different parts of the Town, – at our corner among other places: the proclaimer was the Town-crier, who was accompanied by some of the Corporation . . .

*Sun. 4.* Up at 6½. – Cool but not unpleasant . . . Harriet began her duties as Sunday School Teacher of St Paul's: she takes the Infant department. – Finished reading Whewell's Elegiacs: they show deep piety & a warmth of affection & admiration of his partner wch are unsurpassable . . . This is a copy of 'the Gravestone'

> 'Now that the earth & the Sky have conceal'd the Beloved from our Vision,
> Now we have render'd to earth all that is earthly of Her:
> Give we the spot (how dear!) its due memorial honors;

[30] The criticisms of Goodwin appeared in the April issue of the *Christian Observer*, pp. 250-268, in a review of his Hulsean lectures of 1855. The writer acknowledges his popularity and influence in the university, but 'his theology is not the distinct theology of St. Paul, or of the Fathers of the English Church. His avowed object is to check the inrolling flood of Rationalism; but his plan is to accomplish this by breaking down the old embankments and throwing up new ones of his own construction.' Warming to his theme, the reviewer observes that 'to many of his opinions we are utterly repugnant' and urges Goodwin 'to weigh the tremendous responsibilities of his present position, and the immeasurable evil of which he may be the author'. Despite publishing Goodwin's reply ('you have made me say precisely what I wish to contradict . . . blame me for obscurity if you will'), the editor stuck to his guns (pp. 374-6).

Lay we a stone on the grave; mark we the place of our grief:
Lay we a stone that may speak of *her* to our friends & our children
Lay we a stone that may speak even as she would have willed.
Clearly she spoke her will 'Mark thou, she said, on my tombstone
Not mere wailings of grief, sorrow that knows not of hope;
Let hope shine thro the grief, let faith illumine the sorrow;
For I go to my God parting in faith & in hope.
Yea, O Beloved, I cried, thine own sweet wisdom shall teach me;
Words thou has uttered oft, these shall be fittingly traced . . . '[31]

To Barnwell Church at 11. – A most appalling dismal Mr Young with a look that would turn Vinegar more sour read prayers: he spoke in a tone as severe & mournful as if he thought it a sin to be cheerful. Mr Titcomb preached in a manner thoroughly to my satisfaction . . . He said that the Peace might bring one great blessing in the opportunity wch it offered for the Missionary in Turkey as the Sultan has proclaimed religious toleration in his dominions . . . In the dusk Cooper looked in: – he wanted Whewell's Elegiacs to show to Maddison: – I had quite done with them, & we had a good long chat about them & about poor Mrs Whewell's goodness & the Master's deep attachment to her: he could not stay tea, being engaged to the Maddisons.

*Tu. 6.* Up at ¼ to 7 – Frosty – Bright sunshine – Walk in the Botanic Garden. – At last a letter from Mrs Percy: it was very grateful: – she dissuades me from a life of solitude: – I certainly shall not offer to her, for (like Tony Weller) I have a horror of widows . . . Dr Guest called & brought (– at last) his accounts wch he ought to have sent me 3 months ago: – he brought me a part of his vouchers. He eulogised Willis & Stokes as the 2 great men of genius at Cambridge: – I told him that Whewell was my bright star, & I considered his wide field of knowledge as quite marvellous . . .

*Wed. 7.* . . . Also a visit from Dr Guest & his man with a lawyers bag holding the remainder of the Vouchers: he sat a good long time & we had an agreeable conversation about all his brother-heads: – he is obviously afraid of Whewell & doesn't like him: I told him plainly my profound admiration for Whewells head & heart . . . A comfortless day with piercing East wind & beating rain: – I didn't come home for Tapioca but bought a Sausage-roll & heated it in my shovel . . .

*Sun. 11. Whit Sunday.* Up at 7 – Delightful morning. – Walk in the Cemetery. – The Chapel scarcely got on at all.[32] – Did not go to Christ Church today, it being my turn to preach in Chapel. The Master was there & his two brothers-in-law Lord Monteagle & H.V. Elliott: Mr & Aubrey Spring-Rice

---

[31] Such has been the change in sensibilities that it is now difficult to read Whewell's verses without embarrassment; but he was far from alone in attempting a pseudo-classical prosody (indeed it was fashionable) which has rarely been successful in English, and even more rarely for his chosen theme.

[32] See R. Wolfe, '"Quite a Gem": an Account of the Former Mortuary Chapel at Mill Road Cemetery, Cambridge', *Proceedings of the Cambridge Antiquarian Society* 84 (1995), 143-53. Whewell was much involved in this and contributed to its cost. It was demolished in the 1950s during the first great period of cemetery despoliation in England.

& Lady Monteagle were also there: – I am such a poor creature that tho I preached a very short sermon I was bathed in perspiration & had to mop myself continually; Martin & myself assisted the Master & the Chaplain in the Sacrament . . .

*Wed. 14.* Up at ¼ to 7. – Poor Dosia lay awake most of the night from the pain of the whitloe on her Finger . . . The Grace for confirming Selwyn's noble offer of £700 a year to the Norrisian Professor was (to my astonishment & indignation) opposed: the divisions were in Black Hood House 23 to 6: Bashforth gave the 1st Non Placet: – in the White Hood House the division was 14 to 5: Todhunter gave the 1st Non Placet.[33] – Of these malcontents 10 were Johnians: the 11th was Westmorland (Jesus). I presume the feeling of the Johnians is that the Margaret Professorship is a sort of heirloom with them, & that they do not relish its value being diminished . . . In the Senate House Elliott came & eulogised the sermon wch I preached last Sunday; he thought it very sound & agreed with every word but one, – *it* instead of *He.* I told him that was a blunder in the reading & not in the writing . . .

*Sun. 18.* . . . To Christ Church at 11: Mr Monk read prayers & Mr Titcomb preached an intensely hard missionary sermon from Ephesians IV. 16: – the Church was ill filled (the weather being stormy): but of those present the great majority might have answered like the Scotchwoman who when asked if she understood the sermon of her minister said 'Would I presume sae?' . . .

On the 21st Romilly, on his way to a day in London, was surprised to learn from J.C. Franks, formerly Chaplain of Trinity 'that Browne (the Norrisian Professor) & Selwyn had talked together before the Election & had agreed wchever of them was elected to allow the Norrisian Prof £700 a year!'. In Cornhill he ordered silver boxes to contain Whewell's 'beautiful verses to the Queen on the Peace', visited his bank, and then at the Academy liked the Exhibition 'very much'. Two vehement pages of the Journal are devoted to the pictures he most enjoyed and to detailed criticisms of those most talked of but 'which I can't endure' – Holman Hunt's *Scape Goat* and F.W. Burton's (the water-colourist and later Director of the National Gallery) *Wounded Cavalier.*

*Th. 22.* Up a little before 7. – Walk to Trumpington in the rain: the air most soft & balmy: the nightingales singing. – Called Congregation for the Address to the Queen (wch is excellent: – the Oxford one is (I am told) milk & water) . . . Copied (for my office) Whewell's Address to the Queen & set Welsford about making 2 fair copies (on paper) for the V.C. to send to the Prince & some other Official[34] . . . The V.C. told me he shall appoint our new Trinity Organist (Hopkins, late of Rochester) to be University Organist . . . Met Mrs Clark: she was wearing a preposterous sombrero hat slouching over her face: she drives herself daily in a one-horse phaeton: she is so much better that she is going to give a ball next Thursday! . . .

*Tu. 27.* Up at ¼ to 7. Delicious morning – walk on Hills Road. – Visit from Selwyn (to return Whewell's Elegiacs): he today begins Ely-residence: he

---

[33] For the Norrisian chair see *Endowments*, pp. 58 and 108.

[34] The address congratulated the Queen on the re-establishment of peace. See 5 June.

& Mrs S. are sadly out of sorts, for Dudu has left them! this is a great grief to them, as the dear little maiden has been with them more than 4 years & was as much their darling as if she had been their child . . . Interview with Potts who showed me the alterations to be proposed in the University Bill next Friday by Heywood & L.T. Wigram: they are very sweeping: – e.g. – to have prayers fitted for all religions equally!!!³⁵ – Worked in the Office till 5. Punctually at 7 arrived Grim & Bertha with plenty of baggage but no children: – they were looking very flourishing: Grim does but little in the shaving line: – however he does not venture on a moustache – I had had a fire lighted for my guests. After tea & cold meat we had a good cose:³⁶– & afterwards I read loud Cockburn (Attorney General)'s final speech in Palmer's trial: – it is most effective & must produce conviction. Cockburn is very severe upon several of the medical witnesses for ascribing Cooks death to Epilepsy, Apoplexy, etc etc or some unknown disease. As for Taylor's not finding strichnine in the body' – neither did he in 2 rabbits wch he killed by strichnine. – Bed at 10½.

*Wed. 28.* . . . one of these eundems (an Irishman, a Dr Abraham Hume) came to the House, just as I was starting & offered to drive me to College: – I thankfully accepted: he told me that Palmer was yesterday condemned & sent down to Staffordshire for Execution: he says that there is a strong impression in London that he will contrive to poison himself³⁷ . . . At 12 to the V.C.'s for the Hebrew Scholarship Election . . . I had sent a message home telling them to lunch without me & come to Senate House at 2. – I began my lionising by exhibiting the Senate House & market, then my College Rooms, then the Trinity Kitchens, Combination Room, Hall etc etc. . . . I took Bertha & Grim into the Gallery to see our youngsters & the Fellows at dinner . . . Grim read loud after dinner the 1st day's summing up of Lord Campbell: – then Bertha played & sang: – she sang 'Tom Bowling', 'Ye Banks & Braes', & 2 nigger songs. – Bed ¼ to 11.

³⁵ The Commons went into committee on the much delayed bill on 30 May, when Pleydell-Bouverie opened with a swingeing attack on low academic standards at Cambridge and the consequent need for a statutory commission, while Walpole replied by defending the university's ability to reform itself. Many amendments were proposed, including some minor ones by L.T. Wigram, the university's M.P., but only two major ones, put forward by James Heywood, were accepted. Dissenters were no longer required to make a declaration of faith on obtaining college scholarships or other endowments, and they were to be eligible for membership of the Senate. The latter measure, however, was reversed in the Lords; see 25 April 1857.
³⁶ i.e. 'spell of relaxation'? *O.E.D.* does not know the noun, although it records a verb meaning 'to make oneself cosy'.
³⁷ William Palmer (1824-56), the infamous Rugeley poisoner, was arrested on only one charge of doing away with a friend whose name he had forged to obtain money, but strong circumstantial evidence pointed to his having poisoned several members of his own family including his wife and brother. Such was the local furore that an act was hurriedly passed to remove the trial to London. He was hanged outside Stafford gaol on 14 June. Like J.B. Rush and the Mannings, to whom Romilly also refers, Palmer enjoyed national fame and was commemorated, fittingly enough, in Staffordshire pottery, ballads, and a place in Madame Tussaud's chamber of horrors. Palmer never confessed and as late as 1957 in *They Hanged My Saintly Billy* Robert Graves argued the thin case for his innocence; a more orthodox view is in G. St Aubyn, *Infamous Victorians* (1971), pp. 1-152 and select bibliography.

*Fri. 30.* . . . After lunch we went sightseeing: we finished off the Fitzwilliam Museum (– seeing the Cromwell Letters, the Missals & some of the choice Engravings). We next went to the Public Library[38] where (in the absence of Power) Wootton did the Honors for us: – we saw the Codex Bezæ & read the Gloss, saw the early printed books (viz Caxtons Book on Chess 1474, the 1st Cambridge book (about 1521), & the 1st Oxford wch has a lying title page dated 1464! – We saw also Edward VI's little book, a Breeches Bible (1598), etc etc . . . Bertha . . . attempts rather hard reading: she bought today Davies & Vaughan's translation of Plato's Republic: – I told her it was the hardest thing Plato ever wrote, & I looked out for Grim to read loud the passage about the Souls chusing Lots (wch was set at the Fellowship Examination 2 years ago): I told them that that was the choicest morsel in the work . . .

*Sun. 1 June.* . . . We had no music in the Evening. – I read loud one of Whewell's Elegiacs, & got Grim to read Whewell's sermon after Mrs W's death, & also an admirable one of Harvey Goodwin's on 'the Call' which all people of every profession & employment have. – We had a curious conversation about Milton: Bertha looks on Milton with a religious abhorrence & thinks he makes Eve at a greater distance from God than Adam: she particularly abominates as blasphemous Eve's calling Adam 'Author & Disposer':

– I explained the meaning to her, but it is a matter of deep feeling with her.[39]

*Mon. 2.* . . . Wrote to F.R. (£10): also an elaborate French letter to Sophie: her Letter informed me that the Enquête had taken place, that all Fanny's witnesses had given evidence (in spite of Mr Bourlet having called upon them & tried to intimidate them) & that the Judge is most favourably disposed to Fanny: – *but* the Pleadings have still to wait till September. That ill-conditioned Mr Bourlet threatens me with a voluminous attack of the Romilly family & vindication of himself: – I hope he will have the common sense to abstain from so useless a labour[40] . . .

*Tu. 3.* . . . Grim & Bertha went away by the Great Northern at 11, leaving Scrope Terrace at 10½: – they seemed greatly pleased with their visit. – Dosia & Harriet plaid their parts so well that I gave them each ½ a Sovereign . . . They are making grand preparations for the Peace-Jubilee on Parkers Piece next Thursday: – it is to be a substantial meal (tea & dinner combined) for all the Sunday Scholars . . .

---

[38] i.e. the University Library, as distinct from private college libraries.

[39] i.e. author , 'the efficient cause of something'; disposer, 'controller'. See *Paradise Lost*, Book IV, 635-8: 'My author and disposer, what thou bidd'st/ Unargued I obey;so God ordains:/ God is thy law, thou mine: to know no more/ Is woman's happiest knowledge, and her praise.'

[40] Fanny (Estéphanie) had been married to Bourlet for fourteen years when she began proceedings for a legal separation early in this year. On 13 January Romilly recorded that 'he has made her sign a paper surrendering her jewels and her dower, he has gone to the length of confining her and insisted on her sharing the house with his mistress !!!!! – What a depraved rascal ! Frank is highly indignant at his having attempted to get a loan from me, what Mr Bourlet (who told him of it) in his elegant language calls a "carrotte".'

*Th. 5.* Up at 20' to 7 – No Early Walk – Off by Express: I was in the same carriage with Philpott, Geldart & Guest. – I went to the National Gallery & did not at all like the new pictures bequeathed by Mr Rogers. – Then to the Athenæum for Bread & cheese . . . At 2½ I started from my hotel (Golden Cross) for Buckingham Palace. There were only 7 Heads of Houses present, viz. V.C. (Whewell) Phelps, Philpott, Cartmell & Pulling, Geldart & Guest: – Dr Fisher represented Bond in the Caput, Geldart was the right person for Law, Philpott represented Divinity instead of Cookson, Mathison & Lamb were the right Non Regent & Regent. – Marquis Camden was the only Nobleman; – no Bishops. – Dean Hamilton was present. – About 3 o'clock the Oxford Address had finished & Prince Albert came into the Waiting Room 'Promenade Gallery' (wch was fitted up with beautiful modern busts but no pictures): he shook hands with V.C. & 3 or 4 of the Heads & with nobody else. He apprised us (what Lord Ernest Bruce had officially told us already) that the V.C. & 4 other Heads & the Proctors were to kiss hands but that I was to name the rest of the Deputation. – I (as usual) stood by the Prince & helped hold the Address while he read it. – By the way he said that Lord Derby had a small copy to read from: so of course hereafter a small copy must be provided with the large one. The Queen was standing: the Duchess of Sutherland, Lady Macdonald & the Prince of Prussia were standing by the Queen: – the P. of P. had a degree conferred on him yesterday at Oxford. – After the 7 right persons had kissed hands I proceded to name the rest of the deputation, beginning with Dr Geldart: he walked confidently forward & kissed the Queen's hand: – I am told that Prince Albert made a slight movement as if to stop him: – all the rest made their bows only: – I was not named. – I was extremely nervous & was obliged to ask Godfray (who was standing next me) the names of the Junior Proctor (Wood) & the Senior Esquire Bedell (Leapingwell). – I did not name C.J. Selwyn (the Commissary). – By the way Professor Selwyn was present & asked me to go with him & Dudu at 4 to see the Bears in the Zoological: – I could not have that pleasure wch I should have enjoyed greatly. – Not finding a cab on quitting the Palace I walked with Godfray in our finery thro the streets. – After putting on my common dress I wrote to Horace Waddington at the Home Office an account of the Deputation . . . At 7 I dined with the Edward Romillys who had kindly asked the Kennedys to meet me . . . Mrs Edward spoke about the impossibility of a person who learned French in childhood (as she did) forgetting gender or accents: – she passed a perfect examination upon my crossquestioning. – She had been very gay, having been at the Queens Ball, & last night at the 1st performance of Ristori (the wonderful Italian tragic actress) in Medea . . .

*Fri. 6.* Didn't get up till 8. – As I was journalising in the Coffee room Grim looked in: he told me that there would be a Concert at the Crystal Palace today, that the cost would be 7/6 & that there was no admittance before 1: – I gladly agreed to meet him & Bertha there[41] . . . I went by Rail to Sydenham

---

[41] On the closing of the Great Exhibition in Hyde Park in 1851 Paxton's glass building was bought by a private company and removed to Sydenham, made even larger, and set among

& found Grim amiably waiting for me on the platform: he had gone by a previous train: – Bertha & her sister (Mrs Peel) were with him. – I treated Bertha to a libretto of the Concert & also to a Guide to the Crystal Palace. – In spite of the expense of Admission (7/6) there was a large number of visitors. The place looked enchanting. The beautiful towers (for supplying water) were new to me; the approach & the grounds are greatly embellished. – Grim treated us with buns to stay the wolves in our stomachs: – the Pompeian House & the Alhambra struck me greatly: – the glass fountain played, & at 4 o'clock 9 external fountains began spouting: – the profusion of sculpture is most extraordinary, & there is now also a gallery with a large no of good pictures . . . I went away at 4.10, & got to Shoreditch at the very nick of time 5' to 5 . . . I found both Dosia & Harriet very tired from yesterdays Peace Festival: – it seems to have been a grand treat: I was glad to hear that the workhouse-children were there, & that dissenters etc etc schools sent their children: – all the Ministers walked with them: – Dosia as well as Harriet went as a teacher to the St Pauls children[42] . . .

*Mon. 9.* . . . I met Cooper & asked him how he had got on with the Regent of Baden & how he had fed the Prince & suite. He told me the whole story wch is highly rich. On Saturday morning came a Telegraphic Message from the Palace to the V.C. saying that the Prince Regent of Baden & suite were coming to Cambridge immediately viz. by the train arriving at 10.10. – The V.C. being still in London (he was at the Opera on Friday), the Butler brought the message to John Cooper who forthwith sent off for Cookson (the deputy V.C.). The Regent is the brother of the imbecile reigning Duke of Baden . . . Cooper asked the party to dine in hall, but they couldn't as they were to return to town by the 5 o'clock train: – so (as Cookson offered no hospitality) Cooper ventured on a grand coup, he ordered lunch for the party at Trinity Lodge!! – the Butler asked what wine he should produce: 'O, said Cooper, they must have the best: bring Champagne'! . . . Since his return Whewell has had an interview with Cooper: – he was very grave & almost severe: – 'so I find that the Regent & party have been feasted in my house without my knowledge or consent: – I must think seriously whether I must not dismiss my servants who have presumed to act without my orders'. – Cooper said 'they are quite

landscaped gardens, fountains and lakes with dinosaurs. Adorned with statues, furnished with courts in every style from the Egyptian, the home of exhibitions and concerts, the Crystal Palace was Victorian Disneyland (appropriately opened by Her Majesty), a museum-cum-showground that attracted visitors by the million. See P. Beaver, *The Crystal Palace* (second edition, 1986).

[42] The *Independent* of 7 June describes the 'Peace Rejoicings' in enthusiastic detail. The weather was ideal, the town was hung with flags and banners, and it was estimated that by 5 o'clock some 20,000 people had crowded on to Parker's Piece. They included 5,000 children, led by their teachers, who processed eagerly towards a sit-down tea provided by a general subscription. However, the mountains of plum cake and other delights diminished so rapidly that it became clear that another 2000 unexpected small guests had contributed to their demolition. Tearful late-comers, many from the villages, found nothing to eat and the mayor had rapidly to promise that they must be entertained at a future date. Yet the evening celebrations went as planned with Isaiah Deck master-minding the firework display and an ascent of fire-balloons, and the town, though not the colleges, being partially illuminated.

free from blame, for I distinctly told them I would take the responsibility on myself'. – It is impossible to say how I would have taken such conduct had I been V.C., but I think I should have told Cooper that I thought he had acted very cleverly & shown much presence of mind in a difficult position & that I was sincerely obliged to him . . .

*Sat. 14.* . . . Letter from Sedgwick saying that a Geologist Mr Milne Horne (Qu: Hume?) & lovely daughter are coming to Cambridge on Monday & want lionising till 1½ when they go on to Norwich: he begs me to make love to the young lady (but in his name) & to come on with them to Norwich . . . Two very different events were to take place today: the christening of the Emperor's son at Paris & the hanging of the poisoner Palmer at Stafford. – Palmer's Solicitor (Smith) & some other persons have made great exertions for a respite . . .

On 16 and 17 June Romilly stayed in Norwich where at a grand dinner-party for 16 people he 'never heard Sedgwicks conversation so brilliant as it was after dinner when the women were gone: his subjects were Gibbon, Porson, Lords Brougham & Abinger, Lord Byron & a very graphic account of the opening the vault of Charles I in Windsor Chapel in the presence of George IV & Sir H. Halford', the physician, '(– King Charles' hair is still brown, – disproving the tale of its having turned white)'. On the eighteenth he again went to the *Belle Vue* hotel in Cromer where he walked and bathed, renewed acquaintance with people he had met during his holiday in September and October 1855 and enjoyed getting to know the family of Joseph Wix, the Vicar of Littlebury, Essex and chaplain to Lord Braybrooke. One day on the shore he 'saw neatly traced in the sand a *tortoise* with the word 'Cambridge' over it: – I think some wag has seen me crawling & means it for me'. At intervals during the day and in the evenings he read Chaucer's tales and Schiller's play *Maria Stuart* and after Mrs Fitch had lent him 'Cath. Winkworths translations of German Hymns called "Lyra Germanica"' transcribed several of those he especially admired into his journal.

*Th. 26.* Up at 6½. Left Cromer at ¼ to 8: – all the Wix family were standing at the window to greet me as the Coach drove by. – I of course was outside the Coach . . . Reached Cambridge at 1.35. – Shortly after my arrival that tiresome Mr Pieritz came about his Creation next Tuesday: – I wrote him a certificate of his degree for AM last year. Immediately after came a most thoroughly unwelcome visitor, viz. one of the lower hangers-on to an attorney: he served me with a subpoena to be in Dublin Courts next Monday in re Moore O'Connor v. Barbara Wallen Proprietress of Londonderry Sentinel. (He is the lying pretender to M.B. degree of Dublin in 1848). I immediately exclaimed that I was very ill used in being given such short notice, that my presence was required at Cambridge, that Monday was the busiest day of our University year, & that no person could do my business but myself: – he told me that I *must* attend at Dublin as he had caught me & served the subpoena on me (he handed over £10): that if I failed I should be fined £100 & punished for contempt of Court. – All this brought me to reason: I had shot off my steam: I told him that I intended being in Dublin as commanded, & shook hands with him & bowed him out. – The next thing was to arrange in this crisis . . . I didn't get to bed till 12½. – Today I had been asked to the Harrow Speeches: – it was a brilliant affair: Lord Palmerston & General Williams (the Hero of

Kars) were there: – after the speeches Gen. Williams laid the 1st stone of a monument to the Harrovians who had fallen in the Crimea . . . Agreeable little letter from Sophie containing the following detestable Conundrum communicated by Franky: 'If King Richard was alone at Cologne what would you say to him?' Answer 'O Dick alone!' (eau de Cologne).

*Fri. 27.* Up at 6½. – My before breakfast walk only to the Post Office. I wrote more instructions to Edleston, Welsford & Hoppett. – Off by the Express at 9 o'clock: – I went by the 2nd Class & had very pleasant company (including a hale white-headed Staffordshire Clergyman): – read 'Railway Anecdotes'. – The Clergyman told me that my journey to Holyhead must be from the Euston Square Station & he told me all the times. – In London by 11! I drove at once to Euston Square & took a bed at Olivers Hotel, preferring the journey tomorrow from 9 A.M. till 5¼ to that this Evening from 5 to 1¼ in the middle of the night . . . At the Athenæum I met John Roget & Charles Romilly: Charles said that his eldest boy was suffering from languor (can neither study nor play) & therefore brought away from school. – Finding that the great actress Ristori was to play tonight I braved the tremendous heat & went to the Lyceum . . . I went in the Pit paying 5/ & 2/6 for a Book of Alfieri's 'Rosmunda': – the greater part of the Pit was made into Stalls. Prince Albert & the Prince of Prussia were in the Royal Box, but not the Queen nor the Princess Royal who has burnt her arm by her dress taking fire. – Rosmunda is an utterly diabolical character: Madame Ristori's acting in the jealous & scornful parts I thought marvellous . . .

*Sat. 28.* . . . Left London in the Holyhead Express at 9.15: as I was standing at the Euston Square Station a person spoke to me by name & said we were going on the same mission . . . This gentleman was a Mr Hales, a sickly clergyman who had been Scholar of Trinity: he is AB of 1828 . . . With this Mr Hales were 2 other Gentlemen subpoena'd in the same matter: one was a goodhumoured Clergyman named Dumergue (he was AB of Corpus Christi in 1842, son of the Dentist & brother to Dumergue of Trinity who died last year): the other a Mr Curry a brother-in-law of Moore O'Connor (whom he thoroughly abominates) . . . We got a hasty dinner at 3½ at Chester. – The day was delightful for travelling: but I was greatly inconvenienced by the smother of dust: – I started in white trowsers, – they became black . . . We embarked at Holyhead at ¼ to 7 (an hour & ¼ after our proper time) in a powerful 350 horse-power Steamer. A very large party embarked, including Sir Charles Wood etc. the wind blew very fresh, & Mr Hales very amiably lent me a great coat (he having 2) . . . We didn't reach Kingstown (7 miles from Dublin) till 11½: there was intense confusion & embarrassment in getting the luggage & then in scudding off a long way to the Station for Railway Tickets: – Also much fuss & difficulty about the luggage in Dublin. – We 4 went in one vehicle to the Imperial Hotel in Sackville St: I took a glass of bitter beer & went to bed at once (it being now 1 o'clock): my 3 companions ordered cold meat & negus.

· *Sun. 29.* Didn't get up till 8. – We had agreed to breakfast at 9: we were kept waiting for Mr Hales more than ½ hour. A friend of his (a Mr Monsarrat, a handsome young Clergyman who married a physician's daughter here) came in the middle of breakfast to tell us about the Churches: – the services all begin at *12* o'clock! . . . At 3 we went under the guidance of Mr Monsarrat to the Irish Missions in the Ragged schools: there were 450 men, women & children present: a large no of them were with bare feet & in miserably tattered, dirty clothes: a large proportion of these people are Roman Catholics: they are grouped into a large no of Classes: – the male classes are examined by men: & the female by women: among the examiners of the male classes was one of the 1st Physicians of the place: 2 of Archbishop Whateley's daughters were among the female examiners: – the verse to be taught was 'If thou knewest the gift of God etc etc'. – I was so greatly pleased with the energy & talent of one of the Examiners that when all was over I went & shook hands with him & expressed my admiration of his teaching: he was himself of the working classes: – some of the people (generally men) made fight for the Romish doctrines: – the female teachers were not half so energetic as the male: – at the end each pauper received bread: – I thought the scene very interesting & very affecting. On going out we wrote down our names & gave something . . .

*Mon. 30.* . . . At 10½ we went into Court Mr Monsarrat kindly taking us in his father-in-laws carriage & afterwards most amiably refreshing us with oranges & biscuits). The Chief Justice of the C.P. (Monahan) tried the cause: Whiteside was Counsel for Moore O'Connor & Brewster for the Newspaper: the nominal Defendant was Barbara H.Wallen (proprietress of a Londonderry paper the Sentinel), but the real one was Mr Odriscol (its Editor) whom Moore O'Connor calls O-dry-skull. – A Demurrer was taken by O'Connor against all the points except one, viz the libel charging him with having habitually got drunk with the Roman Catholic priest & then having shared his bed . . . There was a great deal of most tiresome squabbling about the law of Evidence. Mr Brewster was (by said law) precluded from going into facts & proving them by witnesses: – so we have all been fetched for nothing . . . Whiteside put only one witness in the box (Revd Mr Martin) . . . he made a deplorable figure for Mr Brewster drove him into confessing that 3 bitter libels (against Bishop of London . . . ) etc were dictated by O'Connor & transcribed by himself & wife (poor lady) to be sent to the press. By the way this conduct of O'Connor's is said to be the origin of Bishop of London's known antipathy to Irish curates[43] . . .

*Tu. 1 July.* . . . In Court from 10½ to 7 when to the astonishment & indignation of us all the Jury gave Moore O'Connor £100 on the 1st Libel (wch was not gone into, he having demurred & £200 on the 2d Libel (for getting drunk & sleeping with the R.C. priest Macgill, – a dirty huge animal who was reproved by the Chief Justice for his insolent conduct when in the

---

[43] O'Connor showed astonishing effrontery in suing the *Sentinel* for libel and claiming substantial damages. The Bishop of London had ordained him as a missionary to Canada (to which he never went), and then inhibited him from performing clerical duties. On 5 November 1856 Romilly was asked to send the bishop of Derry an attested copy of O'Connor's signature for an ad-eundem degree of 1848, as the testimonials presented to the bishop were now known to be forgeries. On 9 November Romilly received a notice saying that the demurrer was unanimously overruled, damages were not to be paid, and the defendant was to recover her costs against the plaintiff. Leave was granted for another trial. O'Connor's name disappears from the *Clergy List* in 1858.

witness box). I was (to my surprise) put in the Box: – I took my subscription book & laid it on the Ledge of the Box to attract attention: after being sworn in & asked my name & my duties at Cambridge (in answering to wch I said the Book by me was that in wch applicants for Degrees wrote their names) I was asked 'What rumours about Mr M O'C there were at Cambridge & what proceedings had taken place': – upon wch O'Connors Counsel screamed out 'Don't answer that question': his Lordship said 'You will find it hard Mr Romilly to please both these gentlemen'. – I said 'Yes indeed my Lord'. – The same course was pursued with regard to Mr Hales . . . & Mr Dumergue . . . Mr Curry was not put in the box . . . In the Evening we went to the Irish Missions (in the Ragged Schools) to hear a discussion: a young man named Vickers occupied the Pulpit . . . he proceeded to attack the miracles in the Breviary: he read several of them (St Januarius, St Denis etc etc: he was most clamorously assailed by several men, who declared they believed every word of them . . . When Mr Vickers said that the paper called 'the Telegraph' had published that the Pope himself didn't believe all these legends for he had just appointed a Commission to expunge some of them, one man cried out we don't believe the 'Tell-lie-graph' . . .

*Wed. 2.* Up at 7. – Took leave of Mr Odriscol (the unfortunate editor of the Sentinel) – At 10 o'clock the amiable Mr Monsarrat came in his father in law's carriage & took us 4 to see the College etc . . . We then went into the Library: the under-librarian (a Gownsman) did the honors to us: it contains about 130,000 volumes: Mr Hales was shown (at his request) the French Translation of the Testament printed at Bordeaux in 1686: it is full of false translations in support of the Roman Catholic faith . . . I asked to see the great gem of the library & was shown the Codex Montfortianus (a Greek MS.) – which contains the passage of '3 witnesses' 1. John 5. 7-8): it is of 13th Century: it belonged to a Dr Montfort before Archbishop Ussher obtained it. The Librarian showed us also a Latin *Testament* (I believe) called the Book of Kells & said to have belonged to St Colomba . . . About 2 we started from Kingstown in the Lewellyn Steamer: there was but a small party . . . The sun shone bright & there was a gentle breeze: – nothing could be more delightful: – but Mr Hales & Mr Edwards were afraid to eat: – Mr Dumergue, Mr Curry & I made a good dinner. We reached Holyhead (– a distance of 64 miles) in 4 hrs & ½ . . . fortunately it was high water when we started from Holyhead & coasted along the edge of the sea to Chester . . . We reached Chester shortly before 11 . . . I had a glass of beer & went to bed at once.

*Th. 3.* . . . Mr Dumergue, Mr Curry & I had a carriage to ourselves. – Mr Dumergue communicated the following jokes: 'if the Queen were to knight her coachman what insect would she name?' Answer 'Cochi-neal'. – 'Why is riding on horseback unfashionable in the Isle of Wight?' Answer: 'Because the Queen prefers Cowes to Ryde'! – This last is vastly amusing . . . Reached Town about 4 o'clock & proceeded immediately to Shoreditch Station: here I dined economically, – 2 cold nasty penny sausage rolls & ½ pint of porter (excellent), – 3d in all. – Reached Cambridge at 7 & found Harriet & Dosia quite well . . .

*Fri. 4.* Up a little before 7. – My own house looks beautifully clean & feels most comfortable after having lived at hotels & in steam-boats & railway carriages. – At 10 to the Senate House for dissolution of term. – Had an interview with Edleston to thank him for his valuable services: also with Welsford, to whom I offered 2 sovereigns & made him a pretty speech of gratitude: he would not accept a farthing & said it had been a great pleasure to him to help me . . .

*Sun. 6.* Up a little before 7 – Walk in Cemetery: – the Chapel is advancing rapidly: – the West door is very pretty. – During my absence they have built up again at the beginning of the Wranglers walk over the water Hobson's Conduit wch was removed from the Market. – Wrote today to Grim & to Maggie an account of my adventures in Ireland . . .

*Tu. 8.* . . . After lunch I escorted Dosia & her cousin Sarah Shaw (daughter of the Carpenter at Dulwich!) & S.S.'s fellow-servant to the Fitzwilliam Museum: – it was raining cats & dogs. In my Office I worked till past 5 & smoked a cigar to keep myself warm. – At dinner I had a fire, wch I kept up all the Evening with great satisfaction. – Mrs Wootton (born Rumble) is going tomorrow to town under the protection of Dosia to see her husband who is in the Consumptive hospital: – he was a Compositor: – there are 4 delicate children, – one a baby. – Dearest Lucy used to be very kind to both the families. Another of her protégés called today, William How (whom she prentised to Peck): he is a carpenter in good business at Aldershott: he courted my nextdoor-neighbour Mr Foster's Cook but she held him cheap because he is short of stature & she has now got a tall sweetheart!

*Sun. 13.* . . . After lunch took a long dawdling walk to Cherry Hinton, occasionally sitting down & reading last year's journal: – I was disgusted at seeing a troop of young men bathing in the brook: – the path is close by it & is a great thoroughfare on Sundays . . . There is now a bill in Parliament for accepting the Resignation of Bishop Maltby (aged 86) & Bishop Blomfield (age 71): – there is a savage article in yesterdays Times against inefficient Bishops & against the magnitude of the salaries to these 2 eminent retiring Prelates: the article is unreasonable & mischievous: – £6000 & Fulham Palace is not too much for the Bishop of London whose income was £22,000, nor £4500 for the Bishop of Durham whose income was £15000[44] . . .

*Fri. 18.* . . . I today finished my Index of 'University Papers' & worked away till 5 at 'Graduati': – I was not able to get thro my daily task of one year's verifications: – I could do nothing for V.C.'s Index . . .

On 19 July Romilly, on his way to Ely to stay for two nights with Dean Peacock and his wife, was fed with cake by the footman of an aristocratic old couple who shared his

---

[44] Those few curates who could afford *The Times* for 12 July would have been grateful for its very long leader: 'We are given to understand that we ought to extol to the skies the incredible disinterestedness of these successors of the Apostles, who are content to starve – the one on the pay of sixty curates, the other on the pay of forty-five . . . We are reminded that the Bishop of London having lived in princely magnificence for thirty years, and the Bishop of Durham for a quarter of a century, cannot be expected to adapt themselves at once to the privations implied by such miserable allowances . . . There is, too, the important consideration that the Bishops can do what some other Bishops are doing, – they can retain their sees with that grasp which old age and illness rather tighten than relax, and defy the public opinion of Parliament and people.'

railway carriage. He found that great things had been done in the cathedral since his last visit, 'viz. the building up St Catharine's Chapel, the removal of the Organ, the erection of a beautiful wooden screen (of Rattees workmanship) . . . a grand font with sculptures of the emblems of the Evangelists given by Selwyn, a fine fresco ceiling to the Tower, & above all a superb Reredos of Alabaster (with figures, heads etc etc in the highest stile of excellence'. The reredos by George Gilbert Scott was not yet finished.

*Fri. 25.* Up at ¼ to 7. – There had been a good deal of rain in the night: so the air was cooler. – I walked in the Old Botanical Garden, where there is to be today a sale of the materials of the hot house, greenhouses etc etc etc & of a private house pulled down: – I then roamed about the tidy little streets wch sprung up on the site of Mr Humfrey's grounds[45] . . . A man met me whom I take to be Russell (of Eversden) for whose sermons I subscribed last year but never read one: – he expressed surprise at my being alive, & said that old Time was constantly at work with his scythe: he shook hands as tenderly as if he meant to ask me to subscribe to another Volume. – After dinner I worked (at the V.C.'s Index) in the Garden till dark.

*Tu. 29.* . . . Parliament is to be prorogued today. – Today all the stuffed birds flew from Sedgwick's Museum to my staircase. – Sedgwick himself also came & we smoked a cigar . . . Letter from Mr Johns (of Calliper's Rickmansworth) giving me a very agreeable account of Franky Kennedy: I had asked him his opinion 8 or 9 months ago, but his acquaintance with Franky was then too short for him to have formed a judgment. These are his words 'Frank, generous & upright will give you his moral character: – sweettempered, obligeing, retiring (if not shy), somewhat awkward from his size being disproportionate to his age, indicate his outward deportment. In scholarship he is backward: but his capacity is good & he has quick powers of apprehension: he has not the gift of abstraction, so necessary in public school life: but he is fast acquiring habits of application & being industrious to the full extent of his light. I have no doubt of his performing his school course with credit, if not with something more. Brilliant mental display in a boy whose material structure has been undergoing so rapid a development it would be idle to look for: yet I think it far from improbable that he may eventually turn out as *accomplished* a man as with GOD's Blessing he will certainly prove a *good* man'. – Poor Harriet has been suffering so much from tooth ache that she went this Evening to Mr Jones: he used a white powder to kill the nerves of 2 teeth & will stop them tomorrow: the process of nerve killing thus is a slow one of 2 or 3 hours of considerable pain. – I paid expenses 10/: & gave her 2/6. – After dinner worked at V.C.'s index in the garden.

[45] Banker, architect, and formerly mayor of Cambridge, Charles Humfrey had lived in style in a pseudo-Elizabethan mansion near Parker's Piece until, beset by money troubles in his old age, he left the town and died in London in 1848. Romilly, who knew and liked his family, recorded the decline in his fortunes and property: 'it is quite mournful to see the grounds cut up by a brick wall & all appearance of many tenements springing up on the spot' (1 November 1845, *Romilly 1842-47*, p. 146).

*Wed. 30.* Up at ¼ to 7. – Walk on Sheep Green & saw tribes of bathers. – Saw Joshua Barker (who came to help his brother Frank in the garden): he looks but faint & sickly & does not give a good account of himself: he is quite unfit for hard work: – he was twice ruptured from breaking in horses when in the army: he has a pension of 7d a day for two years . . .

*Wed. 6 August.* . . . Dosia returned after her 4 weeks absence: – she is much improved in health: I was very glad to see her so much better: – she had been to see Betsy (Spink) & reported favorably of her & her belongings, except that little Lucy is rather delicate. – I this morning finished the V.C.'s Index; & I had the pleasure of correcting the 1st proof sheet of my new Edition of Graduati . . . Harriet went in the Evening to the fortnightly meeting of the Sunday School Teachers: she brought back word that there had been great excitement in Cambridge today, because there had been a prophecy circulated that *the world would end today*, that the dissolution of the world would be accompanied by intense heat & a dreadful storm!!! . . .

*Fri. 8.* . . . Mr Hyde has sent me 6 Copies of the 'Cambridge University Act': wrote to thank him & began studying this most important document[46] . . .

*Sat. 9.* . . . Today was the Printers annual holiday, (They usually keep it at Trumpington) but I found one solitary young man who was staying in the premises till 11 o'clock & to him I gave my corrected proof sheet. This annual feast is called 'the Way Goose': the young man showed me a notice of it in 'the Printer's Manual': that book says the origin of the name is doubtful, & that it used to be spelt 'Wayz Goose' & was supposed to mean 'stubble goose': Quaere – has the German for 'wheat' – 'weize' anything to do with it[47] . . .

*Mon. 11.* Up at 20' to 7. Walk in Coe Fen & Sheep Green. – Kind Letter from Walter Scott Dumergue, saying there was a subscription to reimburse the Londonderry Sentinel for the fine of £300 awarded to Moore O'Connor: wrote to Dumergue & sent a Guinea.

*Wed. 13.* . . . Highly pleased with a vigorous attack in 'the Times' of the Satanic authors & particularly of the indecent & demoralising plot of the 'Traviata', the opera wch has been played all the season: – the Traviata is acted by the favorite singer (Piccolomini) . . . Prof. Bennett told me that he had read in Hawkins History of Music that the 1st Cambridge Doctor of Music was Master of Kings College & that he was Doctor in 1401 & named St Wix: I told him that Kings was not a College at that time, & that my records of degrees didn't begin till 1454. – After he was gone I looked up all the information & wrote him a full account of my gleanings. Carter (in his history of Cambridge) mentions *St Viste* or St Just as Master of *Kings Hall* from 1464 to 1467 & says he was on 12 December made Doctor of Music for life *by the King*. – I have no record of mandates before 1558.) – I told him that the 1st recorded degree in Music was that of Dr Cowper in 1507 . . .

---

[46] Royal assent to the Act setting up the Statutory Commission was given on 27 July, after which it was proper to distribute copies. See *Annals*, V, 221-31.

[47] The etymology remains impenetrable. The holiday was given by a master-printer to his men each August, originally to mark the start of work by candle-light, and often, as in this case, out of town. The tradition survived at Cambridge University Press until 1958.

*Fri. 15.* . . . In my office I had a visit from Prof. Bennett: he brought the extract from Hawkins of wch he spoke the other day: – it mentions a Hen. Habington having been Mus B in 1463. After he was gone I poured [sic] over Grace Book A (wch begins 1454) from the 1st page for several years & found that sure enough H.H. had such a degree (– it is the first recorded in the Book): he also took Mus D by Grace on condition of previous residence of a year[48] . . . I wrote to Professor Bennett & mentioned the exercises required in 1516 etc, viz a Mass & Antiphon. of the Virgin . . .

*Th. 21.* Up at 10' to 7. – Walk to Railway Station: – there are 15 front arches: there are 16 coats of arms in front & 2 on each of the sides: – I cannot make out what the 20th can be, the University, the 17 Colleges & the Town furnishing only 19[49] . . .

*Sat. 30.* . . . In my office I had a visit from Bowtell (the bookbinder – worthless son of a worthy father): he is hawking about 'History of France' etc etc coming out in parts: I declined taking any: he said he had not had a regular meal for a fortnight: I gave him 2/, telling him it was for his Fathers sake for whom I had great regard: – he did not look starved: he was as fat as butter: he was decently dressed & humble & civil. – Harriet came home from her 10 days outing. So now I have a grand establishment, Dosia & Harriet, Mary Edwards & Hannah Smyth . . . After 4 hours of Graduati verifications I worked out what I could collect about early Vicechancellors: – the 1st *recorded* name I can find any where is that of Henry Stokton who in 1417 was V.C. when the Chancellor John de Rickingale was attending the Council of Constance:[50]– Vicechancellors are mentioned in the old Statute (No 57) whose date is 1275: – but I suspect these antique V.C.'s were merely deputies, & lost authority & title on the return of the Chancellor . . .

*Wed. 10 September.* Up at 7. – Walk in Botanic Garden – Letter from Selwyn (now at Foxton): he had been made ill by the great heat when he was abroad (where he found no place cool but the Crypt of Chartres Cathedral): he has been recruiting at St Leonards: – he says that dear Dudu is quite well but that she thinks her Mamma overworks her with Lessons! Blank Letter from Henslow enclosing his horticultural Programme: one Regulation amused me 'Babies between 1 & 3 years old, who can eat & drink, are not to be hid under

---

[48]  For this man 'Henry Abyndon', first known recipient of the degree of Bachelor of Music, see A.B Emden, *A Biographical Register of the University of Cambridge to 1500* (1963), pp. 1-2.

[49]  A puzzling enumeration. To the nineteen heraldic devices that he saw the railway company had added (or were to add) those of the High Stewards of the university and town, the Lord Lieutenant, and the Chancellor (the late Duke of Northumberland) at the time when the station was opened in 1845.

[50]  More recent research has awarded the palm to one Thomas Ashwell, a Carmelite friar appointed 'President' of the university while its Chancellor was in Rome in 1412. Despite Romilly's great knowledge of the documents in his care, his lists and dates relating to medieval office-holders were usually hit-and-miss, as indeed were those of his immediate successors as Registrary. The great *Alumni Cantabrigienses* of the Venns is superseded for the period by A.B. Emden, *Biographical Register of the University of Cambridge to 1500* (1963). The early Grace books for 1454 to 1544 were published in memory of H.R. Luard, Romilly's successor as Registrary, but no one has come forward in the last ninety years to edit more of them.

the table! Mothers who can't leave them at home may pay 2d for each to be collected for a Prize at next show & called "Baby Ticket" Prize' . . . After dinner came a Miss Ward (a well-mannered middle-aged person): – she is in distress: she is a milliner & says dear Margaret had employed her: she is taking cod-liver oil: – if she can raise a certain small sum Bishop Maltby will give her £10: – Miss Simpson (who sent her to me) gave £1 & Mr Kerrich (who gives to all cases of poverty) gave £1: – I followed their example. – At night read Colliers 'History of the Stage' & corrected No 26.[51] – Fire in the Evening. – Mary left this morning (having staid 25 days): I gave her 10/: she took away with her my Godson Joseph Spink (to whom I gave a bright shilling & some marmalade: – the child (who is 5 years old) was most eager to go home, having had no Children to play with at grand father Spink's.

*Th. 18.* Up at ¼ to 7. – Walk in Botanic Garden. – Letter from Mrs Morris, who wants to get a boy (age 14) into the Pitt Press: – I made enquiries & find that no apprentices are taken without they have passed 2 years as *reading* boys: – such reading boys are usually taken at the age of 12: – wrote to her & told her that she should call on Mr Clay . . . who has the entire management of every thing . . .

*Sat. 20.* . . . Went to Trinity Lodge & got a fresh loan of the Fellowship Book, & by working steadily at it till 5½ got thro all I wanted. One entry amused me: it was the declaration of 3 Fellows (elected *beyond* the no the College had to maintain) that they would not be burdensome or claim any profits till vacancies occurred. Between 1641 & 1660 the admissions were entered in 'a thin book with strings': in the common Book (wch I worked at) there are the names given of 20 or more who were readmitted & sworn in 1660[52] . . .

*Wed. 24.* . . . Greatly shocked at a letter from Latimer Neville telling me of the death of poor dear Lady Braybrooke: she was attacked with inflammation of the brain & died yesterday at Audley End! She had always been a most kind & dear friend to me . . .

*Sat. 4 October.* . . . A dissenter (Johnson of Corpus Christi) called about taking his AB degree: I told him that he might take it on the 10th: – this is the 1st application I have had from a Dissenter: – I was in hopes that Heywood would have been the 1st as he has been the great agitator for degrees to Dissenters. – I took my list of 120 names of Voluntary Theological Candidates to the press . . .

*Th. 9.* My birthday: I am now 65 complete, & (God be praised) am in very good health for an old man . . . At 6½ to tea at Trinity Lodge: the 8 Examiners were myself, Martin, Grote, Cooper, Edleston, Thacker, Mathison & King: the 8 vacancies were Dr Rothman (death), Atkinson, Gorham, Hedley, Scott, Elwyn (all 5 by marriage), Lushington & Wilbraham (2

[51] Of the *Graduati* proofs.
[52] Trinity suffered little materially during the Civil War, but, like the rest of the university, it was thoroughly purged by Parliament in 1644 when 48 of the fellows and the master were expelled for refusing to take the covenant. Many of the survivors were reinstated at the Restoration. Figures for each college are given in J.D. Twigg, *The University of Cambridge and the English Revolution 1625-1688* (1990), p. 98.

lawyers): – we filled them up with Sale & Farrar (3d year men, Crompton (the Judge's son), Monro & Hudson (2d year men) & Brown, Hardy & Rigby (freshmen) . . .

*Fri. 10.* . . . The degrees were 2 AM (both *declarants* for Church of England), 4 AB, 2 eundem.[53] Today was the beginning of the new system without oaths or declarations: – but those who intend being Members of the Senate must declare: – so I divide each page of MAs into 2 sets of Declarants & Non-declarants. – A dissenter (Leigh Smith of Jesus – a Wrangler in 1852) took his AB degree. At this Congregation the Orator read his Letter of thanks to Sir John Patteson. – There was the *singularity* of one Taxor only: his only use is the Custody of Weights & Measures: – the Town have petitioned the University for use of them, & I hope it will be granted as we may not use them ourselves . . . Dined in the Combination Room: the Master sent some Venison (– the Queen gives him some every year): – it was a magnificent dinner & every body in good humour: the Master's Conversation was brilliant . . .

*Sun. 12.* . . . Home to my tapioca & then to St Mary's to hear Harvey Goodwins lecture: – here my attention was thoroughly on the alert & I was highly delighted & greatly edified: – His text was Matthew. VII. 29 'He taught them as one having authority'. – I then went to College & falling in with Martin & Thacker went with them over Newtons rooms, – wch are being beautified towards the Street: – they now belong to Hotham . . . In the Evening answered Grims very amusing letter giving an account of his reception of Bishop Villiers at the 1st Confirmation at Millom Church remembered by mortal man: about 100 were confirmed . . . The Bishop condescended to slang phrases, & speaking of a fraudulent charge for posthorses said 'it's a bore to be done': – as Grim observes this was much in his own stile; – possibly it was elicited by some kindred remarks of Grims.

*Sat. 18.* . . . In my Office I had a visit from the Vicechancellor (about the Electoral Roll): he directed me to write to Waring, Dr Webster & Gaskin (whom I had recommended as striking out of the roll as non-resident Commorants) & tell them of their approaching fate[54] . . . Sent my List of Graces to be printed with the Vicechancellors: it is the longest list I ever saw by far, it has 41 Graces: – 8 of them in consequence of Sir J. Patteson's Award . . .

[53] Under the new Act graduates proceeding to the M.A. degree who also wished to become members of the Senate had to declare, rather than swear, themselves members of the Church of England. The discrimination was aimed chiefly at dissenters and was removed by another Statutory Commission in the 1870s. Of the excluded men only they were not very rare; few Jews entered the university and as a matter of policy the new Roman Catholic hierarchy prevented its members from entering the university lest they be corrupted.

[54] This Roll was required under the Cambridge Act and included those entitled to vote in the November election for the new Council of the Senate, i.e. Heads of Houses, Professors, Public Examiners, University Officers (if members of the Senate), and other members of the Senate who had resided for at least 14 weeks in the previous academical year within a mile and a half of Great St Mary's church. The final Roll listed 264 names. Trinity (56) and St John's (41) were far ahead of the other fifteen colleges while Downing came last with only 4. Commorantes in Villa numbered 14.

*Tu. 21.* Visit from Mr W. Monk (St Johns), Mr Titcomb's Curate . . .
He told me that he thinks his open-air preaching (– in the back streets of
Barnwell) is successful: he seems to have preached sub dio twice a week all the
summer: his audience varies from about 90 to 150: – Mr Titcomb has only
preached once in the open air this year: – so Mr Monk considers that now as
his own province . . . From 2 till 5 I worked in the Office at statistics of
'Special Constables' for the Vicechancellor – 36 were sworn in by Archdall in
November 1836 (by virtue of Act of 6 George IV. 1825), – these worked
gratuitously: – 24 were sworn in by Dr Tatham in 1846 (at the General-Tom-
Thumb riots) & 21 by Philpott in 1847 (at the attacks on the Proctors
& Kingsley after the death of the unfortunate Elizabeth How who was taken ill
after her dismissal from the spinning house, where she had been confined only
one day)[55] . . .

*Wed. 22.* . . . Last Sunday Evening there was a sad calamity in the Surrey
Gardens: Mr Spurgeon (the young Dissenter about whom the world is mad)
was preaching to 12,000 persons jammed into the Concert-room built for
10,000: – an alarm of fire was given (maliciously it is supposed, for there was
no reason for it) & 7 lives were lost, & many persons grievously injured. This
Mr Spurgeon is only 25: he was teacher in Cambridge in the school of
a Dissenter named Leading. – Philpott thinks also in Mr Luke Jone's
school.[56] – By the way Johnson the Dissenting Schoolmaster took AB degree
today (matriculated at Corpus in 1843) . . . Received from Cartmell an official
announcement of the Syndics having voted me the paper & press work of 500
Copies of my forthcoming Graduati. – I wrote my thanks . . .

*Th. 23.* . . . Letter from Mr Somerby (of Boston U.S.) announcing with
great glee that he had given letters of introduction to 3 other Americans . . . &
that they would be down upon me today. – Vastly tiresome. From 11 to 1 in
the Arts Schools (– the Senate House being occupied with Little-Go Examina-

[55] On 6 March 1846 fighting broke out among the crowds struggling to see Tom Thumb, the
American dwarf, outside the town hall, and by the evening of 9 March bands of townsmen
and gownsmen were brawling ferociously in the streets. The police eventually contained the
students in their colleges, whereupon their adversaries attacked them and broke many
windows. The *Chronicle* reported that the police 'with discriminating vigour battered only the
heads with caps on', and one policeman was later sent to jail for knocking a Trinity lad
unconscious. But it is clear from evidence at the subsequent hearing that many young men had
what they thought was an excellent evening. A Trinity pensioner heard that 'the town were
killing a gownsman and so of course he could not stop in his rooms', and the gownsman
knocked unconscious was heard to say 'Damn you, police, get out of the way. We want to
have a jolly row with these cads.' Special constables were sworn in and the authorities issued
threats of expulsion or rustication. There was no more unrest. See *Romilly 1842-47*, pp. 160-
2. Elizabeth Howe, a prostitute, had been confined for one night in the Spinning House in
November 1846 by Kingsley, the Junior Proctor. It was suspected that there (described at the
inquest as 'a gaol unfit for the worst of felons') she had contracted the fever from which she
died, and there were attacks on the Proctors which only ceased after additional special
constables were recruited in February 1847.
[56] C.H. Spurgeon (1834-92), once usher in a Cambridge school who preached first at the age
of sixteen in the nearby village of Teversham and had been Baptist minister at Waterbeach,
was from the age of twenty-two until his death the most popular preacher of the age. His
sermons were heard by thousands and read by millions.

tion): – the V.C. sat up in state with Dr Philpott & Tozer (the Assessor) to revise the Electoral Roll: – Smedley claimed being within 1½ of St Mary's, a Surveyor having measured the distance to his door at Chesterton: – the distance 1 m. 3 f. 175 yds. – touch & go . . .

*Fri. 24.* . . . In my Office I had a visit from C.C. Babington: he described the ludicrous failure of the meeting last night about fit members for the Council: – it is supposed to have been called on suggestion of Dr Corrie: however the Conservatives were rendered mute by the appearance of Dr Fisher & Professor Pryme etc:[57]– Dr Fisher was voted into the Chair as the Senior Doctor present (on a motion of Pryme's): Fisher asked who had called the meeting & who was responsible for the expense of the room: – no answer was given: – the meeting dispersed without any measure being brought forward or any names proposed . . . Got little or no walk in the middle of the day, having to look out Botanic Garden documents etc etc for the V.C. & to prepare for my 'Family'. – We were a party of 15, viz. Cartmell & brother, Phelps, Paget, Shaw, Thompson & his guest C. Merivale, Packe (who sent brace of pheasants), Bateson, France, Clark, Power, Stokes, Martin & myself. – Hudson sent a beautiful bouquet, the dinner was well cooked & the wines praised by the guests: – there was abundance of good talk till past 9: – I gave as a toast the travellers in Greece (Thompson & Clark)[58] . . . I gave the brides of the year & particularly Mrs Cartmell: this elicited a speech from Cartmell concluding with 'go & do likewise', upon wch we all drank Stokes' health with peels of laughter: – I also gave the health of 'the Historian' Merivale for wch he returned thanks very cordially. We made up 2 whist tables . . .

*Mon. 27.* . . . The Dean of Ely & Mrs Peacock took me over in their fly at 10½ to spend the day at Foxton & keep Dudu's birthday wch really falls on Wednesday. – In the Cemetery there is a very pretty Gothic monument to Rattee (the Carver in wood & stone who died at the early age of 34)[59] . . . The day being most lovely we proceeded on our arrival at Foxton to go round all the gardens etc etc to see all the animals (including the 22 turkeys whom we fed with barley, the grand dog Nero, the donkey called Sancho, the bees etc etc) . . .

*Tu. 28.* . . . Fell in with Ainslie & Cookson going to see the Plate for Sir J. Patteson at Peters', – I joined them: the Candelabrum is very pretty & delicate with much frosted work: – it is for 9 lights: – there are 3 figures, a female with a Civic Mace (for the Corporation), another with a Book for the University, & a 3d representing Justice (for Sir J.P.): – 2 winged snakes of discord are being trampled upon. In the shop looking at the plate was Staples Foster: I didn't know who it was & took no notice of him, Ainslie pointedly & intentionally cut him: – he told me afterwards that he was a very loose

---

[57] Professor Corrie, a narrow Tory in academic and national politics, when Vice-Chancellor in 1850 had been hostile to the Royal Commission and prejudiced against the Chancellor. Presumably he called this meeting to influence the choice of members who shared his views. For his failure to be elected to the Council see 7 November. Pryme had advocated reform as early as 1837 (Winstanley, p. 187 note 3).

[58] They wrote up their trip as *Peloponnesus or Notes of Study and Travel* (1858).

[59] For Rattee see 29 March 1855. His suitably elaborate Gothic crocketed monument on the north wall of the Mill Road cemetery is now (1999) much worn and its inscriptions are partly illegible.

disreputable man . . . Visit from Bateson who . . . described to me the dull heavy affair of his presenting the letter of thanks to Prince Albert for his Picture: – the University Deputation consisted of the V.C. (Cookson) & himself. They were shown into a darkish room, & in due time a folding door opened & the Prince appeared: there was a dull silent pause after the bows: then Bateson spoke a few words in English & presented the Letter & made another bow: after wch there was an awful lull & then the Prince said to the V.C. 'Are Lectures going on?'. – Cookson took time to deliberate & then answered 'Sir, it is Term-time': – another pause, after wch the Prince said to Bateson 'You have not been long in Office': – to which B. replied 'Since last October': – then came more bows, & all was over: – no lunch, no cake & no wine! . . . Wrote to G.T.R. & sent £10.

*Th. 30.* . . . At 3 to Trinity Lodge for the ceremony of presenting the plate to Sir John Patteson.[60] We congregated in the dining room: presently we saw a grand procession of the Corporation crossing the great Court, the Mayor (Ekin) in his red robes, preceded by his 4 maces & accompanied by all the Aldermen etc etc in their robes. – The Vicechancellor received us in the diningroom & led the way upstairs with the Mayor. Some of the University wore Cassocks (viz. the Heads, the Orator, Atlay! & Lamb! etc): I did not nor did any Trinity man: – the V.C. & Doctors were in black gowns. In the Henry VIII room we found Sir J. Patteson & a small sprinkling of Ladies, viz, Mrs Austin, Mrs M.A. Atkinson, Mrs Cartmell, the Miss Okes etc. The Candelabrum was on a table in a conspicuous place. Whewell made a very able & amiable speech to Sir J. Patteson (alluding to his Academic distinctions – he was University Scholar): to wch Sir J.P. replied most agreeably & modestly: he said he had obtained the University Scholarship only by a casting vote, that his were unfortunately times when the Kingsmen were shut out from the competition for Mathematical Honours etc etc . . . Then came the Mayors speech: – in the worst taste possible: he said that the Award in general gave them satisfaction, but one part they did not think equitable & trusted it would hereafter be amended: (he meant the Discommuning):[61] – Mr Ekin has the misfortune not to be able to pronounce the letter (h). – The V.C. then directed the Orator to read his Latin Letter: – after wch Sir J.P. read his answer in Latin: – The Town Clerk was then told by the Mayor to read the Corporation letter: – it was short & sensible: Sir J.P. read his answer to this also. – After which we dispersed. The V.C. gave a grand dinner party to 24.

*Mon. 3 November.* Up at 7. – Walk in Botanic Garden. – Called at Mrs Clark's: I went in & had a chat with her: she thinks Clark better, – but he is unable to take anything but beef tea, & is near fainting away if dressing without help. – John Smyth a little better: – but poor Thacker sadly worse. – At ¼ to 9 to the Senate House to hear Whewell's speech on laying down his

---

[60] Patteson's recommendations to settle differences of town and gown made in August 1855 had been embodied in an act of June 1856. See *Annals*, V, 192-201, 207-21.

[61] The speech of the mayor, Mr Ekin, was reported in the *Chronicle*: 'he was perfectly willing to endorse every expression made by the Vice-Chancellor and he also believed that the award had given almost entire satisfaction. He said almost because there was one clause which he would rather have seen omitted. But from the fair manner in which the University appeared desirous of carrying out the award, and the act of parliament founded thereon, he had every reason to believe that the clause would be found a dead letter.'

Office. It was a well written & noble speech: he spoke of the satisfaction he had felt from every Grace he brought forward having been carried; he touched upon the Award & upon the arrangements he had made for the Election of the Council: he then attacked the Proctors sharply for having broken the ordinances of the University which they were bound to enforce (– by calling without his consent a meeting of the Members of the Senate today in the Arts Schools concerning the Election of the Council on the 7th): & he ended by a very touching allusion to his own sorrows, saying that it had been the most mournful year of his life & that none in the rest of his life could equal it . . . I was unable to attend this meeting at 2 as I had a luncheon at that hour: – I was most glad to have an irresistible excuse. My party consisted of Professor & Mrs Selwyn, Mrs Mathison & her two children Dudu & Archibald, Mathison our Fellow (no relation) & Sedgwick. Everything went off capitally: Sedgwick was in great force & told (most admirably) the story of Elisabeth Woodcock snowed up for 8 days:[62] he then took out the children & treated Dudu with the print of E. Woodcock & a Volume of selections from Wordsworth (bound in green morocco), & Archibald with a book of Natural History . . .

*Tu. 4.* . . . At 10 the new V.C. entered upon Office:[63] the Latin of his speech seemed to me very good: he also read it with such clearness of articulation that one didn't miss a syllable . . . The Senior Proctor brought to me all the papers concerning the Council (at yesterday's meeting): – there were 7 Tellers: the procedings were perfectly quiet & ended in 1½ hours . . . The Conservatives at their 2d meeting this Evening agreed to support for the ordinary Members of Council for 4 years Martin (Trinity), France (John's), Hardwick (Catharine's) & G. Williams of Kings.

*Fri. 7.* Up at 7: to College & my Office: – poor Thacker & Clark rather less well: John Smyth a shade better. This was the day for the Election of the Council: from 9 to 12 was the Election of the 4 year Councillors.[64] The following 8 were elected

| Heads | | Whewell | 186 | Phelps | 47 |
|---|---|---|---|---|---|
| | | Corrie | 115 | Cartmell | 17 |
| Professors | | Selwyn | 129 | Sedgwick | 77 |
| | | Brown | 86 | Thompson | 67 |
| | | | | Grote | 37 |
| Members of Senate | | Martin | 130 | Adams & Clark | 85 |
| | | Bateson | 109 | Gunson | 54 |
| | | Paget | 93 | G. Williams | 30 |
| | | France | 90 | Clayton | 28 |
| | | | | Hardwick | 21 |

[62] She had been buried in a snowdrift for eight days with no more sustenance than her snuff while returning home to the village of Impington from Cambridge in February 1799 and recovered long enough to become a local celebrity before dying of frostbite in July. There is a monument to her at Impington and her tale was written up with embellishments to become current in such anecdotal works as Hone's *Every-Day Book* (1827).

[63] i.e. Henry Philpott, Master of St Catharine's, for the second time, the first being in 1846.

[64] The Council as determined in the 1856 Act was to comprise the Chancellor, the Vice-Chancellor, four Heads of Houses, four Professors, and eight members of the Senate (but not more than two from the same college).

```
                    Woodham _____16 ⎫
                    Campion _____13 ⎬
                    Goodwin _____ 5  ⎪
                    Gell _____ 4 ⎭
```

I voted for Whewell & Cartmell (– Philpott having said that he had taken an opinion & that he himself was not to be voted for), for Sedgwick & Thompson, & for Bateson, Adams, Gunson, W.G. Clark . . . At 1 o'clock the voting began for 2 year Councillors: it ended at 4: the V.C. & 2 Proctors took the votes & I had nothing to do. The persons elected were

Heads     ⎰ Neville _____122
       ⎱ Phelps _____76
Prof.      ⎰ Sedgwick ___113
       ⎱ Grote _____103    Thompson had 100
Members of Senate ⎰ W.G. Clark _____(Trinity) _____119
       ⎱ J.C. Adams _____(Pembroke) _____112
        W.M. Campion __(Queens') _____104
       ⎱ C. Hardwick ____(Catharine's) _____82

I voted for Neville, Phelps, Sedgwick, Thompson, Clark, Adams, Campion & Gunson . . . Wrote to Mr Johns of Callipers Hall sending him the Council. – Shilleto printed some very clever scurrilous Latin Elegiacs on the death of the Caput . . .

*Sat. 8.* . . . Today corrected the Press of the 'Errata', being the 66th sheet & gave the last 6d to the boy who brought it: – I also gave Mr Clay a Sovereign to distribute among the men who had part in the printing . . . The Council held its first meeting today: they sat for about 3 hours: they agreed to have 3 meetings a week . . .

*Wed. 12.* . . . Instead of the Caput (now dead) certain Councillors met at V.C.'s Table to verify degrees: 5 is the smallest no (by the Act) to make a Quorum: – The whole Council are to be summoned for every Congregation: – 4 (Neville, Bateson, Sedgwick & Campion . . . ) have offered to attend personally this Michaelmas Term or send a Deputy . . .

*Th. 13.* . . . Matriculation day. The gross number matriculated was 415, 11 more than last November. There were 4 Fellow Commoners (Lord Pelham, Lord Henry Cecil, Hon. – Cavendish, Hon – Hervey),[65] 376 Pensioners, 35 Sizars . . . The nos at Trinity this year were 3 F.C., 122 P, 10 S: – at St Johns they were 1 F.C., 67 P, 18 S: – Caius has dropt down from its grand 50 to 30: Emmanuel had 30 and Christs 28: as for Queens it had but 4 (including the President's youngest son): Sidney also had but 4: – Kings had 4. – Went to Wright's the pastry-cooks & ate 2 sausage-rolls. – Among the Trinity men matriculated were . . . Wedgewood (as they now write their name – son of Hensleigh the Wooden Wedge)[66] . . . This is the 1st

---

[65] i.e. Edward Cavendish and Augustus Henry Charles Hervey of Trinity. In 1837 noblemen and Fellow-Commoners made up ten per cent of the yearly admissions, but since then had diminished in numbers; see 13 November 1852.

[66] As mathematicians had their wooden spoon so classicists had the wooden wedge facetiously named for Hensleigh Wedgwood who had been bottom of the third class in the first Classical

Matriculation without Proctors: – the former 'Declaration' being now abolished by Act of Parliament. – I had not allowed time enough for Trinity by nearly 20'. Wrote to Town Clerk to mention that Leapingwell is now Member of Watch Committee & Emery auditor of Boro Accounts: Cartmell has resigned these 2 places & also the chairmanship of the Press-Syndics: – I presume the reason is annoyance at not being elected on 'the Council' . . .

*Mon. 17.* . . . Breakfasted with Selwyn at Park House: 2 maids were at prayers: the man-servant not allowed in the premises. The party consisted of Prof. & Mrs Selwyn, Mrs Mathison, Dudu & Archibald, & an elderly cousin of Mrs M's (named Harbord). This cousin never moves without a pedometer at his side: he exhibited this watch-like machine wch has a pendulum like a clock: his daily stint of walking is 12 miles wch he performs at about 3¼ per hour. – Gave Dudu one of the new Cambridge Prayerbooks with red liners . . . By the way the Pound I gave to the Pressmen was put (at Mr Clay's suggestion) into their 'sick fund'. – Visit from Professor Bennett . . . he is very strict: he has rejected several musical exercises: *one* he has accepted & made the composer play it on the Corpus organ . . .

*Tu. 18.* . . . College-meeting at 11: we gave away a Bedesman's place (vacant by the death of old Andrews) to a parishioner of Cooper's (aged 66) who lost 2 sons in the Crimea.[67] At the meeting the Master told me about the Assessment for Paving-rate: – it is arranged by the Heads & their Deputies: it has hitherto been by a capitation tax viz. 6s a year on everybody: it now will probably be on the rateable property of every College, – just as the Poor-rate is since the University property has been valued in consequence of Sir John Patteson's Award . . . Greatly pleased with a letter from G.T.R. announcing his long-coveted transfer to Weedon: he is now there . . . the Superintendent (Mr Elliott) is very highly praised. I wrote to George, strongly urging him to do every thing exactly according to Mr E.'s wishes & instructions . . .

*Fri. 28.* . . . Called on John Smyth in the Hospital & found him surprisingly better: – he looked like a pretty girl. – Gave his Mother 5/6 to buy flannel for him. – Miss Bishop (the Matron) told me that she was over-worked in the Hospital & that her health was giving way . . .

*Sat. 29.* . . . Had a visit from Mr Rumbold (Corpus Christi)) . . . He informed me that Robert Bickersteth of Queens (AB 1841) is the new Bishop of Ripon: – Lord Palmerston seems to have no opinion of any but the Evangelical party: – he also seems to prefer the actual working clergy to the lecturing Divinity Professors: – Selwyn had been talked of for this Bishoprick . . . Very interesting letter from Betsy describing her visit last Sunday Evening to 'the Refuge' to see Ann Spink, who seems sincerely penitent & declares herself very happy. Betsy was present at prayers & heard 2 Hymns sung . . . the Clergyman (a remarkably handsome man) read from the Old & New

---

Tripos of 1824. He was a cousin of George and Edward Allen and had married another of their cousins, both belonging to the vast Darwin-Wedgwood clan.

[67] Henry VIII, who endowed Trinity so magnificently, required it to support twenty poor, aged, and impotent men (not academics) of whom half were nominated by the college and half by the crown.

Testaments & gave an excellent address (on God's mercy to sinners) besides the prayers. He shook hands with Betsy & talked to her . . .

*Mon. 1 December.* . . . Took to the V.C. statistics about Ale house-Licences of the last 5 years: they averaged about 180 per annum, & about 40 transfers p.a.: making 220s or £11 per annum wch is lost to the Yeoman Bedell by the University abandoning the power of licensing in obedience to the Award: – the V.C. is meditating some compensation to Crouch who is in extreme indigence. – Visit from Harvey Goodwin who wanted a little help for his 'Working Men's Lecture' Fund: gave him £2: he says that he used on Sundays to lecture to the Working Men on the New Testament & had a very good attendance . . . Began reading Addison's Drummer wch (to my surprise) I found very lively.[68]

*Tu. 2.* . . . Wiseman sent home the Copy of 'Graduati': it is beautifully bound in Red Morocco & the binding cost 12/6: packed it up carefully & sent it by Rail to Windsor Castle: also wrote to General Hon. C. Grey requesting him to ask P. Albert to condescend to accept it . . .

*Th. 4.* . . . letter from Mrs Percy (born Carnaby): she says in mending her boys coat she found in the pocket a letter wch she had given him to post for me some weeks ago (thanking for my last present): – not one word of this do I believe: she now writes for help to buy a Piano Forte: I stuck to my resolution of having no more to do with her & didn't answer the letter . . . The widow of a poor fellow killed on the line (Carrington) called: – she is very young & just going to be put to bed: gave her 2/6 as others had done. – The College Audit from 10 to ¼ to 2. After it was over & the Auditor (Denman) gone we discussed the 'Assessment' . . . It was decided to adopt a new scheme (in compliance with the views of the dissentients) viz. to levy 2/6 p.a. per head on every name on the boards (about 2400) wch will produce £300: the remainder to be paid out of the College Funds . . .

*Tu. 9.* . . . the Master sent me some letters of Lord Lansdowne & Macaulay to read: Lord L. had intended *bequeathing* money for a statue of *Milton* in our antechapel: – but changed his mind & has offered it in his life time. Whewell told him that Milton would not be appropriate as he was not a Member of the College. – Ld Lansdowne (reluctantly but most amiably) acquiesced, & consulted Macaulay about the names suggested by the Master, – George Herbert, Barrow, Bentley, Dryden etc: – Macaulay wrote a very able & eloquent letter on the subject, saying that Bentley was the right person to select, as his was the greatest name England could boast in Classical Learning, & that (as the reputation of Trinity College now rested mainly on Scholarship) we were the more bound to erect a statue to him, – there being at present not even a tablet to him tho he was buried in the Chapel . . . I was surprised at the bad spelling in Ld Lansdowne's letters: 'antichapel'. 'hommage' etc etc . . .

---

[68] Romilly may have been surprised because he knew that Addison's comedy had failed as a production in 1715, though Steele thought highly of it as a play to read. The story tells of the visit of Joseph Glanvill, the divine, to a house in Wiltshire where he hears drummings and sees strange happenings; these are caused by no more than the witchcraft of a vengeful drummer who has been turned out of the house.

*Wed. 10.* . . . Congregation day . . . No opposition to any of the Graces: the most interesting was one for the waste water from Hobson's stream to run thro the Botanic Garden Pond before it falls into 'Vicars Brook':[69]– another Grace was to allow £25 p.a. to Crouch who loses now almost all his income by the Award Act . . .

*Fri. 12.* . . . In my Office a visit from V.C. about the table of Precedence in University Processions, particularly about the place to be assigned to 'The Council': – he told me that he had consulted Lord Lyndhurst about abolishing the nominal offices of Commissary & Deputy High Steward: Ld Lyndhurst strongly dissuaded the abolition: he said the London Lawyers were eager to hold them & that they kept up their attachment to the University . . .

*Mon. 15.* . . . At 11 to the Commemoration Service in Chapel: the Chapel was crowded: Hensley preached from Ecclesiastes 3. 14 'Whatsoever God doeth it shall be for ever': – it was a very thoughtful & able sermon with much about the studies of the place: – he strongly advocated College Sermons. – I declined hearing the Prize Orations in Hall . . . I sent off a packet of Letters to Paris, 3 French ones to Madame, Fanny & Sophie & 1 English one to Frank: I sent my customary étrennes[70] to Fanny & Sophie. – The topic of all my four letters was the separation of Fanny from her worthless husband, wch is now at length legally established . . . The little Harvey Goodwins have invited me to their dance in honor of the birthday of one of them on the 23d: I was hardhearted enough to refuse . . . Very sleepy in the Evening.

*Wed. 24.* . . . Sedgwick came to my Office in the dusk & smoked a Cigar: we afterwards dined in Trinity Hall Hall at a large & very agreeable party . . . The Master gave toasts but there was no speechifying – among other delicacies there was a Swan: Geldart told me of a smart firing off of wit about a Swan: – a man who wrote in praise of it was called 'Writer to the Signet', & another exclaimed 'Hoc signo vinces':[71]– he told also of a pleasantry of Thesiger when envelopping himself in a railway wrapper 'nobody can say I an't worth a rap' . . . I was rather afraid of this 2d piece of dissipation in one week: but I didn't find myself at all the worse for the Burton Ale & the late hours & the noise.

*Th. 25. Christmas Day.* Up at 10' to 7. – Sharp frost: – walk in Alderman Finch's Walk . . . Preached in Chapel: a very small Congregation, the Vice Master, poor Thacker & his Mother, Lord Althorp & the 2 Members, etc etc. I preached Mr Boyer's Christmas Day Sermon. Munro read the Communion (very distinctly & well): Sedgwick & Munro administered the Sacrament . . . At 2 to St Mary's where I heard a 1st rate sermon from Cowie on the universality of Christianity in meeting the needs of all ages & conditions . . . The Doctors all wore Scarlet. – I then went to Kings & sat in the stalls: – Viceprovost (Williams) read the 1st Lesson (at the Lectern): – the Anthem was

---

[69] Vicars Brook ran parallel to Hobson's brook as far as the Botanic Garden and then turned north west through Coe Fen and fell into the Cam, as it still does, by the footbridge. The Grace proposed that surplus water should reach Vicars Brook by another channel, 'per canalem alium'.

[70] i.e. New Year's gifts.

[71] 'By this sign [i.e. the cross] shalt thou conquer', the motto of Constantine.

that glorious one 'There were Shepherds' ending with 'For unto us' . . . I should have said that before Lunch I called upon Miss Apthorp (who had wished to see me) & gave her maids Christmas Boxes . . . By the way the Leapingwells asked me to dine with them today en famille to meet Shaw & eat roast turkey: – I refused, but still ate roast turkey . . .

*Fri. 26.* . . . A very agreeable letter from Maggy: she gives an excellent account of herself & George & the children: – my little Godson calls himself 'Captain Lomley' . . . Today was kept as a holiday in the Town: – similarly last year the week day after Xmas was kept a holiday. – I worked diligently in my office all day till 4½ & then smoked ½ a Cigar . . .

*Mon. 29.* . . . Very amusing letter from Grim. He & Bertha have been for a week at a wateringplace called Seascale: done them all a power of good . . . His 4 eldest children (Bertha, Lucy, Caroline & Baugh) dined with their Father & Mother on Xmas day: he says of the last – 'Baugh would have done well to imitate Dickens' little Cratchets who shoved their spoons into their mouths lest they should shriek for goose before the time' . . . Much pleased with a visit from Mrs Willis & Maggie in my Office about 3 o'clock. Bob is to take his degree in January . . . Mrs Willis is labouring under her delusion of a fond mother that Bob is a Genius, that it is no fault of his that he has been insufferably idle, that he has no taste for Latin & Greek, but is very clever in Mathematics!!! Not at all sleepy after dinner because I kept constantly writing.

*Tu. 30.* . . . At 11 the Bishop designate of Ripon (Robert Bickersteth came to the Senate House for his Mandate DD: he paid me by a draft on Coots 'Pay the DD Fees or Bearer etc': I said I was addressed by all manner of appellations (such as Clerk of the University, Principal Secretary etc) but this was the first time I had been called 'DD Fees'. It was necessary to turn the Convocation[72] into a Congregation & this metamorphosis required the presence of 4 members of the Council besides the V.C. (– the smallest number allowed for a Quorum by the Act being 5): Dr Corrie, Sedgwick & Martin were present, but a considerable delay was occasioned by having to fetch Phelps. The Senate House was full of ladies . . . & a large no of members of the University, principally of the Low Church party. Jeremie made so beautiful a speech that I went & shook hands with him & expressed my admiration: – he praised Lord Langdale & Edward Bickersteth (the Bishops uncles) & highly eulogised the Bishop's own piety, devoted zeal in a most difficult parish from vice & poverty & disease (St Giles), & his great eloquence as a Preacher . . .

[72] i.e. a Congregation held out of Term.

# 1857

*Th. 1 January.* Up at 7. – Thank God I feel quite well on this 1st day of the year . . . My New Year gifts were on the small scale of 1s to Dosia & Harriet, M.A. Tyler & brother, John & Sarah Smyth & blind Peter. Called to see John Smyth: but he was in bed: – his back is sore from having so long kept his bed in the hospital: – the little shop was full of straw (to stuff a mattress for him). – Fell in with the little Harvey Goodwins: they told me of their annual presents from the President of Queens': – he stuffs his pockets with treasures for them & they have to dive in them . . . Poor dear Lady Romilly is relieved from her sufferings: she died on the 30th in the calmest gentlest state possible: her husband, her son Edward & her sister Lady Belper were round the bed: she died pronouncing the words 'God bless you' . . .

*Tu. 6.* . . . By the way an iron-pillar letterbox has today been set up at Mr Asby's corner, – very convenient for me: there are to be 4 others in the town[1] . . .

*Sat. 10.* Up at 7 – Walk in Queens'. – Letter from the V.C. saying he thinks the Classical Tripos is now open to every body whether going in to Mathematical Examination or not, & if going in to Mathematical Examination whatever Class they may gain[2] . . .

*Tu. 13.* . . . The V.C. sent me a little vol. of 'Foundations of Professorships etc' wch he has just had printed . . . Wrote to him in praise of his great energy in his work. Today is 1st day of Term & the 'Council' met. In the office several laggards for Tickets & Degree: among them the Favorite for Senior Wrangler 'Gorst': – a pleasing-looking clever man: – I told him that I had been wishing to see him & should take a good look at him, wch made him & 2 friends laugh . . . I am sorry at hearing that poor Harriet Gillson's nose is very bad again & that she will probably have to leave Mrs Adcocks: however (to my amazement) she has picked up a sweetheart & is engaged to be married: – of course he is very poor, but he will be a protector to her & I am heartily glad of it . . . A youngster . . . told me that last night at 11 o'clock a Johnian named Ambery was the victim of a Garrotte Robbery near the market place: – happily the robber is in custody.[3] – Read '3 Mousquetaires' & was not sleepy.

---

[1] Experimental boxes in London streets had proved so useful in 1855 that they were soon introduced elsewhere, but were still a novelty. No pillar box from the 1850s survives in Cambridge.

[2] No one hitherto could take the Classical Tripos who had not passed the Mathematical Tripos. See 18 February 1851 and Searby pp. 601-4.

[3] The *Cambridge Chronicle* of 17 January and 21 February reported garrotte robberies. In each case an arm was tightened round the victim's neck from behind. Ambery was found unconscious near St Edward's Passage and one of the robbers was caught after a spirited chase by the Jesus College porter Mr Scott. All three robbers were committed to be tried at the Assizes and sentenced to twenty years' transportation. The second robbery was of a railway clerk in Hills Road, but the accused was discharged as having been wrongly identified. It was stated in court that proceedings would be taken against people who increased anxiety by spreading rumours of assault by garrotting. See 19 January 1857.

*Wed. 14.* . . . Letter from Sir John Walsham[4] sending me testimonials of his son Charles . . . (written in his worst & hastiest scrawl) to show that he is a very poor & most hardworking man & that his son ought peculiarly to be selected for the Tancred Scholarship: that he can't afford to live at Knill in rebuilding wch he has laid out prodigious sums, that his eldest son (who was at Trinity) has a poor place of Clerk in the Foreign Office with only £200 a year, his 2d was educated at Durham & is a Curate without stipend, his 3d was killed at Alma[5] (his military Education having cost £1500), & that his own patrimony is burdened with 2 jointures, – so he is quite a pauper!! Wrote to him – Letter from Cartmell saying the Tancred Election is in November & that he will consider Walsham's case. – I hear that the scene of the Garotte robbery was St Edwards passage: Mr Ambery (going out this January was attacked by 2 men & robbed of his watch) . . .

*Mon. 19.* Up at 7. – Signed my 'Victoria' Paper in behalf of Widow Larkins & took upon myself the delivery of it.[6] The poor widow is not well known in the neighbourhood of *King Street* (her printed place of abode): I began at the Hobson Street end & nobody knew any thing about her existence: towards the middle of the street I was told she lived in the Almshouses next the Horse & Groom (St Mary's Almshouses): – they disclaimed her there . . . I tried the Stokys Almshouses & the University Almshouses etc etc & a great no of shops, walking from one end to the other & back, – all in vain. I of course created quite a sensation. – At last a Baker said he didn't know where she lived but he was going to vote for her & would take charge of my paper, – wch I gladly gave him. As I was marching off a goodhumoured woman ran after me & said she believed she could help me if I would walk with her on to Christs piece: – I went with her, & sure enough she took me to Widow Larkins, who with 2 of her daughters (grown up young women) were just getting up for break fast: – they are all very tidy, respectable-looking people: – I told Mrs L. that I had left my paper for her at a Bakers & that I wished her success . . . A copy of the Londonderry Sentinel arrived. It gives a curious account of the Bishop of Derry inhibiting Moore O'Connor from all duties & profits of Culdaff[7] . . . Shocked at hearing there has been another Garotte Robbery here: – the Victim was a deformed young woman (named Bluntsam) who keeps a small school & lives in Park Street: – she was attacked by 2 ruffians . . .

*Fri. 23.* . . . Took Sedgwick & Grote (whom I met coming from 'the Council') to my office: Sedgwick hates having to attend & says it will kill him.

4  Walsham's aunt Ann had married Romilly's uncle, Sir Samuel, the lawyer.
5  The Russians on the heights above the river Alma barred the road to Sevastopol and the allies lost about 3,000 men, mostly British, in the fierce fighting to dislodge them.
6  The Cambridge Victoria Friendly Societies Institution was established in 1837 to provide homes for elderly members and the main building in Victoria Road was begun in 1841. There were a number of almshouses in King Street. The University Almshouses were opposite the entrance to Malcolm Street and St Mary's at the further end of King Steet on the Christ's Piece side. The dilapidated Stokys Almshouses were sold in 1860 and are not shown on the *Cambridge 1859* map published by Monson.
7  Moore O'Connor, Derry Culdaff, appears in the *Clergy List* for 1857 but not in that for 1858.

I got him to sign his 6 Hospital orders for me . . . After dinner I read '3 Mous-quetaires',[8] wch I thought extremely improper: it represents so detestable a state of immorality as I think never existed. I also read 'Dred':[9]– this pleased me.

*Tu. 27.* Up at 7. – Walk in Botanic Garden: – gentle flakes of snow. Meeting of the 7 to arrange about poor Thacker's funeral next Thursday . . . the singing boys will chant the opening sentences . . . Sedgwick was rather for the Chanting beginning from the Hall Steps, but we agreed that it should begin at the Chapel door. Sedgwick said the chanting in the Court used to be the old custom, & that Davies had a dislike to its being so done for himself & directed that he should be buried in St Michaels. – We were a good deal helped in our arrangements by a very minute account of the proceedings at John Wordsworths funeral[10] which has been drawn up by Rowe (the Chapel Clerk). – In my office I had an interview with Roberts of Queens[11] who degraded in hopes of getting a Travelling Bachelorship: he expects that Okely (appointed in 1855) will be obliged to resign now that he is become a papist . . .

*Th. 29.* . . . At ¼ to 10 to the Little Combination room: there were assembled poor Thacker's brother & 2 young friends of his, Sedgwick, Cooper, Paget, Fisher etc etc etc. Sedgwick, Cooper & Lightfoot were in their Surplices, Martin (being Executor was to walk as one of the mourners: I was the Senior Pall-bearer:[12] the other 5 were Jeremie, Thompson, Grote, Mathison & Cope. Shortly after 10 the body was brought from the Hall (where it had been placed early in the morning) & the Procession (headed by Officials, the 10 singing boys & 4 singing men, the 2 Deans & Vicemaster) moved straight across the Court (to the Lecture-room staircase) & then to the great Gateway (where Mrs Thacker joined it) & so to the Chapel: just before reaching the door the choir boys began chanting 'I am the Resurrection & the Life'. – The Mourners sat (I believe) in the Noblemen's seat.[13] – Cooper (senior Dean) read the Psalm & Lightfoot (Junior Dean) the Lesson: – they read exceedingly well. – On coming to the grave (in the antechapel, – close to John Wordsworth's grave) the choristers again sang 'Man that is born of a woman' etc etc etc. – Sedgwick read the rest of the service: being a very tenderhearted

[8] Alexandre Dumas' *Les Trois Mousquetaires* (1844) was based on the *Mémoires de M. d' Artagnan* (Cologne, 1701-2) by Courtils de Sandras.

[9] Subtitled *A Tale of the Dismal Swamp* this was Mrs Stowe's grim anti-slavery novel of 1856 intended to show the debasing effects of slavery on whites. It sold well, was translated and dramatised, but never had the standing or success of *Uncle Tom's Cabin*.

[10] John Wordsworth, Fellow of Trinity and eldest son of Christopher, brother of the poet and Master of the College from 1820 to 1841, had died aged 34 in 1839 of kidney disease.

[11] Probably Edmund Russell Roberts B.A. 1857. Okeley did not have to resign his Bachelorship. See 5 March 1857.

[12] i.e. Romilly walked by the side of the coffin holding the edge of the pall which had been draped over it.

[13] At Trinity in 1837 noblemen and Fellow Commoners accounted for ten per cent of the admissions. But by November 1854 only one nobleman and ten Fellow Commoners were admitted. This benefited the College as 'many of them did not trouble to take degrees, wasted their time and money, and set a bad example to the other undergraduates' (Winstanley, p. 415).

man he was much affected & I was afraid he would have broken down. – It was a very fine & a very touching service to every body, but especially to an old man like myself, seeing a familiar friend 24 years younger than myself called to his account . . . When my hour comes may I be far better prepared to die than I now feel myself to be! . . . I should have said that poor Thacker's niece (a little girl of 11 years old) was not brought prominently forward among the mourners because her black dress was not made. – After dinner I wrote to G.T.R., enclosing £10 & giving him an account of the mournful pageant.

*Fri. 30.* . . . A Queensman is Senior Wrangler, – Brown Finch: he deserves now to be called Gold-Finch. The 2d Wrangler is Savage (of Pembroke) brother of the Senior Wrangler of 1855 who died suddenly while out walking by himself.[14] – It is a melancholy year for Trinity: our best man is No 11; he was also Hopkins best man!! The Senior Wrangler & the 2d were trained by Parkinson: the 3d (Gorst of St John's – who was the favorite for S.W. by Todhunter) . . . I avoided the Combination room & went to my rooms to sit up in state for the Polloi List . . . a Trinity man (Fryer) rushed into my rooms to ask if he was through: – I shook my head: 'O, it can't be, I must have passed, it must be a mistake!': – I said 'I am very sorry for it, but it is too true': – 'then, he exclaimed, it's that detestable Arithmetic & Algebra' . . . Of the 33 plucked for Polloi 12 alas! are Trinity men. – Poor Ambery of St Johns (the garotted man) was plucked. Amps (the Organist) has this time scrambled thro.

*Sat. 31.* . . . Showed myself for a very short time in the Senate House & had the honor of '3 cheers for the Registrary'. The place was crammed especially with women: among them was Mrs Prest who likes to see all that is going on . . . That idle Bob Willis is plucked: I am very sorry for his Father & Mother's sake . . .

*Sun. 1 February.* . . . Up at 7: Therm at 25: thick fog: walk in Cemetery: the Spire nearly finished . . . I then went to Mr Titcomb's 'Childrens Lecture'. I thought it the best I have heard. His Text was Matthew VI. 11. 12 'Give us this day our daily bread & forgive us our debts etc'. – He said God had not promised to give them luxuries – cakes & barley-sugar – but daily bread. He told 2 very pretty stories . . . The 2d story was a delightful one of a little girl whom he called May. She & her Mother were without bread: her mother had no money & no work: – she sent the little girl out into the fields to take some fresh air: – the child gathered herself some wild flowers, but at the last from weariness & hunger burst out a crying: she presently saw a sparrow hopping near her & picking up something & flying away with it: this gave her a little heart & she recollected that our Lord spoke of God feeding the fowls of the air: so she knelt down & prayed: 'O God! Mother & I have no bread: pray send us some'. She was overheard by a Gentleman (who was walking in his garden & was hid from her by the wall): – he came out, talked kindly to her, called on her Mother & became a great friend & benefactor. – I said to Mrs

14 James Savage of St John's, Senior Wrangler and First Smith's prizeman in 1855, was found by a labourer in a dry ditch at Comberton. He had been botanising and 'died in a fit of apoplexy'.

Titcomb 'I am sure I shall not forget for a very long time that beautiful story of little May'. – Mrs T.'s children (like so many others) have the hooping cough: the eldest one only was at Church & she was looking like a Ghost. – I was sadly sleepy in the Evening.

*Mon. 2.* . . . Leapingwell told me that Bateson[15] was this morning elected & that there is to be a feast in St Johns hall. For some time the fortune of France & Bateson was equally balanced: each had 20 promises: about last Friday No 41 (who had been wavering) promised Bateson, whereupon France immediately wrote a very handsome letter to B. & declined all further contest. – This morning 29 Fellows voted, 26 for Bateson & 3 for Collison!!! . . . Leapingwell . . . told me that he should have to adjudicate (he expected) in a charge of assault against 2 gownsmen by a Gyp.[16] Ces Messieurs soupçonnaient que le Gyp s'entendait avec la servante: ils ont eu la bassesse de guetter par le trou de la serrure, et les ayant trouvés 'in flagrante delictu' ils efforçaient la porte & l'un d'eux avec un gros fouet s'est fondu sur le Gyp & l'a assommé d'une façon brutale! . . .

*Th. 5.* . . . At 11½ to the Senatehouse on the matter of the Oratorship: – Bateson's resignation was read & the V.C. appointed Tuesday 17th February for the Election . . . E.H. Perowne is a Candidate: he was 1st Classic in 1850 & gained a Porson Prize & 2 Members Prizes: Clark was 2d Classic in 1844, 2d Medallist, gained a Porson Prize, 2 Greek Odes & the Epigrams.[17] Clark is so agreeable & so popular that a shy cold person like E.H.P. can run no chance against him . . . Willis in his visit spoke to me of his recent visit (with Mary Anne) to Beresford Hope's magnificent house:[18]– it is on so princely a scale that an addition lately made contains 100 rooms!! . . .

*Sat. 7.* . . . Seniority at 11: we did a great deal of business: – arranged about Foleys bust of Richard Sheepshanks[19] (to be opposite John Wordsworths); – bought a treasure wch had been picked up by Edleston (viz. a

[15] i.e. as Master of St John's on Tatham's death after having been Public Orator since 1848. He was an excellent and industrious administrator and generally regarded as a leading liberal in academic affairs.

[16] Leapingwell's fear seems to have been unfounded. There is no record of proceedings in the Vice-Chancellor's Court or report in the *Chronicle* during the following four months.

[17] The prize in books, named after the great classical scholar Richard Porson, was awarded for the best translation into Greek verse of passages from Shakespeare, Ben Jonson, Massinger, or Beaumont and Fletcher. There were four prizes for the best Exercises in Latin prose, given annually by M.P.s for the University, and the Sir William Browne (d. 1774) Gold Medals rewarded the best Greek and Latin odes and epigrams. The medals bore a likeness of Browne and another of Apollo crowning a scholar with laurels.

[18] A. Beresford Hope was an immensely wealthy author, patron of the arts, co-founder of the *Saturday Review*, and founder member of the Cambridge Camden Society. His wife was the eldest daughter of the second Marquis of Salisbury, and his seat was Bedgebury Park at Kilndown in Kent. The classical mansion had been bought by his stepfather in 1836 and much enlarged by him. Presumably the 'addition lately made' was his, since Beresford Hope himself added only a tower, in 1854-5.

[19] Astronomer and Fellow of Trinity who died in 1855. J.H. Foley's wall tablet is surmounted by a bust.

copy of Bishop Saunderson's Logick[20] which had belonged to Newton when an undergraduate & contains his autograph with the date of 1661) – it cost 50s . . . Went into the Fitzwilliam Museum to see the new hanging: it is very successful & was done almost entirely by Hopkins (the Esquire Bedell)[21] . . .

*Th. 12.* . . . At the Seniority we gave away Bumsted Helion to Le Mottee: – as for St Ippolyts it is still not filled up: – Ingram (Chaplain) had expected to have it & had hired servants etc etc, – probably a lady being in the case. In the mean time Hort (suddenly engaged to be married) steps forward & claims as a Fellow: it is a cruel disappointment to Ingram. – Cooper (Senior Dean) wanted the Master to make a peremptory order against Moustaches:[22]– the Master declined (– I think most judiciously) but said that he objected to 'very pronounced moustaches': – it appears that Cooper had ordered a Bachelor Scholar to remove his, & he has not complied . . .

*Fri. 13.* . . . Very amusing letter from Grim who has taken a Parson's-week's holidays[23] & has been into Pembrokeshire collecting rents & feasting his tenants . . . he visited his great friends the Downtons at Shrewsbury, danced till 4 o'cl. at a ball, went to a Pantomime, etc etc). He has highly delighted little Bertha by writing to her & telling her of a Pork-pie-manufacturer whose white stock of meat consisted of one dead dog . . .

*Tu. 24.* Up at 7 – Walk in the Botanic Garden. – Very feeble on my legs all day . . . The Post Mortem Examination has ended most humanely: – only 2 out of 30 have been plucked (viz. Ives of Caius & Cartwright of Trinity): – some desperate bad hands have scrambled thro, including Fox (of Trinity) & Bob Willis (the Prof's idle son) . . . There has been a dreadful Colliery explosion near Barnsley: – 150 lives lost.

*Ash Wednesday 25.* . . . Letter from Martha Bye (in beautiful handwriting) enclosing a Bookmark with 'token of affection' worked in beads: – in the letter were other 2 bookmarks (containing Scripture Texts) for Dosia & Harriet . . . 24 Dunces[24] were admitted today . . . There was a prodigious din in the Senate House at the admission of the Dunces: – some of them were men of mark in

[20] i.e. Robert Sanderson's *Logicae artis compendium* (Oxford, 1631) now in the Wren Library. 'Isaac Newton' is written in ink on the recto of the title-page and 'Isaac Newton Trin Coll Cant 1661' on the verso. Its provenance before Edleston found it is not known.

[21] William Hopkins, F.R.S., the Senior Wrangler-maker and geologist, was appointed a Syndic of the Fitzwilliam from 12 November 1856 and was not therefore involved in the quarrel with Whewell earlier in the year (see 31 January). He presumably completed 'the new hanging' after consultation with other Syndics.

[22] After the Peace of Paris was signed in March 1856 and officers came home from the Crimea wearing beards it became fashionable to wear a moustache with long and drooping whiskers, despite some prejudice against them amongst the clergy. Members of the new volunteer movement especially (see 6 May 1859) would see themselves as entitled to follow military fashion.

[23] Grim's father, Baugh Allen, Romilly's brother-in-law, died in 1845 and had divided his many properties in Wales between his sons George and Edward (Grim) and his second wife. Grim had arranged for someone to take his Sunday services so that he could enjoy a 'parson's week' holiday of anything up to thirteen days.

[24] Most of the Dunces were probably B.A.s who had failed their examinations in January.

the Boats, & their friends were uproarious at their being free from their troubles . . .

*Fri. 27.* . . . Seniority for 2 hours. We carried the giving up to the Town the space cleared opposite All Saints Church:[25] Edleston & King voting against it: – Preston also & Cope were not hearty concurrents, Preston wanting by some annual ceremony to retain our right & Cope doubtful whether the best *line* was taken for our boundary. – Christ Church is behaving most graspingly about the tripartite connexion of Westminster School, Christ Church & Trinity Coll: – they want to exclude us from any presentation to the Mastership!!. They say our recent scheme (of Exhibitions for the Westminsters)[26] altogether upsets all the footing we were on by Queen Elisabeth's foundation. – Legal opinion is to be taken . . .

*Sat. 28.* . . . Letter from Miss Cotton about sale of the Madingley Books. There is to be on Saturday next (7 March) a sale of John Colets Books in London: & 240 Volumes of the Madingley books are then to be sold also: – they consist of Tracts & Newspapers of time of Charles 1 & 2 . . . She says that Sir St Vincent has passed the winter well & drives out daily in a 'Hansom'.[27] – In speaking of the books she says 'You may believe that it is not without pain that I dispose of any part of a long cherished collection . . . It is necessary to make some sacrifices & not to retain *all* that belonged to more wealthy possessors' . . .

*Sun. 1 March.* . . . At the corner of Burleigh St I heard some open-air preaching: a Fellow Commoner of Christs named Brown was holding forth with a good deal of animation in his cap & gown to about 40 or 50 people: another undergr. in cap and gown was distributing Tracts: I begged him to give me one: he immediately dived into his Pocket & produced one of his bettermost called "the Scarlet Line". At night I read this Tract & thought it very able & persuasive: – 'The Scarlet Line' was that wch marked Rahab's house[28] . . .

*Th. 5.* . . . 3d & last day of voting on the New Statutes . . . One dissenter (Duckworth) & one Roman Catholic (Munster) took AB degrees today. – By the way the letter of the Roman Catholic Travelling Bachelor (Okely) was laid on my table:[29] it is on Italian Architecture: it is in very good Latin & is

---

[25] A photograph in the V.C.H., *Cambridge*, III (1959) facing p. 130, shows the tower of All Saints' in the Jewry in St John's Street supported by an arch over the pavement with tall trees behind the wall opposite to it. The church was pulled down in 1865 when the street was widened.

[26] See 9 January 1854.

[27] Joseph Aloysius Hansom (1803-1882) was a prolific architect and inventor whose 'Patent Safety Cab' had unusually large wheels and a body nearer to the ground than its rivals, thus lessening the risk of accidents.

[28] 'And the city [Jericho] shall be accursed, even it, and all that are therein to the Lord: only Rahab the harlot shall live, she and all that are with her in the house because she hid the messengers that we sent' (*Joshua* VI.v.17). Rahab's house was spared because the grateful messengers told her to mark the window through which they had escaped with a scarlet thread.

[29] Wort's will (see 27 January 1857) stated that these bachelors were 'obliged to write once in a month, a letter in Latin to the Vice-Chancellor' giving 'an account to the University of the

illustrated with very beautiful pen & ink drawings . . . The V.C. sent to me plans of all the Rateable Property of the University & Colleges: – they are superbly bound by Wiseman & are of such gigantic size that they will not go into my biggest box . . .

*Fri. 6.* . . . Letter from C.H. Cooper enclosing a list of names & a prospectus of his 'Athenæ Cantabrigienses',[30] the 1st Vol. of wch is to come out in October: – answered his queries & desired him to put me down as a Subscriber . . . Visits in my office from Selwyn & Whewell: Selwyn gave me an excellent account of Peacock who is now convalescent:[31]– Dudu's Father is returned on a 3 years leave: he is entitled to his full pension & will probably never go back to India.[32] – Whewell's object was to learn the particulars of the rejection of the proposals for degrees in 'Moral Sciences' & 'Natural Sciences'.[33] – I wrote him a letter on the subject: they were rejected in 1854 when the Classical Degrees were agreed to. Dined at the Family at France's: a party of 10 . . . Cartmell talked to me about an obnoxious sermon of Claytons preached (as the title page says) on the Sunday *before the Bachelors Ball*.[34] It says that Palmer (the Murderer) (who had been wild but had begun to think seriously from a friends persuasion) became desperately wicked & altogether reckless from seeing 6 clergymen at a ball (wch his friend had begged him to keep away from)!!! Played 5 rubbers & lost 3/6: the players were Phelps, Bateson, Paget, Clark, Stokes & myself. – Away at ¼ past 11. – Slept at Scrope Terrace.

*Mon. 9.* . . . Wrote to Sophie (a French letter as usual) & Frank (enclosing £15). I sallied out in a snow-gale with my letters to Frank & Sir John in my hand: – the wind blew the capes of my cloke about, & I suppose it was in adjusting them that I dropt my money letter! – the other (wch wasn't worth

religion, learning, laws, politics, customs, manners, and rarities, natural and artificial, which they shall find worth observing in the countries through which they pass'.

[30] In collaboration with his son, C.H. Cooper (d.1866) the Cambridge Town clerk and assiduous antiquary, published by subscription two biographical compilations of University worthies between 1500 and 1609. Patient and persevering in his researches, he frequently needed the Registrary's help in verifying facts and dedicated the second volume (1861) to him. See 16 April 1859.

[31] On 16 February Whewell had told Romilly that Peacock was 'alarmingly ill'.

[32] Dudu's father was a judge in the Madras Presidency.

[33] On 2 and 3 May 1854 the Senate had rejected the University's Studies Syndicate's proposal for 'creating Boards of Studies for theology, natural sciences and moral sciences and for enabling the degree of Bachelor of Arts to be obtained by passing either the Natural Science or Moral Science Tripos'. Philpott thought the rejection was due to the Senate's unwillingness 'to put any other studies on the same footing as the old established studies of mathematics and classics'. See Winstanley pp. 279-81 and Searby pp. 231-3.

[34] Charles Clayton, Tutor of Caius, was one of the most fanatical of the Evangelicals who in a university that mistrusted enthusiasm nevertheless had a greater following than any other part of the English church. (See Winstanley, pp. 405-6.)

'I dreamed we both were waiting in the Hall
Serving refreshments at the Bachelors' Ball.
There gayest trifler in the throng of dancers,
Was Clayton cutting figures in the Lancers.'
(G.O. Trevelyan, *The Cambridge Dionysia 1858*)

a farthing) I had retained a good grip of. I discovered my loss when close to the P.O. & retraced my steps (by the back of the Corn Exchange) to my Office, – looking in vain . . . I then went to the P.O. & told my loss & begged the Post-master to send me word of it if it should be posted in the course of the day. – I then went to Mortlocks & took the nos of the 2 notes & stopped them there & at the Joint-Stock Bank & Fisher's & Foster's. I then went to Andrews Towncrier[35] (who lives in Corn Exchange) & gave him 1s for crying my poor letter. – I went to bed without hearing anything of it & indeed I reckon the letter & its contents gone for ever, & am thankful it was not one of my quarterly large remittances.

*Mon. 16.* . . . A joyful & wonderful event happened in the Evening. A little before 9 came the Clerk of the Post Office with a soiled crumpled letter in his hand & asked if that was the one I lost a week ago: indeed it is (said I), but I never dreamed of seeing it again. – It has just been posted (said he) & seems to have lain in a dirty pocket. – I joyfully gave the man 2/6 for bringing me the good tidings . . . He carried off the letter with him & I then wrote to Frank who will have been inundated with letters from me.

*Th. 19.* . . . Congregation-day: no fighting, – the 6 Graces had nothing to do with the new Statutes . . . The afternoon post brought me letters from Frank & Sophie in answer to mine (wch went off by the morning mail last Tuesday: – how rapid the communication is!) . . .

*Sat. 21.* Up at 7, having (as usual after the Family) slept very ill . . . I was pleased at seeing the trees opposite to All Saints Church being cut down: – so that grand street improvement will soon be completed . . .

*Mon. 23.* . . . This is the 25th anniversary of my Election as Registrary: & I bless God for having granted me the power so long to fulfil the duties of a place so well suited to my taste & in which my heart has always been. – I received a grateful letter from poor Miss Ward (the dressmaker): she has been ill & has therefore been unable to acknowledge my small present sooner: she calls me her Patron!! – Letter from Sedgwick saying that he was yesterday 72, & that having an attack of 'tic' he passed the day in solitude. His letter is highly characteristic: he derives 'cul-prit' from the French, quasi 'cul-pris', – a fellow running away & caught by his behind . . .

*Wed. 25.* . . . Sedgwick called 1st at my house & then at my office to beg me to lunch with him at 2 to meet an antique white-haired ex-maid-of-honor to Queen Adelaide (the Hon. Miss Caroline Courtney Boyle): I tried to fight off but ultimately yielded . . . The party was a very small one; viz. 4: Sedgwick, Miss Boyle & her toady & myself. The toady is a Miss Dixon (a miniature painter – about 30): she is spritely & clever & I was much pleased with her, tho she is not a bit pretty. Miss Boyle was not much to my taste: – she talked about Tom Jones, which she volunteered telling us she had read: she did the coolest thing imaginable, wch none but an Irish woman of rank would have done: – she asked Sedgwick to give her a bottle of Claret to take away with her!! – she said she thought the Inn wine (she is at the Bull) would be sure to be bad! – why didn't she then bring out wine with her? – She wanted to carry

---

[35] See 15 March 1854.

Adam Sedgwick

William Whewell

Joseph Romilly in old age

The manuscript of Romilly's diary for three days in February 1849

Thomas Musgrave, Archbishop of
York 1847-1860

George Thomas Romilly at Trinity College

Trinity College Library and St. John's New Buildings, c1855

The University Volunteers on the lawn of King's College, 5 March 1860

Harvey Goodwin, Dean of Ely
1858-1869

Henry Gunning

Interior of the Senate House, c 1850

off the bottle in her pocket, but could not: so I agreed to encase it well in paper & to disguise its appearance thoroughly & to write on it 'Blacking' & to leave it at her hotel: – all wch I did . . .

*Th. 26.* . . . Harriet was bridesmaid this morning at the wedding of Mrs Foster's housemaid (Martha Hurry age 32 to a well-conducted young man named Hardy age 33). – Mr Foster gave an excellent wedding breakfast in the Kitchen to about 24 (including Harriet & Dosia & Mrs Barron): there was plenty of Beef & Ham & other meats & abundance of sweet things & plenty of Port & Sherry . . .

*Fri. 27.* . . . The degrees today were 1 Mandate DD (Bateson), 4 AM, 16 ABs (all *Classical*) . . . The grand batch of Graces in lieu of the rejected ones all passed: – they were voted on by paragraphs: so 5 or 6 Statutes were split into 35 Graces . . . The eulogy of Bateson by Jeremie was very warm, & clothed in choice Latin: – he cautioned Bateson against sweeping away too much & quoted what he called a "decantatum"[36] passage of Pindar about the ease of destroying & the difficulty of restoring. – I am sorry to say that I made a fierce attack on Skinner for bringing 4 men into the Senate-house & not into my rooms to sign:[37] I told him that the Kingsmen were the most irregular men in the University but that I did not blame them but him: – in the afternoon Congregation I took him aside & apologised for my intemperance . . .

*Sun. 29.* In the 'Times' there have been lately some savage & most unjust attacks on Jeremie (accusing him of ignorance of Latin & of French – having made *voix* masculine etc etc): these letters are signed 'Habitans in sicco' & are dated from 'Broad Phylacteries': he assumes that 'Churchman' is Jeremie . . . The principal end of 'Habitans in sicco' is to rail at the utter inefficiency of Pulpit sermons of Church of England men.[38] – It is however believed that the

---

[36] Dr E.S. Leedham-Green thinks that 'decantatum' may mean either a purple or a cautionary passage.

[37] Romilly would have appointed a day on which men hoping shortly to take their B.A. degrees should have come to his rooms to pay their degree fees. It was only six years earlier that Kingsmen had relinquished their right of exemption from ordinary examinations and Romilly may have felt irritated over the years by this privilege. (See also 25 April 1857).

[38] On 16 March a long letter by *Habitans in sicco* contrasted the inaudible preaching of 'the ancient archbishop' in St Margaret's with that of Spurgeon who could hold 10,000 souls in a magnetic chain for about two hours. Should his Grace be advised to invite 'this heretical Calvinist and Baptist' to 'try his voice some Sunday morning' in St Paul's or Westminster Abbey? The cudgels were taken up in succeeding days. *Cantab* deplored an attack on the truly good man Sumner, archbishop of Canterbury, then in his seventy-eighth year. *Habitans* replied in a prominent letter telling readers to find *Cantab* among the greater prophets and advised Jeremie to read *French in Five Lessons*. His letter then develops into a full-scale attack on the Church of England for neglecting the poor in its preaching and asks it to work with Dissenters 'in the great battle which as soldiers of Christ we are all bound to fight against sin and crime'. On 26 March *Cantab* acknowledged his verbal errors blaming them on 'the copy which I sent hastily and without revision to the post'. If the 'blackguard' ignored Jeremie's plea for gentle dealing with those from whom we differ, he had a case with which Romilly had earlier shown sympathy. On 5 December 1855 he had written to W.W. Cazalet acknowledging the gift of his book *On the Right Management of the Voice* and remarking that 'the great mass of speakers are utterly ignorant of the management of the voice. I think the Clergy of England are most peculiarly and most culpably faulty in this matter . . . '.

blackguard is a man with the ill-deserved name of Dasent: – he is subeditor of the 'Times' . . . At Barnwell Churchill Babington shared my pew & we walked home together. He is one of the Examiners of the 400 Little-go-men (¾ of whom are for Honors!) & has therefore got a friend to take his Sunday duty. He is going to dine in hall with Prof. Thompson today to meet Ranke.[39] – By the way I was yesterday introduced by Prof. Miller to that *little* great man: – he is a dwarf: – he married an Englishwoman & speaks English fluently but with a completely German accent: he is Miller's guest. He dined with the Queen last Friday . . . Read Harvey Goodwin on 'Inspiration'.

*Mon. 30.* Up at 7. – Wet morning. – Gave my vote for Adair & Hibbert at 8 o'clock directly after opening of Poll . . . Finished the fair copy of Grace Book A's Index & then worked away strenuously at entering 'the new Statutes' in my Books. – I worked till I got a dazzling of the sight & was obliged to give up about 5½ & walk about my office for ½ an hour. – Poor Adair is defeated for the Town: both he & Hibbert are beaten by the 2 Tories Kenneth Macaulay & Steuart: – I hope Macaulay has come in with clean hands: – he & Astle [sic] on a former occasion were unseated for bribery[40] . . .

*Wed. 1 April.* . . . I afterwards fell in with Mathison who told me the principal matter was the trial of a pupil of his (named J.R. Mills): – he was had up before us lately for being out all night (he having rode over to Bury about an associate's debt & having excited our intense disgust by his brutal want of feeling for his horse). – This time he has got *expelled*: he frequents pothouses, especially one at Harston & gives great offence by his conduct to the Clergyman (Mr Durbin): – he is also much at the Blue Boar . . . The College is well rid of this unprincipled youth . . .

*Th. 2.* . . . Roberts of Queens has written me a letter to ask what payment out of the University Chest or elsewhere is to be made to him for having written the Senior Proctor's Tripos Verses!![41] Wrote him word, the only compensation is a flourish from the trumpet of Fame. – The Tripos writers used to be entitled to a pair of Gloves: – but he seems not to have applied for them & the system of Gloves is now to end. To Mrs Smith (Mother of J. Hamblin Smith) at 8 o'clock to play whist . . . Letter from R. Robinson (trunkmaker & orange-vendor & poet) enclosing printed verses of his on 'removal of the Conduit'[42] etc etc. – He expressed deep penitence for never having repaid the 10s lent him by dearest Lucy: he is afraid he must go to the Union. – Wrote to him & enclosed 5s/.

---

[39] He was working on his many-tomed *Englische Geschichte*. Evidently his English had improved considerably since 1843 when he and Macaulay, unable to speak each other's languages, conversed nearly as unintelligibly in French.

[40] See 1 March 1853.

[41] Romilly seems most unusually to have confused names. In UP 27 (425) he had as usual pasted in printed copies of the Tripos verses and written the names of the authors beneath them. The writers in March 1857 were C.W. Moule of Corpus and J.B. McClellan of Trinity. Edmund Russell Roberts of Queens' – the only undergraduate whose dates make him a possibility – had an undistinguished undergraduate career and would not have been asked to write the verses.

[42] Hobson's Conduit was re-erected at Lensfield Road corner in 1856. See 23 October 1855.

*Sat. 4.* Up at 7. – Walk in Botanic Garden. – Yesterday the County Members were elected & to my great surprise & contentment Adeane was elected: – Lord George Manners was rejected. – The nos were

$$\left\{\begin{array}{ll} \text{Mr Ball} & 2776 \\ \text{Mr Adeane} & 2615 \\ \text{Hon. E.T. Yorke} & 2494 \\ \text{Ld Geo. Manners} & 2131 \end{array}\right\} \ \ldots$$

*Th. 9.* . . . After dinner wrote to my neighbour (Edmund Foster) to beg a seat in his pew tomorrow Evening to hear Mr Spurgeon. – He called (about 9¼) to say that Mr S: would not preach in the Chapel in the Evening, but in Parkers Carriage repository (– if the weather was not thought favorable for an open-air preaching in Fenners Ground at 3): Mr F. said that if a ticket were sent him he would hand it over to me: – very kind on his part . . .

*Good Friday 10.* . . . After lunch I crawled round the Via Lambertina: – I had the Vulgate Latin Testament in my pocket & twice sat down & read for a long while, finding the weather oppressively hot. – When I got home at 5 I found that Mr E. Foster had most kindly called to say there was a new arrangement & that Mr S. was to preach in the Baptist Chapel: he left the key of his pew (No 31) & recommended my being early. – I accordingly swallowed my saltfish in haste & arrived at the Chapel at 5.25: – Mr E.F. had spoken to the Pewopener who was therefore on the look-out for me: – I was most comfortably placed, close to a window: – I didn't find the hour's waiting at all tedious for I read the Hymn Book all the time. – Harriet also got into the Chapel, – arriving a little before myself. – The Chapel was crammed to suffocation, & outside was a dense mass as near the windows as they could get. – Mr Spurgeon is not attractive in appearance: he has high shoulders, a low forehead & none of the beauty of holiness: his voice is not harmonious, & his appearance ungraceful. He also ventures on very homely phrases & is somehow irreverently familiar in speaking of God, – but he is irresistible in the earnestness of his appeals: his whole heart & soul are evidently in the service of his Saviour: – I can imagine Whitfield to have been just such a man. – He began by reading & commenting (not very effectively) on the 90th Psalm . . . There being now some pushing & quarreling in the gallery. Mr Spurgeon begged that those who were crowding the lobbies would leave the Chapel, he entreated them not to make a noise. The time was when he could have preached in a thunderstorm, but since the dreadful accident he was become very nervous: the mere sight of a crowd distressed him greatly. He feared that he should not be able to address them with the same comfort to himself that he had done in the morning, but he prayed for Unction from above & that his lips might be touched with a coal from the altar & that he might melt some of their hearts. – He made 3 Divisions (1) What is Faith? (2) Arguments for it (3) the Question have you Faith? He said that in the old puritan books there was often more matter in one page than in 50 pages of modern divines: in one of these puritan books he had found the description of Faith being made up of 'Knowledge, assent & affiance'. He worked up these points. He made an illustration from a life-buoy being thrown to a drowning man who knew it, believed in its use, clung to it & was saved. – He had another passage about drowning men: he said 'there were 2 men in the stream being hurried on to the cataract of Niagara: ropes were made fast to a tree & the nooses thrown into the river: one of the men put it round his body & was drawn safely to shore, the other grasped a floating log & was dashed to pieces': – of course the tree was our Saviour, – the floating-log was self-righteousness. – He told a very touching anecdote of a girl who said nothing in a room where people were recounting their experiences: – she was objected to: her answer was sublime 'I cannot speak for my Lord, but I can die for Him!' – His longest story was rather à la 'Uncle Tom': it was about a slave-owner & Cuffee. On buying Cuffee he was warned that 'he prayed': 'O, I shall soon flog that out of him'. – 'Cuffee, I allow no praying on my grounds, the first time you are caught praying you shall have 25 lashes & the next time 50'. – 'Massa I'll work stoutly for you, but I must pray'. 'Very well, I shall start you then with 25'. – In the middle of the night the slave-owner waked up his wife: 'can you pray?' – 'No, I can't'. – 'Can any of my people?' – 'No indeed'. – 'Then I must send for Cuffee, for I can't stand that look of his'. 'Why, did he look defyingly?' – 'No, I could have stood that & flogged it out of him but he looked so gentle & happy & as if he pitied me: – I can't get over that look of his'. – Cuffee was fetched: – 'Cuffee, can you pray for your Master who has treated you so cruelly?' – 'Yes, Massa, I've been doing nothing else ever since' . . . In the 2d part of his Sermon 'the Argument' he had the bad taste to quote Hudibras

'He could distinguish & divide
A hair twixt South & South west side'.

He certainly startles one sometimes by the vulgarity & meanness of his illustrations: for example he talked of 'piety with good weight, 16 oz. to the pound'; then again of 'showy flashy goodness that would not stand & was not *washable*': then he spoke of 'religion in evangelical drawing-rooms': – then he spoke of holding to the profession of faith in a light easy way like a man holding a thing loosely in silk-gloved fingers instead of grasping it firmly in a mail-clad hand. – What gave me most pain was the familiarity of the idea of the sinner who had lain at his Saviours feet not being satisfied till he had his arms round His neck. – In the last division 'Have you Faith'? there was a fine taunting passage against a man who professed his faith & went on in his wickedness & talked of being united to his Master in another world: 'Yes: you will: for the Devil is your Master & you will be united to him'. Mr Spurgeon insisted very eloquently on the 1st test of our faith being the renunciation of all self-righteousness. – In the course of the sermon there was a well deserved eulogy of Mr Jay & a most spirited panegyric of Luther. –

I have not for a great length of time been so much excited as by this sermon . . . The conclusion of the sermon I thought very touching: 'in parting from so large a congregation I cannot but feel the reverse of that tender hymn "Here we part to meet again": for the faithless & the wicked will never reach heaven & from them 'We part to meet no more' . . . On coming home I wrote to Mr Edmund Foster a warm letter of thanks.

*Easter Sunday 12.* . . . After lunch I meant to go round the Via Lambertina but meeting Drosier I turned back with him & gave him an account of Mr

Spurgeon's sermon. – He told me 2 anecdotes of Ranke (when here last week): on being told the Fellows might not marry he expressed astonishment at their being so cheerful as they seemed: – on being told that Selwyn had given away £700 a year from his Professorship to the Norrisean he exclaimed 'it is not true', – at wch people ventured to laugh . . .

*Easter Monday 13.* Up at 7. – A very coarse morning; driving sleet & rain: wrapped myself up in great coat & cloke, hoisted my umbrella & walked in the Botanic Garden. – The good system began today of opening the Fitzwilliam on holidays: – the time too is extended by 2 hours: it is now from 10 till 4.[43] Hannah Smyth & her young man came down today . . . I had no visitor in my Office today & worked away with a good will till past 6. – An emigrating pauper protégé of Mrs Challis came: I gave 2s/6d towards the £5 passage money.[44] Hannah sleeps in my house.

*Wed. 15.* . . . Letter from the would be DD (V.F. Vyvyan):[45] he is frightened to death at the idea of writing a Latin sermon: – wrote, suggesting his borrowing one from some friend who is BD or DD. – The Scholarship Examination began today . . .

*Fri. 17.* . . . 3d day of Scholarship: – Mathematics by Edleston & Mathison: Latin prose by Hodson. I worked very hard till past 6 at the Examination & got thro 5 sets of papers . . . Called at Pullen's to ask matrimonial questions (about licence & *residence* previous) for Hannah: he was out of Cambridge: – by the way I have promised to give Hannah a wedding breakfast . . . The V.C. sent into my office a magnificently bound duplicate of the deed of gift of Pictures by Mr Sheepshanks to a National Gallery & (if that is not built) to the Fitzwilliam Museum[46] . . .

*Tu. 21.* . . . In my office I had a visit from Harvey Goodwin who brought me specimens of the Algebra blunders at the recent Little-Go (at wch he examined). – The richest is this 'What is the sum of $100^{-\frac{1}{2}} + 1000^{\,2/3}$?' – Answer $900^{1}/_{6}$: – the noodle adds the indices & subtracts the nos themselves. – Another good one was making $100-\frac{1}{2}$ to mean $100^{2}$. – Four of the little

---

[43] The Fitzwilliam's picture and sculpture galleries were also becoming increasingly accessible to people unconnected with the University during the week. In 1857 Wednesdays and Saturdays were called 'Public Days upon which all persons respectably dressed shall be freely admitted between the hours of 12 and 4, upon condition that, if required, they give their names and addresses'. By 1858 Tuesdays, Thursdays and Saturdays were Public Days. (See *Cambridge University Calendar* 1857, 1858).

[44] 'Hitherto England has not come forward to bear any portion of the expense of emigration; the great mass of emigrants have been left to provide the cost entirely from their own resources and consequently, as a matter of necessity, they have gone to that country to which a passage was attainable at the smallest cost.' See *Emigration from the British Isles* (1862), p. xxx. £5 would take Mrs Challis's protégé to America.

[45] V.F. Vyvyan, Rector of Withiel, Cornwall (1825-77) wanted to proceed to a *per saltum* degree. A Latin and English sermon were required. Despite, or perhaps because of Romilly's practical but surprisingly irresponsible advice, there is no record of Vyvyan having proceeded D.D.

[46] This was John Sheepshanks, partner in his father's firm of clothing manufacturers and brother of Richard and Anne. He gave his collection of modern pictures by British artists to the South Kensington Museum.

Goodwins began Gymnastics today at Fenners Ground:[47]– their practising time is to be from 8½ to 9½ 3 times a week: – I met them returning in high glee from their first lesson. – Seeing a woman with crutches sitting on the steps opposite my house I went to speak to her: she had no money, came from Lincolnshire, & wanted an in-door order for Addenbrookes: gave her 1/- & an order: – her name was Charlotte Peel & her age 60. – I have contrived to pick up a cold, wch I discovered at night: – I suppose from prematurely beginning cotton stockings & sitting all day without my neckcloth . . .

*Th. 23.* Up at 7 – Met the Harvey Goodwins (Cissy i.e. Helen, Fanny, Edward & George) going to their 2d Gymnastic lesson: so I went with them to Mr Fenner's Gymnasium (at the Market Place): – he very civilly came and explained every thing: – he has engaged Jackson (Crimean Guardsman) to drill the Gymnasts: – very carefully he did it: – it was the motion of the arms wch formed the main part of this callisthenic exercise: – Master George is the strongest of the 4 children tho the youngest: after their drill the children passed along a horizontal pole clinging with their hands . . . I was highly delighted with a dissection of the 47th Proposition wch Airy has just sent to Whewell: it is in wood, in 3 pieces wch are joined by hinges so as to make one mass[48] . . .

*Sat. 25.* . . . At 10 to Chapel for the admission of the 14 Scholars & the 3 Westminster Scholars. – I was much struck with the youthful appearance of Sidgwick (Craven Scholar also): he is indeed the youngest of the party, being only just 18: he has a most intellectual & pleasing countenance: – it is feared that he is in a decline & that his life will be a very short one.[49] – The old Scholarship Oath[50] has (in consequence of the Cambridge University Act) been altered into a 'Professio' by erasing all reference to Religion & eliding the words 'juro' & 'Deo teste'. – Afterwards we had a very long College meeting wch lasted till near 1 o'clock: – we agreed to lend our grounds to the Horticultural Society this year (as St Johns did last): – King (with whom I never agree) opposed it violently. – Martins scheme for modification of the 41st Statute (– with regard to rooms etc etc at Trin. for the 3 Regius Professors) was resisted (without reading a word of it) by Grote (who was infinitely tiresome) & Edleston & King etc: in spite of my cordial support it was decided that no debate should be held on the V.C. & Council's proposal

---

[47] F.P. Fenner played his first match at Lords in 1832 and cricket for Cambridge town club for 23 years after that. He kept a tobacconist's and grocery shop (with which he managed to incorporate a gymnasium) at 6 Market Hill until 1863. For a full account of Fenner's ground see Searby pp. 675-6.

[48] Airy's summary of events in 1855 records, 'Afterwards on October 25th . . . I made a mechanical construction for Euclid I. 47 with which I was well satisfied' *Autobiography* (1896), p. 224. Airy was eminently practical and disliked merely theoretical problems.

[49] Henry Sidgwick's arduous and distinguished career belied these early fears. He died in 1900 aged 63.

[50] i.e. undergraduates were no longer required to make or subscribe to any declaration of faith 'on obtaining any exhibition, scholarship or other college endowment'. The House of Lords, however, restored the original restriction of membership of the Senate to graduate members of the Church of England. See Winstanley, pp. 285-6. See Winstanley also (pp. 329-32) for the 41st statute and the regulations concerning the three Regius Professorships of Divinity, Hebrew and Greek.

& Martin's supplemental scheme, but that the V.C. & Council should be required to send to Trinity Coll. one entire scheme of the 41st Statute: – in my opinion a most unkind & uncourteous mode of proceeding, thus refusing all aid to the Council. I however recommended Martin to give his scheme to the V.C. as a help . . .

*Fri. 1 May.* . . . Wrote a long letter to Grim in answer to a very amusing one of his in which he sent me some Greek M.S. of little Bertha (age 8): it was a copy of the 1st few verses of St John, & was very prettily written: – she is a thorough Whig & dressed out the cat in the Liberal colours & begged to have the cake (in honor of little Lucy's birthday) adorned with 'Plump for Lawson' in sugar plums. Grim himself went to vote with his ponies decorated with blue ribbon & himself with 'a stunning blue cockade' till he found he was transgressing the law, when he put the cockade inside his hat . . .

*Fri. 8.* . . . A 2d meeting of 'the Governing body' of the College (i.e. the whole 60 Fellows): the subject of our debate was the 41st Statute & principally the draft of it sent by the Council & proposing to substitute the Margaret & Norrisian Professors as Electors instead of the 2 Seniors of Trinity . . . Thirty five Fellows were present. We sat 4 mortal hours from 11 to 3! The Electors of the Council's proposing were rejected by 31 to 4 . . . Grote's proposal was carried that we should suggest to the Council their bringing forward a scheme of Electors more fully representing the University. – We then proceeded to the discussion of a revision of our Statutes . . . The Master proposed that all Fellows who wish any changes should communicate to him at least a week before he summons a meeting . . . I cooled my brain by an hours stroll after this stormy meeting . . . Dined at the Family at Christ's Lodge: a party of 18. It was meant to be a party of 20: – but Packe & his wife were unable to come on account of his gout. Mrs Austen (the mother of Mrs Cartmell) was present: she is a fine handsome woman with plenty to say for herself & I got on capitally with her . . .

*Sat. 9.* . . . At St Johns they have been holding meetings of 'the governing body' concerning their statutes: – the proposal for allowing Fellowships to be held by married men for a certain time (if they marry within 10 years of becoming Fellows) was rejected: compulsory ordination after 5 years of MA is to be revised.

*Tu. 19.* Up at 6½. – Walk in Botanic Garden. – Letter from Susan Grounds saying that she is better in health, but that her legs are turned *black* & are so weak she can hardly walk: her husband and little Lucy are quite well: the young creature can say the Catechism as far as the Belief and has knit her Father a pair of garters, of wch he is very proud (& doubtless she also). – Wrote to Susan & promised the small maiden a Sovereign when she knits me a pair of muffettees[51] . . .

---

[51]   i.e. mittens or woollen cuffs.

*Cambridge*

Panorama of the city, c. 1850

*Fri. 22.* . . . greatly shocked to hear of the suicide of Miss Bond (sister of Dr B.): she hung herself from the bedpost & was found apparently sitting on the ground so nearly did she touch it: – her feet were spread out along the floor . . . I hear nothing but dismal tidings: – Swannell (age 57) the late Cook of Corpus has fallen down dead: & Miss Macnaughten (sister of our Fellow) has been burnt to death, she trod upon a lucifer match that happened to be on the ground, it ignited & set fire to her dress. – Dined at the Family at Clarks . . . The painted East window of Ely was talked of, to which Bishop Sparkes (who provided so richly for his sons & son-in-law)[52] left £1500 & Thompson mentioned a witticism of Sydney Smith's about the Bishop 'he is not one of those sparks that fly *upward*' . . . Power played charmingly on the Piano. – I played 8 rubbers & lost 18/: away at 11.

*Sat. 23.* . . . This Evening was the boat-procession: – I allowed Dosia, Harriet & Sarah to go to it: Harriet & Sarah had a regular day's pleasuring, for at 2 o'clock they went to Gompert's Crimean Panorama.[53] – I did not go to the Panorama or the Procession: – but I walked & read for an hour in the garden after dinner . . .

*Wed. 27.* . . . At 2 to the Schools where the V.C. had invited the Senate to hear & give explanations about the proposed Statutes for the Margaret, Norrisean & Hulsean Professorships: the V.C. was in the Moderators Box & conducted the proceedings with great calmness & judiciousness . . . At 3 I went to the Horticultural Show in Trinity Walks. The weather was lovely, there were crowds of well drest men, women & children, the flowers & vegetables were very choice, & there was a fine military band: – I found an hours walk there most enjoyable. At 4 dined in Hall & presided: next me sat Wellington Waterloo Humbly:[54]– he sat next me when I dined in hall in January & neither of us had been in hall since! On my other side sat a good-tempered rosy Mr Childers (of Trinity) who is Vicechancellor of Melbourne (Australia): he is going to take his AM tomorrow . . . The history of my dining in Hall was that I sent Dosia & Harriet & Sarah to the shilling exhibition of the Horticultural Show, wch lasted from 5–8 . . . Read walking up & down the garden till dusk.

*Th. 28.* . . . At 10 to V.C.'s for the Hebrew Scholarship Election:[55] vastly inconvenient: – I was detained more than ½ hour: – I got Welsford to take fees

---

[52]  B.E. Sparke was bishop of Ely from 1812 to 1836. 'It was said that one could find one's way in the fens at night by the little Sparkes planted in all the good livings' (J.A.Venn, *Alumni Cantabrigienses*).

[53]  Matthew Gompertz's 'New and Colossal Panorama illustrating The War with Russia! Painted from Drawings and Military Plans, made on the spot, by both French and English Officers' was to be seen in the Town Hall and was such a success that its run was extended by four nights.

[54]  Providentially for his father who had been badly wounded at Waterloo, William Wellington Waterloo Humbly was born in 1815. He was admitted at Trinity in 1842 and served in the Sikh campaign of 1845-6. He lived in Eynesbury, Hunts and called his son William Wellesley.

[55]  There were six Tyrwhitt Hebrew scholarships, the examinations for which took place in May. Tyrwhitt, late Fellow of Jesus, had died in 1818 and by 1857 correspondence in the *Chronicle* showed that the fund had become inadequate to maintain the scholars. Members of the University subscribed to produce the additional sums required.

during my compulsory absence from my rooms. – There was a throng of people who put off to the last moment & came to sign in the Senate House . . . While I was in the midst of all this bustle . . . that bothering stuttering Phil. Frere 'wanted to have a few words with me': – I gave him a thorough scolding & told him I had already had the signature of his man & that he might perceive I was overwhelmed with business & could do nothing in the way of answering questions: – it appeared that he wanted the fees of his man back again: – I instantly handed them to him . . . Going out of the Senate-house I saw a fine boy climbing on the rails, so I took great notice of him: upon wch his Mother said 'he is one of the twins & when he was born you said of me "O the horrid woman" & Prof. Sedgwick was little more civil for he called me "that dreadful woman!"'. – I was highly amused with all this & shook hands with her heartily & had a thorough good laugh at my abominable old-bachelor speech. – I unfortunately have not an idea who she is . . .

*Whit Sunday 31.* . . . I fell in with Miss Beart (Mr Gunning's kind friend who nursed him for the last year & ½ when he was out of his mind) . . . She talked a good deal about Mr Gunning's last moments & mentioned somebody saying to him 'So I hear you are going to marry Miss Beart' & his answering 'I shall not endanger Miss Beart's friendship by talking to her of love'. – She spoke about the late Bishop of Norwich (Hinds)'s marriage a year & ½ ago to the daughter of a lodging-housekeeper.[56] She was urgent to be brought to the Palace at Norwich, & this may have led to his resignation: he has now taken her abroad . . .

*Th. 4 June.* . . . Today there was a grand voting on the proposed statutes for the Margaret, Norrisean & Hulsean Professorships[57] – the scheme was voted on by paragraphs, making 47 Graces. The Hulsean scheme was rejected by a vast majority . . . Some details about the Margaret and Norrisean were rejected (Selwyn objecting stoutly to some regarding his own Professorship & utterly disapproving the Hulse Professorship) . . .

*Sat. 6.* . . . Went by omnibus to the Station . . . At 5½ arrived G.B.A, Dora & John Romilly Allen (who will be 10 on Wednesday next): they were all 3 in a flourishing condition: – We dined at 6 & in the Evening took a little stroll thro Queens' & looked in at the Chapel (where they were digging a grave

---

[56] Hinds had been a widower for more than twenty years when he embarked on this second marriage and ultimately, in the veiled decencies of the *D.N.B.*, 'domestic circumstances induced him to resign'. He lived in retirement till 1872.

[57] The proposed statutes thoroughly revised the regulations for the existing Lady Margaret and Norrisian professorships of Divinity in the interests of efficiency. Each professor was to live within one and a half miles of Great St Mary's during eighteen weeks annually and to be under the supervision of a board which could prescribe the length, number, and general character of his lectures. The Hulsean Professorship was to be established on the recommendation of the Royal Commission and to be endowed out of benefactions of John Hulse (died 1790) to maintain a Christian Advocate and a Christian Preacher. On 15 December 1857 the Senate passed a revised statute which amongst other modifications assigned the endowment of the office of Hulsean Advocate only to the new professorship, and directed that the professor should lecture on subjects which accorded with Hulse's directions. The maintenance of the Hulsean Preacher was to continue as before. See Winstanley, pp. 324-33 for the difficult negotiations.

for poor Watson):[58] we then walked by the backs of the Colleges to Trinity, & so home thro the Town: – tea about 9¼: – no music so I had the piano tuned for nothing. – Romilly (as he is called) is an active minded child, who asks an infinitude of questions, some of them sufficiently puzzling (– why a man can't have children without a wife, & a woman without a husband?) . . . Dora is fond of discussing questions of theology, such as the eternity of future punishments etc etc: – I told her I thought the practical part of religion was what concerned us & that abstruse points should be left to learned divines . . .

*Mon. 8.* Up at ¼ to 7. George & Romilly accompanied me in my early walk in the B. Garden. The rain having fallen all night every thing looked beautifully fresh. – Directly after breakfast we set out sight-seeing, George being arrayed in my new Gown . . . we went to the Fitzwilliam Museum where Romilly astonished me by his knowledge: on being told that a certain stone had 3 inscriptions viz in Hieroglyphic in Coptic & in Greek, he said 'that must be the Rosetta stone'[59] . . . I gave coffee to George etc at 4½ & at 5 they went off by the omnibus, – George having to attend a meeting of 'the Law amendment Society', where Lord Brougham was to preside . . . My company has done me a deal of good, for my cold is a great deal better.

*Tu. 9.* . . . At 12 o'clock there was a meeting of 'the Governing Body', – 30 (including the Master) . . . I did not get away from this long sitting till ¼ to 4. – The last hour was passed in reading the Report of the Committee concerning a revision of our Statutes (viz. Grote, Munro, Edleston, Luard etc): it was read by the Secretary Blore: it contained proposals concerning marriage of fellows, appointment of Tutors, curtailing of Masters authority etc etc. I went away while Grote was making one of his impracticable worrying speeches. – There was a great noise in the Court during our session & Mathison went out to quell it, – youngsters wheeling a comrade in a barrow & shouting like mad . . .

*Wed. 10.* . . . Visit from Munro about the fracas in our Court: the person who behaved worst was a certain Edward Percy Thompson[60] whose name is off the boards (he having always been insufferably idle) & who is in negotiation about a Commission: – Mathison took him by the arm & he threatened to bring an action for Assault & wrote a most impertinent letter to Mathison: Mr E.P.T. seems to be the only son of a widow. – I wrote a letter (at the suggestion of Munro) . . . 'Mr R. in the absence of the Master & Vice Master is entrusted with the supreme authority in the College. Mr R. is much grieved to hear of the conduct of Mr E.P.T. to Mr Mathison & feels it to be his duty to

58 Richard Watson, Fellow of Queens' 1848-57 had 'a paralytic attack' on 4 June 'from which he never rallied'.

59 The basalt stele inscribed in hieroglyphic, demotic and Greek and found near Rosetta on the Nile in 1799, was ceded to the British in 1801 on the capitulation of Alexandria, and transported to the British Museum.

60 E.P. Thompson had served in the Crimea before coming up to Trinity aged 19 in 1856. His father, the vicar of Aspatria in Cumberland, had died in 1838 two years after his marriage to a daughter of Hugh Percy, Bishop of Carlisle. On 15 June Romilly received an unrepentant letter from Thompson and was relieved to hear that the Master, having returned to Trinity, would now pursue the matter.

inform him that unless he satisfies Mr Mathison by a most ample apology he shall feel it incumbent upon himself to state his conduct to the Horse Guards' . . .

*Sun. 14.* . . . I then called at Sedgwick's & (the door being shut) dropt a card in the letter-box. – I was almost immediately overtaken by Mr Deck coming from Sedgwick's: – Sedgwick unhappily had been again troubled with giddiness & Mr Deck this morning applied leaches behind his ears: – he is considerably better but Mr Deck thinks that he ought to be kept very quiet, & that he was too much excited by talking today with Worsley who got in: – Mr Deck described Sedgwick as being out of spirits & irritable . . . After lunch I walked to Cherry Hinton: – as there was a refreshing air & I crawled I performed the circuit (returning by the fields wch look must luxuriant) without sitting down. After dinner I sent out the maids & walked in the garden reading newspaper & journal.

*Tu. 16.* . . . Dosia astonished me today by telling me that she is engaged to a young man named Johnson: he is younger than herself: he is a tailor & a very good workman . . .

The highlight of Romilly's two days in London from 18 to 20 June was his visit, together with a great many Cambridge friends, to a performance of Handel's *Israel in Egypt* at the Crystal Palace. He went there from Charing Cross in a four-horse omnibus and found his chair number 5554 in a district 'marked P on a pole'. 'I thought the magical spot looked more magical than ever . . . The effect of the Orchestra with its 2500 performers was very striking from the women being all in white'. In the interval he fought for a cup of coffee for Mrs Edward Romilly who told him distressing news. Frank Kennedy, the victim of outrageous bullying by a boy in his house, had been taken away from Harrow where he had been doing well. He 'fell from the top of his class to the bottom because he never knew his lessons: – he didn't venture to come to his room for fear of the ruffian & used for a month to live out in the wood & only come home at lock-up time: – he was twice so ill that he was confined to the hospital. Dr Vaughan immediately ordered the ruffian to be expelled, but on the intreaty of Franky for mercy Miller was allowed to stay & was only severely flogged. – Miller & Frank shook hands & there was an understanding that Frank was not to be at Harris's house. But it turned out that all the boys looked shily on Frank & called him sneak & his position was unbearable'.

*Sun. 28.* Up at 7. – Only as far as the Iron seat in Alderman Finch's walk:[61] there I sat down comfortably in the shade. – Letter from Betsy (Spink) that amused me highly: she is astonished at Dosia's intended marriage: she knows the young man well: she hopes that Harriet wont be such an ass as not to know when she is well off & free from anxiety: as for her own part she wishes she were at liberty to pack up her traps & come & live with me again . . .

*Th. 2 July.* . . . At 1 o'clock John Cooper drove me over in his 4 wheel vehicle to the Selwyns . . . After dinner we turned out on the Lawn & romped

---

[61] Charles Finch (1787-1866) was the last of the Finches, iron-founders of Market Hill. He be-·came mayor in 1848 and the gravel path leading southwards from Brooklands Avenue along Hobson's Brook was called after him.

with the children & with a grand squirt squirted on the trees & flowers. – I made Dudu a present of Miss Henslowe's 'Literary Gleanings'.[62] – On returning home we passed a cart carrying the materials of a booth from Trumpington Feast:[63]– when we had past it about 100 yards we heard a cry of 'Come back': we instantly drove back & found a young man lying on the road: he had fallen from the cart & a wheel had gone over him: he was bleeding at the nose & mouth & was apparently insensible: one of the women out of the cart was standing by him & a farmer came up, who undid his neckcloth, washed his face & poured a little water into his mouth . . . there was no Doctor nearer than Melbourne (– the place he was going to): – nothing therefore seemed practicable but getting him lifted again into the cart (for Cooper's vehicle wouldn't allow of his lying at length) & conveyed to Melbourne: – after some considerable time he moved his legs & gave signs of life tho he was unable to speak . . . I gave the woman 2/6 to put in the poor fellow's pocket. – He was a musician who went about playing at the fairs: he was quite a lad, about 18 seemingly . . .

*Mon. 6.* . . . To College at ¼ to 9 to receive fees . . . The degrees were 91 AM, 2 BD, 2 AB & 2 eundem. – One of the ABs was a *Jew* (Cohen – 5th Wrangler in 1853): – The 2 eundem were Sir W. Fenwick Williams Bart (the hero of Kars)[64] & Sir Charles Nicholson Knight (Provost of the College at Sidney & late Speaker of the Assembly).[65] Both of these men have very lately been made LLD at Oxford: the Soldier was received with rapturous applause while he was signing my book & during the whole of Dr Abdy's speech (who presented him & Sir Charles) . . . People thronged round my table to see Sir Williams signature: it was pronounced to be a *bold* hand. – Sir William had an English speech made to him (directly after the Senate House) in the Townhall by the mayor Patrick Beales: he made a short reply upon his favorite topic – 'liberal grants to the Army': – there was Lunch with Champagne in the Aldermens Parlour to Sir W.F.W. the V.Ch. etc . . . I afterwards met Sir William walking with his hostess Mrs Leapingwell: I joined them: he heartily shook hands with me & I had some pleasant talk with him: – he has been all over the world & talks readily about what he has seen & done . . .

*Tu. 7.* . . . At the *Creation* today of MAs all the mummery was given up:[66] the names were simply called over and answered to . . .

*Fri. 10.* . . . By the way Leapingwell told me that Mrs Shilleto is sometimes out of her mind, shuts up the children in the watercloset & treats them with great severity: her father (Mr Snelgar) was a dissenting Minister & hanged himself, & one of her brothers died in a lunatic asylum. – Her 2d son

---

[62] i.e. Fanny H. Henslow's *Literary Gleanings : by an Invalid* (1848), 2nd Series 1857.

[63] For village feasts see E. Porter, *Cambridgeshire Customs and Folklore* (1969), pp.142-6.

[64] See 14 December 1855.

[65] Sir Charles Nicholson (1808-1903) was a Yorkshireman who emigrated to Australia in 1833 where he practised as a physician and soon interested himself in social and political affairs. He was Provost of Sydney University from 1854 to 1862 and Speaker of the new part-elective Council until 1856.

[66] For details of the 'mummery' see H. Gunning, *Ceremonies observed in the Senate-House*(1828), pp. 121-6.

was offered a Clerkship at Crawshays iron works,[67] but she said she was afraid to let him go among a set of infidels & so he was sent to Christs College: his 1st year is just over, & he was the last in the Examination!! – all this is very sad for poor Shilleto . . . John Cooper kindly took me a drive at 5 o'clock: the weather was charming, the sky delightfully clouded, & a pleasant air blowing: – we went round by Shelford & home by Hills Road: – we ended by seeing his allotments (10 acres among 80 allottees): the allotments are close to the Railway Station: – Cooper himself holds one goodsized allotment where he cultivates flowers as well as vegetables & where he has a very pretty summerhouse with a coloured-glass window & a fireplace: he made me a present of a lettuce, wch (after parting with him at Mr Scotts parsonage) I gave to the 1st woman I met . . .

*Sat. 11.* . . . I should have mentioned that at the entrance to Coopers allotments is a board with 2 Texts on it 'The earth is the Lords & the fulness thereof', & 'Whatsoever ye would that men should do unto you do ye unto them likewise': – after these texts is a warning against *weeds* & a notice of the *rent-days* . . . Symptoms of Long Vacation very pronounced: – I had no visitors during 7 hours in my office . . .

*Tu. 14.* . . . Received Letters from Frank Romilly & Sophie (dated 13 July): the Baths of Enghien have done his eyes good & relieved his rheumatism, but his giddiness in the head & weakness of legs are much the same. – Sophie's was a very warm affectionate letter of gratitude for my present. The prétendant's name is Felix Oger: his family resides in Normandy . . . She seems vastly happy & is obviously heartily in love . . . I had a grand inroad of men, women & children of the working-classes, who had come down by an Excursion-train: – I exhibited all my curiosities to them with great good will for they amused me: one Mechanic was proud of showing that he could read the writing of 200 years ago. – I explained to him (as he was intelligent & enquiring) our mode of passing our laws in Latin & entering them in a Gracebook: he was highly pleased with Welsford's hand & said that was what he called real good writing. – I of course repeated this to Welsford. – Immediately after dinner I went into the garden & read 'Never too late to mend'[68] . . .

*Wed. 22.* Not up till 7¼. – Walk in Cemetery: the interior of the Chapel is much advanced, & indeed nearly finished. – I saw flags flying in Barnwell & learned that it was for the grand Tory dinner,[69] wch is today to be given in

---

[67] George Crawshay, a Trinity graduate, was head of the giant ironworks of Hawks, Crawshay & Co. of Gateshead. He was a staunch free-trader and championed the Poles, Hungarians, and Danes in their national struggles.

[68] The themes of Reade's *It is Never too Late to Mend* (1856) were gold-digging in Australia and abuses of power in prisons, which he had studied carefully, there and in England. It 'laid the pattern for one main variety of sensation fiction; namely the muck-raking novel directed towards the elimination of some crying social abuse' (J. Sutherland, *The Stanford Companion to Victorian Fiction* (1989), p. 522).

[69] On 25 July the *Chronicle* devoted a whole exultant page to the grand Tory dinner when six hundred men and a hundred ladies in the gallery celebrated 'the deliverance of Cambridge from the galling monopoly of Radicalism', and the decision of a Committee of the House of Commons that Stewart had been duly elected despite the smallness of his majority. Liberals

the East-Road Tennis Court[70] in celebration of Steuart not being ousted by Adair in the Election Committee of the House of Commons: – By the way a large raquet-court is building close to the Tennis-Court. – Yesterday Captain Wale gave his usual treat at Shelford to the children of the Union: – they returned in the Evening in an Omnibus & a Waggon shouting like mad. – Mr Titcomb's School-feast (to above 1100) was yesterday . . . I did an unusual thing today: I was away from my Office between 4 & 5: I went to the Butteries & got a glass of bitter beer & then lay down on Clare Hall piece reading the new no. of 'Antiquarian Society'.[71]

*Mon. 27.* . . . I also had a visit from Mr Young (the Clergyman whom I heard preach on Sunday)[72] . . . Mr Young's object was to get my signature to a memorial of Cambridge Householders concerning the immorality of midsummer & Sturbridge Fairs. He wishes the 'tippling & dancing booths' to be put more under the surveillance of the Police, & also that *ten* o'clock should be the hour for closing. He says these booths are positive brothels & that they have a room separated by a curtain. – Mr Titcomb's name[73] & his own were put at the head of the list of memorialists . . . I signed it . . . Caroline How began service with me this morning: – I offered up a prayer for her at our Family prayers. – A very long & interesting letter from Grim describing a 4 days tour in the Lakes . . . he took his own 2 ponies & his trap, occasionally hiring a strong horse for leader, & also hiring a conveyance for half his party: he drove 94 miles up hill down-dale . . .

On 28 July Romilly bought the biggest carpet bag he could find in anticipation of his Long Vacation travels which, with brief spells at home, took him away from Cambridge for nearly two months and are described in 114 closely written pages of the Diary.

He began his holiday in the *Belle Vue* hotel in Cromer where he was 'most amiably given my favorite bedroom'. Romilly was the least self-centred of diarists; people quickly responded to his genuine interest in them and the journal records details of the families, friends and not infrequent Cambridge connexions of his by now large

had alleged in March that the seat had not been fairly won – 'as shabby an assault as was ever made upon an honourable political opponent'.

[70] The real tennis court was built in 1853-4 almost opposite the Zion chapel in East Road and extended along part of one side of Parker's Piece. The game became increasingly popular during the second half of the century. See E.B. Noel and J.O.M. Clark, *A History of Tennis* (1924), vol. I.

[71] Presumably the annual report of the Cambridge Antiquarian Society.

[72] Presumably William Young, Rector of Croxton and Vicar of Eltisley, Cambs.

[73] Mr Titcomb also wrote a letter to the *Chronicle* (4 July) as Midsummer Fair took place in his parish. In it he begged employers of young servants and apprentices to do everything possible to persuade them not to go to the Fair in the evenings. 'Let me entreat them to do so out of kindness to them as their guardians – out of pity for them as being young and inexperienced – from a desire to promote their true social welfare . . . How melancholy then your position, if from motives of false kindness, or cold hearted indifference, you allow the young within your charge to be led into ruin.' He then pleaded on behalf of the parents of the young 'many of whom have committed their sons and daughters to your charge with the reasonable hope that they will be faithfully protected'. Titcomb was indefatigable and he and a number of other clergy addressed crowds at the fair each evening.

acquaintance in the little town. On 30 July old Mr William Sharpe, a former Vicar of Cromer, whose sermon on 'heavenly things' Romilly had heard praised, 'preached over to me the said sermon standing before me in his close little room with the windows shut & holding me by the arm as if to prevent my escaping'; and by 8 August the improvement in his health was such that 'I took a 4 hour walk without resting which I thought a great feat'. Nine days later Romilly enjoyed an unusual sight after a long swim in a 'sea magnificently covered with white waves . . . Two of Lord Suffields whippers-in came with the pack while I was dressing: they were in scarlet & rode into the dashing waves & with the encouragement of the horn & free use of the whip gave the hounds a good washing'.

After one night at home where Romilly found Harriet very weak after a severe bout of diarrhœa he began his visits to the nephews of whom he was fondest. He spent the night of August 20th with George and Maggie in their house at Weedon near Northampton where the children could be swung in the orchard and from which 'there was a very agreeable sight this morning at 7, streams of women & children going out gleaning'. George exhibited his office and the military stores before his uncle left for Manchester where he sightsaw and visited the great Art Treasures Exhibition. *The Queen's Hotel* was 'dreadfully full' and in the morning Romilly discovered he had been 'Fleabit in this grand hotel! – The atmosphere being full of smoke, my quilt was covered with blacks (my windows as usual having been open all night)'. The next day was Saturday, a cheap sixpenny admission day, and 'the people streamed in by thousands . . . Many men & boys in working dresses. – I thought the collection of Rembrandt portraits superb. Among the modern pictures were some of the best Turners I have ever seen'.

Romilly's cheerful endurance as a traveller was well tried on the following day. He left for Cumberland by train at 11.15 and then sat outside on the coach from Milnthorpe to Ulverston except when 'I walked up a long hill (a mile long) in the middle of this journey & had the luxury of drinking & having a good wash at a running stream'. He missed the last train to Broughton in Furness and so took a horse and gig for the ten mile journey there, by which time it was quite dark 'though there was glorious starlight & plenty of summer lightning'. From Broughton another horse & gig took him to Millom where his driver 'knocked up a publican (who was just going to bed) to enquire the way to the Vicarage: – it turned out to be 1½ mile off, so I gave the man 1/ to get into our gig and act as guide. – I reached the Vicarage at 10¼ & was most kindly received by Grim & Bertha. After ½ an hours talk I went to bed, having greatly enjoyed my various modes of travel'.

Romilly stayed for nine days with Grim and Bertha 'who have made me most happy by their constant kindness' and their six children. They visited neighbouring clergy, drove and walked in glorious country under brilliant skies and on 29 August took no less than 92 Sunday School children to Seascale for their annual treat. As Millom lies about a mile from the dangerous Duddon Sands estuary Grim had hired two third-class railway carriages in which to take the children 18 miles north to Seascale (now about two miles south of Sellafield) where the sands and swimming were safe. After a swim and an hour's play on the sands Grim and Romilly and a neighbouring high-church vicar and his family 'handed round the eatables & drinkables'. Grim then proposed that Jenkins, his man servant, who had brought his fiddle with him, 'should strike up & that there should be a dance on the grass: – after some reels by 8 children there was a country dance in wch Grim & Mrs Calthorp led off & I danced with Bertha (the elder): the children afterwards danced a grande-ronde. Every thing went off as well as possible . . . We returned by the 6½ train: – I now deserted Grim & his school-children & came back with Bertha & the children. We of course walked the ¾ mile from Underhill Station. Home at 8¼'.

In London again on September 3rd our indefatigable traveller provided himself with a passport for his first visit for eight years to his brother Frank and his family and took steamer trips to see Guy's Hospital 'tower for ventilating the wards' and the famous 'Great Eastern' transatlantic liner designed by I.K. Brunel. And during the rough crossing to Boulogne he occupied himself in reading 'Jane Eyre all day with immense admiration'.

For the first eight days of his visit Romilly and Frank's family stayed in the *Cheval Blanc* hotel at Montmorency about ten miles from Paris. From there they visited Rousseau's retreat, the Hermitage, boated and took sulphur baths at near-by Enghien, walked in the woods with two asses for transport, little Nini riding courageously, and thought little of Napoléon St Leu to which they went in two open carriages. On 14 September they all returned to Paris, Frank's son Jacques, who 'was very amiable and attentive' having taken a room for his uncle near his father's apartment. Romilly, always careful to spare his comparatively impecunious brother expense, took everyone out to dinner on their first evening. 'I was content with the charge 37 francs but it was thought by the ladies so high that it was agreed that we are to dine in future at Franks – I being allowed to pay the expenses'. Romilly was taken to see the school to which Nini was to go in October at his expense, he and Jacques sight-saw energetically and spent a whole day in the Louvre. In the carriage on his homeward journey 'was an invalide Lady, wonderfully like dearest Margaret, with just the same beautiful nose'. On the morning of the homeward crossing Romilly got 'Up at 6. – Went to bathe in the customary blue drawers: the water very pleasant at 7: there were Humane Society people in a boat cautioning one about dangerous spots'. The *Princess Helena* left Boulogne punctually at 12. 'The day was delicious – bright sunshine & fresh wind: we hoisted a sail & had a delightful passage of 2 hours. The air was so clear that the coasts of England & France were visible to each other all day . . . The no of passengers was between 1 & 200, wch was indicated by 2 balls, one at top of the mast & another a little lower'.

*Mon. 21 September.* . . . I dined off cold meat at the Athenæum & returned to Cambridge by the Express in less than 2 hours . . . I found the maids & Mr Dick quite well. – Very glad to be at home again: – everything looks so neat & so comfortable – Harriet had lighted a fire: – I let it go out.

*Tu. 22.* . . . I set to vigorously at my accumulated letters, & with very hard working answered all but 2 (wch were from Sophie & Maggie). A very large no of the letters related to 'Voluntary Theology': one was a begging one from Beast Bailey (I sent him 2 Guineas), another from Miss Stalleybrass (wanting wine & marmalade & to move into drier lodgings at 1s more per week): – I acceded to all her wishes sending her 2 pots of Marm. 2 pints of Port & 2 Sovereigns: – letters also came from Miss Adeane, C.D. Nix, etc begging for Charities, also from Miss Gibbs (asking me to vote for her for the Governesses), etc etc all of wch I answered. Some letters were about University studies & expenses etc: one of them from 'a poor self-educated *ambitious* young man' . . . At night settled the Accounts during my 8 weeks of absence: Harriet had kept them very neatly & very correctly. – She has had something the matter with her ear for some time & is going to consult Mr Humphry tomorrow. Mr Temple calls it Erysipelas.

*Wed. 23.* . . . Mr Humfrey [sic] says that Harriet is out of health & must be a good deal in the open air & take plenty of exercise & do but very little work . . .

*Sun. 27.* Up at 7. – Walk in the Cemetery: – the Chapel is now finished & is very handsome. – Rain during all my walk. – Went to Trinity Church to hear Carus: the Church was crammed: the sermon was about an hour: Text Revelation XXII. 16, 17. The sermon was delivered with great earnestness & onction. – At 3 o'clock I took Emma Miller to Trinity Church to hear the monthly lecture to the children . . . I do not think the children could have much profited from this lecture which was not enlivened by any stories: – he mentioned indeed a good little boy who died at the age of 7 & who often said to his Mother he hoped he should not live long enough to be wicked . . .

*Wed. 7 October.* . . . At 11 to Barnwell. – Mr Titcomb preached: his Text was Hosea VI. 1. 'Let us return unto the Lord, for he hath torn & he will heal us'[74] . . . I did not find this sermon comparably so interesting as the Lecture to the children last Sunday: – Mr T. dwelt on the opium trade, on the tolerance of idolatry, on the want of missionary labour, on the luxurious lives of the British in India and their worldliness . . .

*Tu. 13.* . . . Jeremie arrived this morning from Guernsey & expected to find a list for him to verify[75] . . . I foolishly got very warm & said that if Professors were not on the spot I certainly (without a special order from the Theological Board) would not take the trouble of writing out Lists for them. I suspect Gell to have been the entire mover & that Jeremie is too indolent to care a straw about this farce of verifying Lectures . . . Today received two things from Whewell: 1st 'A register of "the Cambridge youth" (i.e. Bellringers) from 1724': – I deposited it in the St Mary's Box: – 2dly – his remarks on the proposed changes in our Statutes (– concerning tenure of Fellowships, celibacy etc etc):[76]– I read this pamphlet with great care & agreed

---

74 The occasion of Titcomb's sermon was a 'Day of Solemn Fast, Humiliation and Prayer' after 'the grievous Mutiny and Disturbances which had broken out in India' and was fixed by royal proclamation (24 September). It spoke of the need for national humility 'in order to obtain Pardon of our Sins', and earn divine 'Blessing and Assistance on Our Arms for the Restoration of Tranquillity'. The *Chronicle* (10 October) reported that the day 'was observed in Cambridge with every outward sign of decorum. The shops were closed, business ceased, and large congregations attended the various places of worship in the morning'. (See Chadwick pp. 490-1).

75 Although proposals for a Theological Tripos had been rejected in 1854 a Board of Theological Studies had been created. There were also to be theological examinations which, in 1857, took place at the end of May and in mid-December. Honours were to be awarded to successful candidates, but they could not qualify for a degree. Certificates of having passed were to be obtained from the Registrary who was justifiably cross with Jeremie for expecting him to supply lists of those who had attended his preparatory lectures.

76 Whewell seems to have altered his view of the marriage of certain fellows when in his *Considerations* of 1 January 1858 (see also 31 December 1857) he wrote 'If the Tutor, Assistant Tutors, Lecturers and the like, all live out of College, the greatest security for the good order and discipline of the College is removed. Two hundred young men, living in one house, without restraint or control from any graver neighbour . . . can hardly be expected

with the views . . . The Master seems disposed to allow the Tutors to marry, – but not to allow any other of the Fellows: – he is opposed (naturally & I think reasonably) to the proposed curtailment of his own power: – he is also opposed to the scheme of throwing open the Scholarships & Fellowships to the competition of the whole University, – a scheme wch has so signally failed in the case of Downing[77] . . .

*Wed. 14.* . . . Called on John & Lord & Lady Belper at the Bull: I lionised them to the Schools, Caius Hall & Trinity Chapel: we then went to call on Dr & Mrs Bateson: – they were at home & exhibited their house (wch is beautifully improved, – the white paint scraped off the fine oak panels – the gallery made into a spacious drawing-room – etc) & the Library. – One picture I thought very interesting: it was of Charles 1st when his elder brother Prince Henry was alive: on the picture frame is 'Charles Duke of York' . . . Dinner at 6½ to V.C. & Mrs Philpott, the Marchesa, Lord & Lady Belper, Whewell, Selwyn, Clayton, Sir John Romilly, his son Edward, & his nephew young Trotter. – I got Selwyn to sit at the end of the table. Dinner went off capitally, & there was abundance of sprightly conversation. There was ice after dinner. – One thing however was uncomfortable: poor Edward (whose health seems very feeble) felt so ill soon after dinner that he went away & went to bed. – My party broke up at 10¼ & I slept at the House.

*Th. 15.* . . . I called on Edward at Caius but didn't find him. – His Father called at my office & left with me his poor wife's last letter to her children: it is dated 28 Sept./56: it is very tender & full of admirable good sense: it exhibits the profoundest affection for John & sets up his many excellent qualities as models for them. – Her principal points of advice are: 1st not to grieve too deeply for her death, but to feel convinced that God overrules all for the best: – 2dly to love & reverence their Father, always to consult him, to make him their friend: 'my dying instruction to you is to try & make him happy': 3dly to love each other: – 'be very careful not to expose each others weaknesses & faults to others': – 4thly – to love truth: & 5thly to be earnest in Religion: – 'take the experience of a Mother now lying on her deathbed & who feels every day more strongly that without the hope in Christ & the belief in the never failing love & mercy of God she would now indeed be of all persons the most miserable: – the feeling of resting on your Father wch is in Heaven is the only thing that can sustain you when you come to be where I am . . . 9thly

---

to preserve, by day and by night, the quiet, order and propriety which now reign in our courts.'

[77] Despite the fact that many colleges had far fewer undergraduates than they wanted to house, a royal charter of 1800 had allowed the incorporation in the university of the proposed new college of Downing. The college's comparatively flexible experiment in reform, including allowing competition from the whole university for scholarships and fellowships, might have succeeded had it been able to raise the funds to complete its ambitious building programme, quite wrongly approved by the Court of Chancery. As the Crown would not appoint more than three fellows or allow scholarships to be awarded until suitable buildings existed, the college housed only a handful of undergraduates for many years. 'Thus what was intended to be an encouragement of reform became a warning against it; and the other colleges were strengthened in the belief that the old ways were best or at least less dangerous' (Winstanley, p. 7).

'Talk of me between yourselves to your Father; but let it be cheerfully & happily: this is the only way of showing real submission to God's will: & Oh my children try to live so that we shall not finally be separated in the world to come'. Wrote to John expressing my admiration of the Letter of his poor wife . . .

*Fri. 16.* . . . Grand meeting of 'the Governing Body of the College': – the Master & 48 Fellows present: – We sat from 12 to 4: the question (proposed by Norris) 'shall the compulsory Celibacy of Fellows be modified?' was discussed at very great length: – it was carried that it should by a majority of 1, – 25 to 24. The Master, I, Martin etc. voted in the minority: the question was carried by the votes of the 6 newly elected Fellows 5 of whom voted in the majority: – We also discussed the question proposed by Edleston 'It is desirable to make some modification of the rules concerning Fellows taking orders': – this was carried by 36 to 12. I voted in the majority. – The details of these 2 measures will be debated hereafter. Dined with Sir John at the Bull to meet Edward, Trotter & Walsham: – it was an excellent dinner & the youngsters seemed to enjoy it thoroughly . . . John was exceedingly clever & amusing in his conversation . . . Shilleto has printed a letter in the Times on the new word for a Telegraphic Despatch 'Telegram': – he says the analogy of the derivation fails: he suggests 'Telegrapheme': – it is clear that 'Telegram' will be established.[78]

*Sat. 17.* . . . Letter from Sir John saying Lady Belper wishes to know the receipt for our Trinity table beer: – wrote to him promising to get it . . . Harriet returned this morning much improved in health: – the day she went away she was in so weak & nervous a state that when she got to her friend Mrs Mills she couldn't speak but burst out crying: she went to bed directly . . .

*Sun. 18.* . . . Called at Mrs Pratts: saw Mr P. & the baby: it is the weeest thing of 7 weeks old that ever was seen: it is so weak that the wet nurse is often an hour before she can make the little thing suck: but Mrs P. is too excitable to stand such delay & therefore suckles the nurse's baby wch is a young Hercules & pulls away so vigorously as several times to have made her faint away . . .

*Tu. 20.* . . . In the Evening read Johnson's Falkland Islands;[79] Johnson considers them a worthless possession, while Junius on the contrary had exaggerated their value: – I copied out into the 'Beauties of Johnson' the magnificent passage on modern warfare wch John repeated to me last Friday.

[78] In often heated English and with much Greek correspondents to *The Times* in October argued whether Shilleto was right to condemn the infant noun *telegram* on philological grounds and to prefer *telegrapheme*. The ubiquitous J.W. Donaldson supported him, and the argument turned into another Oxbridge contest. It was settled elsewhere, as this report from the Royal Exchange, printed on 21 October, nicely illustrates: 'Gentleman to "Electric Spark" carrying a message – "Boy; is that a *telegrapheme*?" Boy stares. – "No, Sir; we calls it a *telegram*".' See *Notes and Queries* 21 Nov. 1857, 8 May 1858, 2 March 1889, 6 & 13 April 1889.

[79] i.e. Samuel Johnson's *Thoughts on the Late Transactions respecting Falkland's Islands* (1771), written after Spain and Britain had almost gone to war over their claims to the islands. In 1771 Spain yielded them to Great Britain by convention. Junius was the pseudonym of Sir Philip Francis, the author of political letters to the *London Public Advertiser*.

*Wed. 21. . . .* At 4 to the Butteries to get from Mr Clayton the Receipt for making the Trinity Beer: he had got from the Brewer only the receipt for Ale: – while I staid & drank a glass of bitter beer he sent his son to the Brewhouse & got the receipt for Beer: – For 36 gallons of Ale take 5 quarters of malt & 2 lbs of hops: – for 36 of beer 2 quarters of malt & 2 lbs of hops: – the hops must be put in very hot & the water must be very soft (– we use the River water): – after the ale or beer has done working in the cask 2 good handsful of hops are to be added. Wrote to Lady Belper telling her all this and more.

*Th. 22. . . .* Letter from Mrs Tom Grounds, enclosing a pair of muffetees knitted by her little Lucy (who is not 5) . . . the muffetees are very pretty, but too small.

*Tu. 27. . . .* From 11½ to ¼ to 4 at a meeting of 'the Governing Body of Trin. College . . . The great subject of the day was Westlake's proposal of the marriage of certain Fellows (viz. Tutors & Assistants, Senior & Junior Dean, Senior & Junior Bursar): – Sedgwick was manifestly quite out of sorts, for in his ordinary health he would have made a humourous speech but now he only said in a few words that he was not well & ought not to have been present: – The Celebats greatly predominated: the division was 34 to 12 against matrimony . . .

*Wed. 28. . . .* Another meeting of 'the Governing Body' . . . We debated Hawkins' proposal of terminable Fellowships. Martin made an admirable & most convincing speech against it in wch he cited the answers of Trinity & St Johns to Lord Palmerston's Letter of Dec. 1853 recommending the same measure.[80] – Sedgwick spoke of the scientific advantage of the tenure for life & instanced himself: he could not have carried on his duties as Prof. if he had been impoverished by deprivation of his Fellowship . . . I spoke directly against the proposal. But the Reformers gained a triumph: 21 for the Proposal, 20 against it . . . We then discussed Hawkins' 2d proposal of throwing open Scholarships & Fellowships to all the University: – he was seconded by Grote in a speech most worrying & annoying. They consented to having the proposal limited to throwing open the Fellowships to all BAs of the College (whether Scholars or not) . . . I said that having been an Examiner for Scholarships & Fellowships for many years I had always found a deficiency of rewards for the deserving men & not a deficiency of deserving men & the difficulty would be greatly increased by the scheme: – & as to alluring away the best men from

[80] On 12 December 1853 Palmerston, the Home Secretary, wrote to Prince Albert setting out some essential points on which Parliament might expect plans of improvement to be entertained. Fellowships should not be allowed to degenerate into sinecures and after a reasonable time 'should either be relinquished or should only continue to be held on condition of residence, coupled with a discharge of active duty in discipline or tuition, or with the earnest prosecution of private study'. The Vice-Chancellor then sent a copy of this letter to each of the colleges. Trinity in its reply had declared that the average tenure of a fellowship was less than 12 years anyway, as matrimony and the acceptance of a benefice meant that the average number of vacancies each year was rather more than five. See Winstanley, pp. 274-6 and Searby, pp. 538-44.

other colleges I thought it most cruel & ruinous to them, – taking away all their plums & leaving nothing but the suet . . .

*Fri. 30.* Up at 7. – Rain – Walk with umbrella in Botanic Garden. – Wrote a recommendation for Mr Edmund Foster to be allowed the use of the Public Library & directed it to the Syndics. – Letter from Miss Stalleybrass: she is in consternation at the idea of receiving no more wine & marmalade: – so I shall have to go on sending it to her: – wrote to say so. In my office I had a visit from Edward Romilly: he had a draft from his Father & I took him to the Bank & introduced him to old Mortlock; so the youngster opened an account & had the dignity of a cheque book & a passbook. – Grieved to hear that poor Shaw is in most imminent danger: – he fell down in a fit as he was going to hall . . . I hear he has been most kind to poor relations & maintained 2 in College: – early in life he was engaged to be married & was long in the deepest affliction at the death of his intended: – he has been frequently seen by his bedmaker looking at her miniature & in tears . . .

*Wed. 4 November.* . . . I should have mentioned yesterday the receiving the 'Londonderry Sentinel' containing the degredation of Moore O'Connor at the suit of the Bishop of Derry:[81]– he is now gone over to the Church of Rome. Breakfast at 9 o'clock with the Senior Proctor (Day). – Then to the Senate House: I was highly pleased that the Election was unanimous: 30 votes were given & they were all for Philpott. In spite of the pouring rain we all escorted him to his Lodge . . . It is just 75 years since the same person has been V.C. 2 successive years . . . The Bulletin on Shaw's door was 'had a good night & is better . . .

*Fri. 6.* . . . A long sitting of the Governing Body from 11 to ¼ to 4: the remaining 5 of Edlestons proposals were discussed. – That concerning Fellows who are nominal Professors (their Professorships being worth £400 a year) resuming their Fellowships after 10 years service etc etc was carried by 19 to 11 with the condition that there should not be more than 3 lay Fellows in the Seniority.[82] – It was also carried by very small majorities that Chaplains, Scholars & the Librarian might be married: – I voted in the minority. – The marriage of Professors was thrown out by 26 to 4 . . . It was also carried by 26 to 5 that *childless* widowers might be Fellows or Sizars: unrestricted widowers were rejected by 25 to 8 . . . Finished 1st no of 'Virginians':[83] nothing very striking in it.

---

[81]  See 19 January 1857.

[82]  However in 1861 the University Commissioners' report read as follows: 'At Trinity College . . . A Fellowship is immediately vacated by marriage, except in the case of a Fellow holding a Professorship or Public Lectureship in the University, or one of the three offices already specified . . . But a Fellow who has held a Professorship or Public Lectureship . . . for the space of ten years may be continued in his Fellowship, notwithstanding marriage, after he has ceased to hold such Professorship or Lectureship. In this case a special vote of the Master and sixteen senior Fellows is required'. (Parliamentary Papers: *Report of the Cambridge University Commissioners*, 1861. *Reports from Commissioners Vol. XX.*)

[83]  Thackeray's *The Virginians: a Tale of the Last Century* (illustrated by the author) and published in monthly numbers from November 1857 to October 1859.

*Fri. 13.* Up at 7. – Breakfast at 8: no early walk. – at ¼ to 9 to Senate-house for Matriculation: not over till ¼ to 3: a falling off of 51 from last November . . . Poor Queens had but 3, but Sidney 2, Downing 1 . . . Ferrers (Father of Caius) begged me to speak to my cousin Edward about his bad writing: he says that he has been well trained & that he thinks him the best man in his lecture-room . . .

*Tu. 17.* . . . I saw a great no of good friends in the Senatehouse, Birkett (Jesus), Mills, Maddison, etc: but the most interesting were Edmund Mortlock & Shaw: E. Mortlock wore black glasses, but he has now recovered his sight after having undergone 2 operations for Cataract, the last 3 months ago: tomorrow will be the anniversary of the attack made on his life by his nephew Fred. Mortlock in 1842:[84] J.F. Mortlock was transported for life: – he is now in Jail for being in England without leave: – there is talk of a petition by some foolish people for his pardon. – Shaw came down in a Fly, but he walked up the Senate House without help (except from a stick) & looked nearly as well as ever . . .

*Th. 19.* . . . Visit in my Office from Wolfe . . . Mr Wolfe is an advocate for the marriage of Fellows & is a republican in College-matters: he thinks the Master should only be as a common fellow & that the lodge should be done away with!!

*Sat. 21.* . . . Lunch was prepared in vain for George, Maggie & the Captain at 1½: the cross-country trains didn't fit in nicely: they arrived at Peterboro 10' after the train had started & had therefore to wait till the next & reached Cambridge at 5½ . . . The 'Captain' dined fashionably with us at 6 & went to bed at 7½, Maggie sitting with him till he went to sleep: – he is Harriet's bedfellow.

*Mon. 23.* . . . The rain left off about 12: – George, Maggie & my Godson came to my office a little before 1: I showed the child the Queens handwriting & the illuminations in Hare.[85] Then home to lunch. Afterwards I took all 3 to Emmanuel Lodge & exhibited the Sir Joshua ('hot cockles'): then went to Christs College . . . I borrowed of Cartmell the key of the Fellows garden: he kindly escorted us to the gate of the garden. – I showed the old mulberry tree planted by Milton: besides the props to support the branches there is a mound reaching up to the branches: we also had a look at the path & the wretched busts of Milton, Sanderson & Cudworth. – We then went to Sidney Lodge

[84] John Mortlock, grandson of John Mortlock the banker and M.P., had become obsessively convinced that his uncles Edmund, Fellow of Christ's, and Thomas the banker, were defrauding him of his inheritance of the Bank. On 24 March 1843 he was transported to Australia for 21 years for intending to do grievous bodily harm to his uncle Edmund in his rooms in Christ's although in fact his uncle was scarcely injured. The petition, signed by about 1000 people, was not successful and Mortlock was sentenced to a year in Cambridge gaol before returning to Botany Bay. See A.E. Clark-Kennedy *From Cambridge to Botany Bay* (1983) pp. 109-13.

[85] The Captain was shown Elizabeth's signature in the volume of her statutes and then the magnificent illuminations in the *Libri monumentorum privilegiorum Universitatis Cantabrigiensis*. Robert Hare (died 1611), antiquary and benefactor of the university, devoted his later years to collecting and arranging documents that elucidate the history, rights, and privileges of the university and town. (See University Archives, Hare A 1-2).

where I exhibited the portrait of Cromwell.[86] . . . Dined at 6¼: – my Godson didn't dine with us but came in at dessert. After tea I suggested to George reading loud 'the Pirate':[87]– I wrote my journal all the time.

*Wed. 25.* Up at 7. – Walk in the Botanic Garden: – smart rain: – also bought embroidery Cotton for Maggie. She did not stir out this wretched rainy day: – George bought tin tea-service for the Captain's amusement during this stay-at-home day: he also bought stereoscope views of Fitzwilliam, Senatehouse etc etc. . . . Dinner in my college rooms to Maggie, George & Edward (Sir John's 2d son): it was meant to be a party of 5, but at dinner time came a note from Sedgwick saying he had caught cold & dared not come. My little party went off very pleasantly: the shy Edward gets on far better with 2 or 3 than with a large mixt party . . .

*Th. 26.* . . . Both George & my godson have colds & coughs: the little man was physicked & George staid at home all day . . . Congregation Day . . . there were 52 Graces concerning the new Statutes for Lucasian Professorship etc etc etc: 3 were rejected . . . I was shocked to hear that Skinner a fait grand scandale par sa conduite envers la servante de Thomas Pearce: elle a publié sa conduite criminelle, et il n'est plus Chapelain au Collège du Roi . . . We had a College meeting of The Governing Body . . . It was agreed that the appointment of assistant Tutors should be by the Tutors '*cum consensu* Magistri' instead of 'ex *nominatione* Magistri': – we also passed the allowing of 6 lay fellows (unrestricted to Law or Medicine or anything), only 2 being allowed to be in the Seniority at once . . .

*Fri. 27.* . . . At the College meeting we carried by 13 to 5 Grote's proposal that at Elections of Scholars or Fellows 6 (instead of 8) should carry the Election against the Master. I seconded this proposal. The Master spoke warmly against it . . .

*Mon. 30.* Up at 7¼. – Walk about the Town, to order Omnibus etc etc. – We breakfasted at ¼ to 9: – both George & the little man are rather better this morning. – I accompanied them to the Station, where I had some conversation with Bishop Bickersteth (who was going to see Ely after an interval of 20 years). George & Maggie & child travelled in the same carriage with the Bishop. – Fell in with Westmorland who corrected the extremely erroneous idea I had picked up about Skinner's conduct to a maidservant. From his account S. had been often seen talking to loose characters. The connexion with Pearce's servant is declared by her to have been Platonic tho she professes having granted every favor but the last. After S's return from Paris this summer he ceased paying attention to her: whereupon she used to waylay him coming out of King's: – such conduct on her part was such an open scandal that he could not stand it & gave her in charge of a Policeman: – she of course immediately told her story to her Master & he communicated it to King's college . . .

---

[86] i.e. by Samuel Cooper (1609-72), the eminent miniature painter who painted Cromwell several times.

[87] Scott's *The Pirate* was published in 1822.

*Th. 3 December.* . . . Today a meeting of the Governing Body: it was a very painful one: – Edleston brought forward a motion for 'revising the perquisites & emoluments in kind': he specified only some slight matters (bottles of wine etc) to the Bursar but dwelt on the great expenses of the Lodge (in coals etc etc): the Master took it up as a personal attack & used very bitter language. – Edleston strongly disclaimed all idea of personality, said that he by no means wished to diminish the splendor of the Lodge, that (whoever had been Master) he should have thought it his duty to state his objections to 'perquisites etc', etc etc – Sedgwick manfully got up & expressed his sorrow at the anger wch had been exhibited, that he thought a proposition like Mr Edleston's might honestly & inoffensively be brought forward, especially at a time like the present when all Cathedral & Collegiate Institutions were undergoing such strict & (he thought) hostile scrutiny. Sedgwick however declined voting. – I voted therefore 1st & voted for Edlestons motion: it was lost by 15 to 10. – I should mention that the Master had been greatly exasperated by a flysheet wch Edleston circulated this morning concerning the Lucasian Professor: in it he has introduced a note wch accuses Whewell of falsehood in an affidavit wch he made concerning the said Professorship[88] . . . Letter from Maggie saying that my godson is nearly well & that he made her read loud her letter to hear that his message about a kiss was faithfully given: – George is far from well: the Dr says that he must lie by for some days & that he has something very like bronchitis . . .

*Fri. 4.* . . . Audit from 11 to 2: we got thro all the work . . . At 2 to the Senate-house to hear Dr Livingston: he is MD of Glasgow & has an Oxford degree. He is very short with a thick black moustache: he has a wife & 4 children. The V.C. introduced him in a few words of high praise. – The Lecture lasted from 2 to 3¾:[89] then Sedgwick spoke for 10' in enthusiastic admiration of Livingston & called for hearty cheers (wch had been given already most vociferously). – Dr Livingston went out as a Missionary to Africa. His Lecture was delivered with the accent & language of a person who

---

[88] The offending passage and note in Edleston's *Tenure of the Lucasian Professorship with a Lay-Fellowship* read as follows: 'As to the validity of the Lucasian Letter I will simply quote the words of a Queen's Counsel who was employed in the case of the Greek Professor. He writes . . . "It would certainly be the height of imprudence to run the risk of a future Trinity Lucasian Professor being ejected from his Fellowship by wilfully retaining the same blunder in the statutes (if it was one)* as in the case of the Greek Professor . . . ".'
\* Dr Whewell in an affidavit in the Greek Professor's case, stated that the Lucasian letter was not intended to be repealed in 1844, any more than the letter concerning the Regius Professors, thereby implying that the then Seniority had knowledge of it, whereas the fact is that its existence was not known until some years after 1844, and it first saw the light in 1850, in the *Correspondence of Newton and Cotes*. See pp. xliv and xlv for the Lucasian statutes in *Correspondence of Sir Isaac Newton and Professor Cotes* . . . *with notes, synoptical view of the philosopher's life* . . . by J. Edleston M.A. (1850).

[89] The *Chronicle* of 5 December devoted a special supplement to Livingstone's lecture on the following afternoon, where 'the Town-hall never exhibited its wretched incapacity more strongly: only about a third of the people got in; as it was, gallery, platform and benches were crammed'. The Mayor warmly welcomed 'a gentleman whose explorations in Africa had resulted so beneficially in the advancement of civilisation and natural science'.

had been long absent from his native land & was unused to his Mother tongue: – I believe he was 15 years in Africa. There was great variety in his Lecture: he was scientific in his geological details, playful in talking about habits & customs & earnest in his appeals for zeal in promoting civilisation & Christianity in Africa. He was very amusing in his ridicule of the 'rain-makers' in Africa, whom he compared for absurdity with the homeopathists of Europe. He told of an insect whose bite was fatal to dogs & horses & oxen, but did no hurt to men & donkeys whom he supposed kindred creatures. He said of the African women that they would be pretty if (like pretty women elsewhere) they didn't spoil their beauty: – he mentioned the knocking out of the teeth in the upper jaw, & in other cases filing their teeth into a point like cats teeth: – he ridiculed the mode of showing off their woolly hair by having a hoop on their head to set it out as women in England wear hoops elsewhere. He spoke of his joy in seeing rosy faces again after 15 years absence from them. The youngsters were loud in their applause at all fitting times, especially when women were either quizzed or praised. At 4 o'clock there was a grand dinner in Hall at wch the Master & his Guests (Dr Livingston & Airy the Astronomer Royal) were present. I dined there & Sedgwick made over to me his young friend Mr Barrett who helps him in the Lecture-room: – he is exceedingly goodlooking & very pleasant to talk to . . . he is a relation of Barrett the Crockery man . . . In the Combination room the Master gave 2 toasts exceedingly well, – the healths of the Auditor Denman & of Dr Livingston. – The speech of Dr L. in reply was very amusing: he spoke of the African mode of showing friendship by drinking each other's blood & mentioned an anecdote of an African woman from whose arm he had cut a tumour, – some of the blood spirted into his eye on wch she exclaimed 'before you were my friend, now you are my brother' . . .

*Fri. 11.* . . . Cooper took me a drive at 12¼ directly after the Seniority: we went 9 miles to Over[90] . . . Over Church is a beautiful building with a remarkably pretty porch: the parsonage is situated most conveniently, quite close to the Church: – the Chancel has recently been new floored by Trinity College: the Vicar (Warren) has brought the church into admirable repair: the fittings up look rather popish. He has a good quire of unpaid singers, about 50: – there is an organ (wch is buried in crimson curtains & stands on the floor: – there is a lilliputian organ also (about the size of a writing desk) on wch notes are struck for pitching the voice . . .

*Tu. 15.* . . . In my Office I had a visit from a youngster: he said 'Why, you don't know me!' I answered that I unfortunately knew nobody. He was Bob Willis,[91] who came for a card for Sedgwick's Examination (wch he went into yesterday): – he wants if he passes that Examination to take his B.A. degree tomorrow (last day of term). I told him he could not as there would be no business but the formal dismissal of Term: – he must wait till after Ashwed-

---

[90] Nikolaus Pevsner is equally enthusiastic about St Mary's at Over. The 'frieze of ballflower and other flowers' and 'fat gargoyles and battlements are taken right round the S. porch, and this is the most splendid piece of architecture of the church'. *The Buildings of England: Cambridgeshire* (1954) p. 362.

[91] See 8 February 1858.

nesday & become B.A. of 1859. He is a young man not at all to my taste: – his Mother says he is very clever but that he is *careless*, – what I call shamefully idle: – he was always at the very bottom in all the Caius Examinations: he was plucked for his degree last January but scrambled thro at the Post-mortem . . . He is now 23 & has not yet thought of any profession or pursuit!! – In my Office I read a great deal of Gunning's Mémoirs with much amusement, – of course not for the 1st time: – from 5½ to 6 smoked a Cigar. – Sleepy in Evening.

*Fri. 18.* Up at 7. – Walk in Botanic Garden. – Seniority at 11. – We appointed a Successor to Downton our late Sub-Librarian[92] . . . besides the stipend of £60 there is a payment from 'admission money': 5s of this is paid to the Librarian & 2/6 to the sublibrarian: – each person admitted of the College pays this 7/6. The Master approved of strangers who come to see the Library giving a fee to the sublibrarian . . . Visit from Sedgwick: he brought the list of examined & approved by himself & Liveing: 18 passed, 6 plucked (including Bob Willis, whom he calls a 'slimy sluggard') . . .

*Sat. 19.* . . . Wrote to the V.C. expressing my great admiration for the manner in wch he has this term got thro an incredible quantity of work . . . Wrote to Mrs Barron (the Grocer's widow) sending her £5 as a present & for good luck on entering (as she did yesterday) upon a new house. Meeting Mrs Willis & her daughter Margaret I brought them into my house to see the Canary: I showed them the drawing room also & exhibited all the portraits by George & Bertha etc: – the black profile of Sedgwick was a novelty to Mrs W: – she has a photograph of him & wishes to have one of me, – but I have resolved never to have one taken[93] . . .

*Christmas Day. Fri. 25.* . . . While I was at breakfast E.J. Mortlock (Trinity) MA/57 called & left some clever 'Pickwick' Examination Papers[94] written by Calverley (Univ. Scholar & now Christs) & Ferrers the Senior

[92] William White's niggardly salary (£60) as sublibrarian was to be supplemented by tips from visitors, copying and keeping the Admissions Book. In 1873 his salary was increased to £180 a year, but he was then not allowed to accept tips. See P. Gaskell and R. Robson *The Library of Trinity College* (1971) p. 36.

[93] His resolution wavered as on 1 October 1861 he wrote that 'Harriet has had 4 little copies taken of the French Daguerrotype of me'. However the only known photograph of him is that reproduced in this book (plate 3) from one of the Trinity College albums. For his dislike of having his portrait painted see 23 November 1861. There his confession to Paget that he hated and detested the sight of his face is the only allusion in the diaries to what must have been painful to a man who was so aware of good looks, or the lack of them, in others. His portrait, painted by Miss Hervé in 1836, shows us that he was plain and becoming bald comparatively early. He was also short and by his own description had a 'squeaky' voice. All this he accepted with his customary good sense and there is no evidence that he was envious of those whose looks he admired.

[94] There are thirty questions in 'An Examination Paper, Cambridge, 1857' which enjoyed a tremendous success and was reprinted many times in *Fly Leaves*. The examinee is first asked to 'Mention any occasion on which it is specified that the Fat Boy was *not* asleep: and that (1) Mr Pickwick and (2) Mr Weller, senr., ran. Deduce from expressions used on one occasion Mr Pickwick's maximum of speed'. The first prize, which was open to members of Christ's (Calverley's College) was won by Walter Besant, the future novelist, and the second by Walter Skeat, later Elrington and Bosworth professor of Anglo-Saxon.

Wrangler: the original paper was by Calverley: – people underwent the Examination, & he classed them & gave them prizes: – I believe each Examinee paid 1s fee: – This paper of Calverleys will delight Grim: – the 2d is less good: it has Mathematical questions . . . The dinner in Trinity Hall was very luxurious:[95] the members Walpole & Wigram were there, 5 Heads (viz. V.C., Corrie, Cartmell, Guest, Phillips) beside our Host, the Orator (Clark) etc etc. We sat down about 6½ & didn't rise till past 9! Played 6 rubbers & (tho winning 3 of them) lost 7s: the Master of Tr. Hall & L.T. Wigram played at the same table with me: the 1st very well, the 2d made a revoke & plaid villainously. – The Master was (as usual) very kind to me & gave me Burton Ale, & Mrs Geldart had amiably directed coffee to be brought to me at dessert time. I did not partake of the boars-head supper. – It was just midnight when I got home . . . At Barnwell Mr Titcomb preached from the text 'He shall be great' Luke 1.32: . . . I staid Sacrament. – The organist at Barnwell played the Pastoral Symphony & 'For unto us'. – To St Mary's to hear Calthrop: it was an admirable sermon: his text was Luke 2.20 'the shepherds returned glorifying & praising God' . . . I then walked about King's till the service was about to begin (at 3½). The Viceprovost (Theed) read prayers . . .

*Sat. 26.* . . . Today kept as holiday at request of the townspeople. – Letter from Maggie full of Xmas greetings: she says damp weather brings back George's cold & cough & that she is longing for frost for his sake . . .

*Mon. 28.* . . . Letter from G. Peacock (asking statistics about my payments to the Stamp Office)[96] . . . Wrote to him, lamenting over the dissatisfaction of the Commissioners with our labours in revising the Statutes & deprecating their attempting to force on us 'limited tenure of Fellowships' & 'matrimony' . . . At 9 in the Evening (– having today received a kind invitation from Geldart for today, tomorrow & Wednesday to whist & boars head supper) I went to Trinity Hall Combination room . . . Home at 12.

*Tu. 29.* . . . Meeting of the Governing Body: we were highly disgusted at the manner in wch the Commissioners receive our amendments: – they are prepared to agree to only 1!!!!! – that 1 is of no consequence, – the change of the officer who may depose the Master from 'Vicemaster' to 'Visitor': – we were peculiarly indignant at the tenor of the Secretary Bunbury's *unofficial* letter[97] to the Master. By the way Peacock in his letter speaks of the more

---

[95]  The Trinity Hall dinner had taken place on Christmas Eve.

[96]  One of the duties of the Registrary was 'to take the Books of Degrees and Matriculations to the Stamp Office to be stamped, and to be present at the examination of them by the Inspectors of Stamps' (C U R 20.1). A proportion of fees was paid to government in stamp duty.

[97]  The Governing Body did not meet at all during the Long Vacation and by 10 December Whewell had sent Edward Bunbury, former fellow of Trinity and Secretary of the Commission, only six of the revised statutes. Bunbury's unofficial letter to Whewell of 24 December rebuked the college for sending the statutes at 'the late period of the year' and then only a few partial ones 'whereas many other colleges . . . sent them [the Commissioners] a revised body of statutes as a whole . . . Therefore it will devolve upon the Commissioners (if they think fit) to consider the whole body of the statutes, and suggest changes in them as they deem expedient . . . It is no secret either that the proposals which have actually come from Trinity College are merely the *residuum* after changes of a much more sweeping

satisfactory manner in wch Oxford has acted & cites the example of Magdalene College which has funded 4 Professorships of £600 p.a. tho its income is under 30000. – It looks as if the Commissioners mean to inflict no small burdens upon us . . .

*Th. 31.* . . . Received from Whewell 'Considerations'[98] in reply to the sweeping propositions of the Commissioners as conveyed in their 'General principles in regard to Colleges proposed for consideration'. I think Whewells arguments irresistible & wrote to tell him so. – Worked at 'Questionist Papers' till 6.

character have been proposed and rejected'. (Letters and Papers concerning College Statutes, Trinity College Documents). Not surprisingly many of the leaders of the academic reform party, faced with the prospect of changes which would fundamentally affect their own colleges, became alarmed and in Trinity voted against drastic proposals put forward by Edleston and Grote (both Seniors), Charles King and Westlake in particular. See Winstanley, chapter XV.

[98] In the introductory paragraphs of his *Considerations*, written 'in his individual capacity', Whewell says that 'Most or all of the Colleges . . . have sent their proposed alterations' to their statutes 'to the Commissioners for their approval; some of them several months ago'. But the Commissioners' replies have led 'to the general persuasion that the Commissioners are not disposed to promote self-legislation on the part of the Colleges, but wish to take advantage of the lapse of time which will throw the power of legislation into their hands'. The first of January – the date of the *Considerations* – was the date *before* which the Commissioners allowed colleges to alter their statutes.

A problem paper in the Senate House

# 1858

*Fri. 1 January.* God be praised I enter upon this new year in good health & with no anxiety on my mind about any of my relations . . . Gave the maids new shillings. – Treated myself with a beautiful engraving of Milton as a boy of 12 years old. – Dined in Pembroke at 5: there was a magnificent dinner in Honor of the Foundress[1] to a large party & a very noisy one . . . There were 3 whist tables in the Combination room: the 4 players at my table were Pulling (Master of Corpus), Paget & Arlett & myself . . . I lost every rubber & was guilty of a revoke: – I lost more than I have lost time out of mind, viz 87s. There was supper at 11: – but I didn't partake of it, – one full meal being as much as I can venture on.

*Fri. 8.* . . . Letter from Peter Ouvry giving copies of 3 very interesting letters from Henry (Major Ouvry): he was at the taking of Delhi[2] & commanded the cavalry. He seems to have conducted himself with great ability & great courage. He says that in one place just as he was going to bayonet the seapoys taken in arms a piece of paper was blown to him: he picked it up & found it a page from the Testament & the 1st words he saw were 'blessed are the merciful': – his fierceness gave way & the men were taken prisoners, to be dealt with according to the laws of war . . . I was grieved to see in the Times (of yesterday) an account of the death of that great General Havelock (age 62):[3] he died on 27th November – 2 days after the relief of Lucknow: – he died of dysentery & anxiety of mind . . . Amused by a letter from Dr Corrie: he returns the List of books in 1493, & is sorry that he never had time to copy it till yesterday!!!! – he had my list last January & might easily have copied it in 3 or 4 hours. – Did a great deal of indexing.

*Mon. 11.* . . . I should have mentioned that the last whole packet of French letters was remarkably agreeable: the 5 Letters (from Frank, Fanny & Nini, Sophie & Oger) were most affectionate & gave good reports of every body's health . . . Frank is again about to undergo the worry of a move before he was well settled down: he laments having to move his 5000 volumes! – The day being brilliant the plough-boys beset the streets & danced indefatigably. – Mr Tidd Pratt sent me an Alphabet of Calverley's: it is amusing enough: but I am sorry to find that Calverley won't go to Chapel, that he will smoke in the

---

[1]  i.e. Mary de St Pol, Countess of Pembroke, who died at Denny Abbey near Cambridge in 1377.

[2]  Judging by the comparative infrequency of entries in the diary, Romilly seems hitherto to have been more interested in warfare in the Crimea than in India, although *The Times* was daily reporting the horrors of the mutiny. In May 1857 Delhi, India's chief arsenal, became the mutineers' headquarters and the British officers and residents there were massacred. In September the city was recaptured by British troops outnumbered by three to one.

[3]  In September 1857 General Sir Henry Havelock relieved Lucknow after a siege lasting 87 days. His small force was not strong enough, however, to cut its way out again together with the women, children, and wounded. He died four days after the second relieving army under Sir Colin Campbell enabled the withdrawal from Lucknow to begin.

court, & that he does all he can to vex Cartmell: – shameful conduct on his part[4] . . .

*Th. 14.* . . . Letter from Bunbury (Secretary to the Commissioners) asking whether I had any suggestions to make touching my own Office or any other matters: – wrote back word that I desired no change of the Statute of 27th March 1857, – of wch I thoroughly approved[5] . . .

*Fri. 15.* . . . As I was eating my tapioca the new President of Queens' (Phillips) was announced.[6] I found him marvellously dull & heavy: his words too flowed as slowly & as indistinctly as his ideas . . . Phillips . . . looks like a feeble old man; but he cannot be more than 50 years old, for he was of Philpott's year 1829. – Letter from G.T.R. all his household but himself have had Influenza . . . In my office I arranged the drawer concerning the Council & the Commission: – I have the original Commission of 31 August 1850 with the Queen's signature: – this Commission appointed Bp Graham, Dean Peacock, Sir J.F. Herschel, Sir J. Romilly & Prof. Sedgwick . . .

*Sat. 16.* . . . Before breakfast I posted my letter to G.T.R. & went to College, where I brought up from the cellar 3 dozen of audit of 1854 & told Hoppett to pack them up for G.T.R. . . . At 7 o'clock Grim arrived (by Express Train): he had a nose-blowing cold but was in capital spirits & gave an excellent account of all his belongings[7] . . .

*Mon. 18.* . . . Grim was off for Town by the Express at 9·20 . . . Grim told me that at his brothers they played at Charades etc etc & that the problem was proposed of dividing into 2 equal parts 8 pints of milk with no other measure but 8 pints, 5 pints & 3: – it is a very pretty piece of slopping backwards & forwards . . .

*Wed. 20.* . . . Visit from Mr Somerby (the American) whom I took to dine at 'the Family' at St Johns when he was last here:[8] – I told him that I was now a very poor creature & didn't go any where: – I made the most of my cough that he might clearly see that I didn't mean to offer him any hospitality . . . I handed over to him the piece of Milton's Mulberry tree wch I got for him

---

[4] Calverley with his extraordinary verbal memory, his brilliant gift for Latin versification, his keen wit, fearless high-jumping and incurable indolence, was on the whole careful to behave himself in Cambridge, as distinct from Oxford from which he had been sent down. But many of the older dons never knew quite how to take him and 'his elvish character lay so deep . . . that he could not in the least control it . . . It was a misfortune that with this irrepressible propensity he had to spend so many years in an ancient College where he was expected to conform to a routine more formal than that of ordinary life' (J.R. Seeley in W.J. Sendall's *Literary Remains of Calverley*, 1885, p. 109). See also 25 December 1857.

[5] For the revised statute see Winstanley p. 318.

[6] George Phillips, son of a Suffolk farmer, was just fifty-four and was to be President of Queens' for 34 years. He took a leading part in the establishment of the Semitic and Indian Languages Tripos in the 1870s. Despite his slow speech he 'recognised at once the duty . . . of exercising' as President 'a genial hospitality. In that exercise he was most effectively assisted by Mrs Phillips, whose tender sympathy and winning manners endeared her to all who had the happiness of her acquaintance' (*Cambridge Review*, XIII, 1892, 192).

[7] Grim's high spirits may have been partly due to his being 'just made Rural Dean' and to his 'school now rising from the ground' (*Diary*, 9 December 1857).

[8] Genealogist and author of a *Catalogue of Original Documents in the English Archives relating to Maine* (New York, 1858).

when he was last in Cambridge but he went away before I received it from Dr Cartmell.

*Mon. 25.* Up at 7. – Thermometer at 27. – Beautiful morning: – walk in Botanic Garden . . . There seems to be little done in Cambridge for the poor in honor of the Princess's marriage:[9] St Edwards gives a gratuitous tea-drinking to people furnished with Cards (from H. Goodwin, Dr Geldart etc): H.G. sang: the fiddlers were brought in & they danced till 4 o'clock!!! Benet Parish gives relief (coals or soup) to certain paupers: – & Barnwell gives tea at *1 s 6* per head!!!!!!

*Th. 28.* . . . Seniority, in wch we expelled G.C. Lampson (who ought to have taken his degree on Saturday) for keeping a woman at Harston: – he called himself Lloyd the 3 months he kept there: – the complainant was Mr Durbin the Clergyman of Harston. G.C. Lampson has confessed his guilt: he was not present, being ill with measles: his brother was in attendance . . .

*Sat. 30.* . . . The Senate House (in spite of the wet) was crammed to suffocation: I stayed there a very little time. A very large number admitted viz 271 (123 in Honors & 148 in Polloi). The youngsters seemed to me to behave very well. – I understand from Campion (moderator) that the 1st 4 men (Slesser, Smith, Wace & Hadley) had each above 6000 marks: Slesser was more than 400 above Smith.[10] – Hopkins (Senior Wrangler-maker) is said to have had the very highest opinion of Smith & to have thought it almost impossible for him to be beaten. – Slesser was a Pupil of Routh . . . Campion told me that Smith was 1200 marks above Wace, & Wace about as many above Hadley . . . I then paid a visit to Sedgwick & sat with him an hour, during which he ate his dinner. – He is (I rejoice to say) a great deal better: he has been suffering from gum-boils. He is reading Pepys's Memoirs with intense delight, & say [sic] they have kept him alive during his late indisposition[11] . . .

*Fri. 5 February.* . . . Letter from Sophie most delightful: it contained Franky's solution of the Problem of the 3 measures (8 pints, 5 & 3): it was done quite right & explained by him very clearly. – I wrote to him in praise & told him that 10, 7 & 3 would do equally well for halving the whole quantity . . .

*Sun. 7.* . . . On the road met a good-tempered pauper, who called my attention to her new warm cloke 'A lady gave it me on the day of the Princess' marriage' . . . After dinner I wrote to Frank & to Sophie (Madame Oger): £15 will be put in the letter tomorrow. Sophie says most truly that I should never guess who 1st wished her a happy new year: the child in her womb wch

---

[9] i.e. on the Princess Royal's marriage to Prince Frederick William of Prussia, afterwards the Emperor.

[10] As in 1857 the Senior Wrangler, G.M. Slesser, the son of a Scottish crofter, was a Queensman. C.A. Smith was at Peterhouse.

[11] Pepys was scarcely known even among the educated and his shorthand Diary remained undeciphered in the library at Magdalene until Lord Braybrooke, using a version by the Rev. John Smith, began to issue ever larger and improved editions between 1825 and 1858. Bowdlerised and abridged as they were, the Diary was instantly recognised as a classic of its kind. The early editions are discussed in R.C. Latham, *The Shorter Pepys*, pp. xi-xii of the introduction.

is not to see the light till May! She writes in tearing spirits & seems as happy as possible. – I told her I was sure her baby would be a girl as boys never talked before they were born.[12]

*Mon. 8.* . . . Visit from Willis (about fees etc to be paid for Bob who has now past the Professorial Examination & may take a degree after Ashwednesday): – he says there is no vice in Bob, that he has had bad health & is indolent . . .

*Tu. 9.* . . . To London by Express train (9.22) first class with return ticket, cost 20/3 . . . Hopkins & I went in a cab to Burlington Hotel (Cork St.), the V.C.'s Hotel: he very kindly gave us lunch at 1: Cartmell made it a party of 4: – just as we were going to sit down the Marquess Camden came in . . . the Marquess is very exemplary about attending the University Addresses: as he is a K.G. he adds to the Pageant . . . The Room we were received in at Buckingham Palace was the dining room. There were no Bishops present & I think no Noblemen but Lord Camden. – At a few minutes past 3 we were joined by the Prince: he very graciously shook hands with the V.C., Hopkins & myself & 2 or 3 more. – The Queen stood: – the Prince of Wales was just behind her. – I as usual stood by the Prince & held a corner of the great Vellum Address, but he read from a small paper one with which I had furnished him, & wch he gave me back.[13] – I thought he read with an accent more foreign than usual: the Queen read her reply very beautifully & touchingly. – Two persons only kissed hands, viz the V.C. and Commissary Selwyn: – it was meant that the 2 should be V.C. & Phelps, but I having named Selwyn 2d (according to his precedence in the Procession) he naturally stepped forward & kissed the Q.'s hand: he was highly delighted at the honor wch he had never had before: Phelps had, & took his disappointment very goodhumouredly . . . Reached Cambridge at ¼ to 7. – Had an egg with my tea. – Altogether a most successful day: – I made no mistake in my task & found every thing very agreeable . . . Found a little visiter in the house. – Harriet's youngest sister was put to bed on Sunday night with a little girl: – she has to be kept very quiet: – so Willy Watts (a fine boy near 5) is come to stop with his Aunt Harriet: – I told her to keep him as long as ever she liked.

*Th. 11.* . . . Congregation day: – the Queen's Answer to our Address was read: – 4 AM, 2 LLB, 5 AB (4 of whom had paid before). – There were Graces . . . they all passed unopposed except one, wch was to appoint Dr. Donaldson a Bell Examiner in place of Abdy. The abomination against his heterodoxy flamed up absurdly:[14]– the Grace was non-placeted in B.H.H. by Peter of Jesus: 3 other men (Dr Corrie, C. Clayton & Basil Williams (scrutators) voted also against Donaldson: the Grace was carried by 15 to 4 . . .

*Sat. 13.* . . . Letter from Frank Kennedy . . . he describes himself as very happy at Kings College School: he is reading 'Urania' the 8th Book of

---

[12] The baby was a boy.

[13] On the Princess Royal's marriage.

[14] J.W. Donaldson was a brilliant philologist but an unreliable guide in religious matters. He had compounded the notoriety of *Jashar* (1854) with a statement of his general views on *Christian Orthodoxy reconciled with the Conclusions of Modern Biblical Learning* (1857) in which his transcendental orthodoxy could be seen as scepticism.

Herodotus & likes it: what he finds hardest is taking notes of the Lectures . . . Seniority to elect a Chaplain: we elected Edlin . . . We voted that the skeleton man & monkey & certain snakes in bottles etc etc should be given to the Anatomical Museum (Clark would have liked our Mummies also, but we would not part with them) – So now we shall lose one of our sights for visiters to the Library. – Still there will remain Newton's reflecting Telescope, with the standing joke to any Lady that in it she will see Venus, – & the ossified heart of a woman who jilted a Fellow of the College.[15] – The closet of 'the Man & Monkey' is wanted for a hand-washing place . . .

*Sun. 14.* Up at ¼ past 7. – Cough much the same. – Wet morning: walk under outspread umbrella on Trumpington Road. – Having small taste for 'Jew' sermons I made an excuse of the heaviness of the rain & the dirtyness of the East-road & shirked Mr Titcomb this morning.[16] – I went to Benet Church & sat in Dr Pulling's pew, wch I shared with a beneficent Mrs Preedy (sister of Crick & Mrs Thackeray). – Pullen did all the duty: the Congregation was very small: the sermon was in choice language, but was hard & dry & must have been unintelligible to almost every body . . . At 2 o'clock I went to St Mary's & was delighted with Dean Alford's sermon & greatly regret having missed the 1st of them. His subject for the month is the Parable of the Sower . . . today 'stony places where there is no depth of earth' Luke VIII. 13. – He spoke of religious impressions not being religion itself: – he said the young (especially of the weaker sex whom God had endowed with exquisite sensibility of heart) were peculiarly susceptible of strong impressions for religion, – but not merely for religion, they were equally susceptible for the world, for pleasure & for distinction . . . Letter from Agnes Gilmour (now 18) (6 Upper Penton St Pentonville): she is in most delicate health, has broken a small blood-vessel, is afraid of incessant needlework, & wishes to try a small shop for selling childrens ready-made things: – sent her £5 & a sympathising letter . . .

*Mon. 15.* . . . they have just elected Beard of St Johns to be Chaplain in place of Skinner (resigned): a man of St Johns named Ward had been a Candidate: he is called '*real* Ward' to distinguish him from his brother who

[15] In the seventeenth and eighteenth centuries there were no university museums or laboratories and the college libraries, Trinity's particularly, housed a great variety of curiosities, inscriptions, specimens and instruments which had no other home. By the mid-nineteenth century 'such acquisitions had become a principal part of visitors' experiences of the Library, to be viewed with the manuscripts and printed books' (David McKitterick, *The Making of the Wren Library* 1995, pp. 105-9). A mummy from the Canary Islands remained until 1914 and is now in the Museum of Archaeology and Anthropology; Newton's telescope is in the Whipple Museum of the History of Science, but the whereabouts of the faithless heart is unknown. Hands are however still washed in the closet vacated by the Man and Monkey.

[16] The sermon which Romilly was shirking was presumably in aid of the London Society for Promoting Christianity among the Jews. Founded in 1809, the Society became increasingly influential and international in the missionary field and from 1841 had the archbishop of Canterbury as its patron. See W.T. Gidney's centenary volume, *The History of the London Society for Promoting Christianity amongst the Jews* (1908).

wrote on 'idealism'.[17] – When it was dark I smoked a cigar. – Mrs Parry (who is wild about getting a 2d husband) is not much pleased with a Valentine she had on Sunday, – an ugly flaunty woman with the doggrel 'Mrs Parry who wants to marry. Read a good deal of Clementius[18] in the Evening. Cold better.

*Fri. 19.* . . . When I came home to dinner I was greatly shocked at receiving a letter from M.A. Tyler telling of her youngest sister having fallen into sin: – she writes quite broken-heartedly: she is near her confinement: the young man is fond of her & anxious to marry her: – neither he nor she have a farthing: – Mr & Mrs Tyler are still ignorant of this dreadful infamy of their child tho M.A. has now known it a month & has almost fretted herself to death. – I wrote to M.A. & sent £10 for buying a Licence & setting the guilty pair afloat: – I recommended the young man instantly confessing his wickedness to Mrs T. & offering the only remedy that remains, – marriage.

*Sat. 20.* Up at 7. – Sunny frost. Thermometer at 27. – To College to look about marriage licences: – they are Granted by Surrogates[19] (– I believe J. Cooper succeeded Maddison as Surrogate): 15 days residence is required from one of the couple. – Wrote again to M.A.T. . . .

*Mon. 22.* Ld Palmerston has resigned: having been beaten on his bill upon 'Conspiracy to assassinate'.[20] Lord Derby is to try if he can make a Ministry . . . Received from Roby his pamplet on University Reform & wrote to thank him. – It commends Latham's pamphlet but is almost entirely taken up in answering it: – he (Roby) recommends limited Fellowships, marriage etc etc: he is for the minor colleges restricting themselves to one study, e.g. Caius to Physic, & Trinity Hall to Law. I think the pamphlet able & more temperate than I expected: – but I am not convinced by it[21] . . . The V.C. wanted to see if anything was to be made out about the Government payments to the 7 Professors of Anatomy, Botany, Chemistry, History, Jacksonian, Regius Law, & Mineralogy: – Government declare that they pay in advance & that they have already paid up to next 5 April . . . It seems that 6 out of the 7 consider themselves defrauded: particularly Sir James: – it would seem that

---

[17] Arthur Robert Ward, a great cricketer, was curate of All Saints, Cambridge 1856-60. His elder brother William George, the theologian and philosopher, was received into the Roman communion in 1845, having been censured by Oxford University for his *The Ideal of a Christian Church considered in comparison with Existing Practice*. Venn gives another reason for his being called 'real'. 'A very stout man, of very High Church persuasion, he was known as "The Real Presence", his curate at St Clement's, of which he became Vicar in 1860, as "The Wafer".'

[18] i.e. of the *First Epistle of Clement to the Corinthians*, thought to have been written about 95-6 A.D. and to be the earliest first-hand evidence concerning the preservation of Christian doctrine and practice by the apostles. (See 6 March 1861).

[19] The word is applied especially to a clergyman or other person appointed by the bishop as his deputy to grant licences for marriage without banns.

[20] Largely as the result of Orsini's attempted assassination of Napoleon III the government wanted conspiracy to murder to be classed as a felony, but it was beaten by 19 votes on the second reading of the bill.

[21] i.e. Latham's *Considerations on the Suggestions of the University Commissioners with regard to Fellowships and Scholarships* (1857), and Roby's wider-ranging *Remarks on College Reform* (Feb.1858). The state paid the stipends of certain professors which in 1852 amounted in all to slightly over £1,000. See Winstanley, pp. 262-3.

the Executors of Prof. Smyth certainly received what should have been paid over to his successor – the V.C. saw in my office the correspondence with the Treasury in 1832, wch bears out their declaration that they pay in advance. – It is as Philpott expressively calls it) a *nasty* business: – it requires all his calmness & clearness to get thro it . . .

*Tu. 23.* . . . After dinner had a visit from Dosia (now Mrs Johnson): she sat with me a good ½ hour: – she is as happy as a Queen & speaks in great praise of her little husband, the tailor: – Signed a Petition to the Mayor for suppression of the profligate state of Trumpington Street on Sunday Evenings.[22] – Tea & Cards at Corpus Christi Lodge . . . Plaid 6 rubbers & (for the 1st time this year) came off winner: – I won 19s . . . Mrs Prest & her daughter-in-law Mrs William brought me home at 11: – I sat up an hour reading the Times wch is of course very interesting now that a new Ministry is forming by Lord Derby.[23]

*Wed. 24.* Up at 7: charming morning: bright sun: quite warm in spite of the wind. – Sarah Smyth came for an out-door Hospital order for her Mother: she said '2 of her eyes were bad'. – just as if she had 3 or more. Worked all day at the list of Proctors from 1454: – a deal of complication & difficulty in their history . . . Bought Cock Robin (with pictures) for Willy Watts: – he was highly delighted with it. – Letter from M.A. Tyler: all her anxiety about the present sad business made her very ill last Saturday: – her sisters marriage is to take place immediately: – she says the Licence cost £2.17. –: – not until after the marriage will the disgrace be confessed to Mr & Mrs T. . . . A very agreeable letter from Grim: – the little French Governess gives great satisfaction: she teaches Music as well as French . . .

*Fri. 26.* . . . Walk on Hills Road: breakfast with the Selwyns in their new house: only the Study habitable at present.[24] – Letter from Peacock regretting that he cannot dine with me today: he gives a capitally good account of himself: he is working very hard at Commission work & thinks it will be a long while yet before the Commissioners send the College statutes: he thinks time desireable both for the Commissioners & the Colleges, – for the Commissioners to mature & correct their views & for the Colleges to *enlarge* theirs. Peacock is pleased with Roby's pamphlet, wch he thinks of more than common ability: he thinks it a very successful answer to many of Latham's fallacies & that it gives a higher view of the real object of Colleges . . .

[22] The *Chronicle* of 6 March welcomed the petition which 'has now been extensively signed by the most respectable inhabitants'. It 'sets forth that on Sunday evenings Trumpington Street is frequented by a large number of young persons of both sexes who are subject to no control, and the consequence is that modest persons of both sexes are annoyed and those of the female sex insulted, while much moral damage cannot fail to accrue to the young persons themselves'. The petitioners hoped that it might be within the power of the magistrates 'to cause the streets to assume an appearance suitable to a Christian town on the Sabbath evening'.

[23] A brief interlude of Conservative government under Derby and Disraeli followed Palmerston's defeat.

[24] The Selwyns' new house, 6 Belvoir Terrace, was and still is called Vine Cottage, though by no means a cottage. It is free-standing beyond the Belvoir Terrace archway. See 6 April 1859.

*The Chapel, Trinity College, Cambridge*

*The Hall, Trinity College, Cambridge*

The Chapel and the Hall, Trinity College

*Sun. 28.* . . . By the way I find that my new servant Caroline How has never attended the Sacrament tho she has been confirmed & is 28: – I strongly advised her to attend. – At St Marys Dean Alford finished his course on the Parable of the Sower: I did not like his sermon so well as the other 2 I heard: – it is so much easier to describe vice than virtue: – this concluding sermon was on 'the good ground'. – I thought it rather hard and vague: one idea I thought very beautiful, where (in speaking of Gods dealings with us by sorrow & affliction) he said that the blow which severed our dearest ties filled our chamber with angels . . .

*Th. 4 March.* . . . At 9 to the Senate House for the undisputed return of Mr Walpole (Home Secretary)[25] . . . There is to be a grand party in our hall for him today at wch Sedgwick will preside, the Master being engaged: I shall not go to this party. – I took the Election to the Post & delivered it into the hands of The Post-master. – Congregation day . . . Selwyn nonplaceted the Grace for the new 'Deputation at Addresses'[26] (wch excludes the High Steward, the Commissary, the Heads & the Bedells): the division was 8 to 7 in Black Hood House: unopposed in White Hood House . . . Wrote to little Bertha: – her letter much amused me – 'Baugh can say 40 French words & count up to 60 & can say a little fable & a little hymn all in French: he likes it very much. When we are good Mademoiselle gives us bonbons' . . .

Despite careful searches in the University Library volume 27 of the Diary has sadly never been found. We are therefore without entries between 4 March 1858 and 23 February 1859. However we can follow the course of University reform in two admirable chapters, 'The Statutory Commission and the University' and 'The Statutory Commissioners and Trinity College', in D.A. Winstanley's *Early Victorian Cambridge* which clarify a very complicated story.

Domestically, it is clear from the early entries for 1859 that Romilly had at last been obliged to leave the house in Scroope Terrace to which he was much attached, because his landlord, Mr Fawcett now wanted it for himself and his wife. The prospect of the move must have cast a shadow over some pages of the missing Diary but when it re- sumes Romilly and the devoted Harriet and Caroline appear to be living quite happily at 3 Benet Place which was no more than five minutes' walk from their former home. Benet Place was set a little back from Lensfield Road.

[25] Spencer Horatio Walpole, an original member of the Apostles Club, was to represent the University until his retirement from parliament in 1882.

[26] i.e. 'The Council recommend that upon every occasion the Deputation to be appointed to accompany the Chancellor in the presentation of the address should consist of the Vice- Chancellor, the Public Orator, the Proctors, and the Registrary, together with six other Members of the Senate to be nominated by the Vice-Chancellor.'

Engagements were still being fought between Trinity and the Statutory Commissioners during 1858, although basically the Commissioners wished the College well. On 26 October Whewell alleged at a packed five-hour meeting in the Arts School that the Commissioners intended to destroy the colleges; on 29 October Edward Bunbury suggested a small meeting in London and on 13 November Whewell, Martin, Lightfoot and Montagu Butler had an apparently amicable (unrecorded) meeting with the Commissioners. In December Butler and no less than 21 of the other younger Fellows wrote to the Commissioners and it was clear from the revised draft received by Romilly on 23 February 1859 that their views had been taken into account.

# 1859

*Wed. 23 February.* . . . Received from the Commissioners their new draft of Statutes for Trinity College: – this new code is less offensive, for it leaves the College to the management of the Master & Seniors (– saying nothing about that cumbrous democracy of the whole body of Fellows): – but it still proposes 6 Lecturers in the limited tenure of Fellowships,[1] – allows marriage in certain cases,[2] – & proposes that hateful scheme of having one day (*at least*) every year in wch all the body of Fellows shall meet & propound (if they please) objections & difficulties.[3] – Visit from Mathison (to ask questions about the Classical Tripos): I told him that the V.C. had behaved very kindly about his pupil Pomeroy (Lord Harbertson's son) & recommended stretching a point & allowing him to be a Candidate tho he has resided 10 terms (– 8 being the limit for Honorables who escape Little-Go)[4] . . .

*Mon. 28.* . . . Received a most touching letter from Sedgwick describing minutely all the closing scenes of his brother John's life & the admirable conduct of Isabella: – John Sedgwick died calmly & not in one of those dreadful paroxysms of neuralgia under wch he had been so long suffering . . . Sedgwick communicated one piece of good news: – the landowners unanimously offered Richard Sedgwick the incumbency of Dent & Richard has

[1]  The Commissioners proposed that every Fellow, whether clergyman or layman, should vacate his fellowship after ten years of M.A. standing unless he was a Professor, Public Lecturer, Registrary, Librarian, or Public Orator deriving from his office an income not exceeding £800 a year. In addition, a Tutor, Assistant Tutor or Bursar of at least two years' standing could retain his fellowship for as long as he retained his office.

[2]  The 'certain cases' were few, 'but they were more than enough for a society which desired to remain celibate' (Winstanley, p. 356).

[3]  The Commissioners at the end of May 1858 had sent Trinity a draft code of statutes. The most alarming of their suggestions had however already been made by Grote on 19 November 1857 and rejected by the Governing Body: 'We had a very long & animated debate on Grote's hateful & mischievous proposal of an annual meeting of all the Fellows on Commemoration day to propose amendments in the Statutes: – the Master, Sedgwick & Martin spoke warmly against it: – the proposal was negatived'.

[4]  The Hon. James Spencer Pomeroy was admitted pensioner at Trinity in 1855, and as such would not count as a nobleman for academic purposes. He was bracketed fourteenth in the first class in the 1859 Classical Tripos examination.

accepted it! – Richard had before declared his resolution of not taking it. – So Sedgwick will now be able to make a home as long as he lives of the parsonage in wch he was born . . . Sedgwick tells me that Isabella & her Mother will take a Cottage in Dent close to the Parsonage.

*Sat. 5 March.* Up at 7½ – No early walk . . . Walk to Railway Station (as I had no baggage) & then to London by Express 2d Class . . . My object in going to Town was to receive the unclaimed dividend on Mr Halfords gift of £2000 to the Library[5] . . . I then embarked on the Thames at London Bridge: the river is foully impure like the filthiest kennel, but I perceived no stench[6] . . . I then went to Westminster Bridge: – I did a little bit of novelty, I got into the Terrace of the Parliament House: I had it entirely to myself: – this view of the river shows all the dams etc for the new Bridge: they of course are not very attractive but I was desirous of seeing them.[7] The day being bright the steamers were full of passengers. – I then walked in St James Park which was all alive with thousands of men, women & children . . .

*Mon. 14.* Up at 7¼. – Rainy morning: – took books to be bound by way of early walk. – Grand meeting of Master & Fellows: Sedgwick & Moody were present: Martin & Edleston absent: the chief speakers were Moody, Munro, Butler, Lightfoot & Grote: our main discussion was on the great threatened grievance of restricted tenure of Fellowships: – the Master conducted the business most ably. We sat above 3 hours & are to have another meeting next Friday . . . Harriet works most strenuously both in the new house & the old: she today took down a great many books in the Library.

*Tu. 22.* Up at 7¼. – Walk in Botanic Garden. – Breakfasted with the Selwyns: we were party of 6, for besides Lord George Manners (here as foreman of the Grand Jury) there were 2 ladies no longer young, – one of whom I believe to be the Professor's maiden Sister . . . Superintended the hanging of the Pictures & Prints: this work was not over till 6½: – I went away for ½ hour for dinner: it was a very cheap one: it cost 6d: it was at Wrights the pastry cooks & consisted of 2 Sausage-rolls & 2 Cheesecakes . . . I feel most thankful to God for entering into my new house this day in good health & my servants also. They deserve all praise for their indefatigable exertions . . . I put up in the hall a series of College Views (– they had all been

[5]  He had given money in 1842 through trustees (of whom Romilly was one) towards the completion of the library. It had been transferred to the university in 1851, when it amounted to £2,648, and was still unspent. See Clark, *Endowments*, pp. 456-60.

[6]  The Thames Conservators began their duty of river purification imposed by the Thames Conservancy Act of 1857 amidst daunting difficulties. The river within their jurisdiction was in 'a foul and offensive state due to the enormous quantities of refuse and sewage passed through canals and sewers communicating with the Thames over which the Conservators had no control' (Thames Conservancy, *The Thames Conservancy 1857-1957*, 1959, p. 6). Charles Kingsley, writing on 7 July 1859 to Lord Robert Montagu asks him not 'to talk about the Thames. I have thought and written much on it some years since, but have given it up in despair. There is no adequate demand for the sewage. Till you can awaken the farmers, nothing can be done' (F.E. Kingsley, *Charles Kingsley* 1877, Vol. II, 92).

[7]  'The splendid iron bridge at Westminster was opened in 1860-2 after a long period of obstruction of the water-way by its half-ruined predecessor of 1750' (V.C.H., *Middlesex*, II, 1911, 125).

published as the University almanac):[8]– I did not complete my task – Gave Harriet & Caroline £1 each for their excellent service, especially Harriet.

*Fri. 25.* . . . Letter from Mr Bisset the Clergyman of Upholland telling me of poor Mrs Thomas Grounds (Susan Chune's) death: she had been confined to her bed for only a fortnight: her death was quite unexpected: her husband is very grievously affected: Mr B. speaks in his praise & calls him 'a very deserving fellow' . . . She is to be buried on Sunday. – Her husband is Mr Bisset's Sexton, & it is therefore his melancholy duty to dig his poor wife's grave . . . There was a meeting today of the Master & Fellows concerning the Commissioners Statutes & suggestions for several changes in them:[9]– we discussed a series of M.S. modifications drawn up by Butler (based on those printed by Grote): many of us signed most of them . . . I was agreeably surprised today by the arrival of the oil-cloth to match the Turkey carpet: – I had not expected it to come from town under a fortnight: – the need of sending for more arose from my present dining room being much longer than the late: it is a 3-window room while the other had only 2 . . .

*Mon. 28.* Up at 7¼. – Walk in Botanic Garden wch is now looking beautiful with the magnolias in full flower. – Much pleased with a letter from Mrs Fawcett saying that she is highly delighted at finding the Scrope-Terrace house so clean & in so excellent a state. – In my office I had a very long visit from Kingsley, who confesses himself altogether thrown out by the recent changes & came with a heap of questions.[10] He told me that he inherited a Chancery suit from his Father (who had been defrauded of the prodigious sum of £40,000): the suit had infinitely worried his father & cost him a large sum of money: – he threw all the papers into the fire & so relieved himself from the anxiety & expense of litigation . . . After lunch I called on old Mrs Hayward (my next door neighbour): I did not see her son and son in law, but I saw her grand daughter (the little maiden who broke her thigh by falling out of windows) . . . At ¼ past 7 I went to Mrs Prest's to play Quadrille: the players were Mrs P., Mrs Haviland, Mrs Hopkins & myself. There was one vole only: I plaid in it. I lost 1/6. – We plaid very late & I did not get home till 11½: there was an oyster supper of wch I partook. – Mrs Haviland amused me by saying that she had been nearly stifled with smothering smoke & poisoned with a stench of burning from a neighbouring house: – the Shilletos have been burning all their old clothes!!! . . . I wrote today to Edward to tell him to ask

[8]  *The University Almanac*, a single sheet calendar, was published annually and framed by lists of University Officers, Heads of Houses, Professors and teachers of languages etc. Some of the admirably drawn large prints by Bradford Rudge at the head of the calendars can be seen in the incomplete series in the Map Room of the University Library.

[9]  The Governing Body met four times during March and Whewell was before long 'able to send to the Commissioners batches of protests against several of the statutes, of which many, if not all, bore the signatures of at least half' its members (Winstanley, p. 366).

[10]  Palmerston's letter asking Kingsley to accept the Regius chair of Modern History was not to arrive until 9 May, but Kingsley had presumably known for some time that some of his friends wished to see him in the vacant chair. He may well have wanted information about its duties as well as clarification of the 'recent changes'. The Chancery suit refers to the fact that his father was orphaned and his fortune squandered during his minority. See F.E. Kingsley, *Charles Kingsley*, (1877) p. 3.

his tutor to rectify an error in the Little-Go List about himself: – he is printed without the + indicating a Candidate for Honors.

*Tu. 29.* . . . Letter from Mary Anne Tyler: she is in great trouble: the late Mr King (the Solicitor) had lent her Father £20 (he paying £1 a year for interest): – Mr Tyler has paid off £5, & last night received a letter from Mr King's Executor threatening legal proceedings if the remaining sum of £15 & the accumulated interest of £1 6s. 3d is not paid immediately. – I called on M.A.T. & gave her a cheque for £16.6.3: – both she & her Mother burst into tears. But I spoke cheerfully to them & said I was very happy to help them out of their trouble. I saw Mr Tyler, who seemed to me better. – M.A. was sitting in a close hot room by the fire & looked very ill: her hand felt to me hot & feverish, but her Mother said she was cold: – she was drinking hot brandy & water! – I of course prescribed air & exercise to her. – Her brother (who kept the shop in the Petty-Cury) is gone to try & better himself in America . . . Letter from Thomas Grounds acknowledging my present: he says he is not well & that little Lucy frets very much . . .

*Wed. 30.* . . . A College meeting from 1½ to ¼ to 4: our principal matter was executing the Sheepshanks endowment,[11] for wch purpose Airy (the Astronomer Royal) was present: he & Trin. Coll. are Trustees of the endowment. An application was made by the Observatory syndicate for a grant of £100 for 2 computers to reduce the observations at the Cambridge Observatory (the Meridial observations of the last 17 years are still unreduced): we had a long discussion of the written answer brought by Airy for our approval: it agreed to the grant for this one occasion, but suggested Challis' entirely suspending his observations & using all the force of the Observatory assistants in reducing the old observations: – I entirely disapproved this censure of Challis's mode of proceeding & it was withdrawn.

*Th. 31.* . . . A very warmhearted letter from M.A. Tyler saying how happy they were made: I wrote a few lines in reply & was my own postman: I was glad to find her gone out for a walk . . . Congregation day: 2AM, 1 LLM, 1 LLB, 1 ad eundem & 16 ABs . . .

*Sun. 3 April.* . . . Dr Leapingwell has a Romanist friend (if not pupil) who wanted to be entered at Trinity under the condition of not attending Chapel:[12]– Mathison declined accepting him: – Mrs L. had some talk with Whewell on the matter & pronounces him devoid of all liberality: – I believe she will think no better of me, for I told her that I thought it a disadvantage & a difficulty receiving Romanist pupils who refused to attend Chapel: – that I had never before heard of any of the R.C.'s who have been at College refusing to attend

[11] For details of the Richard and Anne Sheepshanks benefaction 1859, Richard having died in 1855, see pp. 131-6 in Clark, *Endowments*. For the Sheepshanks Exhibition see 27 January 1860.

[12] The unnamed man was undoubtedly Sir Rowland Blennerhasset, an Irish baronet educated at Downside and Stonyhurst, admitted at Christ's aged 19 on 29 April 1859. He kept only a term before migrating to Oxford and thence to the continent where he earned a doctorate 'with special distinction' at Louvain. He later became a friend of Lord Acton and a liberal Roman Catholic M.P. See *D.N.B.* Some of his papers are in the University Library (MSS Add. 4989 ff. 192-3).

Chapel, – it of course not being asked that they should attend Sacrament & they being allowed to attend mass . . . The youth applied to Emmanuel College & (of course) Archdall refused him: – At Christs College he has been accepted by Cartmell . . .

*Wed. 6.* . . . Letter from Mr Johns (of Callippers Hall Rickmansworth asking about Sizarships:[13] his brother in-law is just dead (in the vigour of life, – quite suddenly), leaving 9 children, the eldest of 18 years, the youngest of 10 days. – I got out Martins statistics about the Sizars of Trinity & St Johns (wch show the former to be most valuable & the most easily attainable as there are 16 Foundation sizarships (worth near £50 p.a) at Trin. & only 9 Proper Sizars at St Johns) . . . Visit from Selwyn & his brother the Commissary: I agreed to breakfast at Vine Cottage tomorrow: – by the way Selwyn has had the wall facing Coe-fen prettily painted to look like Trellis work . . .

*Th. 7.* . . . Received a long letter from Mathison answering all my questions about Sizars: – he thinks the *necessary* expenses of a Sizar are £53, & that the *actual* expense of a careful Sizar ought not to exceed £100 a year: – the Sizar receives £50 or more for his sizarship, & every time he is in the 1st Class a prize of £25: – so that the clever sizar costs his family not more than £25 p.a. . . .

*Th. 14.* Up at 7. – Walk in Peterhouse Grove . . . Fell in with Dr & Mrs Cookson: they consulted me about a quarrel they had had: – should their little girl (aged 3) be allowed to say 'bless it!' to a worm?. – I said 'certainly': – it was encouraging a kind feeling to what was one of God's creatures: – & besides it was good to teach her not to be disgusted with or afraid of creeping things or any kind of animal: – my view quite agreed with Mrs Cookson's . . .

*Fri. 15.* . . . Received from the Commissioners a copy of their new Statutes for Trin: College. – Visit from Geo. Williams of Kings . . . I showed him our new Statutes. They have not received theirs at Kings: but he says they had a bad case to start with, & had given every possible explanation: he seems to think there will be no great difficulty in accepting the Commissioners statutes[14] . . .

*Sat. 16.* . . . More enquiries from C.H. Cooper: – it cost me a long time to answer them: I shall never want something to do as long as his Athenae Cantab. is going on. – Met a little boy crying close to the Hospital . . . I stopt him to ask what was the matter: 'O, said his Mother, he is crying for a book he has just seen': – 'let's have a look at the book', said I: – so we walked back & he pointed out to me the object of his longing: it was a coloured alphabet, beginning with '*A* was Aladdin with his wonderful lamp': – I made the urchin happy at the small cost of 6d. – The Little-Go came out this morning: of course Edward Romilly & Walsham were in the 1st Class: that idle vagabond Shilleto

---

[13] Sizarships were awarded on grounds of financial need. Sizars came to work and if they were clever to compete for fellowships. They were no longer much distinguished from wealthier undergraduates and had no menial duties, but they were allocated inferior rooms. See W. Everett *On the Cam* (1867) p. 28.

[14] The Commissioners commended King's for its 'candid and friendly disposition'. See *Letter Books of the Commissioners*, I, 338-40.

(of Christ's) was plucked again, – being his 3d time . . . After dinner did pasting work.

*Mon. 18.* Up at 7. – Walk in Botanic Garden. – Read in the Times an abstract of the Novel called 'Adam Bede': it is written by a person calling himself 'George Eliot': – it is however doubtful whether that is not a 'nom de Guerre' . . . 'The Times' praises this new work most highly[15] . . . As I was coming home to lunch I fell in with Miss Apthorp & Mrs Parry: I brought them back & exhibited the house to them: – Mrs Parry astonished me by never having heard the word 'blue-stocking' & by gravely answering to my expression of dislike of blue-stocking ladies, 'I think no ladies wear blue stockings, – they wear pink'![16] . . . My garden (wch consisted of a large turf with only one oval plot for flowers) was today begun to be laid out as a nice flower garden . . .

*Tu. 19.* . . . Visit from Sedgwick: he was in good health: he showed me 2 very interesting letters from Isabel & from Mrs Guthrie (born Clarke) . . . Mrs Guthrie's was full of warm affection & spritely playfulness: – she says 'talk as they will they never can drive the old Adam out of me'. She says that Sedgwicks residence at Norwich was to her Paradise where she walked with Adam[17] . . . Received from the Vicechancellor my quarters salary & my Clerks

|  | £ | s | d |
|---|---|---|---|
| Own Salary | 100 | - | - |
| Clerk's | 7 | 10 | - |
|  | 107 | 10 |  |

[15] *Adam Bede*, published by Blackwood on 1 February 1859, became a sensational success, the Russian translation alone going through three editions in the same year. *The Times* review by E.S. Dallas on 12 April filled three columns and declared 'that its author takes rank at once among the masters of the art'. It surmised that the author 'must be a lady, since none but a woman's hand could have painted those touching scenes of clerical life . . . can this be a young author?. . . If it is, the hand must be extrordinarily cunning, and the genius must be of the highest order.'

[16] It was Romilly who was out of date. As De Quincey wrote in 1858 'the order of ladies called Bluestockings, by way of reproach, has become totally extinct among us'. (Autobiographic Sketches in *Works* (1862) XIII, 353, note).

[17] For Caroline Clarke's walks with Adam see *Romilly 1832-42*, pp. 96-9. Sedgwick had lost his heart to the 21-year old whilst residing as Prebendary of Norwich in January 1836. In March he invited her and her brother-in-law to Cambridge where Romilly found 'the brilliant "young person" (as she sometimes calls herself) sparkling with joy'. During her six day visit 'Carissima', as Sedgwick called her, charmed the ladies she met as well as Fellows of Trinity, and she allowed Romilly to kiss her 'with the best grace possible' after he had given her a framed print of King's Chapel. 'The departure of so fascinating a creature has left a sad blank in our existence' (14 March). For examples of informality in entertaining ladies see M.E. Bury, 'Early Victorian Ladies in Cambridge', *Cambridge* 33 (1993-4), pp. 49-55. In a letter written a quarter of a century later Sedgwick describes Mrs Guthrie 'once the bright, pretty and rather eccentric Caroline Clarke of Norwich' as 'one of the best and most benevolent of womankind . . . For practical good I never knew her match' (Clark and Hughes, II, 372). The editors, however, deprived of direct experience of her charms, have reluctantly concluded from her many letters, summarised by Romilly, that her admiration of her own skills and benevolence is in no way inferior to that of her admirers.

| Deduct Income Tax | 4 | 9 | 7 |
| --- | --- | --- | --- |
| | £103 | - | 5 | - (Paid by V.C.)

So every alternate quarter I shall receive the amount diminished by Income Tax.

*Good Friday 22.* . . . A grand staff of Clergymen at Christ Church . . . The great preacher Spurgeon preached twice today in St Andrews Chapel, but I did not go to hear him. – I took a long crawling walk & was out nearly 3 hours: I went to Cherry Hinton by the cross-road running from the Via Lambertina & returned by the fields: – I met hundreds of children with their hands full of Pagles (Cowslips) . . .

*Fri. 29.* . . . I sent off the Return (to Charles Romilly Clerk of the Crown) by the midday mail . . . Today was the Town Election: – I did not vote: Macaulay 753 votes & Stewart 750 were elected. – The Votes for Twiselton were 682; for Mowatt 669. – I declined dining in Hall to do the Honors to Walpole & Selwyn for I should have had to preside & make speeches.[18] – Cooper acted Vicemaster . . .

*Sun. 1 May.* Up at 7. – Walk as usual to Railway bridge – Wrote to Bailey (sending him £1) . . . Most importunate letter from Mrs Percy (Caroline Carnaby): sent her £2 & declared that positively I will never answer another letter: – poor thing! she has been making soldiers shirts at 5d a piece . . . Went to St Mary's & heard an excellent sermon from Professor Browne: His sermon (like all other Sermons today) was one of Thanksgiving:[19] His Text was Job. XXXIV. 29 'When He giveth quietness who then can make trouble?' . . . He in the conclusion contrasted Spains fall in the scale of Nations after the acquisition of America with the rise of England after the acquisition of India: – Spain had not sanctified her conquest by her conduct to America, neither had we (with our purer form of Christianity) either set the moral example or given the Christian teaching to India which we ought . . .

*Mon. 2.* . . . Walk in Botanic Garden – the Goat has 2 lovely little kids, just a week old. – Looked over 3 sets of Scholarship Papers (viz. Thucydides, Cicero & Horace) . . . The Streets swarming with May lords & ladies, & the air disturbed by the horn blowing: – as usual I distributed 24 halfpence among the poor children. Paper of queries from Mr Cooper, wch I answered as well as I could.

*Th. 5.* . . . At 6½ to Trinity Lodge to tea . . . We proceeded after tea to the Election of 19 Scholars: we chose 13 from the upper year: among those were Sir George Young & Macfarlan (old George's son): – among the 6 of the lower year were Hubert Airy & Aldis[20] the Mathematician: Hodson voted

---

[18] S.H. Walpole had offered himself for re-election after his appointment as Secretary of State for the Home Department. He and C.J. Selwyn, Commissary to the University 1855-58, were both returned unopposed as members for the University.

[19] i.e. a General Thanksgiving by 'Her Majesty's Special Command for the Successes granted to our Arms in suppressing the Rebellion and restoring Tranquillity in Her Majesty's Indian Dominions'. For the form of service see UP 28 no 745.

[20] W.S. Aldis went on to become first Smith's Prizeman and Senior Wrangler in 1861. An authority on optics and solid geometry, he was also a leading advocate of the higher education of women.

against him as not of the Church of England (– his Father is a Baptist): Hodson was in a minority of one: he said our new Statutes would sweep away all Church distinctions & this was the last opportunity of making a stand . . . Mathison had 14 of the Scholars, Clark 2, Lightfoot 3.

*Fri. 6.* . . . Today there was an enthusiastic meeting in the Townhall for the formation of a Rifle Club: the Mayor presided, the V.C. proposed the 1st Resolution.[21] – Paget proposed the 2d: he mentioned having many years ago arrived at Bonne just after the decision of the Prize for Rifle-shooting: – it was won by a student of the University, – a German Prince, – our present Chancellor.[22] – I did not go to this meeting: but it was eminently successful, & a prodigious fighting spirit was exhibited: – Emery of Corpus is one of the great movers . . . Mrs Leapingwell tells me that her husband is a 1st rate shot.

*Sat. 7.* Up at 7. – Walk in the Botanic Garden – Letter from George Romilly communicating the agreeable tidings that (thro the exertions of his friend Maclean) he has got transferred to the Tower, where his work will be much less severe: – he will not now be obliged to move, & he will be able to send Franky to the School on wch he had set his heart. He will be allowed 5 weeks holiday . . . We then had a Seniority for Bursarial business: – the Master communicated to us that he is going to build a pile opposite Trinity great gate wch will contain 60 or 70 sets of rooms: it will be begun immediately & is to be completed in 18 months[23] . . .

*Mon. 9.* . . . Before breakfast I was introduced to the Bishop & Mrs Tait: I was much pleased with both of them: he looks like the earnest indefatigable man that he is: she is a fine woman on a large scale . . . At my office I was employed about Supplicats of 1636.

*Tu. 10.* Up at 7. – Walk to the Office, from wch I brought away some books: they were so heavy that when I got into Tenniscourt Road I put ½ of them on the ground & walked on with the others for about 100 yards, I then put those on the ground & went back & picked up the others, & so on till I brought them all safely to the house . . . At 11 to a Seniority: it appears that

---

[21] Strains placed on the regular army after the Mutiny and worsening relations with France led to calls for volunteer corps, and before official plans were settled the formation of a local rifle club was mooted by Robert Potts of Trinity and William Emery, tutor of Corpus Christi. When 400 signatures from town and gown had been obtained the Mayor called this meeting which Bateson, who had initial doubts, attended as Vice-Chancellor. The demands of such a corps on time and money made it a middle-class affair, and it was well suited to young and fit students, while their seniors had been assured by the Oxford authorities that it would reduce idleness and divert money from 'amusements, dress, etc.'. See H. Strachan, *History of the Cambridge University Officer Training Corps* (1976), pp. 10-23.

[22] Prince Albert and his elder brother Ernest studied at Bonn University for eighteen months in 1837-8. Despite being an excellent shot, he often said he could never understand people 'making a business of shooting and going out for the whole day'.

[23] The 'pile' contained no less than 100 sets of rooms and Whewell's foresight in buying land opposite the Great Gate meant that Trinity was saved from building on the Backs in later years. 'His gifts and bequests to the College in connection with Whewell's Court were of the value of £100,000 . . . Part of the room rents he left to maintain the Whewell Professorship of International Law, part to found scholarships' (G.M. Trevelyan, *Trinity College, an Historical Sketch*, revised ed., 1972, p. 101). (See 26 May 1860 and 10 March 1863).

our Hall is inconveniently filled on *Sundays* with resident members of other colleges: Martin proposed issuing a recommendation to the Fellows 'to use *sparingly* on the Sunday, especially in the Easter Term, the privilege of bringing in guests 'who are of other Colleges': – the proposal occasioned some warm sparring between Martin, Grote & Cope . . . At 2 to the Senate House to hear that great man Owen's lecture on Mammalia:[24] I had never seen him before, & took great interest in his Lecture: he closed it with a simple exhortation to the young men not to neglect the cultivation of their intellect as they belonged to the highest class of Gods organised creatures . . .

*Wed. 11.* . . . Mr Dennis tells me that Mr Mortlock has left an immense fortune, £330,000! every farthing goes to his nephew John (who was junior partner in the Bank & is now the sole head): – there are no legacies, not even to servants . . .

*Sun. 15.* . . . To my delight I found today my Fathers M.S. 'Thoughts on death': they are dated 1814 . . . the M.S. is in my Father's beautifully clear hand: it consists entirely of extracts from different authors (Latin, Spanish etc) . . . My father never recovered from the grief at my Mother's death tho he survived her 25 years . . .

*Mon. 23.* . . . In my office I had a visit from John Roget & his Mother's brother Mr Hobson: they were going to dine at Magdalene. – Roget's arrival is in consequence of Macmillan's telling him that a 2d Edition of his 'Mathematical sketches'[25] is called for . . . Lunched at 1 at Magdalene Lodge: we were a party of 7, viz Latimer & his wife & his eldest little boy Henry (whose dinner it was), a Mr & Mrs Rowsell & the governess (Miss Packe) & myself . . . The Governess is an elegant gentle young person (seemingly about 18) & I was much pleased with her . . . Latimer has named his 2 boys from his poor brothers[26] who were killed in the Crimea . . .

*Th. 26.* . . . Called upon for my Rifle Club Subscription £1.11.6 (whereof 10s 0d. is entrance money) . . . Congregation Day . . . there were also 10 un-opposed Graces; one of them was for allowing men who began residence in

---

[24] Sir Robert Rede, Fellow of King's Hall (later part of Trinity) and chief justice of the common pleas (d.1519) had founded three lectures in humanity, logic, and philosophy, which had not been given for many years. In 1858 the endowment was reorganised by statute and the first new annual lecture was given by Richard Owen 'On the classification and geographical distribution of the mammalia'. See *Endowments* pp. 261-8, and the *Historical Register*, p.148 for a list of lecturers and their subjects. The *Chronicle* of 14 May reported 'a large audience including many ladies and strangers . . . The graceful flow of the Professor's language and the felicity of his illustrations were hardly less admirable than the perfect possession of his subject'.

[25] i.e. *A Cambridge Scrap-book with an Appendix of Papers on Applied Mathematics* (Cambridge, Macmillan, 1859). The fifteen 'papers' contain 'upwards of one hundred and thirty familiar illustrations of The Language of Mathematics . . . hitherto considered beyond the reach of the Senate-House Examination'. There are nine or ten delightful drawings on each page. A householder illustrates 'Elimination of an Unknown Quantity' by kicking an intruder down his steps; two urchins abuse each other in 'Vulgar Fractions Reduced to their Lowest Terms'; and 'Extraction of a Root' shows a dentist and his victim in the chair. See pp. 21, 25, 27. *Familiar Illustrations of the Languages of Mathematics* was first published in 1850.

[26] i.e. Henry killed at Inkerman 5 November 1854; Grey died of wounds 11 November 1854.

Lent 1857 to go in to the approaching June B.A. Examination tho they will not have entered on their *9th term* (wch was the rule).[27] Today a novelty: – the 1st instance of an AM who wrote his name on the 'Non-declarant' line: the man was Okely (who went over to the Church of Rome):[28] he was Travelling Bachelor in 1855. – After dinner read Nicholas Nickleby in the Garden for an hour . . .

*Fri. 27.* . . . Seniority for 2 hours: – Lord Monteagle & other admirers of Tennyson have offered a bust of the Laureat to Trin. Coll:[29]– we had a good deal of discussion on the matter: Edleston was strongly for accepting it, saying that we had memorials of other living men, viz a bust of Bishop Thirlwall, a picture of Sedgwick & an engraving of Le Bas: the Master, myself, Martin, Mathison & King were strongly opposed . . . it was suggested that it should be given to Tennyson himself on the understanding that after his death the College would accept it . . . Mathison expressed strong disapprobation of the tendency of Tennyson's poetry, & King (who is always violent) spoke in abomination of it . . .

*Sat. 28.* . . . At 1½ Grim arrived with little Bertha; I was delighted to receive them: they were very flourishing except that Bertha has a slight cough: – she has been staying in a state of isolation with Mrs Houghton because poor Miss Darquet (her Governess) is laid up with scarlet fever at George Allen's[30] . . .

*Mon. 30.* Up at 7. – Walk in B.G. – Breakfast at 8½. – Heard Bertha read French, wch she does very nicely indeed. – Gave her a new Shilling, a beautiful little Wedgwoodware box (wch Harriet had put on her chimney piece & told me she admired greatly): the Cambridge red-line prayerbook[31] & a 3 Vol. story called 'Bertha's visit to her Uncle'. – It was very fortunate that I had the power of making her so appropriate a present. – Bertha passed the day at home with her little playfellow Miss Pullen . . . Grim & I called on Walton . . . We went (according to direction) to what used to be the Philo-

---

[27] Hitherto although the statutes only required a poll-man to reside for nine terms before proceeding to his ordinary B.A. degree, in practice, as the examinations were held in the Michaelmas or Lent terms, he had to reside for a tenth term. When, however, in 1858 the Senate approved the taking of the ordinary degree examination in June (as from 1859) candidates were able to go down after nine terms.

[28] The Cambridge University Bill passed by Parliament in 1856 allowed all degrees, except for those in divinity, to be taken without a declaration of faith being made. However no Dissenting M.A. could take part in the government of the University by becoming a member of the Senate.

[29] With his bust of Tennyson of 1857 Woolner, an original member of the Pre-Raphaelites, established a national reputation. He soon cornered the market in busts of Trinity men, viz. Sedgwick, Hare, Henslow, and Kemble between 1860 and 1865, and others later. 'Maud' (1855) had been received by a shocked public with violent antagonism, the unbalanced narrator of the poem being mistakenly thought to be the poet himself.

[30] Scarlet fever in Romilly's day was a common cause of death in children, and Paget told him that it was 'the most dangerous of all diseases except Asiatic cholera' (17 February 1854).

[31] In his entry for 8 July 1835 Romilly had written, 'In this Bible is introduced for the first time a new mechanical process by Parker [the university printer] for introducing red lines which used formerly to be ruled by hand'. Red-lining was also used in other liturgical books such as hymn books and prayerbooks.

sophical Reading Room & there found him with 4 pupils:[32]– he came out & had a chat with us: he seemed heartily glad to see his old pupil Grim. – I of course asked him to dine with us: – but he couldn't. – We then went to Caius to see the Hall & Combination room: we found there A.G. Day examining a class: – he acted the part of Cicerone to us . . . The children got on famously together all day. – After dinner a 'Happy Family' caravan came before the house & we all went out to see the animals: – I several times begged the man not to poke the animals. – Grim & I after dessert smoked a Cigar & I then begged him to read something out of Dickens: – he selected Pickwicks trial for breach of promise of marriage: he read it capitally: – he tells me that Dickens himself often selects it for public reading. – At ¼ to 7 sent Miss Pullen home under Harriet's escort. – I accompanied Grim & Bertha to the Station . . .

*Wed. 1 June.* . . . The New system of the Polloi Examination in June began today: – there are 188 Candidates.[33] – In my office I employed myself in verifying their Matriculations and Little-Gos . . . Drank tea with the Henslows: – the young Ladies invited me for a snug party with themselves alone: but . . . their Father was of the party . . . After tea I was asked to write in a book kept for that purpose answers to 10 Queries: viz.

(1) Favorite Virtue – (2) Favorite Historical Character
(3) Most hated Historical Character – (4) Favorite Flower
(5) Favorite Prose writer – (6) Favorite Poet
(7) Favorite Food – (8) Favorite Employment
(9) Favorite Motto – (10) Idea of highest happiness

I wrote down (1) Gentleness – (2) Lady Jane Grey – (3) King John – (4) Rose – (5) Walter Scott – (6) Shakespeare – (7) Mutton (8) – Talking with young ladies – (9) Persevere – (10) Loving wife & 10 children . . . An agitation is being made by Edleston, Grote etc to reconsider the Seniority's refusal to accept the bust of Tennyson: – the paper was sent to me today, but I declined eating my own words & refused to sign it.

*Mon. 6.* . . . Seniority at 11: then at 12 a meeting of the Governing Body concerning the New Statutes: – we have now got the required proportion of ²/₃ to protest against 4 of the Commissioners' Statutes, viz the 7th (concerning the Vicemaster) the 18th (concerning tenure of Fellowships) the 20th (concerning Livings), & the 35th (concerning the Audit)[34] . . .

---

[32] The Philosophical Society moved from Sidney Street in 1833 to a house specially built for it at the corner of All Saints' Passage. Walton must have lived in the Sidney Street house opposite to Jesus Lane. See E. Leedham-Green *A Concise History of the University of Cambridge* (1996), p. 140.

[33] See 26 May 1859.

[34] The Commissioners had sent revised statutes to the College on 12 April. A simple majority of the society was no longer a sufficient protest against a statute and Romilly had been anxious when some of the younger Fellows had refused to vote against the 18th and 20th statutes. However a very narrow two-thirds majority, against which the Commissioners were powerless, was eventually achieved, and on 10 June Whewell sent the four protests to the Commissioners. The 7th statute concerned the appointment of a deputy for the Vice-Master and the 35th the undesirability of the College being represented only by the Master at the annual audit.

*Th. 9.* . . . Congregation day: – several undisputed graces: the degrees were 1 DD of Dignity (Campbell Bishop of Bangor), 1 MD, 15 MA, & 2 MAs *in their absence.* These last degrees are a grand novelty in our Cambridge system: these today were the 1st degrees so conferred: – the parties were Kempson of Caius & Kendall of St Johns: one teaches a school in India, the other is Professor at Toronto . . . A visit in College from M.A. Tyler: – her brother is safely arrived in America . . . She is under the care of Dr Bayes the homeopathist, who prescribes air & exercise . . .

*Tu. 14.* . . . At 1.20 started with Paget, France & the 2 Powers to spend the day at Denver with Stokes. We arrived at Denver Station at 3 o'clock & found Stokes waiting for us with a couple of one-horse open carriages . . . After lunch Stokes took us out in the 2 open carriages (one of wch he drove himself) to see some beautifully restored Churches. We drove thro the tidy little town of Downham Market to Wimbotsham: it belongs to Mr Dashwood, who has the high-church feeling very strongly & has introduced a stone altar, a credence table, piscina etc:[35] he has built a beautiful Apse to this church: – there is painted glass & every embellishment: – there is a good ancient Norman door-way. – We then drove on to Mr Dashwoods other living Stow-Bardolph . . . it has a large side-chapel full of monuments of the Hare Family, & in a closet is carefully preserved a figure of an elderly lady a Miss Hare: the figure is dressed & the face is of wax (wch is now become sufficiently yellow): if Miss Hare was like her wax figure I am not surprised that she remained unmarried . . .

*Sun. 19.* Up at 7. – Walk to College. – At Barnwell a strange deacon read prayers very well. Mr Titcomb preached a farewell Sermon[36] . . . he spoke of having been 14 years among them & his fears that many had no vital religion: – he spoke with gratitude of the help that he had had in 150 School-teachers, & also praised the district-visitors,[37] but lamented that one very difficult district had had no visitor for the last 18 months . . .

[35] Presumably Dashwood's altar had been officially approved, but it is curious that Romilly makes no reference to the cause célèbre of the Cambridge Camden Society's restoration of the Round Church in 1844-5. See 23 July 1849.

[36] Titcomb was presented with a testimonial on 20 June. 'Perhaps no minister has had greater difficulties to contend against, greater demands upon his time and exertion . . . If the word "Barnwell" has not ceased entirely under his ministry to be "a bye-word and a reproach" at any rate much that was glaring has been removed, and decency and order have begun to predominate over immorality' (*Chronicle*, 25 June).

[37] The General Society for the Promotion of District Visiting had been established in 1828 and was widely supported. Many of its lay middle-class members, especially women, visited the poor and sick to whom they gave tickets for relief in kind from local tradesmen.

The inauguration of the Duke of Devonshire as Chancellor of the University of Devonshire House, 1862

*Mon. 20.* . . . Today we conferred the degree of LLD Honoris causa on that admirable man Sir John Lawrence Bart K.C.B.[38] I was most happy in being introduced to him. He was received with the enthusiasm he so well deserves . . . A great deal of worrying work in my office about certificates for Creation & Vote: – I got sadly waspish with a dull slow Mr Harker of Catharine: (to whom I had written fully explaining every thing about replacing his name & paying arrears etc etc): – I expressed angry surprise at his not knowing who the Vicechancellor was: – wch perhaps was as unreasonable on my part as it would have been in him to scout me for not knowing who is the Squire of his parish or his churchwarden . . .

*Tu. 21.* Up at 7. – Walk to St Catharine College to seek out Mr Harker . . . I told him I was come to apologise for the harshness of my reception of him yesterday Evening . . . Mr Harker said that he had been nearly killed by over-work in the great parish of St Barnabas Kennington: he has now the small living of Pulloxhill (near Ampthill) . . .

*Wed. 22.* . . . Edleston bought the 2 lots at Dawson Turner's sale:[39] he gave 84 Guineas for that containing 13 M.S. letters of Newton: – the British Museum very reluctantly gave way to him. – The eldest son of Sir — Eardley of Trinity called on me about a degree by Royal descent:[40] I asked him from what King & he said 'Edward VI': – I said 'No, that can't be for Edw. VI was never married'. – 'Then it was from Edw. IV': – I told him that I expected he would find it was from Edw. III: – he however broke down in his case from not being the grandson of a peer: – he is *great* grandson of a peer . . .

On 24 June Romilly left Cambridge for Norwich reading *Uncle Tom's Cabin* all the way. He found Sedgwick's nephew Richard, who with his family was soon to leave the incumbency of St Giles, Norwich for the family living of Dent in Yorkshire, still under his uncle's roof. As usual during Romilly's visits Sedgwick gave a 'magnificent' dinner party, this time for 16 people and then in the evening there was a large accession of ladies and the cathedral choristers so that 'it was a complete musical party'. Four days later Romilly, having been misinformed, arrived at the station three hours too soon for his train to Yarmouth. 'So I went and planted myself on the steps of the very pretty new Church (in the Norman stile) of St Matthew . . . & read "Guide to Yarmouth".' He put up in a handsome new Hotel called "the Victoria" and found its surroundings 'improved on a scale of great magnificence since my last visit'. Needless to say,

---

[38] Indian administrator who for his services during the mutiny had already received an annuity, a baronetcy, the freedom of the city of London and the degree of D.C.L. from Oxford.

[39] This banker and antiquary died in 1858 and his collection of many thousand autograph letters was sold the following June.

[40] Young Eardley had entered Trinity in March 1858 and the object of his visit was presumably to inquire how he might gain a degree without examination (see note on 29 January 1857). He had no doubt heard that the Elizabethan statutes allowed grandsons of peers and others to be excused such ordeals. As Romilly explained, he did not qualify as the *great* grandson of a peer, Lord Eardley, but he eventually solved the problem by not graduating. One ordeal in later life he could not however escape. In 1867 he was sentenced to eighteen months' hard labour for bigamy and granted a free pardon in 1868. The statute repealing the old privileges of 'nobiles and tanquam nobiles' was sealed on 24 March 1858 though it reserved the rights of those entered at any college before that date.

Romilly found himself amongst people he knew within a few hours of his arrival. 'On the pier I was spoken to by my neighbour Mrs Edleston who told me that Mr and Mrs George (her niece and nephew in law) had come from Norwich in the same carriage with me. – I was also accosted by Charles Lestourgeon who was walking with a Trinity man named Hurst: – Mr R.H. Hurst is very musical and was a great friend of Prof. Walmesley's. – I went home with Mr & Mrs Lestourgeon & their 3 children . . . to tea. Miss Mary sang in a horrid screaming voice "Angels ever bright & fair"'. Hamnett Holditch, Senior Wrangler in 1822 and Fellow of Caius, was also staying at the *Victoria* and despite his notorious shyness 'immediately came up and spoke to me . . . of his having voted for me in 1832' when Romilly was a candidate for the office of Registrary, 'and said that a non-resident was in want of a gown to vote in & that I stript off mine & said "O take mine & my coat too if you want it"'.

Romilly bathed every day, explored the town thoroughly, transcribed an epitaph that particularly pleased him in the churchyard of St Nicholas

'When shall we meet? when time is o'er
And sorrow past & pain
Where shall we meet? God grant in Heaven,
Never to part again'.

and on his last day 'went & lay down on the sand close to the Britannia Pier to listen to the Band: – the Band of the East Norfolk Rifles plays there, as the Band of the Louth Rifles plays on my pier (the Wellington): – it was a delicious Evening, the pleasantest since I have been here: & I found it very delightful listening to the Music & looking at the calm sea studded with vessels'.

*Tu. 5 July.* I was exceedingly sorry on reaching home to find that poor Harriet is very ill with quinsy: she was taken the very night she wrote to me: – she is attended by Mr Temple: – I afterwards saw Mr Temple: he thinks that her illness has taken a turn & that she will be much better in a few days: – in the mean time she suffers very sadly . . .

*Sat. 16.* (hotter than ever) Up at 7. – Walk in Botanic Garden. – Still worked at the Professors' drawer – While locked in my office after lunch (& in the dishabille of no coat, waistcoat or trousers) a female voice called admission. – I told her I could not see her & asked who she was: she answered 'Me', – with wch answer I was satisfied tho it gave me no information. – Poor Harriet Sandfields mother died this Evening: she never rallied at all, & was insensible to the end. – I hear that Mrs Kingsley is dead, – after 10 days illness: it is feared that it is Kingsley's wife & not his Mother:[41]– it will be very dreadful if it is so: they had been married only a few weeks & had been engaged for very many years . . .

*Sun. 17.* . . . It is but too true that it is Kingsley's wife & not his Mother that is dead . . . Took a volume of Miss Martineau's Political Economy tales in my pocket & went to Coe fen & lay down in the shade of a tree & read. –

[41] W.T. Kingsley, late Fellow of Sidney Sussex, and his fiancée, had presumably waited to marry until he secured a College living. Long and frustrating waiting for college livings was by no means uncommon, but, as Romilly wrote in UP 28 (no. 860) 'This was a sad calamity: the lady had been married about 3 weeks after an engagement of about 17 or 18 years: – she was the daughter of the late Mr Wilkins the Architect'. See 12 February 1857.

There were shoals of naked bathers on the banks besides the shoals in the water.[42] – After dinner went into the garden & read 3 sermons of Swifts.

*Sat. 23.* . . . Got 'Adam Bede' (from Woottons Circulating Library) after dinner today: – I read the 1st vol. thro before going to bed: – I think it a work of great genius. – I found it too cold to drink tea in the garden . . .

*Fri. 29.* . . . They are laying down at Cambridge an electric wire under ground,[43] – as of course they could not erect posts in the street: – It is very interesting to see the work: the electric wire is inside of a thin cable & is coiled round a huge cylinder: when taken from the cylinder it is enclosed in a wooden case . . .

*Sun. 7 August.* . . . I went to the afternoon lecture to the School-children by Mr Robinson: this was his 1st Sermon to the children & I thought it capitally good: there is something very winning about Mr Robinson: he looks the personification of gentleness: his voice is sweet & cheerful, & his manner very earnest: he impresses one with the idea of great piety & great amiability . . . The Church was intensely full. – I fell in with a camp meeting on Jesus Common:[44] I was too late for the sermon: but I heard 10 or 12 men in a cart sing a hymn without any instrumental accompaniment: I thought they did it exceedingly well . . . there seemed to me to be above 150 people collected . . . Found sown up in the waistband of my black trousers 4 half sovereigns!!!!

On the following day Romilly left Cambridge on the first stage of his journey to Grim's vicarage at Millom in Cumberland. He met members of his family at the Athenæum, heard their news and was amused by a 'dairymaids joke "What is the difference between a Cow and a rickety Chair?" – Ans. "One gives milk – the other gives whey"'. By the next evening he had travelled 177 miles to Prees near Shrewsbury where he was to spend four nights with Grim's cousin, Archdeacon John Allen, the vicar and friend of Thackeray and Tennyson and indefatigable improver of the position of his clergy. The Allens were kind hosts and Mrs Allen talked especially about her club-footed only son John whose gaiety and cleverness Romilly was to admire when he came up to Trinity in October 1860.

Grim and his family were 'most flourishing' despite the fact that they were without a cook, their governess was on crutches and the Bishop of Carlisle was arriving on 15 August in order to confirm 102 children. The Bishop, Montagu Villiers, was 'a fine handsome man, the father of 6 children. He is a capital talker, full of anecdote' and in the evening 'told a story of himself when Rector of Bloomsbury: he was going to visit a sick person in the 7 dials & when in Monmouth St. he found his pocket handkerchief

---

[42] Men, of course. Coe Fen being upstream from the town was little polluted, and remained a favourite resort until the increasing delicacy of the twentieth century banished nude bathing altogether.

[43] i.e. presumably for The Electric and International Telegraph Co. which had an office in Cambridge. See D.J. Muggleton *A Postal History of Cambridge.* Cambridge Philatelic Society (1970) p. 94.

[44] 'On Sunday last the Primitive Methodists of this town held their annual camp meetings, upon the Midsummer Common . . . and a great many persons availed themselves of the opportunity of being present. The members and friends of the society met in St Peter's Street Chapel at nine in the morning and the Barnwell Abbey at ten, and from these places they proceeded (singing as they went) to the Common . . . ' (*Independent*, 13 August).

had been picked, so he said to a blackguard boy "I have had my handkerchief stolen": the boy instantly put his fingers in his mouth & produced a shrill whistle, wch immediately called up another boy to whom he said "Parson's lost his wipe": in a few seconds it was given him again. – This anecdote was to show that in the most disreputable localities the clergyman was respected'.

The confirmation service over, Romilly, Grim and Bertha had leisure in which to visit neighbouring clergy, two of them former Fellows of Trinity. Grim also took his uncle with him as he went about his parish duties. On 24 August which was intensely hot, the grown-ups and three of the older children had an adventurous climb. 'The ascent was very steep & the short grass so intensely slippery that we slid about very distressingly & sometimes were obliged to creep on all fours. – The mountain is 1900 feet high: we went quite to the 'Old Man' at the top: unfortunately the air was hazy & we could only see the near mountains . . . Our descent was of course far more rapid than our ascent: we sat down (male & female) & slid at the steepest parts . . . we didn't get home till 8¼.'

Romilly left Millom on 26 August very happy in the knowledge that Grim was 'a zealous hardworking clergyman' who preached an admirable sermon and despite his uncle's and Lucy's early misgivings had married an excellent wife. In London once more, on his way by steamer to inspect Sir James Thornhill's 'Painted Chamber & the Chapel' at Greenwich 'the stench of the river was so foul that I was obliged to hold my handkerchief to my nose'. He sensibly returned to London Bridge by the railway and at home once more found 'Caroline very well, but Harriet out of health and spirits'.

*Mon. 5 September.* At 11¼ to Addenbrooke's to vote for a house surgeon (in place of Carver resigned):[45] the proper chairman (the Mayor Mr Balls) had not arrived, so I was asked to take the chair which I did: – to my great relief the Mayor came in about 20' & took his own place: – I was very glad as the proceedings were to last till 5½. Latimer Neville proposed Mr Carver (a brother of the late house-surgeon), & Mr Dennis proposed Mr Wallis (nephew of Mr Geo. Wallis). Mr Wallis had 137 votes & won by a majority of 74. – Walked up & down Trumpington St. with Latimer Neville & his brother-in-law Arthur Savile while waiting for L.N's carriage: – it had in it a packet of buns for L.N's school-feast at Heydon today . . . A comical incident occurred at the voting at the Hospital: it was told me by G. Williams: G.W. voted for Wallis on the recommendation of Dr Humphrey: he met Humphrey's little boy at the Hospital door where he was brought by the foot-boy (his Father being in Germany). G.W. immediately offered to take charge of the child, who is a Governor: the child could not write without lines, so he ruled lines for him & said 'here you will write your own name & here you will write Mr Wallis's' – 'O no, said the child, I shall write Carver': – & so he did.

*Sat. 10.* Up at 7. – Walk on the Hills Road. – Mary Edwards came today at 3 o'clock: she is looking bilious & ill: – she gives a good account of Betsy

---

[45] Addenbrooke's depended solely on voluntary subscriptions and fund-raising events. Subscribers of 20 guineas became governors for life, but the hospital's main income came from annual subscribers of one or two guineas who could recommend patients and vote at the Quarterly Courts. See A. Rook et al., *The History of Addenbrooke's Hospital Cambridge* (1991) p. 53.

& Jem & the children: – Jem is in work at Stratford & is steady. – Mary is going to be married to a very respectable young man who has been lodging with Betsy: he is a painter (like Jem) . . . Mary is about 33 or 34. – In my office I had little interruption & worked my 7 customary hours at old Supplicats . . .

*Mon. 19.* Up at 7. – Walk to office: met Mrs Leathley's daughter on her road to my house: she told me that her Mother died last night (age 77): I gave her £1 for the funeral & told her that I should not continue to her the allowance I made to her Mother, – who if she had lived to Michaelmas would have received £1 from me. – Jem Spink's Mother wanted to see me today: but I refused to see that very indifferent character. – Wrote to F.R. (£15): wrote a french letter to Sophie. – In my office I not only arranged the AB supplicats of 1647-8; but I copied them into the Gracebook where blank pages have been left for them for 2 centuries: – doubtless preceding Registraries have taken for granted they did not exist: – in Richardson's AB vol. there is an entry 'Nulli A.B. anni 1647 teste Registrario'[46] I also entered the names in my M.S.S. volumes of a copy of Richardson's Catalogue.

*Sat. 1st October.* . . . to College at 9 as today is the 1st day of term, & the Congregation therefore at 10. – Nothing but the Election of Proctors (Woollaston & Cope) & a few degrees (5 AM, 3 AB): the Proctors are no longer sworn:[47] they pledge their Honor: – their 4 men are sworn before the V.C. & another Magistrate (Leapingwell) . . .

*Sun. 2.* . . . Mrs Prest described to me the dejection of Kingsley since his wife's death: he drank tea with her last night: – he is greatly annoyed at the state in wch Henson has left the parsonage: – Henson kept poultry & pigs in the house & has left it an Augean stable . . . On coming over Parkers piece 2 nursemaids called my attention to a lost child: it was a pretty little boy with fine large eyes: he seemed to be about 3 years old: he was utterly helpless: – I could only get out of him that his name was 'Billio' & that he lived in 'my house': – I took him by the hand & walked with him in the direction wch he chose: every person of the lower classes (for it was a poor mans child) I asked 'do you know this poor child?', – not a soul did: – as a last resource I took it to the Police Station: – just as I was knocking at the door, to my great delight 2 little girls said 'why there is Billy!' – 'do you know this child?' said I: 'O yes, we live next door': – 'Where do you live?' – 'in Castle St'. – so the poor child was strayed a long way from home. I gave him 6d, & gave 6d apiece to the little girls, who undertook to take him home. – I was highly delighted at meeting with these girls just at the moment when I had given up all hope.

---

[46] William Richardson, Chaplain to George II and III, Master of Emmanuel 1736-73 and industrious antiquary, compiled the MS. lists of degrees in the Registry. His first AB. volume is in the University Library's Manuscript Room, his second in the Cole Manuscripts in the British Library. See G.J. Gray's *Index to the . . . Cole Manuscripts in the British Museum* (1912) p. 131.

[47] For the Oaths of Allegiance and Supremacy and the Oath of Office hitherto given by the Proctors on election see H. Gunning, *Ceremonies* (1828), pp. 10-13; and for the oaths taken by their men sworn in as constables, p. 25.

*Sun. 9.* . . . Walk to the Railway bridge in a thick fog. – This is my birthday: I have today completed my 68th year, & am (by Gods mercy) in good health. Received from Betsy (Mrs James Spink) a most warm-hearted birthday letter: – wrote to her . . . Met Hopkins the Esquire Bedell who told me a piece of news, viz. that I was going to resign the Registraryship & that there were two Candidates in the field Lamb, & Edleston – I told him that I was by Gods blessing well & that I had not the remotest idea of resigning . . .

*Wed. 12.* . . . Letter from 'the Medical Registration Board' asking (modestly) for an account of our whole Educational system & begging to have it *in duplicate*: – I cut out 36 pages of The Calendar of 1859 & sent them to Dr Hawkins. – I did not buy a fresh Calendar to victimise for a duplicate copy. – dined at the Lodge to meet Lord & Lady Belper . . . The carriage for conveying ladies across the Court to the Lodge is too small for their swelling draperies:[48] many walked by its sides . . .

*Th. 13.* . . . Visit in my office from Leapingwell: he said that after I went away from Trin. Lodge last night there was some miserable squealing singing from Mrs Humphry, playing the Concertina from Miss King, etc. etc. – By the way Mrs Humphry last night told me how well her husbands hostel gets on with the 5 students:[49] they talk German at breakfast: they have a German Lady staying with them these 2 years: her own little boy talks German: – they have hired the old Botanic Garden as a playground . . . Leapingwell . . . told me a melancholy piece of news: last Saturday Mrs Ebenezer Foster (during her husband's absence) absconded:[50] she is said to have joined a man who has seduced her & that she is with child by him: – what a sin on her part, & what grief & consternation to her husband & daughter! . . .

*Sat. 15.* Up at 7. – Walk behind Colleges: breakfast at 9 to Henry Strutt, Waller de Montmorency, & N. Rothschild: breakfast was laid for 5, but my cousin Edward never came, having been so fast asleep that when called he did not awake. – My guests seemed to enjoy themselves for they staid till near 11. – I like what I have seen of Strutt, & am also pleased with the modest, gentle, delicate-looking Irishman Montmorency: – I do not much relish Mr Rothschild, whom I find opinionated & devoid of the bump of veneration: he seems to have a high opinion of himself, & has plenty (rather too much) to

---

[48] The fashion for crinolines came from France about 1854 and disappeared towards the end of the sixties as suddenly as it had arrived. The skirts of the ladies going to the soirée were stiffened by steel and whalebone. If, however, they had been going to a ball they might have made use of the carriage, as their skirts would have been swelled by nothing firmer than a dozen or more muslin petticoats. *The Times* of 5 May 1862, reporting on the International Exhibition, disapproved of crinolines on safety grounds: 'For ladies, in the present days of enlarged skirts, anything like a close inspection of the machinery is most dangerous'.

[49] G.M. Humphry, one of the great teachers of medicine in the nineteenth century, was involved in his students' welfare as well as in their academic progress. Statutes which recognised a house as a University Hostel were at last approved on 31 August 1858 and Humphry soon availed himself of them for the benefit of poor students. See A. Rook (ed.), *Cambridge and its Contribution to Medicine* (1971), p. 98 where it is said that the hostel, 56 Trumpington Street, stayed open for three years, and the *Chronicle* for 2 July 1859.

[50] See 15 December 1860.

say for himself. - He is the nephew of the Baroness Mayer: his Father is Baron Lionel (member for London) . . .

*Tu. 18.* . . . In the Evening went to the Town Hall to hear Dickens read:[51] Willy Prest & wife were kind enough to take me in Mrs P.'s carriage: - The room was quite full & Dickens was received enthusiastically. I had never seen him before: he has great power of changing the expression of his countenance: I preferred him in the pathetic parts. He amused me by prefacing his reading with saying that he had no objection to the audience expressing the feelings wch different parts of the reading might excite. His 2 subjects were the history of little Dombey in 6 Chapters from his birth to his death: I thought his manner of repeating all the childs remarks very touching: it seemed to me perfection: - I liked also his impersonation of the character of Toots. - I was rather disappointed with the 2d part of the performance, viz. that from Martin Chuzzlewit, & prefer Grim's mode of reading Mrs Gamp to Dickens': - I was disappointed at Dickens not giving us the grand tea-drinking scene of Sarah Gamp & Betsy Prigg: - I was however much pleased with Dicken's recitation of the part of Mould the undertaker. - This performance lasted 2 hours: - I got home soon after 10.

*Fri. 21.* . . . Letter from Grim describing an excursion to St. Bees . . . He told me of a rule-of-3 sum wch little Bertha has just proposed: 'if 3 screaming babies can awaken 12 sound sleepers how many can 23 babies with equal screaming powers awake?': - a problem wch bespeaks Grims daughter . . . Again at 2 o'clock to a Seniority (at wch the Astronomer Royal was present) to adjudicate the Sheepshanks triennial Exhibition:[52]- this is the beginning of the Exhibition: its value is £50 & it is tenable for 3 years on condition of Residence or special leave from the Trustees. - The 3 Executors were the Astronomer Royal (Airy), Professor Adams & Mathison . . . Of course Stirling is the winner . . .

*Tu. 25.* . . . Wrote to Mrs H. Haviland sending her the Chess Problem called Phillidors Legacy, as she & Mrs W. Prest worked yesterday at a 3-move problem wch I proposed to them from the Illustrated News . . . In the Evening a letter from Mrs H. Haviland sending the answer to the Phillidor problem, worked out by herself: - I was highly pleased with her cleverness & sent her a 3-move mate for her ingenuity to work on . . .

*Fri. 28.* . . . Dined at the Family at Thompson's: we were a party of 10: the 3 absentees were Phelps, Cartmell & Joseph Power (who is not well). Thompson gave us a recherché dinner: he was more sarcastic than ever, - railed at Colonial Bishops as useless if not mischievous, declaimed against

[51] Romilly sensibly went to the second of Dickens's two readings in Cambridge. The *Chronicle* of 22 October devoted three-quarters of a column to them and reported that on the first night hundreds of people were unable to get into the Town Hall and that it was 'some seconds before the cheering ceased' on Mr Dickens's appearance. See also Peter Ackroyd's *Dickens* (1990) pp.1034-45, for a full description of his readings.

[52] Established at Trinity by his sister in 1858 in memory of Richard Sheepshanks of Trinity. It was to be open to competition among undergraduates and held for three years by the best of them 'versed in Astronomy theoretical and practical'.

Bishop Turton,[53] the Trinity Seniority (in the matter of Tennyson's bust) etc etc, & praised nothing but Tennyson whom he idolises . . .

*Sun. 30.* At Barnwell Mr Collis . . . read prayers & another Irishman preached for the Pastoral Aid: his name is Garbett & he is Minister in Grays Inn Lane: he is a very hideous bullet headed dwarf with a profusion of black hair all over his face . . . he has none of the beauty of holiness . . . At 2 to St Mary's to hear my friend Carus: he made the greatest contrast possible to the wild Irishman with his sanguine complexion, his white hair, his soft persuasive manner, & the clearness & distinctness with wch he handled his subject. I was delighted with his subject & thought it most able & convincing . . . Invitation from Master of Magdalene to dinner tomorrow to meet the Bishop of Oxford & Mr Gladston [sic]: – I declined: – tho I should have liked to break thro my rule.

*Tu. 1 November* . . . At 11¼ to Senate House where there was an extraordinary congregation for conferring LLD degrees 'honoris causa' on the Bishop of Oxford, Mr Gladstone (Chancellor of Exchequer), Sir George Grey (Governor of The Cape) & our own member Mr Walpole. – The Senatehouse was very full: the Orator (Clark) made a very elegant ovation in praise of these 4: they were all received most enthusiastically by the youngsters in the Gallery . . . After the degrees the Senate House was closed to prepare for the grand gathering of the Oxford & Cambridge Mission to Central Africa.[54] – The doors were to open at 12½ & the proceedings to begin at 1: – there was an intense crowd long before the time: – there was an entrance for ordinary Members of Senate on south side: I did not squeeze in till just as orders were being given for closing that entrance as the place was crammed . . . The effect of the Senate House was very striking: it was as full as possible, & a bright sunshine set it off beautifully. – There was no form for me to sit on, so (like very many others, men & women, I squatted on the ground. Selwyn (at the V.C.'s direction) opened the proceedings with prayer. The V.C. then made a clear & very interesting statement of the object of the meeting. – The 1st 2 speakers were Jeremie & the Bishop of Oxford: – the speech of Jeremie was exquisite, every sentence was a gem: – I was delighted also with the speech of the Bishop; parts of it were in a very high strain of eloquence, & parts were very gay & lively. Then came the Chancellor of the Exchequer, whom I had never heard before, & was most anxious to hear. – It was a remarkable

---

[53] Thomas Turton, sometime senior wrangler and professor of divinity, had succeeded Dr Allen as bishop of Ely in 1845. He was a vigorous controversialist and connoisseur of pictures.

[54] Committees had been preparing for this meeting since Dr Livingstone's visit to Oxford, Cambridge and London almost two years before. He had then said, also in the Senate House, 'I go back to Africa to try to make an open path for commerce and Christianity; do you carry out the work which I have begun. I leave it with you.' The Bishop of Oxford, as did other speakers, emphasized the immense importance of the Mission now that the slave trade had been abolished: 'we should seek to impregnate our commerce with Christianity, and to prevent it from becoming an instrument of evil . . . in times past commerce itself with Africa, had, as they all knew, been a special minister of evil'. After Romilly's departure towards the end of the meeting Sedgwick traced the explorations of Livingstone and his predecessors on a map and 'the vast assembly then dispersed, amid the cheers of the undergraduates'. (See the *Chronicle* of 5 November where there is a page supplement and relevant letters.)

rhetorical display certainly, but I was disappointed with it: a good deal of it was dreamy & up in the clouds, there was too much praise of Tennyson & too much about Livingston being equal as a *hero* to those immortalised by Tennyson in his Idylls of the Kings. – The next speaker was our Member (Mr Walpole): a very bad performance it was: a great deal of loud declaiming & vehement gesticulation, but obviously it was a task he was performing in wch his heart was not: I got sick to death of it & was heartily glad when he sat down. Sir George Grey (Governor of the Cape) then rose: his appearance is very prepossessing, he looks thoughtful & wise: he gave an account of the different races (the Hottentots, the Caffres & the Bushmen), described their polity etc etc, & gave suggestions for dealing successfully with them: – his manner is not animated, but he has an unfailing command of appropriate language. An African Bishop then spoke (Cotterell Bishop of Grahams Town). I went away at 4½ while he was speaking . . . I was amused in the Senate House by the High-Churchism displayed by the youngsters in the Galleries: – the Bishop spoke of our 'apostolic church', upon wch they applauded furiously . . . This Evening I received a delightful letter from Sophie Kennedy . . . Also a very agreeable letter from Maggie (acknowledging the money): she says that the Captain is just like a magpie: he lays hold of every thing he can get at & hides it, – sometimes in the water: Franky has developed his humanity in a manner like dearest Lucy: he saw several birds in one little cage, for sale at a penny a piece: & he made a purchase to set the birds free: this charms me.

*Wed. 2.* . . . Lunched with Latimer Neville to meet the Bishop of Oxford, Mr & Mrs Gladstone etc: I enjoyed this party very much for Mr & Mrs Gladstone as well as the Bishop were very kind to me: they had been attending a lecture of Sedgwick's: – he was also of the party; so was John Clark (who was going after lunch to exhibit Trinity Library, of wch he is the deputy Librarian in the absence of Glover): a gentle amiable young man (Packe) was also there with 2 sisters: he is Latimers Curate at Heydon . . . Letter from Miss Cotton: she has just left Sir Charles Rowley & is going (after a week in Town) to St Leonards: she has lately been with Lady Charlotte Neville Grenville & says she is wonderfully well in mind & body after all her trials . . .

*Tu. 8.* . . . At 10 to the V.C.'s where the Heads held a *meeting* (for they are shy of calling it a *Court* on the matter of Ephraim Wayman (Solicitor) who had taken a promissory note for £85 from a Caius undergraduate (named Pearse): with law expenses it amounted to £90: Pearse not having paid at the right time was arrested: Clayton (the Prosecutor before the V.C. & Heads) telegraphed to Pearse's family, & a brother in-law came down, paid the £90 & the young man was set at liberty. – Mr Wayman did not appear (tho the V.C. had served a notice on him that he was *at liberty* to do so): he was discommuned[55] . . . After dinner Edleston called to ask about the salary of the

---

[55] Sir John Patteson's Act restricted certain privileges of the University vis-à-vis the town and marked the beginning of improved relations between them. The jurisdiction of the Chancellor's Court was not now to extend to any case in which one of the parties was not a member of the University, and tradesmen and others were not now forbidden to begin

Librarian (Power): I cannot make out that any change has been made since Lodge became Librarian & Principal Librarian in 1828 with the stipend of £210 . . . Letter from George Romilly: he tells me that 4 of his comrades are going to China, where they will have higher pay: he is most thankful to stay in England . . . Franky had high excitement at his school with fireworks on the 5th: the boys were delighted at 2 holes being burnt in the Masters new coat: – George sent Franky in his worst clothes: he came home redolent of gunpowder & as dirty as a sweep . . .

*Th. 10.* Up at 7. – walk in Botanic Garden – Took my Matriculation Book to the V.C. & paid him £1906·10·–. – The Matriculations have improved a little upon those of 1857 & 1858 (when they were only 364): – for the 11 preceding years they exceeded 400. Trinity however had now the largest no it ever had, viz. 147 . . . St Johns had the smallest no since 1816 (when it had 51, & Trin. only 67) – The following is a table of the decennial averages of the *entire* Matriculations of all the Colleges in the 3 terms of the Academic Year: . . .

| From | 1800 to 1809 | 1803 | averaging | 180 | |
|---|---|---|---|---|---|
| | 1810 to 1819 | 2832 | | 283 | |
| | 1820 to 1829 | 4395 | | 439 | (per annum) |
| | 1830 to 1839 | 4266 | | 426 | |
| | 1840 to 1849 | 4529 | | 453 | |
| | 1850 to 1859 | 4361 | | 436 | |

*Fri. 11.* . . . I hear that Shaw gave £5000 to his bedmaker Lydia immediately after his 1st attack & that she says she might have married him, (she married a Mr Adams a week after Shaw's funeral) that he left £2000 to the Leapingwells, £5000 to Cartmell (one of his Executors), £4000 to the College, £5000 to each of his 2 nephews, etc etc . . . Dined at the Family at Pagets: all the members but Cartmell present: Mr Pemberton (cidevant Hodgson was of the party: he is of an extraordinary height: his Mother was a Pemberton: he married his cousin, the widow Campbell, daughter of Col. Pemberton, & then assumed the name of Pemberton.[56] – Played 6 rubbers & lost 1/: the players were Bateson, Mr Pemberton, Power, Paget, Stokes & myself. – Thompson told me of a rich scene at Trinity Lodge the other Evening (when Bishop of Oxford, Sir G. & Lady Grey etc were there): Lady Grey said to the Master 'I have read with great delight your book proving the Plurality of Worlds': – the Master said 'the book which you ascribe to me was written to prove the reverse' – Thompson recommends my reading the Review (in the Quarterly) of Tennyson's 'Idylls of the Kings':[57] his indignation about

proceedings against persons *in statu pupillari* without giving notice to their tutors. However the award upheld the right of Heads of Houses to enjoin upon tradesmen and others certain rules in their transactions with undergraduates and the penalty for not doing so was still discommuning.

[56] The Pembertons had been seated at Trumpington since the 1680s. For a pedigree see Burke, *Landed Gentry*.

[57] Thompson hoped that the *Quarterly Review* (Vol. 106 July and October 1859 pp. 454-85) might induce Romilly to admire Tennyson's poetry. The review is rather 'disposed to quarrel

Tennyson's bust being placed on the Staircase of the Library continues in all its fervour: the bust is not to gain a place in the Library till after the poets death, – 'it is now too soon'. – One of Tennyson's Idylls has the refrain 'too late, too late': this is parodied in Punch (in this matter of the Bust 'by too soon, too soon' . . .

*Tu. 15.* . . . Lunched with Sedgwick at 2: of course I made it my dinner. It was a very agreeable party of 13, viz. Sedgwick, 4 Miss Adeanes & their German Governess Miss Struve, Dr & Mrs Worsley, Clark, Mathison, Duke of St Albans & Lord Milton & myself. – I was much pleased with Miss Struve: she is gentle & cheerful & has plenty to say & talks excellent English. I had never seen the Duke or Lord Milton: the former is a good looking proud-seeming young man of good height: Lord Milton is an ugly dwarf: they both entered freely into conversation & made themselves very agreeable. – Lord Milton however spoke about shooting at cats with an air-gun: I warmly attacked the barbarity of doing so . . .

*Wed. 23.* . . . Meeting of the Governing Body of Trinity College to discuss the 8 statutes just sent by the Commissioners in place of those wch we rejected[58] (– concerning the Vicemaster, the tenure of Fellowships, & the Presentation to Livings). I thought the Master conducted the proceedings very ably & with much kindliness of manner: – tho thinking the new Statutes were calculated to increase too much the lay element in the Seniority he was not disposed to protest against them: Sedgwick, myself, Martin, Grote etc were for acquiescing: – Luard made a vehement attack of these new statutes, & one or 2 sided with him, but the show of hands was decidedly in favor of acceptance: – so I hope we shall have no more discussions about the Statutes, but quietly accept the Commissioners Statutes (wch are now very much more according to our wishes) tho they are not exactly to our taste. – St Johns has rejected the Statute concerning Contributions to the University: – but we have acquiesced in it[59] . . .

with the title of Idylls: for no diminutive . . . can be adequate to the breadth, vigour and majesty which belong to the subjects'. The bust is now on the west side of the library next to that of Arthur Henry Hallam. The *Punch* parody is of *Guinevere* – a long poem in which Tennyson pleads with Whewell 'to stand at Dryden's Byron's side'. Whewell, unmoved, replies 'Too soon, too soon! You cannot enter now'(vol. 37, 12 November 1859, p. 194).

[58] The long battle was over at last. Winstanley (p. 372) sums up his long account as follows: 'But these and many other salutary reforms would never have been made if the college had been left in control of its own destinies. Trinity was by no means the least enlightened of the colleges, but, if it had been left to itself, it would have remained very much as it had been for the past three hundred years. It would be very hazardous to assert that the University could have reformed itself from within and even more hazardous to say that the colleges could have done so.'

[59] It was left to a subsequent commission to compel the colleges to help the university financially, and the 1856 Commissioners' statutes 'for rendering portions of the college property or income available to purposes for the benefit of the University at large' were interpreted very narrowly. Trinity 'was annually to contribute five per cent of its distributable income to the University Chest and to pay each of the Professors, to be hereafter appointed a yearly stipend of six hundred pounds'. But these proposals were later modified in response partly to the letter sent to the Commissioners in December 1858 by Montagu Butler and twenty-one other younger fellows. See link-passage 1858-9 and Winstanley, pp. 362-5.

*Th. 24.* Congregation day: 17 undisturbed Graces: the degrees were 4 AM & 25 AB:[60]– most of the ABs were dunces who were plucked in June: 57 went in to the Examination & 18 of them were plucked (including again Goodeve the claimant by Blood Royal, who told me he was descended from Edward VI!!) – The brother dunces in the galleries were very uproarious in applauding the successful dunces . . .

*Sat. 26.* . . . College meeting: – we agreed to warm the Library with hot water:[61] we ordered a great no. of books for our Library:[62]– we have lately sold our duplicates: we agreed to try the experiment of gas in the *staircases* of the New Court before venturing it throughout all the staircases. – Edleston agitated in favor of abolishing the charcoal fire in Hall[63] & warming the hall with hot water: he had Grote & King as supporters, but the majority of us were opposed . . .

*Mon. 28.* Up at 7. – Walk in Botanic Garden. – Met there Selwyn, & also 2 girls & their brother whom I often see, but never talked to before: Selwyn talked to them & I was glad to make their acquaintance: the girls seem about 14 & 15: they are nicely dressed & well-mannered: they are parishioners of Grote's: their name is Cawcutt, & their Father is a well-to-do farmer who has the farm opposite to the Mill in the Via Lambertina . . . Read Quevedo's Vision of Hell: it is one of the cleverest & bitterest of these satires.[64]

*Th. 1 December* . . . Letter from Grim . . . Little Bertha sends me two rule-of-3 sums of her own setting ((1) about attorneys worrying people to death; (2) about quantity of sand in brown sugar).

*Fri. 2.* Up at 7. – Some snow. – In the Botanic Garden met Selwyn *carrying* his dog Duky (as dogs are not allowed the run of the place): he told me (as a secret) that the Bishop of Ely had offered him the Archdeaconry vacated by the death of Hardwick: he of course refused, as he had previously

---

[60] No less than eleven names on Romilly's list have a line drawn through them and he writes 'Those elided bolted'. Bolting seems to have been a not uncommon way of evading examinations during the years of the diary and on occasion was resorted to by nervous candidates of considerable ability. Thus in 1843 T.M. Goodeve of St John's, who was expected to be Second Wrangler 'after 3 days was seized with a panic terror & bolted: – in spite of this he is 9th Wrangler' (*R.C.D. 1842-1847*, p. 41). It was not Goodeve who claimed descent from Edward VI but E.G.C. Eardley. See 22 June 1859.

[61] The 'warming apparatus' was mercifully installed by Thomas Potter of London in 1860 and no doubt helped William White, appointed sub-librarian in 1857, to hold his office for fifty years. However pre-warming sub-librarians were admirably hardy and on average held office for 28 years. See P. Gaskell and R. Robson, *The Library of Trinity College* (1971), pp. 41, 58.

[62] 'But thanks not only to further benefactors, but also to different expectations of the libraries of Cambridge as a result of university reforms in teaching, and new impetus in the mid nineteenth century for research in humanities and sciences alike, the collections of books and manuscripts expanded at an unprecedented rate in the mid and late nineteenth century' (David McKitterick (ed.), *The Making of the Wren Library*, 1995, p. 141).

[63] William Everett describes the charcoal fire as 'in the centre . . . an ancient open pan or brazier piled up from November to May with live coals, and expelling the colder air from the whole vast apartment'.

[64] Romilly was reading in Spanish the *Sueños*, usually known in English as *Visions* (1627), a series of burlesque descriptions of the follies of the world and consequent hell and judgement.

refused The Deanery of Ely. – Letter from Betsy (Mrs Ja. Spink) telling of her sister Mary's wedding . . . The V.C. called on me & said the reply of the Council to the application of the Queen's University Ireland for admission to 'ad eundem' was 'It is not the custom of this University to grant such admission except to Dublin & Oxford'. – I am not much surprised at this answer, for Dublin does not recognise these Queen's University degrees any more than we recognise the degrees of the London University. – Wrote to the Secretary of Queens University. – The University of Melbourne has sent its thanks for our present of books:[65]– the letter of thanks is very tasty with flaming red capitals to all the important words . . .

*Fri. 9.* . . . Called at Pullen's: he is still confined to his bed & is in grievous pain: – He unfortunately tried to cure himself by the cold-water system: Paget (who attends him) told me that he had no doubt greatly aggravated the malady by such rashness. – Went to hear Sedgwick's concluding lecture: it had but one fault: it lasted 1 hr. 50':[66] he lamented over the neglect of the Natural Sciences at Camb. & said that they were far more encouraged at Oxford, – he gave much good advice to the young men about their intellectual & moral training, – & he contended C. Darwins book[67] (wch advocates the system of *development* (as culled in the Vestiges of Creation) but now called 'natural selection'. – I then went to the 1st grand public drill of the rifle corps: – I heard that about 500 were expected to be on the ground. The drill took place on the meadow adjoining Jesus College: Major Barker (undergrad. of Magdalene) was in Command:[68] he is a fine handsome man with a very pretty wife. Leapingwell is a private. The men have not yet got their

---

[65] On 22 April 1858 there was a grace to give books to the University of Melbourne perhaps in response to a request from Charles Perry, first Bishop of Melbourne who visited his old college in 1855. Dr. McKitterick presumes that they were recent C.U.P. books.

[66] In one of his inimitable letters to Kate Malcolm (29 November), Sedgwick wrote that 'my concluding lecture . . . may be as long as one of old Kittledrummel's sermons' described in Scott's *Old Mortality*. See Clark and Hughes, II, 354.

[67] On 11 November Darwin wrote to Sedgwick telling him that his publishers would send him a copy of '*On the Origin of Species* which is as yet only an abstract. As the conclusion at which I have arrived . . . is so diametrically opposed to that which you have often advocated with much force, you might think that I send my volume to you out of a spirit of bravado and with a want of respect, but I assure you that I am actuated by quite opposite feelings.' Sedgwick in his long letter of thanks grieves that he has read the book 'with more pain than pleasure. Parts of it I greatly admired, parts I laughed at till my sides were almost sore, other parts I read with absolute sorrow, because I think them utterly false and grievously mischievous . . . As to your grand principle – *natural selection* what is it but a secondary consequence of supposed, or known, primary facts ? Development is a better word, because more close to the cause of the fact. For you do not deny causation. I call (in the abstract) causation the will of God: and I can prove that He acts for the good of His creature.' (Clark and Hughes, II, 356-7).

[68] The corps was not to be finally established until 31 December under James Baker who had entered Magdalene in 1859 after service (probably not in the Crimea) with the 8th Hussars. As the author of three tracts on military training his appointment was fully justified, though he was later criticised for his autocratic command 'and his desire for absolute control over everything'. See H. Strachan, *History of the Cambridge University Officers Training Corps* (1976), pp. 24-31.

uniforms: – they were exercised in marching today: they were without their rifles . . .

*Sat. 10.* . . . Letter from G.B. Allen saying that Dora was confined on the 6th & that she & the little boy are doing well. The Master of the Rolls told him 2 anecdotes about children: – a little girl asked her Mother 'if Tories were born so wicked or became so': another on being asked what she would have done if she had seen the man who fell among thieves answered 'killed him quite'. – This maiden had seen her Mamma smash maimed flies & heard her call it 'putting them out of their misery'! . . .

*Wed. 14.* Up at 7. – Sharp frost: thermometer at 25°: – cutting wind: – walk in Botanic Garden. – The tooth wch Jones stopt having never felt comfortable, I this morning had it out: – it was one of the haling-posts of my false teeth, wch are now become useless: – this 2d set have done duty but a short time . . . Visit from Vicechancellor: he came on a melancholy business: he was on his return from the Spinning house where he saw a young girl (only 15 or 16) who was committed by the Proctors:[69] her Father is Johnson & referred the V.Ch. to me as having employed him as a Carver & Gilder: – it is true that I did so, & then knew no harm of him: now however his family is very disreputable & this is not the only daughter who has gone astray . . .

*Th. 22.* . . . Received from John L. Roget a present of his enlarged edition of his very amusing sketches in what he calls 'Cambridge Scrap Book'.[70] – Wrote to express my warm thanks. – Letter from G.T.R.: he gives an improved account of Cappie: – & means to bring Franky on Saturday . . .

*Sat. 24.* . . . In my office I did registrarial work & amused myself by working Equations from Hind. – At 7¼ arrived G.T.R. & his son Franky: G.T.R. wears a moustache: Franky is very short for his age: he will be 11 on 10th March 1860: they both coughed occasionally, but reported themselves to be very well. I had given careful attention to keeping them from catching cold, having kept constant fires in their bedrooms for several days. We dined fashionably at 7½: we had our turkey today . . . Franky is round faced & has a healthy look: he is an amiable & sensible boy, fond of study, & endowed with a good memory . . .

*Christmas-day* . . . Took George & Franky to dine in Hall: there was a good large party (very unusually so I was told). I was in the Chair: the only red gown was Woodhams. There was a magnificent dinner wch the youngster greatly admired: – he is not at all a greedy child. – the choristers sang capitally in the hall: – I did not know the Anthem – I took my guests into the

---

[69] The Act of Parliament confirming Sir John Patteson's award continued the Proctors' power to arrest suspected prostitutes, of whom at least 200 were known to the authorities, and the Vice-Chancellor's power to try them. The Vice-Chancellor sat in the Spinning House to which, if they were found guilty, they were committed. The court was not open to the public, the prisoner was not allowed counsel, and the court was not surprisingly viewed with mistrust by the town. However in appearing for the Vice-Chancellor in Kemp v. Neville, Sir Fitzroy Kelly said that the prison was under the jurisdiction of the Home Office and of the Visiting Commissioners. See 30 November 1860 and Winstanley, pp. 137, 380-2.

[70] See 23 May 1859.

Combination room. We afterwards went to Chapel: I had (as deputy Vice Master) to read the 1st Lesson: the Master read the 2d. – The anthem was just what I hoped for 'Unto us a child is born', & we were plaid out with Handel's Halleluiah chorus, – so the music was a rich treat . . .

*Wed. 28.* . . . Seniority at wch we appointed Luard College Preacher & allowed him to edit (for the Cambridge Antiquarian Society) Rudd's Journal[71] from our M.S.: – we allowed him also (as Junior Bursar) to warm the Library with hot air & to light the College Staircases with Gas. – At this seniority the Head Lecturer (Beamont) was gently censured for not having read Pringle's Latin Prize Essay: it seems wonderful but it is a fact that Pringle wrote a eulogy of Bentley by the Christian name of William:[72] & in the list of prizes it was printed 'laudes Gulielmi Bentley'! – Dined in Trinity Hall Hall as the guest of my good friend Dr Geldart the Master: it was a large party & every thing went off very gaily. I sat next to Woodham who is a capital talker & I enjoyed the party very much . . . Lord Chelmsford (Thesiger, late Lord Chancellor & Sir Charles Locock (the famous accoucheur) were of the party: Lord C. is the freshest looking man of his age I ever saw: he is very gay & conversible: Sir Charles is a very deaf grey old man. He made a professional joke which amused me: he said he lately got into so ill-constructed a carriage that it should have been called a *miscarriage.* I plaid 4 rubbers with the Master, Lord C. & Sir C.L: I won them all & carried off 20s . . . When the Supper of boar's head etc at 10½ was announced I took my departure . . .

*Th. 29.* . . . Visit from Willie Prest (to put off his Mothers Quadrille party for tonight): – he communicated to me the following riddle: – 'If a pig wanted to make himself a sty how would he set about it?'. – Answer 'He would tie a knot in his tail & there's a pig's tie'. – Willie has just sent to Punch the following 'What is the difference between a man who has murdered his 2 daughters & a naked highlander?' . . .

*Sat. 31.* . . . Letters in the Evening from Dosia, Mrs Gilmour, Carry Helm, C.H. Cooper & Jacques. – Dosia wrote about the trouble she is in: her husband (Johnson a Tailor) has got mixt up in a rascally transaction about false dice: she says he was ignorant of the villainy: however he is to be tried next Thursday: – wrote to her & sent her £2. – Mrs Gilmour wrote to say that she was in great anguish, that Agnes lay a dying & longed to have a letter from me: – I wrote to the poor girl & to her Mother . . .

---

[71] i.e. the diary of Edward Rudd, fellow of Trinity and Norfolk parson who died in 1727, to which Luard added some unpublished letters by the great Master of Trinity, Bentley.

[72] His christian name was Richard!

# 1860

*Sun. 1 January* . . . To Barnwell at 3 ¼ to hear the Children's Lecture from Mr Robinson. It was not much of a New year sermon: but I was greatly pleased with it. His text was Luke 2. last verse 'Jesus increased in wisdom & stature & in favor with God & man' . . . He told 2 instances of children increasing in *worldly* wisdom, viz. Benjamin West when 6 years old drawing his sister's child, & James Watt (also at age of 6) making long calculations with chalk on the stone hearth. He told the touching story of the Scotch girl Margaret Wilson's early growth in heavenly wisdom: she & her aged father were tied to stakes as the tide was coming up to induce them to renounce their faith: they died like brave martyrs: she was only 13: she had the anguish (in the times of Charles I) of seeing her father perish 1st, he having been placed lower down. – Mr Robinson told the affecting anecdote of a girl who was going on in the paths of goodness, but was persuaded & forced in to sin by her parents: she died within the year & her last words to her Father were 'Last year I should have gone to my Saviour, but now I go to destruction'. – After dinner I read Jeremy Taylor[1] & wrote journal. Wrote to Mrs Macfarlan sending her my London Orphan votes.

*Mon. 9.* . . . A dumb peel was rung today for Lord Macaulay (Steward of the Town):[2] he was buried in Westminster Abbey. – Letter from Mrs Gilmour saying poor Agnes died yesterday.

*Sat. 14.* . . . Very agreeable letter from Grim, describing his feast to the Choristers on the 23d, his tea-drinking to 80 school-children (besides 12 teachers & friends) on the 24th, his Xmas dinner on the 25th etc etc . . . Grim tells a story of Close (the Dean of Carlisle): he has a horror of smoking: he sent his pet parrot to see the Bishops pet parrot: the moment his parrot came back it said 'take a pipe' . . .

*Sat. 21.* . . . In my Office I was visited by some youngsters to subscribe & get Professorial Tickets.[3] One came to the door in a fly: I brought down my book & took it to him in the fly to write his name: – he was Horace Smith (Trinity Hall): he put out his knee by a fall in skating: he still goes on crutches: – the Examiners sent the papers for him to work in his rooms & a M.A. sat by all the time. – William Prest having lent me yesterday the 1st

---

[1] Romilly not infrequently 'read Jeremy Taylor' on Sunday evenings, but only on Easter Sunday does he mention one of the great books in particular, *A Discourse of the Liberty of Prophesying* (1646).

[2] Macaulay's last speech was in acknowledgment of his election as High Steward of the borough of Cambridge in May 1858. His health had been poor for some while when he died suddenly aged 59 at his London home on 28 December 1859. The *Illustrated London News* of 14 January has views of him in his library and of the magnificent burial in Westminster Abbey.

[3] These certified that they had attended a course of professorial lectures which were free to undergraduates. Graduates paid for them.

No of the Cornhill Magazine (conducted by Thackeray)[4] I was idle enough to read it this morning, i.e. I read 2 tales in it viz. Thackerays 'Lovell the Widower' & 'the Framley Vicarage': I did not much like the former: I found the 2d more amusing . . .

*Tu. 24.* . . . Before breakfast I fell in with Stokes (Secretary to the Commission) who was going up to one of their meetings: he told me that 6 Colleges have received their Statutes, viz. Trinity, St Johns, Christs, Catharine, Trinity Hall & Clare . . .

*Fri. 27.* . . . Hurrah for Trinity!!! we have got the Senior Wrangler & a thoroughly good one he is: his name is Stirling.[5] He gained the Sheepshanks Exhibition (wch 1st came into existence last term) & was very highly thought of by all the Examiners: he has gained his post triumphantly, for it is said that his marks exceed the 2d Wranglers by 2000 – a sum equal to all the marks of the 5th Wrangler . . . the 1st 12 Wranglers are all of Trin. & St Johns, 6 of each . . . Wedgwood is Wooden-spoon: he is son of W. who took his degree in 1824 (1st year of Classical Tripos) & was Wooden-wedge . . .

*Sun. 29.* . . . At Barnwell . . . Mr Robinson preached: it was the Chevins Obiit. Mr Chevin left £6 p.a. for the poor on condition of 2 sermons being preached annually in the church of the Mayor's parish: – one of the preaching days is the Sunday before the Purification (– today). The Mayor & Aldermen etc etc & the 4 maces were all in Church & the bidding prayer preceded the sermon, & the Congregation were plaid out with God save the Queen . . . Two days ago there was a very interesting leader in praise of Sir S. Romilly[6] as the most distinguished of the French refugees: – it arose from the Master of the Rolls (Sir John Romilly) having to adjudicate in a dispute about the Ministers of the French church in London. – Sadly sleepy in Evening.

*Sat. 4 February* . . . College meeting for near 3 hours: our principal matter was the vacant Butlership. Martin had very carefully drawn up statistics about

---

4   George Smith of Smith Elder & Co in 1859 launched a monthly magazine which would sell cheaply for a shilling and offer the reader at least one and usually two novels in instalments together with high-quality essays, short fiction, poetry, and illustrations from the best writers and artists. He secured Thackeray as a novel writer and persuaded him to take on the editorship after Thomas Hughes refused it. Smith offered Trollope twice the largest sum he had ever received for a novel if he would contribute one on a clerical theme, and *Framley Parsonage* buoyed up the magazine for sixteen months and had, as Trollope said, 'a great effect upon my career'. See L. Eddy Jr., 'The Founding of the Cornhill Magazine', *Ball State Monograph* 19 (1970).

5   James Stirling as a Presbyterian could not be elected into a fellowship. Even had Trinity been prepared, as was asserted, to change its statutes, it was obliged, even under the new statutes of 1860-61, to restrict its fellowships to men who professed to be members of the Church of England.

6   The leader in *The Times* of 26 January was a long one which, after the passage to which Romilly refers, explained the complicated case on which the Master of the Rolls had just given judgement. 'There is no greater name than that of Romilly on the list of those refugees who were driven from their country upon the revocation of the Edict of Nantes . . . Sir Samuel Romilly was by far the most eminent of the descendants of the French refugees, and became the founder of a family which will be respected as long as the recollection of his unblemished integrity and high ability endures.'

all the details of profit[7] . . . The feeling was that the profit was altogether too great: we shall doubtless make some reduction,. – the 2 great sources of profit are the bread & beer. –Visit in my Office from V.C. (about a Carus Prize Examiner etc). – Worked at the old Matriculations of King's College. – Letter from Grim announcing birth of a little girl: she was born on the anniversary of Grim's wedding day 2d Feb: she is the 8th child; Grim has been married 12 years: so (as he observes) the average is a child in a year & ½ . . . Bertha & baby are doing well.

*Wed. 8.* . . . Three hours Seniority! we had a great deal of animated discussion: 6 real Seniors were present, viz. Sedgwick, myself, Martin, Grote, Edleston & Mathison: the 2 quasi-seniors were Luard (Junior Bursar) & Hammond. – We agreed to take the butter out of the Butlers hands as to a source of profit: – he is still to have the ordering & procuring of it: – each pound is to be divided into 24 sizings & each sizing (or 'butter') is to be charged ³/4 instead of a penny. Edleston, Mathison & Luard were urgent for taking the bread & beer similarly out of the Butlers hands as matter of profit: – this however was not conceded: – those 3 men are strenuous for the Butler being altogether paid a fixt salary . . . we agreed at last to appoint W.F. Claydon (who has been his late Fathers assistant for 23 years) till next Audit . . .

*Fri. 10.* . . . Visit from Leapingwell: he gave me an interesting account of the meeting in the Schools yesterday: the feeling was very decidedly in favor of degrees in Moral & Natural Sciences.[8] Another topic was the discontinuance of morning sermons at St Mary's . . . Leapingwell gave the meeting some statistics, showing that the Heads were represented by Dr Guest, the Professors by Pryme & Jeremie (– very irregularly), the MAs average 3 & the under-graduates 6! . . .

*Sat. 11.* . . . Last night Gladston (Chancellor of Exchequer) proposed his budget: – peopled [sic] feared a 9 penny income-tax but he goes beyond their fears & announces a 10 penny one. – Played Morphy[9] & did pasting work in the Evening.

*Mon. 13.* Up at 7. – Thermometer at 26°: snowed during my early walk in the Botanic Garden: – snowed at several times of the day. – Letter from Marquis Camden asking my Infant Orphan votes for his Butler's son: – declined. – A long list of queries from Mr Cooper: it took me all day to answer them . . . Visit from V.C: he told me of his visit to the Queen; she enquired about inundations at Cambridge, about the healthiness of the place, etc, – all looking as if the P. of W. were coming up next October. The V.C. told me of a capture wch the Proctors made at 7 in the Evening of an omnibus on its way to Shelford (I think) where there was to be a dance:[10] the omnibus

---

7    Searby tells us that in 'the mid-1850s the net income of the butler of St John's was £299 a year (about £50 more than a senior fellow's)'. See pp. 143-5 for servants' profits in general.

8    See 23 February 1860.

9    i.e. Paul Morphy (1837-84) one of the greatest masters of chess both in Europe and America
•    where he was born. See his *Games of Chess . . . with analytical and critical notes* (1860).

10   On 30 January 1860 Proctor Blore received a letter signed by 'An Inhabitant of the Town' which led to the stopping of an omnibus near Parker's Piece before it left for a party at the de

contained 5 young women & 2 gownsmen (sons of Graham of Hinxton): the females were all lodged in the spinning house: they were not of the lowest class,
but one of them had been there before: – the V.C. has received indignant
letters from London saying the girls were innocent milliners going out for
a lark . . .

*Mon. 20.* . . . Mrs Hagger (d. of poor Mrs Sayer) called upon me. I asked
her her age: she said 34: 'why your brother told me you were about 40?' 'Well
I don't know rightly: it is all down in a book & I never thought of looking . . .
I booked her 36. Having failed to get her Mother's place as Bedmaker she is
now anxious to get her Mother's other place, – waiter in hall. So I wrote on
her behalf to Edleston the Steward. – She of course is in despair at her
Mother's death as her Mother maintained her & her husband & her 4 children:
the husband (after giving up work as blacksmith from failure of sight) used to
do the hard part of his Mother-in-law's work in College. – There was an awful
accident on the E.C. railway this morning to the Express Train at Tottenham:[11]
the driver & stoker killed: I hear 2 passengers also: – my friend Mr Ellicott
broke both his legs! he was brought to Cambridge by the 5 o'clock Express.
Mrs Ellicott had been telegraphed for directly after the accident . . . Visit from
the V.C. – He told me that the 500 University riflemen are to be sworn in next
Monday in the Senate House: they are then to go to St Mary's & hear a sermon
from their chaplain Mr Emery, & afterwards proceed to Parkers Piece to go
thro their exercises. – The V.C. described to me the wedding of Mr Smith
& Miss King at Madingley:[12] he says that Lady King made an attempt to kiss

Freville Arms in Shelford. Emma Kemp, who had taken her fourteen year old sister with her,
was then committed by the Vice-Chancellor to the Spinning House for a fortnight, but
pardoned after five days as the Master of Corpus vouched for the respectability of her mother.
This case was to be given wide – and from the University's point of view – undesirable
publicity for many months. Reports in the London press in December and January 1858-9 had
provoked protests from parents about the University's lax reaction to fornication with
prostitutes, but now the Town, long suspicious of the Vice-Chancellor's 350 year-old power to
commit to prison 'common women and others suspected of evil' arranged for Emma Kemp
and Sarah Ebbon, another of the girls, to bring actions for wrongful imprisonment against
him. It was the first time the University had been called into court on this matter. The case,
eventually heard on 30 November before Lord Chief Justice Erle, was said by one of the
Q.C.s opening for Emma Kemp to be 'of extreme importance to the liberty of Her Majesty's
subjects'. Fitzroy Kelly for the defendant, thought the protection of young men entrusted to
the care of the authorities of the University of even greater importance. Under cross
examination the Vice-Chancellor said 'he was quite satisfied immorality was intended' and
Kelly asked the jury whether the Proctors 'had not a perfect right to suspect that something
improper was likely to happen . . . when the parties were at that time of life when the
passions were strong and . . . dancing – was an exciting occupation'. The jury found that the
Proctors had reasonable grounds for suspicion but that the Vice-Chancellor should have
inquired into the plaintiff's character. Damages of £25 were then awarded to the plaintiff, but
the Lord Chief Justice stated that 'in my opinion it is an improper verdict' and that there must
be further discussion since 'the case is not decided'. For the further verdict see 12 June 1861.

[11] The *Chronicle* of 25 February gives a detailed account of the accident. Ellicott had been
sitting in the carriage next to the tender.

[12] Fanny King, a niece of Sir St Vincent Cotton and daughter of the late Vice-Admiral Sir
Richard King, was married on the sixteenth at Madingley to William Charles Smith of Short-
grove in Essex.

Mr Smith, but that he dexterously evaded it: – he says Mr Smith (who is just twice his wife's age) looked like a miserable victim . . . Letter from Mrs William Prest regretting that I was not a Lady, as she was collecting from all her Lady friends subscriptions for Colours for the Town Rifles (of wch her husband is Captain):[13] I desired her to consider me as a 'masculine old woman' & sent her 10/ . . . The Colours are to be made of bright green silk with the Town arms worked upon them.

*Th. 23.* . . . There was a great gathering in the Senatehouse because the Graces for degrees to Moral & Natural Sciences & also for abolishing St. Mary's Morning Sermons came on. – The Natural Sciences were unopposed: the Moral Sciences were carried nearly 4 to 1, the nos being 97 to 25 . . . The person who gave the Non Placet was E.H. Perowne: – among the 25 were Donaldson & Luard. – The Mor. & Nat. Sci. Tripos came into existence in 1848 when Philpott wrote a very able pamphlet in favor of the scheme: – there was great excitement on the occasion & the very large no of 238 persons voted, – nearly double of the 122 who voted today[14] . . . The Division on the Sermons was 84 to 22: so they are abolished . . . Letter from G.T.R: Cappy is better, & Bertie also . . .

*Sat. 25.* Up at 7. – Thermometer at 25° – Walk in Botanic Garden. – I was joined by Selwyn, his dog (Duke) having been trodden on by a horse & not being in walking order. – He told me that Mr Ellicott while lying on the ground with both his legs broken & his arm dreadfully scalded asked a porter to look for his little black bag of books: – when it was brought to him he said 'now I am quite contented'. – On the very morning of the accident before starting from Cambridge he said to Mrs E. 'if I should be smashed in the train today I shall be greatly missed, I have so much work on me' – He has some one to sit up with him every night as the scene of the disaster recurs to his mind in sleep & he wakes in horror . . . A tall handsome young Fellow Commoner called to ask if he could not put his name on a blank sheet of paper & be reckoned a Candidate for the Little-Go without doing a single question: – he said that it was done at Oxford & (he heard) here also: – I utterly deprecated it as a fraud, if it were feasible . . .

*Mon. 27.* . . . Frisby (who was one of the painters of my house last spring & who went out of his mind & was confined in the Fulbourne Asylum) called to see Harriet, who had kindly visited him in the Asylum: – he is now quite

[13] William Prest, the son of Samuel of Stapleford and Romilly's old widowed friend, had joined the Sixth Regiment after three terms' residence at Caius. He served for five years and was married to the widow of Commander William Lloyd, R.N.

[14] In 1848 moral philosophy, political economy, modern history, general jurisprudence and the laws of England were included in the Moral Sciences Tripos and candidates could be awarded honours as a result of the examination, but not a degree. The Natural Sciences Tripos, on which candidates could also be awarded honours but no degree, included anatomy, comparative anatomy, physiology, chemistry, botany, and geology. In 1854 the Senate had rejected the Studies Syndicate's recommendation that candidates should qualify for a degree, and W.G. Clark, classicist and Public Orator, described the MST as 'a shabby superficiality of knowledge'. The regulations approved on 23 February led to the creation of two Boards of Studies and the beginnings of reform. For a full account see Winstanley, *Later Victorian Cambridge*, pp. 185-206 and 2 December 1861.

well: gave him 5/: he is a worthy young man. – He gave Harriet a long
account of the great kindness he met with during the 10 months he was in the
Asylum, of the 3 grand balls, of the excellent fare, of the work (in the garden,
& latterly his own business of painting), of the variety of amusement
(bagatelle, drafts etc): by way of return he "grained" the Masters room.

*Mon. 5 March.* . . . Letter from James Heywood (Dissenter) asking when
he could take AM degree & saying that he is agitating about Dissenting AMs
having a vote[15] . . . At 12 to Senatehouse to see the Rifle corps take the oath of
Allegiance:[16]– Mr Eaden (Solicitor) made his appearance with a pair of
portentous bands to claim 1s from each person sworn. The arrangements were
excellent & it was impossible for any thing to go off better. Companies of from
16 to 24 marched up to the V.C. & stood face to face of each other, each
2 having a copy of the Allegiance: the V.C. read the oath very slowly to them
& every one repeated after him. – Dr Haviland is Physician of the Corps,
Mr Mortlock is Treasurer: they were both in the Senatehouse in their uniform:
by the way little Master Haviland was so charmed with his fathers uniform that
he kissed his gaiters this morning. Two of the Esquire Bedells are among the
Riflemen, Leapingwell is Serjeant, Godfray a private. – One of the young
riflemen (who was out of his line) jumped over the barrier in the Senate House
with the lightness of a greyhound. The swearing in took an hour: – before they
marched into the S.H. the 500 riflemen had been drawn up on Kings grass-plot
& produced a gallant show: – their uniform is grey: that of the 70 town
riflemen very dark green. – In front of their caps the University corps wear
a badge on wch the University arms are stamped: – it looks like silver but is
only electro-plated. – Parfit contracted to make the complete uniform for
5 Guineas. An engraving of the University arms was wanted for painting them
on the great drum of the Corps: one was taken from the Public Library: – it
was copied too minutely, for the words 'Liber Academiæ' were retained! – At
1 o'clock to St Mary's: it took about 20' for the 500 riflemen to take their
places in the galleries: the church was crammed: the conduct of the young men
was perfectly decorous. Emery (the Chaplain) preached a most earnest
& eloquent sermon (on purity) from Philippians. 1. 27. – I had a capital view
of the rifle corps (from my office window) as they marched thro the streets to
Parkers piece: – The great-drum was drum & cymbals too . . . The town corps
(with their rifles) kept the ground for the University corps & marched back
preceded by the University band . . .

[15] It took eight years of fierce argument in Oxford and Cambridge and parliament before
religious tests were abolished in 1871. Opponents felt either that abolition would mean the end
of religious life in the university or that it would prevent the serious study of religion. For
James Heywood of Trinity College, Fellow of King's College London 1856-87, and an original trustee of Owens College, Manchester, see Winstanley pp. 210, 221, 286.

[16] The oath, pledging allegiance to the crown and obedience to its military officers, is quoted by
H. Strachan, *History of the Cambridge University Officers Training Corps* (1976), p. 21, who
gives a detailed account of the volunteer movement in Cambridge. There were six college-based companies of which 4,5, and 6 were exclusively made up of Trinity men while no.
2 was made up of Johnians. Emery was a founder member of the corps (9 December 1859).
The uniform was 'somewhat in the style of the French infantry: light grey with red facings'
and the belts and the gaiters kissed by Master Haviland were buff.

*Tu. 6.* Up at 7. – So good an account of Mr Ellicott that I announced my intention of making no more enquiries . . . A very swell youngster (Edgell, Trin) – AB Nov./58) came to ask for a certificate of his degree as it will exempt him from an examination for his commission in the army: I had to state the subjects in wch he had been examined (Cicero's Milo, etc): this is the 1st time of my writing such a certificate. Long visit from Bradshaw of Kings: he did me a service by writing (at my request) the names of the Kings College volunteers. – I wrote letters to the 16 other Colleges & got a return from one of them viz Peterhouse: – they have 19 Riflemen . . . Read the 1st no of Dickens new tale 'journeys of an uncommercial traveller':[17] the 1st visit is to a workhouse: I thought it nasty & uncomfortable.

*Fri. 9.* . . . Visit from Senior Proctor Woollaston: I drew out for him a copy of the Grace (of 1818) instituting Proproctors & also a copy of the Proctors Oath. He & the Proproctor Blore were the Officers who made the Capture in the Omnibus:[18] they are prosecuted on behalf of a girl & the damages laid of £500 against each: – Woollaston says he has evidence of her having repeatedly been at a house of ill fame: – the trial is to be in London . . . Returns of Riflemen from Trinity, Emmanuel, Magdalene etc – Trinity has 3 whole Companies, making 221 men: St Johns has only 1 making 76 . . .

*Sat. 10.* Up at 7. Walk behind the Colleges: – the Trinity riflemen were at their drill both in the Master's & the Fellows' paddock . . .

*Th. 15.* . . . Meeting of the Governing Body about a new Statute (concerning penalty to Fellows for non-observance of discipline & for contumacy): the Commissioners sent a draft, in wch (as in our Elizabethan Statutes) the punishment of expulsion (after fruitless admonition etc) is to be inflicted (with the agreement of Master & 5 Seniors): – Sedgwick & Mathison were vehement against expulsion: they did not carry the meeting with them. We adjourned till next Tuesday. – Worked at the 'Wills' etc.[19] – Began also a paper of queries of C.H. Coopers. – Miss Apthorp ill.

*Fri. 16.* Up at 7. Walk behind Colleges. – Received from Luard a pamphlet of his about St Mary's in wch he remonstrates against the lack of subscription

---

[17] Dickens had made a speech to the Commercial Travellers Association in January and later decided to become an 'Uncommercial Traveller' and write a series of essays for *All The Year Round*, his new weekly journal. He was unwell and haunted by the spectres of his childhood and the subjects of the essays are indeed 'uncomfortable'.

[18] Cross-examined by Sir Fitzroy Kelly on 30 November 1860, Proctor Blore said that neither he nor Woollaston knew any of the women and that 'none of our men [the bulldogs] pointed out any of the girls as bad characters'. See the full report of proceedings in the Court of Common Pleas in *The Times* 30 November 1860.

[19] On 4 March Romilly had been asked (together with other holders of probate records) to surrender the University's valuable collection of some 1,550 wills and other testamentary documents proved in the ancient Chancellor's (latterly, the Vice-Chancellor's) Court to the Registrars of the Queen's Court of Probate at Peterborough. On 19 March having protested strongly in vain, 'The Wills etc. went off in 4 boxes to Peterborough' and Romilly on 27 March told the Keeper of Archives at Oxford who had sent him a draft of their bill for retaining the archives that he 'was now against agitating the matter'. The documents were retained by Peterborough until 21 March 1956. Oxford was allowed to keep its wills on condition that an index be supplied and one was published in 1862. See 18 June 1860.

to the Improvements:[20] at the meeting of the Governing Body he mentioned that the last Fellow of Trinity who was deprived of his Fellowship was Wyvill: his offence was breaking the Masters spoons[21] . . .

*Tu. 20.* Up at ¼ to 7. – Called on Mrs Smyth: she is behind-hand for 2 quarters of Sarah's Schooling, – wch is the history of her having kept her at home this last quarter: – gave her the money (£13.3s 8d) to pay her debt . . . Meeting of the Governing Body at 12: we agreed to an amended statute (for suspending for a year & (after repeated contumacious violation of discipline) of depriving a Fellow of his Fellowship): we allowed the appeal to the visitor with the power of the visitors modifying or even reversing the sentence: – we made a condition that no suspension or expulsion should be inflicted without the voices of the Master & 5 Seniors . . . At Christs they proposed to the Commissioners a similar statute with the extravagant power of the Master & 2 Seniors being able to suspend & expel. – this statute was agreed to by the Commissioners . . .

*Mon. 26.* . . . The letters from Frank & Sophie were satisfactory about everybody but Frank himself, who says he considers himself 10 years older than me: – wrote to him announcing £10 (wch ought not to be sent till next Monday) & £25 for Madame & £5 for Nini: wrote french letters to Madame, Fanny & Sophie (in wch last was a very short English one to loup loup).[22] – To Kings Lawn at 2 o'clock: the University rifles were reviewed there: it was a very pretty sight: they went thro their evolutions very correctly: Major Baker commanded. – he was on horseback: on the other side of the river there were sham skirmishes. – The Band plaid 'God save the Q.' as the riflemen marched off the ground. – At 7¼ to Mrs Prests to play Quadrille . . .

*Wed. 28.* . . . Letter from Luard asking for £20 more for St Mary's I having already *paid* my subscription of £50!!!! I think this is the boldest begging I ever heard of: but he is most enthusiastic in every thing he takes up, & says he cannot raise the necessary funds unless all his friends will give him £20: – wrote to say that I could not afford to give him any thing. Frightened in my office by the arrival of a telegram from Shoreditch: my alarm was only momentary, for it was nothing but a question from a Clare Hall man (Gould) 'can I take my degree tomorrow?': – I returned answer 'yes': – I paid 6d for the telegram received & 2s/ for that sent. – Read the March no of the 'Cornhill Magazine' (the 3d): I liked nothing but Thackerays story of 'Lovell the

---

[20] Luard was Perpetual Curate of Great St Mary's and his pamphlet bewailed the lack of space there because of the room taken up by the gallery ('Golgotha') erected in 1757. The font had been relegated to a corner under the staircase and there was no possibility of celebrating Holy Communion in the chancel if there were more than a few communicants. In order to remove the offending gallery Luard hoped to raise £100 from each college and support from individual members of the university.

[21] Mr Jonathan Smith of Trinity Library tells us that on 5 April 1708 the College conclusion books record 'Ordered by the Master and Seniors that 2 fellowships late of Mr Wyvill and Mr Brevat be declared void'. Monk's *Life of Bentley* vol. 1 p. 215 suggests that John Wyvill was caught cutting up College plate in order to melt it down and sell it, perhaps to pay off debts incurred while travelling. Nevertheless, he was ordained in 1709 and in 1714 became a canon of St Pauls.

[22] The name given to himself by Sophie Oger's little boy.

widower' in wch there was some amusement . . . I thought Frimley parsonage dull: it is written by a son of Mrs Trollope: he has written Barchester Towers & some other Novels that have been successful. – Began reading again Walter Scott's Anne of Geierstein.

*Wed. 11 April.* . . . Sarah Smyth returned to school this morning: gave her ½ a Sovereign last night for her travelling expenses thro the hands of Harriet but avoided an interview. – Visit in my office from Mrs Carpenter: the Master has received her & her daughter very kindly & allowed her to have the 6 rooms in the Lecture Room staircase & to have her daughter as a help: but she is afraid of losing that snug little sinecure wch she has as my bedmaker, so I wrote to the Master in her behalf. – Letter from Mrs Kennedy: a very charming one: she gives criticisms of Adam Bede, of Thackeray's writings, of Turner's paintings etc etc in a most agreeable style . . . Read Macaulay's admirable criticism on Addison.[23]

*Sun. 15.* . . . Called on Mrs Prest & met there Mrs Leapingwell, who (being a clever woman) is most intolerant of those she thinks otherwise, among whom she thinks Mrs Paget preeminent: – she won't even allow her to be pretty. Mrs Paget has 2 twin sisters (Mrs Pinnock & Mrs Bryan King) whom she allows to be most handsome. – Mr Taylor (the handsome Tutor of Peterhouse was assailed by her as a lady-killer & as having trifled with the affections of 3 young ladies very recently: – I said 'Dr Pulling had a bad name in that way': – I had better have let that alone as he is a relation of Mrs Williams . . . Afterwards met Mrs Miller (with Mary & Emma): she had been to see Grote, who (she says) looks beautiful with his new teeth: – she says he is very like Schiller. – After dinner read Goodwin's Commentary on St Mark[24] & Jeremy Taylor's 'Liberty of Prophesying'.

*Sat. 21.* . . . At 10 to Chapel for the admission of the 19 new scholars . . . these were all 19 genuine scholars, as the reserved Westminster Scholarships are come to an end . . . Visit from Mr Johnson (the Dissenting Schoolmaster): he is AB of /57: he wishes to take AM in order to have the privilege of taking books out of the Public Library: – he can't have his name in the University Register, being a dissenter: he can't have books out unless he pays the Library tax: he must therefore have his name on the College boards: but his College (Corpus) refuses to keep his name after he has taken A.M. – I think this very illiberal of Corpus: – I recommended his applying to Dr Bateson as the most liberal head of a house whom I know:[25] he had thought of Philpott . . .

*Th. 26.* . . . Called at Pagets to see the Twins: Mrs P. was out but Dr P was at home & had the little ladies brought down to me, the eldest Rose Emma is sleek & plump & gentle, the youngest Violet Elisabeth is smaller & thin & fierce: gave each of the maids 2/. – In my office I had a visit from

---

[23] Presumably in 'Critical and Historical Essays' contributed to the *Edinburgh Review* (1843).

[24] i.e. Harvey Goodwin's *A Commentary on the Gospel of S. Mark* (1860).

[25] It is to be hoped that Bateson was more helpful than the evangelical Dr Pulling. No one was allowed to borrow books from the University Library unless he had been admitted to the degree of M.B., LL.B., M.A., M.D., LL.D. or D.D., had his names on the Boards of his College, or was a member of the Senate resident in town. Members of the university, excepting sizars, each had to pay a quarterly contribution of 1s-6d to Library funds.

Leapingwell who railed at the folly of strict Sabbatarians. – I read with great delight Macaulay's article on Warren Hastings.

*Wed. 2 May.* . . . The wind has been for the last 3 days in the very point that troubles my Office chimney: it fills the room with dense smoke. – Copied out the Woodwardian Inspector's Report:[26]– I was pleased with one remark: 'it ought now to be called the Sedgwickian & not the Woodwardian Museum': – this remark was justified by Sedgwick's magnificent contributions. – I copied also a most interesting statement of Sedgwicks, in wch he tells of all the presents by himself & his friends during the year & gives details of all the work done by Seeley (whom he employs & pays to arrange a catalogue etc etc). – Visit from the V.C.: he told me that Sedgwick made a brilliant speech after dinner[27] & was very complimentary to the ladies . . .

*Th. 3.* . . . Found a little boy in the back way to the Post Office crying: I stopt to ask him what was the matter: he said 'a boy has pulled off my cap & thrown it in there' – pointing to the grating of a malting: – a girl & boy said it was so. – I shouted out to ask if any one was within: a husky drunken voice answered me: I begged the man to pick up the poor boys cap & give it to me: – he said it was in the malt & he durst not go into the malt to get it, for he might be imprisoned if he trod on the malt: – 'will you let me in if I come round?' 'Yes': – so round I went & he had braved the fear of imprisonment, had trampled on the malt & gave me the childs cap. – Henslow told me that he is going to lecture on Botany to the Royal children: – Owen has been giving 3 Lectures on Natural History to the Queen & her children . . .

*Tu. 8.* Up at ¼ to 7. – Walk in Botanic Garden. – Feeling much out of sorts I called on Paget at 8½: he was already gone to a Patient at Coton: I went in & had a chat with Mrs Paget & her 2 boys Edmund & Charles. – Afterwards Paget came to my office: he recommended 8 leaches at back of my ears: he dissuaded using Dr Bonds pills of 1855 (wch have steel in them) & has prescribed a pill of his own just before dinner every day . . . At 2 o'clock came to my house a very agreeable man from Mr Bumpsteds to put on the leaches: I found him very pleasant & cheerful: the leaches were 2 hours at their meal: – the bleeding did not altogether cease till near 10: – the loss of blood did not make me feel at all faint, tho Harriet kindly came up twice with Salts listening at the door to find if I was overcome: but as she heard me talking cheerfully went away . . .

*Wed. 9.* . . . have no doubt I am better. – I had no rushing of blood yesterday Evening in my head . . . Visit from Selwyn accompanied by my old pupil Sir James Colvile: he is a very fine man of Colossal dimensions: he is a Privy Counsellor: he said he was my pupil as a freshman. – Selwyn has

---

[26] Dr Woodward in his will of 1727 left the University his English fossils and the University then bought the foreign fossils which he had described in printed catalogues. These formed the nucleus of the Geological Museum which as the newly called Sedgwick Museum moved to the Downing Street site in 1903.

[27] i.e. the Woodward Audit dinner.

a dinner party today at wch the Duke of St Albans,[28] the Master of Trinity & Sir James are to be present: – Selwyn wished to learn the precedence: I said it was clear that the Duke must take out Mrs Selwyn, & that I recommended an amiable man like Sir James giving way to Whewell (or Lord Affleck as the wags call him)[29] . . .

*Tu. 15.* Up at ¼ to 7 – Thank God I slept well: – the throbbing in my head is less but is not gone . . . Very affectionate letter of condolence in my illness from Maggie: she is highly pleased with her new house wch is full of accommodation & is surrounded with trees: a blackbird & a thrush are frequent visitors in their garden: their domestic creatures are a goldfish, & cat & 3 kittens: – plenty of mice & black beetles in the house . . .

*Sat. 19.* Up at ¼ to 7. Woke with throbbing in the head: but by God's blessing I slept well. Walk in B.G: the verdure of the leaves is exquisite, & the bloom most beautiful. – Wrote to Phelps declining his 'Family' next Friday & begged him to communicate my leaving the Club & my regret at doing so . . .

*Wed. 23.* . . . Letter from Grim saying he proposes coming about the 5th of June: he is now on Sunday Evenings & nights engaged in the duties of a Policeman, for he sallies out to lay hold of the riotous disorderly drunken people: he is accompanied by the Police: – the Cumbrians are addicted to the brutal sport of cockfighting & he expects severe duty WhitSunday night . . .

*Sat. 26.* . . . Fell in with Peete Musgrave (Canon of York, nephew of late Archbishop) while going to a horrid Seniority wch lasted 2 hr 20': he was coming to pay me a visit: his face is as red as a peony: – he brought as a present to the College Library the Archbishop's copy of the Koran wch had belonged to Tippoo Saib.[30] – At the Seniority Mathison refused to sign the Testimonial for L. Craven (our Fellow's) ordination in the 1st form wch speaks of having lived a sober etc life while resident with us: – so the inferior form (wch omits all allusion to moral conduct) was substituted. We had a great deal of Bursarial business, & the Master entered into interesting details about the Hostel wch he has built:[31] it will contain 28 sets of rooms: Luard will reside there: Martin rather objects to its being called 'Michael Hostel' because it is not in St Michael parish. – Called on Paget as I feel thoroughly nervous & out of sorts . . . he recommends meat every day, lamb, mutton or chicken. – Very kind letter from Phelps telling of the regret felt at my resignation

[28] The Duke of St Albans, William Beauclerk, who had succeeded to the title when he was nine, was in his fourth term at Trinity and, Dr. H.C. Porter tells us, became a prominent member of the Amateur Dramatic Club.

[29] The second Mrs Whewell was the widow of Sir Gilbert Affleck, baronet, and after her marriage was curiously and generally known as Lady Affleck. The hit at Whewell presumably refers to his overbearing sense of the dignity of his position especially in his early years as Master and is perhaps also a reference to the money that his second wife brought to the marriage.

[30] Tippoo Sahib, for many years opposed to British expansion in India, was defeated and killed in 1799. His great library was transferred to the East India Company at Calcutta, and manuscripts from it made an outstanding contribution to the collection of printed editions of native Indian literature in the University Library. See McKitterick, pp. 376-7.

[31] See 7 May 1859 and 10 March 1863.

& begging I would allow myself to be considered an honorary member: wrote to say I should be most happy. – Harriet today went 24 miles in a fly to Wickhambrook to take home a friend of hers Anne Shaw (Cook at Mr Edmund Fosters) who is very ill & has the diphtheria.[32] – She didn't get back till past 10: – it was very kind of her to go for she is not well herself & was a good deal overcome. – The Evening being wet I had a fire.

*Th. 31.* . . . Letter from Cartmell telling me the election of a Tancred student yesterday.[33] The Election took place in London at Mr Koe's chambers (Treasurer of Lincoln's Inn). Of the Candidates examined in Caius Hall (by Gunson & Thorpe of Christs & by Hutt & Croft of Caius) 19 were pronounced to have not done well enough for their cases to be considered . . . The successful Candidate was not the person who was highest in the Examination: – his name is William Page Oldham: his father was a surgeon just getting into good practice at Alfreton in Derbyshire when he was struck dead by lightning 6 years ago leaving a widow & eleven!! children: this W.P.O is the eldest boy: the eldest girl is a Governess: – the case excited so much sympathy that a subscription was made & £800 raised as a fund to educate the children: – but the widow has only £150 a year to maintain herself & family. – It would be very difficult for a more fitting object of Mr Tancred's bounty to be found . . .

*Th. 14 June.* Up at 7. – Hope I am a little better, tho the throbbing is still in my head the moment I lie down . . . Directly after 2 o'clock dinner went back to my office to catch deficient signatures etc etc: – staid there till 7¼. – Then walked behind Colleges. I fell in with Mathison & talked with him about the Examination for 'Minor Scholarships',[34] wch ended today having lasted 2 days & a half: there were 40 Candidates, of whom 32 have been entered: of the 8 not entered one is very good & likely to be successful. – The Father of one of the Candidates *a fortnight ago* made the modest request that Mathison would then furnish him with copies of the papers about to be set!!!

*Fri. 15.* . . . The Vicechancellor then went with me to my office: indeed I had been with him there already in the morning & had looked up for him a variety of documents which he is getting together for the trial (Emma Kemp v Latimer) wch comes on next Monday . . .

---

[32] There were great outbreaks in the nineteenth century of this dangerous, infectious, and often fatal disease. Harriet was not alone in being unaware of the risks she ran in accompanying Anne Shaw. The cause and transmission of streptococcal infection remained unknown, and the pathologist Sir Philip Panton could still write forty-four years later, 'On one occasion a nurse whom I had diagnosed in the morning as suffering from diphtheria was discovered later that night transferred to the children's ward'. (A. Rook, Carleton and Cannon, *The History of Addenbrooke's Hospital Cambridge*, 1991, p. 174).

[33] Christopher Tancred (1680-1754) of the West Riding of Yorkshire and owner of a small property at Newmarket left part of his property in trust for the education of four poor students in divinity at Christ's and four in physic at Gonville and Caius.

[34] The Commissioners had proposed that six minor scholarships, not tied to any particular school, should be competed for annually. The annual value was to be at least £40, and the College hoped that this more open competition would attract an increasing number of able young men. See 21 June 1860.

*Mon. 18.* Up at 7. – No walk. – Thank God I feel better this morning
& had no throbbing in my head when I awoke. At 9½ left Cambs. by the
London Express. I was in the same carriage with Mr Walpole, Drs Corrie
& Philpott & Edleston: – the V.C. came up by an earlier train & Dr Philpott
came direct from Norwich. – Gave Edleston a lift in my cab as far as the
Golden Cross, where I put up. By the way Mr Walpole asked me yesterday if
I would like to recover the University Wills. I said 'very much – but not at the
cost of a private bill': he said 'O! it will be a public bill, & I will put Camb. in
as well as Oxford' . . . At Fendall's Hotel I found the V.C, Drs Philpott
& Corrie & John James Smith: we were afterwards joined by Woollaston,
Blore & Mr Hyde. – I remained with this party till ¼ past 3. – It was then
reported that the preliminary prosecution of Barnard Smith would not come on
before 4; & that in all probability the case 'Kemp v Neville' would not be
heard till Saturday!! So I might well have done my own duty in Cambridge
today. –

I now went to the Athenæum & found Sedgwick who was just emerged
from a medicated vapour bath . . . I then went to see Holman Hunt's famous
picture:[35] I was much surprised at its smallness (sold for £6000 as the Exhibitor
told me): it is painted with the high finish of an enamel, but I dislike the
picture exceedingly: – I can see none of the expression of Divinity in our Lords
face (wch Sophie thought so wonderful) & I found great stiffness & coldness in
the group of our Lord & the Virgin. – I went also to see Rosa Bonheur's
pictures with wch I was enchanted . . . I then went into St James' park & sat
down (on a penny chair) by the water-side: – the weather being beautiful the
park was thronged. I then walked to Westminster & looked at the Victoria
tower etc etc & walked across the make-shift bridge for passengers. I drank tea
at the Athenæum & afterwards walked again in the Park with Sedgwick
& Thompson. Sedgwick 1st took us to Pontet & armed himself & us with
Cigars. – Thompson was very amusing. He says that Lord Palmerston (on
being reproached with the appointment of Kingsley to the Chair of Modern
History, – of wch he knew nothing) exclaimed 'Why! he wrote '2 years ago',
& if that is not modern history what is?'. – Thompson says that Lady Affleck
inherited from her brother R.L. Ellis £60,000: Ellis died worth £140,000: he
left £60,000 to the 2 Children of his late sister Mrs Unwin: – he left numerous
legacies, – & small souvenirs of £50 to himself (Thompson), Sedgwick etc etc
etc. – Whewell is going to found a Professorship of 'international Law':[36]–
perhaps that is the reason of dedicating his Hostel to Peace.

---

[35] i.e. the 'Finding of the Saviour in the Temple'. According to *D.N.B.* it was sold for 5500
guineas to the picture-dealer Gambart who exhibited it in Bond Street with great success.
It was given to Birmingham Art Gallery in 1896. Rosa Bonheur was a painter of animals and
country scenes whose patronage by Queen Victoria helped to make her work sought after
by the English aristocracy.

[36] The chair was founded by Whewell's will in 1867; its holder was to suggest 'such measures
as may tend to diminish the evils of war and finally to extinguish war between nations'.
(*Endowments,* pp. 136-40).

*Tu. 19.* Up at 8 – Thank God I feel very comfortable. – Breakfast at Golden Cross. – I then went to Westminster & got into Court in the case Cattaway v. Barnard Smith:[37] I stood all the time: I heard O Malley, G. Denman etc speak, & the furious final speech of James for heavy damages. I thought Barnard Smith gave his evidence in a remarkably clear stile: the matron (Mrs Johnson) also spoke well to the point. The speech of Mr James derided the laws of Cambridge wch were (he said) utterly unlike the laws of England & interfered with the liberty of the subject: he also made a tirade against the defendant's having stated that Mrs Cattaway washed for one of the prostitutes, – as if these unfortunates were to be debarred from cleanliness . . . The Chief Justice (Erle) (who has a trick of lifting up his eyes to heaven) summed up favorably to Barnard Smith, but said that tho he himself had intended that the 2 known prostitutes should alone be brought into the Spinninghouse, yet he was answerable for the act of his servant (the bulldog): – that Cattaway had indeed been detained only 1 qr of an hour . . . that Cattaway had been passing the Evening with one of these Prostitutes & had accompanied her in her walk – so that there was no case for heavy damages. – The Jury (½ special, ½ common) gave £50: – the damages had been laid at £500. – The Chief Justice & Counsel agreed to the case against the V.C. (Kemp v Neville) coming up next Saturday at 10 . . . Called on Mrs Edward Romilly & had a good chat with her & agreed to meet her & Edward at the British Gallery[38] at 4½ . . . discussed the Pictures, which I thought a less interesting collection than usual: – there is a large no of pictures by the earliest Italian Masters wch gave me no pleasure whatever, tho most valuable in the history of Art: – they belong to a most opulent picture-maniac named A. Barker,[39] – a retired shoemaker: – met at the Exhibition Dr & Mrs Cartmell & their baby! & Mr & Mrs Austen. – I also called on Sophie & had a most agreeable talk with her, principally about Frank (who was at the Examination at King's College):[40] – Frank had been examined in French yesterday, & had been unable to translate 'much ado about nothing' into a french phrase: – I confessed my incapacity . . . Read the 1st Vol of 'the Mill on the Floss': Tom & her [sic] sister Maggie interested me highly.

*Wed. 20.* . . . Breakfast at Golden Cross. Then sallied out in the pouring rain to do a little shopping (buying myself silk handkerchiefs, a satin stock & black silk cravat). – I received Dividends wch were sadly in arrear, I having received none since March 1859 . . . Had some cold meat at the Athenæum. – Came to Cambridge by the 5 o'cl. train: I travelled by 2d Class so was not in

---

[37] This was the second day of hearing the first action against the University in the Court of Common Pleas. Cattaway claimed that her reputation had been injured by having been seen to be taken, mistakenly, into the Spinning House and held there for half an hour. The Chief Justice said that Smith had come forward in a way which did him a great deal of credit and had accepted responsibility for the mistaken action of one of his men. The case attracted considerable publicity, though less than that of Kemp v. Neville. See 13 February 1860.

[38] i.e. the National Gallery.

[39] Alexander Barker's collection of pictures, chiefly by great fifteenth century painters, sold at Christies in 1874 for £38,591. See G.F. Waagen *Treasures of Art in Great Britain* II, 125-9.

[40] King's College School, London.

the same carriage with Bateson etc etc . . . Found the maids well & the house beautifully clean.

*Th. 21.* . . . Visit from Mathison: I learned from him the names & schools of the 6 youths who were yesterday elected 'Minor Scholars': their names etc are as follows

- (1) C.B. Davies (Blackheath) – pupil of Clarks
- (2) W.P. Turnbull (St Peter's York) – pupil of Lightfoot
- (3) W.P. Howard (St Paul's)          do
- (4) F.W.H. Myers (Cheltenham) – pup. of Mathison
- (5) H.J. Purkiss (City of London)      do
- (6) A.R. Vardy (City of London)       do

All these 6 youths did very well, & the 1st two very remarkably so: – they are all lads of excellent promise . . .

*Th. 28.* . . . Visit from Archdall – he tells me that it is now 2 years since he gave up going to parties or giving any: I asked him what year he was born in: he told me 1787. He was a détenu in Paris from 1803 to 1810 & says that he then got a passport[41] signed by the Emperor at the time of his rejoicings at his marriage with the Austrian Princess: – General Clark (Duc de Feltre) was a friend of Archdall's & gave a passport among a heap of official papers to the Emperor to sign . . . After dinner read & had coffee in the garden. – Just as I started for my walk I met Worsley & Madam on their road to my house with a basket full of beautiful roses: – after depositing the roses & resting awhile in my parlour I accompanied them to their own grounds & saw the haymaking & spent an hour very agreeably with them . . .

*Fri. 29.* . . . From 5 to 8 I was out: – I walked from Jesus College by the side of the river to 'River Lane' Barnwell: in this lane are the Abbey-Church Schools for girls & infants: they were erected in 1858: they are in different coloured bricks & have rather a fantastic tower: – I peeped in at the windows & thought the rooms spacious & well-lighted. I then walked thro Barnwell to the Paper-Mills (– where there is no longer a 'Gate'). – I was foolish enough to follow the course of the Paper-Mills brook hoping to get into the Cherry Hinton fields path: – violent rain came on: I was at one place in considerable alarm about being bogged; I was not able to get to the Cherry-Hinton path, & was very thankful at last to reach (after more than an hours most floundering & sinking sort of picking my way thro Coldham Common quagmires) the outskirts of Barnwell. – I got home at 8 & put on dry stockings etc & was rejoiced at finding that Caroline had lighted me a fire – Throbbing when I went to bed.

*Fri. 6 July.* Up at 7. – No early walk. – Feel heavy & uncomfortable. – Summoned again to town in re 'Kemp v Neville': – went in 2d Class & passed my time most agreeably in reading 'Midsummer Night's Dream'. Drove direct to the Guildhall Coffeehouse (kept by Walters) & engaged a bed: – this Coffeehouse (or Hotel) is close to the Guildhall. Mr Hyde had engaged a room there, – in which during the morning I saw the V.C, Philpott, Woollaston,

---

[41] The passport still exists at Emmanuel College.

Mynors Bright, Currey, Blore Hough (Surgeon) etc etc . . . Returned to the Hotel at 3; after about ½ hour word was brought that the trial could not come on today but was fixed for the 1st cause on Tuesday morning! So I have come up a 2d time on a fools errand. – Drove to the Shoreditch station & made my dinner in the Refreshment-room off a very indifferent cold veal & ham pie & a sausage-roll. Down to Camb. by 5 o'cl Express (in 2d Class) . . .

*Sat. 7.* . . . Letter from Maggie . . . she found the air of Hernebay (whither she went on the 26th too keen for poor Bertie so she has moved to Margate: Bertie was on the point of death at Herne Bay, but the Margate Doctor speaks hopefully. – George is not allowed any holidays this year so she & her children will spend their 6 weeks at the sea without him . . .

*Sun. 8.* . . . Paid my usual Sunday visit to Mrs Prest . . . She told me that both Mr & Mrs Maddison were dreadfully overcome by that horrible event in their household,[42] – of the young girl (only 15 years old) cutting her throat with Maddison's razor: – the girl has committed childish pilferings of cakes & sweetmeats & had been reprimanded (very gently) by Mrs Maddison & *forgiven* & continued in her place; – Maddison was at the time so much overwhelmed that he could not give evidence at the inquest: – poor Mrs Maddison had to go thro that painful duty . . .

*Tu. 10.* Up at 7½: – not much throbbing, thank God. – Currey (Orator 28 years ago) called on me & I took a little walk with him before breakfast (he having already breakfasted at his hotel in Aldersgate St.) – In the course of the morning Sedgwick dropt in: he was just fresh down from W. of England: after having been made LLD with so much applause at Oxford & dining with the Vicechancellor (Jeune) he had been to Clifton to see his nephew Westall & had spent a day with Mr Harford of Blaize Castle & 2 days with Mr & Mrs Guthrie (Caroline Clark):[43] he received the most cordial welcome from that most enthusiastic & admirable lady: he had not seen her for above 20 years: she devotes herself most passionately to doing good: she is constant in her visiting the sick (however revolting their complaints may be) & has acquired considerable surgical skill, – using the lancet & the probe freely. – The V.C., Philpott & myself lounged for hours about the Guildhall, occasionally going into the different courts. – At 1 the V.C. gave us Sandwiches, & a little before 3 it was decided that our case could not be heard (– this being the last day of the Courts sitting): – so I have been compelled 3 times to go to London in vain: – the trial is to come on in December. Returned to Cambridge by the 5 o'cl. express . . . Harriet has a visitor, Anne Shaw, who was so dangerously ill with diphtheria: I begged her to stay as long as she liked . . .

On 12 July Romilly left Cambridge for a second visit to the Victoria Hotel in Yarmouth. The weather was often windy and wet – on the day after his arrival at 'dinner time a sailor came in begging for the families of 4 fishermen whose boat was swamped this morning and they drowned'. However, as Romilly's readers would expect, the diary records no grumbles but descriptions of bathes in rough seas and long

[42] George Maddison, Vicar of All Saints, Cambridge 1838-56, was now Vicar of Grantham and we cannot find any account of the tragedy in the Cambridge papers.
[43] See 19 April 1859.

walks in the rain. There were also unusually few people about whom Romilly knew. 'Yarmouth has not been so empty as it is now time out of mind', so he spent many hours reading indoors, or on the beach if fine – T.C. Haliburton's *The Clockmaker or the sayings and doings of Samuel Slick of Slickville*, Montaigne's *Essays*, Ariosto's *Orlando Furioso*, and two plays by the German playwright Lessing. On 17 July, a fine day, 'from 6 to 8 I lay down on the beach wrapt up in my cloke (for it was very cold) & read the "Andria"', Terence's earliest comedy 'with great delight' and then back in his hotel spent an agreeable hour with H.T. Buckle, the author of the 'History of Civilisation in England' which had created 'so intense a sensation'. 'Mr Buckle (as I learned in private from Mr Capel)', the clergyman who had seen the book through the press, 'knows all languages, is a 1st-rate chess player, is about 38, has a library of 20,000 volumes & has never been of any profession. I thought him a capital talker'. August the fourth was also companionable as Charles Howes, a Minor Canon of Norwich Cathedral, took him to drink tea with his brother, the Vicar of Belton, and his family. 'It was a very pretty sight seeing all this happy family party: – Mrs F. Howes was sorry that I missed seeing one of her children (– the baby who was in bed): – a 14th child is expected soon. – After dessert the children and uncle Charles plaid at bowls on the lawn & also at a game (wch I never heard of) called Croquet: the players have long-handled mallets with wch they strike wooden balls along the grass thro 7 iron rings fastened in the ground: – the children also walked on stilts & had a fine game of romps till tea-time'.

Perhaps because of the rarity of such amusements the throbbing in Romilly's head improved and he was encouraged too by satisfactory news of all at Bene't Place where Betsy Spink had been staying with Harriet, a frequent correspondent, and Caroline. He heard too from Maggie Romilly, still on holiday with the children at Margate, who was 'disgusted by the bathing machines of the men and women being close together & abstains from bathing'. In decorous Yarmouth on 21 August the weather 'greatly mended in the Evening and I enjoyed my 2 hours stroll from 6 to 8. – After tea I went on the Pier: the appearance of the sea was exquisitely beautiful: there was a most extraordinarily brilliant phosphorescence, & the effect was the more striking from there being a good deal of motion in the water: people exclaimed with delight at the bursting of the breakers'.

On five of the Sunday mornings on which he was away (he was with Sedgwick in Norwich on the sixth), Romilly went faithfully to the 'glorious' church of St Nicholas which was said to hold 3000 people and on Sunday mornings seemed to be full. But on four Sunday evenings he adventured to the Baptist Chapel, the Wesleian Chapel, the Wesleian Free Chapel and to a 'Love Feast' at the Primitive Methodists 'until I could stand it no longer'. The last three days of the holiday were fine. The Yarmouth rifles went 'thro their manœuvres, hundreds of Sunday school children enjoyed their annual treat on the beach and on the day before his return home Romilly had 'a coloured photograph taken of my phiz by a man named Winter . . . I thought I remained perfectly still, but he declared I did not, & the 2 first sittings he declared failures: the 3d he thought would do: – he put my head in a sort of pillory – a ½ Collar at the back of the chair: – his prices varied from 6d to a Guinea: I paid 7/6. – The no of photographers here is prodigious'.

*Th. 30.* . . . Got home at ¼ to 2: found every thing beautifully neat & clean: rejoiced to find Harriet very much better: indeed she looks perfectly well & gives a good account of herself: Caroline too is quite well . . .

*Sun. 2 September.* Up at 7. – Walk to Railway bridge. – A ludicrous thing happened to me: I bought a new hat yesterday: – I put it on today to go to church: when I had got a hundred yards from my own door a man said 'there's paper on your hat': – & sure enough it was so, – the hat was covered with silver paper according to hatters fashion: – very lucky for me to have been told so early, for I should have excited derision if I had walked thro Barnwell in such a state . . . Mr Roose (who shares my pew) on coming out of church pointed out to me Miss Amy Sedgwick (the famous tragic actress who is going to play all this week):[44] she is very young, very goodlooking, was drest in excellent taste & looks like a Lady: Mr Roose told me that she is married, I think he said her husband is Dr Parker: – she is very charitable . . .

*Tu. 18.* . . . Poor W.G. Watson (chaplain of Grays Inn – grandson of the Bishop) has fallen into a crevasse on the Alps:[45]– there has been a sad no of fatal accidents in the Alps this year. – Poor dear Lucy's favorite Carry Hudson (now Mrs Lane) came with a day-ticket. Her husband & 2 of her 4 children (– she has had 5) came with her; I was exceedingly glad to see her: she looked very nicely, & was quiet & gentle as she always used to be: I was pleased with her husband, who is a very respectable looking man of genteel appearance & good countenance & good address . . . They dined in the kitchen & had a bottle of Audit & a bottle of Port. – Harriet very kindly took charge of them & escorted them to the Railway tavern where they all 4 slept in one bed. – Worked diligently till 2 o'clock at a prodigious list of queries of Mr Coopers . . .

*Th. 20.* Up at 7. – A lovely morning – Walk behind Colleges. – Grateful letter from Joseph & Caroline Lane, saying they arrived quite safely. This was the last regular day for applicants for Voluntary Theological Candidates: – among my personal visitors were Henry John Wale (the man made up of fiery red hair). – One person sent a *parcel* from Peterboro enclosing a letter of application: the parcel was endorsed 'Instant: with all speed': – he was in such a hurry as to forget the carriage wch cost me 6 pence . . . Mrs Prest sent her servants last night to the grand bespeak:[46] the coachman roared of laughter at the farce 'the Boots at the Lion': – the other 2 pieces were 'Still waters etc' & 'Volunteer in difficulties' (written by a Mr Palmer) . . . From 5 to 7¼

---

[44] Amy Sedgwick (1830-97) was the stage name of Sarah Gardiner, daughter of William Gardiner, amateur musician and author of *Sacred Melodies* (1813). Well known on the London stage, she gave dramatic recitals there and in the provinces. Her first husband, Dr W.B. Parkes, died three weeks after her visit to Cambridge. See Searby p. 708.

[45] 'To the exercise taken there is now no limit . . . The quietest sort of people are now uncomfortable unless they, at least once a year, tie themselves in batches and go prowling over the tops of unexplored Alps.' (*Saturday Review* 21 April 1860 Vol. 9, p. 493). See also *The Times* (29 September 1860) for a letter from H.J. Cheals saying that in a letter of 21 December 1857 he 'had warned my countrymen against employing Müller', the Tyrolese guide now on trial for the loss of Watson.

[46] The bespeak was often a benefit night for the leading actor whose friends may have chosen the plays. Mrs Prest's servants had gone to the old Theatre Royal in Barnwell, the present Festival, on the best attended night of a thin week. The *Chronicle* of 22 September thought 'Boots at the Lion' a farce 'that never fails to excite an immeasurable amount of risibility'.

357

walked . . . it was very pleasant: in Chesterton I saw a large field of wheat *uncut*. After tea 'Abbot'.[47]

*Sun. 23.* Mrs Lane (Carry Hudson) kindly sent Harriet yesterday a present of the poems of Poe (the American): the book is a very pretty one with good engravings & is well bound: Mrs Lane bought it in the Crystal Palace. Yesterday after dinner I read the life of this dissipated genius (who died in a drunken fit at 38): – I also read his 'Raven' (– the best known of his poems & admired it) . . . Letter from G.T.R. announcing himself for 7 P.M. next Saturday: wrote to him saying that I should dine at 2 but would give him a strong tea at 7. – wrote also to Mrs Houghton sending her £1. – wrote to Betsy sending her £5 & telling of the state of the childrens saving bank . . . Walk from 5 to 7½ to Cherry Hinton by fields & back by the road. – God be praised I had no throbbing since I got up.

*Sat. 29.* . . . Started at 5 for my walk. I ended it with ¼ hours promenade on the platform waiting for the arrival of the Express, wch brought George Romilly. I was glad to find him very flourishing: he looks quite military, as he wears a moustache. We walked home thro a slight mizzling rain. Gave him a strong tea with sausages, etc etc. – We passed the Evening in Chat & in his reading loud the leaders in the Times (about Garibaldi etc).[48]

*Sun. 30.* . . . Wrote to Mr Lyster (Dean of Leighlin) in answer to a letter just received: – he begs me to use all my influence with the Council for getting him an LLD degree, & asks if it would be advisable to beg Lord Monteagle to use his persuasion & also whether it would not be desirable to get *The Prince Consort to write on his behalf*!!! – This Irishman's effrontery is marvellous. I wrote back that the Council would naturally be highly offended at any one interfering with their judging for themselves, & would think the Prince himself had no business to send recommendations. I told the Dean that we had given very few Honorary degrees of LLD & that we had always *ourselves selected* the men on whom we conferred them, & they were men famous in science or in arms such as Owen and Sir John Lawrence . . . George & I dined at 4: the Goose of course was the cheval de bataille. – We went to the College Chapel (wch was ½ filled with townspeople) – After tea George read loud a pamphlet on 'Keeping the Sabbath holy' by Ryle[49] & that beautiful sermon of H. Goodwin's 'the small & the great are there'.

*Mon. 1 October.* . . . walked with George to the Station: he returned to Town by the Express: – he unhappily slept very ill last night also. – Opening of Term. – A grand scene: – the 2 persons nominated for Proctors were G. Williams of Kings & Basil Williams of St Johns. G. Williams is unpopular & it was well known there would be opposition to him: accordingly Dr Leapingwell (who by the way is just transferred from the Univ. Rifles to

[47] i.e. Walter Scott, *The Abbot* (1820).

[48] *The Times* of 29 September continued its detailed reporting of Garibaldi's campaign. He had just fought the battle of Volturno with his irregular levies . . . 'will courage, intelligence, and self-confidence be more than a match for mechanical discipline and professional appliances? . . . They have been conquerors, but not by the usual means of conquest'. Grim may also have read a devastating attack on the Pope's – 'this political tyrant' – appeal for help.

[49] i.e. *Keep it holy! A tract on the sabbath day* by J.C. Ryle (1856).

the Town & is promoted from Serjeant to Captain) nonplaceted the Grace for Geo. Williams. Martin (of Trinity) & myself were the 2 Senior MAs & as such had to take the votes: the V.C. didn't vote: of the 2 Heads Philpott & Cartmell the latter gave a Non Placet: the other 2 Drs (Leapingwell & Donaldson) gave N. Pl. – Martin & myself didn't vote: I (as Senior) had to announce the result, wch was 'Non placet': the nos were 29 to 26.[50] – This is a great curiousity: – I doubt whether it ever occurred before in the history of the University. – I should think Geo. Williams not likely to remain quiet under this marked expression of public feeling . . .

*Th. 4.* . . . The V.C. called & we had a good deal of talk about University business in wch he is very zealous & intelligent. – Certain friends of G. Williams wrote a memorial[51] to the Council begging them to nominate him & give the University an opportunity of reconsidering the vote . . . The Council met at 9. – The V.C. nominated Brocklebank (of Kings), Whewell nominated G. Williams!!!!!! . . .

*Mon. 8.* . . . Visit from the new Proctor Brocklebank (to bring his bond: visit from V.Ch. (to talk over Graces etc etc): – he is going to give a Harvest Home feast to his people at Heydon next Wednesday[52] . . .

*Tu. 9.* Up at 6½. – By God's mercy I have now completed 69 years of my life & am now entering upon the '3 score years & 10' which are pronounced as the limit of our stay upon earth. – God be praised I feel rather better than I have done lately, tho my ailment of throbbing in the head is not departed . . . Letters of congratulation on my birthday from Betsy who sent me eggs, chicken, apples, pears & potatoes & from G.T.R. & wife. – George amused me by saying that Bertie is getting some flesh on his little limbs & now has *something to whip* . . . Letter of Congratulation from M.A. Tyler (who says her Mother is better): she sent me some crochet work & a watch silk chain: wrote to her & sent her a Sovereign for her own birthday when it comes . . .

*Th. 11.* . . . From 5 to 7 walked on Via Lambertina: a woman with a swelled face stopt me: 'my eye tooth is decayed & that swells my face': – 'You

[50] A new and more severe statute of July 1858 meant that fellows and undergraduates must be reported to the Vice-Chancellor for sexual offences, instead of to their colleges. When, therefore, George Williams, Pro-Proctor, found a Fellow of Caius in October 1858 in a house of ill-fame he correctly reported him to the Vice-Chancellor, Dr Philpott. Summoned before the Court of Sex Viri he was admonished. A few weeks later Francis Jameson, the other Pro-Proctor, found an undergraduate in a brothel and incorrectly reported him first to his college, and only then to the Vice-Chancellor, now William Bateson. Bateson appeared to ignore the new statute and once more the offender was only admonished. Williams and Jameson understandably resigned and published their correspondence with the Vice-Chancellor and outraged parents protested against the moral laxity of the disciplinary authorities. On 31 January 1859 two new Pro-Proctors were elected and Philpott hoped that all would now go smoothly. See 3 November 1860.

[51] The memorial read: 'We the undersigned feeling that the vote of Monday does not adequately represent the opinion of the Senate in general, venture to hope that the Council will by nominating Mr George Williams afford an opportunity for a larger number of our body to record their sentiments on the question at issue'. There were 38 signatures. However the Council did not renominate him and controversy gradually subsided, no doubt to Bateson's relief.

[52] The Hon Latimer Neville had been Vicar of Heydon with Little Chishall in Essex since 1851.

should have it drawn': – 'have my eye-tooth drawn? – I am told that would make me blind'. – this highly amused me, for she was perfectly serious & never dreamt of a joke . . .

*Fri. 12.* . . . Seniority of 2 hours length: the only topic was the mode of settling the Seniority of new Fellows: – we ended at last by a conclusion that it should be according to the present rules of University standing (viz. 1st Wrangler, then 1st Classic of Classical Tripos, the Senior Optimes & so on: up to this time it used to be according to their seniority as Scholars: – Edleston (a great stickler for old observances) would not sign:

*Tu. 16.* . . . Tried in vain to find the Kennedies at the Bull: but they are expected today & have taken 2 beds for themselves & 2 for man & maid: – left a note asking them to lunch tomorrow . . .

*Wed. 17.* . . . Frank . . . is a fine tall young man & is cultivating a nascent moustache. Unfortunately he is as nervous about the entrance exam as Kennedy & Sophie: – their alarm must be needless, for his uncle John examined him & was well pleased with his knowledge. – The Marquis of Bristol called on me at my office: he has brought up another son: we had a very pleasant chat: I asked him to lunch but he had already lunched at Trin. Lodge. – At 3 o'clock Kennedy, Sophie & Frank came to lunch: my other guests were Archdeacon Allen & wife & son, Edward Romilly (jun) & Wilcox (Emmanuel) . . . Mr Hudson sent a capital luncheon & gave me some beautiful flowers (for wch I wrote my thanks): I produced Champagne & Prinz Metternichs Johannisberg.[53] Every thing went off nicely: there were 3 freshmen present, so I gave 'health & prosperity to the freshmen'. – We had coffee & chasse-café[54] & broke up about 5. I went with Kennedy & Sophie & Frank to see that youth's comfortable lodgings at Bays on Kings Parade. – I afterwards walked round the Via Lambertina.

*Sat. 20.* . . . Very busy in Office till ¼ to 1: I then went to see Sophie: to my surprise I found that she & Kennedy had just started by the Omnibus. I wrote to her to express my sorrow at missing her. – An American (Alex Barret) came for a Professorial Card: he said he was the 1st man from the Southern States who had ever been at Cambridge. – Frank Kennedy called just as I was sitting down to dinner to say he had passed (– of wch I never had the remotest doubt): he told me 14 are plucked: – I am surprised there are so few . . .

*Sun. 21.* . . . At 11 to Christ Church . . . Carus gave the history of the Pastoral Aid Society for which he was pleading,[55] of the energy of Mr Simeon & Bishop Perry in the year 1835 & the formation of the Society in 1836: I liked this part of his sermon very much: he dwelt forcibly on the debt of gratitude owed by Barnwell for wch so much had been done, – the Church erected in wch he was now preaching etc etc . . .

---

[53] From the vineyards on Metternich's estate at Johannisberg on the Rhine.

[54] i.e. a liqueur.

[55] The Church Pastoral Aid Society, an evangelical association founded in 1836 to maintain curates and lay workers in densely populated districts, was forward in promoting the holding of services in unconsecrated buildings. See also 12 June 1862.

*Mon. 22.* . . . Fell in with Frank Kennedy: he began his Chapels well yesterday by going to the 11 o'cl. service & hearing a sermon of Whewells. He is the private pupil of Somerset (one of the Junior Fellows) who is AB of /57 having been a Wrangler & in 2d Class of Classical Tripos. – The Greek play is the Iphigenia in Tauris[56] of wch Frank has not read a word . . . After dinner a visit from Carus:[57] he was in great spirits: he says his new church at Winchester will be finished in a fortnight. On a sudden he started up & said 'there's my wife, I'll fetch her in to see you': out he rushed: – when he had reached the lady & looked in her face he found it was somebody else! – about 5' after she really did pass by & he brought her in & she was very chatty & agreeable. They are staying with Dr Guest & his pious wife who has prayer-meetings. – Then came Frank Kennedy & staid ¾ hour . . .

*Th. 25.* . . . Congregation: 24 unopposed Graces: 3 of them were for MA degrees to absentees: one was for appointing a Hindustani teacher with salary of £150 p.a[58] . . . the youngsters in the gallery were riotously noisy, stamping & knocking & shouting like mad: – 2 of the ABs were Blofeld & Steward of Trinity whom we had suspended for that business when they threw down a flowerstand on young Hoppett's head & hurt him so seriously: we took off the suspension last Saturday: – Blofeld is popular with the undergraduates . . .

*Sat. 27.* . . . At 12 to a Seniority to elect a Chaplain in room of Glover who is now Librarian . . . We elected Kingsbury (who gained a Norrisian Essay):[59] Munro (who was on this Seniority) is an enthusiast about Kingsbury whom he pronounces a great divine & altogether a sort of prodigy. – We voted as at Fellowships (by voting on each candidate as Elected, Doubtful or Rejected) . . . Mathison agitated about the nuisance & danger of certain small

[56] By Euripides.
[57] Romilly's opinion of Carus and – by hearsay only – of his wife had changed over the years since Lucy's death. She and many other unmarried Cambridge ladies would dearly have liked to be preferred by the spoilt and strikingly handsome Perpetual Curate of Holy Trinity who had remained a bachelor until he was 49. See link passage 28-30 January 1851, 1 April 1852, 24 September and 11 October 1853. This 1860 entry is the first to indicate that the marriage had presumably become a happy one.
[58] The election of a Hindustani teacher was of particular interest to able young men who were competing for entry to the Indian Civil Service. Entry was now open to public competition and it was agreed that civil and military officers in India lacked sufficient knowledge of Indian languages. The election aroused considerable interest in the town as well as the University. Syed Abdoollah was professor of Hindustani at University College, London, and Majors Ottley and Stephen had passed interpreters' examinations during their service in India. Professor Abdoollah in defeat wrote to the *Chronicle* of 1 December to thank 'the electors of the University of Cambridge who have conscientiously and impartially voted for me . . . This act of liberality on their part will, I am sure, be hailed with the utmost satisfaction by my fellow-countrymen in Hindostan, convincing them, as it will do, that the majority of English-men are no longer imbued with that prejudice against them which was unfortunately, in times past, but too general . . . I beg all my friends at Cambridge to be assured that I shall ever retain the liveliest and most grateful recollection of their kindness.'
[59] John Norris of Gonville and Caius, the founder of the Norrisian Professorship of Divinity, had in 1777 endowed a prize of £12 per annum for the best prose English essay on a sacred subject.

pistols (called 'Saloon Pistols')[60] wch the youngsters fire off in their rooms. –
After dinner pasting-work & indexing. Walk to How House from 5 to 7.

*Sun. 28.* . . . Had up little Willie Watts to read: he had been most carefully
prepared & practised by Harriet & read the parable of the Sower (Matthew
XIII. v. 1–10) very nicely: gave him a 6d. A bearded gentlemanlike Fellow
Commoner (Major Stephen) called on me yesterday about the Hindustani
Teachership . . . Called on Mrs Prest: she had quite a levee; she gave a bad
account of herself, & said poor Mrs Haviland has palpitations of the heart. Mrs
Prest is much annoyed at her nephew's failure at the Voluntary Theology, as
she says there was an excellent curacy with a capital house waiting for him at
Whitby . . .

*Th. 1 November.* Up at 7 – Walk behind Colleges. – Breakfast (at my
house) to Frank Kennedy, John H. Allen (son of the Archdeacon) & his cousin
Herbert J. Allen (son of the Archdeacon's brother Charles).[61] John Allen was
very good company & talked away gaily & cleverly: Herbert & Frank scarce
said a word: they all 3 however seemed to enjoy the breakfast . . . At 11 a Seniority in wch the Commemoration was fixt for the 15th December, & the 14th
December was appointed for the day of the meeting of the Master & the M.A.
Fellows: this will be our 1st meeting of the kind: our new Statutes require such
annual meeting for enquiry into the well working of our system: – 6 weeks
notice must be given. Then a sealing in the chapel. – I went from Chapel with
Sedgwick to his rooms & smoked a cigar with him. He showed me 2 exquisite
letters of Mrs Guthrie's & her portrait (a photograph): it is an admirable work
of art: it is in an oval frame surmounted with a true love Knot. He has hung it
up in his bedroom. – He has also just got from the same charming lady
a gigantic ivory paper-Knife (with Cara on one side & A.S. on the other) in
return for a small one of his wch she broke many years ago: she has also sent
him a very handsome book-tray to put on a table . . . Sedgwick also read to me
a most spritely letter from Mrs Barnes (not his Norwich housekeeper): this
Mrs Barnes was the handsome Georgy Smith (sister of Mrs Airy): Sedgwick
used to call her Hebe, & another of her sisters Juno: Hebe is the wife of
a Liverpool merchant named Barnes & is the Mother of 5 children . . .
Mr Barnes has named one of his ships 'Adam Sedgwick'. – Sedgwick was in
great force & I much enjoyed this tête-à-tête with him. Mrs Barnes told
Sedgwick of a prudish friend of hers who had a portrait of a favorite gentleman
in her bedroom: but she turned it out because she thought it improper of him to
be looking at her when she was undressed!!! . . . From 5 to 7 walk round Via
Lambertina: – by the way Edleston today announced that a portrait of the

---

[60] This was presumably a minor fashion as Mr Jonathan Smith of Trinity College Library tells
us that there are no entries in the relevant College conclusions books, which there would have
been if the youngsters had been admonished for using them.

[61] John Allen, Archdeacon of Salop and his brother Charles were second cousins of G.B. Allen
and Grim. See the pedigree 'Allen of Bicton' in earlier editions of Burke, *Landed Gentry*
(1952).

Greek Professor Lambert[62] (from whom the road is named) is on its way to us. Letter from Maggie saying that . . . Bertie is allowed the pleasure of taking her letters to the *pofe* (as he calls it): he always asks if there is any letter for Mamma, & is much mortified when there is none: – she says he recovers very slowly, & a little matter throws him back.

*Sat. 3.* Up at 7. – Walk about Town. At ¼ to 9 to Senate House to hear Neville's speech[63] on resigning: it was nicely written: he touched on many topics, – Whewells Hostel, the Prince of Wales, the Rifle movement, the new Professors etc . . . Visit in my Office from Campion: he came to talk about ad eundem men & their right to wear the Cambridge Hood: it appears that some Dublin-men who have been ad-eundem at Cambridge & Oxford pass themselves off as Cantabs & Oxonians by wearing the Camb. & Oxf. hood: – I gave my opinion against these usurpers . . . Frank Kennedy came to tea: Sophie still kept in town by cold: Frank plays the Piano . . . he is lazy & never goes to morning Chapel. After he was gone I read G. Williams' letter[64] to the Vicechancellor in complaint of his rejection as Proctor & in vindication of his conduct as Proproctor two years ago. He has not mended his position by this pamphlet: – e.g. this sentence is offensive & mischievous: – 'I would not willingly be deprived of a participation in the honor of having asserted – would I could say established – the principles that whoredom is to be visited as a grave offence, & that the degree of M.A. does not confer a licence to sin with impunity'.

*Tu. 6.* . . . Brace of pheasants sent me by Marquis of Bristol & brought by Lord John Hervey (his freshman son): wrote my thanks to both. Letter from Archdeacon Allen, thanking me for my civility to Johnny: he says that Johnny has been questioned by the Master touching a fire in his staircase & that the Master was 'extremely civil & polite'. – John writes to his Father 'I like this place immensely: every body & every thing seem to unite in making it as pleasant as possible'. – In my office a visit from the V.C. to talk about Graces etc etc: he thinks that perhaps the Prince of Wales will not be entered in any College, but merely belong to the University: – I hope he is mistaken . . . saw Caius kitchen chimney on fire: the porter told me it happens often on the day the chimney is swept, from the soot settling in the flue . . . Mrs Willis proposed 2 old french riddles . . . The other was 'Victor Emmanuel est si enrhumé qu'il a perdu *sa voix* (savoie).[65] – Mrs William Prest sang sweetly. –

---

[62] Mr Jonathan Smith of Trinity College Library tells us that the portrait by Daniel Gardner was given to the College by John Lambert who had been bequeathed it in the will of W.C. Oldham, James Lambert's nephew.

[63] i.e. on coming to the end of a year as Vice-Chancellor. Two days later Latimer Neville was re-elected for a second year by 61 votes to 15 for Phillips.

[64] *The Proctorial Question at Cambridge, a Letter to the Vice-Chancellor of the University on the Vote of the Senate October 1, 1860* (Deighton Bell, Cambridge, p. 12). In general the letter is temperate and in addition to summarising the different ways in which the two Vice-Chancellors dealt with the cases submitted to them, deplores the effect that the adverse vote must have on foreign communities with which 'I am at present actively engaged in an endeavour to extend the benefits of our University education'. The memorial and list of signatories were printed at the back of the letter. See 1 and 4 October 1860.

[65] The treaty of Turin ceding Savoy to France had been ratified in April 1860.

Plaid 4 rubbers with Arlett against Mrs Prest & Power: came off even. – Home 11½.

*Wed. 7.* . . . At 10 to Senate House for Election of Council.[66] I staid only a few minutes to see about the supply of cards & returned at 1 when the V.C. declared the Election: – The 2 Heads were Whewell (with 80 votes), Corrie with 73: the votes for other Heads were Bateson 60, Okes 12, Cartmell 3, Geldart 2, Phelps 1, Phillips 1. – The 2 Professors were Browne (with 80 votes), Ellicott with 76: the votes for other Professors were Thompson 47, Miller 23, Jeremie 4, Birkbeck 3. – The 4 ordinary Members were France (with 85 votes), Paget (with 72), Lightfoot (with 61), Mynors Bright with 50 . . . Martin brought to my office Mr Fuller (now our Solicitor in place of Mr Hyde who is ill): he seems very sharp & intelligent: he asked to see the charter of 3d Elizabeth: – he says that 'pronubis vagabundis' is wrongly printed 'pronubis, vagabundis' & wrongly translated 'prostitutes, vagabonds etc': he says it should be translated 'vagabond procuresses': – there is certainly no comma in the Charter. – He says that such infamous women are called in London 'coaches' . . .

*Th. 8.* . . . Letter from John Allen telling me that the fire on his staircase was confined to the lath & plaster: the Master thinks somebody must have dropt a piece of lighted paper between the wall & a coal-bin . . .

*Sat. 10.* . . . Letter from M.A. Tyler saying the London Doctor has done her good & that she wishes to go to him again so I sent her another Sovereign. – Wrote to Frank Kennedy to tell him the answer to his Father's riddle must be 'scaled': – the riddle should be thus proposed: 'When is a wall like a fish'? Ans. 'when it is scaled' . . . at the end of my walk I was overtaken by Skinner & his dog Fairy who is led by a string: Skinner is fond of metaphysics, much admires Lord Bolingbroke,[67] & talks in a strange manner about religious opinions: – old Hunt used to say of him that he was an Arian. – Frank Kennedy came to tea: while I was ironing my University Papers & indexing them I set him to read loud Smyth's brilliant lecture on Sheridan:[68]– he gaped awfully. – He had this morning breakfast with his private tutor Somerset & met there only 2 Clergymen: – he says that at the Soirée at Trinity Lodge the Master & Lady Affleck were very civil to him, that there was music & that he staid an hour . . .

*Mon. 12.* . . . Vicechancellor came to my office to admit Professor Kingsley, whom he had desired to attend: but the Professor never made his

---

[66] The last Caput was elected on 13 October 1856. For the election of the first Council see 7 November 1856.

[67] Perhaps Bolingbroke's (1678-1751) indifference to orthodox religious belief and attacks on aspects of the Old Testament appealed to Skinner. Arians were members of an heretical sect which denied the true divinity of Christ.

[68] William Smyth, Regius Professor of Modern History from 1807 to 1849, had earned his living by tutoring the playwright's eldest son Tom. His reminiscences 'of this sort of connexion with one of the most extraordinary men of the age' make entertaining reading, though clearly not for Frank. Sheridan was an impossible employer whose 'impetuous feelings of the moment were everything'. See Smyth's *Memoir of Mr Sheridan* (Leeds, 1840) dedicated to Miss Cotton of Madingley, and *Romilly 1832-42*, pp.134-5.

appearance, probably being employed in putting the finishing touches to his inaugural lecture. – At 2 I went to the Senatehouse to hear said lecture. The building was very well filled: the lecture lasted more than 1¾ hour!! It was not at all to my taste: & when he meant to be pious he seemed to me merely solemn. He said that he was aware that many persons thought ill of the tendency of his writings. The lecture excited no applause except when he praised Prof. Pryme & when he expressed a fear that he had trespassed too long on our attention. I did not get home for dinner till past 4. – Took a 2 hours walk in the Evening on the Huntingdon road & was nervous at meeting 2 droves of oxen when I was beyond the region of lamps: – the night was pitch dark. – After tea plaid over some of Cochrane's games of chess.[69]

*Sun. 18.* . . . Called on Mrs Prest: she was looking ill & complained of great suffering from gout. Mrs William is got well: she is disgusted with young Mr Everett (son of the distinguished American Statesman): he is an undergraduate of Trinity: she met him at dinner at Professor Millers: – he said 'Will you send me some turkey wch you have not paid me the compliment of asking me to have?': – he then turned his head & put out his tongue! Certainly this was a low piece of buffoonery. – Mrs William told me also that young Mr Everett said: 'it is quite worth having come all the way from America to hear Lady Affleck tell Dr Whewell to light the gas & to hear Whewell say to the Duke of St Albans 'Duke! ring the bell'. – From 5 to 7 I walked on the Trumpington Road.

*Mon. 26.* . . . In my office I had visits from Majors Stephen & Ottley: they are both obviously very anxious about the Election on Wednesday: Major Stephen told me his age is 41: he says he has between 30 & 40 promises: he takes up the ground of immorality against Abdoollah & says he put away a former wife to make way for the present: I told him that Abdoollah had declared publicly that he had but one wife, & I said our business was to elect the man who could teach Hindustani best. – I did not promise him or Major Ottley: – my present leaning is to Abdoollah. – The maids (in spite of pouring rain) drank tea with Harriet's youngest sister Mrs Coulson: she is 26 today: sent her the magnificent present of 1/. – In the Evening walk to Trumpington: it rained all the time.

*Wed. 28.* Up at 7¼ – Walk to office to look at documents. – At breakfast a visit from Mrs Cranwell: she is the widow of an under-librarian of Trinity: she had 4 very pretty daughters: one died at the age of 16: one is a governess at Mrs Philip Hudson's (the Trinity Cook): the eldest teaches scholars in her Mothers house, & is assisted by the youngest sister. Mrs Cranwell came to ask me to give a vote for the Albert Asylum[70] . . . I have now promised all my 4 votes . . . Today was the Election of a Hindustani teacher: I voted for Major Stephen because I knew his brother & himself when a little boy at the time they lived on the Hills Road. – I however had no doubt that Abdoolah is the better teacher of Hindustani. The religious party was very strong against Abdoollah

---

[69] John Cochrane (1797-1878), a first-rate chess player and author of a *Treatise* (1822) on the game.
[70] See 2 July 1861.

as a Mahometan with the privilege of a Haram. The voting was from 11 to 1: the votes were 74 for Major Stephen, 72 for Abdoollah, & 3 for Major Otley. – Major Stephen has just taken his BA at Catharine Hall: he was plucked for B.A. previously . . . Major Otley wrote to ask me the Votes: – I wrote to him poor man.

*Fri. 30.* Up at 7. – Present of £1 to Harriet who is now beginning her 13th year of service with me. Up to town by Express 1st Class: my companions were Law (Bursar of Kings), Pullen & Ellicott, & we had very agreeable talk. Pullen & I came in the same cab to Westminster. – I engaged a bed at Fendall's Palace Yard. I went into the Common Pleas (wch was crowded, & no accommodation of any kind for me who was subpœnaed & for all my charters): – After some hours Cockerell & Cooper saw me & spoke to the keeper of the Judge's private apartments who said I might put my documents in the Jury room & come in by the Judge's entrance: I rewarded him with ½ Crown. – I laid hold of a little shoe-black & with 6 pence induced him to help me bring my boxes etc. – I missed Mr James' opening speech:[71]– Emma Kemp was in the witness box when I got into Court at ¼ to 12: – the Court sat till 6½ & then adjourned. I heard Emma Kemp & her Mother Mrs Looker & Graham examined – Graham (B.A. Emmanuel) is a bad stile of man: he it was who intended giving the dance at Shelford & asked Emma Kemp to make up the party – & also Blore, Bernard Smith, Woollaston & the V.C. – I thought Edwin James was coarse & offensive in his attack of the V.C. for having (as he alleged) signed a warrant for Emma Kemp's committal in which her name was already written by some other person before he had heard the case against her: the warrant was in the hands of Sir F. Kelly, but he refused to produce it unless required by the Chief Justice. – The Chief Justice will decide that point tomorrow: N.B. it never was produced. – I suspect the warrant calls E.K. hard names. The V.C. was not prepared to say whether he wrote his name or not. – Sedgwick & I dined together at the Athenæum: he was tired to death, having been in court from 10 to 6½. – Shocked to see in the paper the death of C.S. Drake (Jesus):[72] he was found in the Grand Junction Canal: he had been dining with a friend & seemed as usual: – he had become addicted to drunkenness & it is doubtful whether he destroyed himself or fell in. – After dinner went up into the drawing room & read School for Scandal till 9½ when I walked thro the comfortless rain to Fendall's hotel.

*Sat. 1 December.* Up at 8. – Went & bought myself a small pot of currant jelly to eat with my breakfast. – Breakfasted at Fendall's Hotel. A little before 10 I went into Westminster Hall: Denman (who is one of our Council) gave me a comfortable seat in Court just before the Queen's Council: the V.C., Philpott etc were there. Today Philpott & Mr Bowles (Inspector of Prisons) were

---

[71] Edwin James became M.P. for Marylebone in 1859 but in 1861 retired from the Commons and was disbarred after the benchers of the Inner Temple found him guilty of serious financial charges.

[72] The *Gentleman's Magazine* for January to June 1861 reports that Drake 'was accidentally drowned aged 45'. He left Cosgrove Priory, where he had been dining and was in 'his usual health', at 10.20 to walk home to Castle Thorpe. 'His nearest way was along the towing-path of the Grand Junction Canal into which he must have fallen.'

examined: – I was asked to produce the Charter of 3d of Elisabeth but was not put into the witness box. – Our leader Sir Fitzroy Kelly deputed his concluding speech to O'Malley (who is slow & uninteresting & was rash enough to talk about Edwin James having spoken 175 times in Parliament): – E. James made a most vehement final speech in wch he told O'M. that if he were not more lively he would never be listened to in the House of Commons: all this case turns on the words of the Charter 'suspecta de malo', and Mr James made a brilliant tirade against the horrors that have followed on 'la loi des suspects'. – The Chief Justice summed up decidedly in favor of the Vice-chancellor. – It was all over at 2: the Jury were then locked up: after I had waited for an hour . . . I got a cab & went off before the verdict was pronounced . . . Mr Thompson Cooper wanted to retain me for the Monday trial, wch I violently opposed, & Mr Cooper & Mr Cockerell said they would dispense with my appearing. – I hope the V.C. don't expect me to attend: – I never thought of asking: – but I think it scarcely possible that my side can want me: – they certainly didn't today.

*Tu. 4.* . . . Carried to my office charters etc. – The trial of Fri. & Sat. (Emma Kemp v Neville)[73] ended in a verdict – 'the Proctors had reasonable ground for suspicion: – the V.C. should have made further enquiry: damages 40s': – so the result is a confirmation of the Proctorial power. The Plaintiff's party are highly dissatisfied & mean to have the matter argued in the Court of Error. – In the 2d action 'Ebbon v. Neville' it was agreed by the Counsel on both sides not to come to a hearing, but to consent to £25 damages to Mrs Ebbon . . .

*Wed. 5.* . . . Seniority at 10 . . . a most rare occurrence, – the 8 actual Seniors (Sedgwick, Romilly, Martin, Grote, Edleston, Mathison, Hodson & King). We debated whether we should (according to our new Statutes,[74] tho not yet confirmed by Queen in Council) give $^1/_{10}$th of a Fellows Dividend to the Scholars: we had a most warm debate: the 5 Juniors were opposed: it was just carried. – We also voted that the minor Fellows elected last October are to receive next Dec. $^4/_5$ of a major Fellows dividend (instead of the old $^2/_5$). Letter from Mrs Morl (born Barron) asking me to lend her & her husband £20! She having had 2 children before marriage is not a person to be patronised: – I refused assisting her in any way. – Walk from 5 to 7. – After tea worked till bed time at my annual list of 'Officers' etc.

*Fri. 7.* . . . Long visit from Potts (Treasurer of Rifle Club): he is indignant against Lt Col. Baker: he says that Baker is most recklessly extravagant, & that he is all for getting all authority & money into his own hands . . . Today took leave of Selwyn: he & wife leave Cambridge today for Rome. – Fell in with Donaldson & told him that I had met Buckle at Yarmouth who had said to me 'there is only one scholar in England & that is Donaldson': – Donaldson told me this anecdote. Buckle said (in company of himself, Lowcock etc) 'All *inductive* philosophy comes from women': some person thought it was the *deductive*: Donaldson suggested it was the *seductive*, & the Accoucheur hinted that it must be the *productive*.

---

[73] See 13 February 1860.

[74] These revisions to the statutes incorporated the Commissioners' response to the letter they had received in December 1858 from Montagu Butler and 21 other young Fellows. The foundation scholars were also to continue to have the right to free rooms and commons.

# TOWN HALL, CAMBRIDGE.

*By Permission of the Right Worshipful the Vice-Chancellor & the Worshipful the Mayor.*

## IMMENSE SUCCESS.
## FOUR NIGHTS LONGER,

Commencing WEDNESDAY, May 27.

NOTICE.—M. GOMPERTZ respectfully announces that, in consequence of the TOWN HALL being engaged for other purposes on Monday and Tuesday, he will not be able to exhibit his Panorama on those Evenings, but will RE-OPEN on WEDNESDAY, May 27th.

### ILLUMINATED DAY EXHIBITIONS

Will take place on FRIDAY & SATURDAY, at Two o'clock. Doors open each Evening at Half-past Seven—to commence at Eight o'clock.

The Musical Accompaniments will be by the following Performers :—
Cornopean..Mr G. HILL    First Violin..Mr. MATTHEWS    Second Violin..Mr. WILLIAMS
Flute and Concertina..Mr. EXTON Pianoforte..Miss STOLDATZ Double Bass..Mr. JONES Harp..Mr. J. EXTON
The Descriptive Lecture by Mr. J. C. BELL.

### M. GOMPERTZ'S New and Colossal PANORAMA, illustrating
## THE WAR WITH RUSSIA !

Painted from Drawings and Military Plans, made on the spot, by both French and English Officers.
The PANORAMA commences with

#### VIEW OF THE TOWN OF VARNA,
AND EMBARKATION OF THE ALLIED TROOPS FOR THE CRIMEA.
#### THE COMBINED FLEETS AT SEA.
#### CAPE CHERSONESE (Sunset).——SEBASTOPOL.

Beautiful and striking Metamorphosis, the sudden Illumination of the Batteries at the report of a gun fired from H. M. steam-ship, Fury.

#### LANDING OF THE ALLIED ARMIES IN THE CRIMEA.

The whole Bay seems teeming with life—barges laden with horses, artillery, and war munitions of every description ; men-of-war boats crowded by our horse soldiers ; together with a variety of craft peculiar to this stupendous undertaking, are seen leaving the fleet to land their living cargo on the surf-beaten shores of Kalamita Bay.

#### BATTLE OF ALMA.—THE ASCENT OF THE HEIGHTS.

In this striking view, the regiments of the Light Division are seen re-forming after the temporary retreat from the Redoubt.

#### TRIUMPHANT ATTACK of the GUARDS & HIGHLANDERS upon the Principal Redoubt.

#### BATTLE FIELD OF THE ALMA (Evening).——THE APPROACH OF NIGHT.

#### MARCH OF THE ARMY THROUGH THE WOOD, ON THEIR WAY TO BALAKLAVA.

At the head of the advancing column is Lord Raglan and Staff; in the distance, a Russian Division, 20,000 strong, retreating upon the approach of our Troops.—Arrival at the beautiful

#### HARBOUR OF BALAKLAVA.

In the foreground of the view, the Greek inhabitants, who were expelled by order of Lord Raglan, are seen leaving the town.

#### TRANSPORT OF ARTILLERY from Balaklava to the Trenches before Sebastopol.

#### SIEGE AND BOMBARDMENT OF SEBASTOPOL,

Showing the combined attack of the Allied Fleets and Land Forces, on the 17th of October, 1854.

#### CAVALRY CHARGE AT BALAKLAVA.

#### RETURN OF THE REMNANT OF THE LIGHT CAVALRY.

#### FIELD OF BALAKLAVA THE NIGHT AFTER THE BATTLE.

By the glaring light of a burning gun carriage, a native Tartar is seen robbing the body of a Russian soldier, by cutting away the purse of money attached to his knee.

#### BATTLE OF INKERMANN.

Showing in this view the position of the outlying pickets of the 2nd and light Division, at the time the Russian forces were advancing up the valley on the right.

#### DESPERATE STRUGGLE IN THE VALLEY OF INKERMANN.

Representing the fearful encounter which took place when Sir George Cathcart rode down into the valley, and rallied his disorganized troops, who are seen dashing through a forest of bayonets and fighting their desperate way up the hill.

#### THE COMMANDER-IN-CHIEF WATCHING THE PROGRESS OF THE BATTLE.

#### FINAL REPULSE OF THE RUSSIANS FROM THE TWO-GUN BATTERY.

The carnage at Alma did not present anything like the scene round the Sand Bag Battery. The piles of dead here were frightful, upwards of 1,200 dead and dying Russians, mingled with our own soldiers and the French, lying in and around it.

#### CAPTURE OF THE MALAKHOFF by the French, under General Pelissier.

Taken from the Mamelon Redoubt, just as the gallant French, having overcome all opposition, are planting the Tri-colour upon the apex of the Malakhoff.

#### ASSAULT ON THE REDAN BY THE BRITISH.

Representing this fearful Tragedy at the moment when the Light Division, forming the storming party, passing the fatal space between the advanced parallel and the point of attack, through a perfect shower of round and grape shot, are swarming into the ditch and up to the salient angle of the Redan.

Previous to the Panorama, will be exhibited a PICTORIAL CHART of the CRIMEA ; showing the Scenes of our

#### NAVAL TRIUMPHS IN THE SEA OF AZOFF,

and exhibiting, in a bird's eye, the Straits of Kertch and Yenikale ; Sebastopol, with the relative positions of the contending Armies, the towns of Odessa, Perekop, Simpheropol, Yenitchi, Fort Arabat, Kaffa, Kertch, Yenikale, Taganrog, Anapa, and all the other towns and fortifications in the vicinity.

To conclude with M. GOMPERTZ'S DIORAMA, representing the
## CRYPT OF THE HOLY SEPULCHRE, AT JERUSALEM;

Exhibiting THREE DISTINCT EFFECTS.

The First representing the interior of the Structure as it appears by daylight ; the Second Effect showing it in the mysterious gloom of midnight ; and the Last Change displaying the Sacred Edifice in the full blaze of light during the celebration of Midnight Mass by the Franciscan Monks, in the act of Adoration before the Holy Shrine and Altar.

An advertisement in the *Cambridge Chronicle* of 16 May 1857 for Gompertz's successful Crimean 'panorama'

*Sat. 8.* In my early walk caught in rain without cloke or umbrella. – From 10 to 1 at Seniority . . . this was Dies Computi[75] . . . We then discussed the chapel Sunday-sermons:[76] Mathison has always been opposed to them, & so continues: he declines taking any part as a preacher: – Sedgwick agreed to preach & so did Grote: – I had previously told the Master that I begged to decline preaching, tho I approved of the continuance of the Sermons. – King (who is to my mind an uncomfortable person whose opinions are never the same as mine) says that he hears the Junior Fellows meditate an approach to the Visitor on the subject of distribution of our dividends. – We agreed to the V.C.'s application (on the part of St Mary's Syndicate) for leave to take down 'Golgotha' –

*Mon. 10.* . . . At the Seniority we agreed to Edleston's proposal of a Hall-Butler with Salary of £150: we rejected Luards proposal of a huge high Chimney (like a Factory Chimney) to carry off the kitchen smoke (– wch infests the rooms on a certain staircase). – We began discussing the scheme wch Mathison (one of the Committee appointed for the enquiry) most warmly (not to say impetuously) presses on the Seniors for the comfort of the young men in Hall: he proposes widening the tables, having only 4 rows of tables instead of the present 5 (– there used to be 6), making ½ of the Undergraduates (instead of merely the Freshmen) dine at 5 etc etc . . .

*Tu. 11.* . . . Visit from a man named Pinney who intends trying the most unreasonable & impudent of things: he means to go in to Sedgwick's Examination tomorrow & ask him to look over his papers before any body else's & to give him a Certificate in time to take B.A. on Thursday! – I told him my opinion of the attempt, – that it was a great presumption & that it couldn't succeed. N.B. – It did. Sedgw. most amiably agreed . . . found Frank Kennedy when I came home . . . He described to me the 'Assaut d'armes': he opened the fencing bout with a son of Jackson the fencing master . . . it ended with a champagne supper at an inn: professional & amateurs were of the party & it was not over till 12½. From 5 to 7 I walked about the town in the mist.

*Wed. 12.* . . . Application for assistance to a pupil-teacher named Baldrey (son of late Parish Clerk): he bears a high character: the object is to raise £20 to start him in life: – I gave 10s: – many persons (Francis Martin among them) gave 20s . . . A Seniority to discuss Mathison's proposed reforms . . . we agreed to allow the experiment of widening the tables, & ordered more silver spoons etc. – It appears that there are 2 Caterers for each year, & also a Caterer for the Scholars, & one for the Bachelors, making 8 Caterers in all:

[75] The day of the annual audit at Trinity at which the amounts of the Fellowship dividends were declared. (See Winstanley, Appendix A and 6 December 1862).

[76] On 3 December 1856 Romilly reported 'an agitation made about a Sermon in the College Chapel (as they now have at Corp, Kings, Queens, Jesus & Clare – I think): we tried the experiment some years ago: it was a failure & broke down after 2 terms: – we have agreed now to try again'. On 11 October 1859 the experiment was found to have been successful and on 8 December 1860 it was decided to continue preaching a sermon on every Sunday morning in term. On 4 December 1856 Mathison had 'boldly said that he thought it would be very difficult to provide College-Sermons wch would do the youngsters good'. His views had not changed.

these Caterers confessedly make a good thing of it: Mrs Cottrell (one of them) confesses to clearing £116 p.a. after paying her underwaiters: each Caterer has 7 underlings (all women) whom she pays only 2/6 a week: they have 2 extra female waiters on Sundays & one man at 1/ . . . It was proposed that the pay of the underlings should be doubled by making them wait at the 4 & at the 5 o'cl. dinners . . .

*Sat. 15.* . . . The V.C. tells me that (in consequence of suggestions of Philpott) it is now settled that the Prince of Wales is to be admitted of Trinity College: – probably under Mathison (the Senior Tutor): the Prince is to come up early in January . . . I shall order a new Matriculation Book for the occasion. – Mr Ebenezer Foster's[77] divorce from his faithless wife is in todays paper: at the age of 36 he married Miss Edwards (age 17 only): her paramour was a Trinity man named Hale . . .

*Fri. 21.* . . . From 5 to 7 I walked round the Via Lambertina: there was a strong North wind & it snowed all the time: – I could not distinguish the path from the road on account of the depth of snow: I fell into a ditch & had to run after my hat & umbrella! – a walk for health rather than for pleasure. – At 8½ to the Stewarts: I there plaid 4 Rubbers with Heaviside against Phil. Frere & wife (she plays very well): came off even. – Mrs Ellicott stunned me with her singing.

*Mon. 24.* Up at 7. – A sharp Frost: it didn't snow: walk to College only. – Up to town by the Great Northern train at 1·35: my companion was Glover our Chaplain: he lent me an interesting book about China full of Chinese drawings . . . there was a great bustle at Kings Cross Station & it was not easy to get a cab: – my driver was very civil & begged me to direct him as he knew nothing about Hyde Park Terrace & had only just begun driving. – Arrived at the Master of the Rolls at little before 6: – We dined at 6½: the party consisted of Sir John & 2 children only (Anne & Edward), Mr James (Johns brother-in-law) Charles & Lady Georgy, Kennedy, Sophie & myself. – Having kissed Annie & Sophie I also proceeded to kiss Lady Georgy, who did not repulse me: but whether she & Charles thought me very impudent or simply mad I know not. – At dinner I took in Sophie & was therefore very happy. – In the Evening his Honors Company of Actors of the Royal Theatre of Tiburnia plaid the farce of 'John Dobbs' most successfully: – there were playbills distributed: they ended with Vivat Magister. – The Actors were Mary & Lucy, Henry & little Arthur of Sir Johns children, Frank Kennedy, & 2 sons of Charles (one of them was only a mute, being a page): Sophie Romilly presided at the Piano as an Orchestra & was also prompter. – It was highly amusing to see little Arthur (age 7) play a Major & wear a moustache & a Uniform. – There was

---

[77] See the *Chronicle* of 15 December for a full account of the proceedings. Edwin James was one of three counsel appearing for Ebenezer Foster. 'The jury returned a verdict for the petitioner on all the issues.' George Hale, a former Trinity undergraduate, was frequently entertained as were other young people by the Fosters. Various witnesses spoke of Foster's kindness to his wife who was nineteen years younger than he, and of his liking for Hale. Venn records that the young people married after the divorce (no date) and had children. (See 13 October 1860).

a good audience beside the dinner company . . . After the play there was a good game of French Blindmans buff[78] . . .

*Christmas Day.* Up at 7½. – Walk in Hyde Park before breakfast: – the cold was very intense: – the Thermometer in many places last night fell below Zero: at the Observatory at Cambridge 4° below Zero: Challis says it was the greatest degree of cold ever recorded at the Observatory . . . Between 6 & 7 John heard a Christmas Carol: he was highly pleased with the beauty of the singing & opened his window to throw out a shilling to the Minstrels: – the Carollers however were Mary, Lucy & Sophy! Of course they were received with open arms: – a charming & touching incident in a Father's life. – John is a very early riser & was up & at his books. –

We breakfasted at 9 (as is always the case on Sundays & holidays): We went to the Rolls chapel:[79] John, Mary, Edward & Henry walked: I came luxuriously in the carriage with Annie, Lucy & Sophie & the amiable Governess Miss Griffin. – The Chapel has been greatly embellished lately: there is a nice little organ & a very good choir: there had been a tendency to entone the whole service, & John told me that he had stopped it by making a scene: when they were beginning to entone the Lords Prayer he said he would leave the chapel if they persisted. – The seats of the Master of the Rolls & household are in a little gallery (– the only one). – The window over the Communion Table has the arms of the Masters of the Rolls in painted glass: over them is 'Sacrorum Seriniorum Magistri': – the Rolls used formerly to be kept in the Chapel: – very recently a large building has been erected for them adjoining the House of the Master: among the documents there preserved is Doomsday-book. – The chapel walls & the pulpit were hung with holly & with artificial red & white flowers in festoons. – Two clergymen officiated . . . After lunch I went to call on Mrs Sibson & Francisca Ouvry (at 40 Lower Brook St): – the Doctor or Frank as they call him was out: my cousins gave me a most hearty & affectionate welcome: I staid chatting with them for an hour at least: – Sarah went out of the room & brought in a coral sort of a coronet to wear on the head & asked me what I thought of it: I said 'I think it very pretty indeed': – she was highly delighted at having caught me in this trap & exclaimed 'you gave it me'. – After this very pleasant visit I went into the park to see the skating on the Serpentine: – there were 3 or 4000 people on the ice: little Arthur was skating but I did not see him. – When it was dusk I walked to the Wellington Statue & up Piccadilly etc etc till 5½. – We dined at 6 as the 7 children & Miss Griffin were to be of the party . . . of course Turkey & Roast beef, plum pudding & mince pies made part of the fare; but we began with a service of oysters: – there was delicious ice at dessert & the Banquet was worthy of Apicius.[80] After dinner little Arthur (or the minor

---

[78]   The editors will be grateful to hear from readers who can tell them of any difference between French and English blind man's buff.

[79]   The Rolls Chapel of St Thomas, largely rebuilt in the eighteenth century, was demolished when the Public Record Office was extended in 1896-1900. The site of the Chapel was later occupied by the P.R.O. Museum. See R.C.H.M., *London* II, West London, 117-18 and plates 167-71. The P.R.O. has now moved from Chancery Lane to Kew.

[80]   The Roman author of a cookery book.

Major as I called him) mounted on a chair & proposed the health of the distinguished guest: he went thro his task very nicely & repeated without stammering the words he had been taught. I of course returned thanks. – This was another of the pleasant incidents of my visit. – We afterwards all 10 played a game of pounce commerce[81] . . . to bed soon after 10.

*Wed. 26.* . . . Directly after breakfast John & Henry took their departure for Porthkerry (where they will find Edward & the elder Henry & their wives Sophy & Rosa: – Henry is satisfied with the fortune he has made & is no longer a merchant). When John & Henry were gone Mary, Sophy & Lucy invited me into the schoolroom. I was delighted to go with them. The schoolroom was decked out with holly representing the words 'Unto you is born this day etc I was asked to hear them sing Carols, & very prettily indeed they did it . . . The 2 youngest then exhibited their baby house, their prize-books & all their treasures: – they tried to show me a wooden mouse walking along the table: – they wound him up & did all they could, but he would not walk today having walked a great deal yesterday! . . . At 10 o'cl. Edward & I left Hyde Park Terrace in a Cab & travelled to Cambridge from Shoreditch by the 11 o'cl. train. I read Schlegel's Hamlet[82] & Edward meditated or worked problems in his head . . . Letter from C.H. Cooper & son begging to dedicate the 2d Vol. of 'Athenæ Cantabrigienses' to me: wrote in reply that I should feel most happy in having my name connected with a work of such high merit . . .

*Fri. 28.* . . . Visit from Whewell: – he came to talk about the Prince of Wales who is expected about the 18th January: – W. said that the Prince knows no Greek & probably not much Latin, so he proposes dispensing with the usual preliminary Certificate of 'examined in Latin & Greek & elements of Mathematics': he says the Prince should have some rooms in College where he may put on his gown etc etc: so he means to assign the Judges Apartments to the Prince & will propose to the Seniors the furnishing them suitably . . .

*Mon. 31.* . . . At 12 the Prince Consort arrived: 4 horses from the Bull were put in requisition for him: he went to Madingley without either V.C. or Whewell: he was pleased with the arrangements & with the house[83] . . . And now by Gods mercy I am arrived at the end of another year of great blessings in which no calamity has befallen any of those dear to me.

[81] A children's round game of cards similar to grab or snap.
[82] August Wilhelm von Schlegel's (1767-1845) translations of Shakespeare are thought to be among the best in any language. See also 15 September 1862.
[83] Miss Cotton, the last of the family to live in Madingley Hall, left it in 1855. See 9 November 1855 and 28 April 1857.

# 1861

*Fri. 4. January.* . . . In my office a visit from Sarah Smyth bringing (at my request) the bill of Miss Adams, her music mistress: – it amounted to £6.13.10. Poor girl! she is tender-hearted to a degree: when I gave her a cheque for it she burst out a crying: her wish is to teach drawing!! . . . During my dinner she brought her drawings for me to look at: I was grieved to find them very bad indeed: but if they had been 10 times better she would have found it a hard matter to get pupils. Wrote her a letter saying she had acquired an elegant accomplishment but I feared it would never be profitable . . . A poor orphan boy (Hutt) at the Pitt Press got his arm into the machinery: he was instantly taken to the Hospital & is doing well under the care of Dr Humphrey . . .

*Tu. 8.* Up at 7¼ – Intensely cold: the Thermometer then at 7: it had been down at 6. Walk in Botanic Garden . . . Visit from Sedgwick: he gave me an account of his niece Isabel going 20 miles in an open dogcart on the intensely cold 12 December to Settle: her veil was frozen, the horse & dog were covered with frost & with icycles at their nose. – Mrs Sedgwick & Isabel have quitted Dent & live at Settle:[1]– Sedgwick amused me with his interpretation of L, S, D – Lucifer, Satan, the Devil . . .

*Fri. 11.* . . . My customary New Year's letter from Miss Wilcox (at Tenby): she gives an excellent account of herself & every body else: – at her brother's Xmas dinner 12 of his children sat down to dinner, & the baby was brought in with the sweets . . . Letter in the Evening from Grim describing his Temperance tea at 1s (at wch 120 were present) & his amateur concert at 9d. Grim made an address to the teetotallers & says it had a spice of low humour. At the Concert Bertha was Prima Donna & sang 'Where the Bee sucks', 'the land of the leal', a scene from the Opera Roméo, & duetts with the Governess Miss Darquet. Grim overheard a stout Cumbrian say 't' parson's wife is best singer of 'em a'. – Grim sent me a spirited translation of the Italian scene made by himself, & wch he recited with great emphasis & gesticulation to the audience, who loudly applauded him . . .

*Th. 17.* . . . Harriet's friend Mrs Milligan[2] has the honor of making the Prince of Wales's gown . . . At 6 drank tea with Sedgwick to meet the 4 young Millers: he gave them new-year gifts (books in wch he wrote their names): after tea he had a grand dessert with variety of sweet things . . . He exhibited his brother-in-law Westall's views & a portfolio of engravings (principally portraits of scientific men). He also told in his charming manner stories of his native valley; two of persons escaping drowning in a marvellous way (the intense violence & whirling of the water dashing them ashore), one of them had fallen into a whirlpool called 'Hells cauldron . . .

*Sat. 19.* . . . Letter from Maggie describing the new Magic Lantern & saying that Franky is at home with a bad cold, wch he caught by going

---

[1]  Mrs Sedgwick and Isabel had moved a few miles south to Langcliffe (near Settle) from Dent which Adam thought of as 'home' all his life.
[2]  i.e. of Messrs Milligan and Johnson, Market Hill.

outside an omnibus (having been asked to make way for a Lady): – there were 9 men in the Omnibus at the time, none of whom would go out but suffered a child like Frank! – Wrote to Maggie. A little after 12 I went to Magdalene Lodge & met the Procession of the V.C. etc going to Trinity.[3] – The Prince received the University deputation in his own apartments (the Judges' rooms at the Lodge): the V.C. presented the Heads (of whom 14 appeared . . . ), the Proctors & 2 Bedells. – The Prince shook hands with nobody but the V.C. & Philpott: the P of course was standing. Directly after the University had retired the Mayor (C.F. Foster), the Deputy Mayor (Elliott Smith) Mayor in /60, Mr Balls (Mayor in /59) & Mr Cooper (Town Clerk) presented an Address from the Town. – I staid at Magdalene Lodge ½ hour while these proceedings were going on at Trinity & had a very agreeable chat with Charles Neville . . . Mrs Latimer . . . had set out the great room in the best stile possible & exhibited all the choice bridal presents: 2 of them were inkstands, one being a gold one given by Sir H. Dukinfield, the other beautifully studied with Cameos. – The inkstand set out for the Prince was that given by Sir H.D: it is one of the most exquisite pieces of workmanship I ever saw. – As soon as the Carriage was announced to be driving up the V.C. & myself went to the door to receive the Prince: – he was accompanied by his Governor (General Bruce) & by Whewell. The V.C. introduced me & the P. did me the Honor of shaking hands with me. The Prince wore his gown. The V.C. put a new pen in his hand & begged him to write his name in English: the Prince wrote

Albert Edward P.

It is a good clear signature. – I then presented my 'Graduati' to the Prince begging him to condescend to accept a book in wch he would find the illustrious name of the P. Consort & the names of his great uncles the Dukes of Sussex & Cambridge. The V.C. then presented the Prince with a beautifully bound copy of the 'Statuta & Ordinationes' & told him they were drawn up by the Master of Catharine. The P. accepted the books very graciously (but without words) & handed them over to his Governor, who took charge of them. – Shortly after Whewell introduced me to the Prince as one of the Seniors of Trinity College & I made another little speech to the Prince expressing my happiness at being so on the august occasion when he condescended to be one of us. – Coffee was then handed round & immediately after the Prince & General Bruce & Whewell went away . . . The heading which I wrote in the new Matriculation Book was,

Census 19 o Jan. 1861<br>
coram Hon. Viro L. Neville A.M. Proc.<br>
et Gul. Whewell S.T.P. Coll. Trin Præfecto<br>
me præsente Jos. R. Reg.

---

[3] This was the strenuous preliminary day on which the Prince was to receive the university deputation and the Address from the town, to be admitted a member of Trinity College and matriculated in Magdalene Lodge as its Master, Latimer Neville, was Vice-Chancellor. The Prince already knew Philpott who had been Vice-Chancellor when his father was installed Chancellor and was now his chaplain and university correspondent.

Directly after the Prince was gone Mrs Latimer, Mrs Col. Baker, Mrs Girdleston & Walsham came in, they having caught a glimpse of the Prince from an upper window. – I then went to my office & wrote an account of all these proceedings to Leapingwell (who communicated with 'the Times' . . . By the way Charles Neville told me that the Prince has brought with him a gigantic black dog . . .

*Sun. 20.* . . . Letter from Franky describing the slides of the Magic lantern: – one of a cow that lifts up her head, one of 3 jumpers who leap on each others shoulders, & the last of an old man who unfolds a scroll with the words 'Good night'. – Wrote to Franky & told him all about the Prince. At Christ Church Mr Wortley (Minister of the Abbey Church) read prayers & Mr Collis preached . . . After Church . . . I was overtaken by Mr Collis who talked to me about the Prince, of whom he speaks slightingly as an effeminate youth with no colour in his cheeks . . . Walk from 5 to 7 on Trumpington Rd in fog.

*Tu. 22.* . . . Took the Matriculation Book to the Millers to show the Prince's signature to the 4 children . . . Worked in my office till 1 arranging the Spinning-house documents sent me by Philpott. – At 1 Sedgwick & I drove to Madingley Hall: – the triumphal arch of evergreens with artificial red & white flowers is still at the Park-gate. We wrote down our names & then Sedgwick sent up his card to Mrs Bruce to ask if she would see him: of course she begged him to come up. – Sedgwick persuaded me to accompany him. We went up the back stairs to the apartments of the General & Mrs B. Their room is adorned with beautiful engravings of the Royal children when little bits of things: there is a portrait of the P. of W. in a uniform & representing him now. – The General I had conversed with before at the Prince's Matriculation: he is a brother of Lord Elgin, & is an agreeable affable handsome man: Mrs B. is a fine bouncing portly lady who seems the picture of good-humour. We were very kindly received & staid at least ½ hour . . . The Prince's household consists of his Governor (Gen. Bruce), of Captain Grey (son of Sir George Grey), & of his private tutor Mr Fisher (an Oxonian). To my great pleasure Dr Paget is the Prince's Physician. Capt. Grey is a Trinity man, but was not a reading man & never took a degree. – From 6 to 7½ walk on Trumpington Road – While I was at tea Mathison called & drank tea with me. He came to talk about the Prince. The Prince was today driving himself about in an open carriage & took off his hat to Mathison who was in the Street. The Prince afterwards called on Mathison in his rooms & had a chat with him just before the Hall dinner. Mathison has to find out some person who can talk French perfectly with the Prince: there is not (as far as Math. & I know) any French Master here . . . The Prince (with a chosen few, – about a dozen from different colleges to be selected as not unworthy associates of the P.) will attend Birkbeck's Law Lectures at his house at Downing. – Mathison gave me an account of the Prince's admission in his apartments (the Judge's rooms) last Saturday: The Prince was attended by his Governor: The Master, Sedgwick & Mathison were the only other persons. The Master said 'There is an old college order of 1850 – (meaning 1750, but he was not aware of the slip) requiring this Declaration from all Noblemen etc admitted of the College'. The Prince then read 'I Albert Edward do declare that I will conform to the rules etc & obey the Master etc': he then signed *Albert Edward P.* – The Master said 'Your Royal Highness is familiar with German & probably can read German handwriting'. The Prince assented; & Whewell then pointed out to him the 1st signature in the Volume wch (tho very badly written) he instantly read as that of Blücher:[4] the Master told him that Prince Blücher's name continued a long time on the college boards . . .

*Wed. 23.* . . . To my great surprise & delight I received directly after dinner an invitation to dine with the Prince tomorrow: it ran thus 'Madingley Hall

      Cambridge 23 Jan.

Major General Bruce presents his compliments to Mr R. & by desire of the P. of W. has the honor to invite him to dine with H.R.H. on Thursday next the 24th instant at 7.30'. – Wrote most joyfully to accept & wrote also to Sedgwick . . .

*Th. 24.* . . . Visit from Robert Potts: he began talking in an excited way about the wonderful sermon of Peter Peckard[5] in 1783 – told him I had never heard of it: 'Why it was preached in St Mary's Pulpit, & is the most powerful attack of the slave-trade!'. – I said still that I had never heard of it: – 'Well, I'm going to print it as I think it may produce a powerful effect on brother Jonathan in this dreadful agitation in South Carolina'. – You will not get a soul on the other side of the Atlantic to read it; they & all the rest of the world are too much agitated by self-interest & too much influenced by the present state of public opinion to care what was preached 80 years ago. – 'But the arguments are irresistible & truth must prevail'. – Not against overwhelming interest. – Of course Potts will print & people wont read . . . At 7½ punctual to our time we reached Madingley Hall: we were the 1st: directly after came the V.C. & Philpott in one Carriage, & Whewell by himself. – After we had been received by Gen. & Mrs Bruce, Captain Grey (the Equerry) & Mr Fisher the private Tutor the Prince made his appearance & shook hands with us all: – he did not wear a star or ribbon, & we were all (as instructed) in an ordinary evening dress without gowns. – the lower suite of rooms only was used: we did not go up into the grand saloon, wch I suppose was thought too cold . . . After dinner nothing but Sherry & Claret offered . . . I ventured to talk to the Prince about his gigantic black Newfoundland dog (wch he brought from Canada), saying that I had heard of his upsetting a railway-porter: – the Prince said that he was indeed most powerful: – this grand dog on first landing was bitten by

---

[4] The Duke of Gloucester visited the University at Commencement in 1814 as did Marshal von Blücher 'who was drawn by the populace from the entrance of the town to Trinity College and received with the loudest acclamations'. The University conferred the degree of LL.D. on him. See *Annals*, IV, 507.

[5] Peter Peckard of Corpus Christi, Oxford, became Master of Magdalene, Cambridge in 1781. The sermon on *The Nature and Extent of Civil and Religious Liberty* which Potts especially admired was preached before the University on 5 November 1783. (See Searby pp. 320-1). Lincoln's election as an abolitionist president of the United States in November 1860 caused consternation in the south; in December a state convention at Charleston announced that South Carolina had seceded from the union. It was quickly followed by Mississippi, Alabama, and other states.

another dog, but he killed his assailant offhand . . . I got on vastly well with Mr Fisher: he described to me the Prince's residence at Oxford (Frewen's Hall):[6]– he intends taking an ad-eundem here. – Got home about 11, having greatly enjoyed the very high honor of dining with the Prince . . .

*Fri. 25.* . . . Hurrah! We have at Trinity again carried off the high prize. Aldis is Senior Wrangler. It is a very curious thing that the Senior Wranglers of 1860 & 1861 (Stirling & Aldis) are both dissenters & therefore excluded from Fellowships . . . Edward Romilly is alas not so high as he & all his friends expected . . . he & a man named Gabb (Johns) are bracketed 14th. Wrote to Edward to express my great regret . . .

*Sat. 26.* . . . At 10 the conferring the degrees in the Senate House.[7] The Prince was there & all his household: – the Prince of course wore his gown: he sat in a chair on the right of the V.C. & was therefore capitally seen. Mrs Bruce sat next Lady Affleck on back seats on the dais. The place was crammed. The young men behaved very well: they gave abundant cheers for the Queen, the Prince Consort, & the Prince of Wales: the new Bishop of Worcester (Philpott) also had a warm greeting . . . I afterwards fell in with Mr Fisher (the Private Tutor). He told me that he had accompanied the Prince to Mr Birkbeck's today, where the Prince attended his 1st Lecture: the subject was 'the countries wch used the laws of England': the lecture was at Prof. B's house: nobody but the Prince & Mr F. present: – it is intended to select a few students to attend with him . . . Harriet got into the Senate House & had a good view of the Prince.

*Mon. 28.* . . . Visit from Mathison: he came to ask if young de Saumarez (presumptive heir to his uncle the childless peer born in 1789) is entitled to wear a hat:[8]– I said 'yes'. – Mathison tells me that Blore (Senior Dean) has been introduced as the best University Tennis player to the Prince. (Blore has been playing this Xmas in Paris): – the Prince is a poor hand & the Duke of St Albans worse . . .

*Sat. 2 February.* . . . Also a letter from John acknowledging mine: he was not taken by surprise at my fears about Edward not being elected Fellow, for

6   The Prince matriculated at Oxford in October 1859 and lived at Frewen Hall with Colonel and Mrs Bruce to whom Prince Albert relentlessly emphasised his son's need to study, and the undesirability of free contact with undergraduates. Herbert Fisher, student of Christ Church, became his tutor in law and constitutional history and in 1862 his private secretary. It seems clear that the nineteen year-old Prince was at last to be allowed rather more freedom at Cambridge.
7   The *Chronicle* of 2 February crossly having deplored the 'scene of confusion more disgraceful than any that we have witnessed for a long time at the [entrance to the] Cambridge Senate House' described the cries after the acclamation of the Prince's arrival as 'neither uncommon nor witty. Lord Palmerston had a fair number of supporters; but the friends of Lord Derby far outnumbered them. The Pope was not popular; and Mr Edwin James, and men of that sort, excited ridicule rather than any other feeling.' For James see 1 December 1860.
8   The 1570 statutes *De vestitu scholarium* decreed that whereas scholars were forbidden to wear hats, sons of Lords and eldest sons of Knights were entitled to wear them instead of caps whilst they were undergraduates. Dr. Leedham-Green tells us that by 1861 correctness in academic dress was to be defined by ordinance rather than statute, but the ordinance was not yet written. Romilly therefore gave his ruling according to the old statutes.

he had already learned that the new rules of the College exclude all under 12th Wrangler. – He gave me much pleasure by saying that he thought Edward greatly improved & that he had much satisfaction in talking with him . . . At 2 to the same Lecture room (under the East side of the Library): one of the 'Sex Viri',[9] Jeremie, was absent: the 5 present were Bishop Philpott, Dr Geldart (Master of Trinity Hall), Archdeacon France, Prof. Browne & Fr. Martin. – The case was this: on Wed. 23d Brockhurst horsewhipped Dodd[10] (Magdalene) savagely. This brutal assault was in Magd. court at ¼ before 6 P.M. – The said Mr Brockhurst has published a good deal about the Jews & is mad on the subject. – He had heard from his friend Mr Reyner of St John's that on some occasion when a Jew Fellow Commoner was in Hall Mr Dodd omitted the name of our Lord from the Grace. Mr Dodd indeed denied it: – but Mr B. called him a liar & horsewhipped him severely & furiously in the presence of College-servants, giving him 12 or 14 lashes & throwing down the Whip & daring him to do the same to him. – Mr Brockhurst allowed the fact of the horsewhipping & gloried in it as done for the glory of his Saviour. His defence was that of a desperate & incurable maniac. He protested against a court presided over by an interested person like the V.C. – The sentence was 'suspension from his degree for 4 years': he means to appeal to the Senate. The Court commended Mr Dodd for his Christian forbearance . . .

*Th. 7.* . . . The Prince's private Tutor Mr Fisher (of Christ Church) . . . told me that the Prince is attending Prof. Kingsley's Lectures (at his house in Fitzwilliam St.): he began last Tuesday: a class of 8 or 9 has been made up. – I said that I hoped the Master's wish to the Prince on his admission 'that it might be a source of happiness to him' had been realised: – he said it had. Fell in with Bateson & he told me of his dinner with the Prince last Tuesday: he found it very agreeable: it was a party of 12: he (Bateson) & Professor Birkbeck were the only officials: the rest were youngsters: among them were Everett[11] (the ill-mannered son of the distinguished American Minister) & Rothschild[12] . . . Bateson said that the Prince was very conversible, – on subjects of amusement . . .

*Wed. 13.* . . . That madman Brockhurst (in his furious anti-Jew tirade called 'Who is on the Lord's side')[13] has the following brutal attack of Whewell for admitting Rothschild an undergraduate of Trinity

[9]  In 1857 a new court was set up to take cognizance of offences committed by senior members of the University, the Registrary included. It was enlarged from four to six members – hence *sex viri*.

[10]  Edward Dodd, Fellow of Magdalene was Vicar of St Giles with St Peter from 1844 to 1868. The *Chronicle* printed an account of the court hearing and a sympathetic letter to him from his parishioners after the assault. The Rev. Joseph Brockhurst of St John's won the Chancellor's Medal in 1826 with a poem on Venice. For some years from 1841 he was Master of a proprietary school at Camberwell, Surrey, and by 1860 curate of Hinxton, Cambs.

[11]  Henry Sidgwick in an undated letter of 1859 took a very different view of William Everett. 'I have got a young American reading with me – a very nice fellow' (A. & E.M. Sidgwick, *Henry Sidgwick*, 1906, p. 44). Sidgwick and Everett were both 21!

[12]  See also 15 October 1859.

[13]  *Who is on the Lord's side or What think you of Christ?* (1861) runs to 192 pages of often good rhyming couplets. Much of Part I is dedicated to the memory of Brockhurst's soldier son, and

'That Mammoth of ill manners – that Great Bear,
That, constellation'd in the upper air
Of Granta, shineth – to be shunned elsewhere' . . .

*Sun. 3 March.* . . . to St Mary's to hear Rowsell:[14] I could not keep from tears at his description of misery in great cities: he had seen a whole family living in a single rc om & at the time he visited it the husband was laid on the bed of sickness & the dead wife had been lying there for 10 days! – It was a heart rending sermon . . . we must go into the dens of misery, we must spread Christianity by works of mercy (like all our Saviours miracles), we must relieve these densely-peopled, unwholesome, immoral herdings together in one close room . . .

*Th. 7.* . . . The corporation is today beginning an iron fence round their field (wch I always thought belonged to Queens) wch is bounded by Erasmus's walk & Queens' ditch.[15] – A regular Dunces' day as to degrees. 10 AB's . . . who had all been plucked more or less frequently. There were 8 new boards (of Theology) . . . & a Grace passed concerning a Syndicate for increasing some Professors Salaries out of the *surplus* Income of the University. This is a glorious state of things: I never before heard of our having a Surplus: – we are also forthwith to build Lecture Rooms & Museums . . .

*Sun. 10.* Up at 7. – I had been restless & confused in my head for some time before I got up . . . At 2 to St Mary's to hear Mr Rowsell: it was a heart-stirring sermon: he told the young men that they need not fear persecution, – that there was none now, – there was apathy, indifference & sometimes perhaps contempt: – he urged the young candidates for Orders to beware of

of Part II to an attack on Trinity, Whewell, and Lord Lyndhurst (as High Steward) in particular and by name.

'That Holy Name...her Master has ignored...to unite
With him and his, a wealthy Israelite,
Whose son – accepted from the general crowd
Of 'Jews, Turks, Heretics' – he hath allowed,
With Christian youth, to wander up and down –
As they, credential'd with a cap and gown –
Among our Halls and Colleges, and thus
Of setting Christ at naught the stain has stamped on us.'

Bound together with poems and prose by other authors in *Poems* 1858-61, part II, pp. 121-2 (Cambridge University Library, class mark XIV. 24 .56).

14 Thomas James Rowsell practised what he preached. Perpetual Curate of St Peter's, Stepney from 1844 to 1860, he toiled in London parishes all his days. His three sermons before the University in 1859 were entitled *The English Universities and the English Poor.*

15 In 1886 G.M. Humphry in his *Guide to Cambridge* described Queens' island, lying between the river and the ditch, as having on it 'a brewhouse, a fruit garden and the grove. A bridge with an iron gate leads from the grove to "Erasmus Walk" which runs across the common between a row of elm trees and the ditch by King's.' Dr Plumptre (President of Queens' 1760-88) believed the walk to have been 'first made . . . in the year 1685'. The footbridge from the north end of the grove to the path which ran on the south side of the trees between it and the walk to King's bridge is clearly shown on contemporary maps as leading to the Queens' road. However it is nowhere called Erasmus Walk and the bridge no longer exists. For details of the limits of Queens' field see J. H. Gray, *History of Queens' College, Cambridge* (1926).

chasing the Clerical Profession as a genteel & elegant & light work, but to seek Curacies in crowded cities where there was boundless misery & vice to be counteracted . . . Much throbbing in my head all the Evening.

*Wed. 13.* . . . After dinner a carriage stopped at my door, from wch got out Hailstone (the Vicar of Botsham) . . . He last year had a slight paralytic seizure & feels constantly a weight on his head like a mustardplaster: he is much better but thinks it prudent to resign: – he will occupy the comfortable house called Anglesea Abbey[16] (now held by his Curate): Hailstone is a patient of Paget's: – he is of prodigious bulk. – He came to resign his Living before me as a Notary Public: – Harriet got 2 of my neighbours (Clark, the Baker) & Rickett (shoemaker) to attend as witnesses . . .

*Fri. 15.* Up at 7. Walk about Town. – Much head-ache & much throbbing. – my brain was in a muddled state . . . Visit from Prof. Selwyn, he is in great health & spirits. – He and Mrs S. are just returned from 6 weeks at Rome: he had a tête-à-tête with the Pope (with whom he conversed in Italian & Latin). He gave the Pope a photographic facsimile of the M.S. of Clemens[17] . . . He found the Pope courteous & affable & cheerful . . .

*Sat. 16.* . . . In my evening walk . . . I called in at Deightons & copied down the names of the 7 who are called by the dreadful appellation of 'the 7 against Christ':[18]– they are as follows,

(1) 'Education of the World': – by Dr Temple (Hd Master of Rugby)
(2) 'Bunsen's biblical researches': – by Rowland Williams (v. Provost of Lampeter)
(3) 'Evidences of Christianity': – by Baden Powell
(4) 'Séances historiques de Genève' – 'National Church' – by H. Bristow Wilson B.D.
(5) 'Mosaic Cosmogony' – by C.W. Goodwin. M.A.
(6) 'Tendencies of Religious Thought in England' – by Mark Pattison B.D.
(7) 'Interpretation of Scripture' – by the Greek Professor Jowett.

– So Oxford is the Mother of 5 of these mischievous men, & Camb. of 2 (R. Williams & C.W. Goodwin) . . . The Duchess of Kent died this morning.

*Tu. 26.* . . . Just as I had finished dinner came the V.C. & brought The Address of Condolence:[19]– it had been written by Prof. Kingsley, but the

---

[16] For a history of the priory before its modern enlargement by Lord Fairhaven see Edward Hailstone's *History and Antiquities of the Parish of Bottisham* (1873).

[17] This refers to photographic facsimiles of the remains of the Epistles of Clement of Rome made from the unique copy preserved in the Codex Alexandrinus, introduction F. Madden (British Museum, 1856). Dr. McKitterick believes this to be the earliest published complete photographic facsimile of a manuscript.

[18] *Essays and Reviews* (1860), edited by Benjamin Jowett and Frederick Temple was of sensational importance because it was written by clergymen and designed to encourage free discussion of Biblical questions in the light of contemporary knowledge, especially German textual criticism. On 12 February 1861 Archbishop Sumner and the bishops failed, they said, to understand how clergymen holding such views could subscribe to the articles of the Church of England. The doctrinal authority of the church was threatened and the arguments continued for years to come. See Chadwick, II, 75-97.

Council (in a 2 hours sitting today) pared down a good deal of its redundance. – I wrote out instructions for Welsford (about parchment, ruling a black border etc etc) & left them at his house. – I also wrote to C.H. Cooper to ask if the Town Address was to be on parchment, & if he could give me a great black wafer as big as the University seal: – he wrote to say that he didn't believe there were any such large black wafers . . .

*Wed. 27.* Up at 7. – Thank God I feel much better . . . Mrs Prest sent me the following riddle 'How are we punished before birth for original sin? & when is the punishment mitigated?'. – Answer 'By 9 months solitary confinement with hard labour: – but in case of twins it is without *solitary* confinement' . . .

*Fri. 5 April.* Up at 7. – Walk about town. 1st day of term: no Graces. – The 'Census'[20] paper is arrived: the collectors of information are called 'Enumerators': – these decennial Censuses began in 1801; so all 7 will have been in my time . . .

*Sat. 6.* . . . At 7 George Romilly came: he was perfectly well & gave rather an improved account of Bertie. He signed in my census paper: there are 4 signatures, Jos. Romilly (age 69), G.T. Romilly (38), Harriet Sandfield (34), Caroline Howes (31) – scholarship Examining ended today: – 78 Candidates.

*Sun. 7.* . . . We dined in Hall: I was in the Chair. It was a very agreeable talking party: old Pryam [sic] told anecdotes about Rénouard, Porson[21] etc (– one of the Greek translation of '3 children sliding etc', – wch childish rhymes Porson declared to be stolen from the Greek & the next morning produced his well-known Greek version). Pryme was very civil to George & told me that he thought he had a very intellectual look, wch I had much pleasure in repeating to George . . . In chapel was Miss Whewell – a maiden sister of the Masters: Martin told me that this venerable lady is very sensible & gentle . . . After tea George read loud (at my request) Macaulay's admirable Essay on Addison.

*Tu. 9.* . . . Visit from Cookson & his pretty little dr Elisabeth: (he came about the Museums & Lecture Rooms).[22] I showed the little maiden the pen & ink drawing of Qn Elisabeth & her Father made her spell Elisabeth in Greek: she is a learned little puss: she knew who was Elisabeth's sister & whom she married: she also talked about the Nile: – as she is not much more than 5 I wish her little head may not be turned by vanity . . . Dr Clark . . . says that

[19] i.e. on the death of the Duchess of Kent.
[20] The Cambridge census of 1851 showed that there were 13,423 males and 14,380 females, an increase over the previous ten years. For the latest figures see 9 May 1861.
[21] A great many of the wittiest pieces in the *Morning Chronicle* came from Porson's pen. His brother-in-law T.E. Perry was its editor, and the Greek iambic version of '3 children sliding on the ice' was written when W.H. Ireland was eventually denounced as a forger of 'Shakespearian' and other manuscripts. Porson, signing himself 'S. England', ridiculed Ireland's 'discoveries' by asserting that his own iambics were a newly found fragment of Sophocles.
[22] In 1854 Salvin had submitted a plan to build much needed lecture rooms, museums and laboratories, which came to nothing for lack of funds. But in 1861, when the Museums and Lecture-Rooms Building Fund amounted to about £27,000, the professors were asked to revise their requirements and building began on the former Botanical Garden site, i.e. the 'New Museums' Site.

Pryme[23] has a prodigious class and is most popular, for he plucks nobody: he began his Lectures with 'Gentlemen, Political Economy is a noble science': – this was warmly responded to by his Class who exclaimed 'So it is: – 3 cheers for the Professor'. – In the Evening I walked by the road to Cherryhinton & back by the fields.

*Th. 11.* Walk in the B.G. – Letter from Maggie saying . . . that poor Franky is sadly disappointed about the recitation prize: tho he repeated Parnell's Hermit with great correctness & expression & also 50 lines of some other poet (to make up the 300) yet another boy learned still more & gained 20 marks above Franky . . .

*Sun. 14.* . . . Frank Kennedy astonished me last night by talking about being in the 1st Class!!!!! I told him that there could be no chance of it, but he must do his best: I shall be content if he is not in the last. . . . Deserted Mr Robinson to hear my old friend Carus preach for the Colonial & Church School Society: – The Church was well filled . . . Carus seemed to me to be attacking & confuting the authors of "Essays & Reviews": – I have not read a word of them & don't mean. I thought Carus's sermon well argued & most convincing: I listened to it with the greatest attention & thought it calculated to do much good . . .

*Tu. 16.* Up at 7. – Walk on Coe fen: – saw young men bathing. – Letter from Betsy (saying she was weak & lackadaisical & that little Margaret had the hooping cough badly): wrote to her to cheer her up . . . Paid £5.5.– to the Fund for Sedgwick's bust (– wch costs £225!!).[24] – Letter from Mr Somerset saying he sees no reason to believe Frank can be higher than 7th Class!! This completely agrees with my own ideas . . . Very much surprised at a *farewell* visit from Edward Romilly: he is leaving Cambridge & about to be entered at Grays Inn: – so he must have abandoned the scheme of reading for the Natural Science Tripos . . . On my return from my Evening walk (in Chesterton meadows) I found Frank waiting my return . . . I strongly spoke to him of the absolute necessity of his working in earnest & beginning this very night. – He won't work: it is not in his nature: – he is the essence of indolence . . .

*Mon. 22.* . . . Frank Kennedy looked in & had some coffee . . . he had today joined a Trinity cricket club & had its ribbon round his white wide-awake: it is a tricolor, red, yellow & blue: – he had been practising on Parkers Piece from 2 till near 5 & had blistered one hand . . . Fell in again with Paget

---

[23] A personal chair was conferred on George Pryme in 1828 from which his only payment was 'my share of certificate fees, which average about £30 a year'. He continued to lecture until he was 82 and was at last certain that a professorship of Political Economy was to be established with an annual stipend of £300. For the contents of the lectures which 'were intended to facilitate the study of a science hitherto inaccessible without the most arduous perseverance' see *Autobiographic Recollections of George Pryme* (1870) edited by his daughter, and 24 October 1861.

[24] The bust is by Thomas Woolner, an original member of the Pre-Raphaelite Brotherhood. See 27 May 1859 and 20 May 1862.

who told me that poor Henslow's end is fast approaching: he can only communicate by signs[25] . . .

*Tu. 23.* . . . I was much grieved to hear from Hoppett that Sedgwick had another seizure last night. He being the bravest man alive has acted since the 1st of these seizures just as if he was in the hey-day of youth & strength. He went last night to the Philosophical & was there taken ill: happily Paget was present & took care of him: Hoppett sat up with him all night: but poor Hoppett is much worn out by want of rest . . . In my Evening walk by the Via Lambertina I tried to teach little Henry Tyrrell to spell 'William' by repeating it over to him 4 times & making him say after me: – but he failed in saying it alone. The Station-master (Mr Morris) was there & asked me if I would like to walk with him along the line: I told him I should like it of all things: so I walked with him to the Cambridge station: the Express train & its predecessor past us . . .

*Th. 25.* . . . Letter from Mathison saying that the young men were dissatisfied with my poor old ugly dirty uncomfortable bedmaker Mrs Carpenter & asking if I had any complaint to make of her: I had an interview with her, shook hands with her & talked in the gentlest kindest way I could: I told her that the youngsters said she was not cleanly & did not keep the rooms nice: I advised her to do her very best to give satisfaction & to make a point of keeping clean & tidy. I wrote to Mathison telling him she had a dirty complexion wch looked saturated with cinder-dust & was beyond all power of soap . . .

*Th. 2 May.* . . . Congregation day: 8 AM & 2 eundems were the only degrees. – There were Graces for appointing Adams Observer in place of Challis (according to Challis's petition for relief),[26] for giving seats in the Throne to all the Council, & for borrowing money (from the Press & Library) for the new Museums.[27] There was no opposition, tho several people went to the Senate House bent on pugnacity . . . Whewell . . . told me that he had been suffering greatly from rhumatism for 3 weeks (not from gout as I had heard). He told me that he had given the rooms taken from my bedmaker Mrs Carpenter to her daughter of whom he heard a very good character. Mrs Carpenter also came & spoke to me with much gratitude for the letters I had written to her & to the Master: she is very happy under the present arrangement & will be allowed to assist her daughter in the rooms . . .

*Sat. 4.* Up at 7. – A keen N.E. wind. – Walk in Botanic Garden. – Hailstorm at 10 . . . A dunce named Hayward (of Corpus, matriculated /52) came to ask questions about LLB: he was plucked at 5 successive Little-

---

[25] Sedgwick went off on 13 April to see his old friend who was suffering from bronchitis and heart trouble. On 8 May Romilly was to write 'Henslow still lingers on, – in a beautiful calm happy frame of mind'.

[26] After 25 years as Plumian professor Challis wanted to be relieved of 'superintending the Observatory and of taking, reducing and publishing Observations'. It was agreed that J.C. Adams, the Lowndean professor, should take over these duties.

[27] The University Property Syndicate on 16 March reported their findings that the Press and Library Building Fund had surplus University funds 'which might be lent for a limited time at proper interest'.

Goes!!![28] . . . Worked at indexing the Statutes approved by the Queen in Council 16 April 1861 . . . wrote to Frank Kennedy (dated for tomorrow): it was to congratulate him on his birthday. – I gave him earnest advice about reading in good earnest. – Gave him a pretty copy (wch had been dearest Lucy's) of Southey's Life of Nelson.[29]

*Tu. 7.* . . . Feeling uncomfortable about the livid blueness in my hands & my want of perspiration I called on Paget: – he listened to the working of my heart, & declares that it is not diseased, but that the action is slow & feeble: – he recommends warmer gloves & a glass of Claret . . .

*Th. 9.* . . . I am much surprised at finding that the population of Cambridge has decreased in the last 10 years by 1452, for in 1851 it was 27, 803 & is now only 26,351: – the census however of 1851 was in Termtime & this is in holyday . . . Up to town by the Express with a 2d Class day-ticket . . . At 2 o'clock (according to the order of the House of Commons) I came to the Select Committee at the House, in the matter of 'the University Election bill'.[30] – I was there accosted by Dr Rowden (the Oxford Registrary) & Sir W. Heathcote (Member for Oxford) . . . Dr Rowden was 1st examined & then Dr Jeune the V.C. of Oxford & last of all myself: – the Oxford system is different from ours: – the Oxonians have a nomination of Candidates & the votes are give viva voce & not by cards. The Oxford V.C. was much opposed to the bill, – wch I myself approve: – it is for allowing voting by transmitted votes. – To my great satisfaction my Examination was over by 4 o'clock . . . Returned to Cambr. by Express & read Spiritual Quixote all the way[31] . . .

---

[28] The law had long been seen as any easy way for idle men to obtain a degree and Romilly thought nothing of it as an academic discipline. In instructing Luard in his early days as his successor as Registrary he wrote 'Leapingwell is altogether wrong about the Tripos verses. They have always been endorsed with the names of the B.A.s and never with the names of *LLB* . . . As for the Moral and Natural Science folks the University has as yet assigned no precedence to these B.A.s: so they must of course be placed last. But as for *LLB* they are in a different class, – as distinct as Fishes from Birds. – I know indeed that the *LLB* are put on a footing with BAs as to taking their degree on the last Saturday in January: – but Leapingwell should recollect that they are admitted (1st, 2d & 3d Class) after the wooden spoon !!' (Letter of 2 May 1862 in C.U.R. 20.1). Leapingwell was of course a lawyer and LL.D.

[29] The *Life* was published in two volumes in 1813.

[30] Under the existing system for electing burgesses for the university voters gave their cards (in Latin) to the Vice-Chancellor as returning officer, sitting in the Senate House with the two Proctors and the Junior Doctor in Divinity as scrutineers. Replying to George Denman, Romilly gave the total number of eligible voters as 'very nearly 5000', about 250 of them resident. He saw no objection to Denman's suggestion that an act of Parliament should allow people living anywhere to send postal votes which after examination would be 'dropped into the boxes, and everything proceeding just as it does now'. 'You may get a letter from the end of the kingdom in one day'. See Report from the Select Committee on the University Elections Bill; together with the Proceedings of the Committee, and Minutes of Evidence in *Reports from Committees* (10), 1861, XIV, pp. 349-54. Also 21 May 1861.

[31] *Or the Summer's Ramble . . . a Comic Romance* (1772), the only enduring book by Richard Graves, written with a marked distaste for religious enthusiasm, especially that of Whitefield the methodist who is portrayed as a sleek hypocrite.

*Fri. 10.* . . . In my office a visit from Bradshaw:[32]– they have offered to continue him 2 years more in the Manuscript department & to give him a salary of £150 p.a. with the understanding that he is to have nothing whatever to do with the management of the Library: – he is disgusted, but I expect that he will accept . . . In my Evening walk I met the V.C. . . . He told me as a secret that the Prince Consort is coming next Tuesday to hear Willis's Lecture. – Walked in Coton meadows & gathered cowslips – Frank Kennedy drank tea with me. Felt ill all day.

*Tu. 14.* . . . Received from 'the Committee Office' a copy of my evidence last Thursday: – the people who questioned me were the Chairman (Dodson) Mr Walpole (our Member), Lord E. Bruce, G. Denman, Mr Ayrton, Mr Hunt & Mr Lowe . . . Mrs Shilleto & 2 daughters were determined they would be in time: – they came to my office 5' before 1! At 1½ I took them into the Senate-house: we got very good places. – The Prince Consort & the Prince of Wales & V.C. arrived punctually as the Clock was striking 2. – Willis began immediately his lecture on Trinity Coll.[33] (beginning from Kings Hall & Michael House & bringing it down to Whewell's new Court).[34] He delivered this able lecture in so low a tone that it was most imperfectly heard & 2 or 3 times the youngsters in the galleries were disposed to scrape him down. – The young men applauded the Prince Consort & the P. of Wales very heartily: – they groaned for the Pope, for Mr Edwin James, Mr Bright etc. . . .

*Sat. 18.* . . . At 1½ to Parkers Piece where there was a Review of the Riflemen of the Univ. Corps. (C.U.R.V.) & the Riflemen of the Inns of Court (I.C. R.V.).[35] I had the good fortune to fall in with that good-tempered fellow Dr Drosier & I walked with him till the Review was over (about 4): – he has great knowledge about military matters, & explained all the movements to me with a clearness wch gave me great interest in the Review. He told me that the Inns-of-Court Corps is reckoned the best in the Kingdom & the University of Camb. the 2d best . . . The Prince of Wales was on the ground, on horseback. – There were dinners given at 5½ in the Halls of Trin., St Johns, Caius, Magdalene (& perhaps some others). – I was amused at hearing that

[32] Henry Bradshaw, appointed Principal Library Assistant in 1856, an authority on mss and early printed books, lazy or over-active in turn, was temperamentally unsuited to administration. Bradshaw did accept the increase in salary – with a bad grace. See McKitterick pp. 528-30.

[33] King's Hall, founded by Edward II about 1317, was re-established by Edward III on the site of the later Trinity Great Court. Michaelhouse, founded in 1324, also became part of Trinity. See E.S. Leedham-Green, *A Concise History of the University of Cambridge* (1996) pp.22-3.

[34] This was the annual Rede lecture; see 10 May 1859. Undergraduates filling the galleries before it began applauded 'several favourites . . . among whom was Professor Kingsley' whose lectures the Prince of Wales was attending. (See the *Chronicle* for 18 May).

[35] The gallant members of the Inns of Court, the 'Devil's Own' marched to Parker's Piece where the *Chronicle*'s reporter (25 May) thought the estimate of 25,000 people on the ground 'a moderate computation'. Besides those taking part in the review military men from far and wide sported every variety of uniform, and the Prince of Wales, in civilian dress, was only recognised when he rode away from the Piece. *The Times*, too, reported enthusiastically and found the Devil's Own marching slightly superior to that of Cambridge. Cambridge, however, lacking the assistance of Judge Willis, 'showed a decided superiority in file firing and the roar of musketry from their line was deep and continuous'.

Judge Willes (one of the Common Pleas Judges) is a *private* in the I.C.R.V, & that he is so excited that he jumps when he fires. – Harriet & Caroline were at this Review . . .

*Tu. 21.* . . . The Senate House was intensely crammed: the Prince & the Duke of St Albans had on their gaudy gowns[36] & the place was brilliant with red gowns. – The degrees were 9: DD of merit to Gell (Bishop designate of Madras), LLD to Ld Elgin, Ld Stratford de Redcliffe, Dr Robinson of Armagh, Sir W. Hamilton, Sir Roderick Murchison, Grote (the Historian of Greece), General Sabine, & Motley (the American Historian of the Dutch Republic) . . . The 2 persons best received & most loudly cheered were Ld Elgin & Mr Grote, – particularly the last. – Then came the recitations of Poems: – this year there were 2 Porson Prizemen. The English Poem was by Myers of Trin: – the subject was 'the Prince of Wales at Washington's tomb':[37]– several parts of the poem were loudly cheered, but when the Prince was said 'to bow his *awful* head' the gallery laughed, – & very properly: – Myers should have written 'awe-struck'. I was pleased in the Senate H. by Mr Walpole telling me that he thought I gave my evidence very well before the Committee of the House of Commons[38] . . . I was very much struck with the smooth face & the contemplative inflexible look of Ld Stratford de Redcliffe: – a great contrast to his countenance is the goodhumoured round happy face of Ld Elgin . . .

*Sat. 1 June.* Up at 7. – Walk about Town. – Work in Office till near 5 (– having eaten sausage roll at 1½ at Wrights). – A little before 6 arrived (walking from the Station) George Allen & Dora & (to my delight) two of their little girls Mary Catherine Romilly (age 10) & Annie Emma (age 8). – The last time George paid me a visit was in 1858 . . .

*Sun. 2.* Up at 7. – Walk about Town: routed out the pew-opener of St Sepulchres (– his name Edwards, & he lives in a little Court to the East of the Corn Exchange) & bribed him to find seats for myself & my 4 guests at the Round Church. – We all 5 went there at 11: the Church is lovely to look at:

---

[36] i.e. the Prince and the Duke of St Albans were wearing the full-dress robes of noblemen of Trinity. George Grote's 12-volume *History of Greece* (1840-56) was, said the Orator, 'in the hands of every studious youth'. (See the *Chronicle*, 25 May). The Earl of Elgin had only just returned from China where the summer palace at Peking had been destroyed in retribution for the abduction by the Chinese of the *Times* correspondent (later murdered) and of British soldiers carrying a letter from him to the Chinese plenipotentiary.

[37] The Prince of Wales, standing at the tomb during his informal and immensely successful visit to America during the previous summer, believes that Washington speaks to him from the dead.

'In silence bent the Prince an awful head
In solemn silence turned him from the spot
He heard the spirit of the mighty dead
He heard and answered not.'

F.W.H. Myers, *The Prince of Wales at the Tomb of Washington. A Poem which obtained the Chancellor's Medal* (1861), stanza XXV.

[38] Romilly's evidence, clear in every detail and decisive in opinion, reads admirably. His Oxford counterpart's performance was not impressive. See 9 May 1861.

every thing is in perfect order: I much admired the painted glass[39] . . . We were a party of 6 at 4 o'clock dinner, by the addition of Frank Kennedy (who was as mute as a fish). – We all went to Trinity Chapel. On the way there I introduced the children to the deer at Peterhouse . . . The Prince was in Chapel, so I hurried my people out that they might get a good view of him in the Great Court . . . After tea I showed illustrated books, & gave Kate a life of Nelson & Annie the story of Beauty & the Beast. – I was amused by hearing from Harriet that Annie said to her 'I am rather disappointed: I expected Uncle was a young man, & I thought I should have a grand bedroom'. To bed shortly after 11.

*Mon. 3.* Up at 7. Walk only to the Bull to order the Omnibus to call. Before I went I had an interview with the little ladies & made for each a paper purse & put in it a bright shilling . . . My Guests breakfasted with me at 8¼ & went off by the Express train: – the little girls wore very pretty red clokes (wch they called Garibaldis[40] . . . I gave Harriet & Caroline & Miss Bridge's maid Mary 1s each to go to the grand contest of 9 Brass Bands in the Old Botanical Gardens this Evening . . . The 1st admission began at 5: – above 3000 people came by cheap trains. I went in spite of the rain a little before 6 & staid an hour & ½ & was much pleased with the performance: – the Yorkshire Band[41] gained the 1st prize of money: the grand Prize of a Cornet was gained by Large of the Cambridge Rifle Band. – Fell in with Frank Kennedy here. – He drank tea with me. – He was in good spirits about his performance at the Examination today in Euclid & Algebra: I more wish it than believe it. He went away early to read for the Greek Play tomorrow.

*Fri. 7.* Up at 7. – So cold that I had a fire at breakfast. – Walk in Botanic Garden. – A Seniority at 12 about additional light in Trinity College Hall at the centre tables: we agreed to have a grand standard Gas-light near the Brazier . . . Frank Kennedy came & drank tea with me . . . he goes home tomorrow . . . I gave him a set of last year's Little-Go papers & told him the subjects for 1862: – he is very wisely going to read them in the Vacation & has the laudable ambition of being in the 1st Class. – Count Cavour is dead: this is a great calamity for Italy . . .

*Mon. 10.* Feel faint and shortbreathed. – Walk in Queens Gardens, wrapt up in my cloke for it was raining. . . . Wolfe (of Clare) was married today in Cambridge to Miss D'Orsey . . . Clare is one of the Colleges whose new Statutes allow their Fellows to marry . . .

[39] Presumably the six windows inserted under Salvin's direction by the Cambridge Camden Society in 1841-3. Five were by Thomas Willement and one by William Wailes. The Gothic and Renaissance art of painting on glass as distinct from staining it in manufacture had died out by the eighteenth century and owed its revival to the nineteenth-century enthusiasm for Gothic architecture and to artists such as Willement and Wailes.

[40] 'Garibaldi jackets' were originally bright red in imitation of the shirts worn by Garibaldi and his followers. Later they were made in other colours. See *Illustrated London News* 27 September 1862.

[41] i.e. the Balidon Band 'which appeared to be composed of artisans'. For a long account see the *Chronicle* (8 June).

*Wed. 12.* . . . At 11 to the Senatehouse for the Election of a successor to poor Henslow: there was no Candidate but Babington:[42] so it was rapidly over. – At 1¼ I went to Magdalene Lodge to witness the Admission of Babington. – The Vicechancellor was highly delighted at having received a Telegram upon 'the Proctorial Question':[43]– the Judges have decided in favor of the University *on all the points*: – hurrah! Walk in the Evening till 8½ on the Barton Road . . .

*Sat. 15.* . . . The Trin: Coll: Classes came out this Evening: – poor Frank is in the 8th! below him is the Last Class, & a still lower class is 'not worthy to be classed' . . . Wrote to Frank to express my sorrow at his position . . .

*Wed. 19.* . . . Letter from Kennedy (in his very worst hand): he takes very greatly to heart Frank's being in the 8th Class, & cannot bear the thought of his place being owing either to incapacity or to idleness. – I think it is owing to both. I wrote to him saying that I thought Frank quite deficient in all strenuous & earnest application, – that I thought it was a part of his constitution & that I did not believe it could be overcome . . . I did not suggest removing Frank from College; for what can be done with him? . . .

*Wed. 26.* . . . After dinner sat in the garden till 5 & then for 1½ hour nailed up prints in the lumber-room & in the water-closet: I selected for the last water pieces . . .

*Sat. 29.* Up at 7. – Very unwell tho I had a good nights rest. . . . Letters from Maggie & G.T.R. expressing sorrow at my illness. – Also a similar very hearty letter from Grim regretting that little Bertha is not quite old enough to come & nurse me. – He says every body is contented with the will of Mrs Eaton:[44] she leaves her personal property of £3000 to Dora's children & Bertha's with liberty to apply the interest to board & education of said children . . . Letter from the Secretary of the Consumption Hospital at Brompton thanking me for my 3 Guinea subscription & enclosing me one indoor (red) & 6 outdoor (black) orders & a paper of instructions. I filled up the inside & also an outside for M.A. Tyler . . .

*Tu. 2 July.* Up at 7. – Walk to Railway Bridge. Knocked at one of the Albert Almshouses[45] to ask who was elected last Thursday: an old woman showed me over her downstairs accommodation . . . I thought the rooms very comfortable & she spoke very cheerfully & contentedly . . . I yesterday made

---

[42] Charles Babington, botanist and archaeologist, had attended Henslow's lectures between 1827 and 1833. His *Manual of British Botany* (1843) went to ten editions, and informed British botanists of continental developments.

[43] For details of the case see 13 February 1860. It was at last brought to an end by a tortuous summing up by Lord Chief Justice Erle who concluded that the finding for the plaintiff Emma Kemp should be set aside, and a verdict entered for the defendant, and that the same decision must apply to the other parallel case of Ebbon v. Neville (*The Times* 13 June 1861). However, the University had scented danger and subsequently decided to overhaul the procedure in Spinning House cases. See Winstanley pp. 381-2.

[44] Dorothea Eaton, mother of Dora, George Allen's wife, and Bertha, Grim's wife, had died on 10 June aged eighty at George's house. Mrs Eaton's granddaughter (by her deceased daughter) was to inherit Parcglas. Her other (married) daughter was presumably well provided for.

[45] i.e. the new almshouses on the Hills Road built by Peck and Stephens to house elderly members of the Royal Albert Society.

alterations in the will wch I drew up just 7 years ago . . . I have given legacies to G.B. Allen (my Executor) & his wife Dora & 3 of their children (viz. John Romilly, Kate & Nanny), to Grim & his wife Bertha & 3 of their children (viz. Bertha, Lucy & Margaret), to Frank & wife & their 3 children, to George Romilly & wife & their 3 children: – so 3 has been my favorite no . . . I also left . . . legacies to poor Elisabeth Stallybrass, my Gyp & Bedmaker & my maids Harriet & Caroline . . .

*Wed. 3.* Up at 7. – Don't feel any less weak or nervous . . . I today drew up an account of my money in the funds & in foreign securities etc, & put it with my will & instructions to my Executor about my funeral & the house in wch I now live. – Then worked at the degrees of 1731 till 3 o'clock . . . When in the garden read the monthly no of Dicken's 'Great Expectations': – it is very little to my taste.

*Fri. 5.* . . . Fell in with Sharpe (Deputy Senior Proctor) & asked him about the threatened action against Basil Williams: he tells me that Basil Williams saw a woman talking to an undergraduate: – he did not touch her nor take her to the Spinning House: – her husband came up, & was very abusive: – they allege that the woman was so much alarmed that she had a miscarriage. – I hear that husband & wife are so disreputable that the husbands brother (who is Clerk at St Giles) won't speak to him. How an action can be brought against Bas. Williams is to me inconceivable . . . Short Evening walk: – only to St Johns walks where I sat down & read Goldsmith's Essays.

*Sun. 7.* . . . Called on Mrs Prest & saw also Mrs William Prest who exhibited to me her archery prize (a very handsome 'nécessaire'). – I learned that Frank Haviland is to be married on Wednesday to a Miss Papillon: there are at present 8 Miss Papillons (sisters), but 2 of them are to be married on Wednesday . . . One of the Caius fellows is just married & means to avail himself of the new privilege of having a year of Grace after his marriage . . .

*Wed. 10.* Up at 7. – More nervous than ever . . . After dinner I had a letter from Maggie: she says that Frank is highly delighted with a boat made & rigged for him by his Father: Bertie lords it over his brothers, – Frank bears it quietly, Cappie rebels. – Sarah Fordham called to say that her child (for whom I voted) was elected:[46]– Mr Clayton & others are helping her for the poor childs outfit: – gave her 10/. A foolish woman stopt me to say there was a lawyer who could get her money out of Chancery! – just as if the poor wretch could have money there, or (if she had) could ever get it out: – I said to her 'stuff & nonsense' & gave her 6d . . .

On 15 July Harriet searched Yarmouth for lodgings for Romilly, Caroline and herself for the next seven weeks. When Romilly arrived on the following day he found that she had 'in her great zeal for my service overworked herself both in mind & body' but had 'discovered most comfortable & beautifully clean & tidy ones . . . my bedroom & sitting room both look on the sea: the maids at present have only one bed; when they have 2 I am to pay ½ guinea more. Harriet prepared every thing just as if I had been in Benet Place.' For this Romilly must have been especially grateful as there are several

---

[46] Sarah's daughter Rebecca aged ten was blind. Romilly had sent his 'Blind proxy' to her on 14 April.

references to letters which would have been difficult to answer had he not been able to set out the official books he had brought with him.

Romilly's health, as always when he was by the sea, improved rapidly; the weather was better than during the preceding year's holiday and there were more people about whom he knew. He especially enjoyed talking to Hamnett Holditch, Senior Wrangler in 1822 and Fellow of Caius who 'told me that he was bred up for a sailor'; he did however take long walks and trips by river to Norwich and from the Britannic pier to Southwold on his own. 'I enjoyed this trip exceedingly for in spite of considerable wind & a rough sea I was not even squeamish. – At Southwold (where there is no pier) we anchored & were put ashore in little boats wch were greatly tossed by the breakers'. And at dinner at the *Swan* he was able to confirm the reputation of Southwold's soles as 'the most delicate in the Kingdom'.

There was a beautiful day for the Regatta when 'the Beach was crowded, & the Piers decorated with flags, & bands playing in all directions. I went out for an hours sixpenny sail in company with 14 or 15 others men & women, all well-conducted & happy: I enjoyed it greatly . . . while lying on the beach read with delight Sidney Smith's Reform speeches'. The weather was fine too for the visit to Yarmouth of the great evangelical preacher, Baptist Noel. Preachers spoke to large audiences near the jetty on Thursday evenings during the season and Noel was listened to 'with breathless attention'. But towards the end of his holiday, after an exciting morning during which he watched a practice rescue of four men from a boat by rocket, the preacher for the evening became so wet that after speaking for three-quarters of an hour he was obliged to conclude 'much sooner than he intended' although his 'audience were snug under their umbrellas'.

Our intrepid diarist swam in frequently rough seas on every day save one, but on August 25 'the waves so high that I didn't venture to bathe: my 1st failure. – Scarcely a man ventured & no woman: indeed one of the bathing-women said to me "We don't let them in such a sea".'. The maids were in any case nervous of bathing and Harriet a poor sailor, but Romilly saw to it that they enjoyed their leisure. He treated Caroline and a neighbour to a row on Caroline's thirty-second birthday and Harriet and a friend to donkey rides on the same day, and on August 27 was pleased to record 'H. & C. on donkeys to Caistor Castle: – they reached it this time & without mishap'.

*Mon. 2 September*. Up at 7. – Lovely morning: bathed. – I have not seen so many bathe both from machines & à la sauvage any day this year: numerous parties also went out sailing. – Harriet went off by the Express at 6.25: Caroline Howe & I came by the 1.50 train . . . I read Redgauntlet & lent Pilgrims Progress to Caroline . . .

*Wed. 18*. Up at 7. – Walk in Foster's Avenue – Feel very uncomfortable. – Amused with statistics in the Times about railway travelling. – The trains in the last year have run 102 millions of miles i.e. more than 4000 times round the earth). The travellers in the year have been 163 millions: – which averages more than 5 journeys for every living soul in the Kingdom. – The cattle, sheep & pigs have been 12 millions: 267,000 horses, & 357,000 dogs . . .

*Sun. 22*. Up at 7. – Caroline went to the early prayer meeting in the Sunday School-room: the prayers are extempore: they are offered up by Traylen, & other young pious men of the working classes . . .

*Fri. 27.* . . . In my Office I worked at the degrees of 1714. – Had a visit from Dr Archdall: he says that there is a report that the freshmen admission at Trinity is 169 & at St Johns only 40[47] . . . He said that a few years ago there was a great emigration to Australia, & (as it happened) a remarkably small admission to St Johns: – he heard a Trinity fellow-commoner account for the latter fact by saying 'all the lower classes have gone to Australia' . . .

*Wed. 9 October.* . . . By Gods great mercy I have now completed my 3 score years & ten & am entering on my 71st year. Tho I feel my health greatly broken & I am a very poor creature yet I have abundant grounds for the deepest thankfulness, for I am still able to employ myself in the duties of my office, wch gives me great happiness & turns off my thoughts from my bodily infirmities. – Letter of Congratulation on my birthday from Mary Anne Tyler, enclosing a silk watchguard of her making: the letter was very kind & affectionate: – she alas! gave a sad account of her own health: – wrote to her & sent her a sovereign. – . . . to my great surprise & very great pleasure Betsy (Mrs James Spink) came at 5 o'clock: she brought with her her youngest child Margaret, a very pretty fair joyous creature with large eyes: I thought Betsy looking very flourishing tho she complained of weakness. – In my Evening walk I bought a dressed doll for little Margaret & a china small basket for little Lucy (who had sent me some birthday-verses printed on Satin & in a gilded frame looking like a Valentine): the last 2 lines amused me,

'May we be dearer friends than ever,
That nothing but the pangs of death may sever',
Corrected the last sheets of the 'Register'.[48]

*Fri. 11.* . . . The 3 new Fellows are very mediocre people: Sedley Taylor was 16th Wrangler, Coutts Trotter was penultimate Wrangler & 2d in 2d Class of Classical Tripos . . . Kirby never got a Scholarship: he took his degree in Classics & was 7th of 1st Class.[49] – It is a wretched show for Trinity College, especially as we had 2 Senior Wranglers of 1860 & 1861 (Stirling & Aldis) who are Dissenters & could not sit . . .

*Wed. 16.* . . . Felt very unwell all yesterday Evening & not much better this morning. – Hearing the bells ringing I went to St Catharine's & learned to my great pleasure that Mr Robinson is elected.[50] – Wrote to wish him joy. Issued a notice of my resignation as Registrary next Xmas. Robinson called on

[47] On 9 November, Matriculation Day, Romilly entered the correct figures in his diary. 134 young men were admitted at Trinity and 64 at St John's.
[48] Presumably of his lists of degrees conferred in the eighteenth century.
[49] Sedley Taylor became president of the University Musical Society and Musical Club, and a road on Trinity property is called after him. Coutts Trotter became a university administrator 'to whom more than any other single person were due the indubitable improvements effected in university matters during his short academic career' (*D.N.B.*). T.F. Kirby was called to the Bar four years after becoming a Fellow and then became bursar of Winchester College from 1877 to 1907.
[50] Romilly could not have foreseen that as a result of what became regarded as the scandal of his election, Robinson would become ostracised, his rival Jameson be caused much unhappiness, and the reputation of St Catharine's suffer during the almost fifty years of Robinson's mastership. Robinson had been guilty of no more than an error of judgement during the election.

me in my Office to thank me for my congratulations: he has been a good deal overcome by the excitement of suspense & the joy of success: I told him that he had now to bring a Lady to preside over his house: – he said that perhaps that would not be long hence . . . he starts today for Scotland where I suspect his lady-love lives . . . To Mrs Prest's to play Quadrille . . .

*Fri. 18.* . . . Letter from Francisca Ouvry: she has cut out of yesterdays Times a eulogistic article on me as Registrary:[51] she has cut it out to keep among her valuables. – I saw this praise of my services at night in Mrs Prest's paper – I suppose it to be written by Leapingwell or Woodham . . .

*Sun. 20.* Up at 7. A heavy fog. – Walked to College & then in the college walks. – Found letters from 2 fresh Candidates for the Registraryship . . . there are now 4 who have printed letters, viz. Campion, Field, Luard & Parkinson . . . Wrote to Luard saying I rejoiced that he was a Candidate for my place & wishing him success.

*Wed. 23.* . . . Grieved to hear that Sedgwick had a fit of giddiness in the night & a very severe one this morning at 8½: Paget ordered leaches & he was immediately greatly relieved, but Paget says he must not lecture this week & that somebody must sit up with him at night . . . Letter from Master of Rolls: he has sent my easy Math. Paper to Henry who is on honor to answer it without assistance[52] . . . John asks me whether a Nobleman can be admitted a *Pensioner* at Trinity: for Viscount Hereford is a Ward in Chancery & his estate is worth only £700 a year . . . I wrote to Mathison to ask his opinion but did not mention Ld H's name. My Evening walk was short as my visit to Sedgwick took up part of my usual 2 hours.

*Th. 24.* . . . A nice letter from young Henry Romilly the Etonian . . . he sent me answers to my Mathematical Questions, – all right & neatly written out. Wrote to him. Wrote also to Sir John telling him I was abundantly pleased with Henry's performance, that I had written a certificate & given it to Mathison who would admit him immediately: I also told John that Mathison & the Master said there was no objection to a Peer being a pensioner:[53] if Ld

---

[51] 'The members of the University have been surprised this morning by an announcement from the Registrar, the Rev. Joseph Romilly, of Trinity College, that he shall resign his office at Christmas. It may truly be said that the regret at losing such an officer will be universal. He was elected in the year 1832, when he found the Registry in a state of great confusion. He will leave it as perfect as it can be made by a judicious and methodical arrangement of all the documents under their respective heads. His uniform kindness and courteous bearing towards all who had occasion for his official assistance or advice have deservedly obtained for him universal esteem and regard.' (*The Times* 17 October, p. 8).

[52] On 19 October Romilly had received a letter from his cousin the Master of the Rolls saying that he wanted his third son Henry to be entered at Trinity 'for next October'.

[53] In 1862 W. Emery of Corpus, late Senior Proctor, gave a paper in Cambridge *On the Past and Present Expenses and Social Condition of University Education*. 'The estimates for the expenses of students at present for three terms a year were on three scales – the lowest being about £120, the second £180 and the highest £250. If private tutors were engaged, a sum of £8 or £10 a term must be added . . . Some men of great economy lived in the University for £100 a year. These rates included all University charges and private expenses as derived from the tradesmen's bills sent in to the tutors . . . It had been shown that . . . one of the sources of extravagance in undergraduates was the habits acquired by them at public schools.' So the estimate for Lord Hereford's expenses allows him a margin. See *Report of the Thirty-Second*

Hereford comes up as a *Pensioner* he cannot spend less than £300 a year: Lords Feilding & Nelson (who were admitted as Noblemen) were very careful & economical & contrived to spend only £400 a year . . . Old Pryme told me that he meant to lecture as long as life was in him: – he is past 80 & looks good for 10 years more. He is very indignant that his Professorship was neglected at the recent increase of stipends . . . After dinner I had a joyous letter from Grim expressing delight at my resignation & hoping that I meant to pass a great deal of my time with him: – wrote to him. – Frank Kennedy looked in before my dinner . . .

*Fri. 25.* . . . Visit from Leapingwell: he says there is talk in the town of Jameson's complaint of ill usage from Robinson in the recent election for the Mastership of Cath: viz. that Robinson did not vote for him (Jameson) as he expected him to do because he (J.) had voted for Robinson: – I can't imagine that Robinson ever gave ground for such expectation on J.'s part. – What an absurd farce for rivals to vote for each other![54] . . .

*Mon. 28.* Up at 7. Called on Sedgwick: he had not slept so well & was greatly dejected: – he had been annoyed by a letter from Dent proposing that some one (I suppose that uncomfortable, disagreeable, dissatisfied gloomy Richard)[55] should come to be with him: he wrote a few lines to Mary (Dicks amiable wife) in opposition, & begged me also to write to give the best account I could of him . . . Letter from Inverness containing the wedding cards of C.K. Robinson (Master of Cath.) & Miss Stewart. Wrote him a letter of warm good wishes. – In my office I had a visit from T. Field (one of the Candidates for my old shoes): he wanted to know what were the duties of Registry: – I told him that I had thought them to require 6 hours daily attendance at the office . . . I am disturbed about the state of my hands, which seem to me to be in a very bad way & to be losing their tenacity.

*Wed. 30.* . . . Called on Sedgwick & found him better & in good spirits: he read me a delightful letter of Cara's wch he had just received. – He was angry

*Meeting of the British Association for the Advancement of Science* (1863), Appendix II, p. 193.

[54] At the time of the election there were only five fellows of St Catharine's and it had become clear that the result would depend on the votes of the candidates themselves – Robinson, the reserved yet kindly bursar and his better-liked and more outgoing friend Jameson the tutor. On 26 October Robinson received a letter from Jameson expressing dissatisfaction with his conduct in the election, and by the time that Robinson and his wife, detained by the death of his father, returned to Cambridge on 23 November he found opinion hardened against him. Winstanley in his chapter on the affair (*Later Victorian Cambridge*, pp. 1-19) says that 'no completely satisfactory explanation for the change in his [Jameson's] attitude has ever been offered' and that many questions remain unanswered. See also 2 December 1861.

[55] i.e. Sedgwick's nephew and brother of Isabella, his favourite niece. Romilly's description of Dick foreshadows the tragic persecution mania (see 19 February 1863) which in April 1864 led to his committal to an asylum for many years. In a letter to Isabella Herschel of 12 November 1852 Sedgwick describes the extraordinary prelude to Dick's marriage. He and Mary had fallen in love when very young: since then 'as Sedgwicks are all like tinder' . . . 'the faithless dog has been in love a dozen times'. A chance meeting on a train in September 1852 led to Dick's tracing the faithful Mary and within a month his uncle had married them and lent them his house in Norwich where Dick was an incumbent. See Clark and Hughes, II, 233 and 15 April 1864.

at a letter from his sister in law Mrs James begging & praying to come & nurse him: – he wrote to scold her & said the idea worried him & made him ill. – He is going out in an open carriage. Gave 1/s to Harriet for a ticket to see the Prince open the Rifle-Ground[56] (on Barton Road) & also to Miss Bridges & Mary . . .

*Sat. 2 November.* Up at 7. Slept better, thank God. – A very kind letter of George's saying that Maggie & her babe Florence Sophie born 15 Oct. are going on famously & the 3 other children are flourishing. He proposes my discontinuing my monthly allowance: – I wrote to him saying that I should go on with it as long as I live . . . I was much surprised today by a letter from a poor scholar of Trinity who subscribes himself 'Alpha': he had (under that disguise) asked me this day 2 years ago for help to pay his Tutor's bill & I had sent him the trifling sum of £1. He now writes a very warm-hearted letter of gratitude (– I had at the time requested him not to write): he tells me there is universal sorrow at my resignation. He will take his degree in January. I have no idea who he is –

*Mon. 4.* . . . College meeting: I had to preside at the latter part of this meeting when the Master went off by the rail: we voted various sums to different beggars, & arranged some leases. I was sorry to hear that some youngsters had behaved very ill at the feast in Hall on the 1st of November: – they had shouted & knocked down benches during the anthem. Read today a 2d King William Essay:[57]– we thought there was only one & have already assigned the Prize to Edwards: this 2d one has been just discovered by the Senior Dean (Blore) to whom it was sent in June! I thought it poor stuff: – he talked of 'solving' King William (as if he had been an equation) . . .

*Th. 7.* . . . Walk by moonlight round the Via Lambertina. Sedgwick sent me 2 letters in the Evening about Mrs Guthrie: – one from Mr G. who fears her illness will become a gastric fever: the other from the maid who says her mistress is too ill to read but begs to have a 6 penny picture-book sent to amuse her.[58] – Of course Sedgwick sent her a packet. – I was sorry to hear from him that he had broken down in the morning: – happily he was much better when he wrote. – The Prince of Wales, the Duke of St Albans etc are this term lectured on Political Science by Whewell: – I hope Pryme will not hear of it: he would be greatly annoyed.[59]

[56] The University Corps of Rifle Volunteers now had their own ground with a range of 1250 yards instead of sharing the Cambridge Rifle Club butts on Mill Road. The Prince presented the corps with a challenge cup, Mrs Neville presented a set of electric targets on behalf of the ladies connected with the university, and E.C.R. Ross of Trinity and Rossie Castle fired the first shots at the target. He had shot his first stag at the age of ten and won the Queen's Prize in 1860 aged twenty. For his portrait and an article on 'The Champion Shot of England' see *The Illustrated London News* 21 July 1860, p. 66.

[57] See 3 November 1854.

[58] The late Dr D.J. Bruce told us that there were six or eight large colour plates and usually very little reading matter in these popular children's books, largely published by Dean and Son and Routledge and Warne. Among titles perhaps acceptable to adults were *John Gilpin*, *Modern Cries of London*, Watts's *Divine and Moral Songs*, and *Royal Procession*.

[59] The Duke of St Albans's scholarship left much to be desired. On 15 June 1861 when Frank achieved a place in the eighth class in the Trinity examinations, the Duke 'is said to have been

*Tu. 12.* Up at 7. Called on Sedgwick: he is none the worse for yesterday's lecture, but is in good force & good spirits about himself. He has received a most kind invitation to meet the Queen & Prince Consort at dinner tomorrow at Madingley . . . However a telegram came in the course of the morning to say the Queen must defer her visit as the King of Portugal (age 24) is dead[60] . . . In my office had visits from the Vicechancellor (Phillips), Martin etc etc., by the way Latham has a humorous way of accounting for Phillips slowness in answering,[61] – that he translates what one says into Syriac & then parses it before he replies. – In the Evening very improved tidings of Mrs G . . .

*Th. 14.* . . . Breakfast to Frank Kennedy, lame merry John Higgins Allen, & nervous sickly Wilcox (who devotes himself to reading to the sick poor) . . . A very kind & charming letter from Sophie Kennedy: she amused me with an anecdote about an Irish parrot which used to say when there was a pause in the conversation 'What a bore! go to bed'. – Wrote to her. At night walked to Trumpington.

*Mon. 18.* . . . Selwyn astonished me prodigiously by showing me a circular 'The friends of Mr Romilly are requested to attend in Clare Hall Combination-room tomorrow concerning a testimonial'!!!! This is the age of testimonials, but I certainly never dreamt of one to myself . . .

*Sat. 23.* . . . I wrote to Paget[62] & told him that I hated & detested the sight of my own face, that I utterly deprecated the idea of my portrait, that I would rather have that of a Gorilla, & that I was too nervous to sit for my Portrait . . . Letter from G.T.R. – it was very satisfactory & very amusing: his baby Florence has been christened & slept thro the ceremony. – there is an little black kitten; Bertie the other day gave it a thorough good washing with soap & water, rough dried it with flannel & put it into the coal-skuttle to sleep: the nurse in replenishing the fire pitched him on it: he began miauing & was rescued with a singed coat & damaged tail! . . .

*Tu. 26.* . . . In my office I had a visit from J.L.F. Russell & a nice little daughter: he came to talk about his position as incorporate A.M: – poor man! I hope he does not know that the sight of him throws me into a nervous fever. I pity him greatly: he is poor & willing to work, but cannot get any body to give him preferment: – he is not popular: living with him would soon make me mad. – Received a packet containing 5 letters, – one from Dora, 3 from her children Nanny, Kate & Romilly & one from little Bertha who is going to pass the winter with them . . . I was amused with Romilly's letter: he told me that his schoolmaster pronounces Cicero *Kickero*, that some boys saw his sisters in their red clokes with Bertha in black & called out 'Hulloh! Boys, there goes Red-Riding Hood & the Wolf' . . . After dinner I wrote 5 letters in answer to these 5. – Little Bertha is learning Greek & German! . . .

examined in nothing but Greek Testament & to have gained only 10 marks! – he is to be reexamined.' It was Pryme, not Whewell, who was Professor of Political Economy.

[60] Pedro V of Portugal, husband of Princess Stephanie of Hohenzollern, had died of cholera during the epidemic which ravaged the whole kingdom in 1860-1.

[61] See 15 January 1858.

[62] Paget was secretary of the testimonial committee.

*Th. 28.* . . . In my Office I worked at my annual list of officers: wrote to a Mr A. Withers undergraduate of Corpus: he was astonished at Emery being the 1st Senior Proctor of Corpus for 100 years: explained to him that Corpus is a Divinity College & therefore the Fellows have to proceed to BD, & it is only since 1858 that BDs can be Proctors[63] . . .

*Fri. 29.* . . . Harriet Sandfield has been 13 years with me this day: she told me she had lately had an offer from the Widower Troughton, but that she never meant to leave me. – Call from a poor Milanese (Gallera by name): he wrote Barrister at Law on his card, so I admitted him supposing he was an Englishman on University business: he told me 'en simple langage je suis en détresse', to wch I answered 'en simple langage voila un scheling': – bon jour' . . . Lord Alwyn Compton told me today that one Fellow of Trinity had said that he saw no good in education!! I wonder whether it was King . . .

*Sun. 1 December.* . . . In the Evening walked by moonlight to Trumpington Church: – the greater part of the time I had Ainslie for my companion: he is a complete idolater of the late Bishop Kaye[64] & says that he would willingly have laid down his life for him, – & I am convinced he would . . . Ainslie is as honest a man as lives: he is for correcting all abuse in our church matters as well as every thing else. – He has however a morbid feeling of dissatisfaction.

*Mon. 2.* Up at 7. – Call on Sedgwick. – His head had been so distressing (doubtless in great measure from a long letter he wrote to Mrs G.) that he sent for Paget who put on a mustard plaster on the back of his head . . . To the V.C.'s at 10½ about the 6 Candidates for Natural Sciences:[65] my cousin Edward Romilly is one: there are 3 B.A. Candidates & 3 undergrad. The examination begins today: it lasts 6 hours for 6 following days . . . At 11 called on Mr & Mrs Robinson at Barnwell Parsonage: – they are not yet gone to Catharine Lodge. I found her a very pleasing affable highland young lady from Inverness . . . Mr Robinson walked with me when I quitted his house. – I told him that I was deeply pained by the treatment he had met with, & that I believed as firmly in his integrity as in my own existence. He said that he had been so harassed & afflicted that he often wished he had never been Master. He told me the details of the Election: – the day before the Election Jamieson [sic] said to him 'I shall vote for you': Robinson replied 'You should not do so: you wish for the Mastership: you should vote for yourself'. – The day of Election Jameson again said he should vote for Robinson, who replied 'you had

---

[63] The tide of Evangelicalism began to flow strongly in Corpus towards the middle of the century. In the reign of Dr Pulling 'the tide reached full flood. The college attracted the sons of Evangelicals from all over the country, and became more than at any other time in its history primarily a nursery for the training of clergymen of the Church of England' (Patrick Bury, *Corpus Christi College Cambridge. A History 1822 to 1952* (1952) p. 58).

[64] John Kaye (1783-1853), Senior Wrangler and Senior Chancellor's medallist, Master of Christ's aged 30, Regius Professor of Divinity and reforming Bishop of Bristol and Lincoln, worked constantly to raise the character of the clergy by his example. 'No prelate stood higher in the esteem of the English church at his death' (*D.N.B.*).

[65] Between 1851 and 1860 the greatest number of candidates was six, the lowest three, three fewer than the number of examiners! Candidates no longer needed to be graduates in mathematics or classics and their numbers not unnaturally gradually increased. See note for 23 February 1860 and Searby pp. 232-3.

better not'. – The end was this: – Milner, Robinson, Jameson voted for Robinson who of course was elected: – Jameson threw his arms round Robinson & wished him joy: Jameson also readily accepted from the new Master the office of President. – This seems to me to prove the thorough honesty of Robinson's proceedings . . . Frank Kennedy & Edward Romilly (junior)[66] drank tea with me: I thought the latter looked ill & unhappy & distrait: – he seems to think too much, – wch certainly is not a fault of his Cousins.

*Wed. 4.* . . . Audit from 10 to 1½: – we agreed (but far from unanimously) to admitting the dissenting Schoolmaster Johnson on our boards for A.M. degree . . . At 3 I went to Fenners ground to see the 6 mile foot-race: the Candidates were 'Deerfoot',[67] Brighton, & 2 others: one gave in after 3 or 4 miles: 'Deerfoot' won by a few yards only. – The Prince of Wales shook hands with him & gave him £5. The 6 miles were run in 55' . . . Beamont took Deerfoot to dine in hall: the Prince dined there.

*Mon. 9.* . . . Called on Sedgwick: he was agitated at the thought of today's Lecture being his last & complained that his head had given way yesterday . . . Went to Sedgwick's concluding lecture: he was in great force: but his feelings rather overcame him in taking leave. – His lecture was far too long: it lasted nearly 2 hours: I thought the account of his own labors from 1818 & his eulogies of those whom he had employed highly interesting: – but I was very weary of his long attack of Darwin & the 'development' theory[68] . . .

*Tu. 10.* . . . At 1 Sedgwick drove me over to Madingley. Fortunately the Prince was at home: he received us very graciously & stood talking with us in the Hall for 10': – General Bruce was also there. – We saw too Mr Fisher the Tutor. After the Prince was gone out riding, we had a very agreeable chat with Mrs Bruce: she & the General have promised to lunch with Sedgwick on Thursday after going over his Museum. – On taking up a book in the drawing-room I was much pleased with seeing on the fly-leaf 'to her dear Bertie from his affectionate sister Helena': – I like greatly that familiarising of Albert into Bertie: – it is delightful to see the royal family on such affectionate unceremonious terms . . .

*Fri. 13.* . . . Very kind invitation from Master of Rolls asking me to spend Xmas with him & offering me as a bribe a copy of part of Domesday Book: – I swallowed the bribe, but declined the visit. – C.K. Robinson & F.J. Jameson have printed a short statement[69] (dated 12 Dec.). – I do not think it a very

---

[66] Edward was clearly not robust as an undergraduate, but he became a master of the supreme court from 1870 to 1886 when he died aged 48. See Joseph Foster, *Men at the Bar* (1885), p. 400.

[67] Deerfoot's opponents were J. Brighton, the four-mile champion of England, Lang of Middlesborough and S. Barker of London. As the son of an Indian chief he wore a racoon headdress, cloak of opossum skins, and moccasins of embroidered cloth, but raced in tights, a short skirt with bells, and a single feather on his head. The race was run in 55 minutes and at its end 'everybody crowded round "Deerfoot" and his spirited opponent to congratulate them on the endurance they had evinced' (*Chronicle* 7 December 1861).

[68] See 9 December 1859.

[69] Both Winstanley in *Later Victorian Cambridge* (chapter 1) and E.E. Rich and Oliver MacDonagh in E.E. Rich (ed.), *St Catharine's College Quincentenary Essays* (1973), agree in

satisfactory document: it runs thus 'Mr R. gives full credit to Mr J's assertion that he, not wishing to vote for himself, gave his vote to Mr R. under the expectation that Mr R. would abstain from voting for himself'. – Mr J. gives full credit to Mr R's assertion that he had no intention of taking any unfair advantage of Mr J's vote, but that he believed at the time that Mr J's vote was given in his favor without the expectation that he should abstain from voting for himself' . . . The P. of Wales was called to Windsor tonight by Telegram: his Father has a fever.

*Sat. 14.* . . . Call on Sedgwick: found him pretty well: he thinks with me that too much fuss has been made about Beamont's taking Deerfoot into Hall last Sunday. In todays Cambridge Chronicle is a letter of Beamonts[70] in excuse of his conduct: he says that Deerfoot is a religious man, that he had seen him in Church & Kings Chapel, & that Deerfoot is in constant communication with the Missionary who instructed him in his own country: that Deerfoot is a stranger in a foreign land, etc. – The lame Statement of Robinson & Jameson is printed in todays paper: it will scarcely give satisfaction to anybody: – it greatly annoys Sedgwick, who is peculiarly interested in the matter as the Master of Catharine is (ex officio) Prebendary of Norwich . . .

*Sun. 15.* . . . Went to Trinity Church to hear Bishop McIlvaine (Bishop of Ohio) . . . before the sermon Mr Clayton begged his Congregation to offer up prayers to God that He would avert from us the horrors of a war with America[71] . . . I was greatly shocked on coming out of church to hear that the poor Prince is dead![72] – the Bulletin in Saturdays Times had been very hopeful: – There was a leader in the Times highly eulogistic of the Prince as a counsellor & guide of the Queen . . .

*Mon. 16.* . . . In my Office wrote out copies of the notices issued by Philpott in Feb. 1847 to declare the vacancy of the Chancellorship (by death of the Duke of Northumberland) . . . Visit from Leapingwell: he thinks Dr Corrie

thinking the statement probably correct and that both decent agitated men had genuinely misunderstood their conversation on the eve of an election which meant so much to them. 'As far as the issue of a broken agreement was concerned that [the statement] should have been the end of the matter and in fact the hubbub died down' (Rich, p. 206) only to be revived in 1867. But so much damage had by then been done that those who read the statement would inevitably have found it unsatisfactory.

[70] On 13 December Romilly 'thought it clear that the agitation against Beamont's goodnatured folly originated with Mathison, who is a stern guardian of discipline'. In this letter Beamont stated his belief 'that we should often do better if we associated more with persons of a different rank, and less with those of the same rank whose character is notoriously bad. Unless I hear more to the disparagement of Deerfoot's character than I ever have heard, I should not shrink from asking him to my own rooms.' The *Independent* of 17 January 1863 reports that Deerfoot was 'in trouble'. He and his abusive opponent were both sentenced to small fines or short terms of imprisonment for assault arising out of a dispute over a foot-race at Hackney Wick on 29 December 1862.

[71] See 9 January 1862.

[72] 'Although the sad intelligence of the Prince Consort's death arrived in Cambridge at 12 on Saturday night, and was known at the railway station at that hour, no steps were taken to promulgate the intelligence until nearly half past eleven on Sunday morning when it was announced by telegraphic message; and in most of the Churches the prayer for his Royal Highness was read as usual' (the *Chronicle* 21 December).

& the Conservatives will bring forward the Duke of Rutland (born in 1815: – pupil of Prof. Selwyn): he thinks the Duke of Devonshire (born in 1808, 2nd Wrangler in Philpott's year) is the right man: I think so too . . . A young Author G.F. Page left his 1st work (a penny tract with 2 pretty engravings) 'the Widow & her son': put down my name for 30 copies . . .

*Th. 19.* . . . Up to Town by the Express . . . Called at Bennetts (62 Cornhill) & gave him instructions for 2 Silver Seal Boxes . . . Went to Lower Clapton to see Mrs George: I found her as usual very joyous & happy . . . there was a very nice simple dinner, cold roast beef, mutton chops & a toad in a hole: by way of pudding there was what Mrs George called 'spotted Dick': it was a batter roll pudding with plums . . . I of course saw baby: she is very pretty & good humoured, but is wondrous small. I gave her a Sovereign to buy a coral to poke her infant gums. – Frank came home for his holidays today: I like the boy much: – he looks strong & healthy: he showed me his character: – (he is in 3d Class): – Greek & Divinity (satisfactory), Latin, History & German (very satisfactory), French (impatient & fussy!!) . . . In the Omnibus from the Station to my house I found Mathison. He told me that Bishop Philpott, Professors Birkbeck & Kingsley & himself were dining with the Prince at Madingley last Friday: at 8½ while they were at dinner a telegram was brought to General Bruce; he showed it to the Prince: no allusion was made to its contents. – The party went on as if there was nothing particular: the Prince played whist with his young friends. – Shortly after 10 the General said to Mathison that a Telegram was come desiring the Prince & himself to go up to Windsor. – Mathison said 'had we not better go at once?' so carriages were ordered & the company was gone by 10½. – Directly after the Prince & the General departed by special train. – About 24 hours after (viz at 10' past 11 on Sat. night) the Princes Father was no more! – Mrs Paget & Maud called to ask me to dinner on Xmas day: – I declined.

*Fri. 20.* Lord Palmerston declines the Chancellorship: probably the Duke of Buccleuch will not be opposed . . . In the afternoon Sedgwick called on me in my office: he had had a visit from Mrs Bruce today . . . Mrs Bruce told Sedgwick that when the General came into the sick room the Queen took his hand & kissed it & then pressed it on the Princes – Some short time before the Prince died a sudden hope sprung up in the Queen's mind & she started up from her knees & exclaimed 'he has not left us'! When he had breathed his last she flung her arms about his neck & kissed him repeatedly most passionately. After the first long burst of bitter grief she said that she should not yield to her affliction but should devote herself to the welfare of her children & her people. – She is indeed a high minded heroic Queen. – the Natural Sciences Tripos is come out: there is no 1st Class, but Edward Romilly is the 1st in the 2d Class . . . Wrote to Sir John to tell him of Edwards good place . . .

*Sat. 21.* . . . Received a very well written & well spelt letter from Martha Bye . . . enclosing a hideous framed photograph (– wch does justice without mercy) of herself & sister Paulina: they are standing up side by side, each with her hands folded, looking like ugly & dismal quakers: Martha is lame but has good health: she is head & shoulders taller than poor sick Paulina. – It was very kind of Martha to give me the photograph, but I was very glad when

Harriet asked me for it. – Wrote to Martha & enclosed ½ Sovereign between her & her sister . . .

*Sun. 22.* . . . Letter from Sophie: it was  mostly about Frank: she is disappointed at his again being in the 7th class & is now nervous about the Little-Go . . . she wishes me to get the real opinion of Mr Girdlestone his Private Tutor. So after church I called on Mr Girdlestone . . . He does not think meanly of Frank's abilities, but finds him insufferably idle: he sometimes has staid away for a whole week together: he promises more diligence, & then falls back: Mr G. sees no reason why Frank should not get thro the Little-Go respectably if he will work steadily: unless Frank will engage to come regularly & to work hard Mr G. declines continuing him as a Pupil.

*Mon. 23.* . . . At 2 to St Mary's to hear Jeremie's exquisite sermon on the death of the poor Prince:[73]– his text was 'All Judah & Jerusalem mourned for Josiah'. The parallel between Josiah & the Prince was very beautiful . . . He made a sublime conclusion on the Resurrection. – The Church was intensely full: I shared the Clerk's seat: very many men & women (including my maids & little Lucy Spink) stood the whole while. – Of course the pulpit & the throne & the maces were in mourning. On coming out I had some conversation with Mrs Geldart: she says that the Prince had a feeling that he should die & begged that they would write to the Princess of Prussia[74] to prepare her. Mrs Geldart told me also that the Princess Louisa exclaimed 'O that God would take poor useless me & spare Papa'! – very touching . . . After dinner read a sermon of Dean Godwins for the Industrial School: – the subject was the boyhood of our Lord. – Walk to Trinity.

*Tu. 24.* . . . At 12 to a Meeting of the supporters of the Duke of Devonshire[75] in Trinity Combination Room: Whewell was voted into the chair, & 3 motions were carried unanimously (about the Dukes fitness, – the naming the Committee, etc): Sedgwick moved the 1st in an animated warm hearted speech: he was seconded by Hopkins (Senior Wrangler maker):the other movers & seconders were Prof. Stokes, Dr Cartmell, Martin & Dr Phelps. Paget made a very good speech, saying that political opinions ought not to influence one at such a time, & that he should support the D. of D. tho he did not agree with his politics. – I afterwards met Prof. Selwyn: he told me there was a hitch about the Duke of Buccleuch & that they had started the Duke of Northumberland . . .

*Wed. 25.* Up at 7½. – Walk to Railway. Wrote to Grim asking him to come & vote for the D. of D. & stay as long as he can: also wrote to Sir John & J.L. Roget. – Had a grand Turkey & Ham for my solitary Xmas dinner . . .

---

[73] The *Chronicle* of 28 December devotes almost three columns to the scene in Great St Mary's and to Jeremie's sermon. His text from 2 Chronicles XXV, 24 likened the good King Josiah and Prince Albert for 'the purity of their lives', 'the cast of their character', 'the patriotic and beneficent direction of their efforts' and the 'startling suddenness of their deaths'. Real popularity said Jeremie, 'now-a-days was only won by real worth . . . and the example of piety, morality and virtue set by the Court had had its influence in every stratum of society'.

[74] The Princess Royal had married Prince Frederick of Prussia in 1858.

[75] i.e. as Chancellor.

*Th. 26.* . . . On going to the Committee-room I was rejoiced to find that the Duke of Northumberland has declined . . . I think it is now too late to hunt up another Tory Candidate: – the D. of D. will be unopposed . . . Left with the V.C. my M.S. account of the last 4 Elections & Installations: the last 3 Installations (in 1835, 1840, & 1847) were in London . . .

*Fri. 27.* . . . Letter from Sir John saying he would do all he could for the D. of D. & come & vote for him tho it would spoil his short Xmas holidays . . . Wrote to him telling him that Drosier had informed me that (on acct of the new regulations about Natural Science Tripos) the 2d Class now requires far more reading than the 1st used . . . Wrote to D. of Dev. (at 78 Piccadilly) sending a list of his titles & asking if it was right . . .

*Mon. 30.* . . . Wrote to V.C. giving him an account of the details of tomorrow's election: – wrote to the Orator saying that I ought to have a copy of his letter to the Duke of D. this very day . . . Visit from the V.C. – it is highly important to expedite matters as the letter of Condolence to the Queen must wait for the Installation of the new Chancellor . . .

*Tu. 31.* Up at 7½ – By way of early walk went to Welsford & read over the Orator's letter, wch he was working at by candlelight. – At 10 the undisputed election of D. of Dev. as Chancellor in the Arts Schools . . . So ends another year of much happiness & of great mercies. – The infirmities of old age are very strongly warning me that my departure from this life is fast approaching & that I should set myself in earnest to prepare for death. – God grant that I may do so.

"Full" M.A.'s.

'Full' M.A.S

VISIT OF THE PRINCE AND PRINCESS OF WALES TO CAMBRIDGE: THE DEJEUNER WITH THE VICE-CHANCELLOR AT PETER HOUSE.

Visit of the Prince and Princess of Wales June 1864: Luncheon with the Vice-Chancellor at Peterhousr

# 1862

*Wed. 1 January.* . . . I hear that the day of Nomination for Registrary is to be on the 28th & of course the Election on the 29th . . . Leapingwell set off with the Orator's letter (beautifully copied by Welsford) to the D. of Devonshire at Holker[1] in Lancashire . . . Dined in Hall at 4¼ where I presided. – Martin, Jeremie, Thompson etc were there . . . I went into the Combination room & remained till the party broke up about 7½. – I made 3 short speeches; one of good wishes for this new year; a 2d when the wedding cake of the Master of Harrow & Mrs Montague Butler was brought in by Kemp with 'the compliments of Mr Butler';[2] & the last, to thank the party for drinking my health wch was given by old Pryam [sic] . . .

*Mon. 6.* . . . I had a long visit from Leapingwell about proceedings at Installations. – I read him my minute details about the Installation of Marquis Camden[3] . . . the Duke wants to know what points he is to touch on in his speech – wch is always in English & read by him directly after his Installation. I said he should take up the matter of the Orators *letter* (wch he has) & dwell on the virtues of the late Chancellor; I think Leapingwell will do well to remind the Duke that the Prince founded a new Prize (– the Legal medal). – The 2 Cambridge papers have ludicrously misconstrued the Orators Letter: – they translate 'summo ascriptus ordini in civitate'[4] – 'made high Steward of the Town'!!!!!!!! . . . In the Evening came the silver seal boxes (wch were promised for Saturday) . . .

*Tu. 7.* . . . Letter from Betsy (thanking me for kindness to little Lucy who will have been with me 8 weeks tomorrow, & who is to go home on Saturday next, – *at my suggestion* & not at all at Betsy's or little-uns . . . Walk by moonlight to Trumpington.

*Th. 9.* . . . Wrote to G.T.R. to wish him joy of his birthday: he is now entering on his 40th year . . . Highly rejoiced to hear that Federal America has agreed to give up Mason & Slidell (whom Capt. Wilkes seized aboard our Mail-steamer the Trent):[5]– so we shall escape the horrors of war with our

---

[1]  i.e. Holker Hall near Grange. The seventh Duke, brilliant academic and great industrialist, and endowed 'with a deep moral earnestness', devoted himself to scientific and industrial concerns and became first president of the Iron and Steel Institute. He presented the Cavendish laboratory to the University and remained its Chancellor until his death in 1891. See C.N.L. Brooke *A History of the University of Cambridge*, vol. 4 (1993), p. 175.

[2]  Montagu Butler became headmaster of Harrow in 1859 when only 26. His bride was daughter of Hugh Elliot, late Governor of Madras.

[3]  The election of John Jeffreys Pratt, Marquis Camden, in 1834 was the first with which Romilly was concerned as Registrary.

[4]  i.e. 'elevated to the highest order in the city'.

[5]  In November 1861 the British mail steamer the *Trent* had been intercepted near Cuba, and two Confederate commissioners on their way to enlist the support of Britain and France forcibly removed. Great indignation was expressed by the European powers and the British government became increasingly bellicose. Ill as he was, Prince Albert worked hard to avoid war, notably by softening the tone of communications with the North, and the prisoners were released and allowed to proceed to Europe in December.

kinsfolk . . . Little Lucy had a friend (Miss Wheaton) to spend the day: – I had given the maids a pheasant & it furnished the feast. In the Evening I walked to Trumpington.

*Fri. 10.* . . . Leapingwell tells me that the Tories invited 5 persons to become Candidates for Chancellorship (who all declined) viz. Duke of Buccleugh, D. of Northumberland (who is said to have illegitimate children innumerable), D. of Rutland (who has 2 Mistresses, one the wife of a Baronet), Marquess of Exeter (who has a bad name for a profligate) & a 5th (whose name he forgot) . . .

*Fri. 17.* . . . To London by Express: I went in 1st Class taking a return ticket for tomorrow (cost 20/3) . . . Paget was very good company: he told the Story of Perry (a farmer near Audley End) being attacked in his house by burglars & shooting one of them dead: Paget received soon after a letter from Farmer Perry (whose daughter had been his patient) saying 'you may have him if you like. I'll send him by a horse & cart'. – Paget accepted the offer to anatomise the body: in a day or 2 a brother of the burglar came & wanted to have a look at the corpse: he was told 'he an't fit to be seen just now, but in a week you'll find him a clean skeleton' . . . Went to Stratton Street where I was very kindly received by Mrs Edward . . . At 1½ I went (in Cassock & Silk stockings, but not with buckles in my shoes) to the Burlington Hotel, carrying the Duke's Patent. There was a large gathering: many Doctors with red gowns: the 2 members for the University, Lord Monteagle etc etc: – I think there were few noblemen (except Lord M.), if indeed there were any. – We left the Burlington Hotel *on foot* at 10' before 2: I walked (as in duty bound) by the side of the V.C. When we arrived (at 2 punctually) at Devonshire House, we went up the grand stair-case: at the bottom of it is the billiard table so that all people on the staircase may see the playing. The rail is covered with glass (wch I took for silver). We were shown into a fine long [sic]: the walls were covered with pictures, but I was not struck with them. The chair of state was a small one of little pretence. Of course the D. of Dev was not in the room. The V.C. & Proctors wore their caps. The Proctors (as in the Senate House) stood on the left of the state chair: – there were 4 or 5 reporters at a table just in the corner opposite. The V.C. sat down for a moment in the state chair & presently Leapingwell was sent for the Duke: the Duke walked up the room having his train carried by his brother & carrying his cap in his hand. The Duke stood before the Chair. The V.C. (who had been standing close to the Registrary) crossed over & stood before the Proctors. The V.C. now made his speech (wearing his cap): it was very sensible & well expressed: it was approved by the Audience: it was spoken distinctly: it was (perhaps) too long, & (certainly) too slowly delivered. I then handed the Patent to the V.C. to put in the hands of the Senior Proctor who read it aloud, he & his colleagues wearing their caps. When it was read the V.C. gave it to the Duke, who immediately put it down. – I think the Duke did not wear bands but had a laced frill to his shirt. The V.C. now administered the 'Declaration of Office' to the Duke 'dabis fidem etc': the Duke replied 'ita do fidem'. The V.C. then took the Duke by the hand & placed him in the Chair & the Bedells saluted by turning their maces. The maces were not in crape – the V.C. presented the Duke with a bound copy of our *new* Statutes. – The Duke put on his cap & the

Orator (preceded by a Bedell) advanced (wearing his cap): he *read* his Latin speech. – It was different from the Letter read in the Senate & sealed. – In this speech he touched upon the University having been till this ceremony unable to send to Her Majesty an address of condolence. The Duke now rose & made an able & manly speech in which he alluded to his having been Chancellor of the University of London, wch he trusted would not be a prejudice against him: – he spoke in a most liberal manner upon the extension of Education & warmly eulogised the late Prince Consort. – The Duke's Garter had not been well fastened & it fell off at the beginning of his speech: – I was afraid that he would put his foot on it: – but fortunately he did not. I had the Honor of a little conversation with the Duke at the end of the Ceremonies when he put into my hands his official speech written on Vellum & signed by himself. – I had a good deal of talk with my amiable old pupil Lord Wriothesley Russell: he was deeply affected at the ceremonial, for he had brought his eldest boy to witness the last, – the poor fellow caught cold & died! – That coxcomb T.J. Phillips ventured to come to this Installation without a gown. – There was no luncheon – I believe there were about 150 persons present. – Lord Monteagle offered to drive me home: but I had only a few steps to go. As soon as I had taken off my dress of ceremony I sallied out . . . When I got back to Stratton Street I found that Edward was returned from Somerset House: so I had a pleasant talk with him & Sophy for an hour: she is wild about Professor Tindal who lectures on Heat etc (in the Royal Institution): she was going this Evening at 9: the Professor is a wild Irishman, immensely energetic & a very successful experimenter: he seems to be the rage in London . . . At 7 I went to the Clarendon Hotel, where we all wore our Gowns (Drs their red ones). The party consisted of 25 . . . The Duke sat in the middle of one side: on each side of him was one of the Members: opposite to him was the Vicechancellor. The Esquire Bedells were at the ends of the Table: I sat between Paget & Hays . . . The Plateau[6] & all the ornaments of the table were silver gilt . . . It was a superb dinner: I had ½ a glass of the 1834 Port, having declined some Burgundy (wch I took for Claret). There were grapes & ice handed round after dinner: the good old fashion was observed of putting the wine on the table after dinner . . . We had coffee & liqueurs about 10½ & then made our bows. – On returning to Stratton Street I found Sophie returned from Tindall's lecture: Edward seems to avoid these nocturnal scientific meetings,[7] – in wch I heartily agree with him. Sophy had brought back with her Mr & Mrs Pollock: the party was at tea & I readily joined in the social meal . . . I have not enjoyed an hours talk so much for a long time for they are gay lively conversers. – The excitement of the day was too much for me: I was very feverish & restless in bed.

[6]  i.e. a decorative tray or dish usually placed in the middle of a large table.
[7]  John Tyndall, F.R.S.(1820-93), friend of Faraday and Huxley and prolific author of scientific papers for the Royal Society, was Professor of Natural Philosophy at the Royal Institution 1853-87. His writings made the chief scientific ideas of the century intelligible to ordinary people. On 5 January Sophie Kennedy had told Romilly in a letter that her brother Edward 'does not get repose enough and that his wife has too much of the Marcet restlessness and thinks movement and liveliness the cure of everything'.

*Fri. 24.* Up at 7. – Walk in the Town to get 1st tidings of Senior Wrangler: – the publishing of the List is now at 9 (not as of old at 8): to my great joy Trinity has the S.W: his name is Barker: this is the 3d successive year; – Sterling, Aldis, Barker: – & we expect Aldis's brother to be S.W. next year! This is the order of the first 5: Barker (Tr), Laing (Johns), Dale (Trin), Torry (Johns), Sephton (Johns) . . . At 11 to V.C. (to examine Supplicats): we waited 3 qrs of an hr before a Quorum of the Council could be collected. – The V.C.[8] exhibited to me his servants Hall: it is decorated with curious old pannelling (of the folded linen pattern): it is highly interesting: there are carved heads of men & women. – At Queens they have 2 Holbeins (Erasmus & Bishop Fisher): – the small portraits of their 2 Queens are close to each other (with one green curtain) . . .

*Sat. 25.* . . . To the Senate House at 10: in spite of the rain it was well filled with ladies . . . The youngsters behaved unusually well in the galleries. They gave 3 cheers for me at the beginning of the proceedings, & also 3 cheers for me when my resignation was pronounced by the Senior Proctor. – In my Office a long visit from Leapingwell, who abused every body (as knave or fool): he is a patient of Dr Bayes & a firm believer in homeopathy[9] . . . That awful calamity at Hartley Colliery has ended in the death of all the men & boys, 219![10]

*Tu. 28.* . . . At 8 to Senate House: the Councillors had 2 Scrutinies & ended by nominating Luard & Power[11] . . . At 9½ arrived Grim: he slept last night at Peterborough: he is out for a parsons fortnight,[12] having had a friend to do duty for him last Sunday . . . We dined in Hall at 4 o'cl. Sedgwick presided. – It was very pleasant. – I made a tirade against Shilleto's publishing in the Independent Press his most libellous Greek verses against Robinson:[13]– Edleston took up the matter so warmly that I suspect he was the publisher: he declared that he knew positively that Shilleto was not . . .

[8] i.e. George Phillips, D.D. of Queens' College. Queens' was founded in 1446 by Queen Margaret of Anjou, consort of Henry VI, and refounded in 1465 by Elizabeth Woodville, consort of Edward V. See E. S. Leedham-Green, *A Concise History of the University of Cambridge* (1996), p. 24.

[9] Dr. F.H.F. Quin (1799-1878) introduced homeopathy into England having studied it in Germany, and by 1857 there were in the U.K. more than 200 practitioners and chemists for dispensing homeopathic medicine. T.R. Bryant of 19 Market Street was 'By appointment to the Cambridge Dispensary' one of these.

[10] On the morning of the sixteenth the gearing had fallen into the single shaft of this pit near Newcastle. The sides collapsed and 200 men and boys were entombed. The seam where most of them had taken refuge was reached a week later; all had been gassed and were lying together as if asleep, many having scratched last messages on their belongings. The Queen sent repeated inquiries. 'Her tenderest sympathy is with the poor widows and mothers, and her own misery only makes her feel the more for them. Her Majesty hopes that everything will be done as far as possible to alleviate their distress, and her Majesty will have a sad satisfaction in assisting in such a measure.' About £80,000 was raised.

[11] i.e. for the office of Registrary.

[12] See 13 February 1857.

[13] See the *Independent* for 4 January 1862. The verses are printed in Greek without any indication of the subject matter or any comment in English.

*Wed. 29.* Up at 7. – Grim & I walked in the Botanic Garden in our Gowns. At ¼ to 10 I took the voting cards to the Senate House: I stood in Scrutiny for ¼ hour till relieved by Glover: the other scrutineer was Fuller. I was the 1st to give my vote . . . After lunch I took Grim to the Fitzwilliam & exhibited Chantrey's bust of Horne Tooke[14] etc: – I also showed him over the beautiful new townhall: we went into the School of Art:[15] several ladies were working in both rooms . . . The numbers at 4 were Power 222, Luard 316. – Walk about my rooms in the Evening. – To my great pleasure the Master of the Rolls came about 8 o'clock: – he had been in his Court at 4 & had voted for Luard & shaken hands with him at the Evening polling (between 7½ & 8½). Grim joined us at tea: he staid to the end, when the nos were, Luard 396, Power 253 each divisible by 11. – The Master of the Rolls left me soon after 9 & went off by the 10 o'cl. train . . .

*Th. 30.* Up at 7: breakfast at 8¼. – We could not breakfast with the Worsleys (as they asked us) . . . Luard called at the Office: I had great pleasure in installing him in the state chair & wishing him a long & happy reign. – I also wished him joy of his approaching marriage.[16] He told me that it would not be till the summer: his intended is a daughter of Archdeacon Hodson who died suddenly of Cholera on one of the Italian lakes (where he & his 2 daughters were touring) about 5 years ago: the daughters also took the disease, the fiancée has been in very delicate health ever since . . . Called on Bumpsted to say that I feared I was going blind: he said 'no' – 'it is a congestion of the eye': – he would send me a pill for 2 successive nights & a bottle of Physic for 2 days & recommended a mustard plaster at night behind my head . . .

*Fri. 6 February.* . . . Luard came for a couple of hours & I explained to him all the details about signing for different degrees. – Finished the fair copy of the Index of 'University Papers': so (by God's blessing) I have now completed every thing relating to the Office up to the end of my 30 years most happy tenure . . . Walk by moonlight to Trumpington. – Frank Kennedy looked in for ¼ hour before my dinner: he declares that he is working very steadily with Mr Girdleston every Evening till 8: Mr G. said that he did his last Paley paper pretty well, tho there were 2 questions that he had not understood & had of course made hash of.

[14] It is a second bust of Horne Tooke, whom Sir Francis Chantrey much admired, that is in the Fitzwilliam. It was made during Tooke's last illness.

[15] In 1842 'the municipal buildings consisted of the upper storey of the old Shire-House and the Guildhall erected by Essex'. In 1859 part of the scheme for new and enlarged premises was at last begun: 'an Assembly room to hold 1400 people, Free Library and Reading Room, Town Clerk's offices, Committee Rooms, Telegraph Office and a School of Art'. The roof of Essex's Town Hall was raised to accommodate the School of Art which, sponsored by Ruskin in 1858, moved from cramped quarters in Sidney Street. See T.D. Atkinson, *Cambridge Described and Illustrated* (1897), pp. 91, 223.

[16] Luard's fiancée was sister of William, the brilliant and controversial commander of 'Hodson's Horse', killed in Lucknow in 1858 during the Mutiny. Luard was the first Fellow of Trinity to marry and retain his Fellowship, and, loving his wife and his college 'thought it calamitous that he was allowed to have them both' (C.N.L. Brooke, *A History of the University of Cambridge* Vol. 4, (1993) pp. 4-7).

*Sat. 7.* . . . I left . . . the Office at 1½ & called at home & armed myself with a piece of bread & glass of beer & walked to the railway bridges on the Shelford & Hauxton Roads: the last is one of the skewest I ever saw . . . Letter from Grim: all prosperous: when in Town he went to the Pantomime. He begs me to conceal the fact from his Bishop & Dean. He was highly pleased with Mother Hubbard . . .

*Wed. 12.* . . . In the office received some fees etc for Luard. – He arrived about 12½. – Walk from 1½ to 3½: went to Cumbarton Gate.[17] – The last ½ hour I was joined by Prof. Babington: he says that Parkinson is immensely cut up at not having been nominated: had Ellicott given a Plumper for him & not also pricked for Luard he would: – so the Dean of Exeter is at discount at St Johns. – Wolfe (the Tutor of Clare) married not long ago the pretty Miss d'Orsey (aged 16!) whose Father lectures on English Literature: – complete case of Wolf & Lamb[18] . . .

*Th. 13.* . . . Harriet received a letter saying that her great friend Jesse Theobald is just arrived from India with wife & 2 children. – She told me that the 3 brothers had all offered to her! She was engaged to one (who died): the *other 2* wanted to take her into India or Australia: she refused to leave England as long as her parents were alive . . . The Queen (thro her Privy Purse Sir Ch. Phipps) has sent Sedgwick photographs of herself & the poor Prince 'in memoriam': – 2 were sent also to Lightfoot (the Prince's Chaplain). – Sedgwick wrote a very touching outpouring of his heart in sympathy for the Queen & admiration for the noble qualities of the Prince.[19] – The Queen was shown this letter by Sir Charles & she wept greatly in reading it, but they were the least bitter tears that she had shed. – I went with Sedgwick to the meeting in Queens' Hall for a memorial to the Prince. – The V.C. made one of the dullest conceivable speeches in opening the proceedings . . . But Whewell, Jeremie & Sedgwick spoke admirably . . . Paget's very few words were hesitating & not judicious, for he said 'there should have been unanimity in the choice of such a Chancellor': Bateson replied that he had never regretted the part he had taken in supporting Lord Powis,[20] that he greatly admired the late Prince & highly approved a memorial to him . . . Sent a Valentine to Lucy Spink (herself a Valentine).

*Sat. 15.* . . . Sedgwick called at my house & wrote a letter to Mrs Guthrie. – We then walked to the Fitzwilliam: I wanted to see if his picture by Lawrence was yet hung up: – it was given by Whewell & accepted by the

[17] Cumbarton (Comberton) was the parish immediately to the west of Barton.
[18] Arthur Wolfe was some 26 years older than his bride. There is no mention of Miss d'Orsey in Boase or Venn – only of his second marriage in 1873.
[19] For the substance of Sedgwick's letter to Sir Charles Phipps and his speech at the memorial meeting see Clark and Hughes, II, 375-6. Sedgwick 'made a profound impression on his hearers by recounting, in his most graphic and picturesque style, a number of details about the Prince which he had observed during frquent interviews with him'.
[20] The Duke of Northumberland had been elected Chancellor in 1840 and on his death on 11 February 1847 the Master and Seniors of St John's asked his brother-in-law, Lord Powis, to be a candidate. For a full description of the election of Prince Albert see *Romilly 1842-47*, pp. 194-201.

Senate last Thursday.[21] – I never liked this picture, wch gives S. a severe & ungenial look, – almost ferocious. – I never liked Lawrence's other picture, of Worsley . . .

*Fri. 7 March.* . . . Walk on Madingley Road: on my return I was joined by the Vicechancellor & Bright: when the V.C. parted from us Bright told me the Prince of W's opinion of the V.C. (Phillips) Claret: he said to Neville 'It is Vinegar': – I hope Phillips is in happy ignorance of this royal estimate of his wine. – In the Evening I was amused by hearing the children playing at 'hide & seek' & shouting out 'keep still, keep still wherever ye be: the rats & mice are coming to see' . . .

*Sat. 8.* . . . Letter from Maggie announcing 4 pots of marmalade, wch have arrived safely: she sent also a machine for keeping the feet warm in bed: it is a mackintosh cushion for holding hot water. – Wrote to her . . .

*Th. 13.* Up at 7 . . . Went to Office about 12: on my return I was attacked with another very bad bleeding at the nose: by bad luck I was without a handkerchief, so my hands (in protecting my nose) got covered with blood & I was a ghastly spectacle to the passers by: – I sent for Paget, who luckily was at home & came instantly: he said 'I have already made my diagnosis, for I saw drops of blood at your door.' He prescribed for me a pill, rhubarb & mutton broth: he also said he would send me a lotion for my eyes. – Letter from Grim, enclosing 2 small photographs of himself & wife: that of himself was good, but I thought Bertha was made old & dismal., Grim is a Candidate for the Living of Narberth & had made application to Lord Palmerston (the Premier)[22] . . . his brother George has been exerting himself in the matter. – He characteristically describes the photographs as likenesses of 'a member of the swell mob[23] & an elderly female' . . .

*Tu. 18.* . . . To a College meeting from 12 to 2. We accepted 2 presents, viz (1) a collection of letters from Simson[24] (editor of Euclid & friend of Dr Smith (the Master of Trinity) . . . & (2) Woolners bust of Sedgwick:[25] this last was made at the request of several Fellows & friends & by them presented: – by the way this bust is going to be exhibited at the Great International Exhibition . . . At the Seniority we agreed to having next year an English paper on Shakespeare –, selecting some one play & asking questions on English literature & on the language: – it is to be for the 2d-year-men. – We agreed to have flowers along the Chapel wall. More Jelly from my good friend Mrs Prest.

---

[21] Mr David Scrase tells us that Mr Samuel Lawrence's portrait had a label on its back: 'Professor Sedgwick by Lawrence, for Dr. Whewell, and deposited by him in the Fitzwilliam Museum there to remain to the death of the Professor. Then to be placed in the Woodwardian Museum.' In 1904 it was transferred to the Museum of Geology.

[22] The patron of the good living of Narberth, Pembrokeshire, was the Crown. The successful candidate (see 8 April), H.C.D. Chandler, had been curate of St Mary's, Haverfordwest.

[23] i.e. pickpockets who dressed and behaved like respectable people.

[24] Robert Simson (1687-1768), professor of mathematics at Glasgow University, in 1756 made an edition of the *Elements* of Euclid which formed the basis of many later textbooks. Dr Robert Smith, Bentley's successor as Master of Trinity, founded the prizes that bear his name.

[25] See 27 May 1859.

*Fri. 21.* Up at 7. – God be praised. I have had no fresh bleeding. – Last night (at Harriet's strong urgency) I tried Maggie's present of the hot-water cushion in bed: – I found it very comfortable, tho I rather object to its india-rubber smell (like a Mackintosh) . . . Wrote to Sedgwick (sending him Mrs G's letter): he will tomorrow be 77 complete: the 22d March is a great day of joy to me, for on that day 30 years ago I was nominated to the Office of Registrary, wch has given me so much happiness for so large a part of my life . . .

*Wed. 26.* . . . Letter from Sarah Ouvry . . . She says the Camden Society are publishing lists of Hugonots naturalised in England & giving short accounts of their families: her brother Frederic has furnished an account of the Ouvrys, but knows not the name of my grandmother (Aimé Garnaults sister): she says the names of Romilly & Delahaize are not in the lists, & that they probably allowed naturalisation to come without seeking it. – Wrote to Sarah saying I was in Boetian darkness: by the way I am equally ignorant of the Christian name of my dear Mother's Mother . . .

*Th. 27.* . . . Visit from Sedgwick who brought 3 Letters on his birthday by Mrs G., Mary (his nephew Dick's pretty amiable wife) & Fanny Cooper (born Hicks: – Sedgwick's brother James married the widow Hicks): – these letters were excellent & showed their writers to be active wives of country clergymen, for they all described cases of grievous sickness & sorrow wch they had attended. Sedgwick & I took 3 turns in the Botanic Garden & I then accompanied him to his rooms to see the magnificent lithographs of the Queen & the late Prince Consort given him by her Majesty: they are the size of life. He has had the words 'From her Majesty the Queen' put on both the frames & the words 'In memoriam' on that of the Prince . . .

*Fri. 28.* . . . Harriet was amused yesterday with Sedgwick's address to me: 'Well! how are you?' – 'I am but a poor creature': 'Say rather that you are a *jolly companion*'. – He has taught the children of Richard & Mary to shout out 'jolly companions every one'. The fire being today in the Library, I sorted the drawers of the glass bookcase & was very glad to find the frame with 3 miniatures of my grandmother & 2 of her children . . . Walk from 2 to 4 in the College walks: there is a grand improvement in St Johns by substituting a light iron fence for the brick wall on the North side of Priors walk.[26] – Called at Frank Kennedy's to enquire about his pinched finger: – his room gave me the idea of his being a thorough votary of mere amusement, – many novels – a book on billiards – cigars – whips & sticks & caps in superfluity: – I saw no inkstand & no scribbling paper. – I hope most heartily that he will be able to go in to the Little Go on Monday & that he will pass.

---

[26] Mr Jonathan Smith of Trinity College Library tells us that this appears to refer to all or part of The Wilderness and bowling-green area of St. John's. White's *Visitor's Guide to Cambridge* (1892) seems to suggest that this area was laid out by Matthew Prior, and Willis and Clark confirm that some work was done in this area while Prior was a fellow. (Vol. II 322-3).

*Sun. 30.* . . . Walk to College to look for Letters . . . my advice of visiting the family vault at Paddington was good . . . John Ouvry North sends me the following particulars on our *Family buried in Paddington.*[27]

*Mr Romilly's Family Vault 1779*

(1) Cath. Hunter – died 16 Dec. 1778 – aged 64
(2) Margaret Farquhar – died 19 Jan. 1781 – aged 64
(3) Peter Romilly – died 29 Aug 1784 – aged 72
(4) Anne Hunter – died 18 March 1793 – aged 56
(5) Margaret Romilly – died 30 April 1796 – aged 81 – my Fathers Mother
(6) Geo. Tho. Romilly – died 4 Feb. 1798 – aged 10
(7) Jane Anne Romilly – died 6 Mar. 1803 – aged 47
(8) Tho. Pet. Romilly – died 7 Dec. 1828 – aged 74
(9) Sam. Romilly – (Lt Col.) died 2 Nov. 1834 – aged 51
(10) Cuthb. Ste. Romilly – died 1 Feb. 1837 – aged 47.

---

I should have mentioned yesterday going into Trinity Chapel to see the new Memorial window: it is by Wailes:[28] one half is in memory of Dr Mill & is given by Mathison, the other is in memory of Campbell the Scholar & is given by his family . . .

*Tu. 1 April.* . . . Letter from Sophie thanking me for my last 3: she thinks my maternal grandmother was named Judith: I do not think it was any more so than my maternal grandfather was named Punch . . . Sophie tells me Lord Overston (– the parsimonious millionaire) said the other day of the American Peabody (who has just given £150,000 for the poor of London) that 'such men ought to be put down by Act of Parliament'![29] Wrote to Sophie. – Sedgwick called at 1½ to go with me to lunch at the Selwyns . . . during dinner Selwyn saw a girls hat blown off into the run of water & rushed out to recover it:[30]– the exploit however was performed by a Carter who fished it out with his whip . . . After lunch (dinner) Selwyn exhibited his beautiful Alderney cow & her calf to us . . . Frank Kennedy came to tea (by invitation) so he had the pleasure of being introduced to the Professor. – Frank said he came out of the Arithmetic Examination dog-tired: he answered respectably & would have done more if he had had more time – he did not find the paper hard . . .

*Fri. 4.* . . . To the Senate House to vote for the Museum & Lecture-rooms.[31] A. Long (of King's – a clever & fastidious amateur artist) gave the

27  See Appendix 1.
28  For Wailes see 2 June 1861.
29  Samuel Jones Loyd, first Baron Overstone, pre-eminent authority on banking and finance died in 1883 as one of the wealthiest men in England. George Peabody, self-made merchant and financier lived in London from 1837 and devoted his wealth to philanthropic causes in England and in his native America. He worked tirelessly for Anglo-American friendship and his funeral service in 1869 was held in Westminster Abbey.
30  Selwyn's dining-room at 6 Belvoir Terrace must have looked out on Trumpington Road down the sides of which ran cleansing water (see 6 April 1859). The cow and her calf were presumably grazing on Coe Fen.
31  Willis's plans when first submitted to the Senate on 16 December 1861 met with almost universal disapproval. But Salvin's amended design, 'the withdrawal of the obnoxious lecture

1st Non-placet: his objection (& that of many more) is the ugliness of the Architecture: the scheme was carried easily – 74 to 14: – several Trinity men . . . declined voting . . . A crossing sweep (to whom I gave a penny) amused me by asking me to buy a stamp: – I did so: somebody had given it to him instead of a penny. – Read Caleb Williams.[32]

*Sat. 5.* . . . Looked for Frank Kennedy's company at tea in vain. – Sedgwick sent me a letter from Mrs Admiral Warren: she is very clever & amusing, but too familiar for my fastidious taste: – Sedgwick she made into Sedgy & (tho she never saw me except on her recent visit to Sedgwick) calls me Romilly without any Mister: – for a short time she called me Josephus – she is passionately fond of her sister Mrs G . . .

*Sun. 6.* . . . Letter from G.B.A. sending me the Pedigree I asked for:[33] his grandfather was John Bartlett Allen of Cresselly: in early life he was engaged to Miss Barlow of Slebitch (a clever woman as appears from her love-letters): – that fell thro: he did marry 'a very good, clever & sensible woman, from whom much of the worth of the Allens is said to have come'. She was an heiress, Miss Hensleigh of Pentenge, daughter of an Attorney: she had 11 children,

(1) Elisabeth – married to Josh. Wedgwood of Etruria . . . died 1828
(2) Cath: – married to Sir James Mackintosh . . . died 1832
(3) John Hensleigh – married to Honorable Gertrude Seymour – died 1843
(4) Caroline – married Rev. Mr Drewe . . . died 1834

rooms' and 'the consequent reduction of expenditure' meant that the design, with the approval of the scientific professors 'whose want of such buildings . . . has become more pressing year by year' was at last adopted. See Willis and Clark, III, 175-6.

[32] By William Godwin (1794); an early example of the novel as social propaganda and as a study of the psychology of crime. The plot is summarised in *Oxford Companion to English Literature*.

[33] For the prolific and much intermarried branches of the Allen family of Pembrokeshire see Burke's *Landed Gentry* (1952) and Appendix I below. J.B. Allen's first wife brought him Cresselly, a fine estate on the coal-bearing headland east of Milford Haven in South Pembrokeshire. His physical strength and harsh, violent temper were legendary, and his unpopularity so great that the matrimonial prospects of his nine daughters were bleak despite their good looks, charm of manner, and admirable upbringing by their mother. The visit of Josiah Wedgwood and his sister to Cresselly during the Haverfordwest races of 1792 was providential. Josiah and Elizabeth Allen soon married and the other sisters then paid frequent visits to the hospitable Wedgwoods. Jane Allen married Josiah's elder brother John, a banker, and these two marriages produced sixteen young Wedgwoods. At the Wedgwoods Catherine Allen met her husband, the widowed James Macintosh, friend of Fox and Sheridan who became Recorder of Bombay. Jessie married the distinguished Swiss historian Jean Charles Leonard de Sismondi. The sons too married well. John inherited Cresselly and at the age of forty-three married a daughter of Lord Robert Seymour, while Baugh married a Romilly – a remarkable record for one family. After the death of Josiah, the sisters' kindest of brothers-in-law, Jessie wrote 'I have often thought that our connection with the Wedgwoods was one of the blessed circumstances of our lives'. J.B. Allen's second wife was Harriet Rees, daughter of one of his colliers. See Elizabeth Inglis-Jones, 'A Pembrokeshire County Family in the Eighteenth Century', *National Library of Wales Journal* XVII (1971-72), 136-60, 217-37, 321-42.

(5) Lancelot Baugh – married (1) Miss Romilly (2) Miss Bayly . . . died 1845

(6) Jane – married John Wedgwood

(7) Harriet – married Revd Mr Surtees . . . died 1845

(8) Jessie – married Mr Sismondi . . . died 1852

(9) Emma Augusta

(10) Frances

(11) A daughter who died young. – In his latter-days J.B. Allen married a young woman of no position, 'of whom the less said the better'. J.B. Allen was in the Life Guards.

*Tu. 8.* . . . Letter from Grim saying that he has not got Narberth Rectory: – he ascribes his 'plucking' to the undue influence of Sir Hugh Owen Bart (Member for Pembroke): his father Sir John (member for the County) ruled every thing, having £23,000 a year & being a flaming tory: he became a ruined man: his son is also a flaming Tory but is poor . . . still he has every thing his own way. – Wrote to Grim. – At the Office from 10 till 2 . . . Walk to Cherry Hinton & back by the road: most of the walk was with that slow-talking V.C. (Philipps): he talks very much to the point when his words do come out. – This was the 4th & last day of Frank Kennedy's Little-Go (Classics & Greek Testament) . . .

*Fri. 11.* . . . The Little-Go List came out today: Frank Kennedy (to my very great joy) has got thro: he is indeed only in the 2d Class – 1st Class 264: 2d Class 78: Plucked 57: – but I never dreamt of his being higher . . . I wrote to his dear Mother & proposed his success should be celebrated in a bowl of Punch. – I called on the said youth to tell him of the result: I found him busy packing up for his departure this Evening: – Walk round Via Lambertina: half cut in 2 with the wind. –Took my Journals (from 1844) to be new backed & lettered & made uniform. – In the Evening received a magnificent present from the Master of the Rolls of his 4 Volumes of his Publications: that of 'Letters in the time of Henry VIII' was as big as that monster[34] . . . A little girl said to me today 'how is your Mamma?'

*Sun. 13.* . . . At Christ Church a stranger read prayers: Mr Robinson preached his 5th Sermon on the words of our Lord when on the Cross . . . I thought it a very able & striking sermon. – Called on Mrs Prest whom I thought a little better: Mrs Leapingwell, Mrs Francis & Mrs William were with her. – Met Mrs Hopkins walking with her daughter Ellis: she is an admirable person: tho in very delicate health she every week teaches & preaches to the men & boys of Barnwell: I believe her Congregation is entirely masculine . . .

---

[34] When the Public Record Office's publications were extended to State Papers it was decided that priority should be given to documents from the time of Henry VIII. In 1856 Sir John Romilly appointed the Rev. J.S. Brewer editor of *Letters and Papers of Henry VIII*, an immense task made all the more difficult because the documents were held in so many different places. See *The Public Record Office 1838-1858* (1991), pp.170-2, David Knowles, *Great Historical Enterprises* (1963), chapter 4, and P. Levine, The *Amateur and the Professional* (1986), chapter 5.

*Sat. 3 May.* . . . Letter from Maggie giving a very agreeable account of the children's visit to the Zoological, where they saw Hippopotamus, 2 baby bears etc etc . . . Walk with Mathison in the new Cricket Ground (of 9 acres) wch Trinity has taken on a lease from St Johns:[35]– the Ground was opened today: – a match was going on. – : we are building on the ground a large establishment for refreshments. – I afterwards went to St John's Racquet Courts & looked on at the play in the inclosed Court. – At 7 o'clock G.T. Romilly arrived . . . after tea he kindly (at my request) read loud to me all the details of the opening of the Great Exhibition on 1st May.

*Sun. 4.* . . . Took George to Trinity Church: – Mr Clayton preached . . . I disapproved of the end in which he made a tirade against the *sinful dissipation* (as he called it) of the next 3 weeks & spoke of the *poisoned* cup of pleasure:[36]– I suppose therefore he means to keep away from the Mayor's déjeuner next Wednesday . . . From 3 till 4 George & I strolled behind the colleges: Mr Hadley took us into the Fellows' walks of St Johns & pointed out to us how the design of them was to represent the nave & transept of a Cathedral . . .

*Tu. 6.* . . . fell in with Robert Potts: he told me the history of Shilleto marrying Miss Snelgar: Shilleto was at the chapel in Green Street when Mr Snelgar was holding forth: Shilleto & Miss Snelgar were in the same pew: there was an alarm of fire: Miss Snelgar fell down from terror: – a fire was kindled in his bosom: he proposed & was accepted & she has borne him 13 children[37] . . .

*Wed. 7.* Up at 7. – Quite hot even then – walk in Botanic Garden: the nightingales sang gloriously. College meeting at 12 . . . At 2 o'clock to the grand breakfast to the High Steward (Duke of Dev.) who was sworn in this morning. The banquet was in the beautiful new Town Hall (now 1st used). I believe the party was 300 men (besides Ladies in the orchestra & gallery who were refreshed with ices & champagne). Every thing was magnificent: – fresh strawberries & all luxuries: – a London toast-master with powerful voice & great gesticulation. The Mayor (who gave the Feast) is Charles Finch Foster, a man made of money . . . The worst speech was the egotistical one of Ball (County Member): people grew impatient & began to scrape him. – The party broke up at about 6. – On going away Whewell & the Duke overtook me in the street: & the Duke kindly shook hands with me & spoke a few words . . .

*Tu. 13.* . . . Prof. Willis has received the Gold Medal of the Royal Institute of British Architects[38] . . . The Mayor most kindly gives concerts on Th. &

[35] Trinity's 'Old Playing Field' lies in the angle between Grange Road and Adams Road.

[36] It is hard to imagine many opportunities for sin during the celebrations of the Duke of Devonshire's installation as Chancellor (see 31 December 1860 for his election), and of his decision to continue to hold the office of High Steward of the Borough. But the poisoned cup may have been sipped more frequently by the young during the May-week celebration despite Charles Clayton's denunciation of balls in particular. See 6 March 1857.

[37] For fire as Cupid see also 15 March 1863.

[38] *The Times* of 3 May describes the presentation by the President of the R.I.B.A. to Willis. Since 1843 the Queen as patroness of the institution 'had placed at the disposal of the Council

Fri. next to the poorer Classes free, gratis. – Harriet went for tickets for self & Caroline How this morning: but there was such a crowd of riff-raff round the door of Mr Wood (the music-seller & ticket-giver) that she came away in disgust & despair . . . So I posted off to Mr Wood Senior: – the rabble was still about the door: – some lad kindly communicated to Mr Wood that I was without & wishing to speak with him. – He was good enough to come out & talk with me: he told me that it was not the intention to admit a single maid-servant (for the Hall would not hold one from each family): – the Concerts were for the lower classes *who paid scot & lot*.[39] – Now that the maids can't go I confess I should not have liked them to be squeezed into the Hall with a crowd of low people, – many of whom would not be fit associates for them . . .

*Tu. 20.* . . . Letters from George Romilly & his Frank: Frank wrote to thank me for my present of a book & told me of what he called 'a grand piece of news' . . . 'on Tuesday the servant laid the cloth for dinner at 12½: the back-gate & side-door were both open: I was in the study doing some work; Mamma & 2 of the servants with Cappie, Bertie & baby were upstairs: at ¼ to 1 when Mamma came down all the silver forks, spoons & mugs together with a bunch of gold seals were gone! They had been stolen!!' – George tells the same tale with wonderful calmness & placidity . . . 'Every person to whom I have told my loss caps it with a similar one: so I infer that it is an episode in domestic life, & as every family seems to have suffered more than ourselves I look upon it as I would upon an attack of measles or hooping cough in children: – it must come & we have had it favourably' . . . There has been (by J.O.) a fierce attack of Mr Palgrave's 'Handbook' of the International Exhibition[40] & it has ended in Mr Palgrave's withdrawal of his book: – Mr Palgrave & Mr Woolner (the Sculptor) live in the same house: Mr Palgrave eulogises to the skies Mr Woolner far above all living sculptors: – 2 of Woolners busts (those of the Laureate Tennyson & of Professor Sedgwick) are in this exhibition: Mr Palgraves words about these 2 are '*the well-known humour & rugged force of the Geologist*, – the majestic, calm & profound feeling to wch we owe the Idylls & In Memoriam'. – Grieved to hear that Mrs

a gold medal to be given every year to any distinguished British or foreign architect or eminent person who might have contributed to the science of architecture by any works or publications of acknowledged merit'.

39 i.e. a tax levied by a municipal corporation on all members of the parish according to their ability to pay.

40 *The Times* devoted many columns to the International Exhibition and on 1 May three to the English collection of pictures which 'is of the highest interest and merit'. On 15 May, however, it printed a long letter from an outraged 'J.O.' which quoted F.T. Palgrave's "A Handbook to the Art Collections" . . . Mr Palgrave is, evidently in his own opinion, a thorough master of arts . . . those whom he praises . . . he praises to the skies; those whom he condemns . . . he damns beyond the possibility of any future redemption'. Thus the sculptor Marochetti's Turin group is classed with the 'centrepieces of a confectioner' and he is denounced as a 'mountebank'. J.O. asks the Commissioners to prohibit sales of the *Handbook* in the Exhibition. In the ensuing correspondence Thomas Woolner denies that he dishonestly influenced Palgrave's opinion of him, and Palgrave defends the critic's right to criticise when 'Art is not only demonstrably bad but injurious from its bad qualities'.

H.J. Haviland finds Dr. H's temper so unbearable that she has left him & gone to live with her Mother Mrs Hughes!! . . .

*Fri. 6 June.* . . . Maggie gave Bertie a pictorial alphabet on his birthday: the 1st letter has an Ass braying thro it. Cappie undertakes to teach Bertie in the satisfactory way 'A stands for Donkey' . . . Wrote to . . . Frank telling him it was high time for him to fix what Professor he would attend: I suggested his chusing Political Economy & reading during the long vacation 'Mrs Marcet's Conversations on Political Economy' & 'McCulloch' (wch are recommended by Pryme'[41] . . .

*Tu. 10.* . . . I lunched at a brilliant party in Caius Hall of ladies & gentlemen . . . I then went to the Horticultural show in Trinity & St Johns: it was a beautiful sight: – as the flowers, the refreshments & the band were in Trinity the grounds of St Johns were but little thought of. – I staid there till past 5, hunting in vain for the Master of the Temple,[42] who was hunting for me . . . Robinson & I dined at the grand dinner at Trinity . . . I was at the high Table as Vice Master & read Grace with the Master. My righthand neighbour at dinner was Mr Walpole & my lefthand neighbour was my good friend Sir W. Page Wood: Mr Chevalier was to have been my lefthand neighbour, but he went away yesterday: – so I missed seeing that distinguished writer on Political Economy: – but I also missed having to talk French to a man who is deaf. I much enjoyed Sir William's lively talk. The Master asked me if I would like to propose any of the Toasts: I declined. He discharged the duty admirably. – He grouped the Honorary degrees. Of course the 1st 3 Toasts were the Queen & the P. of W. & the Chancellor (who spoke most sensibly): – then came the House of Lords for wch the D. of Argyll returned thanks, & capitally well he did it –. Next was the House of Commons for wch Lord Stanley responded. Then came the University: the V.C. replied in his slow manner: he had a very impatient audience; under show of vociferous applause they made his speech a short one. – Lord Lyttelton responded to the Toast of 'Trin. Coll.' in his rough, uncouth, but clever way: – he ended by proposing the Master's health. I was glad to find it very well received: – was it quite gracious for the Master to thank them for the *somewhat unacademic* manner in which they received the toast? – Sir W. Armstrong was very warmly received: Sir Henry Rawlinson, Sir E. Head & the Astronomer Royal (Airy) moderately[43] . . . We went up into the Combination room for tea: Robinson & I staid but few minutes in the combination room: – it was near 12 before we got home. – I should have said that 'Non nobis Domine' was capitally sung after dinner. – The gallery was filled with ladies & made the coup-d-oeil beautiful . . .

---

[41] Macaulay said that 'Every little girl who has read Mrs Marcet's little dialogues on political economy could teach Montagu or Walpole many lessons in finance'. J.R. McCulloch's *Principles of Political Economy* (1825) went through many editions.

[42] i.e. Romilly's old friend and guest Thomas Robinson, Master of the Temple since 1845.

[43] i.e. Sir William Armstrong, inventor, captain of industry and armaments manufacturer; Sir Henry Rawlinson, soldier, linguist in Persian and Indian vernaculars; Sir E.W. Head, Governor-General of Canada 1854-61; and Sir George Airy for 46 years an Astronomer Royal of extraordinary energy.

*Th. 12.* . . . Seniority to elect a brewer in place of William King deceased (age 86): we appointed his grandson Wm King: old King was grandfather of the pretty girl of damaged reputation who became Countess of Stamford.[44] – We agreed to give (to the extent of £50) half the salary of a Curate for the district of Victoria Road & Histon Road: this is a part in great spiritual destitution: the population is above 1000: – the Industrial school will be used for Church services. – We agreed to build for Blore the new Tutor a room at the back of his rooms in Neville's Court: – I asked if it would be an eyesore & Blore said it would only be visible from the Master's kitchen garden: 'O! said the Master, but my potatoes have eyes' . . .

*Tu. 17.* . . . The Classes came out: poor Frank Kennedy is posted! – his papers (Matheson says) had wonderfully little in them, & he had manifestly *copied*!! He utterly denies the copying. This is very sad: but the disgrace of his being posted is not made public, for the printed list does not mention the plucked men . . . I am not without fear that Frank gambles, for he applied to Mathison for £5 the other day and could give no account of what he wanted it for as he confessed that he had money enough to take him to town! All this will be bitter anguish to his Mother. I wrote to her & said that if he could not make a manly resolution of diligence & have firmness to keep it, I should dissuade his coming back as I should doubt his getting thro his 2 Examinations. It was pain & grief to me to write such a letter & it will half break her heart to receive it . . .

*Wed. 18.* Up at 7. – Walk in Botanic Garden. – Letter from Sophie (in answer to mine): Frank has received a very kind & excellent letter from Mr Mathison: Frank's paper was so like his neighbour's (Kempson) that it was certain there had been copying: both were plucked: but as Kempson had been in the 1st Class of Little Go & Frank in the 2d the suspicion naturally attached to him . . .

*Sat. 21.* . . . Letter from Sophie saying that . . . Frank . . . has (at Sophie's dictation) written a letter of sorrow to his private Tutor Girdleston begging him still to keep him for a pupil. – The charge of copying has not been told to Mr Kennedy: but the being plucked & the bet have: – so things are now quiet. – Frank persists in his innocence: he says that Kempson wanted aid in his Euclid paper & that he (F.) said 'if you like to copy – you can': Frank proposes writing this exculpation to Mr Mathison . . .

[44] Venn mysteriously states that the Earl of Stamford married as his first wife Elizabeth, daughter of John Billing of Wincanton, Somerset. However, the *Gentleman's Magazine* 1854, II, 644, recording her death at Brighton in October, adds 'Her ladyship was of humble parentage, her father being a shoemaker at Cambridge. Her personal attraction captivated the Earl when pursuing his studies at Trinity College: and on the 23rd December 1848, they were married at the old church at Brighton. She leaves no issue by her marriage.' In UP 17 (635) Romilly makes a manuscript note of rumours in an unidentifiable newspaper cutting about the marriage: 'her mother is a help to a Trinity Coll: Bedmaker viz. Old Mrs King widow of a Brewer. Some 3 or 4 years ago she bore a child to a Magdalene undergraduate (of the name of Child). She was sent out of town' . . . Romilly calls the girl Billage and it seems clear that she was Elizabeth, daughter of John and Susan Billage, baptised at Holy Trinity in 1825.

On 23 June Romilly stayed for two nights in Stratton Street with the Edward Romillys and as usual wasted no time in visiting galleries and exhibitions. On the twenty-fourth, together with 62,000 other people 'the fullest day they have had yet', he greatly enjoyed a second visit to the Great International Exhibition in Kensington, but on the following morning thought poorly of the Royal Academy pictures. In the National Gallery however, he found in 'the Turner room . . . a collection of Masterpieces & I looked at them with immense admiration'. His two family dinners with Edward and his wife were 'vastly pleasant', but his long visit to the Kennedys was distressing as although 'they both declared that I had been a great comfort to them' the talk was entirely about Frank. Thomas Kennedy had by now been told that his son's 'loss to Lord Pollington (betting on horses) was above £100 . . . Frank had intended paying by instalments: – Kennedy instantly sent the money to Lord P: Frank must break with so dangerous a companion'. It appeared that Frank and his Father, presumably on the previous day, had 'dined together tête à tête: directly after dinner he slept or pretended to sleep till his Mother returned from dining with Lady Georgina', her sister-in-law, 'at 11!!!' Romilly had another cause for indignation on his journey home for 'The Cabman who drove me from the Strand to Shoreditch was a shameless cheat: I asked his fare & he said 2s/6d: – I exclaimed "that is the most impudent charge I ever heard: you know it is 1/6". He said "one must live by impudence": – he took the 1/6.

*Th. 26.* . . . Sedgwick gave a most interesting account of his interview with the Queen: – when he was backing out of the room the Queen smiled & said 'you wont find the way' & opened the door in the corridor for him. He dined with the Lords & Ladies in waiting . . . Sedgwick slept only one night at Windsor. The Queen graciously expressed much gratitude for his coming so far to see her. I have no doubt the long conversation about the Prince Consort did her heart an infinitude of good . . . A slice of Luard's wedding cake was brought me by Major Stephen (Hindustani Teacher).

*Mon. 7 July.* . . . At 1·20 went with Sedgwick to Ely . . . At the Cathedral we were taken in hand by Mr Evans: he is a very agreeable, sensible man & is an attorney in 1st rate practice: he went home & brought an opera-glass & also a flat mirror that we might see Mr L'Estrange's painted ceiling without tiring ourselves by looking up:[45]– I had seen none of this painted ceiling of the clever amateur artist Mr L.E: it is about half finished, & will require 3 or 4 more years for completion. – There are several new painted windows since my last visit . . . One of the most interesting novelties to me was the recumbent bronze monument to my friend & contemporary Mill:[46]– it is a costly & noble monument: the resemblance to Mills features is very striking: a very interesting part of the monument is the representation of 2 students (a Hindustani & a Cantab) at his feet: I have not been so much pleased with a monument for a very long time . . .

[45] After the boarding-in of the ugly timbers of the nave roof Henry Le Strange of Hunstanton was asked to design a decoration for it. He began painting in 1858 but died suddenly three weeks after Romilly's visit and his friend T. Gambier Parry completed his work.

[46] W.H. Mill's recumbent effigy in electroplated copper surmounts a fine tomb chest designed by G.G. Scott and executed by J.B. Philip. From 1820 to 1838 Mill was first principal of Bishop's College, Calcutta – hence the Hindustani student.

*Th. 10.* . . . In the office all the morning. – To my great delight I found the Index to Alpha . . . I found also the Certificate Book of Professorial Examinations (wch Luard had lost & put in a wrong drawer viz 18. – So today has been a very auspicious one to me. – It was my grand day of Honor. I have long past the bright 'golden' time of life, & had thought that I was fallen into dull 'leaden' days, but to my great joy this is to me the 'silver' age, – not from my scanty locks being white but from receiving a most costly present of plate (manufactured by Garrard of London). It consisted of a silver Teapot & Coffeepot in the fashion of Queen Anne's reign & a truly magnificent salver with an exquisite border of Heads, bunches of Grape, etc in alto relievo:[47]– 'materiam superabat opus': – all this was under the direction of Dr Woodham (a great authority in matters of Plate). – Paget was the Secretary & (I believe) the originator of the Testimonial to me: Archdall was the Chairman of the Committee: – 111 friends subscribed: among them were the Master of the Rolls & 2 of his sons (William & Edward) & 2 of his brothers (Henry & Edward) & his nephew Frank Kennedy . . . I had one subscription from the Town viz C.H. Cooper (Author of Athenæ Cantabrigienses). All the Heads (but Whewell, Guest, Pulling, Robinson & Worsley): Whewell did not subscribe to Sedgwicks Bust & is (I believe) opposed to all such testimonials . . . At 3 o'clock Drs Archdall & Cartmell etc etc met together at Pagets: – Mrs Paget & son Edmund were present: we were refreshed with strawberries & coffee & cake & wine: my good old friend Archdall then presented the plate & made a very affectionate warmhearted speech which was well received. – In reply I was rather choky at 1st & was afraid of breaking down: but I turned out to be like a lame horse that has had some go in him: I halted at 1st but when I got warm (wch I did directly) I went along at a good pace. – My speech was principally taken up with statistics about the Registraryship & my predecessors: there have been 16 Registraries from Hobys in 1506 to myself[48] . . . averaging 22¼ years for each: all my predecessors except Halman & Caryl died in harness: those 2 became Masters of Colleges[49] . . . I was elected by a majority of 40 at the age of 40: – I was the 1st Trinity man: there have been 5 Johnians . . .

*Fri. 11.* Walk about Town. – Breakfast in honor of the new plate: my guests were my Chairman (Archdall) & wife, my Secretary (Paget) & wife & 2 children Maud & Edmund: I gave a grand breakfast & had Hoppett to wait: – I think the children wont easily forget the good fare, & the visit to the printroom, & the play in the garden . . .

*Sun. 13.* . . . Mr Weldon . . . preached an ultra low-church sermon with great force & eloquence . . . But the sermon seemed to me to be far beyond the grasp of most of his flock: it certainly had the defect of not being practical, & seemed to be the discourse of an anythingarian. – However Harriet was so

[47] i.e. high relief. The firm of Garrard, founded about 1730, had become royal goldsmiths to William IV and jewellers in ordinary to Queen Victoria in 1843. They showed Queen Anne style pieces in the 1851 Great Exhibition.

[48] For a list of Registraries see *Historical Register of the University of Cambridge to the year 1910* (1917) p. 51.

[49] James Halman became Master of Caius in 1700 and Lynford Caryl Master of Jesus in 1758.

struck with the sermon that she is going to the 2d part of it this Evening. – I called on Mrs Prest & met there Dr & Mrs Leapingwell: the Dr (as usual) was for pulling every body to pieces & was making a furious attack on Lodge for changing to a Tory & calling him vain & silly.[50] I stoutly took up the cudgels for him & said that he was the most intimate & amiable friend I had ever had . . .

Only two days later than the previous year Romilly, Harriet and Caroline again left Cambridge for Mrs Wright's excellent lodgings in Yarmouth. By good luck Harvey Goodwin, now Dean of Ely, and his wife and seven children were also there and their frequent society and that of other friends greatly increased the pleasure of the holiday. John Sykes, Fellow of Pembroke, and Romilly 'had a good deal of talk' on the pier, H.A. Woodham of Jesus and his brother-in-law Dr Fisher and his family visited him, as did his friends' children and on 22 July he met several college servants on a day excursion from Cambridge. On the following day he 'fell in with my old Clerk Richard Rowe' & the Trinity combination room Butler, Kemp. They 'were neither of them free from ailment'.

Romilly's health was equal to the ascent of the 'Nelson monument: 203 steps (as I was told by James Sharman the showman who was in the Victory when Nelson died & is now a hale man of 77)' and to a more than three hour journey by steamer to Cromer. 'The landing at Cromer was uncomfortable, for we arrived at the worst time of the tide & were obliged to anchor some way off: the wind had freshened & the little boats were not easy to get into from the steamer & there was a good deal of alarm & crying out from the middle-aged women: – from these boats the men were carried ashore pickaback, & the women & children in the beachmen's arms'. Once ashore he heard news of earlier holiday friends, by two of whom he was asked to dinner, and 'was glad to see Cromer again after my desertion of it 4 years ago'. Another successful day was spent with Sedgwick in Norwich to which Romilly and the Harvey Goodwins went together by train. Romilly took little Marybel, Sedgwick's great-niece, 'some small presents, a locket, a coral heart, & a scallop-shell pincushion and when she emerged from school at five 'Sedgwick . . . took us a charming excursion on the river . . . the weather was delicious & we staid out till sunset'. There were thirteen of them in two boats – 'the larger boat was pulled by Mr Bulmer', presumably Edward, an assistant minor Canon of Norwich Cathedral and a waterman, the smaller by a waterman. – Dean Goodwin sang two songs, a comic one abut "Guzzling Jem & Gluttonous Jack", the other "the fine old English Gentleman": he has a fine powerful voice & sang capitally: it made quite a sensation among the pleasure boats we met. At 7½ there was a grand tea-drinking with chicken etc etc, tea & supper combined, with a cloth laid: I suspect none of the children had ever seen such an Evening meal: all manner of good things were offered them (Champagne & Audit Ale not omitted). We returned to Yarmouth (by the train wch arrived at 10) after a most successful day's pleasuring. – the Dean gave me a bill to interpret: it ran thus

---

[50] Lodge was neither vain nor silly and for a tribute to him as University Librarian (1822-45) under whom the collections expanded rapidly 'in just that diversity of subjects which the times seemed to demand', see McKitterick, pp. 445-50 and 507-7. Romilly cared for Lodge almost daily during his spells of often hypochondriacal illness, but as a staunch Whig could not tolerate 'his horrid conservative politics'. See *Romilly 1832-42*, 4 and 15 May 1832 for arguments during the excitement over the Reform Bill.

"A wooden barrow a wooden do _____9s 6d
A wooden barrrow a wood do _____9s 6
                    Total _____9s 6"
An ingenious way of spelling "wouldn't" & "would".

As in 1861, Romilly went to Sunday evening services in many different churches and sometimes in the week as well. In the Wherryman church (St Andrews) 'there were "easy" sermons on Tuesd. & Fri. nights' and the singing was good: 'there is no instrument except a pitch pipe to give the key note'. Baptist Noel preached a Thursday evening sermon on the pier and at St Nicholas's C.K. Robinson, the Master of St. Catharines either bellowed or was inaudible so that 'no soul could have given a farthing for the sermons sake'.

On the morning of 28 August Romilly took his '29th Bath' and then devoted the day to saying goodbye to his younger friends. 'After my dinner came Helen, Katey & Fanny & Mary Miller to take leave of me: I gave them cake & claret & they described to me their picnic at Gorlstone'. It had indeed, as he wrote just after his return to Cambridge, been '6 weeks of health & happiness'.

*Mon. 15 September.* No early walk. – To Town by the Express (return-ticket) 2d Class: companions silent: read Shlegel's Hamlet.[51] – Went to Hungerford Market Office & received another Instalment on my 4 shares of £100 . . . I then went by a penny steamer to London Bridge & from thence by rail to Crystal Palace: – I was very stingy (because I happened to have only a very few shillings in my pocket: I went by 3d Class carriage with a return ticket, for wch I paid 1/6 (including the shilling admission to the Palace)!!! I dined equally economically in the 3d Class refreshment room, paying 6d for plate of cold beef, 1d for bread, 2d for ½ pint of ale!!! . . . the people behaved very quietly & well: – no smoking allowed. – The day was brilliant with glorious sunshine. I was enchanted with the view inside & out: there are a great no of very pleasing pictures by modern artists[52] . . . I think this Crystal Palace with its beautiful walks incomparably more attractive than the Great International. – All the Fountains plaid today but not till after my departure . . .

*Th. 18.* Feel very ill . . . Visit from Captain Prest to take me to Fenners Ground to see the athletic sports: I was highly amused with them, especially by the jumping over hurdles & by the race of 9 boys under 12 which was capital: they were pretty boys & nicely got up: it was a 1-mile race (i.e. 4 times round): it was excellently contested: the youngsters ran as if for dear life & won in 5'. 58": the winner (Coward) was so much excited that he burst into hysterical crying. There was a collection made & I gave the trifle I had about me (3s). This collection (£5) was for Lane (the 10 mile Champion): his cup was exhibited: he ran a mile with an amateur . . . Sadly sleepy in Evening.

---

[51] See 26 December 1860.
[52] i.e. Turner, Bonnington, G.S. Newton, Constable, Copley Fielding, J.S. Cotman, Birket Foster and many others. *The Times* of 2 May agrees with Romilly: 'for extent, for convenience, for elevation, for beauty of forms and lines, and for charm of colour, the present building is far, far superior, to that in Hyde Park'. The Crystal Palace, with elaborate additions, had moved to a 200 acre site at Sydenham in 1852.

*Fri. 19.* . . . The day being magnificent I walked for 3 hours at my crawling pace: – I went by the Barton Road to Coton & thence home by the fields: - between Coton & the Barton road they are digging for Coprolites.[53] After dinner read 'No name'.[54] – Very sleepy.

*Fri. 26.* . . . Wrote to Grim who wants a railway ticket card from the British Association secretaries by wch he may travel at single expense backwards & forwards . . .

*Sat. 27.* . . . Directly after breakfast resolved to do all I could to save Grim's money: – called on Professor Liveing (one of the 3 local Secretaries: – he lives at 112 Hills Road): he was unluckily out. Posted off to Ferrers (another of the local Secretaries): met him on Kings Parade & made a sad exhibition of the infirmity of age: I could not recollect Grim's Living & had to go into McMillans to look at the Clergy List. – Immediately after Ferrers despatched a Card for the said Grim by the midday-post. – Bought a photograph of 2 Asses: put it in my book & wrote under it 'Self & Friend' . . . Went to Trin. Library to see Woolner's bust of Hare[55] (given by the Master of Harrow H. Montague Butler): think one profile good: did not like the other . . .

*Wed. 1 October* . . . The Trinity Fellows elected: they were Barker (Senior Wrangler), Crosthwaite (8 Wrangler), Eve (11 W) Whiting (6 of 1st Class of Classical Tripos), & Sir G. Young Bart, (a Senior Optime & 2d Class Classic) . . . Sedgwick returned from his Residence at Norwich: went with him to his office: he gave a Sovereign to the wife of the Porter at his Museum because she had been his servant for 10 years: she has been 10 years married & has 8 children; she is goodlooking & her children pretty. Shilleto is just returned: he can't take Henry Romilly for a pupil – very unfortunate & vexatious. – Wrote to Sir John to tell him & to say that I had therefore written to Jebb to ask him: Jebb was 1st in Classical Tripos this year & was both Porson & Craven Scholar . . .

*Th. 2.* Grim & I breakfasted with the Pagets: I was very glad that little Maud was of the party & had the honor of sitting next to Professor Owen . . . Earnshaw talked in a very interesting manner about the trades-unions at Sheffield[56] & their enormities in blowing up the houses of obnoxious

---

53 William Buckland, geologist and Dean of Westminster, most usefully concluded in 1829 that 'fossil fir cones' and 'bezoar stones' were fossilised excrement and bones of extinct animals and that the calcium phosphate they contained might be useful as manure. It was and huge quantities of 'coprolites' were found in Cambridgeshire and other eastern counties. Half the 98 acres of Coldham's Common, for example, had been dug up by 1859. See the *Chronicle* 12 November 1859 and J.J. Harris Teall, *The Cambridge Coprolite Mining Rush* 1875 (Sedgwick Prize Essay for 1873).

54 Wilkie Collins's *No Name*, the latest of his 'sensation' novels, was serialised in 1862 in Dickens's periodical *All the Year Round*.

55 i.e. one of those on pedestals in front of the bookcases in the library.

56 Only 12 out of 60 trades unions were implicated and 'in no important case were the culprits found at the time; but the motive was clearly industrial and not personal'. In these years when in many towns trades unions were uncertain of their own legality these attacks were by trades unionists violently attempting to enact laws for their own protection. (See Sidney Pollard,

Masters: – the miscreant who performs the deed is always unknown: – the committee summon 8 persons: lots are drawn & the workman who draws the fated lot must needs perpetrate the crime & conceal it: – the great manufacture at Sheffield is 'steel' . . . Grim diligently attended lectures on Geology etc etc.[57] – We dined at 4½ & he went at 8 to hear Prof. Tyndall's lecture on 'Water' in the Townhall: he was delighted with the brilliant experiments.

*Fri. 3.* Grim & I breakfasted with the Selwyns: Selwyn is going today to read a paper on his favorite subject 'the Sun's spots' . . . Took Grim to dine at the great banquet in Trinity at 5. Of course he could not sit with me: he was at table D (the Stewards table): I was at the high table . . . on one side of me was a Belgian Geologist (Köninck) on the other Hepworth Dixon (writer in the Athenæum). Mr Dixon is a cool hand for he boldly planted himself next me in another man's place who had to go & hunt for a place. He wrote a furious article in the Athenæum complaining of inhospitality.[58] He was not invited to St Johns dinner . . . Sedgwick today gave the health of the foreigners who had visited us & particularly mentioned Köninck – Köninck was quite taken by surprise: he returned thanks very well in French & made a warm eulogy of Sedgwick as a great benefactor to Science . . . The Duke of Dev. spoke ably & very modestly of himself as a former President:[59] he paid deserved compliments to the Master (his private tutor) . . . Grim & all the rest of the world went to the grand soirée in the Town hall: – I took a refreshing walk under the influence of a brilliant moon & the splendor of Jupiter.

*Wed. 8.* . . . The British Association is to meet next year at Newcastle under the Presidency of the great gun Sir William Armstrong.[60] – After dinner Grim read loud that very clever squib of Kingsley's entitled 'Speech of Lord Dundreary on the great Hippocampus question' in Section D. last Friday – concerning the fight between Owen & Huxley about the brains of men & apes.[61] Grim read also a leader in yesterday's Times about the said fight. – He read also the 2d Paper of Boz (in 1838) on the Mudfog Association.[62]

---

*A History of Labour in Sheffield* (1959) pp. 252-8). Samuel Earnshaw, Senior Wrangler in 1831 and native of Sheffield, was chaplain of St. Peter's there from 1847 to 1888.

[57] Richard Owen, who by now had a European reputation, gave three lectures at this third meeting in Cambridge of the British Association. There were 34 communications in the geology section. For Tyndall see 17 January 1862. His lecture was a 'Discourse on the Forms and Action of Water' and Selwyn's 'On Autographs of the Sun'. See *Report of the Thirty-second Meeting of the British Association for the Advancement of Science Held at Cambridge in October 1862* (1863).

[58] Dated 8 October the article criticised the *organisation* of the Meeting 'which cannot be called a successful one as to numbers, splendour or results . . . The various Colleges opened their doors very liberally; but through the want of order and arrangement many of their rooms remained to the last day unoccupied. Now Cambridge hotels are bad enough and dear enough at any time; during the past week they have been intolerably bad and dear.'

[59] The Duke, then Earl of Burlington, was President of the British Association meeting in Liverpool in September 1837.

[60] Armstrong was a leading inventor of armaments. See 10 June.

[61] In 1857 Owen had announced that because the human brain possesses a unique lobe, the hippocampus minor, and larger cerebral hemispheres than any other mammal, man was 'as different from the chimpanzee as the ape was from the platypus' (A. Desmond and J. Moore, *Darwin* (1993), p. 453). *The Times* leader was on his side: 'We must not be

*Th. 9.* This is my birthday. – By God's great mercy I have been spared another year & now enter upon the 72d year of a life full of great blessings. I am indeed vastly weak & have the clearest warnings of my fast approaching end, but I am free from pain & am able to get about. – Grim gave me today 'Westward Ho!' or 'Adventures of Sir Amyas Lee' by Professor Kingsley. Mrs Paget brought me a present of fine pears & little Maud Paget a photograph of her papa. – Mary Anne Tyler wrote me a very pious letter & sent me a silk watch guard of her making. Wrote to her & sent her 20*l*. – Grim left me this morning directly after breakfast: he has been with me 9 days & has worked like a dragon at the Sections: – he has enjoyed his visit highly . . .

*Wed. 15.* . . . Letter from Jebb: he don't mean to reside this term, so that scheme for Henry fails: I consulted with Mathison, who recommends either Jackson or Wilson (3d & 4th in 1st Class of Classical Tripos/62) . . .

*Th. 16.* Went to College to look for Jackson's answer: fortunately he is able to take Henry: so I went to Henry's rooms where his Father was breakfasting with him & took Sir John to Jackson & introduced him. – I thought it an interesting sight this lovely morning seeing the 151 Trin: freshmen in the Great Court going to the 2d days preliminary Examination. Sir John leaves Cambridge today. – Letter today from G.T.R. . . . my godson Samuel (who used to be called Cappie) is now no longer dressed in a kilt, but is promoted to tunic & trowsers:[63]– George wants an Æneid with notes that he may read with Franky of an Evening to keep him at the top of his class . . . After dinner read 'Westward Ho':[64] I find a good deal of it heavy & tedious.

*Fri. 24.* . . . Call on Edleston (Bursar) to receive the Michaelmas payment (about £16): I begged him to show me the Muniment Room: it is a dirty comfortless most untidy place without a fireplace: the only interesting object to my taste was the iron-bound Chest (wch is much smaller in point of height & breadth than the University Chest & does not stand on wheels): I remonstrated at its being hidden by boxes & recommended bringing it forward conspicuously. – Adjoining the Muniment Room is 'Sky Parlour',[65]

surprised therefore at the indignation which the "Darwinian theory" represented by the Professor [Huxley] never fails to provoke . . . how unspeakable must be the suggestion that we are lineally descended from the most hideous animal that can be found in our menageries or museums.' If *The Times* leader-writer was not entirely clear about the "Darwinian theory", 'Lord Dundreary' in his speech was glad to have heard the learned gentlemen quarrel, 'though of course we don't understand what is the matter . . . but were very much delighted . . . to find that we all had hippopotamuses in our brains'. Lord Dundreary, the brainless peer originally conceived by Tom Taylor, became the talk of London as developed and played by E.A. Sothern from November 1861 at the Haymarket.

[62] Dickens wrote the *Mudfog Papers* for *Bentley's Miscellany* 1837-9. They contain reports of two meetings of the 'Mudfog Association for the Advancement of Everything' which were attended by such distinguished characters as Mr Muddlebranes, Mr Drawley, Professor Muff, and Mr X. Misty.

[63] Samuel Joseph Maclean had now reached the advanced age of eight.

[64] Written at Bideford where the Kingsleys were staying in 1855.

[65] Mr Jonathan Smith of Trinity College Library tells us that the muniment room was then in King Edward's Tower on the floor immediately beneath the clock. He suggests tentatively, from Farrar's description of the view from Julian's rooms, that "Sky Parlour" is today C4 Great Court.

where Bishop Watson & 'Saint' Brown used to live: – it was abandoned – Edleston recommended me to read Farrar's book called 'Julian Home' or 'College Life': it gives an account of different inhabitants of 'Sky Parlour': Farrar was 4th Classic in 1854 & was Fellow of Trin: – he is now one of the Masters at Harrow . . .

*Sat. 25.* Hoar frost this morning. – Walk on Sheep Green. – In the Office till 12. Then a Seniority in wch we agreed to alter the dinner hour for the comfort of the youngsters for the October & Lent Terms, viz. the weekday dinner hour to be 4½ (instead of 4) & the dinner hour of the Freshmen to be 5½ (instead of 5), & the Evening Chapel on weekdays to be 6½ . . . I was much relieved by receiving from Sophie Oger an answer 'to mine of Wednesday': – she describes my dear brother as far less alarmingly ill than I had feared from her former letter . . .

*Tu. 28.* . . . Harriet returned from her visit to Mrs James Spink: – her visit was nominally for the International Exhibition, but mainly for the sake of her dear friends the Theobalds in their trouble[66] . . . I have no doubt that Harriet's tender heart has been much soothed by seeing her mourning friends: but she is looking very poorly & sorrowful . . . Commemoration proceedings at Christs today. – My good friend poor Joseph Shaw was commemorated: he died worth near £40,000!![67] He was an only child & had some patrimony: he held the sole Tutorship for many years in palmy days when there were numerous Fellow Commoners & he used to clear about £1200 a year by the Tutorship.

*Mon. 1 December.* . . . G.T.R. left me at 9 to return to London . . . Seniority at 12 & afterwards a sealing of the presentation of Glover (our Librarian) to Brading, which became vacant by D.I. Heath's deprivation for heterodoxy:[68]– Brading is worth more than £300 p.a. (viz £319) & cannot therefore (by our new Statutes) be held with a Fellowship: of course it had been offered to all the clerical fellows. – Walk to Red-Cross Gate. Read 'Men of the Time'.[69]

[66] The Theobalds and Harriet were old friends and Frederick Theobald had died suddenly of 'a brain fever' aged 32. For Harriet's engagement to one of the brothers see 13 February 1862. Also 2 December 1848.

[67] Joseph Shaw was tutor of Christ's from 1814 to 1828 and presumably had many private pupils amongst the high proportion of noblemen and fellow commoners then admitted to the college. He gave £200 for buildings in 1823 and left the College £3,000 in his will. See J. Peile, *Biographical Register of Christ's College* II (1913), 353, and the references to him in A. Steele, *The Custom of The Room* (1949), based on the wager books at Christ's.

[68] D.I. Heath held the College living of Brading, Isle of Wight from 1842 to 1862. His *Sermons on Important Subjects* (1860) were alleged to be derogatory to the Thirty-Nine Articles and he was deprived of his benefice, his subsequent appeal to a judicial committee of the Privy Council being rejected. Heath lived in retirement until his death twenty-six years later. For the Clerical Subscription Act of 1865 which enabled the clergy to perceive a difference between the conscientious and the legal attitude to subscription see Chadwick, II, 131-6.

[69] A biographical dictionary of notable contemporaries just published in its fifth edition. Romilly was not included but the Master of the Rolls and his cousin Peter Mark Roget were.

*Th. 4.* . . . Letter from Betsy (Mrs James Spink): a rascally agent to the 'Building Society'[70] has bagged 3 months of her payments & the Society ignore his existence & demand of her £4. 3. 5 . . . wrote to her sending £5 to pay the debt . . . I believe she will after a few more years payments to the 'Building Society' be owner of No 4 Hawksworth Terrace. I charged Betsy to make all her future payments to the Society with *her own hands* . . .

*Fri. 5.* . . . At 8½ to John Power's 'Family': I plaid 7 rubbers & lost 5 of them & 15/s. I became a Member of 'the Family' in 1834 when I succeeded Thirlwall: the party at this dinner on 16 Dec. /34 consisted of Paradox Davy,[71] (the Host), Dr Haviland, The Provost (Thackeray), Tom Mortlock, Lodge, myself & Mr Horseman. – Not home till 11½.

*Sat. 6.* Dowdy & warm – Walk in Queens' grounds. Letter of thanks from Betsy: she says I have taken a ton weight off her mind . . . Mrs Kennedy is anxious about Frank's examination: – his indolence is a sad disease: he had passed the Examination above a week ago (as I pumped out of him) but had never found time to write to his mother!!! I wrote her a long letter telling her that he was *through*, but that Mr Mathieson says he appears to be living with idle expensive associates & to be rather fast . . . A 2 hours Seniority: this was the 'dies Computi': our affairs are most flourishing & we the Seniors are to have the magnificent sum of £650 each[72] . . .

*Tu. 9.* . . . Caroline Howe was one of the Sunday School Teachers at St Pauls: – Mr Scott has sent her a parting present (on his quitting St Pauls for Tydd St Giles): it is Angell James' 'Anxious Inquirer':[73]– I dipt into it & thought it far above all ordinary pious Christians & likely to make the reader mad from intense anxiety . . .

*Th. 11.* Coughed a good deal in the night. – Walk in B. Garden. – Escorted the Shilletos to the distribution of the Rifle prize-cups on King's Lawn:[74] there was 1st a parade & the band plaid . . . All this part went off well, for the

---

[70] The Building Society movement had spread rapidly since the 1830s, and it is clear from Romilly's 'Directions' list (the leaves of his diary which he used as an address book) that the Spinks were already living at 4 Hawksworth Terrace, Stratford, London, in 1859.

[71] The Master of Caius had been a member of the 'Family' since 1787 and Romilly referred to him only as 'Dr Davy' and not 'Paradox' during his lifetime. He describes him at the Family on 6 March 1835 as 'more absurd than ever' and on 30 October 1835 'as tiresome as ever'. He says 'that the Alps were either formed in the air or thrown out from the moon', and it was presumably such opinions that led to his nickname. See Gunning's *Reminiscences* (1854), II, 189-202, 359-66.

[72] i.e. as dividends. Francis Martin, the Senior Bursar, had told the Statutory Commissioners in 1858 that 'the average gross income of the college for the last seven years was considerably greater than that for the ten years before and that an increase in the net income of the college, amounting to £2500, might be expected by the end of the year 1870' (Winstanley, p. 427).

[73] J.A. James's *The Anxious Enquirer after Salvation directed and encouraged* (1834) was reprinted many times and translated by the Religious Tract Society.

[74] The Volunteer movement 'had from the first been associated with the art of shooting and many units could trace their origins to rifle clubs' (H. Strachan, *History of the Cambridge University Officers Training Corps*, 1976, pp. 27-8), where he also quotes from a financial report of 1861 – 'There are Silver Challenge Cups in the possession of the Corps to the value of £450 . . . and it is found that the competition excited for the possession of these Cups gives a very great stimulus to Rifle Shooting'.

weather was fine: but now heavy rain came on, & the finale of making & crossing the pontoon bridge was rather a failure: Colonel Baker indeed rode his horse over, & the greatest part of the riflemen got across: but the bridge was ill made, several who managed to get across were up to their knees in the water, & the last company (on the middle of the bridge) turned right about & retreated, to the derision of the company. The youngsters were all delighted with this mishap . . .

*Fri. 12.* . . . Letter from G.T.R: – Bertie got a marble in his throat & was rescued from choking by well-applied thumps on the back: – afterwards his Mamma gave him a lecture & took away (as she thought) all his marbles: he bore the loss with great fortitude, for they were his brother Cappies (he having secreted his own in an undiscovered nook)! . . .

*Sat. 13.* . . . Seniority from 2 to 3½ about preoption to livings[75] in general, but specially about the case of Luard & Beamont . . . all but Grote sided with the Master in giving the precedence (in preoption to livings) to Beamont: Grote is to write out his reasons . . . We all agreed that the Mathematical part of the Examination for Minor Scholarships is too hard: – Differentials, Mechanics & Hydrostatics are to be excluded in future . . .

*Tu. 16.* . . . At 11 to Chapel for the Communion service: Luard was the preacher and of course his wife came to hear him . . . I liked pretty well all the early part: but I thought he was guilty of indiscretion (not to say impertinence) in reproaching the College for not having the Sacrament administered every Sunday[76] . . . Went to the distribution of prizes in the Hall: – the Latin Oration was by Sidgwick (brother of our Fellow): the subject was Umbra Periclis alloquitur Græcos',[77] it was in choice Latin: Sidgwick is remarkably prepossessing in looks & manners: he (as is usual) read his Oration. The English speech was by Everett (son of the distinguished American): his subject 'the genius of Daniel Wester' [sic] . . . He repeated his Oration by heart (having forgotten to bring the M.S.): it was a great trial of memory.[78] It was

---

[75] The greatly valued right to a Trinity living was offered to fellows in order of seniority, and the case of Luard and Beamont concerned their seniority under the old and new statutes. Luard had put himself under the new statutes, while Beamont remained under the old. Beamont thought he should have priority over Luard who, although above him on the electoral roll, was married and under the new statutes could retain his fellowship as Registrary. Luard persisted in contesting the decision and both sides took legal advice: see 9 February and 17 April 1863. On 24 November 1863 in the Court of Chancery the Lord Chancellor, representing the Crown as visitor of Trinity, declared that Luard's electing to be subject to the new statutes did not affect his seniority, and so he won. See *UP* 33 no. 751.

[76] On 8 December 1860 the Seniority had agreed to continue the experiment begun in October 1859 of having a sermon in chapel every Sunday in term. The *University Commission Report* (1852) said, however, (pp. 145-6) that Holy Communion would be administered 'on one day at least during each of the three Terms' and on one day only seems to have been the normal practice at Trinity.

[77] i.e. The Shade of Pericles addresses the Greeks.

[78] Dr H.C. Porter suggests that William Everett meant to 'forget' his text so that he might emulate his father's astonishing memory as an orator. Edward Everett and Daniel Webster were close friends who abhorred slavery but considered it a lesser evil than disunion. It was thought that Webster's arguments for compromise probably postponed the Civil War for ten years. Romilly objected to William Everett's reference to Lazarus's sisters saying to Christ

427

one of the ablest Orations I ever heard, & was delivered with a rapidity & fervor of empassioned eloquence that I never saw equalled . . . He of course did not satisfy me in every respect: I thought he trod on holy ground when he said of Dan. Webster (in allusion to the fratricidal war in America) 'if thou hadst been here my brothers had not died', & still more objectionably when he said (in praise of Eloquence) that our Lord had been called 'the Word'. – Of course Everett shocked the Tories by his speaking of Charles 1st as a tyrant that tried to rule without law or parliament: he also gave offence by sneering at the pomp & long preparation of months for the funeral of Wellington & contrasting it with the simplicity of Dan. Websters funeral wch was a few days after his death in 1852. – Dan. Webster was never President: he was the most eloquent of all advocates & the most influential of Statesmen . . . I was glad that the Master congratulated him in the name of his Fathers friend. – Young Everett is rather short, he is yellowfaced, very ugly & has a repulsive countenance as of a rude illmanned man . . .

*Christmas Day – Thursday.* Walk about Town: got the Porter of Peterhouse to exhibit the Library to me . . . Letters from G.T.R. & Maggie: Maggie has cut fingers & thumbs in cutting holly to adorn the church: – George has declined (I think wisely) a Turkey for civility to some one at the Tower. Wrote to G.T.R. sending £1 for Xmas boxes for the children . . .

*Tu. 30.* . . . Walk on Hauxton Road: overtaken by Lord Neville (driving to his living): he & his brother Ld Braybrooke were at a concert last night given by Lady Hardwicke for the Lancashire distress: she sang & £70 was collected for the sufferers.[79] – On my return I fell in with Leapingwell: he was (as usual) loud upon the folly of most men's choice in wife, & selected 3 wives in particular to rail at, viz. Mrs Willis, Mrs Miller, & Mrs Besant . . .

*Wed. 31.* . . . So endeth another year of my long life. I have great reason to bless God for the mercies vouchsafed to me in it: I have indeed the added infirmity of bad sight, but otherwise I am in better health at the close of the year than I was at the beginning. But I have great grief at my poor brothers affliction in weakness of limbs & alas! in weakness of intellect.

'Lord, if thou hadst been here, my brother had not died' and to the opening of St John's Gospel, 'In the beginning was the Word'. Whewell had made friends with Edward Everett when he was Minister to Great Britain from 1841 to 1845. See W. Everett, 'The Character of Daniel Webster' in his *College Essays Delivered in Trinity College Cambridge* (1863). For Everett's low opinion of public speaking in Cambridge see his *On the Cam* pp. 142-4.

[79] Owing to the American Civil War supplies of cotton to the mill towns of Lancashire had almost ceased, causing acute distress. Many thousands existed on parish relief and the national relief fund set up in July raised huge sums in the following three years. In Cambridge on 10 November the Senate agreed to urgent measures for collecting subscriptions and clothing and the Vice-Chancellor reminded members that undergraduates also were warmly 'determined to share resources with their distressed brethren'. See 13 January 1863.

# 1863

*Sun. 4 January.* . . . At Barnwell Mr Weldon . . . thought it very wrong that people should come to church without making some contribution (however small) to the support of the services etc: he should from next Sunday have always a collection at the door, when he hoped every body would give something, – a penny or even a farthing: – he said no part of the money would ever be for his enrichment, but would be given towards the maintenance of 2 additional Curates, towards the church repairs, charities etc etc. – I think this a bold & doubtful measure: I fear that people won't give & that they will stay away . . .

*Wed. 7.* . . . In the Evening read with very great interest De Tocqueville's letters:[1] he had a warmth of heart to his friends & a tenderness of affection for his wife & a purity of soul & a devotedness to the public good wch remind me of my uncle Sir Samuel.

*Sun. 11.* . . . Today the new idea of a weekly collection was 1st acted on: – between the Communion & the sermon wooden boxes (like kitchen salt-boxes) were handed round: many more people gave than I expected: – the free seats were very thinly occupied, probably from fear of the money-box & the expected penny . . .

*Plough Monday 12.* . . . Skimmed thro the Mémoir of the Prince Consort: I read it in Deighton's shop: I did not read the Prince's speeches: I found the Mémoir exceedingly interesting: – the anonymous writer confesses that it is very much derived from communications of the Queen, & it is almost insinuated that some parts in praise of the Prince were written by her. – The Mémoir acknowledges one defect in the Prince, – his shyness. – I bought a book of 'Thoughts on Death & Eternity' wch is printed with the Queen's permission: – the fly-leaf contains these words "The Meditations" contained in this vol. form part of the well-known German devotional work 'Stunden der Andacht'[2] . . .

*Tu. 13.* . . . French letters arrived: God be praised! they give an improved account of dear Frank . . . All the letters are full of the warmest praises of Madame for her devotedness to Frank. – Letter from Grim describing his labours: he collected from house to house for the Lancashire distress & got the tidy sum of £32: he has been printing 'New Years Words' to his flock: he has given a school tea-party to '100 brats with plum-cake till they were like so many boa constrictors': he has also given a tea-total party with Magic Lantern & reading Dickens' Christmas Carols: & he has made his report as Rural Dean, – (thinks his own church the best of the lot). – Wrote to him.

---

[1] On 22 October 1862 Archdeacon Allen had recommended Alexis de Tocqueville's letters, i.e. the translation from the French of his *Memoirs, Letters and Remains* (2 vols, 1861), as 'the best book of the year'.

[2] Probably *In Memoriam of His Royal Highness the Prince Consort* (11 pp.) of which a copy exists bound up in *Theological Pamphlets* in the University Library. J.H.D. Zschokkes's *Stunden der Andacht* was translated into English in 1830 by E.J. Burrow as *Hours of Devotion* and in 1843 by J.D. Haas as *Hours of Meditation and Devotional Reflexion*.

*Sun. 25.* Beautiful springlike morning . . . At Christ Church Mr Wortley read prayers & Mr Weldon preached very eloquently from Matthew 7. 11 on the goodness of God. He said he was horrified the other day in seeing a book for children: it had the following passage 'What does God do to naughty children'? – Ans. 'He sends them to Hell'! . . .

*Fri. 30.* Walk to Senate House to hear the Honors published at 9 o'cl. Profusions of lists were showered from the galleries & there was great pushing & hustling. – Trinity Hall has won: Romer is Senior Wrangler:[3] he is immensely popular: he is a great boater & cricketer & is a thorough gentleman & given to literature. The 1st 6 are Romer (Tr. H.), Leeke (Trin), Hockin (Johns), Ledger (Corpus Christi) & Moore (Peterhouse) equal, Aldis (Trin) . . . Wrote to Geldart & Latham to congratulate . . .

*Sat. 31.* . . . Learned the marks of the 1st 3 Wranglers: – Romer 4500; Leeke 4000; Hockin 3700: I have given them in round numbers . . . Routh (Peterhouse) was the private tutor of 9 out of the 1st 10 Wranglers including the Senior Wrangler: Routh seems to have taken the place of Hopkins as Senior Wrangler maker.

*Tu. 3 February* . . . Walk for 2½ hours on Hills Road: – fell in with Mr Girdlestone: recommended him to scold Frank roundly & give him no peace if he dont work: he says he will at the end of this term give me an account of his chances . . .

*Wed. 4.* . . . Seniority at wch we made an interpretation concerning præoption to Livings . . . Case 'A & B are both Fellows in Orders: A. is Senior, B Junior: A puts himself under New Statutes, B remains under Old: we adjudged that B has the præoption'. The Master & 7 Seniors (viz, Romilly, Edleston, Mathison, King, Cope, Munro & Hotham) signed this Interpretation: Grote signed as Dissentient. So Grote was like Prince Napoleon who at the Address of the Senate to the Emperor the other day was the only dissentient (– he objects to his Cousin the Emperor's views concerning Rome) . . . In my walk I fell in with Fawcett the blind Fellow of Trinity Hall, who is Candidate for the Town on the ultra-liberal opinions: he is supposed to be a nominee of the Fosters, who think Adair not up to the mark & have pitched him overboard: – told Mr Fawcett I should vote for him[4] tho I objected to his views on the Ballot. – At ¼ to 7 to Mrs Prest's & plaid quadrille . . . Oysters after the Cards. – Mrs William Prest worked.

*Mon. 9.* . . . Visit from my Godson Clement Francis Romilly Allen (½ brother to George & Grim). The more I see of this youth the more I like him . . . His recent examination (with 17 others) for Chinese Interpreter was in

---

[3]   For Romer being congratulated by the Master (Geldart) see the Trinity Hall group in Robert Farren's 'Senate House Hill: Degree Morning (1863)' reproduced in Charles Crawley's *Trinity Hall 1350-1975* (1976) plate 13. Romer was the college's first Senior Wrangler; Latham was senior tutor.

[4]   i.e. for Henry Fawcett, fellow of Trinity Hall, blinded when he was twenty-five, professor of political economy 1863-84, and M.P. and Postmaster-General. He was a life-long radical and advocate of proportional representation of which Romilly did not approve. He was beaten in Cambridge owing to a split in the Liberal party. See Leslie Stephen's *Life of Henry Fawcett* (1885).

4 rules of Arithmetic, writing from Dictation, making an Abstract of a given paper, translating from Latin & French: – he was examined medically & pronounced of a sound constitution . . . Clement will soon depart for China by the overland route . . . College Meeting of 2 hours: Luard has declared his intention of appealing to the Visitor (concerning our interpretation as to pre-option to livings.) . . . Heard a good joke about Bp. Colenso: 'Colenso has examined Moses in Arithmetic & plucked him'.

*Wed. 11.* Before breakfast gave my Vote for Mr Fawcett in the Town Hall

$$\left.\begin{array}{l}\text{Powell } 708 \\ \text{Fawcett } 627\end{array}\right\} \qquad \left\{\begin{array}{l}\text{Powell (Tory)} \\ \text{elected}\end{array}\right.$$

. . . Today Myers (relation of the Master) was convened: he is a very clever young man: he was elected minor-scholar, & is a Scholar of the College & gained the English Poem. He is self willed & perverse & rebellious: Mathison says he never had so unmanageable a pupil. – The offence of Myers was reading Grace irreverently & with an obvious intention of giving disgust. – He had been punished by the Dean & he thus exhibited his anger. – The fire-brand Edleston was for expelling him: Mathison & King were for rustication: Grote was not present: I pleaded stoutly for a milder punishment wch should not blast his prospects in life:[5]– milder counsel ultimately prevailed & Myers was admonished 1st time previous to expulsion.

*Th. 12.* . . . A very gay letter from Sedgwick at Norwich: his guests (Dick & wife & Addie) have left him . . . talks of coming to Camb. in a week. – Wrote to him & also to Maggie. – Saw The Codex Sinaiticus Petropolitanus:[6] found at Mount Sinai, possessed by Emperor of Russia, edited by Tischendorff: I saw it most advantageously: Bradshaw of Kings took me into Kings Library & exhibited it to me most admirably. The M.S. is supposed to be of 4th century: it contains no part of the pentateuch: it has a little of Chronicles; has Job, Isaiah, part of Jeremiah, none of Daniel & Ezekiel, & has some of the minor prophets: it has the whole of the New Testament & also the epistle of Barnabas & the Shepherd of Hermas. – Wright was with Bradshaw & gave a very interesting account of his attack of Simonides (a lying Greek who was here at the meeting of the British Association last Autumn): – this vagabond pretends that the Codex Sinaiticus is all humbug & that he himself wrote it! – This Simonides skilfully imitates any handwriting, is learned in the characters of different epochs & has been detected in forgery . . .

---

[5]  Romilly's pleading was amply justified by F.W.H. Myers' subsequent career. The holder of six University prizes and two scholarships he became a fellow of Trinity in 1865, when he was also probably the first Englishman to swim across the Niagara below the Falls. From 1872 he was H.M. Inspector of Schools. An occasional poet and essayist, he was also a founder member of the Society for Psychical Research.

[6]  In 1844 Count von Tischendorff found in a basket of fire-kindling in St Catherine's convent on Mount Sinai 43 leaves of the Septuagint. In 1859 he returned with an introduction from the Tsar and the Codex was brought to him for copying. The monks agreed to his taking it to the Tsar at St Petersburg in return for roubles and decorations. Simonides had tried to discredit Bradshaw, the University Librarian, and other experts who detected his frauds. See the introduction to H. and K. Lake, *Codex Sinaiticus Petropolitanus* (1911). In 1933 the Soviet government sold the Codex to the British Museum.

*Tu. 17.* Walk on Hills Road: met Mortlock & wife in phaeton and had some chat with them. In the 'Times' of yesterday there is a dashing leader making light of Colonial Bishops (whom it calls 'Colonials'),[7] handling Colenso very roughly as a man who had never read the Bible till he wrote against it & was so ignorant as not to know of difficulties which every body else knew from their childhood: – this leader sneers a good deal at the Lower House of Convocation. – In the evening read Pickwick.

*Th. 19.* . . . Visit from Sedgwick . . . He read me the 2 letters he had written to Mrs Bruce on the Queen's giving him a copy of 'The Prince Consort's speeches etc' with her own writing in it . . . This consolation was nominally to Mrs Bruce on her own bereavement, but was meant principally for the Queen herself . . . Sedgwick is greatly distressed about the state of mind of his gloomy nephew Dick: he is in a morbid frame of mind & has armed himself with a revolver & thinks there is a conspiracy against him (– he won't say by whom): he sent 2 nights ago for the Police to watch his house all night as he expected an attack. – Poor fellow! this is palpable derangement . . .

*Fri. 20.* . . . A calculating boy (nearly blind) has been exhibiting at the Town Hall:[8] he showed wonderful powers in extracting Cube-roots etc etc, & at the end of the performance repeated in order all the different questions wch had been proposed to him. – Met that queer Skinner: I asked him who the young man was that I had seen with him the other day . . . his name is Palmer & he is nephew of Mrs Palmer landlady of the Hoop: he has feeble health & gives himself up to literature: his great delight is Arabic wch he writes with great facility . . . Skinner very kindly gives him gratuitous instruction every Evening in Greek, Hebrew, Arabic & Syriac. – Read Macaulay's admirable essay on Addison.

*Tu. 24.* . . . Walk on Barton Road: met Dr & Mrs Phillips: they mean to illuminate Queen's gate on the Prince's wedding-day: – there will be a grace tomorrow for illuminating the Senate House & Fitzwilliam . . . Sedgwick drank tea with me: he proposes going to Dent to look after Dick . . .

*Fri. 27.* Feel very poorly. – Went to the Office for an hour (between breakfasts) & wrote out for Luard all details about getting Silver Boxes for addresses etc . . . On Tuesday Mr Newdegate asked Lord Palmerston to an-

---

[7] Unlike Romilly, we read *The Times* leader as defending 'Colonials'. 'Convocation is fortunate this year . . . The sport is easy and excellent, the ground light, and there is every promise of a good run. The vermin has broken cover in a most unexpected quarter. A "Colonial" think of that! – A "Colonial" has attacked the Bible! . . . It would not make the smallest difference if he had converted a hundred thousand Hottentots or Feefees with an entire Roman Catholic Church into the bargain, he would still be a colonial . . . '. However, although *The Times* considers *The Pentateuch and the Book of Joshua: Critically Examined* 'a very foolish book' it advises Convocation not to go too far in its criticisms and recommends 'that candidates for consecration should be examined in the Holy Scripture' thus providing 'against a recurrence of this untoward affair'. See Chadwick, II 90-7 and Searby pp. 110-111.

[8] The calculating boy's performance was sadly not reported by the *Chronicle* and the *Independent* whose journalists' attention was focussed on the royal wedding.

nounce publicly whether the Princess Alexandra was a Protestant:[9] Ld P. replied 'When the question arose of selecting a Princess the following conditions were thought requisite, – (1) that she should be young, (2) – that she should be handsome, – (3) that she should be agreeable, (4) that she should be amiable in disposition, (5) that she should have been well brought up, – & lastly that she should be a Protestant'. – What a gay offhand wag our Premier is! . . .

*Sat. 28.* . . . Commissioned Harriet to buy 6 Wedding Favors for 10th of March, for herself, Caroline Howe, Mary Edwards, M.A. Tyler, Elisabeth Stallybrass & me: I meant them to be all alike, but Harriet brought me one with a small brooch containing portraits of the Prince & Princess: – this cost double, viz. 2s . . .

*Tu. 3 March.* . . . Received from Leslie Stephen a copy of his pamphlet on the 'Poll degree' (objecting to the pamplets of Mayor & Girdleston:)[10] . . . he is for abolishing the Poll Examination altogether: he repudiates the idea of its being the duty of the University to 'make men work', & considers it an absurdity to talk of men's working 5 hours a day. L.S. is of the 'muscular' Christianity school. I was amused by the vigour of his attack on the 'Poll': he says 'Every one admits that it does not give any mental training of the least value'. But it seems to be considered as a negative merit that it does not try to teach any body any thing that he can ever want to know afterwards . . . Seniority about the Massam houses at York . . . this very tiresome business is arranged at last: – Grote & Edleston were infinitely worrying: – the College receives £1800 for these houses (wch are to be pulled down for beautifying the view of the Cathedral) & the College gives £300 towards the improvement. – Meeting in Clare Combination room of the London & Camb. committees for the Albert Statue[11] . . . The Marble party won by 11 to 7. I was a Bronzite. – Scarcely any walk.

9   C.N. Newdegate (Warwickshire, North) at the third reading of Bill 30, the 'Prince and Princess of Wales' Annuities', said that he 'had been requested to ask the noble Lord at the head of the Government to announce distinctly whether Her Royal Highness the Princess Alexandra was a Protestant'. Palmerston's answer was as reported by Romilly and he ended by trusting 'therefore that the choice will be as satisfactory to the nation as I am sure it will be conducive to the happiness of the Prince of Wales' (Hansard, *Paliamentary Debates* , Third Series, 169 (1863), 790.

10   J.B. Mayor in *Considerations upon the Poll Course* (1862) and W.H. Girdlestone in *The Poll Course considered from another Point of View* (1862) proposed a matriculation examination which would exclude the least able men and more examinations to make those in residence work harder. Stephen's revolutionary counter-proposals argue that even a dull young man 'may gain a great deal . . . by constant intercourse with most high-spirited and ablest young men of his own age', and that instead of continuing to acquire a smattering of Greek and Latin the University should provide courses of study for which there may be some desire on the part of the men themselves . . . I am not anxious to try simply to make Poll-men work . . . but I am anxious that we should indirectly appeal to the best class of them, by adding some better motive for work to the only one which can possible stimulate a Poll-man now – the ignoble fear of being plucked.' See L.Stephen, *The Poll Degree from a Third Point of View* (1863).

11   Mr David Scrase tells us that the marble was by J.H. Foley R.A. who sculpted the Prince's seated figure in the Albert Memorial. In 1878 it was at length unveiled by the Prince of Wales in the foyer of the Fitzwilliam Museum and in 1956 moved from there to the grounds of Madingley Hall – a disgraceful removal when one remembers the debt owed to the Prince by the University.

*Fri. 6.* Sunny morning with brisk wind. – In many places there is 'feed the poor' chalked on the pavement: – I quite agree with the recommendation of that mode of keeping the 10th of March. – At Corpus they have a transparency with cyphers Æ & A as if the Princes name were Æneas[12] . . . Harriet went to a 3 penny reading in wch there was singing also.

*Tu. 10.* Fog before breakfast: – the Botanic Garden was shut (on account of Prince of Wales wedding day . . . The best decorations are in Fitzroy Street: a profusion of arches etc covered with festoons & ribbons . . . Sussex Street & Malcolm Street are also profusely adorned with festoons & Chinese lanterns. Went for a short time on Parkers Piece to see the review of the Riflemen. – At 7 sallied out to see the Illuminations (having also sent out the maids under male escort). I thought the effect of the Fitzwilliam (from the Gas) beautiful[13] . . . The lighting up of the Fountain in the Market-place was very pretty indeed: the transparencies at the Townhall produced little effect: – in Benet St. I saw a small transparency of 'the rising sun', – but I hope it will be a long time rising & that the Queen will shine for many a long year. – There was a brilliant effect from blue & red lights in the Senate-house Area, wch lighted up most gloriously Kings Chapel & St Marys & the Library & Senate House. – The greatest attraction was at Trinity, where the outlines of the Masters Court & of the East End of Chapel (showing the tracery of the window) was lighted with lamps: – there were 2 flaming torches atop of the Chapel: – Beamont fastened a huge red carpet (covered with pious texts) in front of the Masters Court: the piety was unquestionable, the taste doubtful: – it looked frightful by day & was scarcely visible at night. – I got home about 8½: I didnot go to Parkers Piece for the fireworks, but saw plenty of rockets in the air: – there was a great bonfire in the Market Place. – There was feeding the poor today[14] in the Corn

---

[12] The *Chronicle* and *Independent* reporters (14 March) thought Corpus Christi's display 'a very novel design' and 'superb'. The papers had also sent journalists to London. The *Chronicle* (14 March) reports that 'Like Caesar' Princess Alexandra 'may exclaim "veni, vidi, vici!" Yes, her youth, her beauty, her gentleness, love and amiability were stamped upon her brow – a brow worthy of England's diadem and she conquered all who saw her; all hearts were in her favor . . . The Prince's choice has found universal favor . . . Her Majesty says that no one can help loving her . . . '.

[13] The *Chronicle* of 14 March devoted two columns to 'The Illuminations'. The Fitzwilliam was lit by a 'row of Jets, the whole length of the building, and a gas Torche on each of the stone blocks' and its reporter, unlike Romilly, thought that the seven transparencies on the Guildhall 'reflected great credit on the town'. The lamps in Trinity were said to number 2,880 and on Market Hill 'the glorious bonfire . . . attracted large crowds round it', while that on Castle Hill 'might well be seen a great many miles distant'. For the Master's (Whewell's) Court see 7 May 1859. Beamont's pious decoration 'neatly framed in evergreens and painted white', read 'God bless the Prince and Princess of Wales. Give the king Thy judgements, O Lord, and Thy righteousness to the King's Son. He shall judge Thy people with righteousness and Thy poor with judgement. Blessed be the Lord God, who only doeth wondrous things.' The *Chronicle* ended by congratulating the crowds on their conduct: 'Everybody seemed ready to oblige everybody else, and there were few who had allowed their animal nature . . . to deprive them of their senses.'

[14] See the *Independent* of 14 March for the parish dinners of roast beef, mutton, pork, and plum puddings or the sums of money for those who were not fed. St Giles's parish, for example, feasted 1,083 adults and 770 children and 'with ten gallons of pickles . . . and plenty of good beer a capital repast was provided'.

Exchange, Industrial school etc etc: those who were not fed received 1/6 for adults & /9 for children. – All the proceedings of the day highly successful.

*Fri. 13.* Walk about the Town. – having received a Card from the new 'Roman Bath' in Jesus Lane I went over the establishment.[15] I was made to take off my boots & wear slippers: I saw the great swimming bath, & went into one room heated up to 84 escorted by 2 men almost naked: they offered to take me into another room at the heat of 140: but this I declined: – these men were shampooers. I thought every thing got up in excellent stile, & was pleased with the architecture inside & out . . .

*Sun. 15.* . . . Went to St Mary's to hear Dean Goodwin preach on the miracle of feeding . . . The end was in behalf of the Old Schools (wch are burdened with a debt of £120):[16] Goodwin was sanguine enough to hope the collection would clear it away: it only half did so, & that was an uncommon success. – . . . Short walk with Woollaston who was one of the plate-holders. – Woollaston told me that F.A. Paley (now a Roman Catholic) rescued a young lady from her house wch was on fire, & 6 weeks after married her:[17] he lives in Cambridge & is very successful as a crammer for the Classical Tripos . . .

*Mon. 23.* . . . Seniority: – a youngster named Bateman (– a very goodlooking gentlemanlike young man) was had up for having disturbed the Congregation at the R.C. Chapel:[18] a letter of the Priest Mr Quinlivan was

[15] On 15 September 1860 the *Chronicle* described Turkish baths as 'springing up in most of the large towns in the Kingdom' and asked 'Where is the enterprising individual who will establish a Turkish bath in Cambridge?'. On 21 March 1863 the *Independent* declared the Roman baths 'in full operation' and benefiting many cases of sciatica and rheumatism. The poor on a doctor's recommendation were admitted at half price until noon each day. However, the baths, in the former coachyard of the Hoop Hotel, became unprofitable and in December 1863 the premises were let to the Pitt Club. See F.A. Reeve, *The Cambridge Nobody Knows* (1977), pp. 15-16.

[16] The 'Old Schools' founded in 1704 as the result of S.P.C.K. propaganda did more for popular education in Cambridge than any other organisation. Until the early nineteenth century when the Old Schools trust began to support Church of England schools they consisted of free dame schools. The 1863 report listed 11 schools teaching an average of 1,252 children, the whole cost of which had to be met from subscriptions, collections and fees. They had to wait ten more years for an inadequate government grant. See *Guide to Education Records in the County Record Office Cambridge* compiled by Angela Black (1972), 'The Old Schools of Cambridge' pp. 15-16.

[17] F.A. Paley remained in Cambridge as a private tutor from 1860 to 1874 when he became Professor of Classical Literature at the Catholic University of Kensington. In 1854 he married Ruth Burchell of Bramley, Surrey.

[18] On 3 May a more serious disturbance took place, surprisingly unrecorded by Romilly. The *Times* of 7 May reported that despite Mr Quinlivan's remonstrations undergraduates had behaved so outrageously on the previous Sunday that their ringleaders were taken into custody by the police and two Pembroke undergraduates were sentenced to prison for seven days without hard labour. 'On their exit from the Town-hall they were greeted with a sympathetic cheer from their brother undergraduates, but at the entrance to the gaol a different reception awaited them. The mob there also cheered lustily, but it was because they saw two gownsmen going to prison.' Yet in a letter to *The Times* on 11 May the tutor of Pembroke was convinced that the undergraduates concerned 'were not guilty of any misconduct in chapel . . . and that their offence consisted in joining in an attempt, after the service, to rescue another undergraduate from the custody of the police'.

read: on Sunday Ev. the 8th of March some ill conducted University youth came into the Chapel smoking & talking: the Evidence against Bateman rather broke down: he confessed to having gone out & come back: he said that he disliked something in the Priest's sermon & said to another young man 'let us go out & come back for the incense". – it is notorious that many unfortunate women hover about the place: – the doorkeeper said that on a former occasion (a year and ½ ago) Bateman had threatened to punch his head: – Bateman denied having been one of the smokers: – he was admonished 1st time previous to expulsion . . .

*Th. 26.* . . . Letter from Elisabeth Stalleybrass acknowledging my present, but begging for Shoes & London Porter: scolded her & sent 10/: she enjoyed the festivities at Royston 10th March & especially an excellent dinner to 1580 where there was coffee for the teetotallers . . . The Classical Tripos was out today: Kings has the 1st Classic (Wilson the Craven Scholar /61), Trinity the 2d (Arth. Sidgwick (Porson & Craven Scholar): – Kings has 4 in the 1st 6 & Trinity 2: – 3 cheers were given for Eton[19] . . .

*Sun. 29.* . . . Letter from Mr Girdlestone saying that Frank's diligence had fallen off greatly, wch he ascribes partly to a cold: his College Examination is allowed as ægrotat:[20] Mr G. says that Frank has yet a great deal to do before he will be fit for the Degree Examination . . .

*Sat. 11 April.* Walk in Peterhouse . . . Saw at the Press the magnificent copies of the Bible & Prayer Book to be presented to the Prince as a marriage gift: they are superbly bound with silver corner-pieces & are adorned with Bristol Stones[21] of large size. – Mr Temple the Surgeon took me in to the shop of Neck the Tailor who uses a sowing machine:[22] he very obligingly exhibited & explained its working . . . Went into St Mary's to see the progress of the destruction of the Doctors Gallery:[23]– Sedgwick said (when it was resolved on) he hoped to be present at the last crash, & if a Rope was used to help pull it . . .

[19] 'Apart from an eclipse in the 1820's' Kingsmen had 'distinguished themselves in the prestigious competitions for the University Scholarships in Classics'. But under the statutes of Henry VI all scholars of King's came from the sister college of Eton and until 1854 no one could take the Classical Tripos who had not passed the Mathematical Tripos and mathematics were virtually non-existent at Eton. Now however that Kingsmen could take the Classical Tripos cheers were given for the teaching of classics at Eton. See L.P. Wilkinson, *A Century at King's, 1873-1972* (1980), pp.1-5 and 3 May 1851.

[20] See 13 January 1856.

[21] i.e. a kind of transparent rock crystal found in the Clifton limestone near Bristol which resembles diamonds in brilliancy.

[22] Although many inventors worked on its development from the 1750s onwards, it was not until 1850 that Isaac Merritt Singer perfected the first practical sewing machine in America.

[23] 'Above the entrance to the chancel was another gallery for the heads of houses, doctors, professors and noblemen. It was commonly called the throne and was first opened in 1754 . . . Another gallery for the undergraduates and bachelors of arts, was built by the university at the western end of the church in 1819 . . . ' A faculty having been approved in May 1862 'this gallery, the enclosed seats under it, and the throne were happily removed in 1863'. See C.H. Cooper, *Memorials of Cambridge* III, (1866) 306-7 and on page 315 an engraving of the 'throne'.

*Fri. 17.* . . . A very agreeable letter from Mrs Kennedy . . . She is tired of the preaching against Colenso: she says controversies are the order of the day: one only escapes Colenso to fall into the similitude (or dissimilitude) of man & apes – hateful doctrine . . . College-meeting: – Roundell Palmer has given his opinion in our case concerning Preoption to Livings: – I skimmed over it and thought it seemed much in favor of Luard . . .

*Mon. 20.* . . . Seniority to try a Mr Dixon for firing a pistol down the bowling green from the room of a Mr Jenkins: both the youngsters are freshmen: Dixon fired at a bird on a tree: the ball glanced, broke a window in the Masters Greenhouse & passed close to the head of the gardener . . . they were both reprimanded & Jenkins was deprived of his College rooms . . .

*Wed. 6 May.* . . . Letter from Sophie Kennedy: – Franks majority is to be celebrated at Dalquharran by a grand dinner of tenants & friends in the School-room: 90 asked & 80 accepted: & all the labourers & colliers & numerous *ladies* are to have a ball & supper . . .

*Fri. 8.* . . . To the Family at 8½: the Host was Joseph Power: the room was insufferably hot, but fortunately we played our Whist without any music. – The newly elected Physician at the Hospital (Dr Latham) was of this party . . .

*Th. 14.* . . . To Town by Express (2d Class). Read Thackerays 'Humourists'.[24] – Received Dividends . . . Bought stockings for myself & maids: 12 Pair for self cost 48/s: 12 for maids cost 33/s . . . I went to the Royal Academy Exhibition. The Picture which seemed to excite most attention was a Picture (by Phillips) called 'the House of Commons': it gave Portraits of the Speaker & several members.[25] – There are 3 pictures by Millais: one is called 'My 1st Sermon': it represents a little girl sitting demurely in a Pew with her prayer-book near her: she is the only figure in the picture: there is nothing at all striking: the child exhibits neither attention or drowsiness. The 2d is called 'the Eve of St Agnes'. I thought it utterly detestable: the subject is taken from some lines of Keats . . .

*Wed. 20.* Walk about Town. – Letter from Kennedy (inclosing 2 letters of Girdeston's [sic] & wishing me to see both Girdleston & Frank . . . Called on Frank Kennedy at 11: the lie-a-bed was not up! – wrote him a note. – His landlady Mrs Bays begged an interview with me:[26] she grieved me much by saying that Frank has struck up an intimacy with Miss Pratt daughter of the

---

[24] i.e. *The English Humorists of the Eighteenth Century: a series of lectures* . . . (1853).

[25] 'The House of Commons 1860' by John Phillip, R.A., three of whose pictures are in the Tate Gallery. Millais, no longer a prominent pre-Raphaelite, was now painting with much greater breadth and freedom; readers of the diary would be astonished if Romilly *had* enjoyed a 'misty' picture inspired by Keats's great romantic poem. The wonder is that he had become a fervent admirer of J.M.W. Turner.

[26] It is interesting that Mrs Bays and Mrs Morls (26 September) should have taken the initiative in approaching Romilly and Mrs Hammond. If they wanted to retain their licences as lodging-house keepers it was important that they should be aware of the behaviour of their young lodgers, and if necessary be able to answer questions put to them by parents and senior members of the university. Their information network was clearly detailed and far-reaching and must have added considerable interest and enjoyment to their lives, as perhaps did the warfare waged between landlords of some inns and the lodging-house keepers. See Searby pp. 128-9.

landlord of the Blue Boar, that she believes he passes his Evenings there & that he never comes home before 11½ or 12: Mrs Bays says that he has lately received a ring from London, wch she suspects is intended for Miss P. – I called at the Blue Boar & begged to speak with Mrs Pratt: she showed me into a room where her daughter was at the Piano: – she left the room when I said I wished for some confidential conversation. – She admitted that Frank was a great deal in the house, that he plaid billiards there, & often had dinner: I told her that I heard her daughter kept company with Frank: she admitted that they might perhaps have walked together but utterly denied his ever having taken her a drive, & said she knew nothing of his ever having made her any present. I earnestly intreated her to break off the intimacy, that it could not end in marriage, but might end in shame & sin. – I then called on Mr Girdlestone. – He showed me one of Frank's papers in the Acts: the 1st half was pretty good: the last abounding in mistakes: Frank only attempted the *translation*. – Mr G. said all his other papers were equally faulty: he obviously thinks that Frank can't pass now. – I asked if he would take him as a pupil in the long Vacation as I thought his chance in November desperate if left to himself during the holidays: he will be willing to do so at his living in the Isle of Wight. – Wrote to Kennedy. Seniority at 1 . . . After the Seniority I had an interview with Frank (whom I found at my house): he read me 2 letters of his Father & Mother & showed me a pretty green enamel ring wch his M. gave him on his birthday. – I got him to construe the 17th of Acts, & thought his performance very indifferent: urged him to construe one or two chapters every day. – I then spoke to him about the degree Examination, saying that as his Father & himself had a great horror of failure it would be wise to defer the Examination till November & to go to Mr G's during the long Vacation & read hard during the summer: he agreed to all this. – I then talked to him very seriously about Miss Pratt, saying the connexion must be broken at once & for ever. – Afterwards walk in Garden. Received a Card for Stowells Lecture on 'Sound Churchmanship' at Town Hall: didn't go.

*Th. 21.* . . . Harriet took Lizzie Mills home today: she came 12th March & is very loathe to go away now tho fond of her Father & of her brother Harry . . .

*Fri. 22.* Letter from Kennedy: he is anxious to know whether the sons of Lord Fitzwilliam & Carington are safe companions for Frank: – wrote to Mathison to ask if they were well-conducted or fast men & took my letter to College . . . Mathison wrote me word that I need not fear to let my cousin be with Carington & Fitzwilliam:[27] they are (he says) generally very idle, but are very nice gentlemanly fellows & bear a good character – Wrote to Kennedy . . .

*Sat. 23.* Walk in Botanic Garden. – Went to the 'Christy Minstrels' in the Townhall at 2, & also sent the maids. Sat next to Mrs Peacock & 2 nice lads (sons of Mr Henderson) whom she brought with her from Ely: – I was much

---

[27] The Hon. W.H.W. Fitzwilliam, second son of the sixth earl, found time for sufficient work to take his B.A. five years after admission to Trinity. The Hon. C.R.W. Carington was admitted at Trinity in 1861 and took his B.A. in 1864.

pleased with the performance wch was not too long for it ended about 4. The proprietor is Collins:[28] he sung 'the pretty Gal in blue' & 'riding in a railway car' with much liveliness: the favorite singer (Wambold) is a Tenor: he sung 'blue-eyed Nelly' & 'Annie Lisle' with great sweetness & tenderness. – There was a burlesque of Swiss singing & of the Italian opera which I thought very rich. – Four, including Wambold (with turn-down collars & drest in black) excited great laughter by enacting 'We're a Band of Brothers', they were the quintessence of dismalness & kept making ridiculous curtsies as they repeated 'We're a band of brothers'. The energy with wch 2 instrumentalists plaid the tamburine & castanets I thought wonderful. – Howard danced a jig with great activity to the delight of the Spectators. There was also a very clever performance on a 'tin whistle'. – In the Evening was the procession of boats: I did not go, but I sent Harriet & Caroline.

*Tu. 26.* . . . The great confederate General (Stonewall Jackson) is dead: he was wounded in the shoulder, underwent amputation & died. – his death was from a blunder: he was shot by his own men. – Walk by Via Lambertina, as I was sitting at the foot of a Telegraph Post Dr & Mrs Archdall passed in their carriage: they picked me up & brought me home.

*Fri. 29.* . . . Mary Edwards (late maid of my landlady Mrs Bridges) has come to my house till she gets a new place: – sent her & Harriet & one of her sisters to a 2penny reading at night: the 'turned Head'[29] was read with much applause . . . Letters from Madame & Sophie: they give a very mournful account of my poor brother . . . the Dr says it is a progressing paralysis & that the organs will become weaker & weaker: they have a sort of bed (wch Sophie calls mechanical) in wch my poor brother can be turned & attended to without pain . . .

*Mon. 1 June.* Walk in Botanic Garden. – Letter from Grim: he is disgusted at the living of Narberth (after 14 months agitation) not having been given to him, but bestowed on a young Curate about 2 years in orders (a harmless quiet man (he thinks), slightly Puseyite in a hotbed of rabid dissent: Grim says that the man's case is that a cousin or uncle did a good deal of dirty work for the unsuccessful liberal candidate at the last County Election: Grim says that his own misfortune is that his friends are honorable men who give their votes according to their conviction (& don't sell them) & so get nothing. He says it is a dreary look-out for a man with a wife & 9 small children, wch used to be an indefeasible claim to a beadelship . . .

*Tu. 2.* Walk in Botanic Garden. – Trinity Examination began this morning. – Having seen in the 'Academy Exhibition' a group of 'Young Romilly' & his greyhound by A. Munro I read thro 'the White Doe of Rylston': the tale is not there; but it is alluded to . . . The tale is told in 'the Force of Prayer, or the founding of Bolton Priory'[30] . . . Read Wordsworth's

---

[28] Probably Samuel Thomas Collins, a well known comic singer in the chief music halls of London and the provinces. He was proprietor of Collins Music Hall from 1862 until his death aged 39 in 1865.

[29] i.e. *The Turned Head : a farce in one act* by Gilbert Abbott à Beckett (1811-1856).

[30] Romilly could scarcely have hoped to find any connexion between his own family and the young man in the poems Wordsworth wrote in 1807 after a visit to Bolton Priory in

Ode on 'Intimations of immortality from recollections of early childhood': I believe his admirers think it his masterpiece: I tried in vain to like it: I found most of it unintelligible . . .

*Mon. 15.* . . . Going out of my own house I fell in with Dr and Mrs Clark & accompanied them to the Anatomical Museum, where John Clark exhibited the Gorilla skeleton wch he has just bought for his father: it cost £32, & (being a very fine specimen) is reckoned cheap. John Clark is an invaluable assistant to his Father & the Museum is in beautiful order . . .

*Tu. 16.* . . . Theodosia called in the Evening to ask me to write a character of her (– she was my servant for 12 years:) her brute of a husband[31] (Johnson a tailor) beats her & behaves in the most reprobate way: she is afraid of her life & is going to swear the peace against him tomorrow: – I gave her 20/ & wrote her a flaming character.

*Wed. 17.* . . . At the Townhall today that beast H. Johnson was bound over to keep the peace towards his wife for 3 months: – what a pity the wretch does not enlist & rid the place of his bad company!

*Th. 18.* . . . Letter from Burn (Head Lecturer) giving me the statistics of Henry's place in the Classes: he is alas! only in the 3d Class (of wch however he is Captain): I am immensely mortified as I had never doubted his being in the 1st. – These are the particulars. –

{ Full marks 3100: highest obtained 1999
{ Marks of H.R. 911

| | | |
|---|---|---|
| Euclid | 121 out of | 500 |
| Algebra | 100 | 600 |
| Trig. | 22 | 350 |
| Sophocles | 329 | 550 |
| Demosth | 97 | 550 |
| Tacitus | 242 | 550 |
| | 911 | 3100 |

Henry's precise place was 35th for the 1st Class was 26 & the 2d 8: – 135 were examined . . .

*Fri. 19.* . . . Letter from George Allen offering to come tomorrow for 2 nights . . . Frank Kennedy called to bid me goodbye: he will go to Mr Girdlestones at Ryde in the 1st week of July: walked with the youth for ½ hour till he went home to pack up. After dinner read Oliver Twist.

*Sun. 21.* . . . George & I went to Christ Church: poor George had an indigestion & went & sat in the free seats near the door . . . Mr Weldon

Yorkshire. *The Force of Prayer* tells of the founding of the Priory in 1151 by the distraught widowed mother of young Romilly, drowned in the Wharfe whilst attempting to leap from one side to the other. His greyhound on a leash checked his jump. *The White Doe* recounts the legend of the gentle animal which each Sunday crossed the fells from Rylstone to listen to the service from Bolton Abbey churchyard. Alexander Munro occasionally executed subject groups.

[31] On 23 February 1858, newly married, 'she was as happy as a Queen and speaks in great praise of her little husband the tailor'. They lived at 8 Sussex Street.

preached ably from 1 Timothy IV. 8 'do all to the glory of God':[32]– he spoke of the great good that had been done to his flock by what seemed a very weak instrument: he meant Miss Hopkins,[33] but I thought the epithet *weak* savoured a little of masculine pride . . .

*Tu. 23.* . . . Betsy's letter was very characteristic: she says if she had been in Dosia's place without children she would have boxed her husbands ears & gone into service, but (she adds) Dosia never had the spine of a mouse . . .

*Fri. 26.* . . . A very sad letter from Sophie Oger saying she thought her Father would not live thro the night: wrote to her. – A brilliant letter from Mrs Guthrie, who is vastly happy at the prospect of Sedgwick coming to see her: she talks of the great good wch her husband (or as she always calls him 'the Canon') does . . . Wrote her a short & melancholy letter, being out of spirits. Mrs Fuller (Harriet Gillson) called yesterday & brought her baby, a pretty black-eyed maid christened Helen Ann.

*Sat. 27.* . . . Letter from Jacques to say that his poor Father died last Thursday night . . . I am now alas! the sole survivor of my Fathers 9 children. Frank was born 28th August 1793, & so had nearly reached the age of 70. – I wrote to Madame, sending her £20 for mourning, & saying that as long as I lived I should continue the monthly & the quarterly remittances. – Took a stroll in the garden. After dinner read 'The Bible & Modern Thought'.[34]

*Mon. 29.* . . . After my dinner Professor Selwyn & dear Dudu called: I was very glad to receive them: – Selwyn walks more lamely than myself: the young lady is getting into the debatable land of incipient womanhood: she looked very pretty . . .

On 1 July Romilly and the maids again left Cambridge for Yarmouth and Mrs Wright's lodgings. The holiday was however less enjoyable than that of the previous year as Romilly was saddened by the death of his younger brother Frank – 'Letters from Paris . . . they were all tender affectionate letters: they sent me a lock of my poor brother's hair: I was surprised at its not being grey' – and a sprained ancle meant that 'I can't as yet venture as far as Gorlston or even as Nelson's Column: I content myself with crawling to the Pier or Jetty & read there'. The Harvey Goodwins were unfortunately only in Yarmouth for about half the holiday and his other Cambridge friends very briefly, so the diaries record the conversation of Yarmouth acquaintances,

[32] 'For bodily exercise profiteth little: but godliness is profitable unto all things, having promise of the life that now is, and of that which is to come' (I Timothy, 4. 8).

[33] Miss Ellis Hopkins was a very able and courageous lady and an excellent example of the major part played by middle and upper class women in the social movements of the fifties and sixties after a century in which their horizons had narrowed. See J. Roach, *Social Reform in England 1780-1880* (1978), pp. 156-7, and 28 December 1863 and 8 April 1864. The *Independent* of 8 June 1863 wrote that 'for two or three years past a young lady [unnamed] . . . has delivered sermons, Sunday after Sunday, to the labourers employed at coprolite digging, and has produced upon them a moral and lasting effect, resulting in the reformation of the drunkard, and endearing some to their homes (whose habitations were once pictures of human depravity) . . . '.

[34] T.R. Birks's *The Bible and Modern Thought* (1861) was a refutation of *Essays and Reviews*. Fellow of Trinity, he succeeded F.D. Maurice as Professor of Moral Philosophy, to the dismay of Maurice's liberal followers.

the sermons he hears and the news contained in frequent letters from his family. Between 14 and 17 July there was however a great excitement: 'The Channel fleet is come into these roads: it is going northward round Scotland: there are 3 wooden ships (including the Flag-ship (the *Edgar*), & 5 iron-clads "the Warrior", the "Black Prince", the "Defence", the "Royal Oak" & Resistance. The Warrior & Black Prince are the largest iron-clads existing.' Romilly of course with his delight in ships and the sea took a shilling trip to the *Edgar* as soon as he could after the fleet's arrival and the next day, despite the sea being too rough for bathing, 'got into a steamer & went all round the fleet'. The *Edgar* was a '91-gun ship: she carries one magnificent Armstrong gun wch throws a ball (so shaped [drawing follows]) of a cwt. – The complement of men is 800: we heard the most interesting of daily sounds, the piping to dinner'. On the seventeenth Romilly was escorted all over the *Warrior* by the brother-in-law of Frances Wilderspin, one of the family's early protégées. Harriet had asked Mr Roper to take care of him and 'he gave me his arm & conducted me with the greatest skill & gentleness. He took me all over the Warrior & showed me everything: he was quite the making of me: "The Warrior" is 425 feet long & has a complement of 700 men'.

A comparatively minor event took place in the evening of 3 August when Romilly went 'to the Britannia Pier to see swimming: the Performers were Professor Woodbridge (who calls himself the champion scientific swimmer), J.P. Jones (the fastest swimmer in the world), the *renowned* Beckwith Family (Miss Jessy aged 9, Master Fred aged 7 & Master William aged 5 (the wonder of the world)'. He watched 'the exploits of the 2 men with great admiration' but went away after the children were put into the boat as he disapproved of young children being exhibited.

Romilly took his 31st bathe on 11 August and the following day 'after a last look at the sea' he and Harriet caught the 9.25 for Cambridge where he 'thought the house & garden looked beautiful'.

*Fri. 14 August.* . . . Sedgwick drank tea with me & gave me a most interesting & mournful detail of poor Dick's malady & his being placed under Dr Wood (at Kensington): Dick communicated his imaginary grievances (about a conspiracy against him, about the murder of a baby of Mary's – when she had not been confined) to Mr Powell (Member for Cambridge) who had been his schoolfellow[35] & to whom he was warmly attached: Mr Powell assisted Sedgwick in the arrangements by wch he was at last put in restraint . . .

*30. 8.* . . . At Christ Church . . . I staid the Sacrament & was glad to see among the communicants a black: he was the more conspicuous from wearing a white jacket: I heard afterwards that he is an open air preacher . . .

*Th. 3 September.* . . . Letter from Grim . . . Grim & his brother went to the British Association at Newcastle but George bolted before the end: Grim says there was a rich scene one day: – a lecturer descanted on the subject of 'the Blacks',[36] declaring that they were of a lower type than the whites. Up got a great he black who answered him triumphantly & was highly applauded . . .

[35] See also 15 and 19 April 1864. Richard and F.S. Powell had both been at Sedbergh.

[36] The lecturer in the Geography and Ethnology Section on 28 August was J.Craufurd F.R.S. 'Mr Craft (a gentleman of colour) who was loudly cheered on rising, defended the African race. In spite of the laws of the Southern States prohibiting intermarriage between the negro and the white there was a large population in the States claiming affinity with both races . . . Whenever the African race had had equal opportunities with the whites, they had shown that

*Sat. 19.* Walk about town – Letters from Sophie & Kennedy. – Sophie tells me that Mr Girdlestone reports very favorably of Frank & thinks him fit to pass the Examination. – Frank however has wisely confessed to his Parents his entanglement with Miss Pratt & has written to her to break it off. – It is therefore resolved that Frank shall not return to Cambr. this October; – his uncle Henry & Aunt Rosa have taken him abroad with them. – Whether Miss Pratt will submit quietly to this dismissal remains to be seen: – her sisters are successful in winning the hearts of gownsmen: one is already married to Mr Gamble (Trinity) A M 1860 & another is engaged to Geo Hammond (Trin) (a freshman last October). I fear that Frank may have promised marriage, but I should think him too lazy to have written any love letters wch could be made the foundation of an action for breach of a promise of marriage. Frank hopes to come up some future time: – this I think a mere delusion, for he will never have energy enough to get up another set of classical subjects. Wrote to Sophie, dissuading Frank's *ever* coming back to Cambridge. Kennedy's letter was of course on the same painful matter: – he has a firm belief that nothing criminal has taken place between Frank & Miss P. – Kennedy begs me to communicate with Mathison, so I wrote to him & also to Mrs Bays, desiring her to let her lodgings. – Sophie's maternal fondness makes her write 'there is no discredit to Frank in the affair: on the contrary there is a great deal that does the utmost honor to his heart & to his principles . . . in fact nothing has saved Frank but his intense love for his Father & Mother & his sense of filial duty'. Walk in Botanic Garden. – in the Evening read 'Vanity Fair'. Ancle so much better, that Harriet rubbed it today for the last time.

*Mon. 21.* . . . Entered names of 3 Candidates for Voluntary Theology at the Pitt Press. – Called (at her request) on Mrs Bays: she has received a letter from Mrs Kennedy about Franks things: I spelt out the letter for her: she told me that 3 weeks ago she saw Frank in Cambridge walking with Miss Pratt . . . In the afternoon a letter from Kennedy: he & Sophie are far from well, wch is quite natural:[37] it appears that Frank had told him of his trip to Cambridge: it does not seem to agree with his declaration of having broken off with her. – Kennedy is anxious to know about Mr Hammonds proceedings, whether he has broken up the connexion & forbidden his son to return to College. – Wrote a long letter to Kennedy asking what things should be sent, & suggesting that the glass & crockery should (as usual) be given to Mrs Bays . . .

*Sat. 26.* . . . Called on Mrs Bays . . . Called also at Mrs Morls (next door to Mrs Bays): I learned that Geo. Hammond (who is engaged to one of the Miss Pratts) & his twin brother do not return to her lodgings: they are however coming back this October & will lodge at Stearn's in Bridge St.[38] – Mrs Morl

---

they possessed considerable intellectual ability and many of them had risen to very high position in society.' *The Times* 29 August 1863.

[37] Sophie and Thomas Kennedy had been childless for twenty-two years before the birth of Frank and the fact that Kennedy was now seventy-five and Sophie sixty-three may have contributed to their feeling 'far from well'.

[38] There is no record in Venn of G.H. Hammond's graduation or marriage. His twin brother did however graduate in 1866. How-house, later Howe-house, was an ancient farmstead with land

told me that the Miss Pratts are fine riders: that their father has a farm at How-house, & that young men used to go over there to drink tea with the Miss Pratts. Mrs Morl declares that she warned Mrs Hammond against her son's goings-on. Mr Hammond lives at 47 Rutland Gate Hyde Park. Clark (the Orator) is the young man's Tutor. – Called on Bulstode (Upholsterer) & requested him to take back a certain writing table (or Oxford desk) wch he furnished 3 years ago. – Picked up by Mrs Clark who drove me down Nightingale Lane & thro Granchester & Trumpington: we were caught in a very heavy shower, but she wrapt me up snug in a great plaid & I didn't get wet. – She sent me some stewing pears. – After dinner wrote to Kennedy.

*Fri. 2 October.* Walk about town – College meeting at 11: bursarial business . . . Wrote to Kennedy telling him that . . . Blore (G. Hammond's tutor) wrote to Mr Hammond *before Easter* telling of his son's acquaintance with Miss Pratt but that Mr Hammond sent his son back to Cambridge for the Easter Term on the son's promise that he would break off entirely with Miss P.: Mr Hammond Père seems to me to have acted like an idiot.

*Fri. 9.* . . . Received from M.A. Tyler as a birthday present a beautiful novel kind of anti-maccassar of her own knitting: it is red on a black ground. She wrote also a very pious letter wch pleased me greatly: she writes, 'I hope you feel better & stronger this birthday than the last, & if it pleases God that you may have many more birthdays; & as each year brings you nearer to a state when we shall have no more change of seasons, I trust you will every year enjoy a brighter foretaste of that happiness wch will be eternal.' – Wrote to M.A. Tyler & gave her a Sovereign . . .

*Fri. 16.* Walk on Hills Road . . . Received from J.B. Mayor his new pamphlet called 'further considerations on the Poll Examination': he attacks (I think successfully) Stephen for saying that idleness is inherent in men, that the idea of Poll-men reading 5 hours a day is mere nonsense, that it is absurd pelting them with examinations, & that Parents do not expect any intellectual training (but only a moral one) for their dull sons . . .

*Mon. 19.* Walk about Town – Heard from Prof. Babington a good story about the British Association this year: they went to Durham (being taken by Sir W. Armstrong who provided omnibusses) to hear the service: one of the Canons mounted the pulpit, but to the surprise of everybody very soon came down again with his sermon in his hand: he was directly replaced by another canon who not only brought a sermon but preached it: – the 1st Canon's sermon was a furious attack on the Essays & Reviews, but seeing Jowett among the crowd he was struck with a consternation & made a precipitate retreat![39] . . . After breakfast I went with Sedgwick into the Old Botanic Garden to see the progress of the New Museums . . .

*Fri. 6 November.* Bright sunny morning: walk about town. Seniority at 12½ . . . Then went to Sedgwicks & had a basin of broth: he has just had

in Impington and Chesterton. It was off the Huntingdon Road near the site of the present Country Centre and Howes Close presumably takes its name from the farm.

[39] .For Jowett's contribution to *Essays and Reviews* see 16 March 1861.

the Copley Medal assigned him:[40] this is a glorious triumph, as it is the highest scientific honor in the land: – it is a great delight to myself & all other admirers of the dear Professor . . .

*Th. 12.* . . . Letter from Mrs Kennedy: she is very happy about Frank: he has had a charming tour in the Pyrenees, to Toulouse, to Montpelier, Avignon, Nimes etc . . . this tour was with his uncle Henry & his aunt Rosa.[41] – They are now returned to England, but Frank is left at Geneva with a Clergyman . . . no one in the house can speak a word of English, so Frank must of necessity learn to speak French . . . Sophie is anxious for him to go into plenty of society, balls & parties: she says '2 or 3 flirtations wouldnt be amiss, – when he once learns what women are & that he has worth in the eyes of more than one, his love for Miss P. will die out: – in the meantime I fear she has no intention of letting go her hold & that she will persecute him as much as she can' . . . The Classes Frank has chosen at Geneva are Natural Philosophy, Chemistry, & French Literature & History: – too much by far in my opinion . . . Leapingwell is very ill: he has an abscess in the Liver.

*Fri. 13.* . . . Read Wilhelm Meister: the only character I take any interest [in] is Mignon.[42] – Called at Mrs Morls to ask about the goings on of the Miss Pratts: she believes that the Hammonds are very much there & play a great deal of billiards at the Blue Boar. – Happened to meet Mr Girdlestone: he believes that Miss P. is doing all she can to procure Frank's Address: if she don't learn it from Frank himself she will never know it . . .

*Sat. 21.* . . . Shilleto has printed a letter (in the Cambridge Chronicle) against Macleods arrogant & conceited 'Thoughts on the approaching Election of a Professor of Political Economy'[43] – Shilleto hopes that he will get *no* vote but his own. Grote also has printed a letter attacking another which had said that Mayor had been brought forward to facilitate his marriage with the niece of a Professor & Incumbent of a neighbouring village:[44] Grote is justly indignant that his supposed family arrangements should be thus discussed. The

---

40 Sir Godfrey Copley (d.1709), M.P., F.R.S., bequeathed one hundred pounds to the Royal Society 'for improving natural knowledge, to be laid out in experiments or otherwise for the benefit thereof as they shall direct or appoint'. In 1736 the Society converted the bequest into a gold medal to be awarded annually. The medal was awarded for Sedgwick's 'observations and discoveries in the Geology of the Palaeozoic Series of Rocks, and more especially for his determination of the Devonian System'. See Clark and Hughes, II, 395-8.

41 i.e. the diarist's cousin, admitted pensioner at Christ's 1824, merchant of Liverpool and Manchester, writer on secret ballots and on the death penalty, and Rosa his wife (née Morris).

42 Goethe's *Wilhelm Meisters Lehrjahre* (1795-6) had an immense influence on romantic fiction. Mignon, bought as a child by Wilhelm from acrobats who maltreat her, is the most ethereal of all Goethe's characters.

43 This was the first of three chairs for which H.D. Macleod was to be an unsuccessful candidate.

44 J.B. Mayor was not an economist and in 1870 became professor of classics at King's college, London. His wife, who knew Russian and Icelandic, was the daughter of John Grote, Vicar of Trumpington and Knightbridge Professor of Moral Philosophy, and niece of George Grote, author of the *History of Greece*. Romilly thought her 'charming'.

Cambr. Chr. of today contains also a scurrilous attack of Mr Fawcett & of Pryme:[45] the 4 following blackguard lines are revived

> Mr Counsellor Pryme
> Is a waster of time
> And the length of his prose
> Is the length of his nose

*Mon. 23.* . . . It is reported that Dr Corrie complained of the Duke of Devonshire giving the University a pothouse dinner at his Installation as Chancellor: he obviously thought that none but a Whig Nobleman could have done such a thing: – by the way the Pothouse was the Clarendon & the dinner one of the most costly ever set upon a table.) – It is highly amusing therefore & vastly pleasant to the said Dr Corrie to learn that one of his model Tory peers Lord Powis is going to give a pothouse-dinner tomorrow in honor of his Institution as High Steward, & at the very same pothouse (the Clarendon)! . . . Harriet & Hannah George went this Evening to a lecture of Dr Humphrys on the brain: Frances Wilderspin went also with her sister Mrs Roper.

*Th. 26.* . . . Felt very uncomfortable all day with shortness of breath & pain in the chest. – Chancery has annulled the Trinity interpretation about preoption to livings: Hammond & Burn were the agitators.

*Fri. 27.* Passed a very restless & distressing night. – Consulted Paget. – He says it is my old complaint, a feeble action of the heart: – he wrote me eatable & drinkable physic: recommended quiet & Claret. – Today was the Election of Political Economy Professor: the final numbers were Fawcett 90, Mayor 80, Courtney 19, Macleod 14. – Wrote to wish Fawcett joy – Fawcett makes the 2d instance of a blind Professor: Sanderson (Christs) Lucasian Prof. in 1711 was the 1st.

*Tu. 1 December.* . . . Visit from Paget: he found my pulse very low & has again recommended a glass of Claret. He advises raising my head in bed by a 3d pillow (– I already use 2), & recommended my getting a Cotton Wool coverlet to put over my feet at night . . .

*Wed. 2.* . . . Harriet took poor Frances to the Hospital, where we thought she would perhaps have her thumb lanced: – it was however found necessary to remove part of the nail etc . . . she did not faint but trembled greatly: one young surgeon held her shoulders & another her knees: Humphrey performed the operation . . . I am truly glad this very painful matter is over before her going to Mrs Collis. – Wrote to Mr Bateson (of 1 Maddox St.) about Coverlets: the price list arrived this Evening: the Cotton famine has raised the price: – what before cost 14 s now costs 26/8 . . .

---

[45] The tory *Chronicle* was doing its best to prevent the radical Fawcett's election to the chair of political economy. On 14 November it had printed a letter from Pryme refuting the allegation that political economy had a connection with party politics. The letter from 'A Conservative' quoting the verses, in vogue when Pryme was elected Professor of Political Economy (1828), maintained that his title helped his election as M.P. for Cambridge borough in 1832.

*Wed. 23.* Better night happily. – Very uncomfortable account of poor Leapingwell . . . Took 20 turns in the Garden. – A most agreeable letter from Mrs Kennedy: this being her 1st Christmas without Frank (ever since his birth) she says she shall miss him sadly: he is thoroughly well & writes long interesting letters. Sophie astonished me (as she had been herself) by saying that he has developped a poetical turn!!! . . .

*Fri. Christmas Day.* Thank God! I had a good night. Let Frances spend the day with the Ropers & sent them 2 bottles of Ale: Caroline dined at home to meet her married brother from Aldershott: – sent a bottle of Ale . . . I remained at home & read a Christmas sermon of Burders, & Bp Jackson's 'sins' of the Tongue.[46] Took 20 turns in the garden. Mr & Mrs Luard wanted to come & have a chat: Harriett wisely wouldn't let them.

*Mon. 28.* Went with Harriett & Frances (in the Omnibus) to the Station to see them start for London: – Harriett has kindly undertaken the charge of Frances, to deliver her at Mr Collis's on Wednesday (at Maidstone)[47] . . . Letter from the admirable Miss Hopkins, stating her scheme for a 'Barnwell's working-men's Hall:[48]– the men themselves have subscribed £40: her Father is to be President: Her Father, the V.C., Dr Humphry have each given £20 . . .

*Tu. 29.* Thank God! another good night. – Letter from G.T.R. (dated 27th) saying that Maggie was put to bed with a fine girl on the 26th . . . Wrote to George wishing him joy & enclosing the monthly draft for £10 on 1st January: I also sent £3 for the children . . . Mr Mayor & Miss Grote were married today at Trumpington: above 100 people at the breakfast: the poor (young & old) were feasted: – that is a good Christian wedding!

*Wed. 30.* Thank God! I slept well. – Nice letter of thanks from Miss Hopkins. – Poor Leapingwell buried today: – the riflemen met on Parkers Piece & accompanied the funeral procession to the Cemetery[49] . . .

---

[46] i.e. 'Sins of the Tongue': Sermon 5 in *The Sinfulness of Little Sins* (1849), p. 108 by John Jackson, later bishop of Lincoln and then London.

[47] Frances Wilderspin had stayed in Romilly's house since 25 August whilst waiting to begin work as nurse to Mrs Collis's new baby.

[48] Perhaps the Working Men's Club and Institute in Fitzroy Street.

[49] Despite Romilly's dislike for Leapingwell's unsparing criticism of almost all the people he knew *The Gentleman's Magazine* (1864.1 p. 264) pays tribute to his 'high social qualities . . . distinguished alike by dignity, amenity and courtesy'. See also the *Independent* for 26 December and the *Chronicle* for his unbounded charity and 'cheerful and kindly humour' (30 December).

# 1864

*Wed. 6 January.* . . . . Caroline went to the annual party given by Mr Haywards servants to their friends & to the trades-people: there was a good deal of singing, & the party was highly successful.

*Mon. 18.* . . . . To my great surprise Betsy made her appearance today: she was anxious to judge of my health from her own eyes. – She came in the Eastern style with gifts in her hand, – a chicken & some potatoes . . . she gave a very good account of Jem, who seems now to be a sober steady man & they live very happily together . . .

*Sat. 23.* . . . . The rumour is rife that the Bishopric of Ely has been offered to Prof. Browne & accepted: it was suggested to me that Lord Palmerston might mean this as a sort of compensation for the harsh & injudicious recall of Prof. Browne's brother from his Government of New Zealand.[1] – Gunson said to me that it could never have been expected that the Bishopric should have been offered to Professor Selwyn whose brother had twice put the ministry in a minority . . .

*Sun. 24.* Bright sunny morning: – happily I slept better. – Letter from Maggie: she has been churched & Alice christened (on 22 Jan): I suspect the clergyman is a Puseyite, for he flung 3 handsful of water over her: Alice seems not to have disapproved, for whenever she gets an opportunity she souses herself. – Frank is about to be confirmed (on 29th Jan.). Wrote to Maggie, recommending George to get for Frank 'Vaughan on Confirmation'[2] . . .

*Fri. 29.* Slept poorly . . . Hurrah for Trin! We have the 2 first Purkiss & Turnbull & 14 other Wranglers. – St Johns had only 4 Wranglers & their best was No 5. Visit from Selwyn: Dudu takes much to heart his not being made Bishop of Ely: she had quite counted on being confirmed by him & speaks very violently against Lord Palmerston . . .

*Mon. 15 February.* . . . . Harriet had a letter from Frances Wilderspin: she grumbles about old Mrs Collis coming & wakening up the baby . . . She is of a most restless & discontented mind, & (I fear) always will be so. – In one of my recent letters to Grim I had said that I thought his 'Good words for 1864' were very biting & severe; so he says in his last to me 'to our north-country folks there is no use in mincing matters except a little at Christmas' . . .

---

[1]  On 29 March 1864 E.H. Browne, fellow of Emmanuel, Norrisian Professor of Divinity and a moderating influence during the Colenso and *Essays and Reviews* controversies, was consecrated Bishop of Ely after the death of Thomas Turton. His brother, Thomas Gore Browne, had been succeeded as Governor of New Zealand by Sir George Grey in 1861 in the vain hope of containing further war with the Maoris over a land purchase. William Selwyn's brother, the Primate of New Zealand, was strongly opposed to the reckless procedures of the English land companies and C.J. Selwyn his youngest brother and Member for Cambridge University spoke critically and at great length on the subject (8 columns in Hansard) on 11 and 12 April 1861. See *Parliamentary Debates* Vol. CLXII 1861. Selwyn also secured the rejection in 1859 of the Endowed Schools Bill and the withdrawal of the Ecclesiastical Commission Bill.

[2]  Presumably C.J. Vaughan's *Notes for Lectures on Confirmation with Suitable Prayers* (1859).

*Sun. 6 March.* Slept indifferently – Thermometer at 42. – Letter from Mrs Kennedy . . . Frank is coming home in about 2 weeks. The reports of him are excellent: Professor de la Rive says of him that he is a 'brave & excellent garçon' . . . Did not venture to Church or to take any walk . . . I read 2 Sermons of Burders & one of Saurin.[3]

*Th. 10.* . . . Letter from G.B.A. saying he has received my Will . . . I gave him my Journal in 32 vols, saying he must not print a word of it, but that if he found it an encumbrance might burn it as soon as he got hold of it . . .

*Sun. 13.* . . . Thank God I feel sufficiently well to venture to Christ Church: it is the 1st time this year, indeed the 1st time since 22 Nov, not far short of 4 months! . . .

*Mon. 14.* . . . Yesterday Mr Weldon scolded his flock for having complained that some of them had been sick & that no clergyman had been to see them: 'when you are ill don't you immediately send for the Doctor? – why don't you send also for the Minister? either I or one of those who assist me in the duty of the parish would come to you immediately'. – Walk in Botanic Garden.

*Fri. 18.* . . . Seniority at 11½, for wch Harriet fortified me with elder wine. – We made arrangements for the Sizars dinners: allowing them (besides the remains of the Fellows tables) 1½ lb meat each & 5d each for pastry: – this is imitated from St Johns, where it is said to work well: (a 2s sealing) – I got a lift on my return home in Mrs Clarks phaeton . . . Letter from Selwyn saying that the sight of my Saurin makes him feel like Ahab coveting Naboth's vineyard:[4] the copy just harmonises with his Bourdaloue etc: would I part with it at a price or exchange it for another book. Wrote in reply that I gave it him with all my heart, & that all my life long I had thought Naboth an unamiable churl . . .

*Sat. 19.* Slept indifferently: thermometer at 42°. – wrote to decline being one of the Stewards at the anniversary dinner of the London Orphan. – Walk in the Botanic Garden. – The boat-race between O. & C. was today.[5] – Oxford won by 46": this is their 5th successive victory: – Camb. has beaten O. at Billiards, but that is not a matter to be proud of, as Billiards are not a manly

---

[3]  Presumably George Burder (1752-1832), the congregationalist minister and one of the founders of the British and Foreign Bible Society, who published many volumes of sermons. For Saurin see 18 March.

[4]  Ahab the wicked king of Samaria coveted Naboth's vineyard and said, 'Give me thy vineyard . . . and I will give thee for it a better vineyard than it: or, if it seemeth good to thee, I will give thee the worth of it in money. And Naboth said to Ahab, The Lord forbid it me, that I should give the inheritance of my fathers unto thee.' (1 *Kings* 21 v. 2). Jacques Saurin (1677-1730), the celebrated refugee Protestant preacher at the Hague talked with unfashionable passion about moral questions and the Calvinist dogma. Louis Bourdaloue (1632-1704), a Jesuit, succeeded Bossuet as the finest preacher of his day in Paris.

[5]  The first university boat race took place at Henley in June 1829, the second in 1836, the third in 1839, and then nearly annually. See Searby, pp. 648-67 for a full account of the increasing popularity of rowing.

exercise & lead to much idleness & gambling[6] – Sedgwick called: but I was out.

*Palm Sunday 20.* . . . At Christ Church a stranger read prayers: Mr Weldon preached very ably . . . the topic was 'care of the souls as well as the bodies of the poor'. He told a touching anecdote about Dr Guthrie (founder of the Edinburgh ragged schools): he was calling on a miserable old woman who complained of cold & hunger: – he said to her 'there is something worse than cold or hunger' – 'Yes, said she, but if you were as cold & hungry as I am you would be unable to think of any thing else' . . .

*Sat. 2 April.* Slept pretty well. – Thermometer at 45°. Lizzie Mills came this morning on a visit to Harriet. – Dosia brought her from Town. Dosia is trying again (at his request) the experiment of living with her reprobate husband . . . Yesterday there was an attempt to prevent Myers (the Plagiary) from taking his degree:[7] I am happy to say the Persecution failed egregiously: 25 to 3 . . .

*Th. 7.* . . . Visit from Luard: he wants me to act for him M. T. & W. next week: he is going to Malvern to fetch back his wife. – Walk about Town & saw the advanced state of St Johns Chapel & Lodge[8] . . .

*Fri. 8.* . . . After dinner the Vicechancellor (Cookson) called: he had been spending yesterday with The Prince & Princess at Sandringham to make arrangements about their visit to Cambridge next June. – I was much pleased at learning that the Prince did me the Honor of enquiring particularly after me & expressing interest in my health. Treated Caroline & Mrs Watts to a 6d reading (at wch Miss Hopkins was expected to read.) – she gave a *Lecture* on *doing good*. The proceeds were for the Sheffield Deluge.[9]

*Fri. 15.* . . . In the morning Sedgwick called & read me a beautiful letter of Mrs Guthrie's: he described minutely the proceedings last Wednesday before the Master in Lunacy (Warren): poor Dick had demanded that his case

6  See the indefatigable John Brown's *Sixty Years Gleanings from Life's Harvest* (1858) Chapters 5 and 6 for a full account of the establishment of his pool and billiards rooms in Cambridge. These were given a 'tacit licence for the future' in 1843 (p. 398) after the Senior Proctor had 'put down billiards' as a game prohibited by the University and a court case. See also *Romilly 1842-47*, p. 88.

7  In a letter to the *Chronicle* of 5 April Shilleto says he non-placeted the supplicat for Myers's degree because of the 'reticence' with which the V.C. had dealt with the allegation that Myers 'Had borrowed from Oxford Prize Poems'. Myers 'was allowed to disavow any improper motives but requested to return the medal'. The *Cambridge Calendar*, writes Shilleto, which always listed university prizes, had this year made no mention of the Camden medal and the ordinary reader must have wondered whether it had not been awarded or whether there had been no candidates.

8  A sentence in William Selwyn's Commemoration of Benefactors sermon in 1861: 'And is there not one improvement more desired than all? long-talked of, long delayed, for which perhaps the time is now come', hastened the building of G.G. Scott's new chapel. The foundation-stone was laid in 1864 and Scott's new Master's Lodge begun a year earlier. For a full account see Willis and Clark, 2, pp. 315, 324-44.

9  The Bradfield reservoir above Sheffield burst one night in March sweeping away whole villages and passing through the town with great loss of life and property. Noting the defective structure of the dam, the coroner's jury urged the government to introduce regular and thorough inspections of such works.

should be brought before a jury: – the Master in Lunacy behaved with the greatest gentleness & forbearance & the Jury were sensible discreet men: the Master told them they had nothing to do with the medical view of the case & what had led or might have led to the condition of Richard Sedgwick; he greatly objected to the production of letters & allowed only one to be read. – Mr Powell (M.P. for Camb.) was in Court as well as Sedgwick: poor Dick now hates him peculiarly (tho once his dear friend) as he assisted in the capture of poor Dick & his conveyance to the Asylum – Every word that Dick uttered in Court showed that his delusions were unaltered: he offered to show the Jury the hollow walls at Kensington in wch the Conspirators lurked. – the Jewry [sic] immediately gave a verdict 'that he was not in a state to manage his own affairs'.[10] – Sedgwick was a good deal overcome in telling this sad tale . . . Introduced Lizzie Mills to Sedgwick who kindly gave her 2/6: she never had so large a coin before & asked Harriet if it was a Guinea. – Lizzie was carried off by the Robinsons of Shelford for a weeks visit: she was delighted to go as there are chickens & a pet dog & Master Robinson!

*Tu. 19.* . . . Sedgwick drank tea with me: he read me letters of Mrs G. & of Mr Bignoll the Surgeon at Kensington: before the Court . . . broke up the other day Richard became very violent & offered to strike Mr Warren, so that it became necessary to remove him by the Policemen: it appears that he attended this Court under a firm conviction that it would be a triumph for him & that he should be instantly set at liberty . . .

*Th. 21.* Sophie Kennedy . . . told me that her brother John met Garibaldi the other day at a small dinner-party of 10 at Panizzis: she says the conversation was lost to most of the guests as Gladston (placed by Lord Shaftesbury next to Garibaldi) chose to speak Italian all the time, tho Garibaldi prefers speaking English.[11] When Lady Russell saw Garibaldi she asked what language he would prefer speaking & he answered 'I like better to speak my bad English than good French': Sophie says he speaks French very well but has never forgiven the French their acquiring his birth place (Nice) and their protection of Rome . . .

*Tu. 26.* Slept but so-so. – Thermometer at 54°. – Mrs Clark offered me a drive, but I had to attend a Seniority: the Master finds unexpected difficulties in our building a ball-room in Nevilles Court, so the present idea is borrowing the Town Hall . . .

[10] Clark and Hughes state that soon after his removal to Dent Richard became an invalid and 'Sedgwick took upon himself the care of his entire family'. Poor Dick seems to have remained insane as there is no mention of him when his family visited his uncle in Norwich in 1862 and '72, although his name continues to appear in the Clergy List. Sedgwick's letters show that he was devoted to Isabella and her children and felt great delight in their company. See Clark and Hughes, II, 387.

[11] Panizzi, the great Principal Librarian of the British Museum and Italian patriot, was all his life in contact with those who worked for the liberation of Italy. Gladstone should have known that Garibaldi might wish to share his 'bad English' with Panizzi's other guests as in 1849, after escaping from the Austrians, Garibaldi had worked in New York as a chandler and trading skipper and had not returned to Italy until 1854.

*Th. 28.* . . . Seniority at 12: a youngster was reprimanded for having come in at 20' to 11 when he was gated. There was agitation at this meeting concerning the Prince & Princess dining in hall as well as having a ball: the idea of the dinner was given up as it was conceived by some: – not by me, that the rest of the University would think Trin. Coll. by giving 2 entertainments took too much upon itself & would be envious[12] . . .

*Fri. 29.* . . . My notion of the University (with the exception of Kings College) . . . is that they would like to grumble a good deal, but would wish to keep clear of all expense & all responsibility . . . In the Evening went luxuriously in a Fly to Cope's: won 2 / . . . Fuller & John Power kindly walked home with me.

*Sat. 30.* . . . Luards man called on me on a begging speculation: his name is Abraham Newland . . . he has 13 children (9 of whom he has placed out without help): he is begging for help for his other 4: gave him the same sum as almost every body else, viz 10/ . . . I afterwards called & left my card at Caius Lodge: the Master in going over one of the model cottages (wch he is building) stept on a loose plank & severely strained himself: he is going on well . . .

*Sun. 1 May.* Slept well. Thermometer at 56°. – Letters from Maggie & George & Mrs Hooker: wrote to the 2 last. Maggie amused me by saying 'your servants live in clover: if George were to ill-use me I should try for the place instead of going to the divorce court'. She thinks Alice's cough proceeds from undigested milk & (as the doctor lets her have her own way) means to bring her up on Cream as she did Flossie: the new nurse is a great treasure . . .

*Mon. 2.* . . . Harriett took Lizzie to Town by the Parliamentary train:[13] Lizzie was a good deal downcast at going away & would have willingly staid all the summer: – gave her 6d as a May Lady: – she is very generous & means to give her brother Harry half of her little stock of money. – She wore today a new straw-hat given her by Mrs Robinson of Shelford. – Walk in Botanic Garden: strong wind.

*Fri. 6.* . . . My crab-tree is in more beautiful bloom than any of the trees of my neighbours. – Seniority at 12: the Master presided: in spite of the alarm about fire felt by Grote & Hammond we at last determined that the Ball shall be in Neville's Court: we rejected Grote's idea of making the undergraduates pay for their tickets . . . Today the 1st stone of St John's Chapel was laid[14] . . .

*Sat. 7.* . . . At Selwyns I saw the 4 pictures wch he bought at Bishop Turton's sale[15] (– all the proceeds of wch, like the rest of the Bishop's property, were to be devoted to different charities): one was the Yarmouth Regatta by Crome (a Yarmouth artist): another was a Virgin & Child (said to

[12] See 6 June for Carus's report that many of the *Clergy* objected to the giving of a ball.
[13] So called since by statute the cost was no more than a penny a mile.
[14] The choirs of St John's and Trinity sang at the service of dedication and the Vice-Chancellor and 'a select but somewhat numerous company was present'. (*Chronicle* 7 May).
[15] For Thomas Turton, sometime Senior Wrangler, Lucasian Professor of Mathematics, Regius Professor of Divinity, and from 1845 to January 1864 Bishop of Ely, see *D.N.B.* He was well known for his taste in the fine arts and his valuable picture collection.

be by Vandyk: – but quære?): a 3d was a pleasing picture of a child, said to be by Sir Joshua: the 4th was a good head of Buonaparte . . .

*Tu. 10.* . . . College meeting at 12: 2 youths Babb & Stephen were had up by the Dean for irregularity at Chapel: they had both been idle dogs, having been posted at the College Examination: we rusticated both of them till Jan. 1865: the latter of them however is to be excused the rustication *if he gets the impending examination for his degree* . . . At 2½ went to the Rede Lecture in the Senate house. – The Lecturer was the Astronomer Royal: his subject total eclipses . . .

*Tu. 17.* . . . Letter from F.O. Martin asking me to get tickets for himself & eldest daughter[16] – wrote to say I could do nothing for him . . . Sedgwick brought also Bishop Mansel's witty but profane verses on Harry Gordon (the Combination Butler & father of the notorious Jemmy Gordon): the following is a copy of them:–

> 'When news was brought down to the sulfurous lake
> That old Harry was whitewash'd again & restor'd,
> The devils huzza'd & got drunk for his sake,
> And brimstone & brandy were push'd round the board.
> Old Satan himself with a voice that shook hell
> In rapture of congratulation to all,
> Cried, courage, my lads, since things turn out so well
> I've hopes now myself of recov'ring my fall' . . . [17]

After West's picture of the overthrow of Satan by Michael was hung up in the chapel people chaffed Harry Gordon by saying Satan's face was vastly like his: Harry Gordon was enraged & complained to Backhouse the Dean who very gravely accompanied H. Gordon to the Chapel & nearly drove him mad by saying 'the likeness is certainly prodigious'.

*Fri. 20.* Slept but so-so – Thermometer at 68°. – Very satisfactory letter from Sophie. She seems very happy about Frank; he has been presented at Court by his Father: he has mixt a great deal more in Society than he ever did before, & has seemed to enjoy it . . . A heavy thunderstorm in the Evening with very vivid lightening & beating rain & driving wind . . . both Harriett & Betsy are greatly affected by thunder-storms.[18] Betsy repeated to me a beautiful hymn of Rob. Grant's (Lord Glenelg's) . . . One Stanza she peculiarly admired

> 'When vexing thoughts within me rise,

[16] Presumably for the Trinity ball.

[17] See Charles Whibley, *Cap and Gown* (1898) pp. 80-82 for the whole poem. Mr Jonathan Smith of Trinity College Library tells us that Gordon was being mocked as a purveyor of such bad wine that the junior fellows persuaded the seniors to sack him. He was however soon whitewashed and reinstated. Gordon, a man of some means, gave his son Jemmy a good classical education and articled him to a respectable attorney. For Jemmy's talents, audacity, profligacy, drunkenness, and spells in prison see Gunning, *Reminiscences*, I, pp.190-8 and *D.N.B.* W.L. Mansel, Bishop of Bristol, public orator and in 1798 Master of Trinity, was the chief wit of academic society.

[18] Betsy Spink and her 'dear little Margaret' were staying with Romilly. Robert Grant, fellow of Magdalene, M.P. and Governor of Bombay, was the *brother* of Lord Glenelg by whom a volume of his sacred poems and hymns was edited posthumously.

And sore dismay'd my spirit dies,
Yet He who once vouchsaf'd to bear
The mortal agony of fear,
Shall sweetly soothe, shall gently dry,
The throbbing heart, the streaming eye'. –

All 6 stanzas of this hymn are printed in the 'Comprehensive Hymn Book' . . . Harriet called my attention to a favorite hymn of hers (in the Cottage Hymn Book): it is called 'Deliverance from the Storm'. – This is the 1st stanza

'Hark! the God of glory thunders!
Swift his vivid lightnings fly!
Who is this that works these wonders?
Who is this that shakes the sky?
Oh! what mighty hand is this!
Moving all unseen it is'.

*Sat. 21.* . . . After coffee Selwyn drove me in his trap to the Foxton Station, where he got into a Carriage with me & returned to Cambridge: (he is the St Mary's Preacher tomorrow) . . . I was so clumsy in getting out of the Railway carriage at Cambridge tonight as to stop short & fall against the Kerb stone, whereby I broke the skin of one of my shins.

*Sat. 28.* Slept well – Therm. 52°. – Leg (I presume) going on right: but it is very painful. Mr Temple called: he recommends the poultice being half linseed . . . When I returned from the drive at 5 I found Grim arrived . . . He is very flourishing.

*Th. 2 June.* . . . My balcony is decorated with 2 flags. (Danish & English): the cost is trifling: only 8s for 3 days, Th. Fri. & Sat. exclusive of 2/6 for putting up. – Miss Chapman & an invalide lady friend came to my house to look from the drawing-room windows at the Prince & Princess as their carriage drove by: – they had a good view[19] . . . At 12½ Grim & I started in a fly for Trinity: we had to make our entry by the Hostel-Gate. At 1½ the Prince and Princess arrived. There was a small platform for them just before Trinity Lodge: it had in it 2 chairs of State. The Royal carriage drove up to the Lodge door: The Court was well filled: when the P. & Pss had taken their seats, all the assemblage (Heads of houses, Noblemen, Bishop Lonsdale, Dr Kennedy, Doctors, Professors, M.A., B.As & undergraduates) filed before the P. & Pss. – I had a capital view of the Princess's pretty face: – she was in mourning (for the late King of Denmark).[20] After the University had filed past the P. & Ps the duke of Devonshire read the Address: then the Princess presented the Prizes to the Riflemen: the Band plaid 'See the Conquering Hero comes' as the Champion received his prize . . . of course Grim joined the Procession as a Trin. M.A. – I took Grim into the beautiful Marquee in Neville's Court where the Trin. Ball is to be given tomorrow. Grim went to

---

[19] See the *Illustrated London News* for 11 June for good illustrations of the visit.

[20] The childless King Frederick II had died in November 1863 and been succeeded by Christian IX, Alexandra's father.

the Senate House at 3 to see the Prince & his suite presented with Honorary Degrees. The enthusiasm manifested for the Princess & for Denmark was prodigious . . . Grim went at 10 to the Fitzwilliam Ball & thought it far the most beautiful he had ever seen. – He outstaid the Royal people: he was only a spectator & feeder: he did not dance . . .

*Fri. 3.* . . . After breakfast Grim was left pretty much to his own devices. I started (in a fly) at 9·30 for Kings, to attend the Chapel service at 10: the Prince & Princess had however begged a delay of an hour: so I had to while away an hour in walking on the lawn or sitting on the Chapel steps. – I was introduced to Professor Wheatston, to Dean Stanley & his wife Lady Augusta, etc etc. As soon as the Chapel-doors were open we all rushed in & took our marked places. The service consisted of the Litany (without any sermon): it ended with an Anthem of Boyces from the Dedication of the Temple . . . After Chapel I went home, not venturing on the crowd & heat of the Senate House (where Degrees were conferred on Wheatstone, Dean Stanley, Lord Palmerston etc etc): there was a little hissing of Dean Stanley but it was overwhelmed by triumphant shouts of applause[21] . . . At 2 o'cl. I went again to Kings for their magnificent luncheon (served by Gunter) . . . There was only one toast given, 'the Queen': the Grace after lunch was sung charmingly from the Gallery by the Choristers: – the gallery was prettily filled with ladies & flowers. – As the Prince quitted the Hall he did me the Honor of shaking hands with me. – The liquids supplied at this lunch were Sherry & Champagne & Seltzer water: I asked for a glass of Beer, but Mr Gunter did not allow so base a beverage:[22] Shilleto had made a similar demand & met a similar refusal: but (being thoroughly at home at Kings) he went to the butteries after lunch & got a draft . . . After the lunch was the procession of boats wch of course was well seen from King's Lawn. The P. & Princess & suite had a small Marquee to themselves . . . The Trinity Ball to the Prince & Princess was tonight: it was in Neville's Court & was most brilliant.

*Mon. 6.* Slept very so-so: but Mr Temple thinks my leg going on very well. – Visit from Carus who last night preached to his old flock: – he was very flourishing & was not accompanied by his wife: – he generally indeed travels en garçon! He says many of the Clergy have taken offence at Trin. Coll. having given a ball to the P. & Princess: I think that many of the Clergy have thereby shown themselves very narrowminded & bigoted . . .

*Tu. 7.* . . . Shilleto sent me the following Latin & English verses (concerning Shilleto's & my asking for beer at the grand luncheon at Kings) by the Provost . . .

[21] The 'little hissing' of A.P. Stanley, Dean of Westminster, presumably arose from his refusal to commit himself to the intolerances of either high or low church parties and he was therefore suspect to both. The applause was for a man who outside his own church commanded immense respect and affection.

[22] Romilly undaunted also asked for beer at the grand dinner at Buckingham Palace after the installation of Prince Albert as Chancellor. Gunter would have disapproved of the palace servant who soon returned with 'some beer in a short glass with a handle (much like a tea cup). This success of mine excited the envy of the Orator [Crick] . . . he having been cautioned against asking for his favourite beverage'(*Romilly 1842-47*, 25 March 1847).

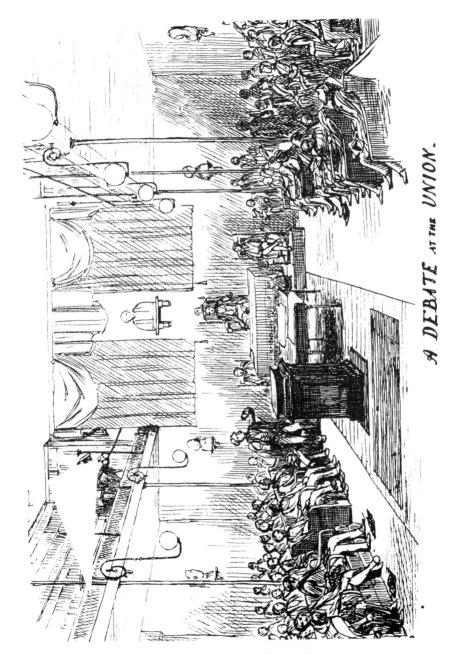

*A DEBATE AT THE UNION.*

An illustration from J. L. Roget, *A Cambridge Scrapbook* (1859)

*To Richard Shilleto M.A.*
When late a Guest in K.C. Hall
For beer as usual you did call
You had, 'tis said, my worthy Malter,
A flat refusal . . .
It chanc'd that Romilly, dear Man,
Was near & under the same ban,
In midst of Sherry, Champagne, Hock,
And other wines wch only shock . . .
'I say, let's go, we're both alike

Against the Gunter we must strike.
You thirst as I do, for some beer;
Without it we both shall be queer:
We must remove th' absurd obstruction
This rascal puts to our free suction . . .
If we must die (we must some day)
I'd rather die with moisten'd clay'.
. . . O generous pair! Forgive us all
Who quite forgot to have the Hall
Provided with some College Small –
. . . Of dear old Romilly I ought
In common conscience to have thought
And my friend Malter's great delight
Should have been better kept in sight.
If ever I am call'd again
To King's Coll. feast to ask you twain
(Familiars both & worthy men)
I promise I will be more heedful –
You, Romilly, shall have your needful,
And you, most constant friend of Ale
Shall have your 'usual' without fail.

K.C. June 4. 1864

These verses (both English & Latin) of the Provost's run off charmingly & are very playful. I am not surprised that he should have thrice gained the Epigram Prize.

*Th. 9.* . . . The Princess is said to have expressed herself as much gratified by *the good-humoured* (meaning *kind*) reception she had met with. – Beamont[23] has given offence to the D. of Devonshire & the V.C. by his obstinacy: he consulted the V.C. about the Prince asking Sir Charles Eastlake to address the pupils of the 'school-of-Art' after the Princess gave them the prizes at the Horticultural Show in St Johns. – The V.C. told him that both himself & the Chancellor would highly disapprove of such a liberty being taken with

[23] W.J. Beamont had played the main part in founding the Cambridge School of Art in 1858 and was a courageous if obstinate man. He had educated missionaries in Palestine and Egypt, been chaplain to the British forces before Sebastopol and had ministered in the camp hospitals.

the Prince. In spite of this Beamont went up to the Prince & made his request & gained his point, for Sir. Charles Eastlake made an Address. What a perverse self-willed creature Bt shows himself to be! . . .

*Mon. 27.* Slept well. – Thermometer at 59'. – Leg vastly sore: – said to be going on well, tho not altogether comfortably . . . Mrs Clark kindly took me a drive . . .

*Tu. 28.* . . . Mr Temple told me that Smith (Curator of Fitzwilliam Museum) is dead of drunkenness: the day after the ball he is said to have been found drunk & the doors of the Museum open. – He was dismissed . . .

*Wed. 29.* . . . Mrs Clark took me a drive thro Cherry-hinton. – Leg very sore. – Mrs Clark lent me 2 Books on Missions to the miserable & the abandoned in London & other great cities. – One is called 'the Missing Link' or 'Biblewomen in the Homes of the London Poor'.[24] The book was in its 30th thousand in 1861 . . . I received also (by Book Post) Oger's 2d part of 'Cours d'histoire Générale' it runs from 1328 to 1648. – Poor Harriet had a bilious attack this Evening.

*Sat. 2 July.* . . . Read 2d No. of 'Temple Anecdotes' lent me by Mr Temple: I find the book interesting, as it contains true stories about all the great inventions & discoveries. – Went on with that excellent book ('the Missing Link') . . .

*Mon. 4 & Tu. 5.* Slept pretty well. – Therm. at 60°. – The poultice had given way in the night & my leg was unusually sore this morning . . . I finished 'the Missing Link' (or the Biblewoman): an admirable book & written with such effect as to be likely to induce other women to join in such a noble mission . . . Harriett had a letter from Miss Wright: she & her mother think it very wicked of people to spread reports of Fever & small pox at Yarmouth: they declare that there never was any fever at all, & that there were very few cases of small pox & those several weeks ago . . . Today a Cricket match was plaid on Parkers Piece by Cambridge townsmen against county of York: the match was won by Cambridge: the Cambridge men are just returned from Australia, where they introduced cricket [25] . . .

*Sat. 16.* Slept well – Therm at 59 – Bought at Dixons 'Stories & Lessons on the Catechism (3 Vol. /56/– My Station & its Duties (by Author of 'last day of week')[26] – Life-work or the Link & Rivet (by L.N.R. author of Missing Link) & 'Ragged Homes & how to mend them' (by Mrs Baily). Mr Temple thinks my leg quite fit for travelling & will not look at it again till my return from Yarmouth . . .

*Tu. 19.* . . . Left Betsy & little Margaret in charge of the house & the Canary for the next 6 weeks.

On 19 July, having left Betsy and her little daughter Margaret in charge of the house, Romilly and his devoted maids set out for what was to be his last holiday.

[24] *The Missing Link; or the Biblewomen in the Homes of the London Poor* by L.N.R.[Ellen Henrietta Ranyard] (1859).

[25] Cambridge were in fact following the first visit of an English professional eleven to Australia in 1861-2.

[26] *My Station and its Duties: a Narrative for Girls going into Service* (1836) by Eliza Cheap.

His injured shin was virtually better, Mrs Wright and her daughter 'were obviously glad to receive us' and he met the Harvey Goodwins on the day after his arrival. The weather for the first few days was 'vastly', 'intensely' or 'scorching' hot and on the twenty-second he foolishly sat on the jetty between lunch and dinner. He came 'home faint & sick & oppressed with languor from the great heat'. His landlady recommended brandy and water which 'did me great good' as did a cheerful letter from Sophie Kennedy. Frank had been with the Yeomanry for ten days drilling at Ayr and 'his Colonel was delighted with him & says he will make a 1st rate Cavalry officer'. At last it seemed as though the Kennedys' worries might be at an end.

Romilly's sickness only lasted for a day and he continued to enjoy his holiday quietly, bathing when the water was calm enough, making friends with his fellow-lodgers, talking to his former clerk Richard Rowe and to Cambridge shop-keepers who were also in Yarmouth. Harriet and Caroline also had a sociable time, drinking tea 'with Mrs Brown (the bathing woman) to meet the 2 Miss Clarks the Bakers daughters at Cambridge' and on the following day being guests of the Miss Clarks 'to meet the Ricketts (my shoemaker)'.

The 'Journal' entry for the last day but one of Romilly's life records his eighth bathe and his approval of 'Mrs Bayley's "Ragged Homes & the way to mend them" – an admirable book'. He 'sat on the jetty for 2 hours' and called on new arrivals in his lodgings'. There is no indication of his feeling especially unwell and his death on the evening of the following day allowed him in Sedgwick's words 'to slide gently out of the world'. According to a footnote (doubtless based on information given by the family), in Clark and Hughes, *Life and Letters of the Reverend Adam Sedgwick* 'He lay down on the sofa after dinner and passed away peacefully whilst his servant was fetching something he had asked for'.

Sedgwick was in residence in Norwich when the news of Romilly's death on Sunday 7 August reached him in a letter from Harriet Sandfield to John Sheldrick, Sedgwick's faithful servant. 'Dear John, sad sad news. Our poor dear Master is *dead dead*, – I have just found him dead; pray break it gently to your poor Master. I cant write any more – I am in such trouble. Harriet Sandfield'. Sedgwick went to Yarmouth early the next day and wrote to Whewell that he felt 'certain he had died without any sensation to disturb his happy expression'. He immediately 'sent an Italian artist [Bianchi] to take an impression of his face and I hope his Nephews will approve of what I have done'. They did and a bust was made for Sedgwick from which casts were taken. George Romilly, the family's artist, agreed however in his letter to Sedgwick of 10 October that the cast had been taken too late and that Bianchi's only 'very imperfect aids' had been 'the two photographs'. George however hoped to draw 'such a likeness as my Uncle's dear friends and relatives would like to possess'.

On 12 August Sedgwick described his funeral in a letter to Mrs Richard Sedgwick which, like the letter to Lady Bunbury below, is quoted in Clark and Hughes. 'A very simple funeral, everything quite plain. All in the carriages were mourners in deed, and not in word only. I can speak for one. He was buried in a vault, where his two sisters lay. A place had been reserved for him. The Master of Trinity, the Dean of Ely, Canon Selwyn, and all the resident Fellows of Trinity (in the vacation few in number) were in attendance at the Church door. The service was read with solemnity, and seemed exactly to suit our beloved friend whom God had taken from us – a man of faith and love, mature in Christian grace'.

A week later Sedgwick wrote to Lady Bunbury, the daughter of Leonard Horner, the geologist ' . . . Dear Romilly was the oldest friend I had in Cambridge. Indeed he was the only one left of those with whom I was on close terms of brotherly love during the early years of my academic life. A cross look or a cross word never, I believe, passed between us; and our intimacy became closer and closer as we advanced in life. He was a Christian indeed, without selfishness, without guile, abounding in deeds of active benevolence, and of most angelic temper. And with such loveable qualities he had good sense and an ample store of knowledge, that made his society at once instructive and delightful . . . With a full heart I ought to bless His holy name for having so long given me the treasure of such a friend.'

The inscription that Romilly wanted upon his tomb is, wrote George Romilly to Sedgwick on 9 August, 'very characteristic of his happy disposition and pious mind'. 'Here lies the body of Joseph Romilly M.A. A senior Fellow of Trin. Coll. Cambridge and Registrary of the University. He was the 5<sup>th</sup> son of Thos Peter Romilly Esq, and of Jane Anne his wife. He enjoyed a long life full of comforts, and numberless blessings, and his only hopes of heaven are in the merits of his Saviour.'

On 20 August 1864 the *Chronicle* printed the following poem:

## IN MEMORIAM JOSEPHI ROMILLY

———

The widow weeps! her only friend
    Has laid in peace his silver head;
Her cruize [sic] of oil is running dry,
    And want may touch her daily bread.
      Ah! she will miss him.

The children weep! their smiling friend
    Is pillow'd where the daisies grow;
Brim are their litt[l]e* hearts with grief,
    Full is the measure of their woe.
      Ah! they will miss him.

And round his home the stranger mourns;
    The beggar trembles, sick and sore;
But though they linger on the step,
    Their friend will never ope the door.
      God! how they miss him.

*Hitchin*

*reads 'litte'

The letters of Harriet, Adam Sedgwick, and G.T. Romilly are to be found among papers 'on the death of Registrary Romilly' in a guard-book (class-mark C.U.R. 20.1.: nos. 14, 15, 16), in the University Archives in the manuscript department of Cambridge University Library.

# APPENDIX I: THE ROMILLY FAMILY

There is extensive material on the family, together with a chart pedigree (c.1677-1906) by Henry Wagner in *Proceedings of the Huguenot Society*, VIII (1905-8). The Romilly entries in Burke's *Landed Gentry* (18th edition, I, 1965), and in Burke's *Peerage* (105th edition 1970), continue various lines into recent times. There are entries in the *Dictionary of National Biography* for Joseph Romilly, his uncle Sir Samuel, his cousins John, Lord Romilly, and Dr Peter Mark Roget, Dr and Mrs Marcet, and for his great-nephew, John Romilly Allen. An asterisk below and in the tables indicates a member of Trinity College, Cambridge.

Stephen (or Etienne) Romilly of Montpellier, a Protestant, settled in England about 1701, was naturalised in 1706, and died in 1733 having married Judith (d.1758), daughter and co-heiress of Francis de Monsallier of Shoreditch. They left with other children a younger son, Peter Romilly (1712-84), who married Margaret (d. 1796), daughter of Aimé Garnault, another French refugee, and they had three surviving children, Thomas Peter (the diarist's father), Catherine (Mrs Roget), and Samuel (the philanthropist and lawyer). For the families of Thomas Peter and Samuel Romilly see Tables A and B. Their sister, Catherine (1755-1835) married in 1778 Jean Roget (1751-83) of the French Protestant Church and had, with an unmarried daughter, Anne Suzanne Louise or 'Annette' (1783-1866), a son Peter Mark Roget (1779-1869). He married in 1824 Mary Hobson (d. 1833) and had two children, Catherine Mary (1825-1905), and John Lewis Roget* (1828-1908). J.L. Roget married and had issue, but the family in England died out with his grandchildren at the end of the present century. See D.L. Emblen, *Peter Mark Roget* (1970).

From Francis de Monsallier Joseph Romilly* shared a common descent with the Fludyer family which included Sir Samuel Fludyer, baronet (1800-76), Mary, Baroness Dacre (d. 1808), Caroline, Countess Brownlow (d. 1824), Mary, Countess of Onslow (d.1830), and Elizabeth, Lady Musgrave (d.1861). From Aimé Garnault he shared a common descent with the Ouvry, Gilson, Vautier and other families; see *Proceedings of the Huguenot Society*, XIV (1929-33), and J.J. Howard and F.A. Crisp, *Visitation of England and Wales*, III (1895), 167-9, and the accompanying volume of *Notes*, V (1903), 51-6, and also J. Garnault Ouvry, 'The Ouvry Family in the 19th Century' in *Proceedings of the Huguenot Society*, 24, part 6 (1988), 473-9. For the populous and intermarried Allen families of Wales see Burke's *Landed Gentry* (17th edition 1952) under 'Allen of Bicton' and 'Allen of Rickeston', and also (18th edition, II, 1969) under 'Evans formerly Harrison-Allen', the well-connected Cresselly branch to which belonged Lancelot Baugh Allen*, who married Joseph's eldest sister, Caroline Romilly. There is a good deal about the Allens in the *National Library of Wales Journal,* 17 (1971/2), and in Canon M.G.R. Morris's *Romilly's Visits to Wales 1827-1854* (1998).

Table A. Peter Romilly 1712-84 = Margaret Garnault d. 1796

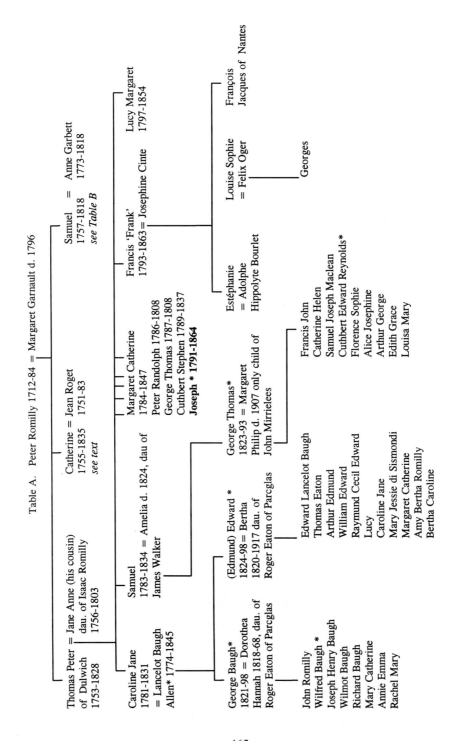

Thomas Peter = Jane Anne (his cousin)
of Dulwich      dau. of Isaac Romilly
1753-1828       1756-1803

Catherine = Jean Roget
1755-1835   1751-83
see text

Samuel     =   Anne Garbett
1757-1818      1773-1818
see Table B

Caroline Jane
1781-1831
= Lancelot Baugh
Allen* 1774-1845

Samuel
1783-1834 = Amelia d. 1824, dau of
James Walker

Margaret Catherine
1784-1847
Peter Randolph 1786-1808
George Thomas 1787-1808
Cuthbert Stephen 1789-1837
**Joseph * 1791-1864**

Francis 'Frank'
1793-1863 = Josephine Cinte

Lucy Margaret
1797-1854

Estéphanie
= Adolphe
Hippolyte Bourlet

Louise Sophie
= Felix Oger

François
Jacques of Nantes

Georges

George Baugh*
1821-98 = Dorothea
Hannah 1818-68, dau. of
Roger Eaton of Parcglas

(Edmund) Edward *
1824-98 = Bertha
1820-1917 dau. of
Roger Eaton of Parcglas

George Thomas*
1823-93 = Margaret
Philip d. 1907 only child of
John Mirrielees

John Romilly
Wilfred Baugh *
Joseph Henry Baugh
Wilmot Baugh
Richard Baugh
Mary Catherine
Annie Emma
Rachel Mary

Edward Lancelot Baugh
Thomas Eaton
Arthur Edmund
William Edward
Raymund Cecil Edward
Lucy
Caroline Jane
Mary Jessie di Sismondi
Margaret Catherine
Amy Bertha Romilly
Bertha Caroline

Francis John
Catherine Helen
Samuel Joseph Maclean
Cuthbert Edward Reynolds*
Florence Sophie
Alice Josephine
Arthur George
Edith Grace
Louisa Mary

Table B.  Sir Samuel Romilly 1757-1818 = Anne 1773-1818, daughter of Francis Garbett of Knill Court, Herefordshire

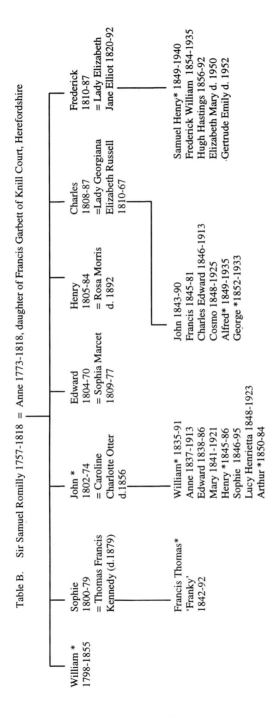

William *
1798-1855

Sophie
1800-79
= Thomas Francis
Kennedy (d.1879)

John *
1802-74
= Caroline
Charlotte Otter
d.1856

Edward
1804-70
= Sophia Marcet
1809-77

Henry
1805-84
= Rosa Morris
d. 1892

Charles
1808-87
=Lady Georgiana
Elizabeth Russell
1810-67

Frederick
1810-87
= Lady Elizabeth
Jane Elliot 1820-92

Francis Thomas*
'Franky'
1842-92

William* 1835-91
Anne 1837-1913
Edward 1838-86
Mary 1841-1921
Henry *1845-86
Sophie 1846-95
Lucy Henrietta 1848-1923
Arthur *1850-84

John 1843-90
Francis 1845-81
Charles Edward 1846-1913
Cosmo 1848-1925
Alfred* 1849-1935
George *1852-1933

Samuel Henry* 1849-1940
Frederick William 1854-1935
Hugh Hastings 1856-92
Elizabeth Mary d. 1950
Gertrude Emily d. 1952

# APPENDIX II: ROMILLY'S WILL

*For the sake of clarity modern punctuation and paragraphs are introduced, and most abbreviations are expanded.*

3 Benet Place, Cambridge 7 March 1864

This is the last will of me Joseph Romilly (Clerk) written with my own hand. I bless Almighty God for the many years of health & happiness which he has vouchsafed unto me & rest my only hope of pardon & acceptance hereafter in the atonement of my blessed Lord & Saviour Jesus Christ. I desire that my funeral may be as plain as possible. My wish is to be buried in the churchyard or public cemetery of the place where I die. If I die in Cambridge (as I hope I shall) I desire to be buried in the churchyard of Christ Church, Barnwell, in the same vault where my dear sisters Margaret Catherine & Lucy Mary are buried. I appoint my nephew George Baugh Allen Esq. my sole Executor. I desire that all my legacies may be free of legacy duty.

I desire my nephew George Baugh Allen to carry out my father (Thomas Peter Romilly's) will as regards a certain sum in bank stock; that sum was originally four thousand pounds; it is now £4030 bank stock (£30 having been purchased when the dividend was above 10 p.c.). This £4030 bank stock is vested in 3 Trustees, Joseph Romilly, Clerk (the present Testator) Edward Romilly, Esquire (now residing at 14 Stratton St, Piccadilly) & Henry Whittaker, Esq. (now residing at 11 Wall St, New York, U.S.). The will of my father Thomas Peter Romilly directs that after the death of all his children (of whom I Joseph Romilly am the last survivor) the aforesaid £4000 bank stock with its accumulation (if any) should be divided equally among their children then living. The grandchildren of the said Thomas Peter Romilly who are now alive are six in number, viz. George Baugh Allen, Esq., Edmund Edward Allen (Clerk) (the two sons of his eldest daughter Caroline Jane), George Thomas Romilly Esq. (only child of his eldest son Samuel), Madame Bourlet (formerly Estéphanie Romilly), Madame Felix Oger (formerly Louise Sophie Romilly) & François Jacques (the 3 children of his youngest son Francis). This F.J. Romilly is always in his family called Jacques. He resides at Nantes where he is Professor of Rhetoric. Madame Bourlet resides with her mother (Josephine Romilly, widow of Francis Romilly) at 21 Rue de Fleurus, Paris. Madame Felix Oger resides at Paris (where her husband is Professor of History) at No 12 Rue de l'Ouest or with her mother at No 21 Rue de Fleurus.

I bequeath to my nephew & executor George Baugh Allen, Esq., five hundred pounds also a small portrait of my dear mother (which hangs in my bedroom) also a framed engraving of that great & good man, my uncle Sir Samuel Romilly, also the red morocco copy of the life of Sir Samuel Romilly,[1] also 2 vols lettered Romilly's speeches (1820), also a copy of Grön-

---

[1] *Memoirs of Sir Samuel Romilly written by himself with a Selection from his Correspondence.* Edited by his sons (1st and 2nd editions, 1840).

464

velts letters written by my uncle and published in 1792, [2] also a small packet endorsed 'M.S.S. of my Father', also the valuable historic documents[3] published by my cousin Sir John Romilly (the Master of the Rolls), also 7 small framed engravings of Garrick &c in different characters.[4]

I bequeath to my niece Dora (wife of G.B. Allen, Esq.), all the jars, table ornaments & chimney ornaments, the little clock that stands on the side board & one of my tea-caddies. I bequeath to John Romilly Allen (son of my nephew G.B. Allen), my "Penny Cyclopaedia".[5] I bequeath to Mary Catharine Allen (daughter of G.B. Allen), my small gold watch. I bequeath to Ann Emma Allen (daughter of G.B. Allen), an ivory inlaid card case that came from India.

I bequeath to my nephew Edmund Edward Allen, Clerk, two hundred pounds, also a pocket communion service, also the Cambridge 2 vol. folio Bible, also Stephens Greek Testament (1549), also Charles Simeon's works (21 vol. 4to), also W. Carus's *Life of Simeon*, also the 4to Cruden's *Concordance*, also 2 vol. 'Sermons de Romilly (1780)',[6] also the framed engravings of Archbishop Musgrave, Bishops Bowstead & Perry & Archdeacon Hare. I bequeath to my niece Bertha Allen (wife of E.E. Allen, Clerk), all the music books of my dear sister Margaret Catherine, also one of my tea caddies. I bequeath to Bertha Allen (Jnr), daughter of E.E. Allen, my pianoforte. (I believe her full names are Bertha Caroline Allen). I bequeath to Lucy Allen (daughter of E.E. Allen), a black silhouette in an oval gilt frame of my dear sister Lucy Mary,[7] also all the books which belonged to my dear sister Lucy Mary. They are contained in 3 bookcases in my house, two of them in the study and one in an attic; also a writing desk & a work-box (with whatever they contain) which belonged to my said dear sister. I bequeath to Margaret Catherine Allen (daughter of E.E. Allen), an octavo edition of Walter Scott's Novels (in 41 Octavo vols) which belonged to my dear sister Margaret Catherine. Also 4 small vols bound in white morocco; they are called 'Specimens of the British Poets'; they belonged to my dear sister Margaret Catherine & were edited in 1809 by my dear brother Cuthbert Stephen; also a framed drawing of my dear sister Margaret Catherine made in her last illness by my nephew G.T. Romilly.

I bequeath to Margaret P. Romilly (wife of my nephew G.T. Romilly), my small quantity of plate (viz. a silver inkstand, a small waiter, tea pot, sugar

---

[2] To the *Letters containing an Account of the Late Revolution in France,* printed in London, which purported to be translated from the German by 'Henry Frederic Groenvelt', Samuel contributed severe criticisms of English institutions. He soon had cause to regret the book as events in France deteriorated, and he destroyed all the unsold copies that could be found.

[3] i.e. the Rolls series.

[4] Garrick's father, like his contemporary Etienne Romilly, was a French Protestant refugee.

[5] Issued by the Society for the Diffusion of Useful Knowledge (1833-46).

[6] Jean E. Romilly (1739-99), a Swiss who was for some years pastor of the French church at Threadneedle Street in London. Peter Romilly, the diarist's grandfather entertained him, and Uncle Samuel visited his family during a continental tour before the French Revolution.

[7] The whereabouts of this is unknown.

basin, cream jug, forks, spoons, cruet stand &c but I beg that (as she already has a silver tea pot) she will give this one to Lucy Allen (daughter of E.E. Allen). I bequeath also to Margaret P. Romilly a patchwork table-cover made by my dear sister Margaret Catherine, also her picture by Jackson, also the hand-skreens & framed drawings of flowers & insects made by her, also the fire-skreens worked by her, also her set of the British Poets 75 small volumes, also 6 vol. folio lettered 'engravings' & 'Cristal [sic] Palace'.

I bequeath to Francis John Romilly, my great nephew (son of G.T. Romilly), my gold watch (which had been my father's), with its chain & seals, also Scott's *Bible* (6 vol. 4to), also Donaldson's *Latin Grammar*, also a vol. lettered Drawings G.T. Romilly, also a volume lettered Prints, also all the drawings & pictures by his father, also a likeness of my uncle Sir Samuel Romilly (in my bed-room). I bequeath to Sam. Jos. Maclean (my godson), son of G.T. Romilly, my silver watch, & also a copy (in greek green morocco) of the life of Sir Sam. Romilly & also 'Punch' bound in more than 20 double vols & also a copy of Grönvelts letters (written by my uncle Sir S.R.).

I bequeath two hundred pounds to my sister-in-law (now residing at 21 R. de Fleurus), widow of my brother Francis. I bequeath two hundred pounds to my niece Estéphanie Bourlet. I bequeath two hundred pounds to my niece Louise Sophie Oger. I bequeath two hundred pounds to my nephew François Jacques Romilly. I bequeath ten pounds to my godchild Georges Oger (son of Felix Oger).

I bequeath to my cousin Francis Thomas Romilly Kennedy, Esq., a snuff box with a portrait of his dear mother on the lid.[8]

I bequeath ten pounds to Elisabeth Stallybrass of Kneesworth St, Royston.[9] I bequeath to my gyp John Hoppett (besides the current quarter's wages) ten pounds, also my cap & gown & hood. I bequeath to my bedmaker Mrs Carpenter (besides the current quarter's wages) ten pounds & the glass & crockery in my rooms & the coals in the cellar of my College rooms. I bequeath to my faithful servant Caroline Howe (besides the current quarter's wages) fifteen pounds, also five pounds for mourning. I bequeath to my faithful & most attentive & kind servant Harriett Sandfield twenty five pounds (besides the current quarter's wages) & 5 pounds for mourning, also my wearing apparel & my linen & the glass & crockery at my house & the coals in the cellar.

I bequeath to my nephew George Thomas Romilly, Esq., the green morocco copy of the life of Sir Samuel Romilly, also the framed engraving of my said uncle at my College rooms, also the portraits of my father & mother by Jackson & Hunt, also a miniature with likenesses of my grandmother & my father & Aunt Roget, also the whole of my estate except what is above otherwise bequeathed. In other words I leave all the rest of my estate after paying my debts, the medical & funeral expenses, probate & legacy duties, to my nephew George Thomas Romilly.

[8] i.e. Sophie Kennedy, née Romilly.
[9] Perhaps an old college servant. Romilly evidently knew her already when she came 'begging for new shoes' three years before he made this will.

Witness my hand the day above written - Joseph Romilly -

Signed sealed & delivered by the Testator Joseph Romilly for his last Will & Testament in the presence of us who at the same time in his presence at his request & in the presence of each other have hereunto set & subscribed our names as Witnesses thereto –

William Henry Besant AM
William Bennett Pike AM                    Witnesses March 7th 1864.

Proved at London 24th August 1864 by the Oath of George Baugh Allen, Esquire, the nephew, the sole Executor to whom Admon was granted.

# INDEX OF PERSONS

Abbreviations:
adm. (admitted), Fell.-Com. (Fellow Commoner), pens. (pensioner), C. (Curate),
R. (Rector), V. (Vicar).

Abdoollah, Syed, Professor of Hindustani at University College, London, 361n., 365-6

Abdy, John Thomas, Fellow of Trinity Hall 1850, Regius Professor of Civil Law, 1854-73, 146, 205-6, 287, 307

Aberdeen, G.H. Gordon, fourth Earl of (d. 1860), adm. nobleman at St John's 1800, M.A. 1804, Conservative Prime Minister 1852-5, 173, 197

Adair, Robert Alexander Shafto, adm. pens. at Trinity 1828, Liberal M.P. for Cambridge 1847-52 & 1854-7, aide-de-camp to the Queen, 108, 276, 289, 430

Adams, Miss, music mistress, 373

Adams, John Couch, Fellow of St John's 1846-52, Fellow of Pembroke 1853-92, Lowndean Professor of Astronomy & Geometry 1859-92, Director of the Observatory 1861-92, 148, 156, 199, 205, 260-1, 331, 383

Adams, Mrs Lydia, before her marriage bedmaker to Joseph Shaw of Christ's, 'neat and comely', 334

Adams, William, a benevolent draper, 56

Adcock, Mrs, *presumably* the wife of Justinian, solicitor of Market St, 266

Adeane, the Misses, the six orphan daughters of Henry & Matilda Adeane, 239, 291, 335

Adeane, Henry John (Jr.), of Babraham Hall, Cambs., like his father Liberal M.P. for Cambs. (1857), 277

Adeane, Hon. Matilda Stanley (d. 1850), second wife of Henry J. (d. 1847) of Babraham Hall, Cambs., 44, 53-4, 66

Adeane, Robert Jones, adm. pens. at Trinity 1849, eldest son of Henry & Matilda, died 1853 aged 23, 53

Adelaide, Queen, widow of William IV, 52, 64, 274

Affleck, Everina Frances, née Ellis, Lady (d. 1865), second wife of William Whewell, 238

Affre, Denis-Auguste (d. 1848), Archbishop of Paris, 42

Ainslie, Miss, daughter of Gilbert, 98, 130

Ainslie, Gilbert, Master of Pembroke 1828-70, 'a great purist about Latin', 54, 59, 74-5, 78, 84-5, 101-3, 105-6, 118, 128, 135, 172, 182, 214, 258, 396

Airy, George Biddell, Senior Wrangler 1823, Fellow of Trinity, Plumian Professor of Astronomy & Experimental Philosophy 1828-36, Astronomer Royal 1836-81, 24, 280, 300, 315, 331, 416, 453

Airy, Hubert, son of George B., Scholar of Trinity 1859, M.D. 1870, writer on sanitation, 318

Albert, Prince, ix, 6n., 15, 17, 24, 32-3, 38-9, 43, 50, 52, 56, 59n., 60-2, 74, 93, 111, 122, 126, 149-56, 159, 172, 181, 188, 229-30, 233, 237n., 245, 259, 263, 319, 372, 374, 377, 385, 395, 398-400, 403, 405, 408, 410, 418, 429, 432-3

Alderson, Sir Edward Hall, Senior Wrangler 1809, Fellow of Caius, Baron of the Exchequer 1834-57 when he died, 76, 103, 119, 204, 207

Aldis, James Arthur, adm. sizar at Trinity 1858, sixth Wrangler 1863, brother of William S., 430

Aldis, William Steadman, Scholar of Trinity 1859, Senior Wrangler 1861, a private coach in Cambridge, 318, 377, 391, 406

Alford, Henry, Fellow of Trinity 1834, V. of Wymeswold. Leics., 1835-53, later dean of Canterbury, 308, 311

Alger, Mrs, daughter of Henry Gunning, 91

Allen, (Lancelot) Baugh (d. 1845), adm. pens. at Trinity 1794, of the Inner Temple, brother-in-law of Joseph Romilly, Master of Dulwich College 1811-20, one of the six clerks in Chancery 1825-42, father of George B. & Edward E., 185

Allen, Bertha (Mrs E.E. Allen), née Eaton, wife of 'Grim' & mother of numerous children (see Appendix I), 2, 4, 52, 60, 185, 202, 222, 243-6, 289-91, 342, 373, 388-9, 409, 465

Allen, Bertha, daughter of Edward & Bertha, died young, 52, 60, 223, 271, 281, 311, 321-2, 331, 336, 388, 395, 465

Allen, Clement Francis Romilly (b. 1844), son of Baugh by his second wife, adm. pens. Trinity 1862, In the Consular Service 1863-98, 430-1

Allen, Dorothea (Mrs G.B. Allen), née Eaton, mother of Catherine, Annie, Kate, Romilly, & others (see Appendix I), 193, 284-5, 338, 386-9, 395, 465

Allen, (Edmund) Edward ('Grim'), second son of L.B. Allen & Caroline Romilly, born 1824, adm. pens. at Trinity 1842, V. of Millom, Cumberland 1854-65, Rural Dean of Gosforth 1859-65, 2, 4-7, 20, 52, 60, 73, 97, 103, 135-8, 150, 171, 178-81, 185, 196, 202, 204, 217, 222-3, 243-6, 265, 271, 281, 289-91, 302, 305, 310, 321-2, 327-8, 331, 340, 342, 350, 373, 388-9, 400, 406-9, 413, 422-4, 429, 439, 442, 448, 454-5, 464-5

Allen, George Baugh, elder son of L.B. Allen & Caroline Romilly, born 1821, adm. pens. at Trinity 1838, practised in the Temple 1846-96, 'the last of the great special pleaders', 6, 10, 45, 63, 83, 94, 96, 175, 179-81, 185, 193, 206-7, 284-5, 338, 386-7, 389, 409, 412, 440-1, 442, 449, 464, 467

Allen, Georgiana Sarah, née Bayly, second wife of Baugh, the daughter of his old school-friend, 'very fair, fat and good humoured', mother of Clement, 413

Allen, Herbert James, cousin of John H., adm. pens. at Trinity 1859, student interpreter in China 1861, 362

Allen, John, Scholar of Trinity 1829, Archdeacon of Salop, one of the three original Inspectors of Schools 1839-46, friend of Thackeray & Tennyson, 60, 104, 327, 360, 363

Allen, John Bartlett (d. 1803), of Cresselly, grandfather of George B. & Grim, 412-3

Birkett, John Parker, Fellow of Jesus 1842, R. of Graveley, Hunts. 1852-80, 60, 297

Bishop, Miss Jane, Matron of Addenbrooke's Hospital, 140, 186, 262

Bisset, Charles, adm. sizar at Clare 1836, incumbent of Upholland, Wigan, Lancs. 1844-81, 314

Blakesley, Joseph William, adm. pens. at Corpus Christi 1827, President of the Union 1829, Fellow of Trinity & member of the 'Apostles', V. of Ware. Herts., 1845-72, 18

Blencowe, Maria, protégée of Lucy Romilly, niece of Mrs Houghton, married 'at last' 1855, to Charles Blencowe, a cousin, 165

Blennerhasset, Sir Rowland, adm. Fell-Com. at Christ's 1859, 315n.

Bliss, Philip, Oxford Registrar, 15n., 214n.

Blofeld, Thomas Calthorpe, adm. pens. at Trinity 1854, B.A., 1859, barrister 1862, 361

Blomfield, Charles James, adm. pens. at Trinity 1803, Bishop of London 1829-56, 'Set himself to reorganise the established Church', 93, 173, 210, 249, 251

Blore, Edward William, Scholar of Trinity 1849, Fellow 1853, Tutor 1857-75, cricket 'blue', Fitzwilliam syndic, son of the architect of the Pitt Press, 'rather too stiff and formal for my taste', 211-2, 229, 235, 285, 342n., 346, 352, 355, 366, 377, 394, 417, 444

Blunt, John Elijah, adm. Fell.-Com. at Trinity 1814, barrister, 23-4

Blunt, John James, Fellow of St John's, Lady Margaret's Professor of Divinity 1839-55, 3, 23-4, 36, 71-2, 94, 121, 123, 173, 191

Bluntsam, Miss, a deformed young woman, perhaps a schoolmistress, 267

Boinville, Vicomte de, friend of George Romilly, 10

Bond, Miss Frances, sister of Henry J.H., daughter of William Bond, rector of Wheatacre, 283

Bond, Henry John Hayles, of 56 Trumpington St., adm. pens. at Corpus Christi 1819, trained at St Bartholomew's Hospital, Regius Professor of Physic 1851, 84, 172-5, 182, 200, 214-6

Bond, Mary, née Carpenter, wife of Henry J.H., 190

Bonheur, Rosa (1822-99), the painter, 352

Borrow, George (d. 1881), the author, 58

Bourdaloue, Louis (1632-1704), French preacher, 80, 449

Bourlet, Adolphe Hippolyte, faithless husband of Estéphanie Romilly, 244, 264

Bourlet, Alexandrine, mother of Adolphe, 41

Bourlet, Madame, Estéphanie (Fanny), daughter of Frank Romilly, 27, 42, 264, 304, 464, 466

Bourlet, Nini, child of Fanny, 291, 304, 347

Bouverie, Hon. Edward Pleydell, adm. Fell.-Com. at Trinity 1834, M.P. for Kilmarnock 1844-74, President of the Poor Law Board 1855-8, 237, 243n.

Bowles, bathing machine proprietor, 112

Bowles, inspector of prisons, 366

Bowtell, worthless son of John the younger, 170, 176, 254

Bowtell, Alicia, daughter of John the younger, 32, 39

Bowtell, John (1743-1813), outstandingly talented bookbinder, 155n.

Bowtell, John (1777-1855), member of the University Library staff for 35 years, nephew of the bookbinder, died at Great Yarmouth, 32, 66, 119, 122, 155, 170, 176

Boyer, James (Bowyer) (1736-1814), Master at Christ's Hospital 1767-99 where Coleridge, Lamb & Leigh Hunt testified to his brilliance & severity as a teacher, as R. of Colne-Engaine (Gainscolne), Essex 1793-1814 kept the private school which Romilly attended, ix, 161, 264

Boyle, Hon. Caroline (1803-83), granddaughter of the Earl of Cork, for many years maid of honour to Queen Adelaide, 274-5

Brabant, Duke of (b. 1835), eldest son of the King of the Belgians, 149-54, 156

Bradford, George A.F.H. Bridgeman, second Earl of, adm. Fell.-Com. at Trinity 1807, 69-70

Bradshaw, Henry, Fellow of King's 1853-86, Superintendent of MSS & rare books in the University Library 1859-67, 346, 385, 431

Braybrooke, Charles Cornwallis Neville, fifth baron, see Neville

Braybrooke, Jane, Lady, eldest daughter of Marquis Cornwallis & wife of R.G.N., 'A sworn enemy to all reform', 17, 19, 21, 30, 40, 122, 145, 149, 189, 191, 236, 238-9, 255

Braybrooke, Richard Cornwallis Neville, fourth baron (1820-61), see Neville

Braybrooke, Richard Griffin Neville, third baron (d. 1858), adm. nobleman at Magdalene 1811. First editor of Pepys' Diary, 17n., 20n., 31, 45-6, 122, 132-3, 189.

Brewster, Irish counsel for the Sentinel newspaper, 249-50

Brewster, Mr & Mrs, son & daughter-in-law of William Brewster the chemist of Sidney St, 16

Bridgeman, Hon. John R.O., son of the Earl of Bradford, adm. pens. at Trinity 1850, 69-70, 126

Bridges, Miss, daughter of the next, 387, 394

Bridges, Mrs., Romilly's landlady in 1863, widow of Ben, bookseller, 311, 439

Bright, Mynors, Fellow & tutor of Magdalene 1853-73, editor of Pepys, 133, 146, 190-2, 195, 228, 355, 364, 409

Bright, Richard, adm. pens. at Peterhouse 1808, distinguished pathologist, 215

Brighton, J., champion runner, 397

Brightwell, Miss, of Norwich, 28, 58

Brimley, Augustin G., wholesale grocer, hop & provision merchant, Market Place, Mayor 1853-4, 148

Brimley, George, adm. pens. at Trinity 1837, Librarian of the College 1845-57, 223

Bristol, Marquis of, see Frederick Harvey

Broadley, Charles Bayles, adm. pens. at Trinity 1819, Deputy Regius Professor of Civil Law 1850-9, disappointed in not being elected Regius Professor, first shows signs of mental illness in 1855, 15, 75, 87, 104, 157, 159-60

Brockhurst, Joseph, adm. sizar at St John's 1828, B.A. 1832, 378-9

Brocklebank, Thomas, Fellow of King's 1847-78, Proctor 1860-1, member of 'The Family', 338, 359

# INDEX OF PERSONS

Hicks, William, adm. Fell.-Com. (aged 30) at Magdalene1819, previously wounded at Trafalgar, R. of Sturmer, Essex 1829-74, 164

Higgin, William, adm. pens. at Trinity 1813, Bishop of Derry 1853-67, 249n., 267, 296

Hildyard, James, Fellow of Christ's 1833-47, R. of Ingoldsby, Lincs. 1846-87, 28

Hiley, Mr, employed at Trinity College, 159

Hillier, Edward John, adm. sizar at Trinity 1843, Fellow 1849-58, schoolmaster, 44

Hind, Miss, *probably* one of two daughters of John, 36

Hind, John, second Wrangler, Fellow of Sidney 1823-4, mathematical author, F.R.A.S., 91, 338

Hinds, the, unattractive neighbours of the Romillys, 46

Hinds, old, 89

Hinds, Samuel, of Queen's College, Oxford, Bishop of Norwich 1849-57, 44, 284

Hinson, the, schoolkeepers of Jesus Lane, 135

Hoblyn, Thomas Hallam, adm. pens. at Trinity 1853, 197

Hobson, Samuel (or Thomas), brother of Mrs Peter Mark Roget, 320

Hockin, Charles, Scholar of St John's, third Wrangler 1863, expert in submarine telegraphy, 430

Hodgson, Christopher (d. 1874), Treasurer to Queen Anne's Bounty, father of Mrs Pulling, 193

Hodgson, Henry Williams (*post* Pemberton), migrated from Trinity to Clare 1838, barrister 1844, married Frances Campbell (née Pemberton) & took her name 1855, 334

Hodson, George, adm. sizar at Trinity 1805, Fellow of Magdalene 1810, Archdeacon of Stafford 1829-55 when he died of cholera, 407

Hodson, George Hewitt, Fellow of Trinity 1841-60, P.C. of Cookham-Dean, Berks. 1845-60, biographer of his brother the commander of 'Hodson's Horse' in the Indian Mutiny, 279, 318-9, 367

Hodson, Louisa Calthorpe, daughter of George, married H.R. Luard in June 1862, 407, 418

Hoffmann, leader of the Organophonic Band, 234

Holditch, Hamnett, Fellow of Caius 1821-67, shy son of harbourmaster of King's Lynn, made freeman of that town on becoming Senior Wrangler in 1822, mathematical author, 390

Home, Charles A.D., adm. pens. at Trinity 1852, M.A. 1855, 180

Hooker, Helen, née Henslow, 452

Hooker, Joseph Dalton (1817-1911), the botanist, assistant Director at Kew 1855, son of Sir William, son-in-law of Professor Henslow, 6, 61, 211

Hooker, Sir William (1785-1865), Director at Kew Gardens, 211

Hope (*post* Bereford Hope) Alexander James, adm. pens. at Trinity 1837, M.P. for Maidstone 1841-52, wealthy politician, author, & patron of the arts, married 1842 Mildred, daughter of Lord Salisbury, 270

Hopkins, Caroline, née Boys, wife of William & mother of Ellis, 314, 413

Hopkins, Miss Ellis, open-air preacher, daughter of William the great coach, 233, 413, 441, 447, 450

Hopkins, John Larkin, adm. pens. at St John's 1842, organist of Rochester cathedral 1841-56, of Trinity College 1856-73, composer, 242

Hopkins, William, adm. pens. at Peterhouse 1823 aged 30, Esquire Bedell 1827-66 when he died, renowned mathematical coach who had nearly 200 wranglers as pupils 15, 36, 74, 87, 98-9, 152, 167, 181, 213, 222, 269, 271, 306-7, 330, 374, 400, 404-5, 430

Hopkins, William Bonner, Fellow of Caius 1844-7, Fellow of St Catharine's 1847-54, C. of Holy Trinity 1846-7, V. of St Peter's, Wisbech 1854-66, 24, 147

Hoppett, son of John, 361

Hoppett, of Silver Street, *perhaps* brother of John, 139

Hoppett, John, Romilly's gyp, of Gifford Place, Green St, 151, 189-90, 212, 214, 224, 248, 305, 383, 389, 419, 466

Hoppner, John (1758-1810), rival of Lawrence as a portrait-painter, 18

Horner, Leonard (1785-1864), the geologist, educational reformer, Factory Act Inspector, 459

Hort, Fenton John Anthony, Scholar of Trinity 1849, Fellow 1852-7, theologian, mountaineer & natural scientist, 11, 114-5, 178, 199, 271

Hose, Frederick, adm. sizar at Queens' 1826, C. of Holy Trinity 1830-45, R. of Dunstable, Beds. 1845-83, 69

Hoskin, Mrs, wife of Peter, author of tracts, 102, 168, 183, 188, 225

Hoskin, Peter Charles Mellish, adm. pens. at Sidney 1835, V. of Whittlesford, Cambs. 1845-62, 168, 183, 186, 188

Hotham, Henry John, Fellow of Trinity 1845, Perpetual C. of St Michael's, Cambridge 1853-7, mathematical & classical scholar, authority on ancient ritual, 208, 215, 256, 430

Hough, James, surgeon of Trumpington St, 355

Houghton, Mrs, loyal Romilly retainer of Highbury Vale, aunt of Maria Blencowe, 119, 321, 358

How, Mrs, of 7 Doric St, *presumably* mother of Caroline, Betsy, William & James, protégés of Lucy Romilly, 16, 20, 23, 26, 50-1, 82, 97, 123, 128, 130, 132, 200, 289

How, Henry, son of a cobbler, 93

How, William, carpenter, protégé of Lucy, 132, 251

Howard, Lord Edward, second son of the thirteenth Duke of Norfolk, Vice-Chamberlain to the Queen 1846-52, M.P. for Horsham 1848, 75

Howard, William Page, adm. pens. at Trinity 1860, died 1862, 354

Howe, Christina, mentally disturbed protégée of Lucy Romilly, 116, 118-9, 141

Howes (How(e)), Caroline, protégée of Lucy Romilly, servant to Joseph from July 1857, 16, 311, 313-4, 328, 354, 356, 381, 386-7, 389-90, 415, 420, 426, 433, 439, 441-2, 447-8, 450, 466

Howes, Charles, Fellow of Clare, Fellow & Chaplain of Dulwich College 1842-58, of the Close, Norwich 1859-80, 356

Howes, John George, Fellow of Peterhouse 1843, P.C. of Little St Mary's 1846-69, 28, 80, 131

Howes, Thomas, of Oriel College, Oxford, R. of Belton, Norfolk 1837, 356

Hudson, a musical prodigy, 207

Ottley, Major, *perhaps* Thomas Henry, candidate for the post of teacher of Hindustani, 361n., 365-6

Outram, Mr & Mrs, 'our opposite neighbours', 36-7

Ouvry, Mrs, *presumably* Sarah Amelia (died February 1857), mother of the following distant cousins of Romilly, 11

Ouvry, the, family, Romilly's distant cousins, 34,

Ouvry, Francisca Ingram (1818-76), author of *Arnold Delahaize* etc., 11, 108, 176, 371, 392

Ouvry, Frederic (1814-81), 11(?), 410

Ouvry, Henry Aimé (1813- 99), Captain in the Indian army, 30, 110, 304

Ouvry, Peter Thomas, adm. pens. at Trinity 1829, C. of Linslade, Bucks. 1848-50, V. of Wing 1850-85, 40n., 73, 304

Ouvry, Sarah *see* Mrs Sibson

Ouvry North, John *see* North

Over, Henry, cook & confectioner, of 3 Union St, 29

Overstone, Samuel J. Loyd, only Baron, adm. pens at Trinity 1813, captain of the Poll 1818, banker, 411

Overton, successful candidate for the Victoria Asylum, 37

Owen, Mrs, Methodist protégée of Lucy, brought up Selina Thompson, 55

Owen, Mrs, friend of Miss Page, 36

Owen, Edward Henry, migrated from Corpus to Jesus 1851, 147

Owen, Sir Hugh, bart. (1803-91), M.P. for Pembrokeshire 1861-8, son of Sir John, 413

Owen, Sir John, bart. (d.1861) of Pembrokeshire, M.P. 1841-61, 413

Owen, Sir Richard (1804-92), naturalist, Hon LL.D. 1859, 6n., 320, 349(?), 358, 422-3

Oxford, Bishop of *see* Samuel Wilberforce

Packe, James, Fellow of King's 1824-48 when he married, of Melton Lodge, Suffolk, 55, 71, 215, 258, 280

Packe, Miss, governess to the children of Latimer Neville, probably sister of William J., 320

Packe, Sarah Martha , née Chapman, wife of James, 55, 215

Packe, William James, of Christ Church, Oxford, C. of Heydon, Essex, 1858-65, 333

Page, Miss, friend of the Romillys, 22, 29, 36

Page, G. F., obscure young author, 399

Paget, Clara, née Fardell, wife of George & mother of ten, 96n., 98, 144, 348-9, 399, 419, 424

Paget, Edmund, son of George, 419

Paget, George Edward, Fellow of Caius 1832-51, Physician to Addenbrooke's Hospital 1839-84, reformed the medical curriculum & examination system, 3, 12, 18, 24, 39, 50, 53, 64, 71, 96, 100, 119, 122, 128, 144, 147, 149, 164, 173, 185, 193, 198, 204, 221, 258, 260, 268, 273, 304, 319, 321n., 323, 334, 337, 348-50, 364, 375, 382-4, 392, 395-6, 400, 404-5, 408-9, 419, 422, 424, 446

Paget, James, surgeon to St Bartholomew's Hospital 1847, Surgeon to the Queen 1858, brother of George, 96

Paget, Maud, daughter of George, 419, 422, 424

Paley, Frederick Apthorp, Scholar of St John's 1836, nephew of the Misses Apthorp, became a Roman Catholic in 1846, classical scholar, 435

Palgrave, Francis Turner (1824-97), critic & compiler of *The Golden Treasury* (1861), 415

Palmer, Edward Henry, Cambridge boy, adm. sizar at St John's 1863, having learnt Arabic from Abdullah, Professor of Arabic 1871, 432

Palmer, Sir Roundell (1812-95), Attorney-General 1863-6, 161, 437

Palmer, William, the Rugeley poisoner, 243, 247, 273

Palmerston, Henry St John, Viscount, adm. nobleman at St John's 1803, M.A. 1806, Hon LL.D. 1864, M.P. for the University in six Parliaments, Prime Minister 1855-8, 1859-65, 11, 146, 159-60, 166, 180, 182, 197, 237n., 247, 262, 295, 309, 314n., 352, 399, 409, 432-3, 448, 455

Panmure, Fox Maule, second Baron, Secretary for War 1855, 197

Pannizi, Sir Anthony (1797-1879), Principal Librarian of the British Museum, 451

Papera, James Philip, Cambridge sculptor, 93n.

Papillon, the Misses, daughters of Thomas of Acrise, Kent, 389

Parfitt, John, tailor, draper, & robe maker, of St Mary's Passage, 168-9, 345

Parke, Sir James, Fellow of Trinity 1804, Judge of Court of Exchequer 1834-55, 110-11

Parker Hamond, William, adm. pens. at St John's 1812, High Sheriff of Cambs. 1852-3, of Pampisford Hall, 64, 110-11

Parkinson, Stephen, Senior Wrangler 1845, Fellow of St John's 1845-71, B.D. 1855, mathematical author, 53, 269, 392, 408

Parry, Mrs Elizabeth, widowed daughter of R.T. Cory (d. 1835), Master of Emmanuel, 49, 229, 309, 317

Parry, Henrietta, daughter of Mrs Parry, 49

Pashley, Miss, a dissenter, 89

Patteson, Sir John, Fellow of King's 1812, barrister 1821, judge of the Queen's Bench 1830-52, 'one of the very best and ablest judges that ever sat in Westminster Hall', 50n., 103, 182, 189, 198, 206, 216, 256, 258-9

Pattison, Mr and family, running a Suffolk workhouse, 108

Payne, Mr, prayer-reader, 140

Peabody, George (1795-1869), American philanthropist, 411

Peacock, Frances Elizabeth, née Selwyn, wife of George, 89, 139, 251, 258, 438

Peacock, George, Fellow of Trinity 1814, Lowndean Professor of Astronomy & Geometry 1837-58, Dean of Ely 1839-58 when he died, x, 35, 59n., 69, 89, 105, 130, 139, 149, 198, 204, 251, 258, 273, 302, 305, 310

Peacock, Thomas, Perpetual C. of Denton, Durham, father of George, 58, 91

Pearce, Miss, rejects G. Williams, 146

Pearce, Henry, farmer, 99

Pearce, Louisa, sister of Henry, 99

Pearce, Thomas, of Cambridge, 298

Pearce, William, of Sawbridgeworth, Herts., 26

# SELECT INDEX OF SUBJECTS AND PLACES

SELECT INDEX OF SUBJECTS & PLACES

# SELECT INDEX OF SUBJECTS & PLACES

# Key to Part of J.W. LOWRY'S CAMBRIDGE MAP

## (*Weekly Dispatch*, 1863)

1. St Peter's
2. St Giles
3. St Clement's
4. St Sepulchre
5. All Saints
6. St Michael's
7. Holy Trinity
8. St Mary the Great
9. St Edward's
10. St Andrew the Great
11. St Benedict's (Ben'e't)
12. St Botolph's
13. St Mary the Less
14. St Paul's
15. Christ Church
16. Abbey Church

### Chapels

17. Castle End
    (Primitive Methodist)
18. Hobson's St
    (Wesleyan)
19. Downing St
    (Independent)
20. St Andrew's St
    (Baptist)
21. St Andrews(R.C.)
22. Zion (Baptist)
23. Eden
    (Particular Baptist)
24. Fitzroy St
    (Primitive Methodist)

### Schools

25. Industrial
26. Pound Hill (Infant)
27. Pound Hill (Girls)
28. Castle End (Boys)
29. All Saints (Sunday)
30. King St (National)
31. Trinity (Sunday)
32. St Andrew the Great
    (Sunday)
33. Perse Free Grammar

34. St Paul's (Infant)
35. St Paul's (National)
36. Barnwell
    (Infant & National)
37. British
38. Ragged
39. Abbey National

### Museums & Libraries

40. Natural & Antiquarian
    Museums
    (Philosophical Rooms)
41. Trinity Library
42. Geolog. & Mineral.
    Museums
    University Library
43. Anatomical &
    Botanical Museums
    Lecture Room
44. Fitzwilliam Museum

### Public Buildings

45. County Courts
46. Senate House
47. King's College Chapel
48. Town Hall
49. Savings Bank
50. Post Office
51. Corn Exchange
52. Pitt Press
53. Police Station
54. Spinning House
55. Addenbrooke's
    Hospital
56. Female Refuge
57. Theatre

### Alms Houses

58. Victoria Asylum
59. Storey
60. Wrays
61. University
62. Jakanetts
63. Knights

64. Kings
65. Queens
66. Perses
67. St Anthony's Hospital

### Societies, etc.

68. Free Library
69. Christian Young Men's
70. School of Art
71. Philo Union
72. Working Men's
    College
73. C. of E. Young Men's
74. Barnwell
    Working Men's

### Hotels

75. Hoop
76. Lion
77. Eagle
78. Bull
79. University Arms

### Colleges

A. Magdalene
B. Saint John's
C. Jesus
D. Sidney Sussex
E. Trinity
F. Trinity Hall
G. Gonville & Caius
H. Clare
I. King's
J. Christ's
K. Queens'
L. St Catharine's
M. Corpus Christi
N. Emmanuel
O. Pembroke
P. St Peter's
   (Peterhouse)
Q. Downing